Nineteenth-Century American Women Poets

ℬLACKWELL 𝒜NTHOLOGIES

Editorial Advisers

Rosemary Ashton, University of London; Gillian Beer, University of Cambridge; Gordon Campbell, University of Leicester; Terry Castle, Stanford University; Margaret Ann Doody, Vanderbilt University; Richard Gray, University of Essex; Joseph Harris, Harvard University; Jerome J. McGann, University of Virginia; David Norbrook, University of Oxford; Tom Paulin, University of Oxford; Michael Payne, Bucknell University; Elaine Showalter, Princeton University; John Sutherland, University of London.

Blackwell Anthologies are a series of extensive and comprehensive volumes designed to address the numerous issues raised by recent debates regarding the literary canon, value, text, context, gender, genre, and period. While providing the reader with key canonical writings in their entirety, the series is also ambitious in its coverage of hitherto marginalized texts, and flexible in the overall variety of its approaches to periods and movements. Each volume has been thoroughly researched to meet the current needs of teachers and students.

Romanticism: An Anthology
Second Edition
edited by Duncan Wu

Romantic Women Poets: An Anthology
edited by Duncan Wu

British Literature 1640–1789: An Anthology
edited by Robert DeMaria, Jr

Nineteenth-Century American Women Writers: An Anthology
edited by Karen L. Kilcup

Nineteenth-Century American Women Poets: An Anthology
edited by Paula Bernat Bennett

Forthcoming
Old and Middle English: An Anthology
edited by Elaine Treharne

Chaucer to Spenser: An Anthology
edited by Derek Pearsall

Renaissance Literature: An Anthology
edited by Michael Payne

The Victorians: An Anthology
edited by Valentine Cunningham

Modernism: An Anthology
edited by Lawrence Rainey

Nineteenth-Century American Literature: An Anthology
edited by Kenny J. Williams

Early African-American Literature: An Anthology
edited by Phillip M. Richards

Native American Women Writers *c.* 1800–1925: An Anthology
edited by Karen L. Kilcup

NINETEENTH-CENTURY AMERICAN WOMEN POETS

AN ANTHOLOGY

EDITED BY **PAULA BERNAT BENNETT**

BLACKWELL
Publishers

Copyright © Blackwell Publishers Ltd, 1998
Introduction, selection, and apparatus
© Paula Bernat Bennett, 1998

First published 1998
2 4 6 8 10 9 7 5 3 1

Blackwell Publishers Inc.
350 Main Street
Malden, Massachusetts 02148
USA

Blackwell Publishers Ltd
108 Cowley Road
Oxford OX4 1JF
UK

All rights reserved. Except for the quotation of short passages for the purposes of criticism and
review, no part of this publication may be reproduced, stored in a retrieval system, or transmitted,
in any form or by any means, electronic, mechanical, photocopying, recording or otherwise,
without the prior permission of the publisher.

Except in the United States of America, this book is sold subject to the condition that it shall not,
by way of trade or otherwise, be lent, resold, hired out, or otherwise circulated without the
publisher's prior consent in any form of binding or cover other than that in which it is published
and without a similar condition including this condition being imposed on the subsequent
purchaser.

Library of Congress Cataloging-in-Publication Data
Nineteenth-century American women poets: an anthology/edited by Paula Bernat Bennett.
p. cm. – (Blackwell anthologies)
Includes bibliographical references and index.
ISBN 0-631-20398-2 (acid-free paper). – ISBN 0-631-20399-0 (pbk.: acid-free paper)
1. American poetry – Women authors.   2. American poetry – 19th century.
I. Bennett, Paula.   II. Series.
PS589.N5   1997
811'.30809287–dc21   97-6863

British Library Cataloguing in Publication Data
A CIP catalogue record for this book is available from the British Library.

Typeset in 9.5 on 11 pt Garamond 3
by Graphicraft Typesetters Ltd., Hong Kong
Printed in Great Britain by
TJ Press, Padstow Cornwall
This book is printed on acid-free paper

To Pam, Lisa, and Bob, and
Anne, Amber, and Mia
for their dedication

Contents

Section II   Poems from Regional, National, and Special Interest Newspapers and Periodicals, arranged chronologically

Alphabetical List of Authors
in Section II

Acknowledgments

Any scholarly project this extensive bears with it a host of debts. My first and greatest debt is to the many scholars, students, friends, and family members who have supported and encouraged me through the seven-year period which went into the making of this text. Their enthusiasm and excitement made what by all rights should have been a lonely labor a shared and pleasurable experience. I wish it were possible to name them all here. There are, however, a few individuals to whom special acknowledgment must be given. In particular I would like to thank Margarett Piatt, Director of the Piatt Castles, West Liberty, Ohio, for giving me access to the Piatt materials in the Castle archives, and I would like to thank Professor Karen Kilcup and Mr Andrew McNeillie of Blackwell who, each in their own way, helped make this anthology happen.

I would also like to thank the following students who put so much time, care, and energy into this project, from typing and proof-reading the poetry to researching and drafting the notes and biographies. From Southern Illinois University, Carbondale, Lisa Day, Pamela Kincheloe, and Robert Alsop, the latter also writing substantively two biographies, those of Frances Kemble and Charlotte Perkins Gilman; from Harvard College, my Radcliffe "Partners:" Mia Bengaris, Amber Ramage, and Anne Stiles. This book would not have been possible without their effort and good faith, and it is dedicated therefore to them.

Finally I wish to thank Southern Illinois University for two ORDA grants supporting my research; the American Antiquarian Society and the National Endowment for the Humanities for a half-year's grant; and The Bunting Institute, Radcliffe College, for their fellowship and intellectual support. In a time of increasingly scarce resources the support given by such awards means more than I can say.

The Editor and Publisher are also grateful for permission to reproduce the following copyright material:

Mary Hunter Austin, "Song of the Basket Dancers," "Lament of a Man for his Son," "Papago Love Songs I and II," "Glyphs I, II, and III," "Neither Spirit nor Bird," "Songs of the Seasons," "Black Prayers," and "On Hearing Vachel Lindsay Chant his Verse" from *The American Rhythm* by Mary Austin. Copyright 1923, 1930 by Mary Austin. Copyright ©

renewed 1950 by Harry P. Mera, Kenneth M. Chapman, and Mary C. Wheelwright. Reprinted by permission of Houghton Mifflin Company. All rights reserved.

Frances Densmore, *Papago Music* originally published in the Bureau of American Ethnology, Bulletin 90.

Emily Dickinson, Poems 334, 339, 391, 479, 593, 601, 613, 709, 721, 754, 822, 1225, 1545, from *The Complete Poems of Emily Dickinson*, ed. Thomas H. Johnson. Copyright 1929, 1935 by Martha Dickinson Bianchi; copyright © renewed 1957, 1963 by Mary L. Hampson. By permission of Little, Brown and Company. Poem 1564 from *Life and Letters of Emily Dickinson*, ed. Martha Dickinson Bianchi. Copyright 1924 by Martha Dickinson Bianchi, © renewed 1952 by Alfred Leete Hampson. Reprinted by permission of Houghton Mifflin Company. All rights reserved.

Poetry is reprinted by arrangement with the publishers and the Trustees of Amherst College from *The Poems of Emily Dickinson*, ed. Thomas H. Johnson, Cambridge, Massachusetts: The Belknap Press of Harvard University Press, copyright © 1951, 1955, 1979, 1983 by the President and Fellows of Harvard College and from *The Complete Poems of Emily Dickinson*, ed. Thomas H. Johnson. Copyright 1929, 1935 by Martha Dickinson Bianchi; copyright © renewed 1957, 1963 by Mary L. Hampson: Little, Brown and Company, Boston.

Alice Ruth Moore Dunbar-Nelson, "You! Inez!" reprinted by courtesy of the University of Delaware Library, Newark, Delaware.

Sarah Louisa Forten ("Ada"), "Look! 'Tis a woman's streaming eye" from the Francis J. Grimké Papers, Box 40–43, Folder 1809, the Moorland-Spingarn Research Center, Howard University.

Sarah Margaret Fuller, "Double Triangle, Serpent and Rays," shelf mark MS Am 1086(4), reprinted by permission of the Houghton Library, Harvard University; "To A. H. B.," Ms. Am. 1450 (145) and "To the Same: A Feverish Vision," Ms. Am. 1450 (145) reprinted by courtesy of the Trustees of the Boston Public Library.

Emma Lazarus, "Assurance" reprinted from the manuscript notebook of Emma Lazarus, from the collection of the American Jewish Historical Society, Waltham, Massachusetts.

Frances Sargent Locke Osgood, "Won't you die & be a spirit" and "The Lady's Mistake," shelf mark bMS Am. 1355, reprinted by permission of the Houghton Library, Harvard University; "The Wraith of the Rose," Griswold Mss. no. 787, reprinted by courtesy of the Trustees of the Boston Public Library.

Lizette Woodworth Reese, "Widower" and "To a Young Poet" from *Pastures and Other Poems* by Lizette Woodworth Reese, © 1933 by Lizette Woodworth Reese. © 1961 by A. Austin Dietrich. Reprinted by permission of Henry Holt & Co., Inc.

Edith M. Thomas, "The Etherial Hunger" and "To Walk Invisible" from *Selected Poems of Edith M. Thomas*, edited with a memoir by Jessie B. Rittenhouse. Copyright 1926 by Harper & Brothers, renewed © 1954 by (Mrs) Louise L. Rittenhouse. Reprinted by permission of HarperCollins Publishers, Inc.

Introduction

When Edmund Clarence Stedman published *An American Anthology* in 1900, he included poems by over one hundred and fifty women poets from Sarah Josepha Hale (1788–1879) to Dora Read Goodale (1866–1953). Within thirty years, the names and contributions of almost all of these women – Emily Dickinson excepted – would be lost. From the standpoint of United States literary history, for most of the twentieth century, it has been as if they never wrote, never were.

There are many reasons for the erasure of one entire field of women's writing. Not all of them have to do with gender. Even more salient in this instance was the profound shift in literary taste resulting from early modernist championship of *vers libre*. "Liberated" from rhyme and from the necessity to adhere to fixed metrical patterns, poets found new, more subtly stringent ways to impose rigor upon themselves and to derive pleasure from their texts. In privileging the musical cadence over the metrical foot, and, even more, in emphasizing "the word," early modernist writers transformed American poetry. From a popular art, self-consciously intended to refine and unify a polyglot and heterogeneous nation, it became a literature that was self-consciously difficult and – despite Whitman's democratizing influence – elite. By the new standards – standards best exemplified by the poetic platform of "New Criticism" – nineteenth-century American poetry not only came to seem "old-fashioned," but, in a profound sense, literarily naive: conventional, timid, and, as Santayana put it, "genteel." Unlike the work of their female peers (the "Sentimentalists"), the poetry of the male "Fireside poets" – Longfellow, Lowell, Holmes – lingered; but the authors themselves were no longer influential. Artistically speaking – Whitman excepted – nineteenth-century men's poetry, no less than women's, had nothing to say to the next generation of American writers, or, at least, so these writers, men and women, claimed.

Since the publication of Cheryl Walker's ground-breaking anthology, *American Women Poets of the Nineteenth Century*, in 1992, six more anthologies – four mixed, one devoted to African American poets, and the most recent, by Janet Gray, devoted, like Walker's, to women – have appeared, signaling a major revival of interest in the field and a shift in previous aesthetic evaluations. Nor should this surprise. Since the 1960s, modernist aesthetics, especially that epitomized in "New Criticism," have come under increasing attack for the exclusionary elitism inherent in their (undeclared) ideological agenda. As the political burden of this agenda has been demystified, so too has the concept of the well-made work of art upon whose filtering capacity New Critics relied.

Disseminated through the school system by means of Cleanth Brooks and Robert Penn Warren's textbook, *Understanding Poetry* (1938), New Critical standards for what constituted "good" poetry, that is, poetry worthy of imitation, study, and preservation, had effectively shaped three academic generations. In the hands of these scholars, a rigorous set of aesthetic criteria evolved, based largely on New Critical readings of seventeenth-century British poetry. More rigid in many cases than Brooks and Warren themselves, critics using these criteria privileged irony, paradox, and ambiguity at the expense of virtually everything else, including any given text's place within its own historical moment. From their perspective, knowing what made a poem "bad" easily became more important than understanding what may have made it "good" to a previous generation of readers. As will be evident from some of my choices and many of my biases, I myself am a recovering New Critic.

But how and by whose standards is the "bad" to be judged, when, as turns out to be the case, even the seemingly "objective" evaluations of the New Critics (like all such aesthetic evaluations) were determined by these critics' own time and cultural milieu and carried with them their own shaping ideological burden? And why should readers so exclusively preoccupy themselves with what is aesthetically "best," in any case? Is not a given culture more than the sum of its "greatest" works? Indeed, does not popular art, which reaches mass audiences, have as much to say about any particular culture as that culture's presumed greatest minds? Perhaps pure (that is, unpoliticized) aesthetic response is not the only reason to engage with art, if indeed such purity is even possible. And perhaps great works of art (like the artists themselves) are not all that separate from the lower forms of culture (and humanity) that surround them. Are Emily Dickinson and Walt Whitman really that exceptional? That utterly "Other," yet somehow that comprehensive, that they should be preserved where the remainder can be safely forgotten?

It is questions such as these, as much as those directed towards issues of gender *per se*, that have opened up nineteenth-century American poetry – a poetry vastly popular in its base – once more for exploration and appreciation. Pointing to what Barbara Herrnstein Smith calls the contingency of (aesthetic) value – its function as a quasi-economic system that attributes worth to some works at the explicit expense of others – these questions direct attention away from the study of art-in-itself to, in Jane Tompkins's phrase, the "cultural work" that specific artistic fashions and art works perform (how they can be situated historically and socially). But as even a cursory glance at the criticism developing around nineteenth-century American women's poetry makes clear, the asking of these questions has yet to resolve all the problems reading this poetry presents. In particular, it has not resolved the issues raised by its close association with the Sentimental. Since the sentimentality of nineteenth-century women's poetry, indeed of their writing generally, continues to delegitimate it as an area of serious academic concern in the eyes of most scholars, it seems best, therefore, to confront the problems it raises head on here.

No group of writers in United States literary history has been subject to more consistent denigration than nineteenth-century women, especially the poets. Beginning with Mark Twain's "Emmeline Grangerford" in *Huckleberry Finn* (1884) and culminating in Ann Douglas's scathing analysis in *The Feminization of American Culture* (1977), their writing has been damned out of hand for its conventionality, its simplistic Christianity, its addiction to morbidity, and its excessive reliance on tears. Equally disturbing, it has been presented, even by those seeking to revive interest in it (most notably, Jane Tompkins, but also Cheryl Walker and Joanne Dobson) as a literature basically without difference. Whether in praise or blame, this writing – Emily Dickinson's excepted – has been reduced to one perspective, that of the conventionally domestic, the "genteel," the "sentimental." Under such rubrics, and despite the power of Tompkins's critique, it has gone unread, except by a small, if growing, number of aficionados.

Having spent the last seven years reading, literally, thousands of poems by hundreds of nineteenth-century American women, I would not deny the existence of the kind of (bad) sentimental art against which Douglas fulminates in *The Feminization of American Culture*. Nor would I deny that this art was meant to fulfill many of the social functions that Tompkins assigns to it in "Sentimental Power," her highly influential essay on Harriet Beecher Stowe. Many nineteenth-century American women, particularly at mid-century, and particularly from the middle class, took their duties as "Angel in the House" seriously, using their writing to project the spiritual and affective values they associated with this (Christian evangelical) interpretation of their sphere. When combined with the nineteenth-century's fondness for regular meters and conventionally poetic diction, and its obsession with death and moral platitudes, the result can be a kind of narrow formulaic verse even sympathetic readers find indigestible. Thus, for example, when speaking of Elizabeth Oakes Smith's "The Sinless Child" (1842) – probably the epitome of this kind of poetry, although an effective poem by its own standard – even Walker becomes uncharacteristically judgmental. Calling the poem "sickly sweet," her anthology reprints only its five-stanza "Inscription," the least, one suspects, she felt she could safely offer, given the poem's historical importance.

But what is lost in such a blanket response to Oakes Smith's poem – whether to damn it (as Walker does) or to recuperate it (as, effectively, Tompkins asks us to do) – is the significance of the fact that within six years of "The Sinless Child's" publication, the author herself rejected the passive, sentimentalized gender values her highly popular poem celebrates. Dropping poetry altogether after the 1840s, Oakes Smith joined the Lyceum circuit, speaking on women's rights and abolition, and she turned to writing pot-boiling, reformist fiction. (Her 1854 novel, *The Newsboy*, is credited with having inspired social legislation on behalf of New York City's street children.) For Oakes Smith, as for many middle-class women of the period, "The Sinless Child" embodied an ideological as well as stylistic moment that was passing even as she wrote. Like the British poet, Coventry Patmore, in the somewhat later, and far more hugely popular "The Angel in the House" (1850), she had given pure expression to one of the century's most popular myths – that of "True Womanhood" – but it was a myth that she, at least, came to see as destructive to women's full realization of their potential before the decade was out.

As the popularity of both Oakes Smith's and Patmore's poems indicates, sentimentality was unquestionably a primary rhetorical mode for many nineteenth-century writers, female and *male*, British as well as American. Despite the difficulties experienced in trying to sustain such unearthly perfection (see, for instance, Julia Ward Howe's "Woman" [1849]), angelized versions of the female Sentimental Subject also unquestionably helped define the social niche to which many young women aspired, particularly at mid-century. Attainable or not, True Womanhood was, at least for a few decades, a dominant social ideal. But, as I will discuss shortly, sentimentality was not the only stylistic or affective option available to women poets during the century, nor did the basic premises underlying sentimentality's appeals to emotion – premises rooted in its alliance not just with domestic ideology, but with evangelical Christianity – go uncontested. What has been eclipsed in the critical debate swirling about sentimentality over the last twenty years is that its deployment both as style and subject position was a fraught issue for many nineteenth-century women writers themselves, Dickinson included.

An anthology introduction is no place to undertake an extended *explication de texte*. However, because of the way in which nineteenth-century women's commitment to sentimentality has been overgeneralized in the scholarly literature, a concrete example of how one woman poet in the second half of the century positions herself critically in respect to it might be helpful here. I would like to take Sarah Piatt's "His Mother's Way" (1880) as exemplary in this respect and as a poem central to an understanding of what was at stake for women and for nineteenth-century society as a whole in the debate over sentimentalism that occurred within the century itself. While Piatt's poem engages a sentimental position, it is not in itself sentimental. It is ironic and bitter. And it raises a vexed social issue – the plight of the homeless – that, from the perspective of the poem's adult speaker, the implied author of the poem, neither bourgeois men *nor* their (sentimental) partners were dealing with effectively, precisely because of the way in which domestic ideology distributed social power and emotional responsibilities between them. (The dilemma Piatt depicts here is being re-played today under the labels Conservative and Liberal, with, I might add, as little success.)

Told until the final stanzas from the limited perspective of a very young boy, "His Mother's Way" describes a woman whose highly sentimentalized reaction to a passing tramp does no more to remedy the underlying social conditions responsible for this man's plight than her husband's macho reaction does to contain the threat to social order his homelessness represents. (The father will "sleep to-night / With both his pistols at his head.") If the husband would use brute force to get his way, all the mother uses is tears to get hers – the same tears, her son tells us disgustedly, she sheds over keep-sake treasures ("old glove[s]" and "ring[s]"), and on clothing she cannot afford to buy ("the shabbiest shawl" [l. 9]). If the child is confused by the excessive lengths to which his father will go not to feel (he would not even cry, the boy says, at his own death), his mother's excessive emotional displays are equally off-putting. Both parents are locked within their respective gender roles, roles that in their rigidity leave the child no room to maneuver. Mother does nothing but weep and wail; father does nothing but posture. Meanwhile, the poet tells us in the final stanzas, speaking in a second voice directly to her readers, the tramp himself goes unhoused, unfed.

To the extent that the mother's tears call attention to the tramp's needs (and would not simply obliterate them with cannon fire or hide them by putting the tramp himself in jail), the mother has the moral high ground of her rather bullish mate. In her capacity to experience another's pain, and in her desire to relieve it, she is closer to her society's normative Christian values (the values, for example, of the sermon on the mount) than are the men who with their "lamp-light leisure, jests, and wine" (l. 46) laugh her to scorn. But Piatt's final speaker – the poem's adjudicating voice – calls the mother "foolish" nonetheless. This is not because she feels – she should feel – but because that is all she does. Action is left to men, and since men have a gendered investment in refusing to feel (being emotional is, after all, the "cultural work" women were supposed to do), there's small chance they will compromise their own comfort to benefit those less fortunate than themselves. Far from remedying the social indifference against which she protests, the mother's excessive tearfulness simply insures that the next generation of males, figured in her son, will continue to behave as their fathers did before them, rather than risk the contempt a cross-gendered expression of sympathy might evoke. (That men are, in fact, permitted to express other kinds of emotions beside the sympathic, most notably rage, is something Piatt does not discuss, but Robert Frost's "Home Burial" could be read as a pendant to Piatt's poem on this issue.)

In a thoughtful article on the keepsake tradition, Joanne Dobson argues that nineteenth-century sentimentality celebrates the preservation of human bonds, the affectional bonds that hold society as well as individual families together, and which sentimentalized artifacts such as keepsakes symbolically embodied. (For examples of "keepsake" poems see Hannah Gould's "The Child on the Beach" [1833], and Ethelinda Beer's "The Baggage Wagon" [1872] in Section II.) When directed, as the wife's sentimentality in "His Mother's Way" is, toward asserting the ties of obligation and common humanity binding the rich and the poor, the privileged and the oppressed, the thrust of nineteenth-century sentimentality could indeed be utopic. As is famously the case with *Uncle Tom's Cabin*, that is, it could help effect progressive social change. Barring that, it could at least make life more difficult for the oppressors – as, for example, Lydia Sigourney tries to do with "The Cherokee Mother" (1831), written at the height of the controversy over President Jackson's Indian Removal policy. Today's readers may find Sigourney's blatant ethnocentrism offensive, but the native editors of the *Cherokee Phoenix*, who published the poem, seemed to have valued its highly sentimentalized portrait of the Cherokee as "brothers under the skin," i.e., just like whites, for what it was: an effective means of eliciting white outrage on their behalf. Certainly, Sigourney – along with other "sentimental" protesters – was a regular on their pages.

Yet when deployed, as the mother's sentimentality in "His Mother's Way" also is, indiscriminately, and without due regard to society's existing power arrangements, sentimentality could also do more harm than good, insofar as, like other positions based on excess, it tended to undermine the credibility of those employing it. For Piatt (as, I might add, for Margaret Fuller in "Governor Everett Receiving the Indian Chiefs" [1844]), sentimental expression was, therefore, a troubled balancing act at best. Too much, and one made oneself appear an idealistic fool, "sloppily sentimental," in today's language, "a bleeding heart liberal;" too little, and one became insensitive to the affective values that presumably make humans "human" – the ability to love, to care, to feel for another's pain. In the latter scenario, "might" would indeed, as Fuller observes, "make right." As she suggests through her reference to "force or fraud," in a world peopled by "Machiavellis," or by his latter-day Jacksonian descendants, Indians did not have a chance. As Piatt's poem suggests, neither did tramps.

I have discussed Piatt's poem at length because it represents the complex way in which one highly intelligent woman poet writing in the second half of the century chose to relate to one of the century's dominant rhetorical modes and to the social and religious values this mode encoded. Sentimentality is an inescapable fact in much nineteenth-century poetry – Emily Dickinson and Walt Whitman not excepted. Like Ophelia's rue, however, it could be worn with a difference. Indeed, as Elaine Goodale Eastman's powerful "The Cross and the Pagan" (1912) suggests, when allied with the missionary spirit that is also integral to evangelical Christianity, nineteenth-century sentimentality's dedication to the victim could turn into a perverse mockery of itself.

If the capacity to experience and endure pain, suffering, self-sacrifice, and loss were, as Jane Tompkins argues, intrinsic to the Sentimental Subject, then Indians (together with African Americans) had undisputed dibs to the highest moral ground. But no less than the guns of oppressors, sentimentality's own imperializing drive, a drive inseparable from its association with Christian missionary labor, was responsible for the suffering and losses Indians and African Americans incurred, as Goodale Eastman's early stint as an instructor at the Hampton Institute and, indeed, as her own efforts on the Indians' behalf may have taught her. Far from being a force for progressive social transformation, in such instances "sentimental power," as critics such as Laura Wexler and Amy Kaplan have recently argued, became a source of oppression in itself.

The point here is that even if much nineteenth-century women's poetry is "sentimental," which it is, what is meant by that term and how it plays out in any particular text or writer's œuvre can be exceedingly complicated, even treacherous, to sort out. Put another way, for those who believe that sentimentality and irony are inherently incompatible, this anthology may contain more than one surprise, coming at them from more than one direction. Nineteenth-century women's literature, poetry as well as fiction, is neither univocal nor transparent. Like any other complex set of artistic encodings of individual and social experience, it needs to be read with care and with due attention to slippage and to ironic reversals. Only then can this poetry be fairly understood both in terms of the "cultural work" it did and the cultural critique it carried. But having said this, it is now time to turn to the anthology itself.

Behind the poems selected for this anthology lies an enormous bulk of material most of which has not been read, let alone seriously studied, in one to two hundred years. To say that the canon which, for better or worse, will sort this material out has yet to be established is a mammoth understatement. Between us, Walker, Gray, and I share seventeen out of two hundred plus writers. When the huge number of poets none of us include is added in, the freedom the anthologist has to maneuver may well seem – to the anthologist, at any rate – more burden than blessing. This anthology could easily have been twice the size it is had it included every poem that at one point or another was considered seriously. Nor was my search, despite the many venues covered, remotely complete. After seven years of hunting, there simply comes a point when the poem on the next horizon must be allowed to go its own way.

Even more to the point, other anthologists might have chosen a different set of poems or poets altogether. Between the six anthologies now in print, there are at least fifteen poets whom I do not include nor would include in any anthology I put together, even if I did have room. They are poets with whom, for a variety of reasons, some, probably quite illegitimate, I do not "connect." Where the poets are the same, moreover, the poems selected are often quite different. Usually this is because there were other poems by the same author I preferred or viewed as more important. There will undoubtedly be times when readers will respond in the same way to selections of mine. ("Now what on earth does she see in that poet or poem!") If values are contingent, they also, all too frequently, boil down to matters of personal experience and taste. But given this, some explanation of how I arrived at the poems I chose does seem necessary, especially since it bears heavily on the anthology's organization.

Nineteenth-Century American Women Poets began in the basement of Widener Library at Harvard University where I was employed for a year, teaching in the freshman writing program. I was collecting nature poems from periodicals as my share in a projected anthology of nineteenth-century women's nature poetry that I and a colleague hoped to publish. For no particular reason I can remember except that, given Widener's enormous resources, it was easy to do, I decided to begin at "A" (the *American Magazine*) and work my way through to "Z" or its equivalent, whatever magazine came last on those seemingly endless rows of shelves (the *Western Literary Messenger*, as it happened). Before the year was out the collegial project collapsed; but I was left with something far more substantial: a thoroughly transformed view of nineteenth-century women's poetry itself.

I have told this story before and have no wish to repeat it here. What matters is that I came away from the experience persuaded not only that nineteenth-century women's poetry was a vastly underrated field, but that to appreciate its vitality, significance, and diversity meant abandoning received notions of how this or maybe any poetry evolved. Like other scholars, I had come to my field assuming that "major" figures would be the heart of it. What I discovered, however – at least where nineteenth-century American women's poetry was concerned – is that the heart lay elsewhere, not in the poet but in the poem. I discovered, that is, that while there might be very few major poets in this field, there were many, many "major" (or, at any rate, very fine) poems; and that it was in these poems, often written by women who, for whatever reason, never seemed to produce anything quite so interesting again, that the heart of nineteenth-century American women's poetry lay. (Milicent W. Shinn's "In a New England Graveyard" [1880], and Margaret Deland's "Noon in a New England Pasture" [1887], are striking cases in point.)

I also came to realize that given the multiplicity of voices creating this poetry, any attempt to restrict the field to a relatively small, manageable number of writers, even the most carefully selected (for diversity and so forth), would profoundly distort it. If I was going to represent nineteenth-century American women's poetry, I had to do it as I found it – poem by poem, voice by voice, from the bottom of the century up. Focal figures there were – writers such as Lydia Sigourney, Lucy Larcom, Rose Terry Cooke, Sarah Piatt, Lizette Woodworth Reese, all of whom created significant bulks of highly interesting poetry, and who were well known within their periods. But finally nineteenth-century women's poetry was most accurately thought of as, figuratively if not literally, an "anonymous" art. That is, it functioned as a craft, where making – not being – was the dominant mode, and where moments of substantive creativity could be discovered not just in a limited number of major writers but scattered diffusely through a population of unknowns.

It was this set of realizations that led me to organize this anthology the way I have. *Nineteenth-Century American Women Poets* is divided into two sections. The first section, which comprises approximately two-thirds of the volume, is devoted to the work of thirty-eight women whom, for want of a better term, I call "principal poets." They are poets who created significant bodies of poetry of such quality that it is appropriate (and useful) to treat them individually. The names of many of these writers will be familiar to readers already from other anthologies if they have followed the field at all: e.g., Sigourney, Maria Gowen Brooks, Frances Osgood, Lucy Larcom, Helen Hunt Jackson, Celia Thaxter, and so forth. The names of others, however, especially from the second half of the century, may be less familiar, at least where their poetry is concerned – Harriet Prescott Spofford, Louise Chandler Moulton, Sarah Piatt, Elizabeth Stuart Phelps, Charlotte Perkins Gilman, Sophie Jewett, and Mary Austin.

Of these, Spofford, Piatt, and Phelps, in particular, were among the most widely disseminated poets of their day, placing hundreds of poems in newspapers and literary periodicals in the United States, Britain, and Ireland. No anthology that attempts to be representative of late nineteenth-century American women's poetry can ignore them, especially since between them they maintained a highly articulated "counter-tradition" to the conventionalized sentimental discourse for which women's poetry of the period is best known.

In this section, the reader will also find selections from the poetry of four significant African American women poets, Sarah Louisa Forten ("Ada"), Frances E. W. Harper, Henrietta Cordelia Ray, and Alice Dunbar-Nelson, and two Native American poets, the Papago medicine woman, Juana Manwell ("Owl Woman"), in Frances Densmore's translation, and the Mohawk poet, E. Pauline Johnson (Tekahionwake), a Canadian who published widely in the United States. I have also included in this section a substantial selection of African American spirituals as transcribed by Christine Rutledge of the Carolina Singers. If these spirituals were not necessarily authored by women (and who is to say that women did not participate equally in their creation?), they were and remain such an essential part of the lives of black women in America, I cannot imagine leaving them out.

Finally, this section also includes significant amounts of lesbian poetry by four writers: Fanny Kemble, Emily Dickinson, Celia Thaxter, and Sophie Jewett. Applying the label "lesbian" to poetry written in an age when women generally felt free to express love for each other is, of course, risky business, especially when the label is one the poets themselves would, in all likelihood, reject for themselves. (Jewett excepted, all these poets seem among other things to have entertained sexual feelings for men as well as women at some point in their lives.) But as Emma Donoghue has recently argued in *Passions Between Women*, more may be lost in not doing so. To restrict the concept of lesbian poetry only to that poetry written by women whose passion for women has evinced itself through explicitly genital behavior or to women who identify as such not only artificially limits (and, not coincidentally, essentializes) lesbian identity, but it leaves contemporary lesbians with an excruciatingly narrow definition of what constitutes a usable past. Idealized and romanticized it may be, but the love these poets inscribe is "lesbian" insofar as it projects a passionate and pervasively eroticized desire between women that parallels similar expressions by other poets when addressing male lovers (compare, for example, Wharton's sonnet sequence "The Mortal Lease" with Thaxter's "Two Sonnets" or Pauline Johnson's "The Idlers" with Kemble's "Noonday: By the Seaside"). Given this, taking the risk of using an anachronistic label for such poetry seems justified.

If the anthology's first section provides depth by focusing on individual women poets, the second section, composed of poems drawn from newspapers and periodicals, arranged chronologically, provides comprehensiveness. Presenting an additional one hundred plus writers, the majority of whom are unknown today – and many of whom were "anonymous" even in their own day – this section reflects the multiplicity and diversity characterizing nineteenth-century American women's poetry as a whole. In this section, readers will find poems drawn from mainstream national and regional publications, e.g., the *Atlantic Monthly*, *Century*, *Overland Monthly*, and the *Louisville Journal*, and from many of the "special interest" journals and newspapers that flourished in the period, including the *Colored American*, *A Wreath of Cherokee Rose Buds*, the *Vindicator* (a newspaper "devoted to the interests of the Choctaws and Chickasaws"), the *Cincinnati Israelite*, *Lowell Offering*, *Shaker and Shakeress*, the *Irish Nationalist*, *Woodhull & Claflin's Weekly*, the *Southern Workman*, *A. M. E. Church Review*, and *New Century for Women*. In its concluding pages, this section also provides a lively assortment of "avant-garde" poems from late nineteenth-century "penny magazines," the harbingers of the so-called little magazines which proved so immensely important to the development and dissemination of early modernist poetry.

Providing a microcosm for the development of women's poetry throughout the century, this section suggests that the consistent denigration of nineteenth-century newspaper and periodical poetry has been very wide of the mark, at least where women's poetry is concerned. Granted these venues published large quantities of bad poetry, they also provided invaluable open spaces where both white women and women of color could bring their most radical, that is, politically charged, writing, as well as that in which they experimented artistically. Thus, for example, not only does one find an astonishing amount of feminist poetry in mainstream periodicals and newspapers (*Atlantic Monthly*, *Galaxy*, *Frank Leslie's Popular Monthly* and so on), but one finds a surprising number of artistically innovative poems as well, poems such as Mary B. Cummings's "Possession" (*Atlantic Monthly* 1875) and Lillie Devereux Blake's "The Sea People" (*Galaxy* 1875). Even more striking, three of the most powerful and innovative poems by black women included in this volume only appear in periodicals, Sarah Mapps Douglass's "The Stranger in America" (*National Enquirer* 1836), Mary E. Ashe Lee's "Afmerica" (*Southern Workman* 1886), of which I will say more later, and Sarah C. Bierce Scarborough's stunning translation of an excerpt from Lamartine's "Toussaint Louverture" (*A. M. E. Church Review* 1888).

As will be apparent from many of these poems, in a way curiously similar to the use of the Internet today, nineteenth-century women used periodicals and newspapers as places to speak, often quite directly, to each other, engaging in a kind of public, yet intimate, dialogue that simultaneously stood in a Bakhtinian sense, in dialogic relationship to the dominant social discourses of their day. (See, for example, the second Ada's "Lines, Suggested on reading 'An Appeal to Christian Women of the South,' by A. E. Grimke" [*Liberator* 1836] and Maria W. Chapman's "The Times that Try Men's Souls" [*North Star* 1848]). To ignore such poetry is to lose touch with much that was most vital and interesting about American women's poetry of the period. Certainly from my perspective this is where the bulk of these women's most important poetry lay – the poetry that best justifies their claim to a significant place in American literary history.

Given both the abundance and the complexity of the material these two sections cover, what then is the best way to go about reading this anthology? Although many readers will probably want to focus on individual poets in depth, I would like to suggest that it can also be profitably read as a whole, especially if it is read in terms of the two basic sets of concerns governing the selection of poems in the first place (for like most anthologies, this one is governed by assumptions). The first set of concerns can loosely be called aesthetic, the second, even more loosely, political. Both hinge on the issue of diversity. I will address the aesthetic concerns first.

Like many other works of feminist scholarship, this anthology participates in the post-structuralist dismantling of absolute standards of aesthetic value. However, as Herrnstein Smith has cogently argued, acknowledging the contingency of values does not necessarily void questions of aesthetic judgment. On the contrary, as long as one admits their contingency, aesthetic judgments are not only possible but inevitable and necessary, particularly when putting a text such as this together. Otherwise, given the enormous volume of material, and the range of accomplishments exhibited by individual writers, one could not get past the starting gate.

In light of this, the criterion of aesthetic selection that seemed to make the most sense (and lock things in the least) was to view poems in terms of how well or poorly they accomplished what they set out to do. While a number of works in this anthology were selected for their cultural interest, with very few exceptions, none were included on this basis alone. As works of art (indeed, looked on purely as verbal constructs) they also had to be effective – well put together, evocative, capable of moving, and so forth. At the same time, however, in selecting for artistic quality, no single standard was applied. Rather, every effort has been made to match the issue of quality to the kind of poem being written, whether neoclassical satire or proto-imagist nature poem, abolitionist "song" or Whitmanesque free verse, epigrammatic quatrain or associatively organized phantasmagoria, the one requirement being that each poem be an "effective" example of its "kind."

Thus, for example, one of the abiding assumptions of this anthology is that even truly popular poetry – that is, poetry written specifically to appeal to and reflect the concerns of a mass audience – can achieve aesthetic excellence when taken on its own terms. Poems such as Alice Cary's "Pictures of Memory" and Lucy Larcom's "Hannah Binding Shoes" may fail this test for many readers today (they are included, largely, as examples of their authors' early work); but poems such as Annie Keely's "The Beautiful Snow" (1859), Elizabeth Akers Allen's "Rock Me to Sleep" (1860), and Ethelinda Beers's "The Baggage Wagon" (1872), all in Section II, are clear cases in point. In their powerful controlling metaphors and precise use of imagery, these poems, which circulated widely through much of the century, spoke with extraordinary eloquence to nineteenth-century readers in ways that, I think, can still be appreciated today, if even the explicit morbidity or sentimentality of their themes makes them less available to modern readers.

If diversity existed in the kinds of poems nineteenth-century women wrote and the skills they brought to them, the way they wrote also underwent profound changes during the course of the century and this too is a matter of aesthetic concern that needed to be represented. As a quick survey of this anthology will demonstrate, far from remaining static stylistically, women's poetry generally moved from the heavily elaborated discursive style of, for example, Lydia Sigourney's "The Alpine Flowers" (1827) and Maria Brooks's "Zóphiël" (1833), to the elliptically pared-down style and perspective of Edith M. Thomas's "The Deep-Sea Pearl" (1903) and Lizette Woodworth Reese's "In Time of Grief" (1896); and these poets have been cited as imagist forerunners by Watts, Walker, and others. By the 1890s, in fact, many women poets, not just the well-known ones – poets such as Florence Earle Coates ("Longing") and Maude Caldwell Perry ("Summer Died Last Night") – were working outside nineteenth-century stylistic frames of reference. In their obliqueness and classical restraint, their delicate and unobtrusive rhythms, and their enigmatic identification of image with meaning, Coates's and Perry's poems are early modernist in everything save their use of rhyme.

Finally, even within the texts of individual authors, working in the same or different lyric genres, a surprising range of different kinds of writing can be found. Along with sentimentality, many other approaches were available to these women at *every* point throughout the century, including but not limited to the romantic, the visionary, the parodic, the aphoristic, the satirical, the erotic, the fanciful, and the tragically ironic. I would also stress – precisely because it runs counter to popular assumptions about nineteenth-century women, be they sentimentalists or "bluestockings" – that some of these poets are wickedly funny, none more so than A. D. T. Whitney and Phoebe Cary, both of whom were gifted comic writers. Poets such as Frances Osgood, Phoebe Cary, Rose Terry Cooke, Celia Thaxter, Sarah Piatt, Henrietta Cordelia Ray, Edith M. Thomas, Louise Imogen Guiney, and E. Pauline Johnson, to name only the most striking, tended to maintain repertoires of styles, examples of which are not always represented here for want of space and, sometimes, because their work in one mode was distinctly more interesting than their work in another. Among the periodical and newspaper poets, diversity is, not surprisingly, even more striking. Indeed, some readers may feel they are on a roller-coaster as they move from one poet's work to the next. If they do that is how it should be.

While diversity was a necessary aesthetic guideline for this volume, it has proved just as important as a "political" guideline. Nineteenth-century women poets came from every walk of life and most ethnic groups within the nation. Working primarily with the short lyric, they used this most flexible and handy of literary forms (one can, after all, write a poem on the back of a cooking chocolate wrapper if one is so inclined – Emily Dickinson did) to express the myriad aspects of their lives. Within the first ten pages of the second section readers will find poems on women's "hard fate," on the denial of natural rights ("Epitaph for a Bird"), on the advantages of spinsterhood, on the "rage" to write, on unwed motherhood, on the fate of Africans, on female education ("The Hot-House Rose"), on taste in men, on how to dominate men ("The Young Girl's Resolution"), on breast-feeding, and on the fate of Jewry. Indeed, by the time I finished collecting poems for this volume, I was persuaded that there was nothing nineteenth-century women poets did not write on. Even abortion is mentioned in one poem ("My Fashionable Mother" [1874]); and wife abuse in its various forms is a persistent theme from one end of the century to the other. Spofford's "Pomegranate-Flowers" (1861), I have argued elsewhere, is one of many nineteenth-century women's poems on masturbation and autoerotic fantasizing. In "Beatrice Cenci" (1871), and in a poem not included here, "Prevented Choice," Piatt may, albeit obliquely, be treating incest. Dickinson has an outhouse poem ("Alone and in a Circumstance" [J1167, 1870]). Why not?

If individual women felt free to raise such presumably "forbidden" topics in their poetry, women poets as a whole felt absolutely no compunctions about debating the issue of their rights. The nineteenth century was a period of seismic shifts in women's lives as the spread of education and the growth of urbanization and industrialization opened up employment possibilities for women that they never before had considered. In publishing alone, as Patricia Okker has recently documented, women editors became major industry players. With the rise of higher education for women, white and black women alike began to prepare for a wide variety of white-collar professions, including medicine, the ministry, and law. Not surprisingly, they brought to their poetry both their excitement at the new possibilities before them and their anxieties over what these changes might mean for their lives. They also brought an increasing determination to express their sense of blockage when deprived of access to the "brave new world" in which they hoped to make their mark. Two long poems written in the late 1880s, equally remarkable and powerful, one by an African American writer, "Afmerica" (1886) by Mary E. Ashe Lee, the other by the sister of President Grover Cleveland, "The Dilemma of the Nineteenth Century" (1887), by Rose Elizabeth Cleveland, both express women's profound frustration with the nation's failed century-old promise of equal opportunity – a promise that had no meaning until extended to men and women, to whites and people of color. To read such poetry today is to hear directly (if not necessarily transparently) how these women felt about their lives, both present and future, what they wanted and expected, and intended to have.

Whichever way it is read, whether as a whole, or in terms of individual writers, *Nineteenth-Century American Women Poets* provides stunning evidence for the complexity of women's subjectivity in the century: the depth and intensity of their passion – autoerotic and homo-erotic as well as heterosexual – their positive as well as negative feelings about marriage, childbirth, and family, their complex relations to children, their loving and detailed obser-vation of nature, their mixed responses to the frontier, their outrage over the decimation of Native Americans and the oppression of African Americans, their awareness of and com-mitment to their own individual racial and ethnic backgrounds, and their abiding, if often conflicted, concern for social inequalities and injustices of all kinds. That is, this anthology provides a highly nuanced, multi-voiced portrait of nineteenth-century American women as a whole in all their differences as well as in what they shared.

At the same time, particularly because of its emphasis on late nineteenth-century American women's poetry (the most neglected aspect of a neglected field), this anthology invites scholars to rethink the origins of modernist poetry, at least where the next generation of women writers is concerned, Amy Lowell, Harriet Monroe, H. D., et al. If this happens, then the study of nineteenth-century American women's poetry will no longer be an idiosyncratic occupation, an affair of aficionados, but – what it should be – integral to the study of the evolution of American poetry as a whole, thus permanently opening this poetry up to the kind of serious academic scrutiny it deserves. Not coincidentally, such a scholarly consequence will also result in the re-situation of Emily Dickinson where she belongs – among the women who were in fact her peers and among whom she was – in fact – no "exception," for all the exceptionality of the genius she possessed.

A Note on Attribution and Editing

American periodicals and newspapers, especially in the first half of the century, played fast and loose with the poetry they published, routinely reprinting without permission, dropping attributions or incorrectly citing them, and editing texts *ad libitum*. Any given "anonymous" work in this text could be by a man or a woman, by an American or not, could have been written in the nineteenth century or earlier, and could represent an accurate version of its original or a heavily edited one. These practices create obvious problems for the anthologist. In one instance, "The Beautiful Snow," published in the editorial pages of *Knickerbocker* in 1859, and other venues, I have knowingly reprinted an edited version because I find its layout more interesting than that of the purported original published in the *Irish Nationalist* some fifteen years later. In another instance, "Woman's Hard Fate" (1800), I have reprinted a poem that was widely circulated through the eighteenth century and which is very possibly British. On the whole, however, if I have made such "errors" I have made them unintentionally as part of the risk I have chosen to take. Since it is virtually certain that readers will recognize some of these poems and their authors or provenance, I would greatly appreciate hearing from them, with any corrections they can make.

When editing these poems I have wherever possible used the earliest available version of a poem as the basis for my text. Where that was not possible I have given both the poem's original date and source, when known to me, and the date of the version I have used. In all cases I have indicated the specific source for my own text. Manifest typographical errors have been corrected, but marked by the insertion of brackets. No attempt has been made, however, to "correct" legitimate nineteenth-century variants such as do'nt for don't and Shakspeare for Shakespeare. In three cases, poems have been excerpted, Brooks's "Zóphiël," Oakes Smith's "The Sinless Child," and Rose Elizabeth Cleveland's "The Dilemma of the Nineteenth Century." Otherwise all texts are presented in their entirety. Dates and texts for Dickinson's poems are based either on Johnson's 1955 variorum edition or, preferably, on the Franklin facsimiles (1981). For ease of reference Johnson-assigned numbers for Dickinson's poems have been provided. Where my texts are based on the Franklin facsimiles, I have followed Dickinson's method for indicating the placement of variants but not her lineation, except in one instance ("Four Trees – upon a solitary Acre" [742]). This decision was difficult and reflects my concerns with space and cost rather than any judgment as to the validity of arguments pro or con the use of Dickinson's own lineation.

Bibliography

Along with works referred to in this introduction, the following bibliography includes many basic texts, such as the *Encyclopedia of American Poetry*, which readers will want to consult. To minimize repetition, full bibliographic details for these latter texts are only given here, not in the supplementary reading lists accompanying individual poets' biographies.

Bain, Robert, ed. *Whitman & Dickinson's Contemporaries: An Anthology of Their Verse.* Carbondale: Southern Illinois University Press, 1996.

Bennett, Paula. "'The Descent of the Angel': Interrogating Domestic Ideology in American Women's Poetry, 1858–1890," *American Literary History* 7 (Winter 1995): 591–610.

———. "Not Just Filler, Not Just Sentimental: Women's Poetry in American Victorian Periodicals, 1860–1900," in *Periodical Literature in Nineteenth-Century America*, eds Kenneth M. Price and Susan Belasco Smith. Charlottesville and London: University Press of Virginia, 1995: 202–79.

———. "'Pomegranate-Flowers': The Phantasmic Productions of Late Nineteenth-Century Anglo-American Women Poets," in *Solitary Pleasures: The Historical, Literary, and Artistic Discourses of Autoeroticism*, eds Paula Bennett and Vernon Rosario II. New York: Routledge, 1995: 189–213.

Brooks, Cleanth and Robert Penn Warren, eds *Understanding Poetry: An Anthology for College Students*, revised edition. New York: Henry Holt and Company, 1958.

Coultrap-McQuin, Susan. *Doing Literary Business: American Women Writers in the Nineteenth Century.* Chapel Hill: University of North Carolina Press, 1990.

Davis, Gwenn and Beverly A. Joyce, comps. *Poetry by Women to 1900: A Bibliography of American and British Women Writers.* Toronto: University of Toronto Press, 1991.

Dobson, Joanne. *Dickinson and the Strategies of Reticence: the Woman Writer in Nineteenth-Century America.* Bloomington: Indiana University Press, 1989.

———. "Reclaiming Sentimental Literature," *American Literature* 69 (June 1997): 263–88.

Donoghue, Emma. *Passions Between Women: British Lesbian Culture 1668–1801.* New York: Columbia University Press, 1995.

Douglas, Ann. *The Feminization of American Culture.* New York: Knopf, 1977.

Foster, Frances. *Written by Herself: Literary Production by African American Women, 1746–1892.* Bloomington: Indiana University Press, 1993.

Gray, Janet, ed. *She Wields a Pen: American Women's Poetry of the Nineteenth-Century.* Iowa City: University of Iowa Press, 1997.

Griswold, Rufus, ed. *The Female Poets of America.* Philadelphia: Carey and Hart, 1849.

———. *The Female Poets of America*, rev. edn R. H. Stoddard. New York: James Miller, 1874.

Haralson, Eric, ed. *Encyclopedia of American Poetry: The Nineteenth Century.* Chicago and London: Fitzroy Dearborn, 1997.

Hollander, John, ed. *American Poetry: The Nineteenth Century*, 2 vols. New York: Library of America, 1993.

Howe, Julia Ward, et al., ed. and comp. *Sketches of Representative Women of New England.* Boston: New England Historical Publishing Company, 1904.

James, Edward T., et al., eds. *Notable American Women, 1607–1950*, 3 vols. Cambridge: Harvard University Press, 1971.

Kane, Paul, ed. *Poetry of the American Renaissance: A Diverse Anthology from the Romantic Period.* New York: George Braziller, 1995.

Kaplan, Amy. Plenary Speech. "The New 19th Century." Conference on 19th-Century American Women Writers in the 21st Century. Hartford, Connecticut: May 30–June 2, 1996.

Kilcup, Karen L., ed. *Nineteenth-Century American Women Writers: An Anthology.* Oxford: Blackwell Publishers, 1996.

Maniero, Lisa, ed. *American Women Writers*, 4 vols. New York: Frederick Ungar, 1979, 1980, 1981.

Mossell, Mrs N. F. *The Work of the Afro-American Woman* (1894). New York and Oxford: Oxford University Press, 1988.

Okker, Patricia. *Our Sister Editors: Sarah J. Hale and the Tradition of Nineteenth-Century American Women Editors*. Athens, Georgia: University of Georgia Press, 1995.

Santayana, George. *The Genteel Tradition; Nine Essays*, ed. Douglas L. Wilson. Cambridge, Massachusetts: Harvard University Press, 1967.

Sherman, Joan R., ed. *African-American Poetry of the Nineteenth-Century: An Anthology*. New York: Oxford University Press, 1992.

——. *Invisible Poets: Afro-Americans of the Nineteenth Century*. Urbana and Chicago: University of Illinois Press, 1989.

Smith, Barbara Herrnstein. *Contingencies of Value: Alternative Perspectives for Critical Theory*. Cambridge, Massachusetts: Harvard University Press, 1988.

Spengemann, William C. with Jessica F. Roberts, eds. *Nineteenth-Century American Poetry*. New York: Penguin, 1996.

Spofford, Harriet P. *A Little Book of Friends*. Boston: Little, Brown, 1916.

——, ed. *Our Famous Women: An Authorized Record of the Lives and Deeds of Distinguished American Women of Our Times*. Hartford, Connecticut: A. D. Worthington, 1884.

Stedman, Edmund Clarence, ed. *An American Anthology, 1787–1900*. Boston: Houghton Mifflin Company, 1900.

Tompkins, Jane. *Sensational Designs; the Cultural Work of American Fiction, 1790–1860*. New York: Oxford University Press, 1986.

Walker, Cheryl, ed. *American Women Poets of the Nineteenth Century: An Anthology*. New Brunswick: Rutgers University Press, 1992.

——. *The Nightingale's Burden: Women Poets and American Culture before 1900*. Bloomington: Indiana University Press, 1982.

Watts, Emily Stipes. *The Poetry of American Women from 1632 to 1945*. Austin and London: University of Texas Press, 1978.

Wexler, Laura. "Tender Violence: Literary Eavesdropping, Domestic Fiction, and Educational Reform," in *The Culture of Sentiment: Race, Gender, and Sentimentality in Nineteenth-Century America*, ed. Shirley Samuels. New York: Oxford, 1992: 9–38.

Yellin, Jean Fagan. *Women & Sisters: The Antislavery Feminists in American Culture*. New Haven and London: Yale University Press, 1989.

—— and Cynthia D. Bond, comps. *The Pen is Ours: A Listing of Writings by and about African-American Women before 1910 with Secondary Bibliography to the Present*. New York and Oxford: Oxford University Press, 1991.

Section I
Principal Poets

Lydia Huntley Sigourney (1791–1865)

Born September 1, 1791 to Ezekiel Huntley, caretaker of the Lathrop estate in Norwich, Connecticut, and to his second wife, Zerviah, Lydia Huntley Sigourney was an exceedingly quick child, whose precocity caught the attention of her father's employer, Mrs Daniel Lathrop. The widowed and childless Mrs Lathrop took the little girl under her wing, giving her access to the Lathrops' private library, guiding her reading, and encouraging her attendance at the local public school. After Mrs Lathrop's death in 1806, the Lathrop family continued to interest itself in Sigourney; and with the backing of Daniel Wadsworth, a wealthy Lathrop relative, she and a friend opened a private school for young women in Hartford, Connecticut, in 1814.

Sigourney's career as a teacher – a vocation for which she claims to have trained since early childhood – came to an abrupt and unhappy end in 1819 with her marriage to Charles Sigourney, a hardware merchant and widower with three children. Much older than his bride, and far more conservative, Charles Sigourney disapproved of women displaying themselves or their talents in public. In the 1820s, however, as her husband's business began to fail, Sigourney, by then a mother herself, defied him – as she had not over her teaching – and turned to writing as her best means of supplementing the family income. Although she already had two books of poetry to her credit (*Moral Pieces, in Prose and Verse*, 1815, and *Traits of the Aborigines*, 1822), her first important collection of poetry, *Poems*, came out in 1827. With it, her career as one of the early nineteenth century's most beloved and best paid women writers was launched.

By 1840, Sigourney had come to be known as "the American Mrs Hemans" after the hugely popular British woman poet, Felicia Hemans. Her reputation rested on twenty-three books whose subjects ranged from "How to be Happy," to "Evening Readings in History." Her poems were regulars in all the leading periodicals (including the *Dial*) and, if one counts reprints in newspapers, the number of her publications in any given year ranges into the hundreds. Indeed, she was so popular that by 1840, Louis Godey paid her $500 a year, just to have her name on the title page of the *Lady's Book*. Ever the shrewd businesswoman, Sigourney fostered her popularity by being extremely generous with her writing, frequently contributing poems for charitable causes, especially those which touched on her own deep-rooted political commitments – temperance, peace societies, missions among the Cherokee and Choctaw Indians, etc.

Sigourney also understood the price she paid for her popularity. In her memoir, *Letters of Life* (1866), she provides a (hilarious) sampling of requests she received, including one for an elegy on "a canary-bird, which had accidentally been starved to death," and another for an elegy on a child who had "drowned in a barrel of swine's food." She was the first American woman poet to make a full-time living out of her writing; but not surprisingly she described her Muse as "a woman of all work, and an aproned waiter" in the kitchen on Mt Parnassus. After Charles died in 1854, Sigourney lived comfortably on her own income until her death in 1865. For a caretaker's daughter, or, as her biographers insist, a "gardener's," she had come a long long way.

In many ways "the case against sentimental poetry" stands or falls on one's reading of Lydia Huntley Sigourney. Pilloried by earlier critics, most notably her biographer, Gordon Haight, as the "Sweet Singer of Hartford," she can be written off as the archetypal nineteenth-century poetess, a writer whose obsession with death, especially child death, makes her the foremother of an entire century of Emmeline Grangerfords. Conversely, she can be viewed – as she is presented here – as a basically political writer, whose particular concerns –

Indians, women, the environment, peace, etc. – make her a highly sympathetic figure for audiences today. In fact, of course, both perspectives are true.

Sigourney's complexity as a writer reflects her complexity as a deeply religious woman who was nevertheless keenly sensitive to the social inequities of class and gender against which she struggled most of her life. (The latter are both areas of tension in her poetry that have yet to be explored.) At the same time, this complexity also reflects the complexity of the sentimental discourse in which she wrote, a discourse that could be used either to support the status quo or to subvert it. At different times, or even at the same time (as in "The Cherokee Mother"), Sigourney does both, making her poetry far less transparent – and far more elusive – than it is generally credited with being.

Even less recognized, Sigourney could also be very witty, not the least at her own expense. "Flora's Party" is a bravura performance that suggests she was an acute observer of the class to which she belonged, what I would call, for want of a better term, the century's *nouveau genteel*. And like sections of *Letters of Life*, this poem's strengths pose the possibility that Sigourney might have flourished as a writer, not just a cultural figure, had she been able to give full rein to her satirical and ironical bent. Had she, however, one doubts the church bells of Hartford would have rung for an hour when she died.

Primary Texts

Moral Pieces, in Prose and Verse, 1815; *Traits of the Aborigines of America*, 1822; *Poems*, 1827; *Poems*, 1834; *Zinzendorff, and Other Poems*, 1836; *Letters to Mothers*, 1838; *Pocahontas, and Other Poems*, 1841; *Scenes in My Native Land*, 1845; *Select Poems*, 1842; *The Western Home, and Other Poems*, 1854; *Letters of Life*, 1866.

Further Reading

Nina Baym, "Reinventing Lydia Sigourney," in *Feminism and American Literary History*, New Brunswick, New Jersey: Rutgers University Press, 1992, 151–5; Patricia Crain, "Lydia Huntley Sigourney," *Encyclopedia of American Poetry*; Ann Douglas, *The Feminization of American Culture*; Mary G. DeJong, "Legacy Profile: Lydia Huntley Sigourney (1791–1865)," *Legacy: A Journal of Nineteenth-Century American Women Writers* 5 (Spring 1988): 35–43; Annie Finch, "The Sentimental Poetess in the World: Metaphor and Subjectivity in Lydia Sigourney's Nature Poetry," *Legacy: A Journal of Nineteenth-Century American Women Writers* 5 (Fall 1988): 3–18; Gordon Haight, *Mrs. Sigourney: The Sweet Singer of Hartford*, New Haven: Yale University Press, 1930; Sandra Zagarell, "Expanding 'America': Lydia Sigourney's *Sketch of Connecticut*, Catherine Sedgwick's *Hope Leslie*," *Tulsa Studies in Women's Literature* 6 (1987): 225–46.

from *Poems* (1827)

THE ALPINE FLOWERS

Meek dwellers mid yon terror-stricken cliffs!
With brows so pure, and incense-breathing lips,
Whence are ye? – Did some white wing'd messenger,
On Mercy's missions trust your timid germ
To the cold cradle of eternal snows?
Or, breathing on the callous icicles,

5

Bid them with tear-drops nurse ye? —
        — Tree nor shrub
Dare that drear atmosphere, — nor polar pine
Uprears a veteran front, — yet there *ye* stand,   10
Leaning your cheeks against the thick ribb'd ice,
And looking up with brilliant eyes to Him
Who bids you bloom unblanch'd, amid the waste
Of desolation.   Man, who panting toils
O'er slippery steeps, or trembling treads the verge   15
Of yawning gulfs, o'er which the headlong plunge
Is to Eternity, looks shuddering up,
And marks ye in your placid loveliness
Fearless, yet frail, and clasping his chill hands
Blesses your pencil'd beauty.   Mid the pomp   20
Of mountain summits rushing to the sky,
And chaining the rapt soul in breathless awe,
He bows to bind you drooping to his breast,
Inhales your spirit from the frost-wing'd gale,
And freer dreams of Heaven.   25

THE SUTTEE[1]

She sat upon the pile by her dead lord,
And in her full, dark eye, and shining hair
Youth revell'd. — The glad murmur of the crowd
Applauding her consent to the dread doom,
And the hoarse chanting of infuriate priests   5
She heeded not, for her quick ear had caught
An infant's wail. — Feeble and low that moan,
Yet it was answer'd in her heaving heart,
For the Mimosa[2] in its shrinking fold

From the rude pressure, is not half so true,   10
So tremulous, as is a mother's soul
Unto her wailing babe. — There was such wo
In her imploring aspect, — in her tones
Such thrilling agony, that even the hearts
Of the flame-kindlers soften'd, and they laid   15
The famish'd infant on her yearning breast.
There with his tear-wet cheek he lay and drew
Plentiful nourishment from that full fount
Of infant happiness, — and long he prest
With eager lip the chalice of his joy. —   20
And then his little hands he stretch'd to grasp
His mother's flower-wove tresses, and with smile
And gay caress embraced his bloated sire, —

THE SUTTEE
[1] *Sati* The Indian funeral practice in which the widow immolated herself on the funeral pyre of her husband.   [2] A subtropical plant whose leaves are sensitive to the touch.

As if kind Nature taught that innocent one
With fond delay to cheat the hour which seal'd   25
His hopeless orphanage. – But those were near
Who mock'd such dalliance, as that Spirit malign
Who twined his serpent length mid Eden's bowers
Frown'd on our parents' bliss. – The victim mark'd
Their harsh intent, and clasp'd the unconscious babe   30
With such convulsive force, that when they tore
His writhing form away, the very nerves
Whose deep-sown fibres rack the inmost soul
Uprooted seem'd. –
                          With voice of high command   35
Tossing her arms, she bade them bring her son, –
And then in maniac rashness sought to leap
Among the astonish'd throng. – But the rough cord
Compress'd her slender limbs, and bound her fast
Down to her loathsome partner – Quick the fire   40
In showers was hurl'd upon the reeking pile; –
But yet amid the wild, demoniac shout
Of priest and people, mid the thundering yell
Of the infernal gong, – was heard to rise
Thrice a dire death-shriek. – And the men who stood   45
Near the red pile and heard that fearful cry,
Call'd on their idol-gods, and stopp'd their ears,
And oft amid their nightly dream would start
As frighted Fancy echoed in her cell
That burning mother's scream.   50

DEATH OF AN INFANT

Death found strange beauty on that cherub brow,
And dash'd it out. – There was a tint of rose
On cheek and lip; – he touched the veins with ice,
And the rose faded. – Forth from those blue eyes
There spake a wishful tenderness, – a doubt   5
Whether to grieve or sleep, which Innocence
Alone may wear. – With ruthless haste he bound
The silken fringes of their curtaining lids
Forever. – There had been a murmuring sound,
With which the babe would claim its mother's ear,   10
Charming her even to tears. – The spoiler set
The seal of silence. – But there beam'd a smile,
So fix'd and holy from that marble brow, –
Death gazed and left it there; – he dared not steal
The signet-ring[3] of Heaven.   15

DEATH OF AN INFANT
[3]   A ring containing a signet or private seal of an
individual or organization.

from *Cherokee Phoenix* (1831)

THE CHEROKEE MOTHER[4]

Ye bid us hence. – These vales are dear,
 To infant hope, to patriot pride, –
These streamlets tuneful to our ear,
 Where our light shallops[5] peaceful glide,

Beneath yon consecrated mounds   5
 Our fathers' treasur'd ashes rest,
Our hands have till'd these corn-clad grounds, –
 Our children's birth these homes have blest,

Here, on our souls a Saviour's love
 First beam'd with renovating ray,   10
Why should we from these haunts remove? –
 But still you warn us hence away. –

Child, ask not where! – I cannot tell,
 Save where wide wastes uncultur'd spread,
Where unknown waters fiercely roll,   15
 And savage monsters howling tread;

Where no blest Church with hallow'd train,
 Nor hymns of praise, nor voice of prayer,
Like angels sooth the wanderer's pain;
 Ask me no more. – I know not where.   20

Go seek thy Sire. – The anguish charm
 That shades his brow like frowning wrath,
Divide the burden from his arm,
 And gird him for his pilgrim-path.

Come, moaning babe! – Thy mothers arms'   25
 Shall bear thee on our weary course,
Shall be thy shield from midnight harms,
 And baleful dews, and tempests hoarse.

THE CHEROKEE MOTHER
[4] When this poem appeared in the *Cherokee Phoenix* it was accompanied by a "Letter to the Delegation of the State of Connecticut," penned by Sigourney on behalf of an "Association of Ladies," protesting President Andrew Jackson's removal policy. In the letter (or "memorial," as such open letters were called), Sigourney states her strategy explicitly: "It will probably be alledged that we have viewed this subject solely through the medium of *feeling*. This was our intention" ([March 12, 1831]: 3). The removal policy was implemented in 1838 when the Cherokee were compelled to make a forced march out to Oklahoma on what has since come to be known as "the Trail of Tears." In 1831, when this poem was written, the Supreme Court had just decreed that the Cherokee would have to leave their ancestral lands.
[5] A light, open boat, used mainly on rivers, propelled by oars or sails or both.

But thou, Oh Father! old and blind,
   Who shall *thy* failing footsteps stay?   30
Who prop thy sorrow-stricken mind
   Driven from thy native earth away?

An exile in thy hoary hairs,
   And hopeless when life's toils are o'er
To mix thy mouldering dust with theirs,   35
   Those blessed sires, who weep no more.

Ye call us brethren. When ye mark
   The grass upon our thresholds grown,
Our hearth-stone cold, – our casements dark,
   Our fated race like shadows flown,   40

Amid your mirth, your festive songs
   Will no remorseful image lower?
No memory of the Indian's wrongs
   Rise darkly o'er your musing hour?

Will a crush'd nation's deep despair,   45
   Your broken faith, – our tear-wet sod,
The babe's appeal, – the chieftain's prayer,
   Find no memorial[6] with our God?

from *Poems* (1834)

FLORA'S PARTY

Lady Flora gave cards for a party at tea,
To flowers, buds and blossoms of every degree;
So from town and from country they thronged at the call,
And strove by their charms to embellish the hall.
   First came the exotics, with ornaments rare,   5
The tall Miss Corcoris, and Cyclamen fair,
Auricula,[7] splendid with jewels new set,
And gay Polyanthus,[8] the pretty coquette.
The Tulips came flounting in gaudy array,
With Hyacinths bright as the eye of the day;   10
Dandy Coxcombs[9] and Daffodils, rich and polite,
With their dazzling new vests and their corsets laced tight,

---

6   Sigourney makes a chilling pun on memorial here.
FLORA'S PARTY
7   A central European primrose having large yellow flowers. Auricula derives from the Latin aurum, for gold. This is one of many puns that make this poem a delight to read.

8   Hybrid garden primrose with many different colored blossoms.
9   Primary meaning, a conceited dandy.

While the Soldiers in Green, cavalierly attired,
Were all by the ladies extremely admired.
But prudish Miss Lily,[10] with bosom of snow,   15
Declared that "the officers stared at her *so*,
'Twas excessively rude," so retired in a fright,
And scarce paused to bid Lady Flora good night.
There were Myrtles and Roses from garden and plain,
And Venus's Fly-trap they brought in their train;   20
So the beaux clustered round them, they scarcely knew why,
At each smile of the lip, or each glance of the eye.
    Madame Damask[11] complained of her household and care,
How she seldom went out even to breathe the fresh air;
There were so many young ones and servants to stray,   25
And the thorns grew so fast if *her* eye was away:
"Neighbour Moss Rose," said she, "you who live like a queen,
And scarce wet your fingers, do'nt know what I mean:"
So that notable lady went on with her lay,
Till the auditors yawned and stole softly away.   30
    The sweet Misses Woodbine, from country and town,
With their brother-in-law, Colonel Trumpet, came down;
And Lupine, whose azure-eye sparkled with dew,
On Amaranth[12] leaned, the unchanging and true,
While modest Clematis appeared as a bride,   35
And her husband, the Lilac, ne'er moved from her side,
Though the belles giggled loudly and vowed "'twas a shame,
For a young married chit such attention to claim;
They never attended a rout in their life,
Where a city-bred gentleman spoke to his wife."   40
    Mrs Piony came in quite late, in a heat,
With the Ice-plant, new spangled from forehead to feet;
Lobelia, attired like a queen in her pride,
And the Dahlias, with trimmings new-furbished and dyed;
And the Blue-bells and Hare-bells, in simple array,   45
With all their Scotch cousins from highland and brae,[13]
Ragged Ladies and Marigolds clustered together,
And gossiped of scandal, the news, and the weather –
What dresses were worn at the wedding so fine
Of sharp Mr. Thistle[14] and sweet Columbine;   50
Of the loves of Sweet William and Lily the prude,
Till the clamours of Babel again seemed renewed.
In a snug little nook sate the Jessamine pale,

---

[10]   The lily is associated traditionally with the Virgin Mary, as a symbol of her chastity.
[11]   The Damask rose; but damask also means a richly patterned fabric, often used for tablecloths, therefore the association with housewifery.

[12]   Any of various annuals that have dense green or reddish clusters of flowers; secondary meaning, an imaginary flower that never fades.
[13]   Steep slope or hillside, especially the steep bank of a river.
[14]   Plant bearing prickly leaves and colored flower heads surrounded by prickly bracts.

And that pure fragrant Lily, the gem of the vale;
The meek Mountain-daisy, with the delicate crest,   55
And the Violet, whose eye told the heaven in her breast;
While allured to their group were the wise ones who bowed
To that virtue which seeks not the praise of the crowd.
But the proud Crown Imperial, who wept in her heart
That modesty gained of such homage a part,   60
Looked haughtily down on their innocent mien,
And spread out her gown that they might not be seen.
    The bright Lady-slippers and Sweet-briars agreed
With their slim cousin Aspens a measure to lead;
And sweet 'twas to see their light footsteps advance   65
Like the wing of the breeze through the maze of the dance;
But the Monk's-hood[15] scowled dark, and in utterance low,
Declared, "'twas high time for Good Christians to go;
He'd heard from his parson a sermon sublime,
Where he proved from the Vulgate[16] – *to dance was a crime.*"   70
So folding a cowl round his cynical head,
He took from the side-board a bumper[17] and fled.
    A song was desired, but each musical flower
Had "taken a cold, and 'twas out of her power;"
Till sufficiently urged, they burst forth in a strain   75
Of quavers and thrills that astonished the train.
Mimosa sat shrinking, and said with a sigh –
"'Twas so fine, she was ready with rapture to die:"
And Cactus, the grammar-school tutor, declared
"It might be with the gamut of Orpheus[18] compared:"   80
But Night-Shade,[19] the metaphysician, complained
That "the nerves of his ears were excessively pained;
'Twas but seldom he crept from the college, he said,
And he wished himself safe in his study or bed."
    There were pictures whose splendour illumined the place,   85
Which Flora had finished with exquisite grace:
She had dipped her free pencil in Nature's pure dies,
And Aurora[20] re-touched with fresh purple the skies.
So the grave connoisseurs hasted near them to draw,
Their knowledge to show by detecting a flaw.   90
The Carnation took her eye-glass from her waist,
And pronounced they were "scarce in good keeping or taste."
While prim Fleur de Lis,[21] in her robe of French silk,
And magnificent Calla, with mantle like milk,
Of the Louvre recited a wonderful tale,   95

---

[15]   A slender erect poisonous herb.
[16]   Latin version of the Scripture, mostly the work of St Jerome in the fourth century CE.
[17]   Drink.
[18]   Legendary Thracian poet and musician.
[19]   Common name for the Solanaceae family of herbs, shrubs, and a few trees. Used for medicinal purposes, including sedatives, from ancient times.
[20]   Roman name for the goddess of Dawn.
[21]   Stylized emblem of a lily long associated with the French crown.

And said "Guido's[22] rich tints made dame Nature turn pale."
Mr. Snowball assented, proceeding to add
His opinion that "*all Nature's colouring was bad*;"
He had thought so e'er since a few days he had spent
To study the paintings of Rome, as he went   100
To visit his classmate Gentiana, who chose
His abode on the Alps, in a palace of snow:
But he took on Mont Blanc[23] such a terrible chill
That ever since that he'd been pallid and ill.

    Half withered Miss Hackmetack[24] bought a new glass,   105
And thought with her nieces, the Spruces, to pass;
But Bachelor Holly, who spyed her out late,
Destroyed all her hopes by a hint at her date:
So she pursed up her mouth and said tartly with scorn,
"*She could not remember before she was born.*"   110
Old Jonquil the crooked-backed beau had been told
That a tax would be laid on bachelor's gold;
So he bought a new coat and determined to try
The long disused armour of Cupid, so sly,
Sought out half opened buds in their infantine years,   115
And ogled them all, till they blushed to the ears.

    Philosopher Sage,[25] on a sofa was prosing,
With good Dr. Chamomile[26] quietly dozing;
Though the Laurel descanted with eloquent breath,
Of heroes and battles, of victory and death,   120
Of the conquests of Greece, and Botzaris[27] the brave,
"He had trod on his steps and had sighed o'er his grave."
Farmer Sunflower[28] was near, and decidedly spake
Of the "poultry he fed, and the oil he might make;"
For the true-hearted soul deemed a weather-stained face,   125
And a toil-hardened hand no mark of disgrace.
Then he beckoned his nieces to rise from their seat,
The plump Dandelion and Cowslip[29] so neat,
And bade them to "pack up their duds and away
For he believed in his heart 'twas the break o' the day."   130
    'Twas indeed very late, and the coaches were brought,
For the grave matron flowers of their nurseries thought;
The lustre was dimmed of each drapery rare,
And the lucid young brows looked beclouded with care;
All save the bright Cereus,[30] that belle so divine,   135
Who preferred through the curtains of midnight to shine.

---

[22] Guido Reni (1575–1642), Italian painter and engraver.
[23] Mountain in France.
[24] Larch. Coniferous tree that is unusual in that it is not an evergreen.
[25] A herb of the genus Salvia; with a pun on having wisdom and calm judgment.
[26] An aromatic herb traditionally used medicinally.
[27] Markos Botsaris (c. 1788–1823), Greek patriot, prominent in the Greek war for independence.
[28] A flower harvested agriculturally for its seeds and oil.
[29] Common meadow flowers typically found on rural land.
[30] Night-blooming flower.

Now they curtseyed and bowed, as they moved to the door,
But the Poppy[31] snored loud ere the parting was o'er,
For Night her last candle was snuffing away,
And Flora grew tired, though she begged them to stay;   140
Exclaimed "all the watches and clocks were too fast,
And old Time ran in spite, lest her pleasure should last."
But when the last guest went with daughter and wife,
She vowed she "was never so glad in her life;"
Called out to her maids, who with weariness wept,   145
To "wash all the glasses and cups ere they slept;
For Aurora, that pimp,[32] with her broad, staring eye,
Always tried in her house some disorder to spy:"
Then she sipped some pure honey-dew, fresh from the lawn,
And with Zephyrons[33] hasted to sleep until dawn.   150

INDIAN NAMES

*"How can the red men be forgotten, while so many of our states and
territories, bays, lakes and rivers, are indelibly stamped by names of
their giving?"*

Ye say they all have passed away,
    That noble race and brave,
That their light canoes have vanished
    From off the crested wave;
That 'mid the forests where they roamed   5
    There rings no hunter shout,
But their names is[34] on your waters,
    Ye may not wash it out.

'Tis where Ontario's billow
    Like Ocean's surge is curled,   10
Where strong Niagara's thunders wake
    The echo of the world.
Where red Missouri bringeth
    Rich tribute from the west,
And Rappahannock[35] sweetly sleeps   15
    On green Virginia's breast.

Ye say their cone-like cabins,
    That clustered o'er the vale,
Have fled away like withered leaves
    Before the autumn gale,   20
But their memory liveth on your hills,
    Their baptism on your shore,

---

[31] A flower with sleep-inducing properties.
[32] There may be a sexual innuendo here.
[33] God of the West wind.

INDIAN NAMES
[34] This solecism appears to be deliberate on Sigourney's
part. See l. 9.
[35] A river in northeast Virginia.

Your everlasting rivers speak
  Their dialect of yore.

Old Massachusetts wears it,   25
  Within her lordly crown,
And broad Ohio bears it,
  Amid his young renown;
Connecticut hath wreathed it
  Where her quiet foliage waves,   30
And bold Kentucky breathed it hoarse
  Through all her ancient caves.

Wachuset[36] hides its lingering voice
  Within his rocky heart,
And Alleghany graves its tone   35
  Throughout his lofty chart;
Monadnock[37] on his forehead hoar
  Doth seal the sacred trust,
Your mountains build their monument,
  Though ye destroy their dust.   40

Ye call these red-browed brethren
  The insects of an hour,
Crushed like the noteless worm amid
  The regions of their power;
Ye drive them from their father's lands,   45
  Ye break of faith the seal,
But can ye from the court of Heaven
  Exclude their last appeal?

Ye see their unresisting tribes,
  With toilsome step and slow,   50
On through the trackless desert pass,
  A caravan of woe;
Think ye the Eternal's ear is deaf?
  His sleepless vision dim?
Think ye the *soul's blood* may not cry   55
  From that far land to him?

from *Family Magazine* (1834)

THE WESTERN EMIGRANT

Amid these forest shades that proudly reared
Their unshorn beauty towards the favouring skies,

---

[36]   An isolated peak in central Massachusetts.   [37]   Mountain in southwest New Hampshire.

An axe rang sharply. There, with vigorous arm,
Wrought a bold emigrant, while by his side
His little son with question and response   5
Beguiled the toil.
                    "Boy, thou hast never seen
Such glorious trees, and when the giant trunks
Fall, how the firm earth groans. Rememberest thou
The mighty river on whose breast we sailed   10
So many days on toward the setting sun?
Compared to that our own Connecticut
Is but a creeping stream."
                          "Father, the brook,
That by our door went singing, when I launched   15
My tiny boat with all the sportive boys,
When school was o'er, is dearer far to me
Than all these deep broad waters. To my eye
They are as strangers. And those little trees
My mother planted in the garden, bound,   20
Of our *first home*, from whence the fragrant peach
Fell in its ripening gold, were fairer sure
Than this dark forest shutting out the day."
    "What, ho! my little girl," and with light step
A fairy creature hasted toward her sire,   25
And setting down the basket that contained
The noon's repast, looked upward to his face
With sweet, confiding smile.
                            "See, dearest, see
Yon bright-winged paroquet,[38] and hear the song   30
Of the gay red-bird echoing through the trees,
Making rich musick. Did'st thou ever hear
In far New England such a mellow tone?"
    "I had a robin that did take the crumbs
Each night and morning, and his chirping voice   35
Did make me joyful, as I went to tend
My snow-drops. I was always laughing there,
In that *first home*. I should be happier now,
Methinks, if I could find among these dells
The same fresh violets."   40
                        Slow night drew on,
And round the rude hut of the emigrant,
The wrathful spirit of the autumn storm
Spake bitter things. His wearied children slept,
And he, with head declined, sat listening long   45
To the swollen waters of the Illinois,
Dashing against their shores. Starting, he spake:

---

[38]   Parakeet.

"Wife! did I see thee brush away a tear?
Say, was it so? Thy heart was with the halls
Of thy nativity. Their sparkling lights,   50
Carpets and sofas, and admiring guests,
Befit thee better than these rugged walls
Of shapeless logs, and this lone hermit-home."
    "No, No! all was so still around, methought,
Upon my ear that echoed hymn did steal   55
Which 'mid the church, where erst we paid our vows,
So tuneful pealed. But tenderly thy voice
Dissolved the illusion;" and the gentle smile
Lighting her brow, the fond caress that soothed
Her waking infant, re-assured his soul   60
That whereso'er the pure affections dwell
And strike a healthful root, is happiness.
    Placid and grateful to his rest he sank;
But dreams, those wild magicians, which do play
Such pranks when reason slumbers, tireless wrought   65
Their will with him. Up rose the busy mart
Of his own native city: roof and spire
All glittering bright, in fancy's frost-work ray.
Forth came remembered forms; with curving neck
The steed his boyhood nurtured, proudly neighed   70
The favourite dog, exulting round his feet,
Frisked, with shrill, joyous bark; familiar doors
Flew open; greeting hands with his were linked
In friendship's grasp; he heard the keen debate
From congregated haunts, where mind with mind   75
Doth blend and brighten; and till morning roved
'Mid the loved scenery of his father-land.

from *Zinzendorff, and Other Poems* (1836)

THE INDIAN'S WELCOME TO THE PILGRIM FATHERS

"On Friday, March 16th, 1622, while the colonists were busied in their
usual labors, they were much surprised to see a savage walk boldly towards
them, and salute them with, 'much welcome, English, much welcome,
Englishmen.'" [39]

Above them spread a stranger sky
    Around the sterile plain,
The rock-bound coast rose frowning nigh,
    Beyond, – the wrathful main:

THE INDIAN'S WELCOME TO THE PILGRIM FATHERS
[39] The source for this epigraph is not known but the incident itself is described by William Bradford in Chapter 11, Book II, of *Of Plymouth Plantation.*

Chill remnants of the wintry snow   5
    Still chok'd the encumber'd soil,
Yet forth these Pilgrim Fathers go,
    To mark their future toil.

'Mid yonder vale their corn must rise
    In Summer's ripening pride,   10
And there the church-spire woo the skies
    Its sister-school beside.
Perchance 'mid England's velvet green
    Some tender thought repos'd, –
Though nought upon their stoic mien   15
    Such soft regret disclos'd.

When sudden from the forest wide
    A red-brow'd chieftain came,
With towering form, and haughty stride,
    And eye like kindling flame: 20
No wrath he breath'd, no conflict sought,
    To no dark ambush drew,
But simply *to the Old World brought*,
    The welcome of the New.

That *welcome* was a blast and ban   25
    Upon thy race unborn.
Was there no seer, thou fated Man!
    Thy lavish zeal to warn?
Thou in thy fearless faith didst hail
    A weak, invading band,   30
But who shall heed thy children's wail,
    Swept from their native land?

Thou gav'st the riches of thy streams,
    The lordship o'er thy waves,
The region of thine infant dreams,   35
    And of thy fathers' graves,
But who to yon proud mansions pil'd
    With wealth of earth and sea,
Poor outcast from thy forest wild,
    Say, who shall welcome thee?   40

from *Select Poems* (1842)

THE VOLUNTEER

Thou'lt go! Thou'lt go!
         In vain, thy stricken wife,
A poor, unconscious infant in her arms,
And thy young children, clinging to thy hand

Implore thy stay. Thine aged parents bend   5
In prayer, and sorrow. Hath the battle-field
Such charms for thee, that thou wilt tread on all
That love and nature give, and rush to reap
Its iron harvest?
          Lo! the roughen'd men,   10
Thy boon[40] companions, 'neath the neighboring hedge
Do wait for thee. The vow hath past thy lips
And thou must go.
            So, hence away, and share
Such pleasures, as thy chosen course may yield;   15
The stirring drum, the pomp of measur'd march,
The pride of uniform, the gazer's shout
Of admiration, the alternate rest
Of idleness in camps, and toil that wastes
The nerveless limb, and starts the sleepless eye.   20
Take too, the stormy joy of deadly strife,
Spill blood, and trample on the mangled form
And like a demon, drink the groans of pain.

Yet sometimes, when the midnight bowl is drained
And thou art tossing in thy broken dream,   25
Bethink thee, soldier, of a cottage home
All desolate, its drooping vines untrained,
Its wintry hearth unfed, and she, with cheek
As pale as penury and woe can make,
(Why dost thou start?) and her once blooming ones   30
Some at hard service, where their bitter bread
Is scantily doled out, and some who ask
Her shuddering heart, for what she cannot give.

– Still doth the vision open?
              There are graves!   35
The white-hair'd father hath his rest in one,
And she, who died lamenting for the son
Who snatch'd the morsel from her feeble hand,
Nor sought her blessing when he went to war,
Sleeps in the other.   40
           Dreamer! wake not yet.
Mar not the sequel. Toward the peaceful shades
Of his own village, comes a poor, lone man
Whom misery and vice have made their own.
His head is bandaged, and his swollen limbs   45
Drag heavily. He hath no threshold stone,
No friend to welcome.

THE VOLUNTEER
[40] *Boon* congenial, intimate, merry.

Is this he who scorn'd
His heaven sworn duties, and his humble home,
And chose his pittance from the cannon's mouth?   50

from *Christian Parlor Magazine* (1844)

A SCENE AT SEA

The summer-moon shone bright upon the deck,
And steadily the vessel o'er the deep
Pursued her way.

             I heard a voice that said,
Death was among us. To the hardy throng   5
Of Erin's[41] sons, who in our little realm
Maintain'd a separate commonwealth, we turn'd,
For there the stern Destroyer wrought his will.
– Stretch'd on his cradle-crib, a boy we found
Of some two summers, nobly form'd and fair,   10
Who slept, to wake no more.

               The mother lay
Upon her face beside him, and replied
Nought, to our soothing words. But at the hush
Of solemn midnight, when the watch was set,   15
Then burst her cry, with startling shrillness forth,
To her dead child.

             "Oh! wherefore did ye die,
My beautiful? Had ye not food enough?
Sweet bread, and purest milk, and tenderest care?   20
Did ye not long your father's home to see,
That emerald isle, the jewel of the world?
And now, when every moment brings us near
To proud Dungannon's[42] cliffs, and green Kinsale,[43]
Why are ye there, so pale, with close-shut eyes?   25
The poor old grandmother, upon her crutch,
Will from the shieling[44] haste to welcome ye –
And I – what shall I say? With empty arms
I'll stand before her, weeping. Oh! my boy!
Why did ye die and leave me?"   30

              Thus she mourn'd,
While but the mocking billows answer'd her.
Yet on the morrow, when the morn was high,

A SCENE AT SEA

[41] *Erin* Gaelic for Ireland.

[42] Rural district in Northern Ireland.

[43] Urban district and seaport in southwest Ireland.

[44] *Shieling* Gaelic for hut or rude shelter.

Up from the steerage came a slow-pac'd train,
And on a plank that thro' the port-hole pass'd   35
Laid the dead child. Then, with a sudden plunge
He went, uncoffin'd, to his wat'ry grave,
Without one hallow'd breath of prayer, or hymn,
To bless the obsequies.

            As day roll'd on,   40
I saw the mother, with red, swollen eyes,
Intent, as usual, on her humble tasks,
Seething[45] the pottage[46] for her husband's meal,
Or with her cronies chatting. And I felt
That Hand was merciful, which still'd so soon   45
The storm of wild emotion, and drew back
The bitter waters from the human heart,
Lest it should drop its burdens ere the time,
And sink, in sad despair.

            But yet, how sad   50
Is death upon the sea! One, at your side,
Faints in his narrow cabin, and is gone.
To-day, you greet the fellow-voyager
With kindly words: – to-morrow stretch your hand,
And touch his vacant pillow. He hath found   55
A couch on ocean's floor.

            Death smiles on land
In broader space. We turn us from his wreck,
To field, or forest, or embroider'd vale,
'Scaping his shafts awhile, and finding still   60
A footing firm. But in the tossing ship
He presseth to your side. You feel the wind
Chill on your bosom, from his sable wings.
He seems to do his work without a veil,
Well-pleas'd that but a single inch of plank   65
Divides the living, and the laughing ones,
From his throng'd empire in the unfathom'd deep.

from *Mother's Assistant and Young Lady's Friend* (1849)

MORNING

See the light mist
That spreads its white wing to the heavens away,
See the fresh blossoms, by the blithe bee kissed,
The hill-top kindling 'neath the king of day,

---

[45] *Seething* boiling.

[46] *Pottage* a dish of meat and vegetables, boiled until tender and seasoned.

    Spire after spire that drinks the genial ray.   5
    The rocks that in their rifted[47] holds abide,
And darkly frown with heads forever grey,
    While the clear stream gleams out in trembling pride,
Through its transparent veil, like a fair, timid bride.

from *The Western Home, and Other Poems* (1854)

FALLEN FORESTS[48]

Man's warfare on the trees is terrible.
He lifts his rude hut in the wilderness,
And lo! the loftiest trunks, that age on age
Were nurtured to nobility, and bore
Their summer coronets so gloriously,   5
Fall with a thunder sound to rise no more.
    He toucheth flame unto them, and they lie
A blackened wreck, their tracery and wealth
Of sky-fed emerald, madly spent, to feed
An arch of brilliance for a single night,   10
And scaring thence the wild deer, and the fox,
And the lithe squirrel from the nut-strewn home,
So long enjoyed.   He lifts his puny arm,
And every echo of the axe doth hew   15
The iron heart of centuries away.
He entereth boldly to the solemn groves
On whose green altar tops, since time was young,
The wingéd birds have poured their incense stream;
Of praise and love, within whose mighty nave[49]   20
The wearied cattle from a thousand hills
Have found their shelter mid the heat of day;
Perchance in their mute worship pleasing Him
Who careth for the meanest He hath made.
I said, he entereth to the sacred groves   25
Where nature in her beauty bows to God,
And, lo! their temple arch is desecrate.

MORNING
[17] *Rifted* cleaved, divided.

FALLEN FORESTS
[18] In an accompanying (Thoreauvian) comment to this poem in *Scenes in My Native Land* (1845), where the poem, in a slightly different version, first appeared, Sigourney writes of environmental conditions in western New York, "Hills and vales are seen covered with stately and immense trunks, blackened with flame, and smitten down in every form and variety of misery. They lie like soldiers, when battle is done, in the waters, among the ashes, wounded, beheaded, denuded of their limbs, their exhumed roots, like *chevaux de frise*, [a wire entanglement, or other moveable barrier, used to hinder cavalry advance] glaring on the astonished eye.... Cromwell advanced not more surely from Naseby to the throne, than the axe-armed settler to the destruction of the kingly trees of Heaven's anointing" (p. 119).
[19] *Nave* center, hub, especially of a church.

Sinks the sweet hymn, the ancient ritual fades,
And uptorn roots and prostrate columns mark
The invader's footsteps.   30
                       Silent years roll on,
His babes are men. His ant-heap dwelling grows
Too narrow – for his hand hath gotten wealth.
He builds a stately mansion, but it stands
Unblessed by trees.   He smote them recklessly   35
When their green arms were round him, as a guard
Of tutelary[50] deities, and feels
Their maledictions, now the burning noon
Maketh his spirit faint. With anxious care,
He casteth acorns in the earth, and woos   40
Sunbeam and rain; he planteth the young shoot,
And props it from the storm; but neither he,
Nor yet his children's children, shall behold
What he hath swept away.
                       Methinks, 'twere well,   45
Not as a spoiler or a thief to prey
On Nature's bosom, that sweet, gentle nurse
Who loveth us, and spreads a sheltering couch
When our brief task is o'er. O'er that green mound
Affection's hand may set the willow tree,   50
Or train the cypress, and let none profane
Her pious care.
                Oh, Father! grant us grace
In all life's toils, so, with a steadfast hand
Evil and good to poise, as not to pave   55
Our way with wrecks, nor leave our blackened name
A beacon to the way-worn mariner.
           (*Scenes in My Native Land* 1845)

BELL OF THE WRECK

The bell of the steamer Atlantic, lost in Long-Island Sound, Nov. 25th, 1846, being supported by portions of the wreck and the contiguous rock, continued to toll, swept by wind and surge, the requiem of the dead.

       Toll, toll, toll,
         Thou bell by billows swung,
       And night and day thy warning words
         Repeat with mournful tongue!
       Toll for the queenly boat,   5
         Wreck'd on yon rocky shore;
       Sea-weed is in her palace-halls,
         She rides the surge no more!

---

[50] *Tutelary*   protecting, guarding.

Toll for the master bold,
  The high-soul'd and the brave,
Who ruled her like a thing of life
  Amid the crested wave!
Toll for the hardy crew,
  Sons of the storm and blast,
Who long the tyrant Ocean dared,
  But it vanquish'd them at last!

Toll for the man of God,
  Whose hallow'd voice of prayer
Rose calm above the stifled groan
  Of that intense despair!
How precious were those tones
  On that sad verge of life,
Amid the fierce and freezing storm,
  And the mountain-billows' strife!

Toll for the lover lost
  To the summon'd bridal train!
Bright glows a picture on his breast,
  Beneath the unfathom'd main.
One from her casement gazeth
  Long o'er the misty sea;
He cometh not, pale maiden,
  His heart is cold to thee!

Toll for the absent sire,
  Who to his home drew near,
To bless a glad expecting group,
  Fond wife, and children dear!
They heap the blazing hearth,
  The festal board is spread,
But a fearful guest is at the gate:
  Room for the sheeted dead!

Toll for the loved and fair,
  The whelm'd beneath the tide,
The broken harps around whose strings
  The dull sea-monsters glide!
Mother and nursling sweet,
  Reft from the household throng;
There's bitter weeping in the nest
  Where breath'd their soul of song.

Toll for the hearts that bleed
  'Neath misery's furrowing trace!
Toll for the hapless orphan left
  The last of all his race!

10

15

20

25

30

35

40

45

50

Yea, with thy heaviest knell
    From surge to rocky shore,
Toll for the living, not the dead,   55
    Whose mortal woes are o'er!

Toll, toll, toll,
    O'er breeze and billow free,
And with thy startling lore instruct
    Each rover of the sea;   60
Tell how o'er proudest joys
    May swift destruction sweep,
And bid him build his hopes on high,
    Lone Teacher of the deep!

Maria Gowen Brooks (1794?–1845)

Dubbed Maria del Occidente by the British poet, Robert Southey, her great admirer, Maria Gowen Brooks (née Abigail Gowen) was born in Medford, Massachusetts, about 1794. Her father, William Gowen, took an active interest in her education and had her reading and memorizing the major British poets (Southey included) by age nine. When her father's death in 1809 left the family in severe financial straits, Brooks's widowed brother-in-law, John Brooks, a man of fifty with two children, helped finance the remainder of her education. She is said to have married him out of gratitude. If so, it was gratitude misplaced.

Plagued by financial reverses during the war of 1812, John Brooks moved his family to Portland, Maine. There, Maria, who was supremely bored, met a Canadian army officer for whom she developed a powerful infatuation. Following her husband's death in 1823, she removed to Mantanzas, Cuba, where her maternal uncle owned a number of coffee plantations. Upon his death shortly thereafter, Brooks, who had inherited the uncle's property, dashed off to Canada to find her officer. They became engaged but the affair ended badly with Brooks making two suicide attempts with laudanum.

Apparently this affair cured any lingering desire Brooks had for romance in the flesh; and she settled down to raising her children – sons and step-sons – and writing her poetry. Now independently wealthy, she divided her time between North America, where she companioned her sons, Horace and Edgar, during their education, England, where she visited with British literary notables, and Cuba, where she eventually died of tropical fever (probably malaria). According to her son Horace, when in Cuba, Brooks always wore white, with a passion flower in her hair.

Brooks published her first book, *Judith, Esther, and Other Poems*, in 1820. A curious mix of biblical retellings and *vers de société*, hitting on the use of laudanum in "good society," *Judith* in no way prepares readers for what is generally considered Brooks's masterwork, *Zóphiël; or the Bride of Seven* (1833), a six-canto Oriental fantasy or erotic epic. Written primarily in a little "Greek" temple, which her brother had built for her, on her coffee estate in San Patricio, *Zóphiël* reflects the lush romanticism Brooks associated with her tropical setting. To my knowledge, the fact that her romantic pleasure in this lushness was dependent on slave labor did not bother her. Indeed, despite slavery having been notorious in Cuba for its brutality, she takes no notice of it anywhere in her printed texts.

Brooks's lack of political awareness sets her strikingly apart from every other major woman poet of the first half of the century and may help account for the fairytale quality of her principal work. Based loosely on the story of Sara and the evil spirit, Asmodeus, in the apocryphal book of Tobit, *Zóphiël* is the extravagantly passionate story of the fallen angel Zóphiël's unrequited love for Egla, a virtuous and beautiful Hebrew maiden. Rather than see Egla marry another, Zóphiël (whom Brooks identifies with the classical Greek god, Apollo) brings about the death of her first six husbands, eliminating each before they can consummate their marriage. The seventh, Helon, the young Hebrew to whom Egla is, in fact, divinely predestined, eludes him; and the defeated Zóphiël is permanently banished from Egla's life.

As a tale of death and erotic obsession, *Zóphiël* is without parallel among the works of nineteenth-century American women poets. It earned Brooks wide admiration among the male literati of her day, from Rufus Griswold, who fulsomely praised it in his watershed 1849 anthology, *The Female Poets of America*, to Robert Southey, who helped Brooks prepare the completed manuscript for publication. Its sales, however, were lukewarm at best; nor does it seem to have had much subsequent influence on other women poets. For all the power of its eroticism, it may, therefore, be best viewed as a curiosity and an interesting index to the kind of passion male readers of the day looked for from strong woman poets, albeit they expressed ritual shock when finding it there.

In the extract reprinted here, Zóphiël comes upon Egla sleeping. Mistaking her for an angel, he falls passionately in love with her but his desire is immediately thwarted by the fortuitous arrival of Egla's maid, Sephora, who has come to lead her to her first husband-to-be, Meles, a nobleman of Medea, where Egla's family lives in exile. The first canto ends when the all-too-eager Meles dies under mysterious circumstances in the bridal chamber where he and his new bride are about to consummate their marriage. Brooks annotated her original text very heavily and I have incorporated some of these annotations in my footnotes, in particular those which illuminate Brooks's strikingly gynocentric and syncretic perspective on religion.

Primary Texts

Judith, Esther, and Other Poems, 1820; *Zóphiël; or the Bride of Seven*, 1833.

Further Reading

Ruth W. Granniss, *An American Friend of Southey*, New York: DeVinne Press, 1913; Jeffrey Groves, "Maria Gowen Brooks," *Legacy: A Journal of Nineteenth-Century American Women Writers* 12 (1995), 38–46; Zadel B. Gustafson, "Maria del Occidente," in *Zóphiël, or the Bride of Seven*, ed. Zadel Barnes Gustafson, Boston: Lee and Shepard, 1879; Geofrilyn M. Walker, "Maria Gowen Brooks," *Encyclopedia of American Poetry*.

from *Zóphiël; or the Bride of Seven* (1833)

FROM CANTO FIRST: "GROVE OF ACACIAS," SECTIONS L–XCVII

L.

It chanced, that day, lured by the verdure, came
  Zóphiël, a spirit sometimes ill; but, ere

He fell, a heavenly angel. The faint flame
    Of dying embers on an altar, where

Zorah, fair Egla's sire, in secret bowed   5
    And sacrificed to the great unseen God,[1]
While friendly shades the sacred rites enshroud,
    The spirit saw. His inmost soul was awed,

And he bethought him of the forfeit joys
    Once his in heaven. Deep in a darkling grot   10
He sat him down; the melancholy noise
    Of leaf and creeping vine accordant with his thought.

LI.

When fiercer spirits howled, he but complained
    Ere yet 'twas his to roam the pleasant earth.
His heaven-invented harp he still retained,   15
    Though tuned to bliss no more; and had its birth

Of him, beneath some black, infernal clift,
    The first drear song of woe; and torment wrung
The restless spirit less, when he might lift
    His plaining voice, and frame the like as now he sung.   20

LII.

"Woe to thee, wild ambition! I employ
    Despair's low notes thy dread effects to tell;
Born in high heaven, her peace thou couldst destroy;
    And, but for thee, there had not been a Hell.

"Through the celestial domes thy clarion pealed;   25
    Angels, entranced, beneath thy banners ranged,
And straight were fiends; hurled from the shrinking field,
    They waked in agony to wail the change.

"Darting through all her veins the subtle fire,
    The world's fair mistress first inhaled thy breath;   30
To lot of higher beings learnt to aspire,
    Dared to attempt, and doomed the world to death.

"The thousand wild desires, that still torment
    The fiercely struggling soul, where peace once dwelt,
But perished; feverish hope; drear discontent,   35
    Impoisoning all possest, – Oh! I have felt

FROM CANTO FIRST: "GROVE OF ACACIAS," SECTIONS
L–XCVII
[1] Brooks's note: The captive Hebrews, though they
sometimes outwardly conformed to the religion of their
oppressors, were accustomed to practise their own in
secret.

"As spirits feel; — yet not for man we mourn,
  Scarce o'er the silly bird in state were he,
That builds his nest, loves, sings the morn's return,
  And sleeps at evening; save by aid of thee.   40

"Fame ne'er had roused, nor song her records kept;
  The gem, the ore, the marble breathing life,
The pencil's colors, all in earth had slept:
  Now see them mark with death his victim's strife.

"Man found thee, death: but Death and dull decay,   45
  Baffling, by aid of thee, his mastery proves;
By mighty works he swells his narrow day,
  And reigns, for ages, on the world he loves.

"Yet what the price? With stings that never cease
  Thou goad'st him on; and when too keen the smart,   50
His highest dole he'd barter but for peace,
  Food thou wilt have, or feast upon his heart."

LIII.

Thus Zóphiël still, though now the infernal crew
  Had gained, by sin, a privilege in the world,
Allayed their torments in the cool night dew,   55
  And by the dim star-light again their wings unfurled.

LIV.

And now, regretful of the joys his birth
  Had promised, deserts, mounts, and streams he crost,
To find, amid the loveliest spots of earth,
  Faint semblance of the heaven he had lost.   60

LV.

And oft, by unsuccessful searching pained,
  Weary he fainted through the toilsome hours;
And then his mystic nature he sustained
  On steam of sacrifices, breath of flowers.[2]

LVI.

Sometimes he gave out oracles, amused   65
  With mortal folly; resting on the shrines,

---

[2]   Brooks's note: It is related also, in the *Caherman Nameh*, that the Peris fed upon precious odours, brought them by their companions when imprisoned and hung up in cages by the Dives. Most of the oriental superstitions harmonize perfectly with the belief of the fathers; and what is there in philosophy, natural or moral, to disprove the existence of beings similar to those described by the latter?

Or, all in some fair Sybyl's form infused,
   Spoke from her trembling lips, or traced her mystic lines.[3]

LVII.

And now he wanders on from glade to glade
   To where more precious shrubs diffuse their balms;   70
And gliding through the thickly-woven shade,
   Where the soft captive lay in all her charms,

He caught a glimpse. The colours in her face,
   Her bare white arms, her lips, her shining hair,
Burst on his view. He would have flown the place,   75
   Fearing some faithful angel rested there,

Who'd see him, 'reft of glory, lost to bliss,
   Wandering, and miserably panting, fain
To glean a joy e'en from a place like this:
   The thought of what he once had been was pain   80

Ineffable. But what assailed his ear?
   A sigh! Surprised, another glance he took;
Then doubting – fearing – gradual coming near –
   He ventured to her side and dared to look;

Whispering, "Yes, 'tis of earth! So, new-found life   85
   Refreshing, looked sweet Eve, with purpose fell,
When first sin's sovereign gazed on her, and strife
   Had with his heart, that grieved with arts of hell,

Stern as it was, to win her o'er to death.
   Most beautiful of all in earth or heaven!   90
"Oh, could I quaff for aye that fragrant breath!
   Couldst thou, or being like to thee, be given

"To bloom for ever for me thus! Still true
   To one dear theme, my full soul, flowing o'er,
Would find no room for thought of what it knew,   95
   Nor picturing forfeit transport, curse me more.

LVIII.

"But, oh! severest curse! I cannot be
   In what I love blest e'en the little span,
(With all a spirit's keen capacity
   For bliss) permitted the poor insect, man.   100

---

[3] Brooks's note: The identity of Zóphiël with Apollo
will be perceived in this and other passages.

LIX.

"The few I've seen, and deemed of worth to win,
  Like some sweet floweret, mildewed in my arms,
Withered to hideousness as foul as sin,
  Grew fearful hags; and then, with potent charm

"Of muttered word and harmful drug, did learn   105
  To force me to their will. Down the damp grave,
Loathing I went, at Endor, and uptorn
  Brought back the dead; when tortured Saul did crave

"To view his lowering fate. Fair, nay, as this
  Young slumberer, that dread witch; when, I arrayed   110
In lovely shape, to meet my guileful kiss,
  She yielded first her lip. And thou, sweet maid –
What is't I see? – a recent tear has strayed,
  And left its stain upon her cheek of bliss.

LX.

"She has fall'n to sleep in grief; haply been chid,   115
  Or by rude mortal wrong'd. So let it prove
Meet for my purpose: 'mid these blossoms hid,
  I'll gaze, and, when she wakes, with all that love

"And art can lend, come forth. He who would gain
  A fond, full heart, in love's soft surgery skill'd,   120
Should seek it when 'tis sore; allay its pain
  With balm by pity prest: 'tis all his own so heal'd.

LXI.

"She may be mine a little year, ev'n fair
  And sweet as now. Oh! respite! while possesst
I lose the dismal sense of my despair: 125
  But then – I will not think upon the rest!

LXII.

"And wherefore grieve to cloud her little day
  Of fleeting life? What doom from power divine
I bear eternally: pity – away!
  Wake, pretty fly! and, while thou mayst, be mine,   130

"Though but an hour; so thou supply'st thy looms
  With shining silk, and in the cruel snare
See'st the fond bird entrapped, but for his plumes,
  To work thy robes, or twine amidst thy hair."

LXIII.

To whisper softly in her ear he bent,   135
   But draws him back restrained: a higher power,
That loved her, and would keep her innocent,
   Repelled his evil touch. And from her bower,

To lead the maid, Sephora comes; the sprite,
   Half baffled, followed, hovering on unseen,   140
Till Meles, fair to see, and nobly dight,
   Received his pensive bride. Gentle of mien,

She meekly stood. He fastened round her arms
   Rings of refulgent ore; low and apart
Murmuring, "So, beauteous captive, shall thy charms   145
   For ever thrall and clasp thy captive's heart."

LXIV.

The air's light touch seemed softer as she moved,
   In languid resignation; his quick eye
Spoke in black glances how she was approved,
   Who shrank reluctant from its ardency.   150

LXV.

'Twas sweet to look upon the goodly pair
   In their contrasted loveliness: her height
Might almost vie with his, but heavenly fair,
   Of soft proportion, she, and sunny hair;
He cast in manliest mould, with ringlets murk as night.   155

LXVI.

And oft her drooping and resigned blue eye
   She'd wistful raise to read his radiant face;
But then, why shrunk her heart? — a secret sigh
   Told her it most required what there it could not trace.

LXVII.

Now fair had fall'n the night. The damsel mused   160
   At her own window, in the pearly ray
Of the full moon: her thoughtful soul infused
   Thus in her words;[4] left lone awhile to pray.

---

[4] Brooks's note: Cœlestes, or the moon, was adored by many of the Jewish women, as well as the Carthaginians. They addressed their vows to her, burnt incense, poured out drink-offerings, and made cakes for her with her [sic] own hands. The goddess is called, in scripture, the Queen of Heaven.

LXVIII.

"What bliss for her who lives her little day,
  In blest obedience, like to those divine,   165
Who to her loved, her earthly lord can say,
  'God is thy law,' most just, 'and thou art mine.'

"To every blast she bends in beauty meek; —
  Let the storm beat, — his arms her shelter kind, —
And feels no need to blanch her rosy cheek   170
  With thoughts befitting his superior mind.

"Who only sorrows when she sees him pained,
  Then knows to pluck away pain's keenest dart;
Or bid Love catch it ere its goal be gained,
  And steal its venom ere it reach his heart.   175

"'Tis the soul's food: — the fervid must adore. —
  For this the heathen, unsufficed with thought,
Moulds him an idol of the glittering ore,
  And shrines his smiling goddess, marble-wrought.

"What bliss for her, ev'n in this world of woe,   180
  Oh! Sire who mak'st yon orb-strewn arch thy throne;
That sees thee in thy noblest work below
  Shine undefaced, adored, and all her own!

"This I had hoped; but hope too dear, too great,
  Go to thy grave! — I feel thee blasted, now.   185
Give me, fate's sovereign, well to bear the fate
  Thy pleasure sends; this, my sole prayer, allow!"

LXIX.

Still fixed on heaven, her earnest eye, all dew,
  Seemed, as it sought amid the lamps of night,
The God her soul addressed; but other view,   190
  Far different, sudden from that pensive plight

Recalled her: quick as on primeval gloom
  Burst the new day-star when the Eternal bid,
Appeared, and glowing filled the dusky room,
  As 'twere a brilliant cloud. The form it hid   195

Modest emerged, as might a youth beseem; —
  Save a slight scarf, his beauty bare, and white
As cygnet's bosom on some silver stream;
  Or young Narcissus, when too woo the light

Of its first morn, that flow'ret open springs;   200
    And near the maid he comes with timid gaze,
And gently fans her with his full-spread wings,
    Transparent as the cooling gush that plays

From ivory fount. Each bright prismatic tint
    Still vanishing, returning, blending, changing,   205
About their tender mystic texture glint
    Like colours o'er the full-blown bubble ranging,

That pretty urchins launch upon the air,
    And laugh to see it vanish; yet, so bright,
More like – and even that were faint compare,   210
    As shaped from some new rainbow. Rosy light,

Like that which Pagans say the dewy car
    Precedes of their Aurora, clipp'd him round,
Retiring as he moved; and evening's star
    Shamed not the diamond coronal that bound   215

His curly locks. And, still to teach his face
    Expression dear to her he wooed, he sought;
And, in his hand, he held a little vase
    Of virgin gold, in strange devices wrought.

LXX.

Love-toned he spoke; "Fair sister, art thou here   220
    With pensive looks, so near thy bridal bed,
Fixed on the pale cold moon? Nay, do not fear!
    To do thee weal, o'er mount and stream I've sped.

LXXI.

"Say, doth thy soul, in all its sweet excess,
    Rush to this bridegroom, smooth and falsehood-taught?   225
Ah, no! thou yield'st thee to a feared caress;
    And strugglest with a heart that owns him not.

LXXII.

"Send back this Meles to Euphrates: – there
    Is no reluctance. Withering by that stream,
Tell him there droops a flower that needs his care.   230
    But why, at such an hour, so base a theme?

LXXIII.

"I'll tell thee secrets of the nether earth
    And highest heaven! Or dost some service crave?

Declare thy bidding, best of mortal birth,
　　I'll be thy winged messenger, thy slave."　　　　　235

LXXIV.

Then softly Egla: "Lovely being, tell,
　　In pity to the grief thy lips betray
The knowledge of – say, with some kindly spell,
　　Dost come from heaven to charm my pains away?

LXXV.

"Alas! what know'st thou of my plighted lord?　　　　240
　　If guilt pollute him, as, unless mine ear
Deceive me in the purport of thy word,
　　Thou mean'st t'imply, – kind spirit rest not here,

"But to my father hasten, and make known
　　The fearful truth: My doom is his command;　　　245
Writ in heaven's book, I guard the oath I've sworn,
　　Unless he will to blot it by thine hand."

LXXVI.

"Oaths sworn for Meles little need avail,"
　　Zóphiël replies: "Ere morn, if't be thy will,
To Lybian deserts he shall tell his tale,　　　　　250
　　I'll hurl him, at thy word, o'er forest, sea, and hill.

LXXVII.

"But soothe thee, maiden; be thy soul at peace!
　　Mine be the care to hasten to thy sire,
And null thy vow. Let every terror cease:
　　Perfect success attends thy least desire."　　　　255

LXXVIII.

Then lowly bending with seraphic grace,
　　The vase he proffered full; and not a gem
Drawn forth successive from its sparkling place
　　But put to shame the Persian diadem.

LXXIX.

While he, "Nay, let me o'er thy white arms bind　　260
　　These orient pearls, less smooth; Egla, for thee,
My thrilling substance pained by storm and wind,
　　I sought them in the caverns of the sea.

LXXX.

"Look! here's a ruby; drinking solar rays,
     I saw it redden on a mountain tip;   265
Now on thy snowy bosom let it blaze:
     'Twill blush still deeper to behold thy lip.

LXXXI.

"Here's for thy hair a garland; every flower
     That spreads its blossoms, watered by the tear
Of the sad slave in Babylonian bower,   270
     Might see its frail bright hues perpetuate here.

LXXXII.

"For morn's light bell, this changeful amethyst;
     A sapphire for the violet's tender blue;
Large opals, for the queen-rose zephyr-kist;
     And here are emeralds of every hue,   275
For folded bud and leaflet, dropped with dew.

LXXXIII.

"And here's a diamond, culled from Indian mine,
     To gift a haughty queen: it might not be;
I knew a worthier brow, sister divine,
     And brought the gem; for well I deem for thee   280

"The 'arch-chymic sun' in earth's dark bosom wrought
     To prison thus a ray, that when dull night
Frowns o'er her realms, and nature's all seems nought,
     She whom he grieves to leave may still behold his light."

LXXXV.[5]

Thus spoke he on, while still the wondering maid   285
     Gazed, as a youthful artist; rapturously
Each perfect, smooth, harmonious limb surveyed
     Insatiate still her beauty-loving eye.

LXXXVI.

For [Zóphiël] wore a mortal form; and blent
     In mortal form, when perfect, Nature shews   290
Her all that's fair enhanced; fire, firmament,
     Ocean, earth, flowers, and gems, – all there disclose

---

[5]   The section numbers skip here; but no text is missing.

Their charms epitomised: the heavenly power
　　To lavish beauty, in this last work, crown'd;
And Egla, formed of fibres such as dower　　　　　　　295
　　Those who most feel, forgot all else around.

LXXXVII.

He saw, and softening every wily word,
　　Spoke in more melting music to her soul;
And o'er her sense, as when the fond night-bird
　　Woos the full rose, o'erpowering fragrance stole;[6]　　300

LXXXVIII.

Or when the lilies, sleepier perfume, move,
　　Disturbed by two young sister-fawns, that play
Among their graceful stalks at morn, and love
　　From their white cells to lap the dew away.

LXXXIX.

She strove to speak, but 'twas in murmurs low;　　　　305
　　While o'er her cheek, his potent spell confessing,
Deeper diffused the warm carnation glow
　　Still dewy wet with tears, her inmost soul confessing.

XC.

As the lithe reptile, in some lonely grove,
　　With fixed bright eye, of fascinating flame,　　　　310
Lures on by slow degrees the plaining dove,
　　So nearer, nearer still the bride and spirit came.

XCI.

Success seemed his; but secret, in the height
　　Of exultation, as he braved the power
Which baffled him at morn, a secret light　　　　　　315
　　Shot from his eye, with guilt and treachery fraught.

XCII.

Nature upon her children oft bestows
　　The quick, untaught perception; and while art
O'ertasks himself with guile, loves to disclose
　　The dark thought in the eye, to warn the o'er-trusting heart.　　320

---

[6]　A nightingale. In the long note accompanying this stanza, Brooks refers readers to the "oriental" fable of the nightingale that fell in love with a rose. Piatt appears to be drawing on the same fable in her far less romanticized version of the nightingale's tale in "A Mistake in the Bird-Market."

XCIII.

Or haply 'twas some airy guardian foiled
    The sprite. What mixed emotions shook his breast;
When her fair hand, ere he could clasp, recoiled!
    The spell was broke; and doubts and terrors prest

Her sore. While [Zóphiël]: "Meles' step I heard –   325
    He's a betrayer! – wilt receive him still?" –
The rosy blood, driven to her heart by fear,
    She said, in accents faint but firm, "I will."

XCIV.

The spirit heard; and all again was dark;
    Save, as before, the melancholy flame   330
Of the full moon; and faint, unfrequent spark,
    Which from the perfume's burning embers came,

XCV.

That stood in vases round the room disposed.
    Shuddering and trembling to her couch she crept.
Soft ope'd the door, and quick again was closed,   335
    And through the pale gray moonlight Meles stept.

XCVI.

But ere he yet, with haste, could throw aside
    His broidered belt and sandals, – dread to tell,
Eager he sprang – he sought to clasp his bride –
    He stopt: – a groan – was heard; he gasped, and fell   340

XCVII.

Low by the couch of her who widowed lay,
    Her ivory hands, convulsive, clasped in prayer,
But lacking power to move; and, when 'twas day,
    A cold black corse was all of Meles, there!

Elizabeth Oakes Smith (1806–1893)

Elizabeth Oakes Smith was the daughter of David and Sophia (Blanchard) Prince of North Yarmouth, Maine. Smith's father, a ship captain, was descended from John Smith, a Massachusetts settler of the 1630s. Prince was lost at sea when Oakes Smith was two years old. A precocious child, Oakes Smith had already learned to read by her second year. She later attended private school and dreamed of one day getting an education equal to that boys received and opening a school of her own. Oakes Smith's mother had other ideas. Convinced that if a girl "did not marry young, [she] would never marry at all," and that for girls there was "nothing outside of marriage," Sophia Prince pushed her sixteen-year-old daughter into marriage with Seba Smith, a Portland journalist and literateur.

Twice his new wife's age and physically unattractive to her, Seba Smith had, according to Oakes Smith's later account, very little idea what to do with a woman except to use her to fill his domestic needs – cooking, cleaning, etc. Oakes Smith bore him five sons, of whom one died in childhood. As a result of unwise land speculations, Seba Smith went bankrupt in the panic of 1837; and the Smiths moved to New York City, where Oakes Smith's career would finally flourish.

In the early 1840s, Oakes Smith published *belles lettres* exclusively, appearing in periodicals such as *Godey's*, and the *Southern Literary Messenger*, which printed "The Sinless Child" in 1842. Through her husband, she became part of a literary circle that included Edgar Allan Poe, the Cary sisters, Horace Greeley, the founder of the *New York Tribune*, and Margaret Fuller. By the late 1840s, however, Oakes Smith's dissatisfaction with her marriage led her to the women's rights movement, and to dropping poetry in favor of explicitly reformist writing. Joining the Lyceum circuit, she spoke mainly on the woman question but also on abolition. In 1851, she published her most important feminist work, *Woman and Her Needs*, a defense of women's right to self-fulfillment beyond the highly circumscribed domestic role that gender ideology dictated for them.

In 1860, the Smiths moved to Long Island. Two of her sons and her husband died, one after the other, the last in 1868. Long attracted to spiritualism, Oakes Smith turned entirely to religion, and by 1877, she was pastor of an independent congregation in Canastota, New York. She died at eighty-seven.

Emily Stipes Watts has identified "The Drowned Mariner," whose power may draw on Oakes Smith's feelings for her dead father, as the writer's most successful poem – a judgment with which I concur. However, "The Sinless Child" is her major contribution to nineteenth-century women's poetry, and an ironic one at that. More fully and clearly than any other American poet of the period, Oakes Smith articulates in this work the moral and spiritual values supporting the domestic ideology of "the Angel in the House" – that is, the very ideology she spent most of her adult intellectual life attacking. The poem's heroine, Eva, who gave her name to the century's most famous avatar of the domestic ideal, little Eva in Stowe's *Uncle Tom's Cabin*, is the living embodiment of what Jane Tompkins calls "Sentimental Power." As pure as she is beautiful, the mere sight of her is enough, it seems, to convert the worldly to good. Like Stowe's little Eva, moreover, Oakes Smith's angelic child seals her miracle of moral transformation by her death, thus underscoring the otherworldliness of the power which inhabits her and which her "true womanhood" represents.

In the excerpt printed here, which reads in some respects as a purified version of the first canto of Brooks's *Zóphïël*, Albert Linne, a mildly dissolute young man, comes upon the pubescent Eva sleeping. Taken by her beauty, he wants, at first, to steal a kiss; but his feckless lust (about which suggestions of rape hover) is almost immediately transformed into adoration. Eva wakes, falls in love with him in turn, and then, having fulfilled her special destiny on earth by joining her soul, if not her body, with his, promptly departs the world in the poem's final section.

"The Sinless Child" should not be read without its headnotes. For all the sentimental vagueness of its ambiance, it is a didactic work. Eva is not a fully rounded human being, nor is she meant to be seen as one. She is a moral/spiritual principle (or Christianized Platonic idea) at work in the mortal and material realm, as Linne's introjection of her values after her death indicates.

Primary Texts

The Sinless Child and Other Poems, 1843; *The Poetical Writings of Elizabeth Oakes Smith*, 1845; *Woman and Her Needs*, 1851; *The Sanctity of Marriage*, 1853; *The Newsboy*, 1854; *The Autobiography of Elizabeth Oakes Smith*, ed. Mary Alice Wyman, 1924.

Further Reading

Robert E. Riegel, *American Feminists*, Lawrence: University of Kansas Press, 1963; Cheryl Walker, *The Nightingale's Burden*; Mary Alice Wyman, *Two American Pioneers: Seba Smith and Elizabeth Oakes Smith*, New York: Columbia University Press, 1927.

from *Southern Literary Messenger* (1842)[1]

FROM "THE SINLESS CHILD: A POEM, IN SEVEN PARTS"

Part VI.

It is the noon of summer, and the noonday of Eva's earthly existence. She hath held communion with all that is great and beautiful in nature, till it hath become a part of her being; till her spirit hath acquired strength and maturity, and been reared to a beautiful and harmonious temple, in which the true and the good delight to dwell. Then cometh the mystery of womanhood; its gentle going forth of the affections seeking for that holiest of companionship, a kindred spirit, responding to all its finer essences, and yet lifting it above itself. Eva had listened to this voice of her woman's nature; and sweet visions had visited her pillow. Unknown to the external vision, there was one ever present to the soul; and when he erred, she had felt a lowly sorrow that, while it still more perfected her own nature, went forth to swell likewise the amount of good in the great universe of God. At length Albert Linne, a gay youth, whose errors are those of an ardent and inexperienced nature, rather than of an assenting will, meets Eva sleeping under the canopy of the great woods, and he is at once awed by the purity that enshrouds her. He is lifted to the contemplation of the good – to a sense of the wants of his better nature. Eva awakes and recognizes the spirit that forever and ever is to be one with hers; that is to complete that mystic marriage, known in the Paradise of God; that marriage of soul with soul, that demandeth no external right. Eva the pure-minded, the lofty in thought, and great in soul, recoiled not from the errors of him who was to be made mete for the kingdom of Heaven through her gentle agency, for the mission of the good and the lovely, is not to the good, but to the sinful. The mission of woman, is to the erring of man.

> 'Tis the summer prime, when the noiseless air
> In perfumed chalice lies,
> And the bee goes by with a lazy hum,
> Beneath the sleeping skies:

FROM "THE SINLESS CHILD: A POEM, IN SEVEN PARTS"

[1] The text for this poem published in the *Southern Literary Messenger* is probably best thought of as a first draft since Oakes Smith went on to expand the poem greatly in the 1843 version. All the poem's main ideas, however, are articulated in this early version and it is an open question whether lengthening it improved it in any substantive way.

When the brook is low, and the ripples bright,   5
   As down the stream they go;
The pebbles are dry on the upper side,
   And dark and wet below.

The tree that stood where the soil is thin,
   And the bursting rocks appear,   10
Hath a dry and rusty colored bark,
   And its leaves are curled and sere.
But the dog-wood and the hazel bush,
   Have clustered round the brook —
Their roots have stricken deep beneath,   15
   And they have a verdant look.

To the juicy leaf the grasshopper clings,
   And he gnaws it like a file,
The naked stalks are withering by,
   Where he has been erewhile.   20
The cricket hops on the glistering rock,
   Or pipes in the faded moss —
From the forest shade the voice is heard,
   Of the locust shrill and hoarse.

The widow[2] donn'd her russet robe,   25
   Her cap of snowy hue,
And o'er her staid maternal form
   A sober mantle threw;
And she, while fresh the morning light,
   Hath gone to pass the day,   30
And ease an ailing neighbor's pain
   Across the meadow way.

Young Eva closed the cottage door;
   And wooed by bird and flower,
She loitered on beneath the wood,   35
   Till came the noon-tide hour.
The sloping bank is cool and green,
   Beside the sparkling rill;[3]
The cloud that slumbers in the sky,
   Is painted on the hill.   40

The angels poised their purple wings
   O'er blossom, brook and dell,
And loitered in the quiet nook
   As if they loved it well.

---

[2] Eva's mother.   [3] *Rill* a small stream.

Young Eva laid one snowy arm   45
    Upon a violet bank,
And pillow'd there her downy cheek,
    While she to slumber sank.

A smile is on her gentle lip,
    For she the angels saw,   50
And felt their wings a covert[4] make
    As round her head they draw.
A maiden's sleep, how pure it is!
    The soul's inwrought repose —
It enters to its chamber in,   55
    Then onward stronger goes.

A huntsman's whistle, and anon
    The dogs come fawning round —
And now they raise the pendent ear,
    And crouch along the ground.   60
The hunter leapt the shrunken brook,
    The dogs hold back with awe,
For they upon the violet bank
    The slumbering maiden saw.

A reckless youth was Albert Linne,   65
    With licensed oath and jest,
Who little cared for woman's fame,
    Or peaceful maiden's rest.
Light things to him, were broken vows —
    The blush, the sigh, the tear;   70
What hinders he should steal a kiss,
    From sleeping damsel here?

He looks, yet stays his eager foot;
    For, on that spotless brow,
And that closed lid, a something rests   75
    He never saw till now;
He gazes, yet he shrinks with awe
    From that fair wondrous face,
Those limbs so quietly disposed,
    With more than maiden grace.   80

He seats himself upon the bank,
    And turns his face away —
And Albert Linne, the hair-brained youth,
    Wished in his heart to pray.

---

[4] *Covert* covering, shelter.

But thronging came his former life,   85
    What once he called delight –
The goblet, oath, and stolen joy,
    How palled⁵ they on the sight.

He looked within his very soul,
    Its hidden chamber saw,   90
Inscribed with records dark and deep
    Of many a broken law.
No more he thinks of maiden fair,
    No more of ravished kiss –
Forgets he that pure sleeper nigh   95
    Hath brought his thoughts to this.

Now Eva opes her childlike eyes
    And lifts her tranquil head,
And Albert, like a guilty thing,
    Had from her presence fled.   100
But Eva held her kindly hand
    And bade him stay awhile; –
He dared not look upon her eyes,
    He only marked her smile;

And that, so pure and winning beamed,   105
    So calm and holy too,
That o'er his troubled thoughts at once
    A quiet charm it threw.
Light thoughts, light words were all forgot –
    He breathed a holier air –   110
He felt the power of womanhood –
    Its purity was there.

And soft beneath their silken fringe
    Beamed Eva's dovelike eyes –
In hue and softness made to hold   115
    Communion with the skies.
Her gentle voice a part did seem,
    Of air, and brook, and bird –
And Albert listened, as if he
    Such music only heard.   120

O Eva! thou the pure in heart,
    Why falls thy trembling voice?
A blush is on thy maiden cheek,
    And yet thine eyes rejoice.

---

⁵ To satiate or cloy.

Another glory wakes for thee,   125
   Where'er thine eyes may rest;
And deeper, holier thoughts arise
   Within thy peaceful breast.

Thine eyelids droop in tenderness,
   New smiles thy lips combine,   130
For thou dost feel another soul
   Is blending into thine.
Thou upward raisest thy meek eyes,
   And it is sweet to thee;
To feel the weakness of thy sex,   135
   Is more than majesty.

To feel thy shrinking nature claim
   The stronger arm and brow –
Thy weapons, smiles, and tears, and prayers,
   And blushes such as now.   140
A woman, gentle Eva thou,
   Thy lot were incomplete,
Did not all sympathies of soul
   Within thy being meet.

Those deep dark eyes, that open brow,   145
   That proud and manly air,
How have they mingled with thy dreams,
   And with thine earnest prayer!
And how hast thou, all timidly,
   Cast down thy maiden eye,   150
When visions have revealed to thee
   That figure standing nigh!

Two spirits launched companionless
   A kindred essence sought –
And one in all its wanderings,   155
   Of such as Eva thought.
The good, the beautiful, the true,
   Should nestle in his heart –
Should lure him by her gentle voice,
   To choose the better part.   160

Her trusting hand, young Eva laid
   In that of Albert Linne,
And for one trembling moment turned
   Her gentle thoughts within.

Deep tenderness was in the glance   165
  That rested on his face,
As if her woman-heart had found
  Its own abiding place.

And when she turned her to depart
  Her voice more liquid fell –   170
"Dear youth, thy thoughts and mine are one;
  When I have said farewell!
Our souls must mingle evermore; –
  Thy thoughts of love and me,
Will, as a light, thy footsteps guide   175
  To life and mystery."

And then she bent her timid eyes,
  And as beside she knelt,
The pressure of her sinless lips
  Upon his brow he felt,   180
Low, heart-breathed words she uttered then:
  For him she breathed a prayer; –
He turned to look upon her face, –
  The maiden was not there.

Part VII.

Eva hath fulfilled her destiny. Material things can no further minister to the growth of her spirit. That waking of the soul to its own deep mysteries – its oneness with another, has been accomplished. A human soul is perfected. Sorrow and pain – hope, with its kin-spirit fear, are not for the sinless. She hath walked in an atmosphere of light, and her faith hath looked within the veil. The true woman, with woman's love and gentleness, and trust and childlike simplicity, yet with all her noble aspirations and spiritual discernments, she hath known them all without sin, and sorrow may not visit such. She ceased to be present – she passed away like the petal that hath dropped from the rose – like the last sweet note of the singing-bird, or the dying close of the wind harp. Eva is the lost pleiad in the sky of womanhood. Has her spirit ceased to be upon the earth? Does it not still brood over our woman hearts? – and doth not her voice blend ever with the sweet voices of Nature! Eva, mine own, my beautiful, I may not say farewell.

'Twas night – bright beamed the silver moon,   185
  And all the stars were out;
The widow heard within the dell
  Sweet voices all about.
The loitering winds were made to sound
  Her sinless daughter's name,   190
While to the roof a rare toned-bird
  With wondrous music came.

And long it sat upon the roof
    And poured its mellow song,
That rose upon the stilly air,   195
    And swelled the vales along.
It was no earthly thing she deemed,
    That, in the clear moonlight,
Sat on the low[l]y cottage roof,
    And charmed the ear of night.[6]   200

The sun is up, the flowerets raise
    Their folded leaves from rest;
The bird is singing in the branch
    Hard by its dewy nest.
The spider's thread, from twig to twig,   205
    Is glittering in the light –
With dew-drops has the web been hung
    Through all the starry night.

Why tarries Eva long in bed,
    For she is wont to be   210
The first to greet the early bird,
    The waking bud to see?
Why stoops her mother o'er the couch
    With half suppressed breath,
And lifts the deep-fringed eyelid up? –   215
    That frozen orb is death.

Why raises she the small pale hand,
    And holds it to the light?
There is no clear transparent hue
    To meet her dizzy sight.
She holds the mirror to her lips   220
    To catch the moistened air: –
The widowed mother stands alone
    With her dead daughter there.

And yet so placid is the face,   225
    So sweet its lingering smile,
That one might deem the sleep to be
    The maiden's playful wile.
No pain the quiet limbs had racked,
    No sorrow dimm'd the brow –   230

---

[6] The whippoorwill. As she notes in a footnote to this stanza, Oakes Smith is drawing on a Native American belief that the night before someone dies, the whippoorwill sings at the person's home.

So tranquil had the life gone forth,
　　She seemed but slumbering now.

They laid her down beside the brook
　　Upon the sloping hill,
And that strange bird with its rare note,　　235
　　Is singing o'er her still.
The sunlight warmer loves to rest
　　Upon the heaving mound,
And those unearthly blossoms spring,
　　Uncultured from the ground.　　240

There Albert Linne, an altered man,
　　Oft bowed in lowly prayer,
And pondered o'er those mystic words
　　Which Eva uttered there.
That pure compassion, angel-like,　　245
　　Which touched her soul when he,
A guilty and heart-stricken man,
　　Would from her presence flee.

Her sinless lips from earthly love,
　　So tranquil and so free;　　250
And that low, fervent prayer for him,
　　She breathed on bended knee.
As Eva's words and spirit sank
　　More deeply in his heart,
Young Albert Linne went forth to act　　255
　　The better human part.

Nor yet alone did Albert strive; –
　　For, blending with his own,
In every voice of prayer or praise,
　　Was heard young Eva's tone.　　260
He felt her lips upon his brow,
　　Her angel form beside;
And nestling nearest to his heart,
　　Was she, THE SPIRIT-BRIDE.

The Sinless Child, with mission high,　　265
　　Awhile to Earth was given,
To show us that our world should be
　　The vestibule of Heaven.
Did we but in the holy light
　　Of truth and goodness rise,　　270
We might communion hold with God
　　And spirits from the skies.

from *The Poetical Writings of Elizabeth Oakes Smith* (1845)

THE DROWNED MARINER[7]

A mariner sat on the shrouds one night,
　　The wind was piping free,
Now bright, now dimmed was the moonlight pale,
And the phosphor gleamed in the wake of the whale,
　　As he floundered in the sea;　　　　　　　　　　　　5
The scud[8] was flying athwart the sky,
The gathering winds went whistling by,
And the wave as it towered, then fell in spray,
Looked an emerald wall in the moonlight ray.

The mariner swayed and rocked on the mast,　　　　　10
　　But the tumult pleased him well,
Down the yawning wave his eye he cast,
And the monsters watched as they hurried past,
　　Or lightly rose and fell;
For their broad, damp fins were under the tide,　　　15
And they lashed as they passed the vessel's side,
And their filmy eyes, all huge and grim,
Glared fiercely up, and they glared at him.

Now freshens the gale, and the brave ship goes
　　Like an uncurbed steed along,　　　　　　　　　　20
A sheet of flame is the spray she throws,
As her gallant prow the water plows –
　　But the ship is fleet and strong:
The topsails are reefed and the sails are furled,
And onward she sweeps o'er the watery world,　　　25
And dippeth her spars in the surging flood;
But there came no chill to the mariner's blood.

Wildly she rocks, but he swingeth at ease,
　　And holds him by the shroud;
And as she careens to the crowding breeze,　　　　30
The gaping deep the mariner sees,
　　And the surging heareth loud.
Was that a face, looking up at him,
With its pallid cheek and its cold eyes dim?
Did it beckon him down? did it call his name?　　　35
Now rolleth the ship the way whence it came.

THE DROWNED MARINER

[7] Melville quoted the first five lines of this poem in the extracts beginning *Moby Dick*. Watts notes however that the "comparative situations of Smith's 'Mariner' and Melville's 'watergazer' on 'The Masthead' (Chapter 35) can be understood only by reading the entire poem."

This poem takes on a special poignancy when one remembers that Smith's own father died at sea, a biographical circumstance that may also help account for its power.

[8] *Scud* loose vapory clouds, mist, or spray.

The mariner looked, and he saw with dread,
   A face he knew too well;
And the cold eyes glared, the eyes of the dead,
And its long hair out on the wave was spread.   40
   Was there a tale to tell?
The stout ship rocked with a reeling speed,
And the mariner groaned, as well he need,
For ever down, as she plunged on her side,
The dead face gleamed from the briny tide.   45

Bethink thee, mariner, well of the past,
   A voice calls loud for thee –
There's a stifled prayer, the first, the last,
The plunging ship on her beam is cast,
   Oh, where shall thy burial be?   50
Bethink thee of oaths that were lightly spoken,
Bethink thee of vows that were lightly broken,
Bethink thee of all that is dear to thee –
For thou art alone on the raging sea:

Alone in the dark, alone on the wave,   55
   To buffet the storm alone –
To struggle aghast at thy watery grave,
To struggle, and feel there is none to save –
   God shield thee, helpless one!
The stout limbs yield, for their strength is past,   60
The trembling hands on the deep are cast,
The white brow gleams a moment more,
Then slowly sinks – the struggle is o'er.

Down, down where the storm is hushed to sleep,
   Where the sea its dirge shall swell,   65
Where the amber drops for thee shall weep,
And the rose-lipped shell her music keep,
   There thou shalt slumber well.
The gem and the pearl lie heaped at thy side,
They fell from the neck of the beautiful bride,   70
From the strong man's hand, from the maiden's brow,
As they slowly sunk to the wave below.

A peopled home is the ocean bed,
   The mother and child are there –
The fervent youth and the hoary head,   75
The maid, with her floating locks outspread,
   The babe with its silken hair,
As the water moveth they lightly sway,
And the tranquil lights on their features play;
And there is each cherished and beautiful form,   80
Away from decay, and away from the storm.

Frances Anne Butler Kemble (1809–1893)

Frances "Fanny" Anne Kemble was born on November 27, 1809 into an illustrious theatrical family. Both her uncle, John Philip Kemble, dubbed "Glorious John," and aunt, Sarah Kemble Siddons, known as "The Tragic Muse," were leading actors of their day. Her father, Charles Kemble, inherited part ownership of Covent Garden Theatre, and her mother, Maria Theresa de Camp, performed in the homes of London nobility as a child. Fanny entered the acting profession at nineteen, playing Juliet in a family production of *Romeo and Juliet*. Her performance was wildly received, helping the family stave off bankruptcy temporarily. When financial difficulties finally forced Charles Kemble to give up the theater's management, he turned to his next most lucrative asset, Fanny, planning her American tour.

Kemble's stage success continued in the States. Her appeal was so great that she set coed fashion trends with the "Fanny cap" and "Kemble curls." Kemble, however, was never enamored of the life and as soon as the tour ended, she traveled to Philadelphia, where she met and soon married Pierce Butler, heir to a Georgian plantation. One year later, Kemble published *Journal of a Residence in America*, a text whose sympathy for abolitionists and satiric treatment of the American leisure class did not endear her to her new family.

In 1838, the Butlers moved with their two daughters, Sarah and Frances, to Pierce's plantation in Georgia. Here, Kemble was able to observe first hand the horrors of American chattel slavery. Although not published until 1863, her *Journal of a Residence on a Georgian Plantation in 1838–1839* is among the most important eye-witness accounts of American slavery. It is noted particularly for its attention to the fate of slave women, on whose behalf Kemble's outrage was fully stirred. Whatever remained of the Butler marriage was unable to withstand either Fanny's politics or her husband's infidelity. In 1845 the couple separated and Pierce Butler received custody of the children. Kemble returned to England and to acting, only to quit the stage permanently after a few years in favor of the less strenuous life of giving readings from Shakespeare. These readings proved phenomenally popular, returning her once more to fame and fortune.

In 1849, the Butlers' divorce, which by then had become notorious, was finalized, and Kemble returned to the States, making her home in Lenox, Massachusetts. Thereafter she shuttled between the States and Britain, finally settling in England with her younger daughter, Sarah. (Kemble's older daughter, Frances, became completely estranged from her mother after the Civil War, when she took up her father's politics along with his estate.) Kemble's final years were as placid as her early years had been tumultuous and she died peacefully in England in 1893 at the age of eighty-four.

Kemble published four volumes of poetry in her lifetime, 1844, 1859, 1866, and 1883, but poetry was clearly a side avocation. Nevertheless she was an extremely good technician and the quality of her writing is unusually consistent in an era when most poets (at least in the United States) tended to be very uneven. That she was deeply influenced by Shakespeare goes without saying, especially in her sonnets (e.g., "What is my lady like? thou fain would'st know –"). Where Kemble contributes most to women's poetry in the United States is in the love poems she wrote to women. Perhaps because of her stage experience, her treatment of erotic desire is unusually frank in a period not noted for its openness about such matters, and these poems are among the boldest and richest lesbian poems to be found in the century.

Robert Alsop with Paula Bennett

Primary Texts

Poems, 1844; *Poems*, 1859; *Journal of a Residence on a Georgian Plantation in 1838–1839*, 1863; *Poems*, 1866; *Poems*, 1883.

Further Reading

 Margaret Armstrong, *Fanny Kemble: A Passionate Victorian*, New York: Macmillan, 1938; Alison Booth, "From Miranda to Prospero: The Works of Fanny Kemble," *Victorian Studies: A Journal of the Humanities, Arts and Sciences* 38 (Winter 1995): 227–54; Dana D. Nelson, "Introduction," in *Power and Privilege: Two Women's Lives on a Georgia Plantation*, Ann Arbor: University of Michigan Press, 1995; Fanny Kemble Wister, *Fanny: The American Kemble*, Tallahassee: South Pass Press, 1972.

from *Poems* (1844)

SONNET

There's not a fibre in my trembling frame
That does not vibrate when thy step draws near,
There's not a pulse that throbs not when I hear
Thy voice, thy breathing, nay, thy very name.
When thou art with me, every sense seems dull,   5
And all I am, or know, or feel, is thee;
My soul grows faint, my veins run liquid flame,
And my bewildered spirit seems to swim
In eddying whirls of passion, dizzily.
When thou art gone, there creeps into my heart   10
A cold and bitter consciousness of pain:
The light, the warmth of life, with thee depart,
And I sit dreaming o'er and o'er again
Thy greeting clasp, thy parting look, and tone;
And suddenly I wake – and am alone.   15

from *Poems* (1859)

LINES

On Reading with Difficulty some of Schiller's[1] early Love Poems

When of thy loves, and happy heavenly dreams
Of early life, oh Bard! I strive to read,
Thy foreign utterance a riddle seems,
And hardly can I hold thy thought's bright thread.

LINES
[1]   Friedrich von Schiller (1759–1805), German dramatist, poet, and historian.

When of the maiden's guilt, the mother's woe,   5
And the dark mystery of death and shame,
Thou speakest — then thy terrible numbers flow
As if the tongue we think in were the same.
Ah wherefore? but because all joy and love
Speak unfamiliar, unknown words to me,   10
A spirit of wishful wonder they may move,
Dreams of what might — but yet shall never be.
But the sharp cry of pain — the bitter moan
Of trust deceived — the horrible despair
Of hope and love for ever overthrown —   15
These strains of thine need no interpreter.
Ah 'tis my native tongue! and howsoe'er
In foreign accents writ, that I did ne'er
Or speak, or hear, a woman's agony
Still utters a familiar voice to me.   20

NOONDAY

By The Seaside

The sea has left the strand —
In their deep sapphire cup
The waves lie gathered up,
Off the hard-ribbed sand.

From each dark rocky brim,   5
The full wine-tinted billows ebbed away,
    Leave on the golden rim
Of their huge bowl, not one thin line of spray.

Above the short-grassed downs all broidered over
With scarlet pimpernel, and silver clover,   10
Like spicy incense quivers the warm air,
    With piercing fervid heat,
    The noonday sunbeams beat,
On the red granite sea-slabs, broad and bare.

And prone along the shore,   15
Basking in the fierce glare,
Lie sun-bronzed Titans, covered o'er
With shaggy, sea-weed hair.

Come in, under this vault of brownest shade,
    By sea-worn arches made,   20
Where all the air, with a rich topaz light,
    Is darkly bright.
    'Neath these rock-folded canopies,
    Shadowy and cool,

The crystal water lies   25
   In many a glassy pool,
Whose green-veined sides, as they receive the light,
Gleam like pale wells of precious malachite.

In the warm shallow water dip thy feet,
Gleaming like rose-hued pearls below the wave,   30
And lying in this hollow, sea-smoothed seat,
Gaze on the far-off white-sailed fisher fleet,
Framed in the twilight portal of our cave;

   While I lie here, and gaze on thee
   Fairer art thou to me   35
Than Aphrodite,[2] when the breathless deep
Wafted her smiling in her rosy sleep,
Towards the green-myrtled shore, that in delight
With starry fragrance, suddenly grew white,
   Or than the shuddering girl,[3]   40
   Whose wide distended eyes,
   Glassy, with dread surprise,
Saw the huge billow curl,
Foaming and bristling, with its grisly freight;
   While, twinkling from afar,   45
With iris-feathered heels, and falchion bright,
From the blue cope of heaven's dazzling height,
Her lover swooped, a flashing noon-tide star.

A mid-day dream hath lighted on thy brow,
And gently bends it down; thy fair eyes swim,   50
In liquid languor, lustreless and dim,
And slowly dropping now,
From the light loosened clasp of thy warm hand,
Making a ruddy shadow on the sand,
Falls a wine-perfumed rose, with crimson glow.   55

Sleep my belovèd! while the sultry spell
Of silent noon o'er sea and earth doth dwell:
Stoop thy fair graceful head upon my breast,
With its thick rolls of golden hair opprest,
My lily! – and my breathing shall not sob   60
With one tumultuous sigh – nor my heart throb
With one irregular bound – that I may keep

NOONDAY
[2] Greek goddess of beauty. According to legend, she
was born of the foam of the sea. See Moulton's "Laus
Veneris" and Piatt's "A Sea-Gull Wounded."
[3] Andromeda, in Greek mythology, a princess of Ethiopia, daughter of Cepheus. After her father offended
Poseidon, the latter sent a sea monster to prey upon
her country. To appease the monster, Andromeda was
chained to a rock at the edge of the sea, from which she
was rescued by Perseus, who later married her.

With tenderest watch, the treasure of thy sleep.
Droop gently down, in slumb'rous, slow eclipse,
Fair fringèd lids! beneath my sealing lips.   65

SONNET

What is my lady like? thou fain would'st know —
A rosy chaplet of fresh apple bloom,
Bound with blue ribbon, lying on the snow:
What is my lady like? the violet gloom
Of evening, with deep orange light below.   5
She's like the noonday smell of a pine wood,
She's like the sounding of a stormy flood,
She's like a mountain-top high in the skies,
To which the day its earliest light doth lend;
She's like a pleasant path without an end;   10
Like a strange secret, and a sweet surprise;
Like a sharp axe of doom, wreathed with blush roses,
A casket full of gems whose key one loses;
Like a hard saying, wonderful and wise.

A NOONDAY VISION

I saw one whom I love more than my life
Stand on a perilous edge of slippery rock,
Under her feet the water's furious strife,
And all around the thunder of their shock;
She stood and smiled, while terror held my breath,   5
Nor dared I speak, or move, or call, or cry,
Lest to wild measuring of the depth beneath,
From her small foothold she should turn her eye.
As in the tyrannous horror of a dream,
I could not look away, but stony, still,   10
Fastened my eyes on her, while she did seem
Like one that fears, but hath a stedfast will.
Around her, through green boughs, the sunlight flung
Its threads of glory like a golden net,
And all about the rock-wall where she clung,   15
The trembling crests of fern with stars were wet,
Bright beads of crystal on a rainbow strung,
Jewels of fire in drops of water set;
And while I gazed, a hand stretched forth to her,
Beckoned her on — and holding firm and fast   20
By this her unseen guide and monitor,
Behind the rocks out of my sight she passed,
And then the agony of all my fears
Broke forth from out my eyes in sudden tears,
And I fell weeping down upon the sod;   25
But in my soul I heard a voice that said

Be comforted – of what art thou afraid?
Nor for the hand she holds be thou dismayed,
The hand that holds her is the hand of God.

Sarah Margaret Fuller (1810–1850)

Sarah Margaret Fuller was born May 23, 1810 in Cambridgeport, a suburb of the city of Cambridge, Massachusetts. Her father, Timothy, was a lawyer and four-term US congressman. Her mother, Margaret Crane Fuller, managed the household and seven children on a relatively small income. Like many poets in this anthology, Fuller was highly precocious; but unlike most of them, she received an early education whose rigor fully matched her ability, learning under her father's tutelage to read Horace, Ovid, and Virgil in the original by the time she was nine.

Although it satisfied her intellectual needs, this education seems to have stranded Fuller in other respects, unfitting her by her own account for the more socially oriented pursuits expected of early nineteenth-century women and causing her a good deal of gender confusion. After two years at Miss Prescott's Young Ladies Seminary in Groton failed to rectify the balance, Fuller returned home to finish her education herself, building on her knowledge of modern and ancient languages and reading widely in the humanities – literature, philosophy, history, and religion.

After her father's death in 1835, Fuller became, effectively, head of household. To earn money she taught, first at Bronson Alcott's school in Boston (1836–7), then at the Greene Street School in Providence, Rhode Island (1837–9). Unlike Sigourney, however, Fuller had no desire to make teaching her life work. By 1839, she had joined the transcendentalist circle around Ralph Waldo Emerson, and when he urged her to edit the *Dial*, his proposed vehicle for transcendentalist literature and ideas, she accepted, putting her own stamp on the journal until her resignation in 1842 to pursue writing full time.

The years between 1839 and 1850 were highly productive for Fuller. Along with serving as correspondent and literary critic for the *New York Daily Tribune* – Horace Greeley's newspaper – she published a series of translations from the German, and both *Summer on the Lakes* (1844) and, her most significant contribution to feminism, *Woman in the Nineteenth Century* (1845). While abroad, she wrote the pieces for her final work, *Things and Thoughts in Europe* (1850), recounting life in Italy during the revolution. It was in the course of covering the revolution that she met and possibly married Giovanni Angelo, Marchese d'Ossoli, by whom she had one son, Angelo. After the fall of the Roman Republic in June of 1849, Fuller, her husband, and child made their ill-fated voyage to the United States. In a storm off Fire Island, New York, their ship went down and all on board were lost.

Like everything in her life, including her putative marriage to the Marchese d'Ossoli, Fuller's poetry is controversial. She wrote a fair amount of it, but much of her poetry is rendered inaccessible to general readers by her reliance on private mythological symbols and by her inwardness and intellectuality. The selection in this anthology is more externally oriented than much of her poetry and, therefore, with one exception, "Double Triangle, Serpent and Rays," not especially representative of what Fuller scholars take as her most interesting poetic work. On the other hand, these poems demonstrate a more earth-bound, less mystical, side of Fuller, that may be of greater interest to non-specialists.

While Fuller's love poems to Anne Hazard Barker have much in common with the erotic poetry to women written by her contemporary, Frances Kemble, her ironic treatment of the fate of Native Americans in "Governor Everett Receiving the Indian Chiefs" stands in sharp contrast to Sigourney's highly emotional appeals. Fuller's distancing of her emotions may come from her desire not to appear "womanish" (that is, like Sigourney), or it may be an index to her own despair. Very possibly, it is both. When taken together with the prefatory poems to *Summer on the Lakes*, this poem's presence in Fuller's travel "journal" suggests that this work is more politically concerned with the detrimental effects of western expansion on both Indians and the land than might first appear. Fuller's poem on Mozart is of interest for other reasons. Poems on music were a genre unto themselves in the nineteenth century but very few of them are successful. Even Dickinson fails when trying to write of Mozart (503, *c.* 1862). Although all readers might not agree, I believe that Fuller captures the sadness and longing that permeate his music with unusual perceptiveness as well as success.

"Double Triangle, Serpent and Rays" provides a sample of Fuller's more private poetry. It articulates clearly the poet's need to resolve the psyche-splitting tensions of her gender identity. According to Jeffrey Steele, who has studied Fuller's poetry most closely, and to whom I am indebted for the transcriptions of all the manuscript poems printed here, the poem "symbolizes the transfiguration of destructive serpent energies into a powerful symbol of androgynous union" (*Encyclopedia of American Poetry*). Fuller used the same figure of interlocking triangles surrounded by a serpent swallowing its tail, and rays, as the frontispiece for *Woman in the Nineteenth Century*.

Primary Texts

Summer on the Lakes, in 1843, 1844; *Woman in the Nineteenth Century*, 1845; *Papers on Literature and Art*, 2 vols, 1846; *The Essential Margaret Fuller*, ed. Jeffrey Steele, 1992.

Further Reading

Stephen Adams, "'The Tidiness We Always Look For in Woman': Fuller's *Summer on the Lakes* and Romantic Aesthetics," *Studies in American Renaissance* (1987): 247–64; Paula Blanchard, *Margaret Fuller: From Transcendentalism to Romanticism*, New York: Dell, 1978; Bell Gale Chevigny, "Growing out of New England: The Emergence of Margaret Fuller's Radicalism," *Women's Studies* 5 (1977): 65–100; Sandra M. Gustafson, "Choosing a Medium: Margaret Fuller and the Forms of Sentiment," *American Quarterly* 47 (March 1995): 34–65; Jeffrey Steele, "Freeing the 'Prisoned Queen': The Development of Margaret Fuller's Poetry," *Studies in American Renaissance* (1992): 137–75; "The Call of Eurydice: Mourning and Intertextuality in Margaret Fuller's Writing," in *Influence and Intertextuality in Literary History*, ed. Eric Rothstein and Jay Clayton, Madison: University of Wisconsin Press, 1991; "Introduction," in *The Essential Margaret Fuller*, ed. Jeffrey Steele, New Brunswick: Rutgers University Press, 1992; "Margaret Fuller," *Encyclopedia of American Poetry*.

Manuscript Poem (1836; Steele, 1992)

To A. H. B.[1]

On our meeting, on my return from N.Y. to Boston, August 1835. –
Written Jany 1836

Brief was the meeting, – tear-stained, full of fears
  For future days, and sad thoughts of the past, –
  Thou, seeing thy horizon overcast,
Timid, didst shrink from the dark-coming years;
And I, (though less ill in mine appears,)   5
  Was haunted by a secret dread of soul,
  That Fate had something written in her scroll
Which soon must ope again the fount of tears;
  Oh could we on the waves have lingered then,
Or in that bark, together borne away,   10
  Have sought some isle far from the haunts of men,
Ills left behind which cloud the social day,
  What grief I had escaped; yet left untried
  That holy faith by which, now fortified,
  I feel a peace to happiness allied; –   15
And thou, although for thee my loving heart
Would gladly some Elysium set apart,
From treachery's pestilence, and passion's strife,
Where thou might'st lead a pure untroubled life,
Sustained and fostered by hearts like thy own,   20
The conflicts which thy friend must brave, unknown, –
Yet I feel deeply, that it may be best
For thee as me, that fire the gold should test,
And that in God's good time we shall know perfect rest!

Manuscript Poem (1835; Steele, 1992)

To the Same: A Feverish Vision

After a day of wearying, wasting pain,
  At last my aching eyes I think to close;
  Hoping to win some moments of repose,
Though I must wake to suffering again.
But what delirious horrors haunt my brain!   5
  In a deep ghastly pit, bound down I lie, –
  About me flows a stream of crimson dye,

To A. H. B.
[1]   Anne Hazard Barker, a friend of Fuller's.

Amid its burning waves I strive in vain;
  Upward I stretch my arms, – aloud I cry
  In frantic anguish, – "raise me, or I die!"   10
When with soft eyes, beaming the tenderest love,
I see thy dear face, Anna! far above, –
By magnet drawn up to thee I seem,
And for some moments was dispelled the fever's frightful dream! –

from *Summer on the Lakes, in 1843* (1844)[2]

"SUMMER DAYS OF BUSY LEISURE"

Summer days of busy leisure,
Long summer days of dear-bought pleasure,
You have done your teaching well;
Had the scholar means to tell
How grew the vine of bitter-sweet,   5
What made the path for truant feet,
Winter nights would quickly pass;
Gazing on the magic glass
O'er which the new-world shadows pass.
But, in fault of wizard spell,   10
Moderns their tale can only tell
In dull words, with a poor reed
Breaking at each time of need.
But those to whom a hint suffices
Mottoes find for all devices,   15
See the knights behind their shields,
Through dried grasses, blooming fields.

TO A FRIEND

Some dried grass-tufts from the wide flowery plain,
A muscle shell from the lone fairy shore,
Some antlers from tall woods which never more
To the wild deer a safe retreat can yield,
An eagle's feather which adorned a Brave,   5
Well-nigh the last of his despairing band,
For such slight gifts wilt thou extend thy hand
When weary hours a brief refreshment crave?
I give you what I can, not what I would,

FROM *SUMMER ON THE LAKES, IN 1843* (1844)
[2] In *Summer on the Lakes, in 1843* Fuller describes her travels through the Midwest, touring the Great Lakes country. Comprised of anecdotes, poems, sketches, dialogues, and reflections, the text has been viewed as incoherent by many readers, but one of its persistent themes is the waste in life and land that western expansion was incurring, bringing Fuller in many ways close to her seeming antithesis, Sigourney.

If my small drinking-cup would hold a flood,[3]   10
As Scandinavia sung those must contain
With which the giant gods may entertain;
In our dwarf day we drain few drops, and soon must thirst again.

GOVERNOR EVERETT[4] RECEIVING THE INDIAN CHIEFS

November, 1837

Who says that Poesy is on the wane,
And that the Muses tune their lyres in vain?
'Mid all the treasures of romantic story,
When thought was fresh and fancy in her glory,
Has ever Art found out a richer theme,   5
More dark a shadow, or more soft a gleam,
Than fall upon the scene, sketched carelessly,
In the newspaper column of to-day?

American romance is somewhat stale.
Talk of the hatchet, and the faces pale,   10
Wampum and calumets,[5] and forests dreary,
Once so attractive, now begins to weary.
Uncas and Magawisca[6] please us still
Unreal, yet idealized with skill;
But every poetaster scribbling witling,[7]   15
From the majestic oak his stylus whittling,
Has helped to tire us, and to make us fear
The monotone in which so much we hear
Of "stoics of the wood," and "men without a tear."

Yet Nature, ever buoyant, ever young,   20
If let alone, will sing as erst she sung:
The course of circumstance gives back again
The Picturesque, erewhile pursued in vain;
Shows us the fount of Romance is not wasted –
The lights and shades of contrast not exhausted.   25

TO A FRIEND
[3]   Fuller's may be alluding to the drinking horn which Thor fails to drain in the hall of the Giants in the *Prose Edda* because its tip goes down into the ocean, filling it with an unending supply of drink.

GOVERNOR EVERETT RECEIVING THE INDIAN CHIEFS
[1]   Edward Everett (1794–1865), American orator and statesman. Everett was governor of Massachusetts from 1836 to 1839. Everett's after-the-fact identity as the notoriously long-winded principal speaker at the dedication of the national cemetery at Gettysburg, at which Abraham Lincoln gave his great (and brief) address, may or may not have bearing on this poem, depending on whether or not one reads Fuller's final lines ironically.

[5]   Wampum were beads made of shells. They were used by North American Indians as aids to memory and as a medium of exchange. Calumets were ritual pipes.
[6]   Uncas was the son of Chingachgook, the Mohican companion of Natty Bumppo in James Fenimore Cooper's *The Last of the Mohicans* (1826); Magawisca was the self-sacrificing Pequod heroine of Catherine Sedgwick's romance, *Hope Leslie* (1827). As highly idealized portraits of Native Americans, both figures were targeted by proponents of Jackson's Indian removal policy as evidence of the fuzzy-mindedness of Indian sympathizers.
[7]   Derogatory terms for persons who aspire unsuccessfully to be poets or wits.

Shorn of his strength, the Samson[8] now must sue
  For fragments from the feast his fathers gave,
The Indian dare not claim what is his due,
  But as a boon his heritage must crave;
His stately form shall soon be seen no more   30
Through all his father's land, th' Atlantic shore,
Beneath the sun, to *us* so kind, *they* melt,
More heavily each day our rule is felt;
The tale is old, – we do as mortals must:
Might makes right here, but God and Time are just.[9]   35

So near the drama hastens to its close,
On this last scene awhile your eyes repose;
The polished Greek and Scythian[10] meet again,
The ancient life is lived by modern man –
The savage through our busy cities walks, –   40
He in his untouched grandeur silent stalks.
Unmoved by all our gaieties and shows,
Wonder nor shame can touch him as he goes;
He gazes on the marvels we have wrought,
But knows the models from whence all was brought;   45
In God's first temples he has stood so oft,
And listened to the natural organ loft –
Has watched the eagle's flight, the muttering thunder heard,
Art cannot move him to a wondering word;
Perhaps he sees that all this luxury   50
Brings less food to the mind than to the eye;
Perhaps a simple sentiment has brought
More to him than your arts had ever taught.
What are the petty triumphs *Art* has given,
To eyes familiar with the naked heaven?   55

All has been seen – dock, railroad, and canal,
Fort, market, bridge, college, and arsenal,
Asylum, hospital, and cotton mill,
The theatre, the lighthouse, and the jail.
The Braves each novelty, reflecting, saw,   60
And now and then growled out the earnest *yaw*,
And now the time is come, 't is understood,
When, having seen and thought so much, a *talk* may do some good.

---

[8] Samson, the Israelite hero in Judges 16. He is said to have lost all his strength after Delilah cut his hair.
[9]Fuller seems to be alluding obliquely here to the famous moment in Book Five of Thucydides's *History of the Peloponnesian War* when a delegation from the invading Athenian army bluntly reminds the citizens of the island of Melos that "the powerful do what they want, the weak do what they must." In effect, Governor Everett is subliminally conveying the same message to the Indian Chiefs in this poem, as they are introduced into the power and wealth of an ever-expanding United States. This message is, of course, consonant with the Machiavellian principle of "force or fraud" to which she will allude shortly (see l. 78).
[10] In western thought, the ancient Greeks and the Scythians have traditionally stood for civilization and barbarism respectively.

A well-dressed mob have thronged the sight to greet,
And motley figures throng the spacious street;   65
Majestical and calm through all they stride,
Wearing the blanket with a monarch's pride;
The gazers stare and shrug, but can't deny
Their noble forms and blameless symmetry

If the Great Spirit their morale has slighted,   70
And wigwam smoke their mental culture blighted,
Yet the physique, at least, perfection reaches,
In wilds where neither Combe nor Spurzheim[11] teaches;
Where whispering trees invite man to the chase,
And bounding deer allure him to the race.   75

Would thou hadst seen it! That dark, stately band,
Whose ancestors enjoyed all this fair land,
Whence they, by force or fraud, were made to flee,
Are brought, the white man's victory to see.
Can kind emotions in their proud hearts glow,   80
As through these realms, now decked by Art, they go?
The church, the school, the railroad and the mart –
Can these a pleasure to their minds impart?
All once was theirs – earth, ocean, forest, sky –
How can they joy in what now meets the eye?   85
Not yet Religion has unlocked the soul,
Nor Each has learned to glory in the Whole!

Must they not think, so strange and sad their lot,
That they by the Great Spirit are forgot?
From the far border to which they are driven,   90
They might look up in trust to the clear heaven;
But *here* – what tales doth every object tell
Where Massasoit sleeps – where Philip[12] fell!

We take our turn, and the Philosopher
Sees through the clouds a hand which cannot err,   95
An unimproving race, with all their graces
And all their vices, must resign their places;[13]

---

[11] George Combe (1788–1858) and Johann Caspar Spurzheim (1776–1828) were two well-known phrenologists of the period. Phrenology was the pseudo-science of reading cranial bumps for clues to personality and behavior. For two more views on phrenology, see "My Head" (1833) and Douglass's "The Stranger in America" (1836) in Section II.
[12] Massasoit (c. 1580–1661) and his son, "King Philip" (Metacomet), were chiefs of the Wampanoag Indians. Metacomet's defeat by British colonial troops in 1676 placed Massachusetts and Connecticut under uncontested Puritan control, not, however, before the Wampanoags had wreaked a large amount of destruction in New England's most costly Indian war.
[13] Fuller is parodying two basic arguments which Americans used to justify their genocidal policies towards the continent's first inhabitants: (1) that the Indians had failed to "improve" upon the land and therefore they did not deserve to have control over it. This argument appears frequently in Puritan writing; and (2) that every race follows a cyclical pattern of development that necessarily ends in disappearance. It was the Indians' unfortunate lot to be on the down side of that cycle now.

And Human Culture rolls its onward flood
Over the broad plains steeped in Indian blood.

Such thoughts steady our faith; yet there will rise   100
Some natural tears into the calmest eyes —
Which gaze where forest princes haughty go,
Made for a gaping crowd a raree show.

But *this* a scene seems where, in courtesy,
The pale face with the forest prince could vie,   105
For One presided, who, for tact and grace,
In any age had held an honored place, —
In Beauty's own dear day, had shone a polished Phidian[14] vase!

Oft have I listened to his accents bland,
    And owned the magic of his silvery voice,   110
In all the graces which life's arts demand,
    Delighted by the justness of his choice.
Not his the stream of lavish, fervid thought, —
The rhetoric by passion's magic wrought;
Not his the massive style, the lion port,   115
Which with the granite class of mind assort;
But, in a range of excellence his own,
With all the charms to soft persuasion known,
Amid our busy people we admire him — "elegant and lone."

He scarce needs words, so exquisite the skill   120
Which modulates the tones to do his will,
That the mere sound enough would charm the ear,
And lap in its Elysium[15] all who hear.
The intellectual paleness of his cheek,
    The heavy eyelids and slow, tranquil smile,   125
The well cut lips from which the graces speak,
    Fit him alike to win or to beguile;
Then those words so well chosen, fit, though few,
Their linked sweetness as our thoughts pursue,
We deem them spoken pearls, or radiant diamond dew.   130

And never yet did I admire the power
    Which makes so lustrous every threadbare theme —
Which won for Lafayette[16] one other hour,
    And e'en on July Fourth could cast a gleam —
As now, when I behold him play the host,   135

---

[14]   Phidias (*c.* 500–*c.* 430 BCE), among the most renowned sculptors of ancient Greece.
[15]   In classical mythology, the abode of the blessed after
death.

[16]   The Marquis de Lafayette (1757–1834), a French
general and statesman.

With all the dignity which red men boast –
With all the courtesy the whites have lost: –
Assume the very hue of savage mind,
Yet in rude accents show the thought refined; –
Assume the naiveté of infant age,   140
And in such prattle seem still more a sage;
The golden mean with tact unerring seized,
A courtly critic shone, a simple savage pleased;
The stoic of the woods his skill confessed,
As all the Father answered in his breast,   145
To the sure mark the silver arrow sped,
The man without a tear a tear has shed;
And thou hadst wept, hadst thou been there, to see
How true one sentiment must ever be,
In court or camp, the city or the wild,   150
To rouse the Father's heart, you need but name his Child.

'Twas a fair scene – and acted well by all;
So here's a health to Indian braves so tall –
Our Governor and Boston people all![17]

Manuscript Poem (1844; Steele, 1992)

DOUBLE TRIANGLE, SERPENT AND RAYS

Patient serpent, circle round,
Till in death thy life is found;
Double form of godly prime
Holding the whole thought of time,
When the perfect two embrace,   5
Male & female, black & white,
Soul is justified in space,
Dark made fruitful by the light;
And, centred in the diamond Sun,
Time & Eternity are one.   10

from Griswold (1849)

MOZART[18]

If to the intellect and passions strong
Beethoven speak, with such resistless power,
Making us share the full creative hour,

---

[17] These final lines smack either of smug self-congratulations or a kind of desperate sarcasm, depending on how one interprets Fuller's view of Everett and his speech-making.

MOZART
[18] Wolfgang Amadeus Mozart (1756–91), Austrian composer.

When his wand fixed wild Fancy's mystic throng,
Oh, Nature's finest lyre! to thee belong   5
   The deepest, softest tones of tenderness,
   Whose purity the listening angels bless,
With silvery clearness of seraphic song.
Sad are those chords, oh heavenward striving soul!
   A love, which never found its home on earth,   10
   Pensively vibrates, even in thy mirth,
And gentle laws thy lightest notes control;
Yet dear that sadness! spheral concords felt
Purify most those hearts which most they melt.

Frances Sargent Locke Osgood (1811–1850)

Frances Sargent Locke Osgood was born in Boston, Massachusetts, in 1811. Her father, Joseph Locke, was a merchant and widower, with four children, when Osgood's mother married him. By him, she had three children, making Osgood sixth in a line-up of seven. Like many girls in middle-class homes of the day, Osgood was educated primarily at home in the family residence in Hingham, Massachusetts. Literary talent ran in the family and two of her siblings, Andrew Aitchison Locke and Anna Maria Foster (Wells), also became writers. Under the pseudonym "Florence," Fanny Osgood published her first pieces at fourteen in Lydia Maria Child's *Juvenile Miscellany*.

Osgood met the Boston artist Samuel Stillman Osgood in 1834 when he invited her to sit for a portrait. They were married in 1835. Shortly thereafter they went to live in England for five years (1835–9). Once there, Samuel Osgood settled down to painting society portraits while his wife settled down to cultivating literary relationships with, among others, Mrs Caroline Norton, Harriet Martineau, and the Countess of Blessington. While in England Osgood published her first two books of poetry, *A Wreath of Wild Flowers from New England* (1838) and *The Casket of Fate* (1839). Both were positively reviewed.

Success abroad insured, as it often does, success at home; and when Osgood and her husband returned Stateside in 1839, Fanny Osgood, now the mother of two children, found herself quickly translated to the upper reaches of America's literary elite. A regular in the most prestigious periodicals of the day, she became a regular at literary salons as well, where she was noted for her wit, and for carrying on an extremely public flirtation with Edgar Allan Poe. Possibly as a consequence of the latter, in 1844, she and her husband became estranged.

Glowing as her early years were, Osgood's final years fell under the shadow of tuberculosis. After her third and youngest child, Fanny Fay, died of the disease, she herself was invalided by it, never to recover. Samuel Osgood had left the East for California and the gold rush in 1849; but he returned not long before his wife's death in 1850 and reconciled with her. Her remaining two daughters, also stricken with the disease, died shortly after their mother.

Scintillating, mercurial, abundantly talented, Osgood led a life that was of a piece with her art. She is among the most elusive of nineteenth-century American women poets, a writer who teases and flirts with her craft and with her readers alike. Osgood is difficult to speak of without falling back on descriptors. She carefully cultivated the childlike and coy persona which she inscribes with such relish in "A Flight of Fancy," and like Fancy herself, Fanny's poems seem too fragile, graceful, and delicate to subject to the ruthlessness of critical analysis. And yet . . .

As Joanne Dobson has recently argued in a watershed article on Osgood's manuscript poetry, there may be a darker side to Osgood or, at any rate, a far more worldly and sophisticated side than readers of her published work have been willing to credit. Read against the three manuscript poems which Dobson discovered, and which are placed first in this selection, Osgood's thematization of gender relationships, in particular, takes on a very different cast. What once seemed airy (if not downright vacuous) in her "sentimental" poetry now appears all too down-to-earth and hard-headed, what once seemed flowery now bears an edge.

Like many poets in this volume, Osgood was a keen observer of social customs, especially the rules governing relationships between the sexes. She was also keenly aware of the degree to which women were rendered vulnerable to masculine dominance by these social conventions. If her poetry is one of flirtation, it also seems, in these respects, to be one of resistance.

As Walker noted in 1992, it is difficult to be certain what Osgood's intentions are. Her ability to walk a fine line between flirtation and disgust, innocence and sophistication, spontaneity and calculation, "naturalness" and artificiality, makes her a master of tonal ambiguity and, possibly, among the century's most difficult women poets. Like Fancy herself, Osgood's genius may be one that forever eludes the scholar's (imprisoning) grasp. Nothing, one suspects, would please her more.

Primary Texts

A Wreath of Wild Flowers from New England, 1838; *The Casket of Fate*, 1839; *Poems*, 1846; *Poems*, 1850.

Further Reading

Mary De Jong, "Her Fair Fame: The Reputation of Frances Sargent Osgood, Woman Poet," *Studies in the American Renaissance* (1987): 265–84; "Lines from a Partly Published Drama: the Romance of Frances Sargent Osgood and Edgar Allan Poe," in *Patrons and Protegés: Gender, Friendship, and Writing in Nineteenth-Century America*, ed. Shirley Marchalonis, New York: Oxford University Press, 1984, 31–58; Joanne Dobson, "Sex, Wit, and Sentiment: Frances Osgood and the Poetry of Love," *American Literature* 65 (December 1993): 631–48; Mary E. Hewitt, ed., *The Memorial: Written by Friends of the Late Mrs. Osgood*, New York: George Putnam, 1851; John Evangelist Walsh, *Plumes in the Dust: The Love Affair of Edgar Allan Poe and Fanny Osgood*, Chicago: Nelson-Hall, 1980; Emily Stipes Watts, *The Poetry of American Women from 1632 to 1943*.

Three Manuscript Poems (*c.* 1845; Dobson, 1993)

"WON'T YOU DIE & BE A SPIRIT"

Won't you die & be a spirit
    Darling, say
What's the use of keeping on
    That robe of clay
If you only were a spirit   5
    You could *stay*

Oh! die & be a spirit
    Darling, do
I should hate to have to go
    If I were you   10
From a being so delightful
    And so true

If you'll die & be a spirit
    You may press
The hand that now you gaze at   15
    And the tress
And the cheek that lips of clay
    Shall n'er caress —

If you'll die & be a spirit
    You may say   20
How tenderly you love me
    Everyday
But *now* I hate to hear you!
    Go Away!

Just think how nice 'twould be   25
    To come & beam
Like a star about my pillow
    Or to seem
A vision — I should love
    To love a dream!   30

THE WRAITH OF THE ROSE

An Impromptu Written on a Visiting Card

The magic of that name is fled,
The music of that dream is dead,
Long since Love's rose, its perfume, shed,
    And what art *thou* to me?
If you have come to clasp again,   5
The fetter of that fairy chain,
You'd better far at home remain,
    And save your time — and *knee*!
And yet that dream was strangely dear,
And yet that name awakes a tear,   10
The *wraith* of Love's sweet Rose is here,
    It haunts me everywhere!
I wish the chain were still unbroken,
I wish those words again were spoken,
I wish I'd kept that last fond token,   15
    And had not burned your hair!
I wish your voice still sounded sweet,

I wish you dared Love's vow repeat,
I wish you were not all deceit,
    And I so fickle-hearted!   20
I wish we might go back again,
I wish you *could* reclasp the chain!
I wish – *you hadn't drank champagne,*
    So freely since we parted!
Alas! While Flattery baits your line,   25
You fish in shallower hearts than mine!
You'll never find a pearl divine
    Like that *my* spirit wasted!
But should you catch a seeming prise,
A *flying* fish you'll see it rise,   30
Away – beyond your wicked eyes,
    Before the treasure's tasted!
Oh! *if* those eyes were splendid now,
As when they spoke the silent vow!
Oh! *if* the locks that wreath your brow,   35
    Were not – but this is idle!
My wish shall be with kindness rife,
I'll wish you all the joys of life,
A pleasant home – a peerless wife,
    Whose wishes, Sense shall bridle!   40

THE LADY'S MISTAKE

That his eyebrows were false – that his hair
Was assumed I was fully aware!
I knew his moustache of a barber was bought
And that Cartwright provided his teeth – but I thought
    That his *heart* was at least true and fair   5

I saw that the exquisite glow
Spreading over the cheek of my beau
From a carmine shell came and I often was told
That his elegant calf by his tailor was sold
    I dreamed not that his *love* was but show   10

I was sure – I could easily tell
That the form which deluded each belle
Was made over his own – but I could not believe
That his flattering tongue too was made to deceive
    That his *fortune* was humbug as well   15

I had made up my mind to dispense
With a figure, hair, teeth, heart & sense
The calf I'd o'erlook were it ever so small
But to think that he is not – a *count* after all
    That's a not to be pardoned offence!   20

from *Poems* (1846)

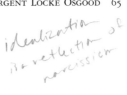
*idealization of
Reflection of
narcissism*

THE LILY'S DELUSION

A cold, calm star look'd out of heaven,
   And smiled upon a tranquil lake,
Where, pure as angel's dream at even,
   A Lily lay but half awake.

The flower felt that fatal smile   5
   And lowlier bow'd her conscious head;
"Why does he gaze on me the while?"
   The light, deluded Lily said.

Poor dreaming flower! – too soon beguiled,
   She cast nor thought nor look elsewhere,   10
Else she had known the star but smiled
   To see himself reflected there.

THE DAISY'S MISTAKE

A sunbeam and zephyr were playing about,
   One spring, ere a blossom had peep'd from the stem,
When they heard, underground, a faint, fairy-like shout;
   'Twas the voice of field-daisy calling to them.

"Oh! tell me, my friend, has the winter gone by?   5
   Is it time to come up? Is the Crocus there yet?
I know you are sporting above, and I sigh
   To be with you and kiss you; – 'tis long since we met!

"I've been ready this great while, – all dress'd for the show;
   I've a gem on my bosom that's pure as a star;   10
And the frill of my robe is as white as the snow;
   And I mean to be brighter than Crocuses are."

Now the zephyr and sunbeam were wild with delight!
   It seem'd a whole age since they'd play'd with a flower;
So they told a great fib to the poor little sprite,   15
   That was languishing down in her underground bower.

"Come out! little darling! as quick as you can!
   The Crocus, the Cowslip, and Buttercup too,
Have been up here this fortnight, we're having grand times,
   And all of them hourly asking for you!   20

"The Cowslip is crown'd with a topaz tiara;
   The Crocus is flaunting in golden attire;

But you, little pet! are a thousand times fairer;
To see you but once, is to love and admire!

"The skies smile benignantly all the day long;   25
The bee drinks your health in the purest of dew;
The lark has been waiting to sing you a song,
Which he practised in Cloudland on purpose for you!

"Come, come! you are either too bashful or lazy!
Lady Spring made this season an early entrée;   30
And she wonder'd what could have become of her Daisy;
We'll call you coquettish, if still you delay!"

Then a still, small voice, in the heart of the flower,
It was Instinct, whisper'd her, "Do not go!
You had better be quiet, and wait your hour;   35
It isn't too late even yet for snow!"

But the little field-blossom was foolish and vain,
And she said to herself, "What a belle I shall be!"
So she sprang to the light, as she broke from her chain,
And gayly she cried, "I am free! I am free!"   40

A shy little thing is the Daisy, you know;
And she was half frighten'd to death, when she found
Not a blossom had even *begun* to blow!
How she wish'd herself back again under the ground!

The tear in her timid and sorrowful eye   45
Might well put the zephyr and beam to the blush;
But the saucy light laugh'd, and said, "Pray don't cry!"
And the gay zephyr sang to her, "Hush, sweet, hush!"

They kiss'd her and petted her fondly at first;
But a storm arose, and the false light fled;   50
And the zephyr changed into angry breeze,
That scolded her till she was almost dead!

The gem on her bosom was stain'd and dark,
The snow of her robe had lost its light,
And tears of sorrow had dimm'd the spark   55
Of beauty and youth, that made her bright!

And so she lay with her fair head low,
And mournfully sigh'd in her dying hour,
"Ah! had I courageously answer'd 'no!'
I had now been safe in my native bower!"   60

A FLIGHT OF FANCY

At the bar of Judge Conscience, stood Reason arraign'd,
The Jury impannell'd – the prisoner chain'd.
The Judge was facetious, at times, though severe,
Now waking a smile, and now drawing a tear;
An old-fashion'd, fidgety, queer-looking wight,[1]   5
With a clerical air, and an eye quick as light.

"Here, Reason, you vagabond! look in my face;
I'm told you're becoming an idle scapegrace.
They say that young Fancy, that airy coquette,
Has dared to fling round you her luminous net;   10
That she ran away with you, in spite of yourself,
For pure love of frolic – the mischievous elf.

"The scandal is whisper'd by friends and by foes,
And darkly they hint too, that when they propose
Any question to *your* ear, so lightly you're led,   15
At once to gay Fancy, you turn your wild head;
And *she* leads you off in some dangerous dance,
As wild as the Polka that gallop'd from France.

"Now up to the stars with you, laughing, she springs,
With a whirl and a whisk of her changeable wings;   20
Now dips in some fountain her sun-painted plume,
That gleams thro' the spray, like a rainbow in bloom;
Now floats in a cloud, while her tresses of light
Shine through the frail boat and illumine its flight;
Now glides through the woodland to gather its flowers;   25
Now darts like a flash to the sea's coral bowers;
In short – cuts such capers, that with her I ween
It's a wonder you are not ashamed to be seen!

"Then she talks such a language! – melodious enough,
To be sure – but a strange sort of outlandish stuff!   30
I'm told that it licenses many a whapper,[2]
And when once she commences no frowning can stop her;
Since it's new – I've no doubt it is very improper!
They say that she cares not for order or law;
That of you – you great dunce! – she but makes a cat's paw.   35
I've no sort of objection to fun in it's season,
But it's plain that this Fancy is *fooling* you, Reason!"

Just then into court flew a strange little sprite,
With wings of all colors and ringlets of light!

A FLIGHT OF FANCY
[1] *Wight* archaic for a person.   [2] *Whapper* whopper, a blatant gross lie.

She frolick'd round Reason – till Reason grew wild,   40
Defying the court and caressing the child.
The judge and the jury, the clerk and recorder,
In vain call'd this exquisite creature to order: –
"Unheard of intrusion!" – They bustled about,
To seize her, but, wild with delight, at the rout,   45
She flew from their touch like a bird from a spray,
And went waltzing and whirling and singing away!

Now up to the ceiling, now down to the floor!
Were never such antics in courthouse before!
But a lawyer, well versed in the tricks of his trade,   50
A trap for the gay little innocent laid:
He held up a *mirror*, and Fancy was caught
By her image within it, so lovely, she thought.
What could the fair creature be! – bending its eyes
On her own with so wistful a look of surprise!   55
She flew to embrace it. The lawyer was ready:
He closed round the spirit a grasp cool and steady,
And she sigh'd, while he tied her two luminous wings,
"Ah! Fancy and Falsehood are different things!"

The witnesses – maidens of uncertain age,   60
With a critic, a publisher, lawyer and sage –
All scandalized greatly at what they had heard,
Of this poor little Fancy, (who flew like a bird!)
Were call'd to the stand and their evidence gave:
The judge charged the jury, with countenance grave.   65
Their verdict was "guilty," and Reason look'd down,
As his honor exhorted her thus, with a frown: –

"This Fancy, this vagrant, for life shall be chain'd,
In your own little cell, where *you* should have remain'd;
And you – for *your* punishment – jailer shall be: 70
Don't let your accomplice come coaxing to me!
I'll none of her nonsense – the little wild witch!
Nor her bribes – although rumor does say she is rich.

"I've heard that all treasures and luxuries rare,
Gather round at her bidding, from earth, sea, and air;   75
And some go so far as to hint, that the powers
Of darkness attend her more sorrowful hours.
But go!" and Judge Conscience, who never was bought,
Just bow'd the pale prisoner out of the court.
'Tis said, – that poor Reason next morning was found,   80
At the door of her cell, fast asleep on the ground,
And nothing within, but one plume rich and rare,
Just to show that young Fancy's wing once had been there.

She had dropp'd it, no doubt, while she strove to get through
The hole in the lock, which she could not undo.   85

TO SYBIL

"Sooth her in sorrow and brighten her smile;
Chide her most gently if folly beguile;
One so unsullied and trustful of heart,
From the good shepherd will never depart.

"Now she adores thee as one without spot,
Dreams not of sorrow to darken her lot.
Joyful, yet tearful, I yield her to thee;
Take her, the light of thy dwelling to be."

Yes! go to him – thy young heart full
    Of passionate romance,
And be the fiat of thy fate
    His lordly word and glance!

Be thy soul's day, his careless smile;   5
    His frown, its clouded night;
His voice, the music of thy life;
    His love, thy one delight!

Sit at his feet, and raise to his
    Those large, pure, dreaming eyes,   10
And tell him all thy lovely thoughts
    As radiantly they rise.

Press to his hand that childish cheek,
    And stroke his stern dark face,
And charm him with thy ways so meek,   15
    Thy glad, aerial grace!

Look for his coming with clasp'd hands
    And hush'd and listening heart,
And strive to hide thy joyous tears
    With woman's bashful art.   20

And in thy low Eolian[5] tones,
    Melodiously wild,
Falter thy fond, sweet welcome out,
    Oh, rare, enchanting child!

To SYBIL
[5] Variation of Aeolian. The [A]eolian harp was a wind harp. Mid-century women poets often adopted this instrument as a figure for their own creativity, since it suggested both their passivity and their responsiveness to the natural world around them.

Then if he coldly turn away,   25
  In silence to him steal,
And touch his soul with one long gaze
  Of passionate appeal.

I know them all — th' endearing wiles —
  The sweet, unconscious art —   30
The graceful spells that nature taught
  Her darling's docile heart.

I know them all — I've seen thee lift,
  At some unkindly tone,
Those dark, upbraiding eyes of thine,   35
  Where sorrowing wonder shone,

And sudden tears would dim the glance,
  And then — the wrong forgiven —
A smile would steal up in the cloud,
  Like starlight into heaven.   40

Go — try them all — those girlish wiles!
  He cannot choose but love,
He cannot choose but guard from ill
  His little, nestling dove!

For rare, my Sybil, 'tis to see   45
  Thy iris-mind unfold;
The magic of thy maiden glee,
  That turns all gloom to gold; —

Th' aurora blush that on thy cheek
  Thy heart's love-story tells;   50
The wondrous world within thine eyes
  Lit up like the gazelle's.

But if thou think'st, dear dreaming child!
  That he will watch as now,
In after years, each smile and shade   55
  That cross thy changing brow;

And modulate his tone to meet
  The pleading of thy soul,
And feel in all his wanderings,
  Thy gentle breast his goal;   60

And daily feed thy mind and heart
  With hallow'd love and lore,
Nor turn from those imploring eyes,
  That wistful look for more;

And watch thee where — as borne in air —   65
   Thou float'st the dance along,
And deem thy form alone is fair,
   Of all the fairy throng;

In transport look and listen when
   Thy light caressing hands   70
Lure forth the harp's harmonious soul,
   From all its silver bands;

Indulgent stoop his falcon-will
   To let it fly with thine,
And smile in manly pride to see   75
   His pet's soft plumage shine;

And yield to every gay caprice,
   And grieve for every sigh,
And grant all airy hopes that play
   On pleading lip or eye;   80

If *this* be thy dream, enthusiast, be,
   I can but idly pray,
Heaven shield thee in thy *waking* hour,
   And keep it long away!

A MOTHER'S PRAYER IN ILLNESS

Yes! take them first, my Father! Let my doves
Fold their white wings in Heaven, safe on thy breast,
Ere I am call'd away! I dare not leave
Their young hearts here, their innocent, thoughtless hearts!
Ah! how the shadowy train of future ills   5
Comes sweeping down life's vista as I gaze!
  My May! my careless, ardent-temper'd May!
My frank and frolic child! In whose blue eyes
Wild joy and passionate wo alternate rise;
Whose cheek, the morning in her soul illumes;   10
Whose little, loving heart, a word, a glance,
Can sway to grief or glee; who leaves her play,
And puts up her sweet mouth and dimpled arms,
Each moment for a kiss, and softly asks,
With her clear, flute-like voice, "Do you love me?"   15
Ah! let me stay! ah! let me still be by,

To answer her and meet her warm caress!
For I away, how oft in this rough world,
That earnest question will be ask'd in vain!
How oft that eager, passionate, petted heart,   20

Will shrink abash'd and chill'd to learn at length
The hateful, withering lesson of distrust!
Ah! let her nestle still upon this breast,
In which each shade, that dims her darling face,
Is felt and answer'd, as the lake reflects   25
The clouds that cross yon smiling heaven! and thou –
My modest Ellen! tender, thoughtful, true;
Thy soul attuned to all sweet harmonies;
My pure, proud, noble Ellen! with thy gifts
Of genius, grace, and loveliness, half hidden   30
'Neath the soft veil of innate modesty,
How will the world's wild discord reach thy heart
To startle and appall!   thy generous scorn
Of all things base and mean – thy quick, keen taste,
Dainty and delicate – thy instinctive fear   35
Of those unworthy of a soul so pure,
Thy rare, unchildlike dignity of mien,
All – they will all bring pain to thee, my child!
And oh! if even their grace and goodness meet
Cold looks and careless greetings, how will all   40
The latent *evil* yet undisciplined
In their young, timid souls, forgiveness find?
Forgiveness, and forbearance, and soft chidings,
Which I – their mother – learn'd of Love to give!
Ah! let me stay! – albeit my heart is weary,   45
Weary and worn, tired of its own sad beat,
That finds no echo in this busy world
Which cannot pause to answer – tired alike
Of joy and sorrow – of the day and night!
Ah! take them first, my Father! and then me;   50
And for their sakes – for their sweet sakes, my Father!
Let me find rest beside them, at thy feet!

from *North American Daily* (1848)

FANNY FAY'S BABY JUMPER[4]

They tell of a ring that is ever enchanted,
By light-tripping fairies in summer nights haunted;
And they say that whoever shall step but within it

FANNY FAY'S BABY JUMPER
[1]   The *North American Daily* in which this poem appeared was a bilingual newspaper published for the largely military American colony living in Mexico City at the opening of the Mexican War. How this poem fell into the editor's hands, and why Osgood wrote it in the first place, are both mysteries. (Was she remunerated by the manufacturer? One suspects so.) Noting that the "labor-saving machine" had become the object of satirical wit on the part of the bachelors in the community, the editor published Osgood's poem, in hopes of restoring domestic peace in the community. Fanny Fay is the name of Osgood's youngest child.

Has only to wish for some treasure to win it!
A fable no longer! behold in its glory   5
The dear fairy thing that they talk of in story,
With its magical music, its toys and its treasures.
A gay charmed circle of exquisite pleasure.
And here sits a fay, with her blue eyes up glancing,
Her tiny hands spread and her little feet dancing,   10
While her soft rippling coo, like a ring-dove's is heard,
To tell her sweet rapture! the beauty! the bird!
   A health, oh inventer, of blest Baby Jumpers –
A health in the richest and rarest of bumpers!
The sage and the seer are foretelling a year   15
When all shall be peace in this sad little sphere,
When the poor shall rejoice and the bondman go free,
But the MOTHER shall owe her mille[n]nium to thee.
   Away with all jolting and tossing forever;
The croon and the lullaby murmur then never!   20
Only leave the babe-queen in the circle enchanted,
Each wish of her dear little heart shall be granted!
Let her mount her gay throne and away in the air,
She rises o'er sorrow and dances off care;
Descending, her tiny f[ee]t but touc[h] the floor,   25
And up through the ring she is floating once more.
Her happy laugh echoes, the silver bells ringing,
She seems a young spirit thro' the air her way winging;
And her soft rippling coo, like a ring-dove's is heard,
To tell her sweet rapture – the beauty! the bird!   30

from *Poems* (1850)

WOMAN

A Fragment

   Within a frame, more glorious than the gem
To which Titania[5] could her sylph[6] condemn,
Fair woman's spirit dreams the hours away,
Content at times in that bright home to stay,
So that you let her deck her beauty still,   5
And waltz and warble at her own sweet will.
   Taught to restrain, in cold Decorum's school,
The step, the smile, tó glance and dance by rule;
To smooth alike her words and waving tress,
And her pure *heart's* impetuous play repress;   10

WOMAN
[5] The Fairy Queen in Shakespeare's *A Midsummer Night's* [6] An elemental spirit of the air.
Dream.

Each airy impulse – every frolic thought
Forbidden, if by Fashion's law untaught,
The graceful houri[7] of your heavenlier hours
Forgets, in gay saloons, her native bowers,
Forgets her glorious home – her angel-birth –   15
Content to share the passing joys of earth;
Save when, at intervals, a ray of love
Pleads to her spirit from the realms above,
Plays on her pinions shut, and softly sings
In low Æolian tones of heavenly things.   20
   Ah! *then* dim memories dawn upon the soul
Of that celestial home from which she stole;
She feels its fragrant airs around her blow;
She sees the immortal bowers of beauty glow;
And faint and far, but how divinely sweet!   25
She hears the music where its angels meet.
   Then wave her starry wings in hope and shame,
Their fire illumes the fair, transparent frame,
Fills the dark eyes with passionate thought the while,
Blooms in the blush and lightens in the smile: 30
No longer then the toy, the doll, the slave,
But frank, heroic, beautiful, and brave,
She rises, radiant in immortal youth,
And wildly pleads for Freedom and for Truth!
   These captive Peris[8] all around you smile,   35
And one I've met who might a god beguile.
She's stolen from Nature all her loveliest spells:
Upon her cheek morn's blushing splendour dwells,
The starry midnight kindles in her eyes,
The gold of sunset on her ringlets lies,   40
And to the ripple of a rill, 'tis said,
She turned her voice and timed her airy tread!
   No rule restrains *her* thrilling laugh, or moulds
Her flowing robe to tyrant Fashion's folds;
No custom chains the grace in that fair girl,   45
That sways her willowy form or waves her careless curl.
I plead not that she share each sterner task;
The cold reformers know not what they ask;
I only seek for our transplanted fay,
That she may have – in all *fair ways* – her way!   50
   I would not see the aerial creature trip,
A blooming sailor, up some giant ship,
Some man-of-war – to reef the topsail high –

---

[7] One of the beautiful maidens believed by some Muslims to dwell in paradise for the pleasure of the faithful. Osgood also seems to be punning on the classical Greek concept of the hours.

[8] Female spirits associated with fallen angels.

Ah! reef your *curls* – and let the *canvas* fly!
   Nor would I bid her quit her 'broidery frame,   55
A fairy blacksmith by the forge's flame:
No! be the fires *she* kindles only those
With which man's iron nature wildly glows.
"Strike while the iron's hot," with all your art,
But strike *Love's* anvil in his yielding heart!   60
   Nor should our sylph her tone's low music strain,
A listening senate with her wit to chain,
To rival Choate[9] in rich and graceful lore,
Or challenge awful Webster[10] to the floor,
Like that rash wight who raised the casket's lid,   65
And set a genius free the stars that hid.
   Not thus forego the poetry of life,
The sacred names of mother, sister, wife!
Rob not the household hearth of all its glory,
Lose not those tones of musical delight,   70
All man has left, to tell him the sweet story
Of his remember'd home – beyond the night.
   Yet men too proudly use their tyrant power;
They chill the soft bloom of the fairy flower;
They bind the wing, that would but soar above   75
In search of purer air and holier love;
They hush the heart, that fondly pleads its wrong
In plaintive prayer or in impassion'd song.
   Smile on, sweet flower! soar on, enchanted wing!
Since she ne'er asks but for *one trifling thing*,   80
Since but *one* want disturbs the graceful fay,
Why *let* the docile darling *have – her way!*

Sarah Louisa Forten ("Ada") (1814–1883)

Sarah Louisa Forten was born in 1814 in the city of Philadelphia, Pennsylvania – "old abominable Philadelphia," as her niece, Charlotte Forten Grimké, referred to it. Forten's father, James Forten, was the great-grandson of an African slave. After serving as a powder boy in the Revolutionary War, he entered the lucrative sail-making business. By the 1830s, he was one of the richest men in Philadelphia, with net assets said to be worth $100,000. A committed abolitionist, James Forten was a principal backer of William Lloyd Garrison's abolitionist newspaper, the *Liberator*, and during Sarah's childhood, her father's home in Philadelphia provided lodgings and hospitality for many traveling abolitionists, Garrison and the poet John Greenleaf Whittier among them.

    Sarah Louisa's mother, Charlotte Forten, was of mixed racial descent, including African, Caucasian, and Native American strains. A charter member of the Philadelphia Female

---

[9] Joseph H. Choate (1832–1917), American lawyer and diplomat.

[10] Daniel Webster (1782–1852), a noted statesman and orator.

Anti-Slavery Society, she, like her daughters (Margaretta, Sarah, and Harriet), remained politically active throughout her life. The Forten women's activities included fund-raising for abolitionist causes, community-organizing, leadership roles on charitable committees, and improving educational opportunities for Philadelphia's black children. In many of these activities, they worked side by side with white women abolitionists, including Lucretia Mott and Angelina Grimké, whom Sarah particularly admired.

In 1838, Sarah married Joseph Purvis, the brother of Robert Purvis, a noted black abolitionist and her sister Harriet's husband. Sarah Louisa and Joseph moved to a farm outside Philadelphia, after which Sarah's public activity was sharply curtailed, probably due to child-bearing and rearing. Joseph Purvis died in 1857, leaving his widow eight children and a large pile of debts. Sometime later Sarah Louisa moved back to her parents' home in Philadelphia, bringing her youngest children, Anne and William Purvis, with her. Publicly speaking all that is known of her thereafter is that she was once again working on anti-slavery fair committees with her two sisters in the early 1860s.

The least well documented of the three sisters (Margaretta was an educator and Harriet, like her husband, an active abolitionist), Sarah Louisa Forten was also, at least for a while, the most literary. Published under the pseudonym "Ada," her poems began to appear in the *Liberator* in early 1831, at which time her father wrote Garrison disclosing her identity as "Ada." By March 1836, when her last known poem appears in the *Philanthropist*, she had published fifteen poems, plus one biting "op-ed" piece, "The Abuse of Liberty," signed Magawisca. This is a slight number, to be sure, but large enough and of such quality that one wishes she had written more. Unfortunately, with the exception of a few manuscript poems, some of doubtful authenticity, it appears she did not.

A good deal of confusion now surrounds Forten's output. In 1837, the *Liberator* began reprinting poems from the *Massachusetts Spy* which were signed by a second "Ada," Eliza Earle, sister of John Milton Earle, the *Spy's* owner and publisher.[1] These poems, to which "Lines, Suggested on reading 'An Appeal to Christian Women of the South,' by A. E. Grimke" probably should be added (see Section II), have traditionally been identified as Forten's. Of them, however, only the status of the Grimké poem, which was written for the *Liberator*, but which is in Earle's densely allusive style, is in any way moot.

In its directness, its limpidity, and poignancy, Forten's poetry is representative of good abolitionist lyrics of her period. "The Grave of the Slave" was set to music and lines from "An Appeal to Woman" were used at the opening of the first Convention of American Women against Slavery (1837). The latter poem is especially notable for its blend of feminist and abolitionist concerns, a blend that typifies Forten's thinking and that of the group to which she belonged, especially the Grimké sisters. On the whole, however, the emphasis in Forten's poems falls where abolitionist sentiment generally fell: on the cruel disruption of family bonds slavery produced and on the hypocrisy of a country that called itself "Christian" and "democratic" but that nevertheless tolerated the holding of slaves (see, for example, the poems by Sarah Mapps Douglass in Section II). Whatever his or her specific theme, the poet's goal in such works was to make the reader (or hearer) *feel* the pain

---

[1]   Whittier identifies Eliza Earle as the "second" Ada when reprinting one of her *Massachusetts Spy–Liberator* poems in the *Pennsylvanian Freeman*. Since Whittier knew both "Adas" personally, it is highly unlikely that his attribution is in error. For help in untangling Ada's many knots, I wish to thank Professors Julie Winch and Todd Gernes. My biography is especially indebted to Professor Winch, who has shared much as yet unpublished material with me, including her transcription of "Look! 'Tis a woman's streaming eye." To Professor Gernes I owe the wisdom of making me find out on my own that a second Ada did indeed exist, improbable as it seemed at first, and unwilling as I was to believe it.

that slavery caused and therefore experience the outrage that feeling such pain inspired. Read in this light, Forten's poems more than accomplish their goal.

Primary Texts

The *Liberator* poems appeared on the following dates: "The Grave of the Slave" (January 22, 1831); "Past Joys" (March 19, 1831); "Prayer" (March 26, 1831); "The Slave" (April 16, 1831); "My Country" (January 4, 1834); "An Appeal to Woman" (February 1, 1834). "Look! 'Tis a woman's streaming eye" is in the Elizabeth Smith Album, Francis J. Grimké Papers, Moorland-Spingarn Collection, Howard University.

Further Reading

Leon Litwack, "The Emancipation of the Negro Abolitionist," in *The Abolitionists*, ed. Richard O. Curry, Hinsdale, Illinois: Dryden Press, 1973; Mrs N. F. Mossell, *The Work of the Afro-American Woman*, Philadelphia: G. S. Ferguson, 1894; Janice Sumler-Edmond, "The Forten Sisters," in *Black Women in America: An Historical Encyclopedia*, ed. Darlene Clark Hine, 2 vols, Brooklyn, New York: Carlson, 1993; Jean Fagan Yellin, *Women & Sisters: The Antislavery Feminists in American Culture*, New Haven: Yale University Press, 1989; Jean Fagan Yellin and Cynthia D. Bond, *The Pen is Ours: A Listing of Writings by and about African-American Women before 1910*; Jean Fagan Yellin and John C. Van Horne, eds, *The Abolitionist Sisterhood: Women's Political Culture in Antebellum America*, Ithaca: Cornell University Press, 1994.

from *Liberator* (1831)

THE GRAVE OF THE SLAVE

The cold storms of winter shall chill him no more,
His woes and his sorrows, his pains are all o'er;
The sod of the valley now covers his form,
He is safe in his last home, he feels not the storm.

The poor slave is laid all unheeded and lone,   5
Where the rich and the poor find a permanent home;
Not his master can rouse him with voice of command;
He knows not, he hears not, his cruel demand.

Not a tear, not a sigh to embalm his cold tomb,
No friend to lament him, no child to bemoan;   10
Not a stone marks the place, where he peacefully lies,
The earth for his pillow, his curtain the skies.

Poor slave! shall we sorrow that death was thy friend,
The last, and the kindest, that heaven could send?
The grave to the weary is welcomed and blest;   15
And death, to the captive, is freedom and rest.

PAST JOYS

The friends we've loved, the home we've left,
   Will ofttimes claim a tear;
And though of these we are bereft,
   Still memory makes them dear.

And deep we feel each trifling ill,   5
   Each sorrow of the soul;
But care we for the painful thrill,
   That o'er some breasts doth roll?

Poor Afric's son – ah! He must feel
   How hard it is to part   10
From all he lov'd – from all that life
   Had twined around his heart.

His is a sorrow deeper far,
   Than all that we can show;
His is a lasting grief, o'er which   15
   No healing balm can flow.

The mother, wife, or child he loved,
   He ne'er shall see again;
To him they're lost – ay, dead indeed:
   What for him doth remain?   20

A feeling of deep wretchedness
   Comes o'er his troubled soul;
The thoughts of home, – of other days,
   In painful visions roll.

His home – ah! That lov'd name recalls   25
   All that was dear to him;
But *these* were scenes he'll know no more –
   He only *feels* they've been.

PRAYER

This sacred right none are denied,
Which makes the soul to Christ allied;
Man bends the heart and bows the knee,
And knows in prayer that he is free.

Yes, free to ask of Him, whate'er   5
The fainting heart alone can cheer;
To worship at that holy shrine,
Where beams thy Spirit, Lord, divine.

And Afric's children they are free,
To breathe their vows, their prayers to Thee;   10
With thought of future joy and gain,
The slave forgets his grief and pain;

Forgets awhile his slavish fear;
Forgets, – that fetters bind him here;
And in that sweet communion rest   15
His hopes, his fears, – for he is blest.

THE SLAVE

Our sires who once in freedom's cause,
    Their boasted freedom sought and won,
For deeds of glory gained applause,
    When patriot feelings led them on.
And can their sons now speak with pride,   5
Of rights for which they bled and died, –
Or while the captive is oppressed,
Think of the wrongs they once redress'd?
Oh, surely they have quite forgot,
That bondage once had been their lot;   10
The sweets of freedom now they know,
They care not for the captive's wo.
The poor wronged slave can bear no part
In feelings dearest to his heart;
He cannot speak on freedom's side,   15
Nor dare he own a freeman's pride.
His soul is dark, ay dark as night,
O'er which is shed no gleam of light;
A cloud of error, doubt and fear,
O'er him is ever hovering near;   20
And sad and hard his lot must be,
To know that he can ne'er be free;
To feel that *his* is doomed to be
A life, and death, of slavery.
But will not justice soon arise,   25
And plead the cause of the despised?
For oh! my country, must it be,
That they still find a foe in thee?

from *Liberator* (1834)

MY COUNTRY

Oh! speak not of heathenish darkness again,
Nor tell me of lands held in error's dread chain!

Where – where is the nation so erring as we,
Who claim the proud name of the "HOME OF THE FREE"?
What a throb do the lov'd ties of country awake   5
In the heart of the exile! – for time cannot break
The sweet vision of home, and all he loved well,
Which has thrown o'er his pathway a magical spell.
Can the name of "MY COUNTRY" – the deeds which we sing –
Be honored – revered – 'midst pollution and sin?   10
Can the names of our fathers who perished in fight,
Be hallowed in story, midst slavery's blight?
When America's standard is floating so fair,
I blush that the impress of falsehood is there;
That oppression and mockery dim the high fame,   15
That seeks from all nations a patriot's name.
Speak not of "my country," unless she shall be,
In truth, the bright home of the "brave and the free!"
Till the dark stain of slavery is washed from her hand,
A tribute of homage she cannot command.   20

AN APPEAL TO WOMAN

Oh, woman, woman, in thy brightest hour
Of conscious worth, of pride, of conscious power,
Oh, nobly dare to act a Christian's part,
That well befits a lovely woman's heart!
Dare to be good, as thou canst dare be great;   5
Despise the taunts of envy, scorn and hate;
Our "skins may differ," but from thee we claim
A sister's privilege, in a sister's name.

We are thy sisters, – God has truly said,
That of one blood, the nations he has made.   10
Oh, christian woman, in a christian land,
Canst thou unblushing road this great command?
Suffer the wrongs which wring our inmost heart
To draw one throb of pity on thy part;
Our "skins may differ," but from thee we claim   15
A sister's privilege, in a sister's name.

Oh, woman! – though upon thy fairer brow
The hues of roses and of lilies glow –
These soon must wither in their kindred earth,
From whence the fair and dark have equal birth.   20
Let a bright halo o'er thy virtues shed
A lustre, that shall live when thou art dead;
Let coming ages learn to bless thy name
Upon the altar of immortal fame.

Manuscript Poem (1837)

"LOOK! 'TIS A WOMAN'S STREAMING EYE"[2]

Look! 'Tis a woman's streaming eye,
These are woman's fettered hands,
That to you so mournfully,
Lift sad glance, and iron bands.
Are not woman's pulses warm,   5
Beating in this anguished breast?
Is it not a Sister[']s form,
On whose limbs these fetters rest?

Julia Ward Howe (1819–1910)

Julia Ward Howe was born in New York City on May 27, 1819, the fourth child of a well-to-do Wall Street banker, Samuel Ward Jr, and his sometime poet wife, Julia Rush (Cutler). Howe's father was a devout Episcopalian with a strong Calvinist bent, and a strict belief in discipline and the rewards of heaven and hell. Between tutors and private schools, Howe received an excellent education, especially in modern languages and German philosophy, and she was already the author of several articles on modern European writers when she met her future husband, Samuel Gridley Howe, director of the renowned Perkins Institute for the Blind. Highly regarded for his work on hospital reform and various other social causes, including abolition, Samuel proposed to the young writer and Howe threw youth's romantic dreams aside to marry him for what she viewed as his nobility of character.

United to a man who was her senior both in years and reputation, and who vehemently opposed the participation of married women in public life, Julia Howe soon stood at risk of withering away in her husband's shadow. That she did not is a testimony to her own powerful willfulness. Husband and wife clashed over everything, including the use of her inheritance. In spite of Samuel's resistance, however, Howe continued to pursue her literary career, publishing her first book of poetry, *Passion Flowers*, anonymously in 1854, and bearing with the marital consequences *post facto*.

Three years later, Howe's first play, *Leonora, or the World's Own*, was produced at the New York Lyceum. Replete with sex and violence (nineteenth-century style), *Leonora* was panned as indecent by the New York theater critics and closed in one week (undoubtedly to her husband's everlasting relief). A second play, *Hippolytus*, written that same year – and suffering from the same disabling features – was never published. That it existed at all, however, says a great deal about Howe's intestinal fortitude – and about the frustration her husband probably experienced when dealing with her.

The turning point for Howe's life – and career – came with the *Atlantic Monthly*'s publication of "Battle-Hymn of the Republic" in February, 1862. Written to the tune of "John Brown's Body," its martial cadences and Old Testament imagery have an overpowering

---

"LOOK! 'TIS A WOMAN'S STREAMING EYE"
[2] Forten copied this poem into a friend's album, under a cut-out picture of the famous abolitionist image of a bare-breasted African American woman holding up her chained hands and asking, "Am I not a woman and a sister?"

effect. By 1864, Howe's poem had swept the North, galvanizing a martial spirit that, in the main, was sadly lacking among demoralized Union forces. Its spiritual zeal and moral idealism – and the stark simplicities of its Calvinist world view – make it the closest thing to perfect poetic expression that abolition's moral certainties would ever receive. Even today, its calling is hard to resist.

"Battle-Hymn of the Republic" brought Howe permanently to public attention as a writer in her own right, giving her the leverage she needed to break from her husband's control. (Even Boston's closed literary society finally acknowledged her.) Thereafter her life in all its multifarious reform activities from woman's suffrage to world peace is inseparable from the life of the age. By the time Samuel Gridley Howe died in 1876, he had long since abandoned any attempt to rein her in. As he lay dying, he confessed to extramarital affairs instead. Clearly, the moral shoe had migrated to the other foot. Howe remained an (increasingly) loved celebrity and active participant in reform movements to the end of her life, still giving speeches on equal rights as late as 1906. The first woman elected to the American Academy of Arts and Letters (1908), she died of pneumonia at ninety-one.

Interest in Howe's poetry has tended – perhaps inevitably – to lag well behind that in her life, yet she was among the stronger women poets of her age. In poems such as "My Last Dance," "Battle-Hymn of the Republic," and "The Soul-Hunter," the darkness that emerges as melodrama in her plays is brought under artistic control. She has selected apt metaphorical vehicles for her emotions, and the impact of the poems is both chilling and exhilarating. It was this same Calvinistically tinged darkness, perhaps, that allowed Howe to accept with such tightly controlled equanimity the harshest judgments of God, in her lament for a dead child, "Remembrance," one of the finest maternal elegies the century would produce. In her excellent analysis of Howe's poetry for the *Encyclopedia of American Poetry*, Wendy Dasler Johnson stresses the complexity of Howe's production as it was mediated through her multifaceted lyric "I." Hopefully this representation of Howe's work – however slight in itself – suggests something of this complexity here.

Primary Texts

Passion Flowers, 1854; *Words of the Hour*, 1857; *Later Lyrics*, 1866; *From Sunset Ridge: Poems, Old and New*, 1898; *Reminiscences, 1819–1899*, 1899; *At Sunset*, 1910.

Further Reading

Leonardo Buonomo, "Julia Ward Howe's 'Italian' Poems in *Passion Flowers*," *Annali di Ca' Foscari* 40 (1991): 27–35; Deborah Pickman Clifford, *Mine Eyes Have Seen the Glory: A Biography of Julia Ward Howe*, Boston: Little, Brown, 1979; Wendy Dasler Johnson, "Julia Ward Howe," *Encyclopedia of American Poetry*; Tracy McCabe, "Avenging Angel: Tragedy and Womanhood in Julia Ward Howe's *The World's Own*," *Legacy: A Journal of Nineteenth-Century American Women Writers* 12 (1995), 98–111; Laura Richards and Maude Howe Elliott, eds, *Julia Ward Howe 1819–1910*, 2 vols, Boston: Houghton, 1915.

from Griswold (1849)

WOMAN

A vestal priestess,[1] proudly pure,
   But of a meek and quiet spirit;
With soul all dauntless to endure,
   And mood so calm that naught can stir it,
Save when a thought most deeply thrilling   5
Her eyes with gentlest tears is filling,
Which seem with her true words to start
From the deep fountain at her heart.

A mien that neither seeks nor shuns
   The homage scattered in her way;   10
A love that hath few favored ones,
   And yet for all can work and pray;
A smile wherein each mortal reads
The very sympathy he needs;
An eye like to a mystic book   15
   Of lays that bard or prophet sings,
Which keepeth for the holiest look
   Of holiest love its deepest things.

A form to which a king had bent,
The fireside's dearest ornament –   20
Known in the dwellings of the poor
Better than at the rich man's door;
A life that ever onward goes,
Yet in itself has deep repose.

A vestal priestess, maid, or wife –   25
   Vestal, and vowed to offer up
The innocence of a holy life
   To Him who gives the mingled cup;
With man its bitter sweets to share,
To live and love, to do and dare;   30
His prayer to breathe, his tears to shed,
Breaking to him the heavenly bread
Of hopes which, all too high for earth,
Have yet in her a mortal birth.

This is the woman I have dreamed,   35
And to my childish thought she seemed
The woman I myself should be:
Alas! I would that I were she.

WOMAN

[1] The Vestal Virgins were the priestesses of Vesta, the goddess of the Hearth and one of the tutelary deities of ancient Rome. Rome's safety was thought to depend upon their obedience to their vow of chastity.

from *Passion Flowers* (1854)

My Last Dance

The shell of objects inwardly consumed
Will stand, till some convulsive wind awakes;
Such sense hath Fire to waste the heart of things,
Nature, such love to hold the form she makes.

Thus, wasted joys will show their early bloom,   5
Yet crumble at the breath of a caress;
The golden fruitage hides the scathèd bough;
Snatch it, thou scatterest wide its emptiness.

For pleasure bidden, I went forth last night
To where, thick hung, the festal torches gleamed;   10
Here were the flowers, the music, as of old,
Almost the very olden time it seemed.

For one with cheek unfaded (though he brings
My buried brothers to me, in his look)
Said, "Will you dance?" At the accustomed words   15
I gave my hand, the old position took.

Sound, gladsome measure! at whose bidding once
I felt the flush of pleasure to my brow,
While my soul shook the burthen of the flesh,
And in its young pride said, "Lie lightly thou!"   20

Then, like a gallant swimmer, flinging high
My breast against the golden waves of sound,
I rode the madd'ning tumult of the dance,
Mocking fatigue, that never could be found.

Chide not, – it was not vanity, nor sense,   25
(The brutish scorn such vaporous delight,)
But Nature, cadencing her joy of strength
To the harmonious limits of her right.

She gave her impulse to the dancing Hours,[2]
To winds that sweep, to stars that noiseless turn;   30
She marked the measure rapid hearts must keep
Devised each pace that glancing feet should learn.

My Last Dance
[2] The Horae. In Greek and Renaissance mythology, the Hours (or Seasons) are typically represented as female goddesses.

And sure, that prodigal o'erflow of life,
Unavow'd as yet to family or state,
Sweet sounds, white garments, flowery coronals   35
Make holy, in the pageant of our fate.

Sound, measure! but to stir my heart no more –
For, as I moved to join the dizzy race,
My youth fell from me; all its blooms were gone,
And others showed them, smiling, in my face.   40

Faintly I met the shock of circling forms
Linked each to other, Fashion's galley-slaves,
Dream-wondering, like an unaccustomed ghost
That starts, surprised, to stumble over graves.

For graves were 'neath my feet, whose placid masks   45
Smiled out upon my folly mournfully,
While all the host of the departed said,
"Tread lightly – thou art ashes, even as we."

from *Atlantic Monthly* (1862)

BATTLE-HYMN OF THE REPUBLIC

Mine eyes have seen the glory of the coming of the Lord:
He is trampling out the vintage where the grapes of wrath are stored;
He hath loosed the fateful lightning of His terrible swift sword:
        His truth is marching on.

I have seen Him in the watch-fires of a hundred circling camps;   5
They have builded Him an altar in the evening dews and damps;
I can read His righteous sentence by the dim and flaring lamps:
        His day is marching on.

I have read a fiery gospel writ in burnished rows of steel:
"As ye deal with my contemners, so with you my grace shall deal;   10
Let the Hero, born of woman, crush the serpent with his heel,
        Since God is marching on."

He has sounded forth the trumpet that shall never call retreat;
He is sifting out the hearts of men before His judgment-seat:
Oh, be swift, my soul, to answer Him! be jubilant, my feet!   15
        Our God is marching on.

In the beauty of the lilies Christ was born across the sea,
With a glory in his bosom that transfigures you and me:
As he died to make men holy, let us die to make men free,
        While God is marching on.   20

(MS 1861)

from *Later Lyrics* (1866)

The Soul-Hunter

Who hunts so late 'neath evening skies,
A smouldering love-brand in his eyes?
His locks outshame the black of night,
Its stars are duller than his sight
    Who hunts so late, so dark.   5

A drooping mantle shrouds his form,
To shield him from the winter's storm?
Or is there something at his side,
That, with himself, he strives to hide,
    Who hunts so late, so dark?   10

He hath such promise, silver sweet,
Such silken hands, such fiery feet,
That, where his look has charmed his prey,
His swift-winged passion forces way,
    Who hunts so late, so dark.   15

Sure no one underneath the moon
Can whisper to so soft a tune:
The hours would flit from dusk to dawn
Lighter than dews upon the lawn
    With him, so late, so dark.   20

But, should there break a day of need,
Those hands will try no valorous deed:
No help is in that sable crest,
Nor manhood in that hollow breast
    That sighed so late, so dark.   25

O maiden! of the salt waves make
Thy sinless shroud, for God's dear sake;
Or to the flame commit thy bloom;
Or lock thee, living, in the tomb
    So desolate and dark, –   30

Before thou list one stolen word
Of him who lures thee like a bird.
He wanders with the Devil's bait,
For human souls he lies in wait,
    Who hunts so late, so dark.   35

Night-Musings

I walk the lonely roofs at night,
The roof-tree creaking as I go;

A farthing taper gives me light,
And monstrous darkness sits below.

What spell is in these feet of mine   5
That binds them so to beat the air?
What tears are in my blood, or wine,
That will not yield to sleep or prayer?

Ah me! the day brought sleep enough;
Its humming pulses drowsed my soul;   10
My ways were spun of funeral stuff,
And every meal was death and dole.

But now my measured footstep seems
A chariot, drawn by burning doves;
Or now my fancy climbs in dreams   15
A ladder of transfigured loves.

Or now I stand as Jacob³ stood,
Matched hand to hand, and knee to knee:
Thou unknown Fate, declare thy good!
Answer, and I will set thee free.   20

And now I walk a garden bed,
Whose flowers contend with fervent airs;
And each fair bell that lifts its head
A look of loved remembrance wears.

Or, last, I sit in some strange isle,   25
Unsexed by Age and Wisdom's might,
And make a pictured parchment smile
With words illegible for light.

A slip, a shock, a distant tone!
The world's pale watchman crying woe;   30
I spin my thread of light alone,
And Darkness whets its shears below.

ROUGE GAGNE⁴

The wheel is turned, the cards are laid;
The circle's drawn, the bets are made:
I stake my gold upon the red.

NIGHT-MUSINGS
³ Both this stanza and the preceding one make glancing allusions to significant events in the life of Jacob:
his dream on the road to Bethel of a ladder ascending
to heaven, and his wrestling match with the angel of
God. Both events occurred at night. (See Genesis 28
and 32.)
ROUGE GAGNE
¹ French: "the red wins," an expression in roulette.

The rubies of the bosom mine,
The river of life, so swift divine,   5
In red all radiantly shine.

Upon the cards, like gouts of blood,
Lie dinted hearts, and diamonds good,
The red for faith and hardihood.

In red the sacred blushes start   10
On errand from a virgin heart,
To win its glorious counterpart.

The rose that makes the summer fair,
The velvet robe that sovereigns wear,
The red revealment could not spare.   15

And men who conquer deadly odds
By fields of ice, and raging floods,
Take the red passion from the gods.

Now, Love is red, and Wisdom pale,
But human hearts are faint and frail   20
Till Love meets Love, and bids it hail.

I see the chasm, yawning dread;
I see the flaming arch o'erhead:
I stake my life upon the red.

REMEMBRANCE[5]

There was a time when thy dear face to me
Was but a dream, with nameless pangs between.
Three happy years upheld the fatal screen
Whose fall left blank and bitterness for thee.

As one who at a gracious drama sits,   5
And builds long vistas in its magic ways,
"For this must come, and this;" and while he stays
The end consigns him to the silent streets:

So did I stand when thy sweet play was done,
Wondering what spell the curtain still should hide,   10
Waiting and weeping, till my saintly guide
Took by the hand, and pitying said, "Pass on."

REMEMBRANCE
[5]   This elegy was probably written for Samuel Gridley,
Jr, b. 1859, d. 1862.

So thou art hid again, and wilt not come
For any knocking at the veilèd door;
Nor mother-pangs, nor nature, can restore   15
The heart's delight and blossom of thy home.

And I with others, in the outer court,
Must sadly follow the excluding will,
In painful admiration of the skill
Of God, who speaks his sweetest sentence short.   20

Alice Cary (1820–1871)

Alice and Phoebe Cary, sister poets, were born in 1820 and 1824 respectively on a farm near Mount Healthy, Ohio, a small community west of Cincinnati. In 1835, their mother died of tuberculosis, which had already claimed two of their five siblings. According to the Cary legend, their new stepmother was unsympathetic to their literary interests. However, as Judith Fetterly observes, if she was, she put no appreciable barriers in their way. Largely self-educated, the Cary sisters knew what they wanted from a fairly young age and with singular determination they went out and got it.

Between the late 1830s, when their first poems appeared in local newspapers, and 1849, when they joined the ranks of "younger" poets, crowding the final pages of Rufus Griswold's anthology, *The Female Poets of America*, the two sisters worked assiduously readying themselves for the literary life – somewhere else besides Ohio. With Griswold's backing, and that of other New York literati, Alice took the first step, moving to New York City in 1850. Phoebe joined her the following spring. Within a matter of years, Alice, who was the workhorse of the pair, had raised enough money by dint of constant publication and strict economy to buy a house on 20th Street in New York City. Here, for fifteen years, the pair presided over their famous Sunday evening receptions.

Alice and Phoebe Cary were staunch Universalists, champions of abolition and women's suffrage, and among the most popular writers of their day. Invalided during the last years of her life by the disease that claimed so many of her family, Alice died of tuberculosis in 1871 in the house that she and Phoebe shared. Unable to recover from the strain and grief of her sister's death, Phoebe, suffering from hepatitis, followed a scant five months later.

Today, Alice Cary's tales of rural life, especially those collected in *Clovernook: or, Recollections of Our Neighborhood in the West* (1852) and its sequel (1853), have drawn the most interest to the poet. Praised for their "realism," they are highly valued as early anticipations of the regionalist movement that would flourish in women's literature in the *fin de siècle*. Despite the fact that in her own day she was identified primarily as a poet, Alice Cary's poetry has attracted much less interest. In this case, understandably.

To a much greater extent than her sister, Alice committed herself to the role of the sentimental woman poet, and in the end she may have paid too dearly for the popularity it won her. Certainly, by Phoebe's account, Alice grew to dislike many of her poems, especially the early ones, like "Pictures of Memory," which was her first big "hit." Rhapsodized over by Edgar Allan Poe in his review of Griswold's 1849 anthology as that text's "noblest" poem, Alice Cary's lament for a dead brother made her reputation overnight.

As Jonathan Hall notes in his fascinating analysis of the Cary sisters' reviews, when the critical "backlash" against such poetry came in the mid-1850s, Alice, who was by then fully identified with the sentimental elegy, was caught in it. What had seemed nobly pathetic to Poe now seemed to somewhat later critics morbidly overdone. Since the market for the morbidly (or piously) overdone remained relatively strong through most of the century, Alice's sales did not suffer. (Together with Lucy Larcom, she and Phoebe were the only nineteenth-century American women poets Houghton Mifflin honored with a prestigious and lucrative "household edition.") But her pride did. As Hall notes, it took over ten years for her to put forth another book, and when she did, it was in a distinctly chastened vein.

Even chastened, however, Alice Cary was never the poet her sister was. Occasionally, however, she touches on that dark, almost pagan vein inside herself that was the source of some of her most chilling stories. In their way, "Summer and Winter" and, even more, "The Seal Fisher's Wife," use ballad conventions of repetition and alliteration brilliantly. The latter poem, in particular, possesses the timeless quality towards which so many traditional British ballads seem to strive, and which the circularity of repetition reinforces, echoing, as it does, the circularity of the seasons themselves. In "Maid and Man," on the other hand, Cary's darkness seems to tip over toward black humor. With its curious and totally unexpected drop into nowhere, this poem seems a fitting way to close this relatively unrepresentative selection of a poet's verse.

Primary Texts

Clovernook: or, Recollections of Our Neighborhood in the West, 1st Series, 1852; *Lyra and Other Poems*, 1852; *Clovernook: or, Recollections of Our Neighborhood in the West*, 2nd Series, 1853; *Poems*, 1855; *Ballads, Lyrics, and Hymns*, 1866; *A Memorial of Alice and Phoebe Cary, with Some of Their Later Poems*, ed. Mary Clemmer Ames, 1875; *The Poetical Works of Alice and Phoebe Cary*, 1877.

Further Reading

Mary Clemmer Ames, ed., *A Memorial of Alice and Phoebe Cary, with Some of Their Later Poems*, New York: Hurd and Houghton, 1875; Katherine Lee Bates, "Alice and Phoebe Cary," in *The Poems of Alice and Phoebe Cary*, New York: Crowell, 1903; Phoebe Cary, "Alice Cary," *Ladies' Repository* (July 1871); Judith Fetterly, "Introduction," in *Alice Cary, Clovernook Sketches and Other Stories*, New Brunswick, New Jersey: Rutgers University Press, 1988; Jonathan Hall, "Alice and Phoebe Cary," *Encyclopedia of American Poetry*.

from Griswold (1849)

PICTURES OF MEMORY

Among the beautiful pictures
    That hang on Memory's wall,
Is one of a dim old forest,
    That seemeth best of all:
Not for its gnarled oaks olden,   5
    Dark with the mistletoe;
Not for the violets golden
    That sprinkle the vale below;

Not for the milk-white lilies,
    That lead from the fragrant hedge,   10
Coquetting all day with the sunbeams,
    And stealing their golden edge;
Not for the vines on the upland
    Where the bright red berries rest,
Nor the pinks, nor the pale, sweet cowslip,   15
    It seemeth to me the best.

I once had a little brother,
    With eyes that were dark and deep —
In the lap of that old dim forest
    He lieth in peace asleep: 20
Light as the down of the thistle,
    Free as the winds that blow,
We roved there the beautiful summers,
    The summers of long ago;
But his feet on the hills grew weary,   25
    And, one of the autumn eves,
I made for my little brother
    A bed of the yellow leaves.

Sweetly his pale arms folded
    My neck in a meek embrace,   30
As the light of immortal beauty
    Silently covered his face:
And when the arrows of sunset
    Lodged in the tree-tops bright,
He fell, in his saint-like beauty,   35
    Asleep by the gates of light.
Therefore, of all the pictures
    That hang on Memory's wall,
The one of the dim old forest
    Seemeth the best of all.   40

from *Beadle's Monthly* (1866)

SUMMER AND WINTER

The winter goes and the summer comes,
    And the cloud descends in warm, wet showers;
The grass grows green where the frost has been,
    And waste and wayside are fringed with flowers.

The winter goes, and the summer comes,   5
    And the merry blue-birds twitter and trill,
And the swallow swings on his steel-blue wings,
    This way and that way, at wildest will.

The winter goes, and the summer comes,
   And the swallow he swingeth no more aloft,   10
And the blue-bird's breast swells out of her nest,
   And the horniest bill of them all grows soft.

The summer goes and the winter comes,
   And the daisie dies and the daffodil dies,
And the softest bill grows horny and still,   15
   And the days set dimly, and dimly rise.

The summer goes, and the winter comes,
   And the red fire fades from the heart o' th' rose,
And the snow lies white where the grass was bright,
   And the wild wind bitterly blows and blows.   20

The winter comes, and the winter stays,
   Ay, cold and long, and long and cold,
And the pulses beat to the weary feet,
   And the head feels sick and the heart grows old.

The winter comes and the winter stays,   25
   And all the glory behind us lies,
The cheery light drops into the night,
   And the snow drifts over our sightless eyes.

from *The Poetical Works of Alice and Phoebe Cary* (1877)

THE SEAL FISHER'S WIFE

The west shines out through lines of jet,
Like the side of a fish through the fisher's net,
   Silver and golden-brown;
And rocking the cradle, she sings so low,
As backward and forward, and to and fro,   5
   She cards the wool for her gown.

She sings her sweetest, she sings her best,
And all the silver fades in the west,
   And all the golden-brown,
And lowly leaning cradle across,   10
She mends the fire with faggots and moss,
   And cards the wool for her gown.

Gray and cold, and cold and gray,
Over the look-out and over the bay,
   The sleet comes sliding down,   15
And the blaze of the faggots flickers thin,

And the wind is beating the ice-blocks in,
　As she cards the wool for her gown.

The fisher's boats in the ice are crushed.
And now her lullaby-song is hushed, —　　　　　　　20
　For sighs the singing drown, —
And all, with fingers stiff and cold,
She covers the cradle, fold on fold,
　With the carded wool of her gown.

And there — the cards upon her knee,　　　　　　25
And her eyes wide open toward the sea,
　Where the fisher's boats went down —
They found her all as cold as sleet,
And her baby smiling up so sweet,
　From the carded wool of her gown.　　　　　　30

A FRAGMENT

It was a sandy level wherein stood
　The old and lonesome house; far as the eye
Could measure, on the green back of the wood,
　The smoke lay always, low and lazily.

Down the high gable windows, all one way,　　　　5
　Hung the long, drowsy curtains, and across
The sunken shingles, where the rain would stay,
　The roof was ridged, a hand's breadth deep, with moss.

The place was all so still you would have said
　The picture of the Summer, drawn, should be　　10
With golden ears, laid back against her head,
　And listening to the far, low-lying sea.

But from the rock, rough-grained and icy-crowned,
　Some little flower from out some cleft will rise;
And in this quiet land my love I found,　　　　15
　With all their soft light, sleepy, in her eyes.

No bush to lure a bird to sing to her —
　In depths of calm the gnats' faint hum was drowned,
And the wind's voice was like a little stir
　Of the uneasy silence, not like sound.　　　　20

No tender trembles of the dew at close
　Of day, — at morn, no insect choir;
No sweet bees at sweet work about the rose,
　Like little housewife fairies round their fire.

And yet the place, suffused with her, seemed fair —   25
   Ah, I would be immortal, could I write
How from her forehead fell the shining hair,
   As morning falls from heaven — so bright! so bright.

MAID AND MAN

All in the gay and golden weather,
   Two fair travelers, maid and man,
Sailed in a birchen boat together,
   And sailed the way that the river ran:
The sun was low, not set, and the west   5
Was colored like a robin's breast.

The moon was moving sweetly o'er them,
   And her shadow, in the waves afloat,
Moved softly on and on before them
   Like a silver swan, that drew their boat;   10
And they were lovers, and well content,
Sailing the way the river went.

And these two saw in her grassy bower
   As they sailed the way the river run,
A little, modest, slim-necked flower   15
   Nodding and nodding up to the sun,
And they made about her a little song
And sung it as they sailed along:

"Pull down the grass about your bosom,
   Nor look at the sun in the royal sky,   20
'T is dangerous, dangerous, little blossom,
   You are so low, and he is so high —
'T is dangerous nodding up to him,
He is so bright, and you are so dim!"

Sweetly over, and sadly under,   25
   They turned the tune as they sailed along,
And they did not see the cloud, for a wonder,
   Break in the water, the shape of the swan;
Nor yet, for a wonder, see at all
The river narrowing toward the fall.   30

"Be warned, my beauty — 't is not the fashion
   Of the king to wed with the waiting-maid —
Make not from sleep his fiery passion,
   But turn your red cheek into the shade —
The dew is a-tremble to kiss your eyes —   35
And there is but danger in the skies!"

Close on the precipice rang the ditty,
  But they looked behind them, and not before,
And went down singing their doleful pity
  About the blossom safe on the shore –   40
"There is danger, danger! frail one, list!"
Backward whirled in the whirling mist.

Phoebe Cary (1824–1871)

In a telling recollection in her autobiography, Elizabeth Oakes Smith comments on what it was like to attend a literary evening at Emma Embury's salon. "I remember Fannie Osgood and Phoebe Carey [*sic*] rather excelled at this small game [engaging in witty repartee], but Margaret Fuller looked like an owl at the perpetration of a pun, and I honored her for it" (p. 91).

The mixture of spite and sophistication in Oakes Smith's comment says much about the New York literary scene into which the Midwest Cary sisters had, with no small amount of dexterity, inserted themselves. Julia Ward Howe found Boston a closed club – at least until "Battle-Hymn of the Republic" opened it up to her – but New York welcomed *parvenus* – if, that is, they could play the game. Belying the carefully cultivated persona of her popular poetry, which made her seem the very model of a model sentimental "poetess," and a country girl to boot, Phoebe Cary not only played the game, she excelled at it.

The more closely one examines Phoebe Cary, the more complex and difficult to assess she becomes. What does one make of a poet too shy to speak in public, whose boldness in verse makes her a parodist without parallel among nineteenth-century American women poets? Indeed, what does one make of a poet who writes half a volume of morbid sentimental treacle, then fills the remaining half with poems of stunning literary revenge? What, that is, does one make of Phoebe Cary? Who was she? and perhaps, even more to the point, what did she make of the poetry she wrote? If there is no way to put together the two halves of *Poems and Parodies*, Cary's 1854 volume of verse, can one put together its author?

In many ways, Cary, like Sigourney, is a test case for the sentimental woman poet; but where for Sigourney sentimentalism was a legitimate strategy which she adopted in the service of the numerous social causes to which she was committed, Cary's adoption of a sentimental voice appears far more enigmatic, calculated, and problematic. Perhaps some of it was sincere; perhaps all of it was economically motivated. Living in New York was expensive then, as now, and although her sister Alice made the lion's share of their income, Phoebe had the more expensive tastes.

What is clear is that Phoebe Cary had an irrepressible satirical bent, which she directed largely at the foibles of gender, and that after 1854, she went to some pains to make sure her readers did not realize it. In his excellent study of the Cary sisters' poetry, to which I am very much indebted, Jonathan Hall explains why. Analyzing reviews of the Cary sisters' poetry, he notes that reviewer reaction to Phoebe's 1854 volume was horror. It was acceptable for "a woman of sentiment" to target Longfellow's "Psalm of Life;" but Bryant's "The Future Life," never – that was "profanation."

What these reviewers were responding to, Hall writes, was the way in which "Phoebe's pomp-puncturing wit is calling into question the very definition of 'a woman of sentiment,' transposing pious pseudo-profundities into light-hearted romps, or reversing the genders of speaker and object as a means of commenting playfully on the masculine bias inherent in extant poetic conventions."

But was this simply light-hearted playfulness? In a revealing comment, Mary Clemmer Ames, the Cary sisters' adoring memorialist, observes that Phoebe Cary was a "disenchanter." "Hold up to her . . . your most precious dream, and in an instant, by a single rapier of a sentence, she would thrust it through, and strip it of the last vestige of glamour." From her choice of targets in *Poems and Parodies* (effectively the nineteenth-century male canon, plus Mrs Hemans), it is clear that Cary knew who and what she was up against; and she lived without illusions. If there was no place in New York City for a country mouse, the publishing world that she and her sister inhabited also had no room for a cocky hen. A deeper critique, had she wished to make one, would not have advanced her cause – nor put bread on the table.

After *Poems and Parodies*, Cary continued to seed her volumes with poems of wit directed toward gender issues, and also, not infrequently, with poems such as "The Rose," "Disenchanted," and "Hidden Sorrow," which treat these same issues much more seriously and complexly, although the last may also be a parody. But she was also very careful never to make herself a target by grouping such poems together again. Like Osgood, with whom Oakes Smith appropriately links her, she left an enigma behind instead.

Primary Texts

Poems and Parodies, 1854; *Poems of Faith, Hope and Love*, 1868; *A Memorial of Alice and Phoebe Cary, with Some of Their Later Poems*, ed. Mary Clemmer Ames, 1875; *The Poetical Works of Alice and Phoebe Cary*, 1877.

Further Reading

Mary Clemmer Ames, ed., *A Memorial of Alice and Phoebe Cary, with Some of Their Later Poems*, New York: Hurd and Houghton, 1875; Katherine Lee Bates, "Alice and Phoebe Cary," in *The Poems of Alice and Phoebe Cary*, New York: Crowell, 1903; Ada R. Carnahan, "Phoebe Cary," *Ladies' Repository* (July 1872); Phoebe Cary, "Alice Cary," *Ladies' Repository* (July 1871); Horace Greeley, "Alice and Phebe Cary," in *Eminent Women of the Age*, Hartford: Betts, 1869; Jonathan Hall, "Alice and Phoebe Cary," *Encyclopedia of American Poetry*; Elizabeth Oakes Smith, *Selections from The Autobiography of Elizabeth Oakes Smith*, ed. Mary Alice Wyman, Lewiston, Maine: Lewiston Journal Company, 1924.

from Griswold (1849)

THE CHRISTIAN WOMAN

Oh, beautiful as morning in those hours,
    When, as her pathway lies along the hills,
Her golden fingers wake the dewy flowers,
    And softly touch the waters of the rills,
Was she who walked more faintly day by day,   5
Till silently she perished by the way.

It was not hers to know that perfect heaven
    Of passionate love returned by love as deep;

Not hers to sing the cradle-song at even,
    Watching the beauty of her babe asleep;   10
"Mother and brethren" – these she had not known,
Save such as do the Father's will alone.

Yet found she something still for which to live –
    Hearths desolate, where angel-like she came,
And "little ones" to whom her hand could give   15
    A cup of water in her Master's name;
And breaking hearts to bind away from death,
With the soft hand of pitying love and faith.

She never won the voice of popular praise,
    But, counting earthly triumph as but dross,   20
Seeking to keep her Savior's perfect ways,
    Bearing in the still path his blessèd cross,
She made her life, while with us here she trod,
A consecration to the will of God!

And she hath lived and labored not in vain: 25
    Through the deep prison cells her accents thrill,
And the sad slave leans idly on his chain,
    And hears the music of her singing still;
While little children, with their innocent praise,
Keep freshly in men's hearts her Christian ways.   30

And what a beautiful lesson she made known –
    The whiteness of her soul sin could not dim;
Ready to lay down on God's altar stone
    The dearest treasure of her life for him.
Her flame of sacrifice never, never waned,   35
How could she live and die so self-sustained?

For friends supported not her parting soul,
    And whispered words of comfort, kind and sweet,
When treading onward to that final goal,
    Where the still bridegroom[1] waited for her feet;   40
Alone she walked, yet with a fearless tread,
Down to Death's chamber, and his bridal bed!

from *Poems and Parodies* (1854)

SAMUEL BROWN[2]

It was many and many a year ago,
    In a dwelling down in town,

THE CHRISTIAN WOMAN
[1] Christ.

SAMUEL BROWN
[2] A parody of Edgar Allan Poe's "Annabel Lee."

That a fellow there lived whom you may know,
    By the name of Samuel Brown;
And this fellow he lived with no other thought   5
    Than to our house to come down.

I was a child, and he was a child,
    In that dwelling down in town,
But we loved with a love that was more than love,
    I and my Samuel Brown, –   10
With a love that the ladies coveted,
    Me and Samuel Brown.

And this was the reason that, long ago,
    To that dwelling down in town,
A girl came out of her carriage, courting   15
    My beautiful Samuel Brown;
So that her high-bred kinsman came
    And bore away Samuel Brown,
And shut him up in a dwelling-house,
    In a street quite up in town.   20

The ladies not half so happy up there,
    Went envying me and Brown;
Yes! that was the reason, (as all men know,
    In this dwelling down in town,)
That the girl came out of the carriage by night,   25
    Coquetting and getting my Samuel Brown.

But our love is more artful by far than the love
    Of those who are older than we, –
    Of many far wiser than we, –
And neither the girls that are living above,   30
    Nor the girls that are down in town,
Can ever dissever my soul from the soul
    Of the beautiful Samuel Brown.

For the morn never shines without bringing me lines
    From my beautiful Samuel Brown;   35
And the night 's never dark, but I sit in the park
    With my beautiful Samuel Brown.
And often by day, I walk down in Broadway,
With my darling, my darling, my life and my stay,
    To our dwelling down in town,   40
    To our house in the street down town.

"THE DAY IS DONE"[3]

The day is done, and darkness
   From the wing of night is loosed,
As a feather is wafted downward
   From a chicken going to roost.

I see the lights of the baker,   5
   Gleam through the rain and mist,
And a feeling of sadness comes o'er me,
   That I cannot well resist.

A feeling of sadness and *longing*,
   That is not like being sick,   10
And resembles sorrow only
   As a brick-bat resembles a brick.

Come, get for me some supper, –
   A good and regular meal,
That shall soothe this restless feeling,   15
   And banish the pain I feel.

Not from the pastry baker's,
   Not from the shops for cake,
I would n't give a farthing
   For all that they can make.   20

For, like the soup at dinner,
   Such things would but suggest
Some dishes more substantial,
   And to-night I want the best.

Go to some honest butcher,   25
   Whose beef is fresh and nice
As any they have in the city,
   And get a liberal slice.

Such things through days of labor,
   And nights devoid of ease,   30
For sad and desperate feelings
   Are wonderful remedies.

They have an astonishing power
   To aid and reinforce,
And come like the "Finally, brethren,"   35
   That follows a long discourse.

"THE DAY IS DONE"
[3] A parody of Henry W. Longfellow's "The Day is
Done."

Then get me a tender sirloin
 From off the bench or hook,
And lend to its sterling goodness
 The science of the cook.   40

And the night shall be filled with comfort,
 And the cares with which it begun
Shall fold up their blankets like Indians,
 And silently cut and run.

THE CITY LIFE[4]

How shall I know thee in that sphere that keeps
 The country youth that to the city goes,
When all of thee, that change can wither, sleeps
 And perishes among your cast-off clothes?

For I shall feel the sting of ceaseless pain,   5
 If there I meet thy one-horse carriage not;
Nor see the hat I love, nor ride again,
 When thou art driving on a gentle trot.

Wilt thou not for me in the city seek,
 And turn to note each passing shawl and gown?   10
You used to come and see me once a week, –
 Shall I be banished from your thought in town?

In that great street I don't know how to find,
 In the resplendence of that glorious sphere,
And larger movements of the unfettered mind,   15
 Wilt thou forget the love that joined us here?

The love that lived through all the simple past,
 And meekly with my country training bore,
And deeper grew, and tenderer to the last,
 Shall it expire in town, and be no more?   20

A happier lot than mine, and greater praise,
 Await thee there; for thou, with skill and tact,
Hast learnt the wisdom of the world's just ways,
 And dressest well, and knowest how to act.

For me, the country place in which I dwell   25
 Has made me one of a proscribed band;
And work hath left its scar – that fire of hell
 Has left its frightful scar upon my hand.

THE CITY LIFE
[1]   A parody of William C. Bryant's "The Future Life."

Yet though thou wear'st the glory of the town,
   Wilt thou not keep the same belovèd name,   30
The same black-satin vest, and morning-gown,
   Lovelier in New York city, yet the same?

Shalt thou not teach me, in that grander home
   The wisdom that I learned so ill in this, –
The wisdom which is fine, – till I become   35
   Thy fit companion in that place of bliss?

JACOB[5]

He dwelt among "apartments let,"
   About five stories high;
A man I thought that none would get,
   And very few would try.

A boulder, by a larger stone   5
   Half hidden in the mud,
Fair as a man when only one
   Is in the neighborhood.

He lived unknown, and few could tell
   When Jacob was not free;   10
But he has got a wife, – and O!
   The difference to me!

THE WIFE[6]

Her washing ended with the day,
   Yet lived she at its close,
And passed the long, long night away,
   In darning ragged hose.

But when the sun in all his state   5
   Illumed the eastern skies,
She passed about the kitchen grate,
   And went to making pies.

SHAKESPEARIAN READINGS[7]

Oh, but to fade, and live we know not where,
To be a cold obstruction and to groan!
This sensible, warm woman, to become

JACOB
[5] A parody of William Wordsworth's "She Dwelt Among Untrodden Ways."
THE WIFE
[6] A parody of James Aldrich's "A Death Bed."

SHAKESPEARIAN READINGS
[7] In order, Cary parodies *Measure for Measure* III.i.117–31; *A Midsummer Night's Dream* II.i.155–64; and *Twelfth Night* II.iv.108–16.

A prudish clod; and the delighted spirit
To live and die alone, or to reside   5
With married sisters, and to have the care
Of half a dozen children, not your own;
And driven, for no one wants you,
Round about the pendant world; or worse than worst
Of those that disappointment and pure spite   10
Have driven to madness: 'T is too horrible!
The weariest and most troubled married life
That age, ache, penury, or jealousy
Can lay on nature, is a paradise
To being an old maid.   15

That very time I saw, (but thou couldst not,)
Walking between the garden and the barn,
Reuben, all armed; a certain aim he took
At a young chicken, standing by a post,
And loosed his bullet smartly from his gun,   20
As he would kill a hundred thousand hens.
But I might see young Reuben's fiery shot
Lodged in the chaste board of the garden fence,
And the domesticated fowl passed on,
In henly meditation, bullet free.   25

My father had a daughter got a man,
As it might be, perhaps, were I good-looking,
I should, your lordship.
And what 's her residence?
A hut, my lord, she never owned a house,   30
But let her husband, like a graceless scamp,
Spend all her little means, – she thought she ought, –
And in a wretched chamber, on an alley,
She worked like masons on a monument,
Earning their bread. Was not this love indeed?   35

from *National Anti-Slavery Standard* (1861)

DEAD LOVE

We are face to face, and between us here
    Is the love we thought could never die;
Why has it only lived a year?
    Who has murdered it – you or I?

No matter who – the deed was done   5
    By one or both, and there it lies:

The smile from the lip forever gone,
    And darkness over the beautiful eyes.

Our love is dead, and our hope is wrecked;
    So what does it profit to talk and rave,   10
Whether it perished by my neglect,
    Or whether your cruelty dug its grave!

Why should you say that I am to blame,
    Or why should I charge the sin on you?
Our work is before us all the same,   15
    And the guilt of it lies between us two.

We have praised our love for its beauty and grace;
    Now we stand here, and hardly dare
To turn the face-cloth back from the face,
    And see the thing that is hidden there.   20

Yet look! ah, that heart has beat its last,
    And the beautiful life of our life is o'er,
And when we have buried and left the past,
    We two, together, can walk no more.

You might stretch yourself on the dead, and weep,   25
    And pray as the Prophet prayed, in pain;
But not like him could you break the sleep,
    And bring the soul to the clay again.

Its head in my bosom I can lay,
    And shower my woe there, kiss on kiss,   30
But there never was resurrection-day
    In the world for a love so dead as this!

And, since we cannot lessen the sin
    By mourning over the deed we did,
Let us draw the winding-sheet up to the chin,   35
    Ay, up till the dead-blind eyes are hid!

from *Beadle's Monthly* (1866)

THE HUNTER AND THE DOE

A lonesome doe, a piteous sight to see,
    Straying about a most unfriendly wold,
Was by a hunter found, who tenderly
    Sheltered her in his bosom from the cold.

Poor desolate one, she had no other choice,   5
   She gave him love, she could not give him less;
In all the world beside, there was no voice
   Whose tones for her dropped into tenderness!

And so it came about, that where he strayed
   Over the hills, she followed far and wide;   10
Nor fields of sweetest flowers, nor pleasant shade,
   Had any power to lure her from his side.

But he, as light and roving hunters may,
   Another season found another mate;
Of her grown weary, pushed her from his way   15
   With careless hand, and left her to her fate.

Now in the dust her head has fallen so low
   She hardly cares to lift it up again;
Another, who had struck the self-same blow,
   Could not have hurt her with so sharp a pain.   20

Therefore, in silent helplessness she lies,
   Crushed utterly with shame, and sore distressed;
Pierced through the heart, and smit between the eyes,
   By the same hand that yesterday caressed.

Oh, faithless master of that faithful doe,   25
   Whose life must end in thee, where it began;
Oh, tenderest friend, oh, cruelest, cruelest foe
   That ever creature had, thou art the man!

from *Galaxy* (1866)

IN ABSENCE

Watch her kindly, stars:
From the sweet protecting skies
Follow her with tender eyes,
Look so lovingly that she
Cannot choose but think of me: 5
   Watch her kindly, stars!

Soothe her sweetly, night:
On her eyes, o'erwearied, press
The tired lids with light caress;
Let that shadowy hand of thine   10
Ever in her dreams seem mine:
   Soothe her sweetly, night!

Wake her gently, morn:
Let the notes of early birds
Seem like love's melodious words;   15
Every pleasant sound, my dear,
When she stirs from sleep should hear,
    Wake her gently, morn!

    Kiss her softly, winds:
Softly, that she may not miss   20
Any sweet, accustomed bliss;
On her lips, her eyes, her face,
Till I come to take your place,
    Kiss and kiss her, winds!

from *Harper's Bazar* (1869)

DOROTHY'S DOWER

In Three Parts

Part I.

"My sweetest Dorothy," said John,
    Of course before the wedding,
As metaphorically he stood,
    His gold upon her shedding,
"Whatever thing you wish or want   5
    Shall be hereafter granted,
For all my worldly goods are yours."
    The fellow was enchanted!
"About that little dower you have,
    You thought might yet come handy,   10
Throw it away, do what you please,
    Spend it on sugar-candy!
I like your sweet, dependent ways,
    I love you when you tease me;
The more you ask, the more you spend,   15
    The better you will please me."

Part II.

"Confound it, Dorothy!" said John,
    "I haven't got it by me.
You haven't, have you, spent that sum,
    The dower from aunt Jemima?   20
No; well that's sensible for you;
    This fix is most unpleasant;
But money's tight, so just take yours
    And use it for the present.

Now I must go – to – meet a man!
  By George! I'll have to borrow!
Lend me a twenty – that's all right!
  I'll pay you back to-morrow."

25

Part III.

"Madam," says John to Dorothy,
  And past her rudely pushes,
"You think a man is made of gold,
  And money grows on bushes!
Tom's shoes! your doctor! Can't you now
  Get up some new disaster?
You and your children are enough
  To break John Jacob Astor.[8]
Where's what you had yourself when I
  Was fool enough to court you?
That little sum, till you got me,
  'Twas what had to support you!"
"It's lent and gone, not very far;
  Pray don't be apprehensive."
"*Lent!* I've had use enough for it;
  My family is expensive.
I did n't, as a woman would,
  Spend it on sugar-candy!"
"No, John, I think the most of it
  Went for cigars and brandy!"

30

35

40

45

from *Woodhull & Claflin's Weekly* (1873)

Was He Henpecked?

"I'll tell you what it is, my dear,
  Said Mrs. Dorking, proudly,
"I do not like that chanticleer[9]
  Who crows o'er us so loudly.

"And since I must his laws obey,
  And have him walk before me,
I'd rather like to have my say
  Of who should lord it o'er me."

5

"You'd like to vote." he answered slow,
  "Why, treasure of my treasures,

10

Dorothy's Dower
[8] John Jacob Astor (1763–1848), a United States fur
merchant and financier. His name was synonymous with
wealth in the mid- to late nineteenth century.

Was He Henpecked?
[9] *Chanticleer* rooster.

What can you, or what should you know
    Of public men, or measures?

"Of course, you have ability –
    Of nothing am I surer;
You're quite as wise perhaps as I,   15
    You're better, too, and purer.

"I'd have you just for mine alone;
    Nay, so do I adore you,
I'd put you queen upon a throne,
    And bow myself before you."   20

"You'd put me! you! now that is what
    I do not want precisely;
I want myself to choose the spot
    That I can fill most wisely."

"My dear, you're talking like a goose –   25
    Unhenly, and improper";
But here again her words broke loose,
    In vain he tried to stop her.

"I tell you, though she never spoke
    So you could understand her,   30
A goose knows when she wears a yoke,
    As quickly as a gander."

"Why, bless my soul! what would you do?
    Write out a diagnosis?
Speak equal rights? join with their crew   35
    And dine with the Sorosis?[10]

"And shall I live to see it, then,
    My wife a public teacher?
And would you be a crowing hen,
    That dreadful unsexed creature?"   40

"Why as to that I do not know;
    Nor see why you should fear it,
If I can crow, why let me crow,
    If I can't then you won't hear it."

"Now, why," he said, "can't such as you   45
    Accept what we assign them?

---

[10]   The first women's club in the United States. Alice
Cary was its first president.

You have your rights, 'tis very true,
But then we should define them!

"We would not peck you cruelly,
We would not buy and sell you;   50
And you, *in turn*, should think, and [be,]
And do, just what we tell you!

"I do not want you made, my dear,
The subject of rude men's jest;
I like you in your proper sphere: 55
The circle of a hen's nest!

"I'd keep you in the chicken-yard,
Safe, honored, and respected;
From all that makes us rough and hard,
Your sex shall be protected."   60

"Pray, did it ever make you sick?
Have I gone to the dickens?
Because you let me scratch and pick,
Both for myself and chickens?"

"O, that's a different thing, you know,   65
Such duties are parental;
But for some work to do, you grow
Quite weak and sentimental."

"Ah! yes, it's well for you to talk
About a parent's duty!   70
Who keeps your chickens from the hawk?
Who stays in nights, my beauty?"

"But, madam, you may go each hour,
Lord bless your pretty faces!
We'll give you anything, but power   75
And honor, trust and places.

"We'd keep it hidden from your sight
How public scenes are carried;
Why, men are coarse, and swear, and fight —"
"I know it, dear; I'm married!"   80

"Why, now you gabble like a fool;
But what's the use of talking?
'Tis yours to serve, and mine to rule,
I tell you, Mrs. Dorking!"

"Oh, yes," she said, "you've all the sense,   85
   Your sex are very knowing;
Yet some of you are on the fence,
   And only good at crowing."

"Ah! preciousest of precious souls,
   Your words with sorrow fill me;   90
To see you voting at the polls
   I really think would kill me!

"To mourn my home's lost sanctity,
   To feel you did not love me;
And worse, to see you fly so high,   95
   And see you roost above me!"

"Now, what you fear in equal rights
   I think you've told precisely;
That's just about the place it lights,"
   Said Mrs. Dorking wisely.   100

from *The Poetical Works of Alice and Phoebe Cary* (1877)

THE ROSE

The sun, who smiles wherever he goes,
   Till the flowers all smile again,
Fell in love one day with a bashful rose,
   That had been a bud till then.

So he pushed back the folds of the soft green hood   5
   That covered her modest grace,
And kissed her as only the bold sun could,
   Till the crimson burned in her face.

But woe for the day when his golden hair
   Tangled her heart in a net;   10
And woe for the night of her dark despair,
   When her cheek with tears was wet!

For she loved him as only a young rose could:
   And he left her crushed and weak,
Striving in vain with her faded hood   15
   To cover her burning cheek.

DISENCHANTED

The time has come, as I knew it must,
   She said, when we should part,

But I ceased to love when I ceased to trust,
  And you cannot break my heart.

Nay, I know not even if I am sad, ·   5
  And it must be for the best,
Since you only take what I thought I had,
  And leave to me the rest.

Not all the stars of my hope are set,
  Though one is in eclipse;   10
And I know there is truth in the wide world yet
  If it be not on your lips.

And though I have loved you, who can tell
  If you ever had been so dear,
But that my heart was prodigal   15
  Of its wealth, and you were near.

I brought each rich and beautiful thing
  From my love's great treasury:
And I thought in myself to make a king
  With robes of royalty.   20

But you lightly laid my honors down,
  And you taught me thus to know,
Not every head can wear the crown
  That the hands of love bestow.

So, take whatever you can from me,   25
  And leave me as you will;
The dear romance and the poesy[11]
  Were mine, and I have them still.

I have them still; and even now,
  When my fancy has her way,   30
She can make a king of such as thou,
  Or a god of common clay.

HIDDEN SORROW

He has gone at last; yet I could not see
  When he passed to his final rest;
For he dropped asleep as quietly
  As the moon drops out of the west.

DISENCHANTED
[11] *Poesy* old-fashioned word for poetry, connotes
dreaminess and romance.

And I only saw, though I kept my place,   5
   That his mortal life was o'er,
By the look of peace across his face,
   That never was there before.

Sorrow he surely had in the past,
   Yet he uttered never a breath;   10
His lips were sealed in life as fast
   As you see them sealed in death.

Why he went from the world I do not know,
   Hiding a grief so deep;
But I think, if he ever had told his woe,   15
   He had found a better sleep.

For our trouble must some time see the light,
   And our anguish will have way;
And the infant, crying out in the night,
   Reveals what it hid by day.   20

And just like a needful, sweet relief
   To that bursting heart it seems,
When the little child's unspoken grief
   Runs into its pretty dreams.

And I think, though his face looks hushed and mild,   25
   And his slumber seems so deep,
He will sob in his grave, as a little child
   Keeps sobbing on in its sleep.

Lucy Larcom (1824–1893)

Lucy Larcom was born in Beverly, Massachusetts, a seaport community north of Boston, on March 5, 1824. Her father, Benjamin, was a retired shipmaster; her mother raised ten children of whom Larcom was the next to youngest. After her father's death when Larcom was nine, her mother moved her large and impecunious family to Lowell, where both she and the children could earn livings. Lois Larcom ran a boarding house for mill girls. At the age of eleven, Larcom began working in the textile mills. From five o'clock in the morning until seven at night, she labored, first as an unskilled "bobbin girl," later as bookkeeper in the cloth room of the Lawrence Mills.

Deplorable as Larcom's situation was, it could have been worse. As part of their employment policy, the New England mills maintained a paternalistic approach to their young workers, overseeing their moral and spiritual welfare, and subsidizing their efforts at self-education. A woman determined to better herself, Larcom took full advantage of the educational and literary opportunities the mills provided. After developing her skills on a manuscript magazine she and her sister Emeline produced, she became a major contributor to the *Lowell Offering* and other mill publications.

In 1846, Larcom left the mills to travel with Emeline, her husband, and child, to Illinois, where Larcom completed her education at the Monticello Female Seminary. Larcom had planned to remain with her sister, but when she broke her engagement to Frank Spaulding, Emeline's brother-in-law, she decided to return East. In the poem "In Vision," Larcom rationalizes her decision in terms of a quasi-religious calling to a higher life than the domestic one for which Emeline had settled.

In 1854, Larcom obtained a teaching position at Wheaton Seminary in Norton, Massachusetts, where she remained until 1862. Thereafter, writing and editing became her chief means of support, as her literary reputation flourished under the sponsorship of John G. Whittier. In 1884, Larcom's complete poetry was given the imprimatur of a Houghton and Mifflin "household edition," making her one of only three nineteenth-century American women poets so honored (the other two were the Cary sisters). A deeply committed evangelical Christian, Larcom turned almost entirely to religious writing in her last years. Never strong, she died in Boston of a heart ailment at the relatively young age of sixty-nine, leaving behind a cache of close to thirty titles.

Interest in Larcom today has focused almost exclusively on her prose reminiscences of her New England childhood and her life as a mill operative. Even those who admire her in other ways have tended to dismiss her poetry as largely conventional and sentimental. Unlike Phoebe Cary, who played brilliantly with the sentimental conventions she despised, Larcom's strongest poetry, however, is of quite a different order, and it warrants much more serious attention than it has received.

Like most nineteenth-century United States poets, Lucy Larcom wrote unevenly. In her own day, her best known poem, and the one that brought her her first taste of literary fame, was "Hannah Binding Shoes," a poem she later disavowed. Larcom's desire to disavow "Hannah" is understandable. When compared to other poems on the same theme (the waiting woman) – Alice Cary's "The Seal Fisher's Wife," Phelps's "The Stone Woman of Eastern Point," or even, albeit from a very different angle, Spofford's "Pomegranate-Flowers" and Dickinson's "I tend my flowers for thee – ," (339) – "Hannah" is not a particularly impressive piece of work. Facile in rhyme, meter, and image, it is also hopelessly stereotyped in its presentation of the principal figure's basic situation.

But "Hannah" is by no stretch of the imagination the best that this serious and deeply religious woman could produce. As poems such as "Weaving" and "In Vision" suggest, Larcom's strength lay in contemplative poetry, and in poetry of moral vision. To such poetry she brought a complicated consciousness, shaped by her exacting Puritan heritage and by her own need to survive in a hostile environment. Like Dickinson's "Soil of Flint" (681), the granite of New England was what she "tilled." And from it she drew a vision of life as paradoxically hopeful and beautiful as that to which Cape Ann gives rise in what I take to be her signature poem, "Wild Roses of Cape Ann." In this densely allusive poem (as difficult and demanding as "Hannah" is easy to read), Larcom explores the origins of her art and of her people's ethos in a way of life made hardy by its precarious perch on rocky headlands never meant to nurture human life:

> But still the hardy huntsmen of the deep
> Clung to their rocky anchorage, and built
> Homes for themselves, like sea-fowl, in the clefts.
> And cabins grouped themselves in villages,
> And billows echoed back the Sabbath bells,

And poetry bloomed out of barren crags,
  With life, and love, and sorrow, and strong faith,
            (*Wild Roses of Cape Ann* 1881)

Few poets, from New England or elsewhere, have captured as movingly the deep embedding of the region's history and spirit in its uniquely fertile yet harsh topography, as has Larcom in these lines from the conclusion of "Wild Roses of Cape Ann." If they are sentimental, they are sentimentalism at its best.

Primary Texts

Poems, 1869; *An Idyl of Work*, 1875; *Wild Roses of Cape Ann and Other Poems*, 1881; *Lucy Larcom's Poetical Works*, 1884; *A New England Girlhood, Outlined from Memory*, 1892.

Further Reading

Nancy Cott, "Foreword," in *A New England Girlhood*, Boston: Northeastern University Press, 1986; Benita Eisler, *The Lowell Offering*, New York: Lippincott, 1977; Philip S. Foner, *The Factory Girls*, Chicago: University of Illinois Press, 1977; Shirley Marchalonis, *The Worlds of Lucy Larcom: 1824–1893*, Athens, Georgia: University of Georgia Press, 1989.

from *The Crayon* (1857)

HANNAH BINDING SHOES

A Rhyme of the Bay State

Poor lone Hannah,
Sitting at the window, binding shoes.
  Faded, wrinkled,
Sitting, stitching, in a mournful muse.
    Bright-eyed beauty once was she,   5
    When the bloom was on the tree:
        Spring and winter
Hannah's at the window, binding shoes.

  Not a neighbor
Passing nod or answer will refuse   10
  To her whisper
"Is there from the fishers any news?"
    Oh, her heart's adrift, with one
    On an endless voyage gone!
        Night and morning   15
Hannah's at the window, binding shoes.

  Fair young Hannah,
Ben, the sun-burnt fisher, gayly woos:
  Tall and clever,

For a willing heart and hand he sues.   20
   May-day skies are all aglow,
   And the waves are laughing so!
     For her wedding
Hannah leaves her window and her shoes.

   May is passing;   25
'Mong the apple-boughs a pigeon coos.
   Hannah shudders;
For the wild southwester mischief brews.
   Round the rocks of Marblehead,[1]
   Outward bound, a schooner sped.   30
     Silent, lonesome,
Hannah's at the window, binding shoes.

   'Tis November.
Now no tear her wasted cheek bedews.
   From Newfoundland   35
Not a sail returning will she lose,
   Whispering, hoarsely, "Fishermen,
   Have you, have you heard of Ben?"
     Old with watching,
Hannah's at the window, binding shoes.   40

Twenty winters
Bleach and tear the rugged shore she views.
   Twenty seasons;
Never one has brought her any news.
   Still her dim eyes silently   45
   Chase the white sails o'er the sea.
     Hopeless, faithful,
Hannah's at the window, binding shoes.

from *Poems* (1869)

WEAVING

All day she stands before her loom;
   The flying shuttles come and go:
By grassy fields, and trees in bloom,
   She sees the winding river flow:
And fancy's shuttle flieth wide,   5
And faster than the waters glide.

HANNAH BINDING SHOES
[1] Massachusetts town built on a rocky promontory
overlooking the Atlantic ocean, fifteen miles northeast
of Boston.

Is she entangled in her dreams,
 Like that fair weaver of Shalott,[2]
Who left her mystic mirror's gleams,
 To gaze on light Sir Lancelot?   10
Her heart, a mirror sadly true,
Brings gloomier visions into view.

"I weave, and weave, the livelong day:
 The woof is strong, the warp is good:[3]
I weave, to be my mother's stay;   15
 I weave, to win my daily food:
But ever as I weave," saith she,
"The world of women haunteth me.

"The river glides along, one thread
 In nature's mesh, so beautiful!   20
The stars are woven in; the red
 Of sunrise; and the rain-cloud dull.
Each seems a separate wonder wrought;
Each blends with some more wondrous thought.

"So, at the loom of life, we weave   25
 Our separate shreds, that varying fall,
Some stained, some fair; and, passing, leave
 To God the gathering up of all,
In that full pattern wherein man
Works blindly out the eternal plan.   30

"In his vast work, for good or ill,
 The undone and the done he blends:
With whatsoever woof we fill,
 To our weak hands His might He lends,
And gives the threads beneath His eye   35
The texture of eternity.

"Wind on, by willow and by pine,
 Thou blue, untroubled Merrimack![4]
Afar, by sunnier streams than thine,
 My sisters toil, with foreheads black;   40

WEAVING
[2] Larcom is alluding to the title character in Alfred, Lord Tennyson's 1833 Arthurian romance, "The Lady of Shalott." Under an evil curse, she must weave day and night and never look out of the window, but only view the external world in images in her mirror. When Sir Launcelot passes by, however, she cannot resist looking at him, sealing her doom. She was a very popular archetype for the passive and fated maiden in Victorian literature.
[3] The woof (or weft) is the threads that were woven across a warp to make a fabric; the warp is the threads stretched lengthwise in a loom to be crossed by the woof.
[4] The Merrimack river flowed through Lowell and Lawrence where Larcom labored as a child.

And water with their blood this root,
Whereof we gather bounteous fruit.

"There be sad women, sick and poor;
    And those who walk in garments soiled:
Their shame, their sorrow, I endure;   45
    By their defect my hope is foiled:
The blot they bear is on my name;
Who sins, and I am not to blame?

"And how much of your wrong is mine,
    Dark women slaving at the South?   50
Of your stolen grapes I quaff the wine;
    The bread you starve for fills my mouth:
The beam unwinds, but every thread
With blood of strangled souls is red.

"If this be so, we win and wear   55
    A Nessus-robe of poisoned cloth;[5]
Or weave them shrouds they may not wear, –
    Fathers and brothers falling both
On ghastly, death-sown fields, that lie
Beneath the tearless Southern sky.   60

"Alas! the weft has lost its white.
    It grows a hideous tapestry,
That pictures war's abhorrent sight: –
    Unroll not, web of destiny![6]
Be the dark volume left unread, –   65
The tale untold, – the curse unsaid!"

So up and down before her loom
    She paces on, and to and fro,
Till sunset fills the dusty room,
    And makes the water redly glow,   70
As if the Merrimack's calm flood
Were changed into a stream of blood.

Too soon fulfilled, and all too true
    The words she murmured as she wrought:

---

[5]   In Greek mythology, the shirt once belonging to the centaur, Nessus. The shirt became poisoned when Nessus's blood stained it after Hercules shot him with a poisoned arrow. Not knowing that it was poisoned, Deianira, Hercules's wife, later gave the shirt to Hercules as a gift, hoping to reclaim his love; hence the shirt became a symbol both for a poisoned gift and for evils that rebound on the evil doer.
[6]   An oblique reference to the Moirae or "Three Fates" who control human destiny in Greek mythology. Clotho spins the thread of life, Lachesis determines its length, and Atropos cuts it.

But, weary weaver, not to you   75
   Alone was war's stern message brought:
"Woman!" it knelled from heart to heart,
"Thy sister's keeper know thou art!"[7]

from *Atlantic Monthly* (1870)

BLACK MOUNTAIN IN BEARCAMP LAKE[8]

A little lake, that in a quiet place,
   Bordered with green home-fields and forest pines,
   Seems to lie dreaming, rippled with soft lines
That glide like smiles across a sleeping face.
In the lake's depth an outline vague you trace;   5
   A shadowy mountain on its breast reclines;
And tremulous with the wonder of its dream
A shape sublime it makes that image seem. –
   So is the greatest man not half so great
In wise men's thoughts, or the world's wondering eye,   10
   Crowned with a grandeur sure to isolate,
   As in some heart where he may mirrored lie; –
He finding in that distant nearness rest;
She with her grand illusion more than blest.

from *Good Company* (1879)

THE WATER LILY

From the reek of the pond, the lily
   Has risen in raiment white, –
A spirit of airs and waters –
   A form of incarnate light;
Yet, except for the rooted stem   5
   That steadies her diadem, –
Except for the earth she is nourished by,
Could the soul of the lily have climbed to the sky?

---

[7] Genesis 4:8. "Then the Lord said to Cain, 'Where is Abel your brother?' He said, 'I do not know; am I my brother's keeper?'"

BLACK MOUNTAIN IN BEARCAMP LAKE
[8] Bearcamp Lake was a favorite recreation spot for the poet, John Greenleaf Whittier (1807–92), who sponsored Larcom in the literary world and also collaborated with her on a number of projects. This poem seems to suggest that Larcom viewed her subordinate position to Whittier with some irony.

from *Wild Roses of Cape Ann* (1881)

Wild Roses of Cape Ann[9]

Wild roses of Cape Ann! A rose is sweet,
No matter where it grows; and roses grow,
Nursed by the pure heavens and the strengthening earth,
Wherever men will let them. Every waste
And solitary place is glad for them,   5
Since the old prophet sang so, until now.
But our wild roses, flavored with the sea,
And colored by the salt winds and much sun
To healthiest intensity of bloom, –
We think the world has none so beautiful.   10
Even from his serious height, the Puritan
Stooped to their fragrance, and recorded them[10]
"Sweet single roses," maidens of the woods,
The lovelier for their virgin singleness.
And when good Winthrop[11] with his white fleet came,   15
Skirting the coast in June, they breathed on him,
Mingling their scent with balsams of the pine,[12]
And strange wild odors of the wilderness:
Their sweetness penetrated the true heart
That waited in Old England, when he wrote   20
"My love, this is an earthly Paradise!"

No Paradise, indeed! the east wind's edge
Too keenly cuts, albeit no sword of flame![13]
Yet have romantic fancies bloomed around
This breezy promontory, ever since   25
The Viking with the commonest of names
Left there his Turkish heroine's memory,
Calling it "Tragabigzanda."[14] English tongues
Relished not the huge mouthful; and a son,

Wild Roses of Cape Ann

[9]   Cape Ann is located on the eastern peninsula of Essex County in Massachusetts, north of Massachusetts Bay. It is famous for its wild roses.

[10]   Larcom's note: Allusions to the early history of Cape "Anne" may be verified by referring to the Narrative of Captain John Smith; to the records of Hubbard, Higginson, Winthrop, and others; and to the local histories of the shoretowns of Massachusetts, northeast of Salem.

[11]   John Winthrop (1588–1649). Appointed Governor of the Massachusetts Bay Colony in 1629, he was in good part responsible for shaping the colony's exclusionary theocratic policy. He arrived on the *Arabella* at what is now Salem, Massachusetts, in the summer of

1630. He described the landing in Cape Ann in his journal, *The History of New England*, and in letters.

[12]   An unusually fragrant evergreen, indigenous to the American northeast.

[13]   Paradise after the fall was guarded by an angel holding a flaming sword.

[14]   Larcom is making a somewhat heavy-handed joke at the expense of John Smith, whose name alone was sufficient to strip him of the romantic aura in which he sought to wrap his "Viking" voyages. Tragabigzanda is the name of the Turkish princess who, Smith claims, saved his life when he was adventuring in the East. King Charles I of England, with eminent good sense, rechristened the cape in honor of his mother, Anne of Denmark.

Christening it for his mother, made Cape Anne   30
Bloom with yet one more thought of womanhood.

But never Orient princess, British queen,
Left on this headland such wild blossoming
Of romance dashed with pathos, – roses wet
With briny spray, for dew drops, – as to-day   35
Haunts the lone cottage of the fisherman,
In hopes half-suffocated by despair,
When the Old Salvages[15] foam and gnash their teeth,
And all the battered coast is vexed with storms
Down the long trend of Maine, to Labrador.   40

Had Roger Conant, patriarch of the Cape,[16]
Who left the Pilgrims as they left the Church,[17]
To seek a fuller freedom than they gave, –
Freedom to worship God in the ancient way,
Clothing the spirit's heavenward flight with form, –   45
Had Roger Conant, kindliest of men,
One forethought of the flood of widow's tears
Wherewith this headland would be drenched, – the sea
Has no such bitter salt! – had he once dreamed
Of vessels wrecked by hundreds, amid shoals   50
And fogs of dim Newfoundland, he had left
Doughty Miles Standish[18] an unchallenged claim
To every inch of coast, from Annisquam[19]
To Marblehead. "What?" said the Plymouth folk,
"Shall Conant seize our fishing-grounds? Shall he   55
Who went out from us, being not of us,
Take from our children's mouths their rightful food
For strangers who might stay at home, unstarved,
Unpersecuted? What does Conant mean?
Let Standish see!" The two met, face to face,   60
Lion and lamb: and first the lamb withdrew,
And then the lion; neither having found
Food for a quarrel on these ledges bare.
Standish sailed back to Plymouth; Conant sought
A quiet place, suiting a quiet man,   65
Lived unassuming years, and fell asleep
Among the green hills of Bass-River-Side.[20]

---

15   Old wrecks.
16   Roger Conant (1592–1679), manager of the
Dorchester Company's fishing settlement on Cape Ann.
The settlement failed and he went on to found Naumkeag
(Salem), which flourished. He was a nonconformist but
not a separatist, and voluntarily left the Plymouth colony
with whose rigid policies he disagreed.

17   The Church of England, from which the Puritans
separated.
18   Myles Standish (1584–1656), military adviser and
hired mercenary for the Plymouth colony.
19   A village and summer resort in northeastern Massachusetts. Today it is a northern suburb of Gloucester.
20   Today, Beverly, Massachusetts, on Boston's North
Shore.

So Tragabigzanda washed her granite feet,
Careless of rulers, in the eastern sea.
But still the hardy huntsmen of the deep[21]   70
Clung to their rocky anchorage, and built
Homes for themselves, like sea-fowl, in the clefts.
And cabins grouped themselves in villages,
And billows echoed back the Sabbath bells,
And poetry bloomed out of barren crags,   75
With life, and love, and sorrow, and strong faith,
Like the rock-saxifrage,[22] that seams the cliff,
Through all denials of east wind, sleet, and frost,
With white announcements of approaching spring:
Or like the gold-and-crimson columbines[23]   80
That nod from crest and chasm, a merry crowd
Of rustic damsels tricked[24] with finery,
Tossing their light heads in the sober air:
For Nature tires of her own gloom, and Sport
Laughs out through her solemnities, unchid.   85

The sailor is the playmate of the wave
That yawns to make a mouthful of him. Songs,
Light love-songs youth and joy lilt everywhere,
Catch sparkle from the sea, and echo back
Mirth unto merriment, – spray tossed toward spray.   90
Hark to the fisher, singing as he rocks,
A mote upon the mighty ocean-swell!

IN VISION[25]

Although to me remains not one regret
     For lovely possibilities that were ours,
     Dreamed out across vast beds of prairie-flowers
Into the beckoning West, where the sun set,
     A glowing magnet, drawing our hearts on   5
As if they were but one heart, after him,
Where all our blending future seemed to swim
     In light unutterable, a new dawn,
An opening Eden, – although it was well
That picture faded, haunts me yet its spell.   10

And I am glad I saw it, and with thee, –
     Then near as my own spirit, – now as far
     Removed into the unseen as that calm star

---

[21] Fishermen, but also, probably, whalers.
[22] *Rock-saxifrage* rockfoils, low rock plants that can grow under very inhospitable conditions.
[23] *Columbines* delicate flowering plants that can grow on rocks.

[24] *Tricked* dressed up.
IN VISION
[25] According to Larcom's biographer, Shirley Marchalonis, this poem addresses Larcom's broken engagement to Frank Spaulding, her sister Emeline's brother-in-law.

Which looked across the undulant grassy sea
   Into our faces, and sank out of sight.   15
We dreamed a dream together: nothing more
To thee; to me a vision that before
   Nor after broke the seals of heavenly light,
And showed me, rapt, life's beaker mystical,
Glimpsed and withdrawn, the untasted Holy Grail.[26]   20

I gazed there at thy bidding; was it wrong?
   I knew a separate path awaited me,
   And I divined another quest for thee,
Under strange skies, where I did not belong:
   But for one hour, letting Doubt stand aside,   25
I saw Life pass, transfigured in Love's form;
The mystery wherewith inmost heaven is warm
   Descended, clothed in whiteness, as a bride.
Though that apocalypse annulled thy claim,
Thine eyes yet burn their question through its flame.   30

Had but that fatal prescience been withheld,
   Whereby To-morrow evermore would rise,
   Laughing To-day down with relentless eyes,
What beauty had we not together spelled
   Out of Life's wonder-book, – or else, what bale!   35
The dream was not fulfilled, – could never be;
Yet is the vision light of light to me,
   Dazzling to blankness the world's bridal tale. –
Elsewhere our orbits meet, receding star,
Lost in the dawn that floods me from afar!   40

from *Atlantic Monthly* (1882)

FALLOW[27]

I like these plants that you call weeds, –
   Sedge, hardhack, mullein, yarrow, –
That knit their roots, and sift their seeds
Where any grassy wheel-track leads
   Through country by-ways narrow.   5

They fringe the rugged hillside farms,
   Grown old with cultivation,
With such wild wealth of rustic charms

---

[26] The lost chalice from which Christ is said to have
drunk at the Last Supper. It stands as a symbol of an
unobtainable spiritual ideal.

FALLOW
[27] Ploughed ground that is left unseeded, allowing
weeds to take over.

As bloomed in Nature's matron arms
   The first days of creation.   10

They show how Mother Earth loves best
   To deck her tired-out places;
By flowery lips, in hours of rest,
Against hard work she will protest
   With homely airs and graces.   15

You plow the arbutus[28] from her hills;
   Hew down her mountain-laurel:
Their place, as best she can, she fills
With humbler blossoms; so she wills
   To close with you her quarrel.   20

She yielded to your axe, with pain,
   Her free, primeval glory;
She brought you crops of golden grain;
You say, "How dull she grows! How plain!" –
   The old, mean, selfish story!   25

Her wildwood soil you may subdue,
   Tortured by hoe and harrow;
But leave her for a year or two,
And see! she stands and laughs at you
   With hardhack, mullein, yarrow!   30

Dear Earth, the world is hard to please!
   Yet heaven's breath gently passes
Into the life of flowers like these;
And I lie down at blessèd ease
   Among thy weeds and grasses.   35

Adeline D. T. Whitney (1824–1906)

Described by one biographer as a "second generation Boston Brahmin," Adeline Dutton Train Whitney was born in Boston, Massachusetts, on September 15, 1824. Her father, Enoch Train, was a wealthy Boston merchant and ship-owner; her mother, Adeline Dutton, was a New Hampshirite, whose seventeenth-century antecedents settled in the Watertown area outside Boston. Whitney attended Lyman Beecher's Congregational Church until her father remarried in 1836. Her stepmother then brought her into the Unitarian Church. Later in life, she, like many Brahmins, became an Episcopalian, her "solid" Puritan ancestry notwithstanding.

---

[28] *Arbutus* an evergreen tree or shrub.

Between the ages of thirteen and eighteen, Whitney attended the George B. Emerson school for girls, a fashionable private school in Boston. Along with a year at a Northampton boarding school, this was the extent of her formal education. Later she was to tell the young women readers to whom she conveyed domestic advice that the study of Latin gave her the discipline she required to carry out her household chores, in particular, "the preparatory processes of cookery." While her original audience may have taken her seriously – and some scholars today certainly have – in light of the poems selected here, it is quite possible she was being droll.

On November 7, 1843, Whitney married Seth Dunbar Whitney, twenty-one years her senior, a trader in wool and leather. The couple settled in his hometown, Milton, Massachusetts, a few miles south of Boston. Whitney proceeded to have four children – three girls and a boy – of whom three survived into adulthood. Her writing career, which consisted mainly of novels and advice books directed toward young women, began only after her children were grown.

With the exception of Habegger, what critical material exists on Whitney has focused attention on her didactic juvenile fiction. Her novels lie in the popular tradition of "Home and Heart." Replete with the standard domestic advice of their era, they urge girls to eschew all work that might lead them outside the home. Beverly Seaton, Whitney's most recent biographer, suggests that Whitney, like other upper-class women, was concerned over the scarcity of good servants. Despite the woman-centeredness of the world they inscribe, Whitney's novels, Seaton argues, are designed to support the status quo – "the most traditional aspects of the lives of upper-class American women of her day." Her poetry, Seaton notes in passing, was designed to promote the same basic set of ideas. But was it? Always?

Like the poetry of Phoebe Cary, whose precise contemporary she is, Whitney's poetry epitomizes the public/private split that makes the work of nineteenth-century women so treacherous to speak about but so fascinating to study. First published 1860, then running through fifteen (!) separate reprintings or editions between 1861 and 1912, *Mother Goose for Grown Folks* suggests that Adeline D. T. Whitney was not quite what she seemed. Or, at any rate, her view of the domestic life was not quite so simplistic and piously dutiful as her advice books, novels, and, indeed, much of her more conventional poetry, make it appear. Rather, it seems that A. D. T. Whitney was possessed of a wicked sense of humor; and the butt of her humor was, by preference, the rules and rites of the very world to which she was, as a woman, assigned.

Insofar as humor involves making "fun" of something, even if it is only an idea or a set of codes, the line between comedy and its dark double, aggressive anger, can be hard to discern. Indeed, joking about something is often viewed as a relatively benign way of relieving one's anger toward it. Are the poems in *Mother Goose* good-natured fun, a venting of steam, not to be taken seriously, or are they the not-so-subtle expressions of one woman's rage?

Poems such as "Jack Horner" (with its very phallic thumb) and "Missions" suggest that despite what she preached publicly, privately Whitney was quite aware that women were socially oppressed by men who benefited directly and indirectly from oppressing them. Indeed, one of Mother Goose's most persistent themes is the way in which men, from Shakespeare down, have enlarged themselves in life by feeding off women, plagiarizing women's works, and then (as in "Bowls") mystifying their own authority and privilege through their power to control discourse.

In her beautiful lament for a dead housewife ("Released") – a poem which begs comparison to Dickinson's masterful "How many times these low feet staggered" (187) – Whitney identifies the domestic sphere as "Four walls / Whose blank shut our all else of life," leaving its female victim trapped in "A world of pain, and toil, and strife." Appearing in *Pansies*, there is nothing to suggest that this poem was meant to be taken as light-hearted fun. But if it is not, then what would ever possess a woman like Whitney to urge others to voluntarily consign and resign themselves to such misery? The final stanza of "Released" suggests that Whitney viewed sanctification in heaven as woman's reward for her martyrdom on earth; but even as I write these words, I can hear Mother Goose laughing.

Primary Texts

Mother Goose for Grown Folks, 1860; *Pansies*, 1873; *Holy Tides*, 1886; *Daffodils*, 1887; *White Memories*, 1893.

Further Reading

Alfred Habegger, *Gender, Fantasy, and Realism in American Literature*, New York: Columbia University Press, 1982; Beverly Seaton, "Adeline Dutton Train Whitney," *American Women Writers*: 406–8.

from *Mother Goose for Grown Folks* (1860)

BRAHMIC

If a great poet think he sings,
   Or if the poem think it's sung,
They do but sport the scattered plumes
   That Mother Goose aside hath flung.

Far of forgot to me is near: 5
   Shakspeare and Punch[1] are all the same;
The vanished thoughts do reappear,
   And shape themselves to fun or fame.

They use my *quills*, and leave me out,
   Oblivious that I wear the *wings*;   10
Or that a Goose has been about,
   When every little gosling sings.

Strong men may strive for grander thought,
   But, six times out of every seven,
My old philosophy hath taught   15
   All they can master this side heaven.

BRAHMIC
[1] British popular humor magazine, here standing in contrast to Shakespeare's "high" art.

JACK HORNER

"Little Jack Horner
Sat in a corner
Eating a Christmas Pie:
He put in his thumb,
And pulled out a plum,
And said, 'What a great boy am I!'"

Ah, the world hath many a Horner,
  Who, seated in his corner,
Finds a Christmas Pie provided for his thumb:
  And cries out with exultation,
  When successful exploration   5
Doth discover the predestinated plum!

  Little Jack outgrows his tire,
  And becometh John, Esquire;
And he finds a monstrous pasty ready made,
  Stuffed with notes and bonds and bales,   10
  With invoices and sales,
And all the mixed ingredients of Trade.

  And again it is his luck
  To be just in time to pluck,
By a clever "operation," from the pie   15
  An unexpected "plum";
  So he glorifies his thumb,
And says, proudly, "What a mighty man am I!"

  Or perchance, to Science turning,
  And with weary labor learning   20
All the formulas and phrases that oppress her, –
  For the fruit of others' baking
  So a fresh diploma taking,
Comes he forth, a full accredited Professor!

  Or he's not too nice to mix   25
  In the dish of politics;
And the dignity of office he puts on:
  And he feels as big again
  As a dozen nobler men,
While he writes himself the Honorable John!   30

  Nay, he need not quite despair
  Of the Presidential Chair:
The thing is not unlikely to be done;
  Since a party puppet now

May wear boldly on its brow   35
The glory that a Webster[2] never won!

Not to hint at female Horners,
  Who, in their exclusive corners,
Think the world is only made of upper crust;
  And in the funny pie   40
  That we call Society,
Their dainty fingers delicately thrust:

Till it sometimes comes to pass,
  In the spiced and sugared mass,
One may compass (don't they call it so?) a *catch*;   45
  And the gratulation given
  Seems as if the very heaven
Had outdone itself in making such a match!

O, the world keeps Christmas Day
  In a queer, perpetual way;   50
Shouting always, "What a great, big Boy am I!"
  Yet how many of the crowd,
  Thus vociferating loud,
And its accidental honors lifting high,
  Have really, more than Jack,   55
  With all their lucky knack,
Had a finger in the *making* of the Pie?

SOLOMON GRUNDY

"Solomon Grundy
Born on Monday,
Christened on Tuesday,
Married on Wednesday,
Sick on Thursday,
Worse on Friday,
Dead on Saturday,
Buried on Sunday:
This was the end
Of Solomon Grundy."

So sings the unpretentious Muse
That guides the quill of Mother Goose,
And in one week of mortal strife
Presents the epitome of Life:

JACK HORNER
[2]   Daniel Webster (1782–1852), lawyer, orator, and
statesman. Any one of the three Presidents preceding
Lincoln in office could represent Whitney's target here;
but more likely she was thinking of all three: Millard
Fillmore (1850–3), Franklin Pierce (1853–7), and James
Buchanan (1857–61).

But down sits Billy Shakspeare next,   5
And, coolly taking up the text,
His thought pursues the trail of mine,
And, lo! the "Seven Ages"[3] shine!
O world! O critics! *can't* you see
How Shakspeare plagiarizes me?   10

And other bards will after come,
   To echo in a later age,
"He lived, – he died: behold the sum,
   The abstract of the historian's page"; –
Yet once for all the thing was done,   15
   Complete in Grundy's[4] pilgrimage.

For not a child upon the knee
But hath the moral learned of me;
And measured, in a seven days' span,
The whole experience of man.   20

BOWLS

"Three wise men of Gotham
   Went to sea in a bowl:
If the bowl had been stronger,
   My song had been longer."

Mysteriously suggestive! A vague hint,
   Yet a rare touch of most effective art,
That of the bowl, and all the voyagers in 't,
   Tells nothing, save the fact that they did start.
There ending suddenly, with subtle craft,   5
The story stands, – as 't were a broken shaft, –
More eloquent in mute signification,
Than lengthened detail, or precise relation.
So perfect in its very non-achieving,
That, of a truth, I cannot help believing   10
A rash attempt at paraphrasing it
May prove a blunder, rather than a hit.

Still, I must wish the venerable soul
Had been explicit as regards the *bowl*.
Was it, perhaps, a railroad speculation?   15
Or a big ship to carry all creation,
That, by some kink of its machinery,
Failed, in the end, to carry even three?

SOLOMON GRUNDY
[5] The reference is to Jacques's "Seven Ages of Man"
speech in *As You Like It* II.vii.139–66.

[1] Mrs Grundy was an imaginary character in a popular
stage play whose name came to stand for those persons
in a community who sought to uphold proprieties.

Or other fond, erroneous calculation
Of splendid schemes that died disastrously?   20

It must have been of Gotham manufacture;
Though strangely weak, and liable to fracture.
Yet – pause a moment – strangely, did I say?
Scarcely, since, after all, it was but clay; –
The stuff Hope takes to build her brittle boat,   25
And therein sets the wisest men afloat.
Truly, a bark would need be somewhat stronger,
To make the halting history much longer.

Doubtless, the good Dame did but generalize, –
Took a broad glance at human enterprise,   30
And earthly expectation, and so drew,
In pithy lines, a parable most true, –
Kindly to warn us ere we sail away,
With life's great venture, in an ark of clay,
Where shivered fragments all around betoken,   35
How even the "golden bowl" at last lies broken!⁵

MISSIONS

"Hogs in the garden, –
    Catch 'em, Towser!
Cows in the cornfield, –
    Run, boys, run!
Fire on the mountains, –
    Run, boys, run boys!
Cats in the cream-pot, –
    Run, girls, run!"

I don't stand up for Woman's Right;
    Not I, – no, no!
The real lionesses fight, –
    I let it go.
Yet, somehow, as I catch the call   5
    Of the world's voice,
That speaks a summons unto all
    Its girls and boys;

In such strange contrast still it rings
    As church-bells' bome   10
To the pert sound of tinkling things
    One hears at home;

BOWLS
⁵ Ecclesiastes 12:6; symbol of the end of all things.

And wakes an impulse, not germane
    Perhaps, to woman,
Yet with a thrill that makes it plain   15
    'T is truly human; –

A sudden tingle at the springs
    Of noble feeling,
The spirit-power for valiant things
    Clearly revealing.   20
But Eden's curse doth daily deal
    Its certain dole, –
And the old grasp upon the heel
    Holds back the soul!

So, when some rousing deed's to do,   25
    To save a nation,
Or, on the mountains, to subdue
    A conflagration,
Woman! the work is not for you;
    Mind your vocation!   30
Out from the cream-pot comes a mew
    Of tribulation!

Meekly the world's great exploits leave
    Unto your betters;
So bear the punishment of Eve,   35
    Spirit in fetters!
Only, the hidden fires will glow,
    And, now and then,
A beacon blazeth out below
    That startles men!   40

Some Joan,[6] through battle-field to stake,
    Danger embracing;
Some Florence,[7] for sweet mercy's sake
    Pestilence facing;
Whose holy valor vindicates   45
    The royal birth
That, for its crowning, only waits
    The end of earth;
And, haply, when we all stand freed,
    In strength immortal,   50
Such virgin-lamps the host shall lead
    Through heaven's portal!

MISSIONS

[6] Jeanne D'Arc (1412?–31), daughter of a French farmer. She led the French army successfully against occupying British forces in the 1420s. She was eventually captured and burnt at the stake as a witch.

[7] Florence Nightingale (1820–1910), the founder of modern nursing. She became legendary as a result of her service under intolerable conditions during the Crimean War.

COBWEBS AND BROOMS

"There was an old woman
Tossed up in a blanket,
Seventeen times as high as the moon;
What she did there
I cannot tell you,
But in her hand she carried a broom.
Old woman, old woman,
Old woman, said I,
O whither, O whither, O whither so high?
To sweep the cobwebs
Off the sky,
And I'll be back again, by and by."

Mind you, she wore no *wings*,
That she might truly *soar*; no time was lost
In growing such unnecessary things;
    But blindly, in a blanket, she was *tost*!

    Spasmodically, too!   5
    'T was not enough that she should reach the moon;
But seventeen times the distance she must do,
    Lest, peradventure, she get back too soon.

    That emblematic broom!
Besom[8] of mad Reform, uplifted high,   10
That, to reach cobwebs, would precipitate doom,
    And sweep down thunderbolts from out the sky!

    Doubtless, no rubbish lay
About her door, – no work was there to do, –
That through the astonished aisles of Night and Day,   15
    She took her valorous flight in quest of new!

    Lo! at her little broom
The great stars laugh, as on their wheels of fire
They go, dispersing the eternal gloom,
    And shake Time's dust from off each blazing tire!   20

from *Pansies* (1873)

"UNDER THE CLOUD, AND THROUGH THE SEA"

So moved they when false Pharaoh's legions pressed, –
    Chariots and horsemen following furiously, –

COBWEBS AND BROOMS
[8] *Besom*   a bundle of twigs attached to a handle and
used as a broom.

Sons of old Israel, at their God's behest,
    Under the cloud, and through the swelling sea.[9]

So passed they, fearless, where the parted wave   5
    With cloven crest uprearing from the sand, –
A solemn aisle before, behind a grave, –
    Rolled to the beckoning of Jehovah's hand.

So led He them, in desert marches grand,
    By toils sublime, with test of long delay,   10
On to the borders of that Promised Land
    Wherein their heritage of glory lay.

And Jordan raged along his rocky bed,
    And Amorite[10] spears flashed keen and angrily;
Still the same pathway must their footsteps tread,   15
    Under the cloud, through the threatening sea.

God works no otherwise. No mighty birth
    But comes by throes of mortal agony:
No man-child among nations of the earth
    But findeth baptism in a stormy sea.   20

Song of the saints who faced their Jordan-flood
    In fierce Atlantic's unretreating wave;
Who, by the Red Sea of their glorious blood,
    Reached to the freedom that your blood shall save!

O countrymen! God's day is not yet done!   25
    He leaveth not his people utterly.
Count it a covenant,[11] that he leads us on
    Beneath the cloud, and through the crimson sea!

                       (1861)

RELEASED

A little, low-ceiled room. Four walls
    Whose blank shut out all else of life,
And crowded close within their bound
    A world of pain, and toil, and strife.

"UNDER THE CLOUD, AND THROUGH THE SEA"
[9] Whitney is comparing the United States's travails in the Civil War with those experienced by the Israelites on the flight of Israel out of Egypt, including the parting of the Red Sea for Moses and his followers and its closing over Pharaoh and his troops. See Exodus 12–14.

[10] The Amorites were a people of Canaan. They were eventually subdued and absorbed by the Israelites.
[11] In Exodus 14, God makes a covenant with Israel, making the Israelites his chosen people in return for their strict obedience to God's law. Like Howe and many other abolitionists, Whitney is framing the Civil War as a holy war.

Her world. Scarce furthermore she knew 5
    Of God's great globe that wondrously
Outrolls a glory of green earth
    And frames it with the restless sea.

Four closer walls of common pine;
    And therein lying, cold and still, 10
The weary flesh that long hath borne
    Its patient mystery of ill.

Regardless now of work to do,
    No queen more careless in her state,
Hands crossed in an unbroken calm; 15
    For other hands the work may wait.

Put by her implements of toil;
    Put by each coarse, intrusive sign;
She made a Sabbath when she died,
    And round her breathes a rest divine. 20

Put by, at last, beneath the lid,
    The exempted hands, the tranquil face;
Uplift her in her dreamless sleep,
    And bear her gently from the place.

Oft she hath gazed, with wistful eyes, 25
    Out from that threshold on the night;
The narrow bourn she crosseth now;
    She standeth in the eternal light.

Oft she hath pressed, with aching feet,
    Those broken steps that reach the door; 30
Henceforth, with angels, she shall tread
    Heaven's golden stair, forevermore!

A RHYME OF MONDAY MORNING

One half the world is wringing wet,
    Or on the lines a-drying;
That so the seven days' smirch may get
    A weekly purifying.

A smoke goes up through all the air, 5
    And dims its summer glory;
Like that which doth the torment bear
    Of souls in purgatory.

Vainly to shun the tax we seek;
    In penance for our sinning, 10

One day is forfeit from the week,
  To make a clean beginning.

For, gathering stain as on we go, –
  Type of our shame and sorrow, –
White robes we wore but yesterday   15
  Are in the suds to-morrow.

Ah, life without and life within
  In unison consenting!
Six days contracting soil and sin;
  One, washing and repenting!   20

O world, once swept with awful flood
  From ages of pollution!
O nations, cleansed with fire and blood
  In day of absolution!

May God assoil[ize][12] all at last!   25
  Of all be loving-heedful!
And place us where, earth's purging past,
  No washing-day is needful!

Frances Ellen Watkins Harper (1825–1911)

All that is known of Frances Ellen Watkins Harper's family background is that she was born to a free black woman, and that her mother died when the poet was three. Thereafter, Harper lived in Baltimore with her aunt and uncle, who ran the Mental Moral Improvement Society, a "school of oratory, literature and debate" for free blacks. She attended this school until she was thirteen or fourteen, when she hired out as a domestic to a Baltimore family.

Harper left the South in 1850 and moved to Ohio, where she taught sewing at Union Seminary near Columbus. Under the influence of the black abolitionist William Grant Still, she became involved in the anti-slavery movement, eventually settling in Maine where she became a full-time lecturer for the Maine Anti-Slavery Society. In an incident that says much about her courage and humanity, when news of the debacle at Harper's Ferry reached the East, she offered financial and moral support to John Brown's family and stayed with Mrs Brown until her husband was executed.

Harper married Fenton Harper, a widower with three children, in 1860, moving with him to a farm outside Columbus, Ohio. About her married life, Harper remarked that her role was to play a "farmer's wife" who "made butter for the Columbus market." They had one daughter, Mary. Harper's husband died in 1864. Like many another nineteenth-century husband in this volume, at his death he left his widow his children and his debts.

A RHYME OF MONDAY MORNING
[12] *Assoilize* to set free from sin, purify, with an obvious pun on laundering.

Active throughout her long career in many political organizations, including the American Women's Suffrage Association, the National Council of Women, the Women's Christian Temperance Union, and the National Council of Negro Women, Harper lived a largely public life, devoting herself to others rather than exploring her own interior world. During a speech in rural Alabama in 1871, she observed that "a room to myself is a luxury that I do not always enjoy." Given her circumstances – and the depth of her political commitments – an art of solitary introspection, such as, for example, Emily Dickinson engaged in, would have been no less a luxury. Did her poetry suffer?

According to Melba Boyd, there were twelve thousand copies of Harper's second book, *Poems on Miscellaneous Subjects* (1854) in print by 1858. According to William Still, as many as fifty thousand copies of her first four books were available by 1872. *Poems on Miscellaneous Subjects* alone went through seven editions. To anyone familiar with the woes of publishing poets, these are impressive figures which most poets of the period would probably have envied. Yet at the same time, critical reaction to Harper's poetry has been mixed, with one article, sympathetic to Harper, tellingly titled: "Is Frances Ellen Watkins Harper Good Enough to Teach?" More than anywhere else, the problem seems to lie in the specific kind of poetry that Harper, a woman who lived her entire adult life in the public arena, chose to write.

Noting that "Harper's literary aesthetics were formed during the first half of the nineteenth century, and her commitment to a literature of purpose and of wide appeal remained constant," Frances Foster, Harper's modern editor, argues – accurately – that Harper intended much of her poetry to be recited publicly, not to be read and studied in private. When she lectured on anti-slavery and other causes, poems would accompany her speeches. When her poems were read privately, it was typically in media such as the abolition press where calls to action – not aesthetic contemplation – were the paramount concern.

In such contexts, Harper's high degree of accessibility, even her reliance on stereotypes (the so-called sentimental images of wailing mothers, shrinking maidens, and courageous black heroes), are strengths insofar as they contribute to the immediacy of her poetry's power to elicit the desired affect: whether pity or outrage. She knew just how to pull her audience's heart strings – and to bring them into a sense of empathic oneness with the broken-hearted husbands, wives, and children whose afflictions she inscribes. But, less obviously, Harper also wrote with a sharp eye to the class and gender issues subtending slavery – in particular the way in which patriarchal institutions (from slavery to government itself) battened on their ability to oppress women across lines of race and class. As much a feminist as an abolitionist, Harper's analysis of the political and economic as well as emotional consequences of the "double standard" for women can still ring a sympathetic chord in feminist audiences today.

Like all good popular poetry, Harper's best poems are vigorous, challenging, and thoughtful in their stands, especially on women's issues, where Harper is, arguably, at her most radical. And her achievement, as a black woman in the nineteenth century, sets a standard for determined yet humanistic political activism few people, white or black, male or female, could match from her day to our own.

Primary Texts

Poems on Miscellaneous Subjects, 1854; *Sketches of Southern Life*, 1872; *Iola Leroy; or Shadows Uplifted*, 1892; *The Martyr of Alabama and Other Poems*, 1894; *Atlanta Offering: Poems*, 1895; *Complete Poems of Frances E. W. Harper*, ed. Maryemma Graham, 1988; *A Brighter Coming Day: A Frances Ellen Watkins Harper Reader*, ed. Frances Foster, 1990.

Further Reading

Elizabeth Ammons, "*Legacy* Profile: Frances Ellen Watkins Harper," *Legacy: A Journal of Nineteenth-Century American Women Writers* 2 (1985): 61–6; Melba Joyce Boyd, *Discarded Legacy: Politics and Poetics in the Life of Frances Ellen Watkins Harper 1825–1911*, Detroit: Wayne State University Press, 1994; Frances Foster, ed., *A Brighter Coming Day: A Frances Ellen Watkins Harper Reader*, New York: Feminist Press, 1990; Maryemma Graham, ed., "Introduction," in *Complete Poems of Frances E. W. Harper*, New York and Oxford: Oxford University Press, 1988; Patricia Liggins Hill, "Let Me Make the Songs for the People: A Study of Frances Watkins Harper's Poetry," *Black American Literature Forum* 15 (Summer 1981): 60–5; Paul Lauter, "Is Frances Ellen Watkins Harper Good Enough to Teach?," *Legacy: A Journal of Nineteenth-Century American Women Writers* 5 (Spring 1988): 27–32; Joan R. Sherman, *Invisible Poets: Afro-Americans of the Nineteenth Century*; William Still, *The Underground Rail Road*, Philadelphia: Porter and Coates, 1872.

from *Poems on Miscellaneous Subjects* (1854)

BIBLE DEFENCE OF SLAVERY

Take sackcloth of the darkest dye,
    And shroud the pulpits round!
Servants of him that cannot lie,
    Sit mourning on the ground.

Let holy horror blanch each cheek,   5
    Pale every brow with fears:
And rocks and stones, if ye could speak,
    Ye well might melt to tears!

Let sorrow breathe in every tone,
    In every strain ye raise;   10
Insult not God's majestic throne
    With th' mockery of praise.

A "reverend" man, whose light should be
    The guide of age and youth,
Brings to the shrine of Slavery   15
    The sacrifice of truth!

For the direst wrong by man imposed,
    Since Sodom's fearful cry,[1]
The word of life has been unclos'd,
    To give your God the lie.   20

BIBLE DEFENCE OF SLAVERY
[1] Genesis 18. The city of Sodom, together with that of Gomorrah, was destroyed by God for its sinfulness in the days of Abraham and Lot.

Oh! when ye pray for heathen lands,
  And plead for their dark shores,
Remember Slavery's cruel hands
  Make heathens at your doors!

from *Liberator* (1861)

TO THE CLEVELAND UNION-SAVERS[2]

(An Appeal from One of The Fugitive's Own Race)

Men of Cleveland, had a vulture
  Clutched a timid dove for prey,
Would ye not, with human pity,
  Drive the gory bird away?

Had you seen a feeble lambkin,   5
  Shrinking from a wolf so bold,
Would ye not, to shield the trembler,
  In your arms have made its fold?

But when she, a hunted sister,
  Stretched her hands that ye might save,   10
Colder far than Zembla's regions[3]
  Was the answer that ye gave.

On your Union's bloody altar,
  Was your helpless victim laid;
Mercy, truth, and justice shuddered,   15
  But your hands would give no aid.

And ye sent her back to torture,
  Stripped of freedom, robbed of right, —
Thrust the wretched, captive stranger,
  Back to Slavery's gloomy night!   20

Sent her back where men may trample,
  On her honor and her fame,
And upon her lips so dusky
  Press the cup of woe and shame.

TO THE CLEVELAND UNION-SAVERS

[2] The title alludes to Cleveland Ohio's Republican party, known as the Union Party. Harper is castigating party members for their hypocrisy in supporting the Fugitive Slave law. In 1861, a slave woman, Sarah Lucy Bagby, was seized by the United States marshal on January 19 in the home of L. A. Benton, where she was employed as a servant. Sympathetic Clevelanders tried unsuccessfully to buy her freedom. After a hearing, the United States commissioner returned her to her owner to take back to Virginia. She was the last slave to be returned South under the Fugitive Slave law.

[3] Belonging to Nova Zembla, a group of islands in the Arctic Ocean north of Archangel in Russia; hence, Arctic.

There is blood upon your city, —　　　　　　　　　25
　　Dark and dismal is the stain;
And your hands would fail to cleanse it,
　　Though you should Lake Erie drain.

There's a curse upon your Union!
　　Fearful sounds are in the air;　　　　　　　30
As if thunderbolts were forging,
　　Answers to the bondsman's prayer.

Ye may bind your trembling victims,
　　Like the heathen priests of old;
And may barter manly honor　　　　　　　　35
　　For the Union and for gold; —

But ye cannot stay the whirlwind,
　　When the storm begins to break;
And our God doth rise in judgment,
　　For the poor and needy's sake.　　　　　　40

And, your guilty, sin-cursed Union
　　Shall be shaken to its base,
Till ye learn that simple justice
　　Is the right of every race.

from *Sketches of Southern Life* (1872)

AUNT CHLOE

I remember, well remember,
　　That dark and dreadful day,
When they whispered to me, "Chloe,
　　Your children's sold away!"

It seemed as if a bullet　　　　　　　　　　5
　　Had shot me through and through,
And I felt as if my heart-strings
　　Was breaking right in two.

And I says to cousin Milly,
　　"There must be some mistake;　　　　　　10
Where's Mistus?" "In the great house crying —
　　Crying like her heart would break.

"And the lawyer's there with Mistus;
　　Says he's come to 'ministrate,
'Cause when master died he just left　　　　15
　　Heap of debt on the estate.

"And I thought 'twould do you good
　　To bid your boys good-bye –
To kiss them both and shake their hands
　　And have a hearty cry.　　　　　　　　　　　20

"Oh! Chloe, I knows how you feel,
　　'Cause I'se been through it all;
I thought my poor old heart would break
　　When master sold my Saul."

Just then I heard the footsteps　　　　　　　　25
　　Of my children at the door,
And I rose right up to meet them.
　　But I fell upon the floor.

And I heard poor Jakey saying,
　　"Oh, mammy, don't you cry!"　　　　　　　　30
And I felt my children kiss me
　　And bid me, both, good-bye.

Then I had a mighty sorrow,
　　Though I nursed it all alone;
But I wasted to a shadow,　　　　　　　　　　35
　　And turned to skin and bone.

But one day dear uncle Jacob[4]
　　(In heaven he's now a saint)
Said, "Your poor heart is in the fire,
　　But child you must not faint."　　　　　　　40

Then I said to uncle Jacob,
　　"If I was good like you,
When the heavy trouble dashed me
　　I'd know just what to do."

Then he said to me, "Poor Chloe,　　　　　　　45
　　The way is open wide:"
And he told me of the Saviour,
　　And the fountain in His side.[5]

Then he said, "Just take your burden
　　To the blessed Master's feet;　　　　　　　50
I takes all my troubles, Chloe,
　　Right unto the mercy-seat."

AUNT CHLOE
[1]　Harper is probably using this name for its biblical resonance. Jacob was a patriarch of ancient Israel.
[5]　The bleeding wound in Christ's side at the time of his crucifixion. Christ's wound itself alludes to the Old Testament scene in which Moses strikes a rock and water pours forth; hence fountain.

His words waked up my courage,
   And I began to pray,
And I felt my heavy burden   55
   Rolling like a stone away.

And a something seemed to tell me,
   You will see your boys again —
And that hope was like a poultice
   Spread upon a dreadful pain.   60

And it often seemed to whisper,
   Chloe, trust and never fear;
You'll get justice in the kingdom,
   If you do not get it here.

THE DELIVERANCE

Master only left old Mistus
   One bright and handsome boy;
But she fairly doted on him,
   He was her pride and joy.

We all liked Mister Thomas,   5
   He was so kind at heart;
And when the young folkes got in scrapes,
   He always took their part.

He kept right on that very way
   Till he got big and tall,   10
And old Mistus used to chide him,
   And say he'd spile us all.

But somehow the farm did prosper
   When he took things in hand;
And though all the servants liked him,   15
   He made them understand.

One evening Mister Thomas said,
   "Just bring my easy shoes:
I am going to sit by mother,
   And read her up the news."   20

Soon I heard him tell old Mistus
   "We're bound to have a fight;
But we'll whip the Yankees, mother,
   We'll whip them sure as night!"

Then I saw old Mistus tremble;   25
  She gasped and held her breath;
And she looked on Mister Thomas
  With a face as pale as death.

"They are firing on Fort Sumpter;[6]
  Oh! I wish that I was there! –   30
Why, dear mother! what's the matter?
  You're the picture of despair."

"I was thinking, dearest Thomas,
  'Twould break my very heart
If a fierce and dreadful battle   35
  Should tear our lives apart."

"None but cowards, dearest mother,
  Would skulk unto the rear,
When the tyrant's hand is shaking
  All the heart is holding dear."   40

I felt sorry for old Mistus;
  She got too full to speak;
But I saw the great big tear-drops
  A running down her cheek.

Mister Thomas too was troubled   45
  With choosing on that night,
Betwixt staying with his mother
  And joining in the fight.

Soon down into the village came
  A call for volunteers;   50
Mistus gave up Mister Thomas,
  With many sighs and tears.

His uniform was real handsome;
  He looked so brave and strong;
But somehow I could'nt help thinking   55
  His fighting must be wrong.

Though the house was very lonesome,
  I thought 'twould all come right,
For I felt somehow or other
  We was mixed up in that fight.   60

THE DELIVERANCE
[6] The firing on Fort Sumpter in South Carolina by   The event marked the official opening of hostilities
Confederate soldiers took place on April 12–14, 1861.   between the North and the South.

And I said to Uncle Jacob,
   "Now old Mistus feels the sting,
For this parting with your children
   Is a mighty dreadful thing."

"Never mind," said Uncle Jacob,   65
   "Just wait and watch and pray,
For I feel right sure and certain,
   Slavery's bound to pass away;

"Because I asked the Spirit,
   If God is good and just,   70
How it happened that the masters
   Did grind us to the dust.

"And something reasoned right inside,
   Such should not always be;
And you could not beat it out my head,   75
   The Spirit spoke to me."

And his dear old eyes would brighten,
   And his lips put on a smile,
Saying, "Pick up faith and courage,
   And just wait a little while."   80

Mistus prayed up in the parlor,
   That the Secesh[7] all might win;
We were praying in the cabins,
   Wanting freedom to begin.

Mister Thomas wrote to Mistus,   85
   Telling 'bout the Bull's Run[8] fight,
That his troops had whipped the Yankees,
   And put them all to flight.

Mistus' eyes did fairly glisten;
   She laughed and praised the South,   90
But I thought some day she'd laugh
   On tother side her mouth.

I used to watch old Mistus' face,
   And when it looked quite long
I would say to Cousin Milly,   95
   The battle's going wrong;

---

[7] *Secesh* derived from secession, one of the rights for which the Southern Confederacy was fighting.
[8] Chloe is mispronouncing the name of one of the major Southern victories at the early stage of the war. The first battle of Bull Run, to which Chloe is referring, occurred on Sunday, July 21, 1861.

Not for us, but for the Rebels. –
  My heart 'would fairly skip,
When Uncle Jacob used to say,
  "The North is bound to whip."   100

And let the fight go as it would –
  Let North or South prevail –
He always kept his courage up,
  And never let it fail.

And he often used to tell us,   105
  "Children, don't forget to pray;
For the darkest time of morning
  Is just 'fore the break of day."

Well, one morning bright and early
  We heard the fife and drum,   110
And the booming of the cannon –
  The Yankee troops had come.

When the word ran through the village,
  The colored folks are free –
In the kitchens and the cabins   115
  We held a jubilee.

When they told us Mister Lincoln
  Said that slavery was dead,[9]
We just poured our prayers and blessings
  Upon his precious head.   120

We just laughed, and danced, and shouted,
  And prayed, and sang, and cried,
And we thought dear Uncle Jacob
  Would fairly crack his side.

But when old Mistus heard it,   125
  She groaned and hardly spoke;
When she had to lose her servants,
  Her heart was almost broke.

'Twas a sight to see our people
  Going out, the troops to meet,   130
Almost dancing to the music,
  And marching down the street.

---

[9]   A reference to the Emancipation Proclamation, announced on September 22, 1862, and put into final effect January 1, 1863. It had application only to slaves being held in rebellious States.

After years of pain and parting,
    Our chains was broke in two,
And we was so mighty happy,   135
    We did'nt know what to do.

But we soon got used to freedom,
    Though the way at first was rough;
But we weathered through the tempest,
    For slavery made us tough.   140

But we had one awful sorrow,
    It almost turned my head,
When a mean and wicked cretur[10]
    Shot Mister Lincoln dead.

'Twas a dreadful solemn morning,   145
    I just staggered on my feet;
And the women they were crying
    And screaming in the street.

But if many prayers and blessings
    Could bear him to the throne,   150
I should think when Mister Lincoln died,
    That heaven just got its own.

Then we had another President,[11] –
    What do you call his name?
Well, if the colored folks forget him   155
    They would'nt be much to blame.

We thought he'd be the Moses
    Of all the colored race;
But when the Rebels pressed us hard
    He never showed his face.   160

But something must have happened him,
    Right curi's[12] I'll be bound,
'Cause I heard 'em talking 'bout a circle
    That he was swinging round.

But everything will pass away –   165
    He went like time and tide –
And when the next election came
    They let poor Andy slide.

---

[10] John Wilkes Booth, who assassinated President Lincoln on April 14, 1865.

[11] Andrew Johnson (1808–75), 17th President of the United States, serving from 1865 to 1869. He came close to impeachment in 1868 because of his lenient policy toward the South.

[12] Chloe's pronunciation of "curious."

But now we have a President,[13]
  And if I was a man   170
I'd vote for him for breaking up
  The wicked Ku-Klux Klan.

And if any man should ask me
  If I would sell my vote,[14]
I'd tell him I was not the one   175
  To change and turn my coat.

If freedom seem'd a little rough
  I'd weather through the gale;
And as to buying up my vote,
  I hadn't it for sale.   180

I do not think I'd ever be
  As slack as Jonas Handy;
Because I heard he sold his vote
  For just three sticks of candy.

But when John Thomas Reeder brought   185
  His wife some flour and meat,
And told her he had sold his vote
  For something good to eat,

You ought to seen Aunt Kitty raise,
  And heard her blaze away;   190
She gave the meat and flour a toss,
  And said they should not stay.

And I should think he felt quite cheap
  For voting the wrong side;
And when Aunt Kitty scolded him,   195
  He just stood up and cried.

But the worst fooled man I ever saw,
  Was when poor David Rand
Sold out for flour and sugar;
  The sugar was mixed with sand.   200

I'll tell you how the thing got out;
  His wife had company,
And she thought the sand was sugar,
  And served it up for tea.

---

[13] Ulysses S. Grant (1822–85), 18th President of the United States, serving from 1869 to 1877. He made active efforts to suppress Klan activities in South Carolina in the 1870s.

[14] Chloe/Harper will return to this subject in "Aunt Chloe's Politics." The post-reconstruction period (also known as the "gilded age") was a time of rampant political corruption.

When David sipped and sipped the tea,   205
  Somehow it did'nt taste right;
I guess when he found he was sipping sand,
  He was mad enough to fight.

The sugar looked so nice and white –
  It was spread some inches deep –   210
But underneath was a lot of sand;
  Such sugar is mighty cheap.

You'd laughed to seen Lucinda Grange
  Upon her husband's track;
When he sold his vote for rations   215
  She made him take 'em back.

Day after day did Milly Green
  Just follow after Joe,
And told him if he voted wrong
  To take his rags and go.   220

I think that Curnel[15] Johnson said
  His side had won the day,
Had not we women radicals
  Just got right in the way.

And yet I would not have you think   225
  That all our men are shabby;
But 'tis said in every flock of sheep
  There will be one that's scabby.

I've heard, before election came
  They tried to buy John Slade;   230
But he gave them all to understand
  That he wasn't in that trade.

And we've got lots of other men
  Who rally round the cause,
And go for holding up the hands   235
  That gave us equal laws.

Who know their freedom cost too much
  Of blood and pain and treasure,
For them to fool away their votes
  For profit or for pleasure.   240

---

[15] Colonel.

Aunt Chloe's Politics

Of course, I don't know very much
About these politics,
But I think that some who run 'em
Do mighty ugly tricks.

I've seen 'em honey-fugle[16] round,   5
And talk so awful sweet,
That you'd think them full of kindness,
As an egg is full of meat.

Now I don't believe in looking
Honest people in the face,   10
And saying when you're doing wrong,
That "I haven't sold my race."

When we want to school our children,
If the money isn't there,
Whether black or white have took it,   15
The loss we all must share.

And this buying up each other
Is something worse than mean,
Though I thinks a heap of voting,
I go for voting clean.   20

Learning to Read

Very soon the Yankee teachers
Came down and set up school;
But, oh! how the Rebs did hate it, –
It was agin' their rule.

Our masters always tried to hide   5
Book learning from our eyes;
Knowledge did'nt agree with slavery –
'Twould make us all too wise.

But some of us would try to steal
A little from the book,   10
And put the words together,
And learn by hook or crook.

I remember Uncle Caldwell,
Who took pot liquor fat

Aunt Chloe's Politics
[16] *Honey-fugle* sweet-talking.

And greased the pages of his book,   15
  And hid it in his hat.

And had his master ever seen
  The leaves upon his head,
He'd have thought them greasy papers,
  But nothing to be read.   20

And there was Mr. Turner's Ben,
  Who heard the children spell,
And picked the words right up by heart,
  And learned to read 'em well.

Well, the Northern folks kept sending   25
  The Yankee teachers down;
And they stood right up and helped us,
  Though Rebs did sneer and frown.

And, I longed to read my Bible,
  For precious words it said;   30
But when I begun to learn it,
  Folks just shook their heads,

And said there is no use trying,
  Oh! Chloe, you're too late;
But as I was rising sixty,   35
  I had no time to wait.

So I got a pair of glasses,
  And straight to work I went,
And never stopped till I could read
  The hymns and Testament.   40

Then I got a little cabin –
  A place to call my own –
And I felt as independent
  As the queen upon her throne.

CHURCH BUILDING

Uncle Jacob often told us,
  Since freedom blessed our race
We ought all to come together
  And build a meeting place.

So we pinched, and scraped, and spared,   5
  A little here and there:
Though our wages was but scanty,
  The church did get a share.

And, when the house was finished,
　　Uncle Jacob came to pray;　　　　　　　　　10
He was looking mighty feeble,
　　And his head was awful gray.

But his voice rang like a trumpet;
　　His eyes looked bright and young;
And it seemed a mighty power　　　　　　　　　15
　　Was resting on his tongue.

And he gave us all his blessing –
　　'Twas parting words he said,
For soon we got the message
　　The dear old man was dead.　　　　　　　　　20

But I believe he's in the kingdom,
　　For when we shook his hand
He said, "Children, you must meet me
　　Right in the promised land;

"For when I'm done a moiling　　　　　　　　　25
　　And toiling here below,
Through the gate into the city
　　Straightway I hope to go."

THE REUNION

Well, one morning real early
　　I was going down the street,
And I heard a stranger asking
　　For Missis Chloe Fleet.

There was something in his voice　　　　　　　　5
　　That made me feel quite shaky,
And when I looked right in his face,
　　Who should it be but Jakey!

I grasped him tight, and took him home –
　　What gladness filled my cup!　　　　　　　　10
And I laughed, and just rolled over,
　　And laughed, and just give up.

"Where have you been? O Jakey, dear!
　　Why didn't you come before?
Oh! when you children went away　　　　　　　　15
　　My heart was awful sore."

"Why, mammy, I've been on your hunt
　　Since ever I've been free,

And I have heard from brother Ben, –
   He's down in Tennessee.   20

"He wrote me that he had a wife."
  "And children?" "Yes, he's three."
"You married, too?" "Oh no, indeed,
   I thought I'd first get free."

"Then, Jakey, you will stay with me,   25
   And comfort my poor heart;
Old Mistus got no power now
   To tear us both apart.

"I'm richer now than Mistus,
   Because I have got my son;   30
And Mister Thomas he is dead,
   And she's got nary one.

"You must write to brother Benny
   That he must come this fall,
And we'll make the cabin bigger,   35
   And that will hold us all.

"Tell him I want to see 'em all
   Before my life do cease:
And then, like good old Simeon,[17]
   I hope to die in peace."   40

from *Atlanta Offering: Poems* (1895)

A DOUBLE STANDARD

Do you blame me that I loved him?
   If when standing all alone
I cried for bread a careless world
   Pressed to my lips a stone.

Do you blame me that I loved him,   5
   That my heart beat glad and free,
When he told me in the sweetest tones
   He loved but only me?

Can you blame me that I did not see
   Beneath his burning kiss   10

THE REUNION
[17] Luke 2:22–34. Simeon was an aged and devout man who recognized the infant Jesus as the long-expected Messiah. His recognition of the child represented the sign which made him feel ready to depart the world "in peace."

The serpent's wiles, nor even hear
 The deadly adder hiss?

Can you blame me that my heart grew cold
 That the tempted, tempter turned;
When he was feted and caressed   15
 And I was coldly spurned?

Would you blame him, when you draw from me
 Your dainty robes aside,
If he with gilded baits should claim
 Your fairest as his bride?   20

Would you blame the world if it should press
 On him a civic crown;
And see me struggling in the depth
 Then harshly press me down?

Crime has no sex and yet to-day   25
 I wear the brand of shame;
Whilst he amid the gay and proud
 Still bears an honored name.

Can you blame me if I've learned to think
 Your hate of vice a sham,   30
When you so coldly crushed me down
 And then excused the man?

Would you blame me if to-morrow
 The coroner should say,
A wretched girl, outcast, forlorn,   35
 Has thrown her life away?

Yes, blame me for my downward course,
 But oh! remember well,
Within your homes you press the hand
 That led me down to hell.   40

I'm glad God's ways are not our ways,
 He does not see as man;
Within His love I know there's room
 For those whom others ban.

I think before His great white throne,   45
 His throne of spotless light,
That whited sepulchres shall wear
 The hue of endless night.

That I who fell, and he who sinned,
   Shall reap as we have sown;   50
That each the burden of his loss
   Must bear and bear alone.

No golden weights can turn the scale
   Of justice in His sight;
And what is wrong in woman's life   55
   In man's cannot be right.

Rose Terry Cooke (1827–1892)

Rose Terry Cooke was born February 17, 1827 on a farm near Hartford, Connecticut. Both her father, who was related to the Wadsworth family (s.v. Lydia Huntley Sigourney), and her mother came from distinguished Connecticut families or, as one biographer puts it, "solid Puritan stock." When Cooke was six, her father moved the family into the Wadsworth homestead in Hartford, where Cooke's paternal grandmother resided. Cooke attended the Hartford Female Seminary, founded in 1823 by Catherine Beecher. There she came under the influence of John Pierce Brace, an advocate of "liberalized" or "feminized" (anti-Calvinist) Christianity.

After graduation, Cooke taught, first in Connecticut and then in New Jersey, until an inheritance from a great uncle in 1848 freed her to return to Hartford and to take up a writer's life. Her first poem, "The Trailing Arbutus," appeared in the *New York Daily Tribune* in 1851. Thereafter, she became a prolific contributor of poems and short stories to a wide variety of periodicals and newspapers. In 1861, she had enough poems of solid merit to publish her first collection. By then, she had also broken new ground for New England regionalist fiction and was in great demand.

In 1873, at the age of forty-six, Cooke, who had been doing very well on her own, inexplicably married Rollin H. Cooke, a widower with two children, sixteen years her junior. As recorded in her letters to her publisher, James Ticknor, the remainder of Cooke's life was a losing struggle against the slide into penury and desperation marriage initiated, as her husband, who seemed incapable of holding a job, proved quite capable of dispersing her entire inheritance. Broken in health and spirit, she died of influenza in 1892, never having been able to reclaim her original reputation.

Recent interest in Cooke's literary contribution has focused primarily on her short stories, which like Alice Cary's can be seen as anticipating the "realism" of *fin-de-siècle* regionalism and local color artistry (Mary Wilkins Freeman, et al.). As Cheryl Walker has argued, however, Cooke's poetry merits serious critical attention as well, certainly a good deal more than has been paid to it to date.

Often witty and ironic, Cooke's strongest poetry is not as readily accessible as her prose; but on that very ground it is, in some ways, more intriguing. The same dark imagination that shapes her depictions of the deadening routine of rural New England life is here applied more abstractly to the life of the psyche. Her tone is frequently enigmatic, and her topics veiled and meant to puzzle – hints and innuendoes replacing the blunt assessments of the narrators of her stories.

There are numerous occasions in Cooke's poetry when one feels that her speaker is speaking to herself, and merely allowing readers to overhear without making concessions to them. A poem such as "Bluebeard's Closet," for example, appears to point, as Walker argues, to a veiled malevolence lurking beneath the surface of everyday life, while other poems, such as "Truths," "Midnight," and "Che Sera Sera," seem to locate the source of evil in the self. There is also a romantic restlessness in Cooke's poetry that is just as difficult to pin down, as in "The Suttee," which comes perilously close to embracing the Indian funeral practice of sati ("widow-burning") as a means of ascension to God. And finally there are those poems, in particular the spectacular "Margaritas Ante Porcos [Pearls before swine]," which suggest the poet's alienation not just from men, but from other women – also a theme in "La Coquette."

Particularly when read against Cooke's stories, with their deeply sympathetic but straight-forward portraits of the hardness and narrowness of rural women's lives, these poems suggest that there were secret springs to Cooke's power that lay in a well-protected imaginative life, a life she only touches lightly even in her verse.

Primary Texts

Poems, 1861; *Somebody's Neighbors*, 1881; *Poems*, 1888; *Huckleberries Gathered from New England Hills*, 1891.

Further Reading

Karen Kilcup, "'Restless, Bold, and Unafraid': Rose Terry Cooke's Poetry," *Encyclopedia of American Poetry*; Susan A. Toth, "Rose Terry Cooke," *American Literary Realism*, 42 (Spring 1971): 170–6; Cheryl Walker, "Rose Terry Cooke," *Legacy: A Journal of Nineteenth-Century American Women Writers* 9 (February 1992): 143–50; "Teaching Dickinson as a Gen(i)us: Emily among Women," *The Emily Dickinson Journal* 2 (February 1993): 172–80; Perry D. Westbrook, *Acres of Flint: Sarah Orne Jewett and Her Contemporaries*, Metuchen, New Jersey: Scarecrow Press, 1981.

from *Poems* (1861)

TRUTHS

> I wear a rose in my hair,
>> Because I feel like a weed;
> Who knows that the rose is thorny
>> And makes my temples bleed?
> If one gets to his journey's end, what matter how galled the steed?   5
>
> I gloss my face with laughter,
>> Because I cannot be calm;
> When you listen to the organ,
>> Do you hear the words of the psalm?
> If they give you poison to drink, 'tis better to call it balm.   10
>
> If I sneer at youth's wild passion,
>> Who fancies I break my heart?

'Tis this world's righteous fashion,
　　With a sneer to cover a smart.
Better to give up living than not to play your part.　　　　　　　　15

If I scatter gold like a goblin,
　　My life may yet be poor.
Does Love come in at the window
　　When Money stands at the door?
I am what I seem to men. Need I be any more?　　　　　　　　20

God sees from the high blue heaven,
　　He sees the grape in the flower;
He hears one's life-blood dripping
　　Through the maddest, merriest hour;
He knows what sackcloth and ashes hide in the purple of power.　　　25

The broken wing of the swallow
　　He binds in the middle air;
I shall be what I am in Paradise –
　　So, heart, no more despair!
Remember the blessed Jesus, and wipe His feet with thy hair.[1]　　　30

La Coquette[2]

You look at me with tender eyes,
That, had you worn a month ago,
Had slain me with divine surprise: –
But now I do not see them glow.

I laugh to hear your laughter take　　　　　　　　5
A softer thrill, a doubtful tone, –
I know you do it for my sake.
You rob the nest whose bird is flown.

Not twice a fool, if twice a child!
I know you now, and care no more　　　　　　　　10
For any lie you may have smiled,
Than that starved beggar at your door.

He has the remnants of your feast;
You offer me your wasted heart!
He may enact the welcome guest;　　　　　　　　15
I shake the dust off and depart.

Truths
[1] The allusion is to Mary Magdalene, one of the most prominent of Jesus's female followers and type for the fallen woman. In Luke 7:37 she is said to have wiped Jesus's feet with her hair.

La Coquette
[2] French: the flirt.

If you had known a woman's grace
And pitied me who died for you,
I could not look you in the face,
When now you tell me you are "true."   20

True! – If the fallen seraphs wear
A lovelier face of false surprise
Than you at my unmoving air,
There is no truth this side the skies.

But this *is* true, that once I loved. –   25
You scorned and laughed to see me die;
And now you think the heart so proved
Beneath your feet again shall lie!

I had the pain when you had power;
Now mine the power, who reaps the pain?   30
You sowed the wind in that black hour;
Receive the whirlwind for your gain!

BLUE-BEARD'S CLOSET[3]

Fasten the chamber!
Hide the red key;
Cover the portal,
That eyes may not see.
Get thee to market,   5
To wedding and prayer;
Labor or revel,
The chamber is there!

In comes a stranger –
"Thy pictures how fine,   10
Titian[4] or Guido,[5]
Whose is the sign?"
Looks he behind them?
Ah! have a care!
"Here is a finer."   15
The chamber is there!

Fair spreads the banquet,
Rich the array;
See the bright torches
Mimicking day;   20

BLUE-BEARD'S CLOSET
3   *Bluebeard* nickname of the chevalier Raoul in a story
by Charles Perrault. He is said to have locked the bodies
of his first six wives in a closet.

4   Tiziano Vecellio (*c.* 1487–1576), Italian Renaissance
artist.
5   Guido Reni (1575–1642), Italian painter and engraver.

When harp and viol
Thrill the soft air,
Comes a light whisper:
The chamber is there!

Marble and painting,   25
Jasper and gold,
Purple from Tyrus,[6]
Fold upon fold,
Blossoms and jewels,
Thy palace prepare: 30
Pale grows the monarch;
The chamber is there!

Once it was open
As shore to the sea;
White were the turrets,   35
Goodly to see;
All through the casements
Flowed the sweet air;
Now it is darkness;
The chamber is there!   40

Silence and horror
Brood on the walls;
Through every crevice
A little voice calls:
"Quicken, mad footsteps,   45
On pavement and stair;
Look not behind thee,
The chamber is there!"

Out of the gateway,
Through the wide world,   50
Into the tempest
Beaten and hurled,
Vain is thy wandering,
Sure thy despair,
Flying or staying,   55
The chamber is there!

The Suttee[7]

Come, thou dead image, to thy rest!
The flashing embers wait for thee,

---

[6] Tyre, the ancient city of Phoenicia, renowned for its textile manufacture, in particular its purple dye.

The Suttee
[7] See Sigourney, "The Suttee."

And heaped above my panting breast
  Lie faggots fit thy couch to be.

I know thee now, cold shape of clay,   5
  Whose life was but a thrill from mine! –
One gasp, and undeceiving day
  Showed the base thing no more divine.

Lo! I have framed a costly pyre;
  There lie those dreams with wandering eyes,   10
And hopes, too ashen now for fire,
  Strew pathways to the sacrifice.

I am a widow, and shall I
  Linger a living death away?
Here on the dead, I, too, will die,   15
  Quick! lest the flesh refuse to stay.

Burn! burn! glare upward to the skies,
  Paint the low hills and creeping night:
Louder the shrieking south-wind cries,
  And terror speeds the lessening light.   20

Slowly these eager tongues aspire;
  I shudder, though they set me free.
Go, coward senses, to the fire –
  But the wing'd soul, oh God! to Thee!

"CHE SARA SARA"[8]

She walked in the garden
  And a rose hung on a tree,
Red as heart's blood,
  Fair to see.
"Ah, kind south-wind,   5
  Bend it to me!"
But the wind laughed softly,
  And blew to the sea.

High on the branches,
  Far above her head,   10
Like a king's cup
  Round, and red.
"I am comely,"
  The maiden said,

"CHE SARA SARA"
[8] Italian: what will be will be.

"I have gold like shore-sand,   15
  I wish I were dead!

"Blushes and rubies
  Are not like a rose,
Through its deep heart
  Love-life flows.   20
Ah, what splendors
  Can give me repose!
What is all the world worth?
  I cannot reach my rose."

MIDNIGHT

The west-wind blows, the west-wind blew,
  The snow hissed cruelly,
All night I heard the baffled cry
  Of mariners on the sea.

I saw the icy shrouds and sail,   5
  The slippery, reeling deck,
And white-caps dancing pale with flame,
  The corpse-lights of the wreck.

The west-wind blows, the west-wind blew,
  And on its snowy way,   10
That hissed and hushed like rushing sand,
  My soul fled far away.

The snow went toward the morning hills
  In curling drifts of white,
But I went up to the gates of God   15
  Through all the howling night.

I went up to the gates of God.
  The angel waiting there,
Who keeps the blood-red keys of Heaven,
  Stooped down to hear my prayer.   20

"Dear keeper of the keys of Heaven,
  A thousand souls to-night
Are torn from life on land and sea,
  While life was yet delight.

"But I am tired of storms and pain;   25
  Sweet angel, let me in!
And send some strong heart back again,
  To suffer and to sin."

The angel answered — stern and slow —
   "How darest thou be dead,   30
While God seeks dust to make the street
   Where happier men may tread?

"Go back, and eat earth's bitter herbs,
   Go, hear its dead-bells toll;
Lie speechless underneath their feet,   35
   Who tread across thy soul.

"Go, learn the patience of the Lord
   Whose righteous judgments wait;
Thy murdered cry may cleave the ground,
   But not unbar His gate."   40

Right backward, through the whirling snow —
   Back, on the battling wind,
My soul crept slowly to its lair,
   The body left behind.

The west-wind blows, the west-wind blew,   45
   There are dead men on the sea,
And landsmen dead, in shrouding drifts —
   But there is life in me.

from *Galaxy* (1866)

IN THE HAMMOCK

How the stars shine out at sea!
Swing me, Tita! Faster, girl!
I'm a hang-bird in her nest,
All with scarlet blossoms drest,
Swinging where the winds blow free.   5

Ah! how white the moonlight falls.
Catch my slipper! there it goes,
Where that single fire-fly shines,
Tangled in the heavy vines,
Creeping by the convent walls.   10

Ay de mi! to be a nun!
Juana takes the veil to-day,
She hears mass behind a grate,
While for me ten lovers wait
At the door till mass is done.   15

Swing me, Tita! Seven are tall.
Two are crooked, rich, and old,
But the other – he's too small;
Did you hear a pebble fall?
And his blue eyes are too cold.   20

If I were a little nun,
When I heard that voice below,
I should scale the convent wall;
I should follow at his call,
Shuddering through the dreadful snow.   25

Tita! Tita! hold me still!
Now the vesper bell is ringing,
Bring me quick my beads and veil.
Yes, I know my cheek is pale
And my eyes shine – I've been swinging.   30

from *Scribner's Monthly* (1879)

SAINT SYMPHORIEN[9]

(Led Out to Martyrdom: His Mother Speaking from the Wall)

Symphorien! Symphorien!
Look up! the heavens are parting wide.
He waits for thee – the Crucified.
The pain is short, the palm is near.
Look up! O God! he cannot hear,   5
    Symphorien! Symphorien!
Where is my voice? my breath is gone:
Symphorien! my son, my son!
Ah – look! – his clear eyes turn to me,
His firm, sweet, smiling lips I see.   10
God will be good to thee and me,
            Symphorien!

Dear Lord, how long I prayed for him,
With trembling tongue, and vision dim:
For baby hands about my breast,   15
For baby kisses on it pressed!
Thou heardest me: – this is the rest!
    Symphorien! Symphorien!
My child! my boy! it is not much,

SAINT SYMPHORIEN
[9] Martyred in Autun *c.* 200 CE for refusing to honor
pagan gods.

Only a sharp and sudden touch,   20
Think on the Master, – not on me:
Remember His long agony.
The lictors[10] will be merciful,
The headsman's axe will not be dull,
Only one moment – then for thee   25
The raptures of eternity,
    Symphorien!

My baby! oh, my baby boy!
A miracle of life and joy:
A rosy, careless, dimpled thing.   30
And now Dear Lord, be comforting! –
Martyr and saint. Let be! let be!
He must not know this agony.
Through my heart, too, the sword hath gone.
Be silent lest he hear me groan –   35
    Symphorien! Symphorien!
One last long look: oh saint! my child.
My boy! my own! – He turned and smiled.
And now behind the crowd of spears,
The whirling dust, – he disappears.   40
    Symphorien!

Martyr and saint? You think I care?
Oh, fools and blind! I am his mother.
What! bless the Lord and turn to prayer?
He is my child – I have no other.   45
No hands to clasp, no lips to kiss.
Who talks to me of heaven's bliss?
    Symphorien! Symphorien!
Come back! come back! Deny the Lord!
Traitor? – Who hissed that burning word?   50
I did not say it. God! be just
I did not keep him; I am dust.
The flesh rebels. I am his mother.
Thou didst not give me any other.
Thine only Son? – but I am human.   55
Art thou not God? – I am a woman.
    Symphorien! Symphorien!
    Come back!

---

[10]   *Lictors* Roman functionaries who carried the
symbols of office before the magistrate in public
appearances.

from *Atlantic Monthly* (1881)

ARACHNE[11]

I watch her in the corner there,
　　As restless, bold, and unafraid,
She slips and floats along the air,
　　Till all her subtile house is made.

Her home, her bed, her nets for food,　　　　5
　　All from that inward store she draws;
She fashions it and knows it good
　　By instinct's sure and sacred laws.

No silver threads to weave her nest
　　She seeks and gathers far or near,　　　　10
But spins it from her fruitful breast,
　　Renewing still till leaves are sere.

Till, worn with toil and tired of life,
　　In vain her shining traps are set,
For frost hath stilled the insect strife,　　　　15
　　And gilded flies her charm forget.

Then, swinging on the shroud she spun,
　　She sways to every wintry wind,
Her joy, her toil, her errand done,
　　Her corse the sport of storms unkind.　　　　20

Poor sister of the spinster clan!
　　I too, from out my store within,
My daily life and living plan,
　　My home, my rest, my pleasure spin.

I know thy heart when heartless hands　　　　25
　　Sweep all that hard-earned web away,
Destroys its pearled and glittering bands,
　　And leave thee homeless by the way.

I know thy peace when all is done, –
　　Each anchored thread, each tiny knot　　　　30
Soft shining in the autumn sun,
　　A sheltered, silent, tranquil spot.

ARACHNE
[11] A Lydian woman so skilled in weaving that she dared to challenge the goddess Athena to a contest. Upon seeing the perfection of Arachne's work, Athena turned her into a spider.

I know what thou hast never known,
　　Sad foresight to a soul allowed, –
That not for life I spin alone,　　　　　　　　　　　　35
　　But day by day I spin my shroud.

from *Poems* (1888)

MARGARITAS ANTE PORCOS[12]

See how they crowd and snort below,
　　And fight for husks all brown and dry;
While at their feet, like beads of snow,
　　The pearls you threw to feed them lie.

Tears that the bruised and breaking heart　　　　　　5
　　Hides in its shell, to jewels turn;
They have their value in the mart,
　　They glitter – when they cease to burn.

Go, take them to the smiling bride,
　　Your life that lives in frozen tears;　　　　　　　　10
They crown her dark hair's odorous pride,
　　The heart-beats swing them in her ears.

Oh, fool! to fling them to the swine,
　　That tramp and snatch and rend below;
You pour away your life divine,　　　　　　　　　　15
　　And think to reap the grain you sow!

Know, then, that all your waste is vain –
　　Vainly these precious gems are thrown;
The snuffling herds that crowd the plain
　　Are hungry beasts, and beasts alone.　　　　　　　20

Alas! what dream of fond despair,
　　What lavish love, hath power divine
To work an answer to your prayer,
　　To make you angels out of swine?

Rosa Vertner Johnson Jeffrey (1828–1894)

The biographical information on Rosa (Griffith) Vertner Johnson Jeffrey is scanty and entirely of the period, making it more unreliable than usual. She was born in 1828 in Natchez, Mississippi. Her father, John Griffith, is described as a man of culture, given to

---

MARGARITAS ANTE PORCOS
[12]　Latin: pearls before swine.

writing light pieces for the popular market (e.g. "Indian stories"). Her mother was the daughter of Dr James Abercrombie, an Episcopal minister from Philadelphia. Jeffrey's mother died when she was nine months of age, and her aunt adopted her, changing her name to Vertner, and taking her to live on the family plantation near Port Gibson, Mississippi. Ten years later, either she or the entire Vertner family moved to Lexington, Kentucky, in order that she might complete her education at the seminary of Bishop Smith.

When she was seventeen, Jeffrey married Claude M. Johnson, a "gentleman of elegant fortune." They had six children, two of whom died in infancy. Johnson died sometime before the Civil War began and about two years after his death, Jeffrey married Alexander Jeffrey, a native of Edinburgh, Scotland, who settled in the United States. According to one biographer, the couple spent the duration of the war in the North, in Rochester, New York, where Jeffrey bore three more children. By 1868, Jeffrey, her husband, and her now sizable family, returned to the South. Despite her circumspect withdrawal to New York during the war, Jeffrey is said to have claimed a strong Southern allegiance.

In 1850, Jeffrey began publishing in the *Louisville Journal*, encouraged by publisher, George Prentice, who was responsible for bringing a number of Southern women poets to national attention (Amelia Welby and Sarah Piatt, among them). Her first volume, *Poems by Rosa*, was published by Boston's prestigious Ticknor and Fields in 1857 – a literary coup for a young Southern writer. While living in the North, she cultivated a number of significant literary relationships, including N. P. Willis, Washington Irving, and George Bancroft. However, possibly because of her Southern background, her national reputation never throve. She died in 1894.

Most of Jeffrey's production is relatively conventional, making "Hasheesh Visions" a one of a kind. Never republished, to my knowledge, in any of her books, it is an oddity of epic proportions, a phantasmagoric dream poem whose meaning, if it has one, is unavailable to modern readers – as, one suspects, it probably was to readers in Jeffrey's own day. (Some of my students have argued that the poem's imagery – in particular, its concluding images of blackness – may reflect Jeffrey's response to the coming war, in which case the poem bears close comparison to Piatt's "Mock Diamonds.")

Clearly influenced by British texts on opium usage, such as Ludlow's *The Hasheesh Eater*, as well as by Coleridge's poems, "Hasheesh Visions" also partakes of a tradition of romantic visionary poems among American women writers that runs from Brooks to Anne Throop (Section II). Like Sigourney's "Flora's Party" and Spofford's "Pomegranate-Flowers," it also partakes of a tradition in linguistic *tours de force*, wherein women writers effect pyrotechnic displays of their own verbal ability. Yet finally it is like none of these poems but only itself. As Julia Deane Freeman ("Mary Forest"), the editor of *Women of the South*, the anthology in which the poem appears, comments, there is no way to know whether the poem was written from "the direct inspiration of the drug itself," but the qualities of "crazy play and prodigality of words" which Freeman identifies in it (and to which she was apparently drawn, against her own better judgment) justify reprinting it here.

Primary Texts

Poems by Rosa, 1857; "Hasheesh Visions," *Women of the South, Distinguished in Literature*, ed. Julia Deane Freeman [Mary Forest], 1861; *The Crimson Hand and Other Poems*, 1881.

Further Reading

Julia Deane Freeman [Mary Forest], ed., "Rosa Vertner Johnson Jeffrey," in *Women of the South, Distinguished in Literature*, New York: Derby & Jackson, 1861; Ida Raymond, ed.,

"Rosa Vertner Jeffrey," in *Southland Writers: Biographical and Critical Sketches of the Living Female Writers of the South with Extracts of their Writings*, 2 vols, Philadelphia: Claxton, Remsenn & Haffelfinger, 1870; "Rosa Vertner Jeffrey," *Magazine of Poetry* 1 (January 1889): 72–5.

from *Women of the South* (1861)

HASHEESH VISIONS

Fiery fetters fiercely bound me,
Globes of golden fire rolled round me,
Jets of violet-colored flame
From ruby-crusted mountains came,
And, floating upward, wreathed on high   5
Like gorgeous serpents through the sky,
To whose rich coils the stars of night
Clung and became like scales of light;
A crimson sea before me blushed,
To which ten thousand rivers rushed –   10
Ten thousand rivers, all of flame,
And as they hissing onward came,
Their burning waters seemed to pour
Along an opalescent shore,
While, in that red deep, far away,   15
A myriad opal islands lay.
With eager, wistful gaze I turned
To where their dazzling splendors burned;
With fearful struggles, stung by pain,
I rent my fiery bonds in twain,   20
And madly (when my limbs were free)
Plunged headlong in that lurid sea,
Whose red and seething billows seemed
To mock me as they hissed and screamed;
While tortured thus, scorched to the bone,   25
I drifted on with ceaseless moan,
Till, near those opal islands cast,
When (dreaming all my anguish past)
I grasped a smooth and glittering shore
In vain, then drifted on once more;   30
On, on, till countless isles were past,
And then a boiling wave at last
Spurned, flung me from its blazing crest,
To *seem* at least one moment blest,
Upon an isle which seemed to be   35
The fairest in that wondrous sea;
But on its cool and polished shore
My agony scarce ceased before

This beautiful and long sought goal,
This Eldorado[1] of my soul,   40
For which I yearned with wild desire,
Seemed thronged with skeletons of *fire*,
That danced around me, shrieked my name,
And scorched me with their tongues of flame,
Till (in unutterable pain)   45
I prayed that lava sea in vain
To bear me from a haunted land,
To save me from that demon band,
That seized me with a fiendish laugh,
And cups of fire then bade me quaff,   50
Until the withered flesh all peeled
From my parched bones, and left revealed
A skeleton like theirs! a shell,
Red as the hottest flames of hell!
Then loud we laughed, and wide and far   55
Rang out that fiendish laugh, "ha, ha!"
In every wave an echo seemed,
Until the sea with laughter screamed;
The blazing billows leaped on high,
And *roared* their laughter to the sky,   60
Whose star-scaled serpents from afar
Hissed back a mocking laugh, "ha, ha!"
We tossed our flaming goblets up,
And danced and laughed, till every cup
Was drained, and still though wrung with pain,   65
We quaffed and danced and laughed again,
Till, faint with agony, a chill
Of *horror* seemed my frame to thrill,
The fire-fiends left me doubly curst
Cold! freezing! yet consumed by thirst.   70
I wore a form of flesh again,
And cried for "water," but in vain;
And then an icy slumber fell
Upon me, till the gushing swell
Of mountain torrents, in their strife,   75
Awakened me to light and life –
To light and life, for now I stood
Beside a cool, deep-shaded flood
Upon a shore so *passing* fair,
Its beauty brightened my despair   80
A moment, while the hope was nursed
That I might quench my frantic thirst.

HASHEESH VISIONS
[1] Fabled city of gold sought by fifteenth-century Spanish invaders of South America.

Enchanting pictures! bright and fine,
Enamelled on my heart they shine;
That fresh green shore, that clear deep tide,   85
Whose waves o'er rocks of sapphire glide,
Until at last, with wildest leap,
Into a gulf more broad and deep
Than *ten Niagaras* swift they whirl
O'er crystal spars and crags of pearl!   90
But lo! when on that moss-grown brink
I stooped my aching head to drink,
And sinking there a lotus-cup,
Raised it in trembling gladness up,
My parching lips gave forth a groan   95
To find the water turned to *stone*!
A chalice heaped with sapphires bright,
To mock me with their liquid light,
Jewels a king might proudly wear,
But which I *cursed* in my despair,   100
And then with bitter anguish, flung
Back to the tide from which they sprung.
The lotus bloom I would have torn
To atoms, but (as if in scorn,
Of my fierce rage, by some weird power)   105
I found an alabaster flower,
Whose leaves and stem with matchless sheen
Of emerald seemed superbly green.
I climbed along the crags of pearl,
To head the waters in their whirl.   110
But when I bent in madness down
To where the white spray, like a crown
Of glory on the torrent gleamed,
(Though o'er my brow its moisture streamed,)
With lips apart that longed to feel   115
A dewy freshness through them steal,
Upon my parched and swollen tongue
A shower of *diamond* gems was flung.
Oh! what were *gems* to one who yearned
For water-drops, and would have spurned   120
Their wealth, to sip the dew that sleeps
Within the hair-bells' azure deeps?
Upon the shore again I rushed,
Where countless fruits in beauty blushed,
Pomegranates, rare and ripe, and one,   125
Whose rind was rifted by the sun,
Revealed unto my ravished sight
The crimson pulp – Oh! what delight
I felt, as quick, with throbbing heart,
I tore it eagerly apart,   130

Expecting then the fruity seed
With red and luscious juice to bleed.
Like those, which, at the far off South,
Distilled their sweetness in my mouth,
Long, long ago, when as a child,   135
By Hope and Love and Joy beguiled,
My trusting heart had never grieved
To find itself at last deceived.
But in that strange enchanted rind
No liquid sweetness did I find,   140
Which (tempting while it half concealed)
A mass of rubies now revealed,
Of royal rubies, flashing there
To mock, and madden my despair.
I plucked an orange, when behold!   145
Within my hand it turned to gold;
And when from loaded vines I tore
The purple grapes, that seemed to pour
Their honeyed juices on the ground,
Clusters of amethysts I found.   150
If in a *desert* I had been,
Where gushing waters are not seen,
Nor luscious fruits (to tempt in vain),
Less terrible had been the pain
Of my fierce thirst; and as I cried   155
For "water," fair forms seemed to glide
Beneath those haunted groves, who quaffed
From crystal cups bright draughts, and laughed
Derisive laughter – soft and clear,
As they approached me – near – so near   160
I almost caught their goblets bright,
When swift they turned in sudden flight,
And from afar, pealed forth those swells
Of laughter clear as silver bells.
Then others came, more fair, who reaped   165
The dripping vines, and gaily heaped
Each one within a jasper urn
Her stores of grapes, which seemed to turn
Beneath *their* hands to sparkling wine,
While useless gems they shone in mine.   170
A vintage by a river's brink!
Yet no one offered me a drink
Of wine or water, and ere long
The chorus of a vintage song
Came stealing to me, whence those maids   175
Had vanished 'mid ambrosial shades.
In quick pursuit, I followed where
Their voices rippled through the air,

Till *blind* with anguish – cold as death,
Chilled (by the south wind's balmy breath),   180
Yet burnt by torturing thirst within,
Fiercer than memories of sin,
Beneath that lustrous summer sky,
I laid me down and *prayed* to die.
But vainly rose my mournful prayer,   185
The "King of Terrors" came not there;
And sudden darkness, like a spell,
Appalling darkness round me fell,
Which reft the earth of light and bloom,
And steeped my soul in utter gloom.   190
I started up – the sun had set,
The torrent poured o'er crags of jet
Its inky waters – and o'er all
A black sky hung its funeral pall –
So black, the clouds that floated by   195
Seemed atoms rifted from the sky.
Black barks before me seemed to glide,
Whose sails were *blacker* than the tide,
Peopled by wild and frantic gholes [*sic*],
Strange skeletons, as black as coals,   200
Who on those ghostly decks had met
To quaff black blood from cups of jet.
The land I found so bright and warm,
Seemed stricken by a scathing storm;
Its fruits and flowers of late so fair,   205
Hung now like ebon cinders there,
And groves which erst were green as spring,
Looked blacker than the raven's wing;
So freezing cold the wind had grown,
I seemed within the frozen zone,   210
And snow came drifting to the earth,
Black as the clouds that gave it birth.
I saw it *all* – though wrapped in night –
Plainly as if revealed by light,
That rayless, dense, unbroken gloom   215
Was suffocating as the tomb
To those who from long trances wake,
And strive their coffin-lids to break,
(Discovered, when too late to save)
Who slept, to wake within the *grave*!   220
Their agony, though keen, is brief,
But death came not to *my* relief,
And years of bitter pain they seemed,
Those torturing hours through which I dreamed.
Upon that cold and dismal brink   225
I stooped my head and strove to drink

The murky waves, when through the dark
Came gliding up a spectral bark;
I climbed the deck, where demons stood,
And quenched my thirst at last, in *blood*!   230
They pledged me in that draught accurst,
And still I drank, to quench my thirst,
Unmindful that our black bark swept
To where those maddened waters leapt,
Into that fathomless abyss,   235
Until I heard them scream and hiss
Within my ears – on, on we dashed,
While 'mid those jetty crags loud crashed
Our sinking ship – on, on we rushed,
Till masts and timbers all were crushed,   240
When, blind with blackness, 'mid the roar
Of inky waves, I heard no more.

Helen Hunt Jackson (1830–1885)

Helen Marie Fiske Hunt Jackson was born in 1830 in Amherst, Massachusetts. Her father, Nathan Fiske, was a professor at Latin, Greek, and moral philosophy at Amherst College. Both he and his wife, Deborah Vinal Fiske, were strict Calvinists and their early influence on Jackson may help account for the often paradoxical melding of radicalism and conservatism her life – and poetry – both demonstrate.

Nathan and Deborah Fiske died of tuberculosis while Jackson was still in her teens, her mother in 1844, her father in 1847. Thereafter, she was cared for by relatives and teachers. She received her education at Ipswich Female Seminary, where Lavinia Dickinson was also schooled, and at Abbott (later Springler) Institute in New York City. During childhood, she and Emily Dickinson, whose exact contemporary she was, played together occasionally, but there was no hint then of the shared interests that would eventually draw them together.

In 1851, Jackson married Edward Bissell Hunt, a lieutenant in the army. Because of his military career, they traveled quite a bit, a lifestyle that Jackson called "scatterdom." In 1855 they moved to Newport, Rhode Island, where Jackson became part of a community of intellectuals, making invaluable connections among the publishing crowd of the day. Among the most important of these connections was that with Anne Lynch Botta, whose literary salons saw the launching of many a young poet (s.v. Edith M. Thomas).

By 1865, a series of tragedies had devastated Jackson's personal life, taking both her husband and her two sons. Jackson turned to writing as a way to express grief and as a source of income. In light of the tendency to sentimentalize women poets of this period, Jackson's hard-nosed comment to James Fields on how she saw her writing is instructive: "I never 'write for money,'" she told the publisher, "I write for love, then after it is written I print for money. . . . 'Cash is a vile article' – but there is one thing viler; and that is a purse without any cash in it." No Emily Dickinson she.

In 1873, on a doctor-advised trip to Colorado Territory, Jackson met William Sharpless Jackson, Quaker banker and railroad executive. They were married in 1875 and set up house in Colorado Springs, where she spent the remainder of her life. In the 1870s, with her husband's support, Jackson finally found an adequate focus for her boundless energy in her championship of the cause of Native Americans, the absorbing interest of the last decade of her life. Her most effective writing on behalf of Native Americans came in *A Century of Dishonor* (1881), an unvarnished report of the US government's long-standing betrayal of America's indigenous peoples. Although a huge "best-seller," her "Indian" novel, *Ramona* (1884), on the other hand, failed miserably of its political goal, probably because Jackson allowed the romance in her story-line to overwhelm the social issues at stake.

Jackson's failure with *Ramona* was, in a sense, symptomatic of her limitations generally as a writer of *belles lettres* (in this reader's opinion she was most successful as a journalist). As much literary figure as writer, Jackson's importance as a late nineteenth-century poet has been greatly magnified by her connection to matters incidental to her poetry – her friendship with Emily Dickinson and her advocacy of Indian rights. Jackson's actual poetic output was surprisingly slight, especially by the standards of the time. And, more important, in her poetry as in her positions on many cultural issues – including women's rights and African American equality – she was surprisingly conservative. A poet who loved to tell stories, she tells them well, with clean lines and precise imagery, but, as with *Ramona*, too often she tells them thinly and moralistically, rarely venturing into new territory, stylistically or thematically, or taking on "hard" subjects.

To judge by the number of reprintings in modern anthologies, "Poppies in the Wheat," with its wonderfully evocative refrain, is considered her best poem; but I find the gothic grotesquerie of "Habeas Corpus," with its medieval challenge to death, equally impressive. Certainly the macabre self-irony of this poem meshes with the Jackson of the Dickinson correspondence; and helps explain perhaps why, in spite of her many limitations, it is difficult not to honor Helen Hunt Jackson simply for being the woman (big, brash, and sassy) she was.

Primary Texts

Verses, 1870; *A Century of Dishonor*, 1881; *Report on the Conditions and Needs of the Mission Indians*, 1883; *Ramona*, 1884; *Sonnets and Lyrics*, 1886; *Poems*, 1892.

Further Reading

Evelyn I. Banning, *Helen Hunt Jackson*, New York: Vanguard, 1973; Susan Coultrap-McQuin, *Doing Literary Business: American Women Writers in the Nineteenth Century*; Joanne Dobson, *Dickinson and the Strategies of Reticence: The Woman Writer in Nineteenth-Century America*; Valerie Sherer Mathes, *Helen Hunt Jackson and her Indian Reform Legacy*, Austin: University of Texas Press, 1990; Ruth Odell, *Helen Hunt Jackson*, New York: Appleton-Century, 1939; Richard B. Sewall, *The Life of Emily Dickinson*, 2 vols, New York: Farrar, Straus and Giroux, 1974; Cheryl Walker, "Helen Hunt Jackson," *Garland Encyclopedia*; Rosemary Whitaker, *Helen Hunt Jackson*, Boise: Boise State University Press, 1987.

from *Independent* (1869)

HER EYES

That they are brown no man will dare to say
He knows. And yet I think that no man's look

Ever those depths of light and shade forsook,
Until their gentle pain warned him away.
Of all sweet things I know but one which may   5
Be likened to her eyes.
          When, in deep nook
Of some green field, the water of a brook
Makes lingering, whirling eddy in its way,
Round soft drowned leaves; and in a flash of sun   10
They turn to gold, until the ripples run
Now brown, now yellow, changing as by some
Swift spell.
          I know not with what body come
The saints. But this I know, my Paradise   15
Will mean the resurrection of her eyes.

MY BEES: AN ALLEGORY

"Oh, bees, sweet bees!" I said, "that nearest field
Is shining white with fragrant immortelles.[1]
Fly swiftly there and drain those honey wells."
Then spicy pines, the sunny hive to shield,
I set, and patient for the autumn's yield   5
Of sweet I waited.
          When the village bells
Rang frosty clear, and from their satin cells
The chesnuts leaped, rejoicing, I unsealed
My hive.   10
          Alas! no snowy honey there
Was stored. My wicked bees had borne away
Their queen, and left no trace.
          That very day
An idle drone who sauntered through the air   15
I tracked and followed, and he led me where
My truant bees and stolen honey lay.
Twice faithless bees! They had sought out to eat
Rank, bitter herbs. The honey was not sweet.

from *Independent* (1870)

POPPIES IN THE WHEAT

Along Ancona's[2] hills the shimmering heat,
A tropic tide of air, with ebb and flow,
Bathes all the fields of wheat, until they glow

MY BEES: AN ALLEGORY
[1] *Immortelles* everlasting plant or flower.

POPPIES IN THE WHEAT
[2] Ancona, major port city in central Italy on the Adriatic.

Like flashing seas of green which toss and beat
Around the vines. The poppies, lithe and fleet,   5
Seem running, fiery torchmen, to and fro
To mark the shore.
                    The farmer does not know
That they are there. He walks with heavy feet,
Counting the bread and wine of autumn's gain;   10
But I − I smile to think that days remain
Perhaps to me, in which, though bread be sweet
No more, and red wine warm my blood in vain,
I shall be glad, remembering how the fleet,
Lithe poppies ran, like torchmen, in the wheat.   15

from *Independent* (1876)

BURNT OFFERING

The fire leaped up, swift, hot, and red;
    Swift, hot, and red, waiting a prey;
The woman came with swift, light tread,
    And silently knelt down to lay
Armfuls of leaves upon the fire,   5
As men lay fagots on a pyre.

Armfuls of leaves which had been bright
    Like painter's tints six months before,
All faded now, a ghastly sight,
    Dusty and colorless, she bore,   10
And knelt and piled them on the fire,
As men lay fagots on the pyre.

Watching the crackle and the blaze,
    Idly I smiled and idly said:
"Good-by, dead leaves, go dead leaves' ways.   15
    Next year there will be more as red."
The woman turned, and from the fire
Looked up as from a funeral-pyre.

I saw my idle words had been
    Far crueler than I could know,   20
And made an old wound bleed again.
    "It is not leaves," she whispered low,
"That I am burning in the fire,
But days! It is a funeral pyre."

from *Poems* (1892)

A DREAM

I dreamed that I was dead and crossed heavens, –
   Heavens after heavens with burning feet and swift, –
And cried: "O God, where art Thou? I left one
   On earth, whose burden I would pray Thee lift."

I was so dead I wondered at no thing, –   5
   Not even that the angels slowly turned
Their faces, speechless, as I hurried by
   (Beneath my feet the golden pavements burned);

Nor, at the first, that I could not find God,
   Because the heavens stretched endlessly like space.   10
At last a terror seized my very soul;
   I seemed alone in all the crowded place.

Then, sudden, one compassionate cried out,
   Though like the rest his face from me he turned,
As I were one no angel might regard   15
   (Beneath my feet the golden pavements burned);

"No more in heaven than earth will he find God
   Who does not know his loving mercy swift
But waits the moment consummate and ripe,
   Each burden from each human soul to lift."   20

Though I was dead, I died again for shame;
   Lonely, to flee from heaven again I turned;
The ranks of angels looked away from me
   (Beneath my feet the golden pavements burned).

                        (MS 1877)

from *Atlantic Monthly* (1881)

TIDAL WAVES

Sudden from out the vast bewildered sea,
Fierce tidal waves, like unchained monsters, break:
In cruel clutch the mightiest ships they take,
Tossing them high in fiendish jubilee;
Leaving them far inland, stranded hopelessly,   5
Worse wrecks than sharpest rock or reef can make.
At record of such wave, strange fancies wake,
Half wake, within me, as if memory
Recalled some life in other world.

There rolls   10

A dangerous sea, unseen, on which are borne
By fiercer tidal waves brave women's souls
To barren inlands, where, too strong to die,
Even of thirst and loneliness and scorn,
Like ghastly stranded wrecks, long years they lie!   15

from *Independent* (1884)

"TOO MUCH WHEAT"

"Too much wheat!" So the dealers say.
  Millions of bushels left unsold
Of last year's crop; and now, to-day,
  Ripe and heavy and yellow as gold,
This Summer's crop counts full and fair;   5
And murmurs, not thanks, are in the air,
And storehouse doors are locked, to wait;
And men are plotting, early and late.
"What shall save the farmers from loss,
If wheat too plenty makes wheat a dross?"   10
"Too much wheat!" Good God, what a word!
A blasphemy in our borders heard.

"Too much wheat!" And our hearts were stirred,
  But yesterday, and our cheeks like flame.
For vengeance the Lord his loins doth gird,   15
  When a nation reads such tale of shame.
Hundreds of men lie dying, dead,
Brothers of ours, though their skins are red;
Men we promised to teach and feed.
O, dastard Nation! dastard deed!   20
They starve like beasts in pen and fold,
While we hoard wheat to sell for gold.
"Too much wheat!" Men's lives are dross!
"How shall the farmers be saved from loss?"

"Too much wheat!" Do the figures lie?   25
  What wondrous yields! Put the ledgers by!
"Too much wheat!"
          O, Summer rain,
  And sun, and sky, and wind from West,
Fall not, nor shine, nor blow again!   30
Let fields be deserts, famine guest
Within our gates who hoard for gold
Millions of bushels of wheat unsold,
With men and women and children dead

And daily dying for lack of bread! 35
"Too much wheat!" Good God, what a word!
A blasphemy in our borders heard!

from *Century* (1885)

HABEAS CORPUS[3]

My body, eh? Friend Death, how now?
    Why all this tedious pomp of writ?
Thou hast reclaimed it sure and slow
    For half a century, bit by bit.

In faith thou knowest more to-day 5
    Than I do where it can be found!
This shriveled lump of suffering clay,
    To which I now am chained and bound,

Has not of kith or kin a trace
    To the good body once I bore; 10
Look at this shrunken, ghastly face:
    Didst ever see that face before?

Ah, well, friend Death, good friend thou art;
    Thy only fault thy lagging gait,
Mistaken pity in thy heart 15
    For timorous ones that bid thee wait.

Do quickly all thou hast to do,
    Nor I nor mine will hindrance make;
I shall be free when thou art through;
    I grudge thee naught that thou must take! 20

Stay! I have lied; I grudge thee one,
    Yes, two I grudge thee at this last, –
Two members which have faithful done
    My will and bidding in the past.

I grudge thee this right hand of mine, 25
    I grudge thee this quick-beating heart;
They never gave me coward sign,
    Nor played me once a traitor's part.

I see now why in olden days
    Men in barbaric love or hate 30

HABEAS CORPUS
[3] Latin: "you must have the body."

Nailed enemies' hands at wild crossways,
   Shrined leaders' hearts in costly state:

The symbol, sign, and instrument
   Of each soul's purpose, passion, and strife,
Of fires in which are poured and spent   35
   Their all of love, their all of life.

O feeble, mighty human hand!
   O fragile, dauntless human heart!
The universe holds nothing planned
   With such sublime, transcendent art!   40

Yes, Death, I own I grudge thee mine
   Poor little hand, so feeble now;
Its wrinkled palm, its altered line,
   Its veins so pallid and so slow –

(Unfinished here.)

Ah, well, friend Death, good friend thou art;   45
   I shall be free when thou art through.
Take all there is – take hand and heart;
   There must be somewhere work to do.

Emily Dickinson (1830–1886)

Daughter of Edward and Emily Norcross Dickinson, Emily Elizabeth Dickinson was born on December 10, 1830 in Amherst, Massachusetts, a rural community approximately ninety miles west of Boston. Her paternal grandfather was a founder of Amherst College, and her lawyer father, Edward, was a member of the state legislature and a United States congressman. Dickinson grew up with two siblings – an older brother, Austin, with whom she was fiercely competitive (they were both in love with the same woman, Susan Gilbert Dickinson), and a younger sister, Lavinia, who spent her life playing Martha to Dickinson's Mary. She also had a sizable circle of friends with whom she socialized, either in person or, more and more as the years went on, through correspondence.

As a child, Dickinson attended Amherst Academy, later going to South Hadley Female Seminary (now Mount Holyoke) for a year. Between these institutions and her father's library – particularly, his dictionary – she had an excellent education. She did some traveling – Washington, Philadelphia, and Boston (for eye treatments) – but on the whole she preferred to keep at home, raising flowers in her conservatory, baking, writing letters and poems. Lacking economic necessity, she chose not to publish her poems, distributing them as "gifts" to friends instead. Hers was, in short, by nineteenth-century standards, a quite ordinary life. Had she not been a genius, no one would have noticed when she lived or died, let alone how "peculiar" she was.

But Dickinson was a genius and her poetry is the single richest body of lyric verse produced by a woman in the English language. And that has changed everything about the way in which she has been treated. Enjoying the unique status of the United States's one unequivocal canonical woman writer – the only one who is invariably taught in the nation's literature classrooms – Dickinson has been pawed over to the exact extent that her women peers have been ignored. No aspect of her life is too trivial to study, no fragment of verse – from chips embedded in her letters to jottings on scraps of paper – too minor to salvage, indeed, to tout as a "poem" in itself. Yet, as Dickinson wrote of "Sister Sue," it would seem "That those who know her, know her less / The nearer her they get" (1400, c. 1877).

The mystery that is Emily Dickinson's poetry (not to mention that which has been woven about her life) has only intensified with the burgeoning of Dickinson scholarship since 1955, when Thomas H. Johnson published his now discredited three-volume variorum edition of her poetry. And both poetry and life appear launched on an infinite series of reconstructions, as scholars of various persuasions attempt to make sense of the vast amorphous body of material she left behind. As these reconstructions multiply, so has the complexity of putting Dickinson's "poems" into print (from simply reading her handwriting to determining the appropriate lineation to deciding which version of a poem to "privilege" to, finally, deciding if a particular text is a poem at all).

For myself, after years of studying Dickinson in print and manuscript, I am persuaded that her "poems" cannot be fairly read apart from her letters, her "fascicle bundles," her cooking chocolate wrappers, her feathers, her roast chickens, her flowers, and her glasses of sherry – in short, apart from the material world in which she located and left them, a world as far apart from the sterility of the published page as one could possibly get. I also know, however, that there is no handy means for publishers to present her work in this way. Even hypertext won't quite do.

Yet there is value in presenting Dickinson here – even if, perforce, in print. In expanding our appreciation for Dickinson's artistic genius, modern scholarship has created a *cordon sanitaire* about the poet, based on her assumed difference from other nineteenth-century women poets. As both Cheryl Walker and Joanne Dobson have eloquently argued, however, and as even a cursory examination of this text demonstrates, Dickinson shared a rich body of themes and images with other women writers of her day. One can, for example, compare her treatment of the dead housewife (187) with Whitney's "Released;" her version of New England's "Soil of Flint" (681) with Larcom's poem on Cape Ann; her "waking dream" poem (518) with Lazarus's "Assurance;" and her shipwreck poem (619) with those by Sigourney ("Bell of the Wreck") and Thaxter ("Wherefore"). Similarly, one can explore how her identification with spiders compares to Cooke's or her treatment of frost and flowers with Osgood's, her hunter and doe with Phoebe Cary's, and so on. (I have included as many such pairings as I can, without thoroughly distorting my presentation of Dickinson or the other poets.)

In almost every instance Dickinson's treatment is far briefer, more pungent, and linguistically more abrasive, yet the tone and even the approach can at times be surprisingly similar. What this suggests – and there is no small amount of irony here – is that Dickinson was far more dependent on her peers than they, needless to say, were on her. Indeed, she can not be fairly read apart from them. She was a (late) nineteenth-century American woman poet, the finest the line produced. If publishing her among these poets establishes this fact, then it will justify Dickinson's appearance in this volume, despite the various compromises printing her entails.

Primary Texts

The Poems of Emily Dickinson, ed. Thomas H. Johnson, 3 vols, 1955; *The Letters of Emily Dickinson*, eds Thomas H. Johnson and Theodora Ward, 3 vols, 1958; *The Manuscript Books of Emily Dickinson*, ed. Ralph W. Franklin, 2 vols, 1981.

Further Reading

Paula Bennett, " 'By a Mouth that Cannot Speak': Spectral Presence in Emily Dickinson's Letters," *Emily Dickinson Journal* 1 (Fall 1992): 76–99; Joanne Dobson, *Dickinson and the Strategies of Reticence: The Woman Writer in Nineteenth-Century America*; Susan Howe, *The Birth-Mark: Unsettling the Wilderness in American Literary History*, Hanover: University Press of New England for Wesleyan University Press, 1993; Jerome McGann, *Black Riders: The Visible Language of Modernism*, Princeton: Princeton University Press, 1993; Richard B. Sewall, *The Life of Emily Dickinson*, 2 vols, New York: Farrar, Straus and Giroux, 1974; Barton L. St Armand, *Emily Dickinson and Her Culture: The Soul's Society*, New York: Cambridge University Press, 1984; Cheryl Walker, *The Nightingale's Burden: Women Poets and Amercan Culture before 1900*.

from Franklin (1981)

187 (c. 1860)

How many times these low feet staggered –
Only the soldered mouth can tell –
Try – can you stir the awful rivet –
Try – can you lift the hasps of steel!

Stroke the cool forehead – hot so often –   5
Lift – if you care – the listless hair –
Handle the adamantine fingers
Never a thimble – more – shall wear –

Buzz the dull flies – on the chamber window –
Brave – shines the sun through the freckled pane –   10
Fearless – the cobweb swings from the ceiling –
Indolent Housewife – in Daisies – lain!

211 (c. 1860)

Come slowly – Eden!
Lips unused to Thee –
Bashful – sip thy Jessamines –
As the fainting Bee –

Reaching late his flower,   5
Round her chamber hums –
Counts his nectars –
Enters – and is lost in Balms.

239 (C. 1861)

"Heaven" – is what I cannot reach!
The Apple on the Tree –
Provided it do hopeless – hang –
That – "Heaven" is – to Me!

The Color, on the Cruising Cloud –   5
The interdicted Land –
Behind the Hill – the House behind
There – Paradise – is found!

Her teazing Purples – Afternoons –
The credulous – decoy –   10
Enamored – of the Conjurer –
That spurned us – Yesterday!

251 (C. 1861)

Over the fence –
Strawberries – grow –
Over the fence –
I could climb – if I tried, I know –
Berries are nice!   5

But – if I stained my Apron –
God would certainly scold!
Oh, dear, – I guess if He were a Boy –
He'd – climb – if He could!

280 (C. 1861)

I felt a Funeral, in my Brain,
And Mourners to and fro
Kept treading – treading – till it seemed
That Sense was breaking through –

And when they all were seated,   5
A Service, like a Drum –
Kept beating – beating – till I thought
My Mind was going numb –

And then I heard them lift a Box
And creak across my ~~Brain~~   10
Soul
With those same Boots of Lead, again,
Then Space – began to toll,

As all the Heavens were a Bell,
And Being, but an Ear,   15
And I, and Silence, some strange Race
Wrecked, solitary, here –

And then a Plank in Reason, broke,
And I dropped down, and down –
And hit a World, at every ˙plunge,   20
And ˙Finished knowing – then –

Crash – ˙Got through –

291 (C. 1861)

How the old Mountains drip with Sunset
How the Hemlocks burn –
How the Dun Brake is draped in Cinder
By the ˙Wizard Sun –

How the old Steeples hand the Scarlet   5
Till the Ball is full –
Have I the lip of the Flamingo
That I dare to tell?

Then, how the Fire ebbs like Billows –
Touching all the Grass   10
With a departing – Sapphire – feature –
As a Duchess passed –

How a small Dusk crawls on the Village
Till the Houses blot
And the odd Flambeau, no men carry   15
Glimmer on the Street –

How it is Night – in Nest and Kennel –
And where was the Wood –
˙Just a Dome of Abyss is Bowing   nodding   after –   unto
Into Solitude –   at the   20
                                       Fashions – baffled –

These are the Visions flitted Guido –
Titian – never told –
Domenichino[1] dropped his pencil –
˙Paralyzed, with Gold –   25

+Is tipped in Tinsel
 +By the Setting Sun
  +Acres of Masts are standing
+back of Solitude   +next to –
+powerless to unfold –

---

291 (C. 1861)
[1] Guido Reni (1575–1642); Tiziano Vecellio or   Domenichino (1581–1641), well-known Renaissance and
Titian (c. 1487–1576); and Domenico Zampieri or   Baroque painters.

334 (1862)

All the letters I can write
Are not fair as this —
Syllables of Velvet —
Sentences of Plush,
Depths of Ruby, undrained,   5
Hid, Lip, for Thee —
Play it were a Humming Bird —
And just sipped — me —

339 (c. 1862)

I tend my flowers for thee —
Bright Absentee!
My Fuschzia's Coral Seams
Rip — while the Sower — dreams

Geraniums — tint — and spot —   5
Low Daisies — dot —
My Cactus — splits her Beard
To show her throat —

Carnations — tip their spice —
And Bees — pick up —   10
A Hyacinth — I hid —
Puts out a Ruffled Head —
And odors fall
From flasks — so small —
You marvel how they held —   15

Globe Roses — break their satin flake —
Upon my Garden floor
Yet — thou — not there —
I had as lief they bore
No Crimson — more —   20

Thy flower — be gay —
Her Lord — away!
It ill becometh me —
I'll dwell in Calyx — Gray —
How modestly — alway —   25
Thy Daisy —
Draped for thee!

391 (c. 1862)

A Visitor in Marl —
Who influences Flowers —

Till they are orderly as Busts –
And Elegant – as Glass –

Who visits in the Night –   5
And just before the Sun –
Concludes his glistening interview –
Caresses – and is gone –

But whom his fingers touched –
And where his feet have run ——   10
And whatsoever Mouth he kissed –
Is as it had not been –

401 (C. 1862)

What Soft – Cherubic Creatures –
These Gentlewomen are –
One would as soon assault a Plush –
Or violate a Star –

Such Dimity Convictions –   5
A Horror so refined
Of freckled Human Nature –
Of Deity – ashamed –

It's such a common – Glory –
A Fisherman's – Degree –   10
Redemption – Brittle Lady –
Be so – ashamed of Thee –

465 (C. 1862)

I heard a Fly buzz – when I died –
The Stillness in the Room
Was like the Stillness in the Air –
Between the Heaves of Storm –

The Eyes around – had wrung them dry –   5
And Breaths were gathering firm
For that last Onset – when the King
Be witnessed – in the Room –

I willed my Keepsakes – Signed away
What portion of me be   10
Assignable – and then it was
There interposed a Fly –

With Blue – uncertain stumbling Buzz –
Between the light – and me –

And then the Windows failed – and then   15
I could not see to see –

479 (c. 1862)

She dealt her pretty words like Blades –
How glittering they shone –
And every One unbared a Nerve
Or wantoned with a Bone –

She never deemed – she hurt –   5
That – is not Steel's Affair –
A vulgar grimace in the Flesh –
How ill the Creatures bear –

To ache is human – not polite –
The Film upon the Eye   10
Mortality's old Custom –
Just locking up – to Die.

from Johnson (1955)

492 (c. 1862)

Civilization – spurns – the Leopard!
Was the Leopard – bold?
Deserts – never rebuked her Satin –
Ethiop – her Gold –
Tawny – her Customs –   5
She was Conscious –
Spotted – her Dun Gown –
This was the Leopard's nature – Signor –
Need – a keeper – frown?

Pity – the Pard – that left her Asia –   10
Memories – of Palm –
Cannot be stifled – with Narcotic –
Nor suppressed – with Balm –

from Franklin (1981)

518 (c. 1862)

Her sweet Weight on my Heart a Night
Had scarcely deigned to lie –
When, stirring, for Belief's Delight,
My bride had slipped away –

If 'twas a Dream – made solid – just   5
The Heaven to confirm –
Or if Myself were dreamed of Her –
The ⁺power to presume –

With Him remain – who unto Me –
Gave – even as to All –   10
A Fiction superseding Faith –
By so much – as 'twas real –

⁺wisdom

520 (C. 1862)

I started Early – Took my Dog –
And visited the Sea –
The Mermaids in the Basement
Came out to look at me –

And Frigates – in the Upper Floor   5
Extended Hempen Hands –
Presuming Me to be a Mouse –
Aground – upon the Sands –

But no Man moved Me – till the Tide
Went past my simple Shoe –   10
And past my Apron – and my Belt
And past my ⁺Bodice – too –

And made as He would eat me up –
As wholly as a Dew
Upon a Dandelion's Sleeve –   15
And then – I started – too –

And He – He followed – close behind –
I felt His Silver Heel
Upon my Ancle – Then my Shoes
Would overflow with Pearl –   20

Until We met the Solid Town –
No ⁺One He seemed to know –
And bowing – with a Mighty look –
At me – The Sea withdrew –

⁺Bosom   ⁺Buckle

579 (C. 1862)

I had been hungry, all the Years –
My Noon had Come – to dine –

I trembling drew the Table near –
And touched the Curious Wine –

'Twas this on Tables I had seen –   5
When turning, hungry, Home
I looked in Windows, for the ⁺Wealth
I could not hope – ⁺for Mine –

I did not know the ample Bread –
'Twas so unlike the Crumb   10
The Birds and I, had often shared
In Nature's – Dining Room –

The Plenty hurt me – 'Twas so new –
Myself felt ill – and odd –
As Berry – of a Mountain Bush –   15
Transplanted – to the Road –

Nor was I hungry – so I found
That Hunger – was a way
Of ⁺Persons outside Windows –
The Entering – takes away –   20

+Things   +to earn   +Creatures

593 (C. 1862)

I think I was enchanted
When first a ⁺sombre Girl –
I read that Foreign Lady –²
The Dark – felt beautiful –

And whether it was noon at night –   5
Or only Heaven – at Noon –
For very Lunacy of Light
I had not power to tell –

The Bees – became as Butterflies –
The Butterflies – as ⁺Swans –   10
Approached – and spurned the narrow Grass –
And just the ⁺meanest Tunes

That Nature murmured to herself
To keep herself in Cheer –

---

593 (c. 1862)
² Elizabeth Barrett Browning (1806–61), one of
Dickinson's favorite women poets, whose death in June
of 1861 had moved her deeply.

I took for Giants – practising   15
Titanic Opera –

The Days – to Mighty Metres stept –
The Homeliest – adorned
As if unto a ⁺Jubilee
'Twere suddenly ⁺Confirmed –   20

I could not have defined the change –
Conversion of the Mind
Like Sanctifying in the Soul –
Is Witnessed – not Explained –

'Twas a Divine Insanity –   25
The ⁺Danger to be sane
Should I again experience –
'Tis Antidote to turn –

To Tomes of solid Witchcraft –
Magicians be asleep –   30
But Magic – hath an Element –
Like Deity – to keep –

+little Girl   +As Moons –
lit up the low – inferior Grass –
+Common Tunes – faintest –
+Sacrament   +ordained   +Sorrow

601 (c. 1862)

A still – ⁺V̶o̶l̶c̶a̶n̶i̶c̶ – Life –
That flickered in the night –
When it was dark enough to ⁺do
Without ⁺erasing sight –

A quiet – Earthquake Style –   5
Too ⁺subtle to suspect
By natures this side Naples –
The North cannot detect

The Solemn – Torrid – Symbol –
The lips that never lie –   10
Whose hissing Corals part – and shut –
And Cities – ⁺ooze away –

+Volcano   +show   +endangering   +smouldering
  +slip – slide – melt –

605 (c. 1862)

The Spider holds a Silver Ball
In unperceived Hands –
       ⁺as He knits
And ⁺dancing softly ⁺to Himself
His ⁺Yarn of Pearl –   ⁺unwinds –   5
          ⁺expends –

He plies from Nought to Nought –
In unsubstantial Trade –
Supplants our Tapestries with His –
In half the period –   10

An Hour to rear supreme
His ⁺Continents of Light –
Then ⁺dangle from the Housewife's Broom –
His ⁺Boundaries – forgot –

+Pursues his pearly strands –   +Coil –
+Theories +perish by +Sophistries

613 (c. 1862)

They shut me up in Prose –
As when a little Girl
They put me in the Closet –
Because they liked me "still" –

Still! Could themself have peeped –   5
And seen my Brain – go round –
They might as wise have lodged a Bird
For Treason – in the Pound –

Himself has but to will
And easy as a Star   10
⁺Look down upon Captivity –
And laugh – No more have I –

+Abolish his –

619 (c. 1862)

Glee – The great storm is over –
Four – have recovered the Land –
Forty – gone down together –
Into the boiling Sand –

Ring – for the Scant Salvation –   5
Toll – for the bonnie Souls –

Neighbor – and friend – and Bridegroom –
Spinning upon the Shoals –

How they will tell the Story –
When Winter shake the Door –   10
Till the Children urge –   ⁺ask –
But the Forty –
Did they – Come back no more?
Then a s̆oftness – suffuse the Story –
And a silence – the Teller's eye –   15
And the Children – no further question –
And only the Sea – reply –

675 (C. 1863)

Essential Oils – are wrung –
The Attar from the Rose
Be not expressed by Suns – alone –
It is the gift of Screws –

The General Rose – decay –   5
But this – in Lady's Drawer
Make Summer – When the Lady lie
In Ceaseless Rosemary –

681 (C. 1863)

On the Bleakness of my Lot
Bloom I strove to raise –
Late – my ⁺garden of a Rock
Yielded Grape – and Maize –

Soil of Flint, if ⁺steady tilled –   5
Will ⁺refund the Hand –
Seed of Palm, by Libyan Sun
Fructified in Sand –

+Acre of   +steadfast
tilled   +reward – repay –

709 (C. 1863)

Publication – is the Auction
Of the Mind of Man –
Poverty – be justifying
For so foul a thing

Possibly – but We – would rather   5
From our Garret go

White – Unto the White Creator –
Than invest – Our Snow –

Thought belong to Him who gave it –
Then – to Him Who bear   10
In Corporeal illustration – Sell
The Royal Air –

In the Parcel – Be the Merchant
Of the Heavenly Grace –
But reduce no Human Spirit   15
To Disgrace of Price –

721 (c. 1863)

Behind Me – dips Eternity –
Before Me – Immortality –
Myself – the Term between –
Death but the Drift of Eastern Gray,
Dissolving into Dawn away,   5
Before the West begin –

'Tis Kingdoms – afterward – they say –
In perfect – pauseless Monarchy –
Whose Prince – is Son of None –
Himself – His Dateless Dynasty –   10
Himself – Himself diversify –
In Duplicate divine –

'Tis Miracle before Me – then –
'Tis Miracle behind – between –
A Crescent in the Sea –   15
With Midnight to the North of Her –
And Midnight to the South of Her –
And Maelstrom – in the Sky –

722 (c. 1863)

Sweet Mountains – Ye tell Me no lie –
Never deny Me – Never fly –
Those same unvarying Eyes
Turn on Me – when I fail – or feign,
Or take the Royal names in vain –   5
Their far – slow – Violet Gaze –

My Strong Madonnas – Cherish still –
The Wayward Nun – beneath the Hill –
Whose service – is to You –
Her latest Worship When the Day   10

Fades from the Firmament away –
To lift Her Brows on You –

732 (C. 1863)

She rose to His Requirement – dropt
The Playthings of Her Life
To take the honorable Work
Of Woman, and of Wife –

If ought She missed in Her new Day,   5
Of Amplitude, or Awe –
Or first Prospective – Or the Gold
In using, wear away,

It lay unmentioned – as the Sea
Develope Pearl, and Weed,   10
But only to Himself – be known
The Fathoms they abide –

742³ (C. 1863)

Four Trees – upon a solitary Acre –
Without Design
Or Order, or Apparent
⁺Action –
⁺Maintain –   5

The Sun – upon a Morning meets them –
The Wind –
No nearer Neighbor – have they –
But God –

The Acre gives them –   10
Place –
They – Him – Attention of
Passer by –
Of Shadow, or of Squirrel, haply –
Or Boy –   15

What Deed ⁺is Their's
Unto the General Nature –
What Plan

---

742 (C. 1863)
³ The line breaks in this poem are unusually ambigu-
ous, even for Dickinson, and have been followed except
where the next line is unequivocally in lower case.

They severally − ˚retard − or further −
Unknown −   20

+signal − notice   +Do reign −
+they bear   +promote − or hinder −

754 (C. 1863)

My Life had stood − a Loaded Gun −
In Corners − till a Day
The Owner passed − identified −
And carried Me away −

And now We roam ˚in Sovereign Woods −   5
And now We hunt the Doe −
And every time I speak for Him −
The Mountains straight reply −

And do I smile, such cordial light
Upon the Valley glow −   10
It is as a Vesuvian face
Had let it's pleasure through −

And when at Night − Our good Day done −
I guard my Master's Head −
'Tis better than the Eider-Duck's   15
Deep Pillow − to have shared −

To foe of His − I'm deadly foe −
None ˚stir the second time −
On whom I lay a Yellow Eye −
Or an emphatic Thumb −   20

Though I than He − may longer live
He longer must − than I −
For I have but the ˚power to kill
Without − the power to die −

+the   +low   +harm   +art

from Johnson (1955)

822 (C. 1864)

This Consciousness that is aware
Of Neighbors and the Sun
Will be the one aware of Death
And that itself alone

Is traversing the interval   5
Experience between
And most profound experiment
Appointed unto Men –

How adequate unto itself
It's properties shall be   10
Itself unto itself and none
Shall make discovery –

Adventure most unto itself
The Soul condemned to be –
Attended by a single Hound   15
It's own identity.

from Franklin (1981)

872 (C. 1864)

As the Starved Maelstrom laps the Navies
As the Vulture teazed
Forces the Broods in lonely Valleys
As the Tiger eased

By but a Crumb of Blood, fasts Scarlet   5
Till he meet a Man
Dainty adorned with Veins and Tissues
And partakes – his Tongue

Cooled by the Morsel for a Moment
Grows a fiercer thing   10
Till he esteem his Dates and Cocoa
A Nutrition mean

I, of a finer Famine
Deem my Supper dry
For but a Berry of Domingo   15
And a Torrid Eye –

937 (C. 1864)

I felt a Cleaving in my Mind –
As if my Brain had split –
I tried to match it – Seam by Seam –
But could not make them fit –

The thought behind, I 'strove to join   5
Unto the thought before –
But Sequence ravelled out of 'Sound –
Like Balls – upon a Floor –

+tried   +reach

1059 (c. 1865)

Sang from the Heart, Sire,
Dipped my Beak in it,
If the Tune drip too much
Have a tint too Red

Pardon the Cochineal —   5
Suffer the Vermillion —
Death is the Wealth
Of the Poorest Bird.

Bear with the Ballad —
Awkward — faltering —   10
Death twists the strings —
'Twas'nt my blame —

Pause in your Liturgies —
Wait your Chorals —
While I ⁺repeat your   15
Hallowed name —

＋recite

from Johnson (1955)

1136 (c. 1869)

The Frost of Death was on the Pane —
"Secure your Flower" said he.
Like Sailors fighting with a Leak
We fought Mortality.

Our passive Flower we held to Sea —   5
To Mountain — To the Sun —
Yet even on his Scarlet shelf
To crawl the Frost begun —

We pried him back
Ourselves we wedged   10
Himself and her between,
Yet easy as the narrow Snake
He forked his way along

Till all her helpless beauty bent
And then our wrath begun —   15
We hunted him to his Ravine
We chase him to his Den —

We hated Death and hated Life
And nowhere was to go –
Than Sea and continent there is   20
A larger – it is Woe

2. Secure] Protect   12. Yet] But
7. Yet] But   12. the] a
8. begun] began   15. begun] began

1138 (c. 1869)

A Spider sewed at Night
Without a Light
Upon an Arc of White.

If Ruff it was of Dame
Or Shroud of Gnome   5
Himself himself inform.

Of Immortality
His Strategy
Was Physiognomy.

1167[4] (1870)

Alone and in a Circumstance
Reluctant to be told
A spider on my reticence
Assiduously crawled

And so much more at Home than I   5
Immediately grew
I felt myself a visitor
And hurriedly withdrew

Revisiting my late abode
With articles of claim   10
I found it quietly assumed
As a Gymnasium   ·
Where Tax asleep and Title off
The inmates of the Air
Perpetual presumption took   15

1167 (1870)

[1]   According to Johnson, Dickinson transcribed this remarkable poem on a sheet to which she had already pasted an unused 1869 three-cent postage stamp and "two small strips clipped from *Harper's Magazine* for May 1870. One bears the name 'George Sand' and the other 'Mauprat' – the title of the novel by George Sand published in 1836." Since Dickinson then made the poem's lines accommodate to the already occupied space, Johnson believes that the poem is "autobiographical" and that "'in a circumstance reluctant to be told' ED had been guided to *Mauprat* and had found the book a 'larceny of time and mind.'"

As each were special Heir –
If any strike me on the street
I can return the Blow –
If any take my property
According to the Law   20
The Statute is my Learned friend
But what redress can be
For an offense nor here nor there
So not in Equity –
That Larceny of time and mind   25
That marrow of the Day
By spider, or forbid it Lord
That I should specify.

1. in] of   12. As] for
4. Assiduously] deliberately /   14. inmates] Peasants
   determinately / impertinently   15. presumption] complacence
7. a] the   16. special] lawful / only
8. hurriedly] hastily   19. take] seize

from Franklin (1981)

1201 (C. 1871)

So I pull my Stockings off
Wading in the Water
For the Disobedience' Sake
Boy that lived for "Ought to"
                        "or'ter"   5
Went to Heaven perhaps at Death
And perhaps he did'nt
Moses was'nt fairly used –
Ananias[5] was'nt –

1225 (C. 1872)

Its' Hour with itself
The Spirit never shows.
What Terror would enthrall the Street
Could Countenance disclose

The Subterranean Freight   5
The Cellars of the Soul –
Thank God the loudest Place he made
Is licenced to be still.

1201 (C. 1871)
[5] Acts 5:1–11. Ananias fell dead after lying to Peter
about the amount he gave to the Church. His punishment – like that of Moses, who was denied entry into
the promised land by God – was, in Dickinson's opinion, an instance of God's proclivity to mete out unfair
punishments.

from Johnson (1955)

1377 (C. 1876)

Forbidden Fruit a flavor has
That lawful Orchards mocks –
How luscious lies within the Pod
The Pea that Duty locks –

2. Orchards] Damsons

1545[6] (C. 1882)

The Bible is an antique Volume –
Written by faded Men
At the suggestion of Holy Spectres –
Subjects – Bethlehem –
Eden – the ancient Homestead –   5
Satan – the Brigadier –
Judas – the Great Defaulter –
David the Troubadour –
Sin – a distinguished Precipice
Others must resist –   10
Boys that "believe" are very lonesome –
Other Boys are "lost" –
Had but the Tale a warbling Teller –
All the Boys would come –
Orpheus' Sermon captivated –   15
It did not condemn –

1564[7] (C. 1883)

Pass to thy Rendezvous of Light,
Pangless except for us –
Who slowly ford the Mystery
Which thou hast leaped across!

1670 (DATE UNKNOWN)

In Winter in my Room
I came upon a Worm

1545 (C. 1882)

[6] This poem was sent as a message to Dickinson's
nephew, Edward Dickinson ("Ned"); it was accompanied
by the line " 'Sanctuary Privileges' for Ned, as he is unable to attend –" Johnson suggests that Ned was home
sick from school, but it is also possible (given the poem's
subject matter) that he skipped church, a lapse with
which Dickinson would have been sympathetic. In the
poem's semi-final draft Dickinson gives fifteen different
alternatives for "warbling" in line 13, including "bonnie,"
"typic," and "pungent."

1564 (C. 1883)

[7] This is one of a small group of elegies that Dickinson
wrote after the death of her eight-year-old nephew,
Gilbert, in 1883. Eighteen months later Dickinson re-
used them in a letter to Thomas Went-worth Higginson
in reference to George Eliot's death.

Pink lank and warm
But as he was a worm
And worms presume   5
Not quite with him at home
Secured him by a string
To something neighboring
And went along.

A Trifle afterward   10
A thing occurred
I'd not believe it if I heard
But state with creeping blood
A snake with mottles rare
Surveyed my chamber floor   15
In feature as the worm before
But ringed with power
The very string with which
I tied him – too
When he was mean and new   20
That string was there –

I shrank – "How fair you are"!
Propitiation's claw –
"Afraid he hissed
Of me"?   25
"No cordiality" –
He fathomed me –
Then to a Rhythm *Slim*
Secreted in his Form
As Patterns swim   30
Projected him.

That time I flew
Both eyes his way
Lest he pursue
Nor ever ceased to run   35
Till in a distant Town
Towns on from mine
I set me down
This was a dream –

1677 (DATE UNKNOWN)

On my volcano grows the Grass
A meditative spot –
An acre for a Bird to choose
Would be the General thought –

How red the Fire rocks below 5
How insecure the sod
Did I disclose
Would populate with awe my solitude

1722 (DATE UNKNOWN)

Her face was in a bed of hair,
Like flowers in a plot –
Her hand was whiter than the sperm
That feeds the sacred light.
Her tongue more tender than the tune 5
That totters in the leaves –
Who hears may be incredulous,
Who witnesses, believes.

4. sacred] central   5. tune] tone
5. tender] timid / magic

Adah Isaacs Menken (1835–1868)

The one fact all Adah Isaacs Menken's biographers agree on is that she was born on June 15. Beyond that, her origins and the story of her early life, at least until recently, were a matter of myth – myth generated largely by Menken herself. According to Menken's most recent biographers – John Cofran, who did the digging, and Dorsey Kleitz, who accepts Cofran's findings – hard evidence for Menken's "real" origins has at last been discovered and the truth revealed. Menken came into the world on June 15, 1835, in Memphis, Tennessee, Ada C. McCord, the daughter of an Irish businessman, Richard McCord, and his wife Catherine.

The prosaic conclusion to the great Menken mystery almost leaves one wishing that the myth – that she was a Jewess, that she was a mulatta, that she was somehow exotica whether born in Ohio, Tennessee, Louisiana, or Texas, in 1835 or some other year – could be restored; yet the debunking, the ordinary conclusion to the flamboyant tale, is of a piece with everything else in Adah Menken's life, a life that, like the stage on which she played, flourished only by being something it was not.

Menken first went on the stage in New Orleans, where her family had moved following her father's death. And it was through her stage work that she met the first of her four husbands, the man who gave her the name she is known by – Alexander Isaac Menken (she would add an "s"). Following her marriage, Menken converted to Judaism, possibly sincerely or possibly to win over her new husband's wealthy parents. Whichever the case, she can next be found publishing heartfelt articles and poems on Jewish issues in the *Cincinnati Israelite*.

The Menkens separated in 1859, after Alexander Menken suffered severe financial losses. The enterprising Adah went to New York City, where she hobnobbed with Walt Whitman and his crowd and married John Carmel Heenan, a pugilist known as the Benicia Boy. Out for revenge, Alexander Menken announced publicly that he and Adah were still married (this, despite the fact that they had a rabbinical diploma of divorce, something he failed to mention). Heenan chose to believe the outraged former husband and abandoned Menken in 1860, declaring their marriage void. Kleitz contends, probably rightly, that Menken's rage over these events fueled her strongest poem, "Judith," written at this time.

In 1861, Menken achieved the acme of notoriety in *Mazeppa*, a dramatization of Byron's verse epic, in which she played the youthful male lead. In the play's final scene she appeared on stage strapped to the back of a horse and to all appearances in the nude (her costume is variously described as a flesh-colored body stocking, with loin cloth or tunic). Garbed in her new reputation as "the naked lady," Menken took *Mazeppa* on a highly successful road tour, first in the States, then in Europe. Scandal followed her wherever she went, a well-publicized affair with an aging Alexander Dumas capping her European reputation. After returning to England in 1867, however, Menken found her popularity on the wane. One year later, she collapsed during a rehearsal in Paris and died shortly thereafter, from what was later diagnosed as cancer. *Infelicia*, her only book, appeared eight days after her death. A collection of monodies, two-thirds in free verse, the book was savaged by reviewers who, not unjustifiably, found it overwrought and melodramatic. Kleitz, with equal justice, describes it as "a kind of nineteenth-century feminist *Howl*."

In her style as in her life, Adah Menken was the closest nineteenth-century America would come to an in-your-face woman poet (Victoria Woodhull, co-editor of *Woodhull & Claflin's Weekly*, might lay a rival claim for prose). Even if she was not the Jewess or the mulatta she said she was, her identification with these socially marginalized groups permeates her writing in ways that cannot be ignored. Like her idol, Whitman, she claims to be one with those for whom she speaks, a Jew for the Jews, a black for the blacks, an outcast with the outcasts. And into these identities, or personae, she pours her own sense of outrage, using the Whitmanian catalog to list the various crimes which society committed against its own. Like Whitman, Menken also fashions herself as the voice of the prophet, making effective use of hypnotic biblical cadences to reinforce the power of her Jeremiadic indictments.

Where she differed, it seems, was in her fundamental right to such a magniloquent self. For all his bombast, Whitman knew he was a man with man's "representative" right to claim his privilege and speak for whom he chose; he does so with nonchalant aplomb. But Adah Isaacs Menken knew that at bottom she was only Ada C. McCord, an Irish girl from Memphis, Tennessee, and in the intense excesses of her self-preoccupation as in her determination to speak for everyone in the loudest voice possible, there is all too often an ominously hollow ring.

Primary Text

Infelicia, 1868.

Further Reading

John Cofran, "The Identity of Adah Isaacs Menken: A Theatrical Mystery Solved," *Theatre Survey* 31 (May 1990): 47–54; Barbara Foster and Michael Foster, "Adah Menken: An American Original," *North Dakota Quarterly* 61 (Fall 1993): 52–62; Dorsey Kleitz, "Adah Isaacs Menken," *Encyclopedia of American Poetry*; Wolf Mankowitz, *Mazeppa, the Lives, Loves, and Legends of Adah Isaacs Menken: A Biographical Quest*, New York: Stein and Day, 1982; Joan Sherman, "Introduction," in *Collected Black Women's Poetry*, vol. 1, New York and Oxford: Oxford University Press, 1988.

from *Infelicia* (1868)

JUDITH[1]

*"Repent, or I will come unto thee quickly, and will fight thee with the
sword of my mouth." – Revelations ii.16.*

I.

Ashkelon is not cut off with the remnant of a valley.
Baldness dwells not upon Gaza.[2]
The field of the valley is mine, and it is clothed in verdure.
The steepness of Baal-perazim is mine;
And the Philistines spread themselves in the valley of Rephraim.[3]   5
They shall yet be delivered into my hands.
For the God of Battles has gone before me!
The sword of the mouth shall smite them to dust.
I have slept in the darkness –
But the seventh angel[4] woke me, and giving me a sword of flame, points
to the blood-ribbed cloud, that lifts his reeking head above the mountain.   10
Thus am I the prophet.
I see the dawn that heralds to my waiting soul the advent of power.
    Power that will unseal the thunders!
    Power that will give voice to graves!
    Graves of the living;   15
    Graves of the dying;
    Graves of the sinning;
    Graves of the loving;
    Graves of despairing;
And oh! graves of the deserted!   20
These shall speak, each as their voices shall be loosed.
And the day is dawning.

II.

Stand back, ye Philistines!
Practice what ye preach to me;
I heed ye not, for I know ye all.   25
    Ye are living burning lies, and profanation to the garments which with
stately steps ye sweep your marble palaces.
    Your palaces of Sin, around which the damning evidence of guilt hangs
like a reeking vapor.

JUDITH
[1] In the Apocrypha Judith saves her people from
Nebuchadnezzar's forces by stealing into the camp of
his general, Holofernes, and beheading him.
[2] Ashkelon and Gaza are two cities in southwest
Palestine.

[3] Baal-perazim and the valley of Rephraim are sites
where David conquered the Philistines in 2 Samuel 5:18–
25.
[4] See Revelations 10:7–11.

Stand back!

I would pass up the golden road of the world.

A place in the ranks awaits me.   30

I know that ye are hedged on the borders of my path.

Lie and tremble, for ye well know that I hold with iron grasp the battle axe.

Creep back to your dark tents in the valley.

Slouch back to your haunts of crime.

Ye do not know me, neither do ye see me.   35

But the sword of the mouth is unsealed, and ye coil yourselves in slime and bitterness at my feet.

I mix your jeweled heads, and your gleaming eyes, and your hissing tongues with the dust.

My garments shall bear no mark of ye.

When I shall return this sword to the angel, your foul blood will not stain its edge.

It will glimmer with the light of truth, and the strong arm shall rest.   40

III.

Stand back!

I am no Magdalene[5] waiting to kiss the hem of your garment.

It is mid-day.

See ye not what is written on my forehead?

I am Judith!   45

I wait for the head of my Holofernes!

Ere the last tremble of the conscious death-agony shall have shuddered, I will show it to ye with the long black hair clinging to the glazed eyes, and the great mouth opened in search of voice, and the strong throat all hot and reeking with blood, that will thrill me with wild unspeakable joy as it courses down my bare body and dabbles my cold feet!

My sensuous soul will quake with the burden of so much bliss.

Oh, what wild passionate kisses will I draw up from that bleeding mouth!

I will strangle this pallid throat of mine on the sweet blood!   50

I will revel in my passion.

At midnight I will feast on it in the darkness.

For it was that which thrilled its crimson tides of reckless passion through the blue veins of my life, and made them leap up in the wild sweetness of Love and agony of Revenge!

I am starving for this feast.

Oh forget not that I am Judith!   55

And I know where sleeps Holofernes.

---

[5]   Mary Magdalene, female follower of Jesus. Traditionally she has come to represent the repentant prostitute. See Luke 7:36–50.

WORKING AND WAITING

Suggested by Carl Müller's Cast of The Seamstress,
at the Dusseldorf Gallery

I.

Look on that form, once fit for the sculptor!
  Look on that cheek, where the roses have died!
Working and waiting have robbed from the artist
  All that his marble could show for its pride.
      Statue-like sitting   5
      Alone, in the flitting
And wind-haunted shadows that people her hearth.
      God protect all of us –
      God shelter all of us –
From the reproach of such scenes upon earth!   10

II.

All the day long, and through the cold midnight,
  Still the hot needle she wearily plies.
Haggard and white as the ghost of a Spurned One,
  Sewing white robes for the Chosen One's eyes –
      Lost in her sorrow,   15
      But for the morrow,
Phantom-like speaking in every stitch –
      God protect all of us –
      God shelter all of us
From the Curse, born with each sigh for the Rich!   20

III.

Low burns the lamp. Fly swifter, thou needle –
  Swifter, thou asp for the breast of the poor!
Else the pale light will be stolen by Pity,
  Ere of the vital part thou hast made sure.
      Dying, yet living: 25
      All the world's giving
Barely the life that runs out with her thread.
      God protect all of us –
      God shelter all of us
From her last glance, as she follows the Dead!   30

IV.

What if the morning finds her still bearing
  All the soul's load of a merciless lot!
Fate will not lighten a grain of the burden
  While the poor bearer by man is forgot.

Sewing and sighing! 35
Sewing and dying!
What to such life is a day or two more?
God protect all of us —
God shelter all of us
From the new day's lease of woe to the Poor! 40

V.

Hasten, ye winds! and yield her the mercy
Lying in sleep on your purified breath;
Yield her the mercy, enfolding a blessing,
Yield her the mercy whose signet is Death.
In her toil stopping, 45
See her work dropping —
Fate, thou art merciful! Life, thou art done!
God, protect all of us!
God shelter all of us
From the heart breaking, and yet living on! 50

VI.

Winds that have sainted her, tell ye the story
Of the young life by the needle that bled;
Making its bridge over Death's soundless waters
Out of a swaying and soul-cutting thread.
Over it going, 55
All the world knowing!
Thousands have trod it, foot-bleeding, before!
God protect all of us —
God shelter all of us,
Should she look back from the Opposite Shore! 60

ANSWER ME

I.

In from the night.
The Storm is lifting his black arms up to the sky.
Friend of my heart, who so gently marks out the lifetrack for me,
draw near to-night;
Forget the wailing of the low-voiced wind:
Shut out the moanings of the freezing, and the starving, and the dying,
and bend your head low to me: 5
Clasp my cold, cold hands in yours;
Think of me tenderly and lovingly:
Look down into my eyes the while I question you, and if you love me,
answer me —
Oh, answer me!

II.

Is there not a gleam of Peace on all this tiresome earth?   10
Does not one oasis cheer all this desert-world?
When will all this toil and pain bring me the blessing?
Must I ever plead for help to do the work before me set?
Must I ever stumble and faint by the dark wayside?
Oh the dark, lonely wayside, with its dim-sheeted ghosts peering up
through their shallow graves!   15
Must I ever tremble and pale at the great Beyond?
Must I find Rest only in your bosom, as now I do?
           Answer me –
           Oh, answer me!

III.

Speak to me tenderly.   20
Think of me lovingly.
Let your soft hands smooth back my hair.
Take my cold, tear-stained face up to yours.
Let my lonely life creep into your warm bosom, knowing no other rest
but this.
Let me question you, while sweet Faith and Trust are folding their white
robes around me.   25
Thus am I purified, even to your love, that came like John the Baptist
in the Wilderness of Sin.
You read the starry heavens, and lead me forth.
But tell me if, in this world's Judea, there comes never quiet when once
the heart awakes?
Why must it ever hush Love back?
Must it only labour, strive, and ache?   30
Has it no reward but this?
Has it no inheritance but to bear – and break?
           Answer me –
           Oh, answer me!

IV.

The Storm struggles with the Darkness.   35
Folded away in your arms, how little do I heed their battle!
The trees clash in vain their naked swords against the door.
I go not forth while the low murmur of your voice is drifting all else
back to silence.
The darkness presses his black forehead close to the window pane,
and beckons me without.
Love holds a lamp in this little room that hath power to blot back Fear. 40
But will the lamp ever starve for oil?
Will its blood-red flame ever grow faint and blue?
Will it uprear itself to a slender line of light?

Will it grow pallid and motionless?
Will it sink rayless to everlasting death?   45
        Answer me –
        Oh, answer me!

V.

Look at these tear-drops.
See how they quiver and die on your open hands.
Fold these white garments close to my breast, while I question you.   50
Would you have me think that from the warm shelter of your heart
I must go to the grave?
And when I am lying in my silent shroud, will you love me?
When I am buried down in the cold, wet earth, will you grieve that you
did not save me?
Will your tears reach my pale face through all the withered leaves that will
heap themselves upon my grave?
Will you repent that you loosened your arms to let me fall so deep,
and so far out of sight?   55
Will you come and tell me so, when the coffin has shut out the storm?
        Answer me –
        Oh, answer me!

Celia Thaxter (1835–1894)

Celia Laighton Thaxter was born on June 29, 1835 in Portsmouth, New Hampshire. Her father, Thomas Laighton, came from a seafaring family. After trying out a number of different careers, including lighthouse keeper and politician, he found his niche as owner/manager of a resort hotel on Appledore Island, the largest of the Shoals Islands off the New Hampshire coast. Still famous today, "Appledore" became a summer mecca for New England's glitterati, including Hawthorne, Emerson, Lowell, Twain, Larcom, Elizabeth Stuart Phelps, Annie Fields, and Sarah Orne Jewett.

If Thaxter's father provided fertile ground for his daughter's growth as an artist, Thaxter's mother, Eliza Rymes Laighton, was the emotional lodestone of her life. In particular, the two shared a deep love for gardening and for the rugged life of the coastal islands. Eliza Laighton's death in 1877 devastated Thaxter and some, at least, of the latter's many passionate love poems to women are probably addressed in whole or part to her mother.

When Celia was twelve, her father hired Levi Thaxter, a Harvard graduate, to tutor her. Levi Thaxter introduced his young charge to the works of the standard British and American poets – Longfellow, Lowell, Keats, Arnold, Tennyson, and the Brownings. On September 30, 1851, he and the sixteen-year-old Celia were married. Their union ranks among the unhappiest made by the various poets in this volume (no mean trick), separating Thaxter from all she knew and loved, including her mother and life on the coastal isles. (Her profound sense of loss for the latter surfaces in her first published poem, "Land-Locked.")

The couple had three sons, the first of whom, Karl, was brain damaged from birth and a burden on Thaxter for the rest of her life. Levi himself turned out to be meanly parsimonious in the best New England fashion and refused to provide his young wife with paid help. In a bitter letter to Annie Fields, her one confidante at the time, Thaxter calls her Newtonville home "Bachelor's Hall" and says she is fed up with waiting on Levi and his Harvard cronies. After thirty-three years of marriage, marked increasingly by differences and separations, Levi's death in 1884 freed Thaxter to live the rest of her life as she chose, in peace and calm, among her books, flowers, and friends, and well within the "sad caressing murmur" of the sea. She died unexpectedly at Appledore in August, 1894. Annie Fields and Sarah Orne Jewett were with her.

Celia Thaxter wrote largely to make money since Levi was loath to give her any. After the highly acclaimed appearance of "Land-Locked" in the *Atlantic Monthly* in 1861, she was a regular in the major periodicals. Her nature poetry was especially admired, probably because it drew so deeply on her knowledge of New England's granite shoreline. As a consequence of having witnessed as a child a shipwreck in which all hands were lost, Thaxter's treatment of nature, and of the ocean in particular, is not naive. She rejoiced in the flora and fauna which the ocean sustained; but she was also keenly aware of how quickly the sea could turn on those who made their living by it. She was also profoundly troubled, as poems such as "Wherefore" and "At the Breakers' Edge" indicate, by the questions which the apparent irrationality of life – and death – at sea raised. (It is illuminating, for example, to compare Sigourney's "Bell of the Wreck" with Thaxter's "Wherefore" and Dickinson's "Glee – The great storm is over" [619].)

At the same time, however, Thaxter epitomizes many of the limitations as well as the strengths one can expect from a late nineteenth-century American woman poet writing for a genteel magazine market. Thaxter was not naive nor was she mindlessly sentimental although she did write many sentimental lyrics, especially her songs. Many of her best poems, like "Wherefore," are meditative; others, like the love poems, "Two Sonnets," are deeply passionate and brilliantly controlled. But her primary concern was to make her poetry conform to the expectations of the audience for whom she wrote. The qualities this audience encouraged – didacticism, moral uplift, conventional language and metrics – discouraged risk-taking and render much of her poetry relatively uninteresting to readers today.

There are times, to use images deployed by Dickinson and Piatt, when one longs for the tiger to break out, for the snake to reveal itself, and they do not. Insofar as Thaxter believed it was her duty to hide her miseries behind a mask of good cheer, sharing them only with a very few who were nearest to her and on whose silence she could rely, the poet was at one with the expectations she fulfilled. In this case, unless a "private" cache of poetry is discovered more revealing than the public work she left behind, it was her art that lost.

Primary Texts

Poems, 1872; *Among the Isles of Shoals*, 1873; *Poems*, 1874, 1876; *The Cruise of the Mystery and Other Poems*, 1886; *Poems*, 1896; *The Heavenly Guest*, ed. Oscar Laighton, 1935.

Further Reading

Celia Thaxter Issue, *Colby Library Quarterly* 6 (1964); Rosamond Thaxter, *Sandpiper: The Life and Letters of Celia Thaxter*, Francestown, New Hampshire: Golden Quill Press, 1963; Jane E. Vallier, *Poet on Demand: The Life, Letters, and Works of Celia Thaxter*, Portsmouth, New Hampshire: Peter E. Randall, 1994.

from *Atlantic Monthly* (1861)

LAND-LOCKED

Black lie the hills, swiftly doth daylight flee,
    And, catching gleams of sunset's dying smile,
    Through the dusk land for many a changing mile
The river runneth softly to the sea.

O happy river, could I follow thee!   5
    O yearning heart, that never can be still!
    O wistful eyes, that watch the steadfast hill,
Longing for level line of solemn sea!

Have patience; here are flowers and songs of birds,
    Beauty and fragrance, wealth of sound and sight,   10
    All summer's glory thine from morn till night,
And life too full of joy for uttered words.

Neither am I ungrateful. But I dream
    Deliciously, how twilight falls to-night
    Over the glimmering water, how the light   15
Dies blissfully away, until I seem

To feel the wind sea-scented on my cheek,
    To catch the sound of dusky flapping sail,
    And dip of oars, and voices on the gale,
Afar off, calling softly, low and sweet.   20

O Earth, thy summer-song of joy may soar
    Ringing to heaven in triumph! I but crave
    The sad, caressing murmur of the wave
That breaks in tender music on the shore.

from *Atlantic Monthly* (1874)

IN KITTERY CHURCHYARD[1]

"Mary, wife of Charles Chauncy, died April 23, 1758, in the 24th year
of her age."

Crushing the scarlet strawberries in the grass,
I kneel to read the slanting stone. Alas!
How sharp a sorrow speaks! A hundred years

IN KITTERY CHURCHYARD
[1] Kittery, a seacoast town on the Maine–New Hampshire border, settled in the late seventeenth century.

And more have vanished, with their smiles and tears,
Since here was laid, upon an April day,   5
Sweet Mary Chauncy in the grave away, –
A hundred years since here her lover stood
Beside her grave in such despairing mood,
And yet from out the vanished past I hear
His cry of anguish sounding deep and clear,   10
And all my heart with pity melts, as though
To-day's bright sun were looking on his woe.
"Of such a wife, O righteous Heaven! bereft,
What joy for me, what joy on earth is left?
Still from my inmost soul the groans arise,   15
Still flow the sorrows ceaseless from mine eyes."
Alas, poor tortured soul! I look away
From the dark stone, – how brilliant shines the day!
A low wall, over which the roses shed
Their perfumed petals, shuts the quiet dead   20
Apart a little, and the tiny square
Stands in the broad and laughing field so fair,
And gay green vines climb o'er the rough stone-wall,
And all about the wild birds flit and call,
And but a stone's-throw southward, the blue sea   25
Rolls sparkling in and sings incessantly.
Lovely as any dream the peaceful place,
And scarcely changed since on her gentle face
For the last time on that sad April day
He gazed, and felt, for him, all beauty lay   30
Buried with her forever.   Dull to him
Looked the bright world through eyes with tears so dim!
"I soon shall follow the same dreary way
That leads and opens to the coasts of day."
His only hope! But when slow time had dealt   35
Firmly with him and kindly, and he felt
The storm and stress of strong and piercing pain
Yielding at last, and he grew calm again,
Doubtless he found another mate before
He followed Mary to the happy shore!   40
But none the less his grief appeals to me
Who sit and listen to the singing sea
This matchless summer day, beside the stone
He made to echo with his bitter moan,
And in my eyes I feel the foolish tears   45
For buried sorrow, dead a hundred years!

WHEREFORE

Black sea, black sky!   A ponderous steamship driving
    Between them, laboring westward on her way,

And in her path a trap of Death's contriving
   Waiting remorseless for its easy prey.

Hundreds of souls within her frame lie dreaming,   5
   Hoping and fearing, longing for the light:
With human life and thought and feeling teeming
   She struggles onward through the awful night.

Upon her furnace fires fresh fuel flinging,
   The swarthy firemen grumble at the dust   10
Mixed with the coal — when suddenly upspringing,
   Swift through the smoke-stack like a signal thrust,

Flares a red flame, a dread illumination!
   A cry, — a tumult!   Slowly to her helm
The vessel yields, 'mid shouts of acclamation,   15
   And joy and terror all her crew o'erwhelm;

For looming from the blackness drear before them
   Discovered is the iceberg — hardly seen,
Its ghastly precipices hanging o'er them,
   Its reddened peaks, with dreadful chasms between,   20

Ere darkness swallows it again!   and veering
   Out of its track the brave ship onward steers,
Just grazing ruin.   Trembling still, and fearing,
   Her grateful people melt in prayers and tears.

Is it a mockery, their profound thanksgiving?   25
   Another ship goes shuddering to her doom
Unwarned, that very night, with hopes as living,
   With freight as precious, lost amid the gloom,

With not a ray to show the apparition
   Waiting to slay her, none to cry "Beware!"   30
Rushing straight onward headlong to perdition,
   And for her crew no time vouchsafed for prayer!

Could they have stormed heaven's gate with anguished praying,
   It would not have availed a feather's weight
Against their doom.   Yet were they disobeying   35
   No law of God, to beckon such a fate.

And do not tell me the Almighty Master
   Would work a miracle to save the one,
And yield the other up to dire disaster,
   By merely human justice thus outdone!   40

Vainly we weep and wrestle with our sorrow –
  We cannot see his roads, they lie so broad:
But his eternal day knows no to-morrow,
  And life and death are all the same with God.

from *Poems* (1874)

AT THE BREAKERS' EDGE

Through the wide sky Thy north-wind's thunder roars
  Resistless, till no cloud is left to flee,
And down the clear, cold heaven unhindered pours
  Thine awful moonlight on the winter sea.

The vast, black, raging spaces, torn and wild,   5
  With an insensate fury answer back
To the gale's challenge; hurrying breakers, piled
  Each over each, roll through the glittering track.

I shudder in the terror of Thy cold,
  As buffeted by the fierce blast I stand,   10
Watching that shining path of bronzèd gold,
  With solemn, shadowy rocks on either hand;

While at their feet, ghastly and white as death,
  The cruel, foaming billows plunge and rave.
O Father! where art Thou? My feeble breath   15
  Cries to Thee through the storm of wind and wave.

The cry of all Thy children since the first
  That walked Thy planets' myriad paths among;
The cry of all mankind whom doubt has cursed,
  In every clime, in every age and tongue.   20

Thou art the cold, the swift fire that consumes;
  Thy vast, unerring forces never fail;
And Thou art in the frailest flower that blooms,
  As in the breath of this tremendous gale.

Yet, though Thy laws are clear as light, and prove   25
  Thee changeless, ever human weakness craves
Some deeper knowledge for our human love
  That looks with sad eyes o'er its wastes of graves,

And hungers for the dear hands softly drawn,
  One after one, from out our longing grasp.   30
Dost Thou reach out for them? In the sweet dawn
  Of some new world thrill they within Thy clasp?

Ah! what am I, Thine atom, standing here
  In presence of Thy pitiless elements,
Daring to question Thy great silence drear,   35
  No voice may break to lighten our suspense!

Thou only, infinite Patience, that endures
  Forever! Blind and dumb I cling to Thee.
Slow glides the bitter night, and silent pours
  Thine awful moonlight on the winter sea.   40

from *Atlantic Monthly* (1877)

MUTATION

About your window's happy height
  The roses wove their airy screen:
More radiant than the blossoms bright
  Looked your fair face between.

The glowing summer sunshine laid   5
  Its touch on field and flower and tree;
But 't was your golden smile that made
  The warmth that gladdened me.

The summer withered from the land,
  The vision from the window passed: 10
Blank Sorrow looked at me; her hand
  Sought mine and clasped it fast.

The bitter wind blows keen and drear,
  Stinging with winter's flouts and scorns,
And where the roses breathed I hear   15
  The rattling of the thorns.

from *Lippincott's Magazine* (1878)

ALONE

The lilies clustered fair and tall;
I stood outside the garden wall;
I saw her light robe glimmering through
The fragrant evening's dusk and dew.

She stooped above the lilies pale;   5
Up the clear east the moon did sail;
I saw her bend her lovely head
O'er her rich roses blushing red.

Her slender hand the flowers caressed,
Her touch the unconscious blossoms blest: 10
The rose against her perfumed palm
Leaned its soft cheek in blissful calm.

I would have given my soul to be
That flower she touched so tenderly!
I stood alone outside the gate,   15
And knew that life was desolate.

from *The Cruise of the Mystery and Other Poems* (1886)

BETROTHED

Softly the flickering firelight comes and goes;
    The warm glow flashes, sinks, departs, returns,
And shows me where the delicate red rose
    In the tall, slender vase of crystal burns.

The tempest beats without. The hush within   5
    Is sweeter for the turmoil of the night;
Ice clatters at the pane and snow-flakes spin
    A web of woven storm, a shroud of white.

Its secret the wild winter weather keeps,
    No sound transpires except the tempest's breath;   10
Locked in the frost the muffled pathway sleeps,
    For any human token still as death.

My eyes the room's familiar aspect hold,
    Its quiet beauty and its sumptuous gloom,
Its glimmering draperies of dull rich gold,   15
    The gleam upon the burnished peacock's plume.

My rose, my book, my work, I see them all,
    With my whole soul surrendered to one sense,
My life within my ears, for one footfall
    Listening with patience breathless and intense.   20

'T is my heart hears, at last, the silent door
    Swing on its hinges, there 's no need the fire
Should show me whose step thrills the conscious floor,
    As suddenly the wayward flame leaps higher.

Thou comest, bringing all good things that are!   25
    Infinite joy, and peace with white wings furled,

All heaven is here and thou the morning-star,
Thou splendor of my life! "Thou Day o' the world!"[2]

from *Poems* (1896)

TWO SONNETS

Not so! You stand as long ago a king[3]
    Stood on the seashore, bidding back the tide
That onward rolled resistless still, to fling
    Its awful volume landward, wild and wide.
And just as impotent is your command   5
    To stem the tide that rises in my soul.
It ebbs not at the lifting of your hand,
    It owns no curb, it yields to no control;
Mighty it is, and of the elements, –
    Brother of winds and lightning, cold and fire,   10
Subtle as light, as steadfast and intense;
    Sweet as the music of Apollo's lyre.
You think to rule the ocean's ebb and flow
With that soft woman's hand? Nay, love, not so.

And like the lighthouse on the rock you stand,   15
    And pierce the distance with your searching eyes;
Nor do you heed the waves that storm the land
    And endlessly about you fall and rise,
But seek the ships that wander night and day
    Within the dim horizon's shadowy ring;   20
And some with flashing glance you warn away,
    And some you beckon with sweet welcoming.
So steadfast still you keep your lofty place,
    Safe from the tumult of the restless tide,
Firm as the rock in your resisting grace,   25
    And strong through humble duty, not through pride.
While I – I cast my life before your feet,
And only live that I may love you, sweet!

Harriet Prescott Spofford (1835–1921)

Harriet Prescott Spofford was born on April 3, 1835, in Calais, Maine, into a prestigious family tracing its roots to seventeenth-century settlers. Historically, the Prescott males

---

BETROTHED
[2] Spoken by Antony to Cleopatra in Shakespeare's tragedy, Act IV.viii.13.

TWO SONNETS
[3] King Canute of England, Norway and Denmark (995?–1035).

distinguished themselves in many different capacities, including positions in the military, merchant shipping, and the church. The War of 1812, however, brought a major reversal in family fortunes, one that fell most heavily on the shoulders of Spofford's father, Joseph Newmarch Prescott, a lawyer and lumber merchant. Hoping to stave off ruin, Joseph Prescott left the East in 1849 to try his fortunes in California; Spofford's mother, Sarah Bridges Prescott, moved the remaining family to Newburyport, Massachusetts, to live with relatives. There Spofford attended the Putnam Free School for four years, followed by two years at the prestigious Pinkerton Academy in Derry, New Hampshire. At both schools, her bent for literature was recognized and encouraged.

Spofford began publishing in the late 1850s to help support her family. She attracted the interest of Thomas Wentworth Higginson, and with his assistance, her stories began appearing in prestigious Eastern periodicals. Higginson introduced Spofford into the charmed inner circle of Boston literary society. Once admitted, she developed close personal and professional relationships with many of the significant women writers of her day, including Celia Thaxter, Annie Fields, Gail Hamilton (Mary Abigail Dodge), and Rose Terry Cooke. Always a prolific writer, as well as an abundantly talented one, Spofford produced continuously for sixty years, working in all the popular genres from sketches to travel literature.

In 1865, Spofford married the lawyer and politician Richard S. Spofford, also from old New England stock. The marriage was an exceptionally good one. Fully his wife's intellectual peer, Richard Spofford not only admired her work but left her free to do it. She, conversely, loved him but did not make him her life. Together they purchased Deer-Island-in-the-Merrimack, and here, in the house they built, they provided a home for Spofford's family as well as Richard's sister and the orphaned children of friends. Richard Spofford died in 1888; Harriet lived another thirty-three years, ever active, ever productive, her one tragedy, other than Richard's death, the loss of their only child in infancy.

Although Spofford valued her poetry more highly than her stories, most of which she wrote to make money, contemporary scholars have reversed this valuation – in keeping with the modern taste for narrative structures. In Spofford's case, this has resulted in substantial loss. Spofford wrote a good deal of conventional poetry, certainly, but at her best, she is one of the most powerful poets of her period, with "Pomegranate-Flowers" unequivocally her strongest poetic work and among the most important women's poems the century produced.

Spofford's greatest strengths are all in this poem: the lushness, the passion, the deep concern for women and, above all, for women's creativity, the spectacular ability to handle language, and the wildness of her imagination – a wildness that led Emily Dickinson to say of one Spofford story ("Circumstance") that it was the only thing she had read that she did not believe she could have written herself (given Dickinson's thorough knowledge of Shakespeare, no small compliment even if meant to be taken as hyperbole).

Set in a seaport town, near the docks (Newburyport?), "Pomegranate-Flowers" tells the story of one day in the life of a young, unnamed seamstress. As her "daedal fingers" sew a wedding veil, the "glad girl" engages in an Oriental fantasy, focusing on the pomegranate flower that blooms on her garret window ledge – the gift of a long-departed lover.

To be fully appreciated, Spofford's poem must be read against the many "deserted women" poems that punctuate this anthology, including Dickinson's "I tend my flowers for thee" (339). It must also be read against Brooks's Oriental fantasy, Zóphiël, and against those poems in which other women poets, again including Dickinson, use the production of textiles (from spider webs to Belgian lace) as a metaphor for women's creativity. Finally, it must be read against that very long tradition in which women have served not as artists themselves but as the source of inspiration for men – as in Dickinson's bitter comment to

Thomas Wentworth Higginson on Maria Lowell, "You told me Mrs Lowell was Mr Lowell's 'inspiration.' What is inspiration?" (*Letters* 481).

In creating the image of a self-sufficient woman artist – a woman who draws her inspiration from her own, profoundly autoerotic, connection to femaleness, figured in the pomegranate flowers – Spofford appears to be answering Dickinson's question, before the question itself was asked. In doing so, she wrote one of the most important texts by a woman artist on the sources of her own creativity extant in American women's literature. Although not every woman artist is likely to concur with Spofford's vision, the vision itself is one feminist scholarship should not afford to ignore.

Primary Texts

"Pomegranate-Flowers," *Atlantic Monthly* 7 (May 1861): 573–9; *The Amber Gods and Other Stories*, 1863; "The Price," *Harper's New Monthly Magazine* 35 (October 1867): 664; *Poems*, 1882; *In Titian's Garden and Other Poems*, 1897.

Further Reading

Alfred Bendixen, ed., "Introduction," in *"The Amber Gods" and Other Stories*, New Brunswick, New Jersey: Rutgers University Press, 1989; Paula Bennett, "'Pomegranate-Flowers': The Phantasmic Productions of Late Nineteenth-Century Anglo-American Women Poets;" Anne Dalke: "'Circumstance' and the Creative Woman: Harriet Prescott Spofford," *Arizona Quarterly: A Journal of American Literature, Culture, and Theory* 41 (Spring 1985): 71–85; Robin Riley Fast, "Killing the Angel in Spofford's 'Desert Sands' and 'The South Breaker,'" *Legacy: A Journal of American Women Writers*, 11 (Spring 1994): 37–54.

from *Atlantic Monthly* (1861)

POMEGRANATE-FLOWERS

The street was narrow, close, and dark,
  And flanked with antique masonry,
The shelving eaves left for an ark
    But one long strip of summer sky.
    But one long line to bless the eye –   5
    The thin white cloud lay not so high,
    Only some brown bird, skimming nigh,
    From wings whence all the dew was dry
Shook down a dream of forest scents,
Of odorous blooms and sweet contents,   10
    Upon the weary passers-by.

Ah, few but haggard brows had part
  Below that street's uneven crown,
And there the murmurs of the mart
    Swarmed faint as hums of drowsy noon.   15
    With voices chiming in quaint tune
    From sun-soaked hulls long wharves adown,

The singing sailors rough and brown
Won far melodious renown,
Here, listening children ceasing play,   20
And mothers sad their well-a-way,
In this old breezy sea-board town.

Ablaze on distant banks she knew,
Spreading their bowls to catch the sun.
Magnificent Dutch tulips grew   25
With pompous color overrun.
By light and snow from heaven won
Their misty web azaleas spun;
Low lilies pale as any nun,
Their pensile[1] bells rang one by one;   30
And spicing all the summer air
Gold honeysuckles everywhere
Their trumpets blew in unison.

Than where blood-cored carnations stood
She fancied richer hues might be,   35
Scents rarer than the purple hood
Curled over in the fleur-de-lis.
Small skill in learned names had she,
Yet whatso wealth of land or sea
Had ever stored her memory,   40
She decked its varied imagery
Where, in the highest of the row
Upon a sill more white than snow,
She nourished a pomegranate-tree.

Some lover from a foreign clime,   45
Some roving gallant of the main,
Had brought it on a gay spring-time,
And told her of the nacar[2] stain
The thing would wear when bloomed again.
Therefore all garden growths in vain   50
Their glowing ranks swept through her brain,
The plant was knit by subtile chain
To all the balm of Southern zones,
The incenses of Eastern thrones,
The tinkling hem of Aaron's train.[3]   55

The almond shaking in the sun
On some high place ere day begin,

POMEGRANATE-FLOWERS
[1] *Pensile* hanging loosely, suspended.
[2] *Nacar* orange-red.

[3] As priests, Aaron and his sons ritually burned incense (1 Chronicles 23:13) and wore garments on which
were sewn golden bells so as to announce their comings
and goings (Exodus 31:33–5).

Where winds of myrrh and cinnamon
  Between the tossing plumes have been,
  It called before her, and its kin   60
  The fragrant savage balaustine[4]
  Grown from the ruined ravelin[5]
  That tawny leopards couch them in;
But this, if rolling in from seas
It only caught the salt-fumed breeze,   65
  Would have a grace they might not win.

And for the fruit that it should bring,
  One globe she pictured, bright and near,
Crimson, and throughly[6] perfuming
  All airs that brush its shining sphere.   70
  In its translucent atmosphere
  Afrite[7] and Princess reappear, –
  Through painted panes the scattered spear
  Of sunrise scarce so warm and clear, –
And pulped with such a golden juice,   75
Ambrosial, that one cannot choose
  But find the thought most sumptuous cheer.

Of all fair women she was queen,
  And all her beauty, late and soon,
O'ercame you like the mellow sheen   80
  Of some serene autumnal noon.
  Her presence like a sweetest tune
  Accorded all your thoughts in one.
  Than last year's alder-tufts in June
  Browner, yet lustrous as a moon   85
Her eyes glowed on you, and her hair
With such an air as princes wear
  She trimmed black-braided in a crown.

A perfect peace prepared her days,
  Few were her wants and small her care,   90
No weary thoughts perplexed her ways,
  She hardly knew if she were fair.
  Bent lightly at her needle there
  In that small room stair over stair,
  All fancies blithe and debonair   95
  She deftly wrought on fabrics rare,
All clustered moss, all drifting snow,

---

[1] *Balaustine* flower of the wild pomegranate.
[5] *Ravelin* a detached structure with two embankments.
[6] *Throughly* this appears to be a rather awkward coinage on Spofford's part for "all through."

[7] *Afrite* in Arabian mythology a powerful evil demon or monster.

All trailing vines, all flowers that blow,
   Her daedal[8] fingers laid them bare.

Still at the slowly spreading leaves   100
   She glanced up ever and anon,
If yet the shadow of the eaves
   Had paled the dark gloss they put on.
   But while her smile like sunlight shone,
   The life danced to such blossom blown   105
   That all the roses ever known,
   Blanche of Provence, Noisette, or Yonne,[9]
Wore no such tint as this pale streak
That damasked half the rounding cheek
   Of each bud great to bursting grown.   110

And when the perfect flower lay free,
   Like some great moth whose gorgeous wings
Fan o'er the husk unconsciously,
   Silken, in airy balancings, —
   She saw all gay dishevellings   115
   Of fairy flags, whose revellings
   Illumine night's enchanted rings.
   So royal red no blood of kings
She thought, and Summer in the room
Sealed her escutcheon on their bloom,   120
   In the glad girl's imaginings.

Now, said she, in the heart of the woods
   The sweet south-winds assert their power,
And blow apart the snowy snoods
   Of trilliums in their thrice-green bower.   125
   Now all the swamps are flushed with dower
   Of viscid pink, where, hour by hour,
   The bees swim amorous, and a shower
   Reddens the stream where cardinals tower.
Far lost in fern of fragrant stir   130
Her fancies roam, for unto her
   All Nature came in this one flower.

Sometimes she set it on the ledge
   That it might not be quite forlorn

---

8   *Daedal*   adjectival form of Daedalus, the mythological architect of the Cretan labyrinth in which the
Minotaur was confined. In later literature he comes to
stand for the archetypal artist or maker. Spofford's seamstress thus becomes a type for the artist also.

9   *Blanche of Provence. Noisette. Yonne*   names of individual species of roses, also evocative of Provençal ladies,
who served as the inspiration for troubadour poetry,
thus once again reinforcing the idea that the seamstress
is a figure for the artist and that the pomegranate flower
is the homoerotic-autoerotic source of her inspiration.

Of wind and sky, where o'er the edge,   135
   Some gaudy petal, slowly borne,
   Fluttered to earth in careless scorn,
   Caught, for a fallen piece of morn
   From kindling vapors loosely shorn,
   By urchins ragged and wayworn,   140
Who saw, high on the stone embossed,
A laughing face, a hand that tossed
   A prodigal spray just freshly torn.

What wizard hints across them fleet, –
   These heirs of all the town's thick sin,   145
Swift gypsies of the tortuous street,
   With childhood yet on cheek and chin!
   What voices dropping through the din
   An airy murmuring begin, –
   These floating flakes, so fine and thin,   150
   Were they and rock-laid earth akin?
Some woman of the gods was she,
The generous maiden in her glee?
   And did whole forests grow within?

A tissue rare as the hoar-frost,   155
   White as the mists spring dawns condemn,
The shadowy wrinkles round her lost,
   She wrought with branch and anadem,[10]
   Through the fine meshes netting them,
   Pomegranate-flower and leaf and stem.   160
   Dropping it o'er her gold-stitched hem,
Some duchess through the court should sail
Hazed in the cloud of this white veil,
   As when a rain-drop mists a gem.

Her tresses once when this was done,   165
   – Vanished the skein, the needle bare, –
She dressed with wreaths vermilion
   Bright as a trumpet's dazzling blare.
   Nor knew that in Queen Dido's[11] hair,
   Loading the Carthaginian air,   170
   Ancestral blossoms flamed as fair
   As any ever hanging there.
While o'er her cheek their scarlet gleam
Shot down a vivid varying beam,
   Like sunshine on a brown-bronzed pear.   175

And then the veil thrown over her,
   The vapor of the snowy lace

---

[10] *Anadem* a garland or filet.   [11] *Dido* in Virgil's *Aeneid*, the Queen of Carthage.

Fell downward, as the gossamer
   Tossed from the autumn winds' wild race
   Falls round some garden-statue's grace.   180
   Beneath, the blushes on her face
   Fled with the Naiad's shifting chase
   When flashing through a watery space.
And in the dusky mirror glanced
A splendid phantom, where there danced   185
   All brilliances in paler trace.

A spicery of sweet perfume,
   As if from regions rankly green
And these rich hoards of bud and bloom,
   Lay every waft of air between.   190
   Out of some heaven's unfancied screen
   The gorgeous vision seemed to lean.
   The Oriental kings have seen
   Less beauty in their daïs-queen,
And any limner's pencil then   195
Had drawn the eternal love of men,
   But twice Chance will not intervene.

For soon with scarce a loving sigh
   She lifts it off half unaware,
While through the clinging folds held high,   200
   Arachnean[12] in a silver snare
   Her rosy fingers nimbly fare,
   Till gathered square with dainty care.
   But still she leaves the flowery flare
   – Such as Dame Venus' self might wear –   205
Where first she placed them, since they blow
More bounteous color hanging so,
   And seem more native to the air.

Anon the mellow twilight came
   With breath of quiet gently freed   210
From sunset's felt but unseen flame.
   Then by her casement wheeled in speed
   Strange films, and half the wings indeed
   That steam in rainbows o'er the mead,
   Now magnified in mystery, lead   215
   Great revolutions to her heed.
And leaning out, the night o'erhead,
Wind-tossed in many a shining thread,
   Hung one long scarf of glittering brede.[13]

---

[12]   *Arachnean*   like Arachne's work (both the mytho-   [13]   *Brede*   archaic variant of braid.
logical figure and the spider).

Then as it drew its streamers there,   220
    And furled its sails to fill and flaunt
Along fresh firmaments of air
    When ancient morn renewed his chant, —
    She sighed in thinking on the plant
    Drooping so languidly aslant;   225
    Fancied some fierce noon's forest-haunt
    Where wild red things loll forth and pant,
Their golden ant[h]ers wave, and still
Sigh for a shower that shall distil
    The largess gracious nights do grant.   230

The oleanders in the South
    Drape gray hills with their rose, she thought,
The yellow-tasselled broom through drouth
    Bathing in half a heaven is caught.
    Jasmine and myrtle flowers are sought   235
    By winds that leave them fragrance-fraught.
    To them the wild bee's path is taught,
    The crystal spheres of rain are brought,
Beside them on some silent spray
The nightingales sing night away,   240
    The darkness wooes them in such sort.

But this, close shut beneath a roof,
    Knows not the night, the tranquil spell,
The stillness of the wildwood ouphe,[14]
    The magic dropped on moor and fell.   245
    No cool dew soothes its fiery shell,
    Nor any star, a red sardel,[15]
    Swings painted there as in a well.
    Dyed like a stream of muscadel[16]
No white-skinned snake coils in its cup   250
To drink its soul of sweetness up,
    A honeyed hermit in his cell.

No humming-bird in emerald coat,
    Shedding the light, and bearing fain
His ebon spear, while at his throat   255
    The ruby corselet sparkles plain,
    On wings of misty speed astain
    With amber lustres, hangs amain,
    And tireless hums his happy strain;
    Emperor of some primeval reign,   260

---

[14] *Ouphe* elf or goblin.
[15] *Sardel* from sard, a deep orange-red variety of chalcedony.

[16] *Muscadel* either a brown, red-yellow in hue, from the French *muscade*, or a printer's error for muscatel, a rich sweet wine made from muscat grapes. Possibly a play on both.

Over the ages sails to spill
The luscious juice of this, and thrill
   Its very heart with blissful pain.

As if the flowers had taken flight
   Or as the crusted gems should shoot   265
From hidden hollows, or as the light
   Had blossomed into prisms to flute
   Its secret that before was mute,
   Atoms where fire and tint dispute,
   No humming-birds here hunt their fruit.   270
   No burly bee with banded suit
Here dusts him, no full ray by stealth
Sifts through it stained with warmer wealth
   Where fair fierce butterflies salute.

Nor night nor day brings to my tree,   275
   She thought, the free air's choice extremes,
But yet it grows as joyfully
   And floods my chamber with its beams,
   So that some tropic land it seems
   Where oranges with ruddy gleams,   280
   And aloes, whose weird flowers the creams
   Of long rich centuries one deems,
Wave through the softness of the gloom, –
And these may blush a deeper bloom
   Because they gladden so my dreams.   285

The sudden street-lights in moresque[17]
   Broke through her tender murmuring,
And on her ceiling shades grotesque
   Reeled in a bacchanalian[18] swing.
   Then all things swam, and like a ring   290
   Of bubbles welling from a spring
   Breaking in deepest coloring
   Flower-spirits paid her minist'ring.
Sleep, fusing all her senses, soon
Fanned over her in drowsy rune[19]   295
   All night long a pomegranate wing,

---

[17] *Moresque* characteristic of Moorish art or architecture, North African.
[18] *Bacchanalian* orgiastic. From Bacchus, the Greek god of wine.

[19] *Rune* a poem or incantation of mysterious significance, especially in a magic charm.

from *Harper's New Monthly Magazine* (1867)

THE PRICE

I.

The velvet gloss of the purple chair
Deepened beneath her yellow hair;
Idly she folded and fluttered her fan,
Nor deigned a glance at the haughty man.

Soft was the robe she wore that night,   5
Softly her jewels shed their light;
In lace like the hoar-frost, fine and thin,
Rested the curve of her soft round chin.

Rich was the shadow of the room,
And warm the shifting fire-light's bloom   10
That lofty wall and ceiling sheathed,
Heavy the perfumed air she breathed.

The panel-picture, half descried,
Opened a summer country-side;
The statues in the ruddy gleam   15
Seemed happy spirits lost in dream.

From a tripod's crystal vase
Full-blown blossoms filled the place
With their fragrance and delight,
Floated forth in day's despite.   20

Sumptuous sense of costly cheer
Pervaded the bright atmosphere,
As if charmed walls had shut it in
From all the dark night's gusty din.

II.

The sad old year went out with rain,   25
The new year tapped upon the pane —
Tapped in a whirl of frozen snow,
And shrouded all the earth below.

Chill, as it silvered her casement o'er,
The pitiless wind blew over the moor,   30
Into the great black night o'erhead
The wild white storm forever fled.

Bitter, she knew, the stinging sleet
Far away on the moor-side beat —

Beat on a hillock hidden there,   35
And heaped on a broken heart's despair.

She shivered as though one touched the dead,
That grave-mound lay on her hope like lead;
Round her the light and the warmth of breath,
Round him the desolate dark of death.   40

Oh, if she lay in that silent tomb –
If she were wrapped in that rayless gloom –
If those dear arms but clasped her in
Out of the black night's storm and sin!

But here a creature bartered and sold,   45
Bound by the baseness of hard red gold,
Held by the master, whose gloating eyes
Hovered like hawks above their prize.

III.

He leaned his arm on the mantle there,
He looked at her with her shining hair,   50
With her drooping eyes and her rosy chin
And the dimples for smiles to gather in.

His from the dainty foot's slight tip
Up to the crimson of the lip –
His from the halo of the hair   55
To the white hand's magic in the air.

But never his the tender thought,
Not his the sigh with yearning fraught,
The conscious blush that flits and flies,
The lingering of impassioned eyes.   60

All her bearing seemed to say,
"I am yours. Bid me obey.
But the rebel in my soul
Spurns to answer your control!"

Of women she the peerless flower   65
So scornfully defied his power;
The smouldering anger burned his heart,
Then blazed and tore his lips apart.

IV.

"Madam," said he, "since you are mine,
Lift those eyes and let them shine.   70

Sometimes, when you hear me speak,
Let the smile impinge your cheek."

"When you bought me, Sir," said she,
"You bought and paid for simply me;
No one bargained for my smile –   75
'Twas not thought of all the while."

Said he, "Owe you naught beside –
Home, nor peace, where still hours glide?
Morn means sunshine, song, and dew –
Are not smiles a part of you?"   80

"Once, indeed, perhaps they were,"
She replied. "Now, should they stir,
Smiles would be, with all their blooms,
Like the funeral lamps in tombs."

"Though one shut you dungeon-deep   85
In his heart, awake, asleep –
Though he claim of you no more
Than the beggar at the door –"

But the lightnings of her eyes
More than swift and low replies,   90
Whose music hid the word they said
Sharper than an arrow-head,

Hushed and told him all was loss,
All his wealth but gilded dross;
Bars retain nor rubies buy   95
Love, whose light wings cleave the sky.

"Ah! 'tis well you stand away –
Fire and flint disturb my clay;
Else, although I am a slave,
Every day I dig your grave."   100

"Cruel words!" he answered her.
"Kinder eternal silence were.
Am I before you so unclean –
Easy to put a world between?"

"Nay," she said, "make no ado;   105
Be to me as I to you.
When I pass you mind no more
Than a shadow on the floor."

Ah! how fair th' unruffled face!
How complete the weary grace!   110
How remote the quiet tone —
She that should be all his own!

"See," he said, "I can not sue.
Never was I taught to woo.
Yet I love you, though you make   115
Heart and soul within me ache!"

She lifted both her snowy arms,
Loaded with his golden charms.
"If you love me, Sir," said she,
"Take your chains and set me free!"   120

from *Harper's New Monthly Magazine* (1869)

MAGDALEN[20]

If any woman of us all,
    If any woman of the street,
Before the Lord should pause and fall,
    And with her long hair wipe his feet —

He whom with yearning hearts we love,   5
    And fain would see with human eyes
Around our living pathway move,
    And underneath our daily skies —

The Maker of the heavens and earth,
    The Lord of life, the Lord of death,   10
In whom the universe had birth,
    But breathing of our breath one breath —

If any woman of the street
    Should kneel, and with the lifted mesh
Of her long tresses wipe his feet,   15
    And with her kisses kiss their flesh —

How round that woman would we throng,
    How willingly would we clasp her hands
Fresh from that touch divine, and long
    To gather up the twice-blest strands!   20

MAGDALEN
[20]   Mary Magdalene, woman follower of Jesus and type
for the fallen woman. See "Judith" by Adah Isaacs
Menken.

How eagerly with her would change
 Our idle innocence, nor heed
Her shameful memories and strange,
 Could we but also claim that deed!

from *Harper's New Monthly Magazine* (1872)

REPRIEVE

Over the brink of the place I bent,
 And glanced in the darkling pool below –
Darkling with heavy hemlock shadows,
 And the gloom where sunbeams never go.

And a low, slow wind stirred the veiling branch   5
 With a ghastly twilight downward thrown,
And I saw a face, the face of a woman,
 A white dead·face I had thought my own!

from *Atlantic Monthly* (1880)

INTERMEZZO[21]

Sheer below us, as we stand to-night
 Leaning on the balustrade, the river
Flows in such still darkness that the stars,
 Painted on its bosom, scarcely quiver.

Far above us, through the violet depths,   5
 All those silent stars sweep in their places;
What a solemn shining flight they soar,
 From court to court of the eternal spaces!

Oh, how beautiful you are, my love!
 How your heart bounds with its tender yearning!   10
How upon your lips, your cheeks, your eyes,
 The fragrant flame of your full life is burning!

Yet alas, alas, the flame shall fall,
 Love and lover shall be dust and ashes,
While those stars move mercilessly on,   15
 And the tide still paints their awful flashes!

INTERMEZZO
[21] *Intermezzo* a brief entertainment between two acts
of a play.

Louise Chandler Moulton (1835–1908)

Born April 10, 1835, on a farm near Pomfret, Connecticut, Louise Chandler Moulton came from old Yankee Calvinist stock. Her well-to-do parents, Lucius Lemuel and Louisa Rebecca Clark Chandler, provided her with an excellent education. At the local school in Pomfret, her classmates included the celebrated American painter James McNeill Whistler and Edmund Clarence Stedman, the poet and anthologist. Both men remained friends for life. A verbally precocious child, Moulton edited her first book, *The Waverly Garland, a Present for all Seasons* in 1853, at fifteen. Two more books quickly followed, *The Book of the Boudoir; or a Memento of Friendship* (1853) and *This, That, and the Other* (1854). The latter volume, the first containing her own poems and sketches, purportedly sold 20,000 copies. The same year Moulton entered Emma Willard's Female Seminary in Troy, New York. One wonders what her classmates made of her.

After graduation from Emma Willard's, Moulton married William Moulton, editor and publisher of *The True Flag*, a Boston literary journal. The couple settled in Boston, and her husband introduced Moulton into the upper echelons of Boston literary society. Visitors to their home at 28 Rutland Square included some of the brightest luminaries of the era: Whittier, Longfellow, Holmes, and Emerson, among them. Moulton had one daughter, Florence, and a son who died in infancy.

Between 1860 and 1870, Moulton published very little. But in 1870, she accepted a post as the Boston literary correspondent for the *New York Tribune*. At the same time she began submitting poems and stories to the major periodicals – *Atlantic Monthly, Harper's, Galaxy*, etc. In 1877, she met with gratifying social and literary success in London, where her newly published volume, *Swallow-Flights*, elicited the inevitable comparisons to Mrs Browning and Christina Rossetti.

Thereafter, Moulton split her life between England and the United States, hosting a salon in Boston for six months of the year and summering in Euston Square, London, for the remainder. By the end of the 1870s, she was a full-fledged professional literary figure, with a remarkable set of connections on both sides of the Atlantic. Through the vigorous application of her pen, she maintained this position until her death in 1908, leaving behind an invaluable treasure of correspondence with most of the major literary figures of the *fin de siècle*. Not just in her assiduous correspondence but in her notorious flamboyance (her genius was for graveyard poetry and she acted the part), she could be viewed as an early prototype for Marianne Moore.

Stylistically as well as in lifestyle, Moulton ranks, in fact, among transition figures. Her juvenilia came out of the sentimental tradition of keepsake books and memorabilia, but in her mature poetry craft, not sentiment, is paramount – this despite the (playful) morbidity of her themes. She delighted in writing in a variety of difficult verse forms – rondels, sonnets, triolets, etc. – and her emphasis was on the word. Indeed, as she lamented, her thematic range was exceedingly narrow, being largely confined to love and death. But what she said, she said (or tried to say) well, in a clean, lucid, uncluttered style that sounds very modern next to the work of some of her stronger and more complex contemporaries, Spofford and Piatt, for example. In a way quite unlike theirs, one hears in her voice the twentieth century calling. It is no accident that she is credited with introducing the pre-Raphaelites and the Symbolists to the States. Like them, in her lifestyle and in her art, she is a forerunner of literary movements to come.

Primary Texts

Evaline, Madelon, and Other Poems, 1861; *Swallow-Flights*, 1877; *Poems*, 1882; *In the Garden of Dreams*, 1891; *At the Wind's Will*, 1900; *Poems and Sonnets of Louise Chandler Moulton*, ed. Harriet Prescott Spofford, 1908.

Further Reading

Harriet P. Spofford, ed., *Our Famous Women: An Authorized Record of their Lives*, 1884; *A Little Book of Friends*, Boston: Little, Brown, 1916; Lilian Whiting, *Louise Chandler Moulton, Poet and Friend*, Boston: Little, Brown, 1910.

from *In the Garden of Dreams* (1891)

A GIRL'S FUNERAL IN MILAN

There in the strange old gilded hearse
    With a mound of paper-flowers on her breast,
Her life being over, for better or worse,
    They bore her on to her final rest.

And the women followed her, two by two,   5
    And talked of how young she was to die;
And the cold drops drenched them through and through,
    As under the pitiless, frowning sky

On they marched in the drizzling rain
    To the little old church in the Milan square,   10
Where the choir-boys chanted with shrill refrain,
    And the toothless Padre muttered his prayer;

Then straight to the waiting grave they went;
    And the rain rained on, and the wind was still;
Since, all her treasure of life being spent,   15
    It was time Death had of the girl his will.

And they left her there with the rain and the wind,
    Glad, I think, to have come to the end;
For the grave folds close, and the sod is kind,
    And thus do the friendless find a friend.   20

LAUS VENERIS

A Picture by Burne Jones[1]

Pallid with too much longing,
    White with passion and prayer,

LAUS VENERIS

[1] *Laus Veneris* Latin for "In Praise of Venus." Moulton alternatively titled this poem, "The Venus of Burne Jones," after a work by the pre-Raphaelite artist, Edward Burne-Jones (1833–98).

Goddess of love and beauty,
   She sits in the picture there, –

Sits with her dark eyes seeking   5
   Something more subtle still
Than the old delights of loving
   Her measureless days to fill.

She has loved and been loved so often
   In her long, immortal years,   10
That she tires of the worn-out rapture,
   Sickens of hopes and fears.

No joys or sorrows move her,
   Done with her ancient pride;
For her head she found too heavy   15
   The crown she has cast aside.

Clothed in her scarlet splendor,
   Bright with her glory of hair,
Sad that she is not mortal, –
   Eternally sad and fair,   20

Longing for joys she knows not,
   Athirst with a vain desire,
There she sits in the picture,
   Daughter of foam and fire.[2]

WHEN DAY WAS DONE

For L. W.

The clouds that watched in the west have fled;
   The sun has set and the moon is high;
And nothing is left of the day that is dead
   Save a fair white ghost in the eastern sky.

While the day was dying we knelt and yearned,   5
   And hoped and prayed till its last breath died;
But since to a radiant ghost it has turned,
   Shall we rest with that white grace satisfied?

The fair ghost smiles with a pale, cold smile,
   As mocking as life and as hopeless as death –   10
Shall passionless beauty like this beguile?
   Who loves a ghost without feeling or breath?

---

[2] In Greek mythology Venus (Aphrodite) is said to have been born of the sea foam that arose when Uranus's testicles hit the water, after the god was mutilated by his son, Kronos.

I remember a maiden as fair to see,
  Who once was alive, with a heart like June;
She died, but her spirit wanders free,   15
  And charms men's souls to the old mad tune.

Warm she was, in her life's glad day, –
  Warm and fair, and faithful and sweet;
A man might have thrown a kingdom away
  To kneel and love at her girlish feet.   20

But the night came down, and her day was done;
  Hoping and dreaming were over for aye;
And then her career as a ghost was begun –
  Cold she shone, like the moon on high.

For maiden or moon shall a live man yearn?   25
  Shall a breathing man love a ghost without breath?
Shine, moon, and chill us, you cannot burn;
  Go home, Girl-Ghost, to your kingdom of death.

A PARABLE[3]

I longed for rest and, some one spoke me fair,
  And proffered goodly rooms wherein to dwell,
  Hung round with tapestries, and garnished well,
That I might take mine ease and pleasure there;
And there I sought a refuge from despair,   5
  A joy that should my life's long gloom dispel;
  But ominously through those halls there fell
Strange sounds, as of old music in the air.

As day went down, the music grew apace,
  And in the moonlight saw I, white and cold,   10
A presence radiant in the radiant space,
  With smiling lips that never had grown old;
  And then I knew the secret none had told,
And shivered there, an alien in that place.

LOVE'S GHOST

Is Love at end? How did he go?
His coming was full sweet, I know;
  But when he went he slipped away
  And never paused to say good-day –
How could the traitor leave me so?   5

A PARABLE
[3] This poem is the initial poem in a sonnet sequence
entitled "His Second Wife Speaks."

There 's something in the summer, though,
That brings the old time back, and lo!
   This phantom that would bar my way
      Is dead Love's ghost.

His footfall is as soft as snow,   10
And in his path the lilies blow;
   He quenches the just-kindled ray
   With which I fain would light my way,
And bids me newer joys forego,
      This tyrant ghost.   15

THE SHADOW DANCE

She sees her image in the glass, –
   How fair a thing to gaze upon!
   She lingers while the moments run,
With happy thoughts that come and pass,

Like winds across the meadow grass   5
   When the young June is just begun:
She sees her image in the glass, –
   How fair a thing to gaze upon!

What wealth of gold the skies amass!
   How glad are things 'neath the sun!   10
   How true the love her love has won!
She recks not that this hour will pass;
She sees her image in the glass.

from *Chap-Book* (1895)

WHERE THE NIGHT'S PALE ROSES BLOW

Ah, the place is wild and sweet
Where my darling went –
If I chase her flying feet,
When the day is spent,
Shall I find her as I go   5
Where the Night's pale roses blow?

from *At the Wind's Will* (1900)

WHEN YOU ARE DEAD

A Lover Speaks

When you are dead, my dainty dear,
   And buried 'neath the grass,

Will something of you linger near,
    And know me if I pass?

Last night you wore a wild, sweet rose,   5
    To match your sweet, wild grace –
The only flower on earth that grows
    I liken to your face.

I would that I that rose had been,
    To bloom upon your breast!   10
One golden hour I should have seen –
    What matter for the rest?

To-day you will not grant my prayer,
    Or listen while I plead –
But when you dwell alone, down there,   15
    It may be you will heed;

And then your silent heart will stir
    With some divine, sweet thrill,
To know that I, your worshipper,
    Through death am faithful still;   20

And something of you, lingering near,
    May bless me if I pass –
When you are dead, my dainty dear,
    And buried 'neath the grass.

AT NIGHT'S HIGH NOON

Under the heavy sod she lies –
I saw them close her beautiful eyes –
She lies so still, and she lies so deep,
That all of them think she is fast asleep.

I, only, know at the night's high noon   5
She comes from the grave they made too soon:
I see the light of her cold, bright eyes,
As I see the stars in the wintry skies.

The scornful gleam of an old surprise
Is still alive in those wonderful eyes –   10
And the mocking lips are ripe and red,
Smiling, still, at the words I said.

She mocks me now, as she mocked me then: –
"Dead is dead," say the world of men –
But I know when the stars of midnight rise   15
She shines on me with her cold, bright eyes.

Sarah Morgan Bryan Piatt (1836–1919)

Born on a plantation outside Lexington, Kentucky, in 1836, Sarah Morgan Bryan Piatt came from Kentucky's bluest blood. Her father, Talbot Nelson Bryan, was a descendant of Morgan Bryan, who migrated west with Daniel Boone in the late 1700s. Equally prolific, the Boones and Bryans intermarried over a number of generations, making Boone, as Sarah notes in "The Grave at Frankfort," several times her "kinsman" through marriage. Piatt's mother, Mary Spiers, came from a less well-known but no less well-established Kentucky family of slave-holding plantation owners.

Piatt's mother died when she was eight, the first of many deaths that reverberate through her poetry. As was the custom, she and her two siblings were parceled out among relatives, Piatt and her younger sister, Ellen, going to their maternal grandmother's, on the latter's plantation near Lexington. (One of Piatt's poems, "A Child's Party," is set shortly after her arrival there.) After the grandmother's death, Piatt lived briefly with her father and new stepmother on their plantation in Versailles. When this arrangement failed, she was settled permanently on her father's sister, Aunt "Annie" Boone, in New Castle, Kentucky. Piatt's only constant through all these changes was her mother's nurse – an elderly black slave woman. Piatt celebrates and mourns their relationship, with its double legacy of love and guilt, in a number of poems, but most notably in "The Black Princess."

While in New Castle, Piatt completed her formal education, graduating from Henry Female Seminary, in 1855, with a solid background in the classics and a more-than-passing acquaintance with the British romantics, above all Byron, whom she idolized. At about this time, she started writing poetry – yards of it – for local newspapers, bringing herself to the attention of George Prentice, the publisher of the *Louisville Journal*. Despite its volume (approximately one hundred and fifty poems), almost all of this early work is interesting only as juvenilia. In its youthful high spirits and romantic naiveté, it suggests that Sarah ("Sallie") Bryan still had a great deal to learn.

It was Prentice who introduced Piatt to her future husband, John James Piatt, a young Ohioan, also from a large pioneering family, and a poet of sorts. The two were joined in June of 1861 at Aunt Annie's house in New Castle and then moved North to Washington, D.C. just as the Civil War broke out. It was against the backdrop of this war in which she could not take sides without betraying someone or something, and in the crucible of a marriage that brought far more pain than joy (including the deaths of six of her eight children, three of them in childhood), that Sarah Piatt the poet was formed.

After Emily Dickinson, Piatt is arguably the most difficult and, at the same time, most rewarding woman poet writing in America in the course of the century. In terms that seem uncannily apt for Dickinson herself, one reviewer describes Piatt's poetry as "wayward, abrupt, enigmatic . . . prolific in hints, and innuendoes, and questions it neglects to answer." She demands, he growls, "more intelligence than is possessed by one reader in a hundred." Within this reviewer's framework of values, this was not a compliment; but as a (hyperbolic) observation it is not that far off from being true.

Although she published prolifically throughout her life – twenty-seven of her poems appeared in the *Atlantic Monthly* alone – Piatt was, in fact, little liked. In an age that revered popular poets, she wrote poetry manifestly difficult to read and impossible to sing. In a period that wanted to view (good) women as angels, she repeatedly described herself as a snake. To a society that wanted to see itself as virtue incarnate – a land of innocent Adams or chivalrous knights of the Lost Cause – she brought the mirror of war-wasted death, urban poverty and homelessness, and endemic bourgeois corruption. To a people who saw themselves as Christians, she brought Christ's words. She had, her reviewers mourned, gone the way of the Brownings, both Robert with his rough meters and twisted syntax, and Elizabeth with her intellectualism, feminism, and high-minded social zeal. This time the inevitable comparison to presumptively superior British poets was not meant as praise. Nor was it ungrounded.

The sources of Piatt's difficulty are manifold, deriving as much from what she says as the sometimes tortured way she says it. Like her life, her poetry is everywhere and always bisected temporally by the war. On the one hand there was the ante-bellum (Southern) past, a childhood "fairyland" of myth and romance which, as she says in one poem, hid "snakes in its bright sands" ("A Hundred Years Ago"). On the other was the post-bellum North, a nightmare of industrial pollution and urban poverty where, according to another poem, the homeless died of exposure in full view of those well-off enough to help them but too indifferent to care ("A Neighborhood Incident"). Within both these geo-temporal locations she was alienated. Not only were these worlds not what they claimed – or seemed – to be, but she herself was not what she seemed to be in either of them.

It was from this last bitter realization – that neither as Southern "belle" nor Northern bourgeois matron could she escape the consequences of her white skin and class privilege – that Piatt's most powerful and important poems come, including, among those published here, "Giving Back the Flower," "Shapes of a Soul," "A Hundred Years Ago," "Beatrice Cenci," "The Grave at Frankfort," "Over in Kentucky," "Mock Diamonds," "A Ghost at the Opera," "There was a Rose," "A Child's Party," and "The Palace-Burner," the last of which I take to be her signature poem. In these poems, as through much of her work, neither past nor present provide a refuge for the speaker since in both she must confront the reality of her own complicity in evil. Like an incest survivor, for whom restored memories of the past radically alter the present, the adult Piatt's understanding of the corruption on which her "fairytale" Southern childhood was based, ironizes all that comes after it, leaving her no stable point on which to stand.

And it may be for this reason that Piatt, to a degree unmatched by any other poet with whom I am familiar, relies on dialogue (and on "hints, and innuendoes, and questions [she] neglects to answer"), when writing. Unlike most of her nineteenth-century poet peers, Piatt rarely preaches, "His Mother's Way" being a striking exception. Rooting her poetry in the social world, she mediates her themes through dialogue instead, letting the moments she depicts stand as they are, for readers to do with as they may. Like Dickinson's poetry, therefore, Piatt's demands that one interact with it to read it at all. In some poems, such as "Beatrice Cenci," this means working between the present moment's dialogue and the speaker's consciousness, which is locked in the multiple time frames of the past; in others, such as "Mock Diamonds," it means piecing the entire poem together from hints two people (in this case, a man and wife) drop in conversation.

Far from being the "sweet singer" that literary history has chosen to paint her as (see, for example, James B. Colvert's biography of her in *Notable American Women*), Sarah Piatt is one of the truly great singers of domestic and social infelicity – of wives who long for lovers from the dead, of women who lack the courage to act on their own political convictions, of husbands who are utterly indifferent to the social and personal misery around them, of children whose very games and stories inculcate in them the morbid and destructive values of the society in which they live. If I had to name a nineteenth-century author she was like, it would probably be Ibsen. But by that very token, she was, as noted earlier, not the kind of woman poet nineteenth-century audiences were likely to like. Although her broken style and rough meters helped prepare the public ear for Dickinson, and her urban settings, use of fragmentary dialogues, and ironic, even cynical, perspective helped prepare the way for modernists such as T. S. Eliot, she herself was forgotten. It is more than time for her poetry to receive the attention it deserves.

Primary Texts

The Nests at Washington and Other Poems, 1864; *A Woman's Poems*, 1871; *A Voyage to the Fortunate Isle and Other Poems*, 1874; *Poems in Company with Children*, 1877; *That New World and Other Poems*, 1877; *Dramatic Persons and Moods with Other New Poems*, 1880; *An Irish Garland*, 1885; *In Primrose Time*, 1886; *The Witch in the Glass*, 1889; *An Irish Wildflower*, 1891; *An Enchanted Castle*, 1893; *Pictures, Portraits, and People in Ireland*, 1893; *Child's World Ballads*, 1895.

Further Reading

Paula Bennett, " 'The Descent of the Angel': Interrogating Domestic Ideology in American Women's Poetry, 1858–1890;" "John James and Sarah Morgan Bryan Piatt," *Encyclopedia of American Poetry*; James B. Colvert, "Sarah Morgan Bryan Piatt," in Edward T. James et al., eds, *Notable American Women, 1607–1950*; Jean Allen Hanawalt, "A Biographical and Critical Study of J. J. and Sarah Morgan (Bryan) Piatt," Unpublished dissertation, University of Washington, 1981; Emily Stipes Watts, *The Poetry of American Women from 1632 to 1943*.

from *Galaxy* (1867)

GIVING BACK THE FLOWER

So, because you chose to follow me into the subtle sadness of night,
    And to stand in the half-set moon with the weird fall-light on your
        glimmering hair,
Till your presence hid all of the earth and all of the sky from my sight,
    And to give me a little scarlet bud, that was dying of frost, to wear,

Say, must you taunt me forever, forever? You looked at my hand and
    you knew   5
    That I was the slave of the Ring,[1] while you were as free as the wind
    is free.
When I saw your corpse in your coffin, I flung back your flower to you;
    It was all of yours that I ever had; you may keep it, and – keep
    from me.

Ah? so God is your witness. Has God, then, no world to look after
    but ours?

GIVING BACK THE FLOWER
[1] Her wedding ring.

May He not have been searching for that wild star, with trailing
        plumage, that flew   10
Far over a part of our darkness while we were there by the freezing
        flowers,
    Or else brightening some planet's luminous rings, instead of thinking
        of you?

Or, if He was near us at all, do you think that He would sit listening
        there
Because you sang "Hear me, Norma,"[2] to a woman in jewels and lace,
While, so close to us, down in another street, in the wet, unlighted air,   15
    There were children crying for bread and fire, and mothers who
        questioned His grace?
Or perhaps He had gone to the ghastly field where the fight had been
        that day,
    To number the bloody stabs that were there, to look at and judge
        the dead;
Or else to the place full of fever and moans where the wretched
        wounded lay;
    At least I do not believe that He cares to remember a word that you
        said.   20

So take back your flower, I tell you – of its sweetness I now have
        no need;
    Yes, take back your flower down into the stillness and mystery to keep;
When you wake I will take it, and God, then, perhaps will witness indeed,
    But go, now, and tell Death he must watch you, and not let you walk
        in your sleep.

SHAPES OF A SOUL

White with the starlight folded in its wings,
    And nestling timidly against your love,
At this soft time of hushed and glimmering things,
    You call my soul a dove, a snowy dove.

If I shall ask you in some shining hour,   5
    When bees and odors through the clear air pass,
You'll say my soul buds as a small flush'd flower,
    Far off, half hiding, in the old home-grass.

Ah, pretty names for pretty moods; and you,
    Who love me, such sweet shapes as these can see;   10

---

[2] Piatt is quoting loosely from the opera *Norma* (1832) by Vincenzo Bellini (1801–35). Presumably, like the Druidic heroine of the opera, who carries on a secret liaison with the Roman proconsul of Britain, the speaker has taken a lover from among the enemy. The meeting narrated in the poem occurs in Washington, D.C., where Piatt and her husband spent time during the Civil War. The lover in this poem also figures in a number of other Piatt poems; typically he has given her a flower and he dies of a chest wound in the war (see, for example, "The Grave at Frankfort" and "A Ghost at the Opera").

But, take it from its sphere of bloom and dew,
　　And where will then your bird or blossom be?

Could you but see it, by life's torrid light,
　　Crouch in its sands and glare with fire-red wrath,
My soul would seem a tiger, fierce and bright   15
　　Among the trembling passions in its path.

And, could you sometimes watch it coil and slide,
　　And drag its colors through the dust a while,
And hiss its poison under-foot, and hide,
　　My soul would seem a snake – ah, do not smile!   20

Yet fiercer forms and viler it can wear;
　　No matter, though, when these are of the Past,
If as a lamb in the Good Shepherd's care
　　By the still waters it lie down at last.[3]

from *Galaxy* (1870)

A HUNDRED YEARS AGO

You wrong that lovely time to smile and say
　　Sharp desolation shivered in the snow,
And bright sands nursed bright serpents, as to-day,
　　A hundred years ago.

The world was full of dew and very fair,   5
　　Before I saw it scarr'd and blacken'd so;
There was wide beauty and flush'd silence there,
　　A hundred years ago.

No child's sweet grave, with rose-buds torn away
　　By the most bitter winds the falls can blow,   10
Before my tears in freezing loneness lay
　　A hundred years ago.

No phantom stars, one night in every Spring,
　　Saw my faint hands, with pallor wavering slow,
Give back the glimmering fragment of a ring,   15
　　A hundred years ago.

I did not feel this dim far-trembling doubt
　　Of Christ's love in the sky, or man's below,

SHAPES OF A SOUL
[3] Piatt's point is not that after death her sins will be
forgiven but that the speaker's interlocutor (presumably
her husband) will get what he wants (an "angel-wife")
only when she is dead. (That is, she is mocking the
concept of "True Womanhood" inscribed in texts such
as Oakes Smith's "The Sinless Child.")

And hold my heart to keep one Terror out,
   A hundred years ago.   20

The shadow Life may wither from the grass,
   Back to God's hand the unresting seas may flow;
But what shall take me where I dream I was
   A hundred years ago?

Ah, would I care to look beyond the shine   25
   Of this weird-setting moon, if I could know
The peace that made my nothingness divine
   A hundred years ago?

from *Overland Monthly* (1871)

BEATRICE CENCI[4]

(In a City Shop-window)

Out of low light an exquisite, faint face
   Suddenly started. Goldenness of hair,
A South-look of sweet, sorrowful eyes, a trace
   Of prison paleness – what if these were there
When Guido's hand could never reach the grace   5
   That glimmered on me from the Italian air –
Fairness so fierce, or fierceness half so fair?

"Is it some Actress?" a slight school-boy said.
Some Actress? Yes. —
               The curtain rolled away,   10
Dusty and dim. The scene – among the dead –
   In some weird, gloomy, pillared palace lay;
The Tragedy, which we have brokenly read,
   With its two hundred ghastly years was gray:
None dared applaud with flowers her shadowy way –   15
Yet, ah! how bitterly well she seemed to play!

– Hush! for a child's quick murmur breaks the charm
   Of terror that was winding round me so.

BEATRICE CENCI
[1] This is among the most complex, multi-layered and difficult poems that Piatt wrote. Briefly, the poem turns on a quadruple reference to "Beatrice Cenci:" (1) Beatrice Cenci (1577–99), the historical personage, daughter of Francesco Cenci (1549–98). With the aid of her brothers, and possibly a lover, she murdered her father after he imprisoned her and her stepmother in a tower. Although it was popularly believed that he incested her, she and her fellow conspirators were put to death; (2) the famed portrait, possibly by Guido Reni, said to be Beatrice Cenci, which hangs in the Barberini Palace and was much copied in the nineteenth century. It is one of these copies that the speakers in the poem view in the store window; (3) Beatrice Cenci, the heroine of Percy Bysshe Shelley's verse drama, *The Cencis* (1819); and (4) an imagined actress who plays Beatrice Cenci's role in the drama. The speaker identifies so strongly with the latter (the woman who "played" Beatrice Cenci's "role") that she begins hallucinating her own presence on the stage. Only her child's question recalls her to "reality."

And, at the white touch of a pretty arm,
   Darkness and Death and Agony crouch low   20
In old-time dungeons:
               "Tell me, (is it harm
To ask you?): is the picture real, though? –
And why the beautiful ladies all, you know,
Live so far-off, and die so long ago?"   25

from *Capital* (1872)

THE FUNERAL OF A DOLL

They used to call her Little Nell,[5]
   In memory of that lovely child
Whose story each had learned to tell.
   She too was slight and still and mild,
   Blue-eyed and sweet; she always smiled,   5
And never troubled any one
Until her pretty life was done.
And so they toll'd a tiny bell,
   That made a wailing fine and faint,
As fairies sing, and all was well.   10
   Then she became a waxen saint.

Her funeral it was small and sad.
   Some birds sang bird-hymns in the air.
The humming bee seem'd hardly glad,
   Spite of the honey every-where.   15
   The very sunshine seem'd to wear
Some thought of death, caught in its gold,
That made it waver wan and cold.
Then, with what broken voice he had,
   The Preacher slowly murmur'd on   20
(With many warnings to the bad)
   The virtues of the Doll now gone.

A paper coffin rosily-lined
   Had Little Nell. There, drest in white,
With buds about her she reclined,   25
   A very fair and piteous sight –
   Enough to make one sorry, quite.
And when at last the lid was shut
Under white flowers, I fancied — but

THE FUNERAL OF A DOLL
[5] Highly sentimentalized figure in Charles Dickens's novel *The Old Curiosity Shop* (1841). Like Dickens's other women of this type, Little Nell epitomizes many of the *Angel in the House*'s most salient traits – passivity, spirituality, goodness, etc. – making Piatt's reference to a "waxen saint" a bitter jibe.

No matter. When I heard the wind   30
   Scatter spring-rain that night across
The doll's wee grave, with tears half-blind
   One child's heart felt a grievous loss.

"It was a funeral, mamma. Oh,
   Poor Little Nell is dead, is dead.   35
How dark! – and do you hear it blow?
   She is afraid." And, as she said
These sobbing words, she laid her head
Between her hands and whisper'd: "Here
Her bed is made, the precious dear –   40
She cannot sleep in it, I know.
   And there is no one left to wear
Her pretty clothes. *Where did she go?*
   See, this poor ribbon tied her hair!"

THE GRAVE AT FRANKFORT[6]

I turned and threw my rose upon the mound
   Beneath whose grass my old, rude kinsman lies,
And thought had from his Dark and Bloody Ground[7]
   The blood secured in the shape of flowers to rise.

I left his dust to dew and dimness then,   5
   Who did not need the glitter of mock stars
To show his homely generalship[8] to men
   And light his shoulders through his troubled wars.

I passed his rustling wild-cane, reached the gate,
   And heard the city's noisy murmurings;   10
Forgot the simple hero of my State,
   Looked in the gaslight, thought of other things.[9]

Ah, that was many withered springs ago;[10]
   Yet once, last winter, in the whirl of snows,

THE GRAVE AT FRANKFORT

[6] Daniel Boone's (1735–1820) grave is located in Frankfort, Kentucky, the State capital.

[7] "Dark and bloody ground" was the preferred meaning attributed to the Indian name for "Kentucky" in the nineteenth century and served as a rather grim soubriquet for the State. Time, Piatt argues in this poem, gave it proof.

[8] Piatt's note: General Boone, backwoodsman of Kentucky – Byron.

Boone was never given an official military commission. The unstated comparison is to General Ulysses S. Grant (1822–85), 16th President of the United States and leader of the Union forces during the Civil War.

[9] One of the things Piatt's speaker is presumably thinking about is the difference between Kentucky-then (a wilderness) and Kentucky-now (a gas-lit "civilization").

[10] In this as in many other poems, Piatt is playing on multiple time frames: (1) the moment in which the poem itself is spoken; (2) the moment "many withered springs ago" when she threw down the rose; (3) the moment "last winter" when she hallucinated her vision of Boone in front of his cabin door; (4) and Boone's own mythological time. The rose ties the latter three times together, and in all likelihood is the same flower that she gives back to her former lover in "Giving Back the Flower." Viewed typologically, that is, Boone and his Indian "troubles," as the Indian wars were called, are an antetype which the Civil War fulfills, and Boone himself is an antetype of the speaker's soldier-lover, who ultimately will wear a bloody rose upon his chest.

A vague half-fever, or, for aught I know,   15
    A wish to touch the hand that gave my rose,

Showed me a hunter of the wooded West,
    With dog and gun, beside his cabin door;
And, in the strange fringed garments on his breast,
    I recognized at once the rose he wore!   20

MOCK DIAMONDS

(At the Seaside)

The handsome man there with the scar? —[11]
    (Who bow'd to me? Yes, slightly) —
A ghastly favor of the War,
    Nor does he wear it lightly.

Such brigand-looking men as these   5
    Might hide behind a dagger
In — ah, "the fellow, if I please,
    With the low Southern swagger?

"One of the doubtful chivalry,
    The midnight-vengeance meetings,   10
Who sends, from ghostly company,
    Such fearful queer-spell'd greetings!"

No — but a soldier late to throw
    (I see not where the harm is)
Lost Cause and Conquer'd Flag below   15
    The dust of Northern armies.

What more? Before the South laid down
    Her insolent false glory,
He was, at this fair seaside town,
    The hero of — a story.   20

And painted Beauty scheming through
    The glare of gilded station,
Long'd for the orange flowers — that grew
    Upon his rich plantation.

MOCK DIAMONDS

[11] The speaker is echoing a question someone (her husband, as it turns out) asks her. They are at a "fair seaside town" (probably a South Carolina resort) and he is interrogating her about other vacationers, some of whom he thinks may have been her lovers prior to their marriage. Of the first (the man with the scar) she says she only knew him "slightly." Of the second, "the fellow . . . with the low Southern swagger," she admits to having had a relationship but one broken off by his subsequent pursuit of another woman (an heiress). Both the former lover, who for all his air of chivalry ends up a guerrilla raider in the Confederate forces, and the "heiress," who turned out not to have any money, are the "mock diamonds" of the poem's title.

I knew him then? Well, he was young   25
    And I was – what he thought me;
And there were kisses hidden among
    The thin bud-scents he brought me.

One night I saw a stranger here, –
    "An heiress, you must know her,"   30
His mother whisper'd, sliding near.
    Perhaps my heart beat lower.

The band play'd on, the hours declined,
    His eyes looked tired and dreamy;
I knew her diamonds flash'd him blind –   35
    He could no longer see me.

Leave your sweet jealousy unsaid:
    Your bright child's fading mother
And that guerrilla from – the dead?
    Are nothing to each other.   40

He rose before me on the sand
    Through that damp sky's vague glimmer,
With shadows in his shadow, and
    All the dim sea grew dimmer.

He spoke? He laughed? Men hear of men   45
    Such words, such laughter never.
He said? *"She wore Mock-Diamonds"* – then,
    Pass'd to the Past forever.

from *Independent* (1872)

OVER IN KENTUCKY

"This is the smokiest city in the world,"[12]
    A slight voice, wise and weary, said, "I know.
My sash is tied, and if my hair was curled
    I'd like to have my prettiest hat and go
There where some violets had to stay, you said,   5
Before your torn-up butterflies were dead –
            Over in Kentucky."

OVER IN KENTUCKY
[12] This line is spoken by the speaker's young daughter. The bulk of the poem is spoken by the child's mother, a former Kentuckian now living across the Ohio river in the Cincinnati area, which, by the 1870s, had become thoroughly polluted with coal dust. As in "The Grave at Frankfort," Piatt is playing on the gulf between real time (the modern city of industrialized pollution) and mythological time (fabled Kentucky, which hid its pollutions in old home grass).

Then one, whose half-sad face still wore the hue
  The North Star loved to light and linger on[13]
Before the war, looked slowly at me too,   10
  And darkly whispered: "What is gone is gone.
Yet, though it may be better to be free,
I'd rather have things as they used to be
      Over in Kentucky."

Perhaps I thought how fierce the master's hold,   15
  Spite of all armies, kept the slave within;
How leaden chains, when broken, turned to gold
  In empty cabins, where glad songs had been,
Before the Southern sword knew blood and rust,
Before wild cavalry sprang from the dust,   20
      Over in Kentucky.

Perhaps — but, since two eyes, half-full of tears,
  Half-full of sleep, would love to keep awake
With fairy pictures from my fairy years,
  I have a phantom pencil that can make   25
Shadows of moons, far back and faint, to rise
On dewier grass and in diviner skies,
      Over in Kentucky.

For yonder river, wider than the sea,
  Seems sometimes in the dusk a visible [moan][14]   30
Between two worlds — one fair, one dear to me.
  The fair has forms of ever-glimmering stone,
Weird-whispering ruin, graves where legends hide,
And lies in mist upon the charméd side,
      Over in Kentucky.   35

The dear has restless, dimpled, snowy hands,
  Yearning toward unshaped steel, unfancied wars,
Unbuilded cities, and unbroken lands;
  And something sweeter than the faded stars
And dim, dead dews of my lost romance found   40
In beauty that has vanished from the ground,
      Over in Kentucky.

THE BLACK PRINCESS

A True Fable of my old Kentucky Nurse

I knew a Princess: she was old,
  Crisp-haired, flat-featured, with a look

---

[13] Piatt's black nurse, who will reappear in "The Black Princess" and "A Child's Party."

[14] In the *Independent* this word is "moon," which appears to be a printer's error. In remaining versions of the poem, Piatt has "moan."

Such as no dainty pen of gold
    Would write of in a fairy book.

So bent she almost crouched, her face   5
    Was like the Sphinx's face, to me,
Touched with vast patience, desert grace,
    And lonesome, brooding mystery.

What wonder that a faith so strong
    As hers, so sorrowful, so still,   10
Should watch in bitter sands so long,
    Obedient to a burdening will!

This Princess was a slave – like one
    I read of in a painted tale;
Yet free enough to see the sun,   15
    And all the flowers, without a vail.

Not of the lamp, not of the ring,[15]
    The helpless, powerful slave was she;
But of a subtler, fiercer thing –
    She was the Slave of Slavery.   20

Court-lace nor jewels had she seen:
    She wore a precious smile, so rare
That at her side the whitest queen
    Were dark – her darkness was so fair.

Nothing of loveliest loveliness   25
    This strange, sad Princess seemed to lack;
Majestic with her calm distress
    She was, and beautiful, though black.

Black, but enchanted black, and shut
    In some vague giant's tower of air,   30
Built higher than her hope was.   But
    The true knight came and found her there.

The Knight of the Pale Horse,[16] he laid
    His shadowy lance against the spell
That hid her self: as if afraid,   35
    The cruel blackness shrank and fell.

Then, lifting slow her pleasant sleep,
    He took her with him through the night,

THE BLACK PRINCESS
[15] The slave of the lamp is the genie in the story of   [16] Death.
Aladdin; the slave of the ring is a married woman.

And swam a river cold and deep,[17]
And vanished up an awful hight.   40

And in her Father's house beyond,
    They gave her beauty, robe, and crown:
— On me, I think, far, faint, and fond,
    Her eyes to-day look, yearning, down.

THE PALACE-BURNER[18]

A Picture in a Newspaper

She has been burning palaces. "To see
    The sparks look pretty in the wind?"   Well, yes —
And something more.   But women brave as she
    Leave much for cowards, such as I to guess.

But this is old, so old that everything   5
    Is ashes here — the woman and the rest.
Two years are oh! so long.   Now you may bring
    Some newer pictures.   You like this one best?

You wish that you had lived in Paris then?
    You would have loved to burn a palace, too?   10
But they had guns in France, and Christian men
    Shot wicked little Communists, like you.

You would have burned the palace?   Just because
    You did not live in it yourself! Oh! why?
Have I not taught you to respect the laws?   15
    You would have burned the palace. Would not *I*?

Would I? Go to your play. Would I, indeed?
    I? Does the boy not know my soul to be
Languid and worldly, with a dainty need
    For light and music?   Yet he questions me.   20

Can he have seen my soul more near than I?
    Ah! in the dusk and distance sweet she seems,

---

[17]   Jordan. There is an echo here of the spiritual "Michael
Row the Boat Ashore."
THE PALACE-BURNER
[18]   A striking illustration of the execution of a *petroleuse*
– or "palace-burner," as the female members of the Paris
Commune were called – appeared in *Harper's Weekly*,
July 8, 1871. The principal speaker here is a bourgeois
mother, who is talking with her young son, probably
about this illustration. The Paris Commune (March 18–
May 28, 1871) was Europe's first experiment in com-
munism. Coming at the end of the Second Empire under
Louis Napoleon (see Chapman's translation of Hugo's
"Souvenir of the Night of the Fourth of December" in
Section II), it was an insurrectionary government led by
urban workers who, among other acts, burned down the
Tuileries palace. Over 17,000 men, women, and children were executed by government forces following a
three-month seige. The execution of the female commu-
nards, in particular, elicited outrage in the United States
and much pondering of women's roles in such affairs.

With lips to kiss away a baby's cry,
   Hands fit for flowers, and eyes for tears and dreams.

Can he have seen my soul?   And could she wear   25
   Such utter life upon a dying face,
Such unappealing, beautiful despair,
   Such garments – soon to be a shroud – with grace?

Has she a charm so calm that it could breathe
   In damp, low places till some frightened hour;   30
Then start, like a fair, subtle snake, and wreathe
   A stinging poison with a shadowy power?

Would *I* burn palaces?   The child has seen
   In this fierce creature of the Commune here,
So bright with bitterness and so serene,   35
   A being finer than my soul, I fear.

from *Atlantic Monthly* (1872)

THERE WAS A ROSE

"There was a Rose," she said,
   "Like other roses, perhaps, to you.
Nine years ago it was faint and red
   Away in the cold dark dew,
   On the dwarf bush where it grew.   5

"Never any rose before
   Was like that rose, very well I know;
Never another rose any more
   Will blow as that rose did blow,
   When the wet wind shook it so.   10

"'What do I want?' – Ah, what?
   Why, I want that rose, that wee one rose,
Only that rose.   And that rose is not
   Anywhere just now?   God knows
   Where all the old sweetness goes.   15

"I want that rose so much:
   I would take the world back there to the night
Where I saw it blush in the grass, to touch
   It once in that fair fall light,
   And only once, if I might.   20

"But a million marching men
   From the North and the South would arise?

And the dead – would have to die again?
And the women's widowed cries
Would trouble anew the skies?   25

"No matter.   I would not care?
Were it not better that this should be?
The sorrow of many, the many bear, –
Mine is too heavy for me.
And I want that rose, you see!"   30

from *Capital* (1873)

A GHOST AT THE OPERA

It was, I think, the Lover of the play:
    He, from stage-incantations, turned his head,
And one remember'd motion shook away
    The whole mock fairyland and raised the dead.

I, in an instant, saw the scenery change.   5
    Old trees before me by enchantment grew.
Late roses shivered, beautiful and strange.
    One red geranium scented all the dew.

A sudden comet flung its awful vail
    Around the frightened stars.   A sudden light   10
Stood, moon-shaped, in the East.   A sudden wail
    From troubled music smote the spectral night.

Then blue sweet shadows fell from flower-like eyes,
    And purplish darkness droop'd on careless hair,
And lips most lovely – ah, what empty sighs,   15
    Breathed to the air, for something less than air!

Oh, beauty such as no man ever wore
    In this wan world outside of Eden's shine,
Save he who vanished from the sun before
    Youth learn'd that youth itself was not divine!   20

I might have touch'd that fair and real ghost,
    He laugh'd so lightly, look'd so bright and brave –
So all unlike that thin and wavering host
    Who walk unquiet from the quiet grave.

Myself another ghost as vain and young,   25
    And nearer Heaven than now by years and years,
My heart, like some quick bird of morning, sung
    On fluttering wings above all dust and tears.

But some great lightning made a long red glare:
  Black-plumed and brigand-like I saw him stand –   30
What ghastly sights, what noises in the air!
  How sharp the sword seemed in his lifted hand!

He looked at me across the fading field.
  The South was in his blood, his soul, his face.
Imperious despair, too lost to yield,   35
  Gave a quick glory to a desperate grace.

I saw him fall.   I saw the deadly stain
  Upon his breast – he cared not what was won.
The ghost was in the land of ghosts again.
  The curtain fell, the phantom play was done.   40

from *Independent* (1873)

HER BLINDNESS IN GRIEF[19]

What if my soul is left to me?
Oh! sweeter than my soul was he.
  Its breast broods on a coffin lid;
Its empty eyes stare at the dust.
  Tears follow tears, for treasure hid   5
Forevermore from moth and rust.

The sky a shadow is; how much
I long for something I can touch!
  God is a silence: could I hear
Him whisper once, "Poor child," to me!   10
  God is a dream, a hope, a fear,
A vision – that the seraphs see.

"Woman, why weepest thou?"[20] One said,
To His own mother, from the dead.
  If He should come to mock me now,   15
Here in my utter loneliness,
  And say to me, "Why weepest thou?"
I wonder would I weep the less.

Or, could I, through these endless tears,
Look high into the lovely spheres   20
  And see him there – my little child –

HER BLINDNESS IN GRIEF
[19] In a letter to E. C. Stedman dated August 20, 1873,
J. J. Piatt gives a vivid description of the death of Sarah's

four-day-old infant. It was her first such loss (many others
would follow) and she was inconsolable.
[20] John 20:15, spoken by Christ to Mary.

Nursed tenderly at Mary's breast,
   Would not my sorrow be as wild?
Christ help me. Who shall say the rest?

There is no comfort anywhere.   25
My baby's clothes, my baby's hair,
   My baby's grave are all I know.
What could have hurt my baby? Why,
   Why did he come; why did he go?
And shall I have him by and by?   30

Poor grave of mine, so strange, so small,
You cover all, you cover all!
   The flush of every flower, the dew,
The bird's old song, the heart's old trust,
   The star's fair light, the darkness, too,   35
Are hidden in your heavy dust.

Oh! but to kiss his little feet,
And say to them, "So sweet, so sweet,"
   I would give up whatever pain
(What else is there to give, I say?)   40
   This wide world holds. Again, again,
I yearn to follow him away.

My cry is but a human cry.
Who grieves for angels? Do they die?
   Oh! precious hands, as still as snows,   45
How your white fingers hold my heart!
   Yet keep your buried buds of rose,
Though earth and Heaven are far apart.

The grief is bitter.   Let me be.
He lies beneath that lonesome tree.   50
   I've heard the fierce rain beating there.
Night covers it with cold moonshine.
   Despair can only be despair.
God has his will. I have not mine.

from *Independent* (1874)

WE TWO

God's will is – the bud of the rose for your hair,
   The ring for your hand and the pearl for your breast;
God's will is – the mirror that makes you look fair.
   No wonder you whisper: "God's will is the best."

But what if God's will were the famine, the flood?   5
   And were God's will the coffin shut down in your face?
And were God's will the worm in the fold of the bud,
   Instead of the picture, the light, and the lace?

Were God's will the arrow that flieth by night,
   Were God's will the pestilence walking by day,[21]   10
The clod in the valley,[22] the rock on the hight –
   I fancy "God's will" would be harder to say.

God's will is – your own will. What honor have you
   For having your own will, awake or asleep?
Who praises the lily for keeping the dew,   15
   When the dew is so sweet for the lily to keep?

God's will unto me is not music or wine.
   With helpless reproaching, with desolate tears
God's will I resist, for God's will is divine;
   And I – shall be dust to the end of my years.   20

God's will is – not mine. Yet one night I shall lie
   Very still at his feet, where the stars may not shine.
"Lo! I am well pleased"[23] I shall hear from the sky;
   Because – it is God's will I do, and not mine.

from *Independent* (1880)

HIS MOTHER'S WAY[24]

"My Mamma just knows how to cry
   About an old glove or a ring,
Or even a stranger going by
   The gate, or – almost anything!

"She cried till both her eyes were red   5
   About *him*, too. (I saw her, though!)

WE TWO
[21] Psalm 91:5–6: "Thou shalt not be afraid for the terror by night, nor for the arrow that flieth by day, nor the pestilence that stalks in the darkness, nor the destruction that wastes at noonday."
[22] Job 21:33, "The clods of the valley are sweet to him," spoken by Job of the wicked who are nevertheless favored by God. The centrality of the Book of Job to this poem can not be overstressed, despite the fleetingness of this allusion. The "rock" which follows appears to be a more general allusion to the safety and security enjoyed by those in God's favor.

[23] Matthew 3:17, "and lo, a voice from heaven, saying, 'This is my beloved son, with whom I am well pleased.'" Given that these words are spoken by God at the baptism of Christ, it appears that Piatt, like Dickinson, may be adopting the role of the female Christus, along with that of a female Job; but, like Dickinson, if so, she does so ironically. Neither her suffering nor her death will lead her to accept God's will, even if in the end she must obey it. This is among Piatt's angriest poems.
HIS MOTHER'S WAY
[24] Piatt's note: Written after reading certain newspaper discussions as to the treatment of the "tramp."

And he was just a —, Papa said.
    (We have to call them that, you know.)

"She cried about the shabbiest shawl,
    Because it cost too much to buy;   10
But Papa cannot cry at all,
    For he's a man. And that is why!

"Why, if his coat was not right new,
    And if the yellow bird would die
That sings, and my white kitten too,   15
    Or even himself, *he* would not cry.

"He said that he would sleep to-night
    With both the pistols at his head,
Because that ragged fellow might
    Come back. That's what my Papa said!   20

"But Mamma goes and hides her face
    There in the curtains, and peeps out
At him, and almost spoils the lace.
    And he is what she cries about!

"She says he looks so cold, so cold,   25
    And has no pleasant place to stay!
Why can't he work? He is not old;
    His eyes are blue – they've not turned gray."

So the boy babbled. . . . Well, sweet sirs,
    Flushed with your office-fires, you write   30
You laugh down at such grief as hers;
    But are these women foolish quite?

I know. But, look you, there may be
    Stains sad as wayside dust, I say.
Upon your own white hands (ah, me!)   35
    No woman's tears can wash away.

One sees her baby's dimple hold
    More love than you can measure. . . . Then
Nights darken down on heads of gold
    Till wind and frost try wandering men!   40

But there are prisons made for such,
    Where the strong roof shuts out the snow;
And bread (that you would scorn to touch)
    Is served them there. I know, I know.

Ah! while you have your books, your ease,   45
    Your lamp-light leisure, jests, and wine,
Fierce outside whispers, if you please,
    Moan, each: "These things are also mine!"[25]

from *Independent* (1881)

A NEIGHBORHOOD INCIDENT

"Did you know, Mamma, that the man was dead
    In that pretty place, there under the hill?"
"So, with only the clouds to cover his head,
    He died down there in that old stone mill;
He died, in the wind and sleet, and – mark   5
This truth, fair sirs – in the dark.

"(Yes, a pretty place!) In the summer time,
    When the birds sing out of the leaves for joy,
And the blue wild morning-glories climb
    On the broken walls, it is pretty, my boy: 10
But not when the world around is snow
And the river is ice below.

"Men looked sometimes from the morning cars
    Toward the place where he lay in the winter sun,
And said, through the smoke of their dear cigars,   15
    That something really ought to be done.
Then talked of – the President, or the play,
Or the war – that was furthest away."

"Do you know when his father wanted some bread,
    One time, by the well there? Wasn't he old!   20
I mean that day when the blossoms were red
    On the cliffs, and it wasn't so very cold."
"And I gave him the little I well could spare
When I looked at his face and hair.

"Then we met him once – it was almost night –   25
    Out looking for berries among the briers,
So withered and weird, such a piteous sight,
    And gathering wood for their gypsy fires.
'No, the young man is no better. No, no.'
He would keep on saying, so low."   30

---

[25] Possibly a rendering of Isaiah 66:1–2, "All these things my hand has made, and so all these things are mine;" but also suggestive of Jesus of Nazareth's deep identification with the poor and outcast.

"But the women there would not work, they say."
    "Why, that is the story; but, if it be true,
There are other women, I think, to-day
    Who will not work, yet, their whole lives through,
All lovely things from the seas and lands   35
Drop into their idle hands.

"But they would not work, so their brother – and ours –
    Deserved to die in that desolate place?
Shall we send regrets and the usual flowers?
    Shall we stop and see the upbraiding face,   40
As it lies in the roofless room forlorn,
For the sake of a dead man's scorn?

"He did his best, as none will deny,
    At serving the Earth to pay for his breath;
So she gave him early (and why not, why?)   45
    The one thing merciful man call death.
Ah! gift that must be gracious indeed,
Since it leaves us nothing to need.

"As for us, sweet friends, let us dress and sleep,
    Let us praise our pictures and drink our wine. 50
Meanwhile, let us drive His starving sheep
    To our good Lord Christ, on the hights divine;
For the flowerless valleys are dim and drear,
And the winds right bitter, down here."

from *Wide-Awake* (1883)

A CHILD'S PARTY

Before my cheeks were fairly dry,
    I heard my dusky playmate say:[26]
"Well, now your mother's in the sky,
    And you can always have your way.

"Old Mistress[27] has to stay, you know,   5
    And read the Bible in her room.
Let's have a party! Will you, though?"
    Ah, well, the whole world was in bloom.

"A party would be fine, and yet –
    There's no one here I can invite."   10

A CHILD'S PARTY
[26] The speakers in this poem are a young white child   [27] The grandmother, who owns the plantation.
who has just lost her mother and her "dusky playmate,"
a slave child.

"Me and the children."   "You forget –"
"Oh, please, pretend that I am white."

I said, and think of it with shame,
   "Well, when it's over, you'll go back
There to the cabin all the same,   15
   And just remember you are black.

"I'll be the lady, for, you see,
   I'm pretty," I serenely said.
"The black folk say that you would be
   If – if your hair just wasn't red."   20

"I'm pretty anyhow, you know.
   I saw this morning that I was."
"Old Mistress says it's wicked, though,
   To keep on looking in the glass."

Our quarrel ended. At our feet   25
   A faint green blossoming carpet lay,
By some strange chance, divinely sweet,
   Just shaken on that gracious day.

Into the lonesome parlor we
   Glided, and from the shuddering wall   30
Bore, in its antique majesty,
   The gilded mirror dim and tall.

And then a woman, painted by –
   By Raphael,[28] for all I care!
From her unhappy place on high,   35
   Went with us to the outside air.

Next the quaint candlesticks we took.
   Their waxen tapers every one
We lighted, to see how they'd look; –
   A strange sight, surely, in the sun.   40

Then, with misgiving, we undid
   The secret closet by the stair; –
There, with patrician dust half-hid,
   My ancestors, in china, were.

(Hush, child, this splendid tale is true!)[29]   45
   Were one of these on earth to-day,

---

[28] Raphael Sanzio (1483–1520), Italian Renaissance painter, here used generically for a great artist. In a later version of the poem Piatt demotes him to "ignotus," that is, anonymous.

[29] In a letter to an admirer, written in 1886, Piatt verifies the basic authenticity of the incident described in this poem.

You'd know right well my blood was *blue*;
    You'd own I was not common clay.

There too, long hid from eyes of men,
    A shining sight we two did see.   50
Oh, there was solid silver then
    In this poor hollow world — ah me!

We spread the carpet. By a great
    Gray tree, we leant the mirror's glare,
While graven spoon and pictured plate   55
    Were wildly scattered here and there.

And then our table: — Thereon gleamed,
    Adorned with many an apple-bud,
Foam-frosted, dainty things that seemed
    Made of the most delicious mud.   60

Next came our dressing. As to that,
    I had the fairest shoes! (on each
Were four gold buttons) and a hat,
    And the plume the blushes of the peach.

But there was my dark, elfish guest   65
    Still standing shabby in her place.
How could I use her to show best
    My own transcendent bloom and grace?

"You'll be my grandmamma," I sighed
    After much thought, somewhat in fear.   70
She, joyous, to her sisters cried:
    "Call me Old Mistress!   do you hear?"

About that little slave's weird face
    And rude, round form, I fastened all
My grandmamma's most awful lace   75
    And grandmamma's most sacred shawl.

Then one last sorrow came to me:
    "I didn't think of it before,
But at a party there should be
    One gentleman, I guess, or more."   80

"There's uncle Sam, you might ask him."
    I looked, and, in an ancient chair,
Sat a bronze gray-beard, still and grim,
    On Sundays called Old Brother Blair.

Above a book his brows were bent.   85
   It was his pride as I had heard,
To study the New Testament
   (In which he could not spell one word).

"Oh, *he* is not a gentleman,"
   I said with my Caucasian scorn.   90
"He is," replied the African;
   "He is. He's quit a-plowing corn.

"He was so old they set him free.
   He preaches now, you ought to know.
I tell you, we are proud when he   95
   Eats dinner at our cabin, though."

"Well – ask him!"   Lo, he raised his head.
   His voice was shaken and severe:
"Here, sisters in the church," he said,
   "Here – for old Satan's sake, come here!   100

"That white child's done put on her best
   Silk bonnet. (It looks like a rose.)
And this black little imp is drest
   In all Old Mistress' finest clothes.

"Come, look! They've got the parlor glass,   105
   And all the silver, too. Come, look!
(Such plates as these, here on the grass!)"
   And Uncle Sam shut up his book.

The priestess of the eternal flame
   That warmed our Southern kitchen hearth[30]   110
Rushed out. The housemaid with her came
   Who swept the cobwebs from the earth.

Then there was one bent to the ground,
   Her hair than lilies not less white,
With a bright handkerchief was crowned: 115
   Her lovely face was weird as night.

I felt the flush of sudden pride,
   The others soon grew still with awe,

---

[30]   The cook. Piatt is playing on the subtle power relationships within the plantation household, wherein the white child has power by virtue of white skin privilege but the cook has power by virtue of her position at the top of the hierarchy for "house slaves," and "brother Blair" has the de facto power which the slave community itself has attributed to him as its spiritual leader. Insofar as the white child is a child and a guest on the plantation to boot, she is subordinate to the latter two adults. Only the support of her nurse, who claims equal or greater status to the cook and brother Blair, rescues her from this situation. (For a very different perspective that still asserts the black caretaker's household power, see L. Virginia French's "Mammy" [1869] in Section II.)

For, standing bravely at my side,
    My mother's nurse and mine, they saw.   120

"Who blamed my child?" she said. "It makes
    My heart ache when they trouble you.
Here's a whole basket full of cakes,
    And I'll come to the party too.". . . .

Tears made of dew were in my eyes   125
    These after-tears are made of brine.
No sweeter soul is in the skies
    Than hers, my mother's nurse and mine.

from *Atlantic Monthly* (1884)

THE CHRISTENING

In vain we broider cap and cloak, and fold
    The long robe, white and rare;
In vain we serve on dishes of red gold,
    Perhaps, the rich man's fare;
In vain we bid the fabled folk who bring   5
    All gifts the world holds sweet:
This one, forsooth, shall give the child to sing;
    To move like music this shall charm its feet;
    This help the cheek to blush, the heart to beat.

Unto the christening there shall surely come   10
    The Uninvited Guest,
The evil mother, weird and wise, with some
    Sad purpose in her breast.
Yes, and though every spinning-wheel be stilled
    In all the country round,   15
Behold, the prophecy must be fulfilled;
    The turret with the spindle will be found,
    And the white hand will reach and take the wound.

from *An Enchanted Castle* (1893)

IN THE ROUND TOWER AT CLOYNE[31]

{C. L. P., Ob. July 18, 1884}

They shivered lest the child should fall;
    He did not heed a whit.

IN THE ROUND TOWER AT CLOYNE

[31] Piatt wrote this elegy after the death of her sixth child, Louis, born 1874, in a boating accident in Cork Harbour, Ireland, where J. J. was serving as American consul. The Piatts had presumably visited the round

They knew it were as well to call
    To those who builded it.

"I want to climb it any way,   5
    And find out what is there!
There may be things — you know there may —
    Lost, in the dark somewhere."

He made a ladder of their fears
    For his light, eager feet;   10
It never, in its thousand years,
    Held anything so sweet.

The blue eyes peeped through dust and doubt,
    The small hands shook the Past;
"He'll find the Round Tower's secret out,"   15
    They, laughing, said at last.

The enchanted ivy, that had grown,
    As usual, in a night
Out of a legend, round the stone,
    He parted left and right.   20

And what the little climber heard
    And saw there, say who will,
Where Time sits brooding like a bird
    In that gray nest and still.

. . . About the Round Tower tears may fall;   25
    He does not heed a whit.
They know it were as well to call
    To those who builded it.

from *Child's World Ballads* (1895)

A SEA-GULL WOUNDED

Ah, foam-born, beautiful!³² So looked, I know,
    The Mother of Love, when her caressing arm

---

tower at Cloyne among many tourist sights in the area;
and it is to this location that she transfers Louis's death,
turning it into a quest for secret knowledge. The round
towers of Ireland were stone structures built in the first
century CE to provide protection against Viking raiders.
They are extremely difficult to climb.

A SEA-GULL WOUNDED
³² Aphrodite, born of the sea after Uranus's testicles
fell into it. Foam gathered about the dismembered parts
and Aphrodite emerged. In classical times, the white
dove was sacred to Aphrodite. Piatt has transferred this
association to the white seagull.

Felt the stung blood stain its immortal snow,
    After the fight there on the plain.[33] . . . What charm,
Of all the blind Greek gave to her, had she   5
That you have not – her sister of the sea?

And this young Diomed, who gave the wound
    With his first gun, if truth the bitter need
Be told (man's race is pitiless), looks round –
    His eye is used to blood – and sees you bleed.   10
Fly to Olympus, with your broken wing,
And Jove will laugh at you, fair, hapless thing!

from *Century* (1898)

A MISTAKE IN THE BIRD-MARKET

A Persian in the market-place[34]
    Longed for, and so took home, a wren.
Yes, his was but a common case;
    Such always are the ways of men!

Once his, the brown bird pleased him not;   5
    Almost he wished it would take wing.
He loosed the cage-door, and forgot
    The dark, unsinging, lonely thing.

Night came, and touched with wind and dew
    (Alone there in the dim moonshine)   10
A rose that at the window grew –
    And oh, that sudden song divine!

His children started from their sleep,
    Their Orient eyes with rapture lit;
Their pale young mother hid to weep;   15
    Their father did not care a whit.

He only heard the impassioned wail
    From that small prison overhead.
"My wren is but a nightingale!
    I'll wring its noisy throat!" he said.   20

---

[33] In the *Iliad*, Homer has Diomedes accidentally wound Aphrodite as she steps between him and Paris, whom she is protecting.

A MISTAKE IN THE BIRD-MARKET
[34] This poem turns on the Oriental fable, popular in the nineteenth century, of the nightingale that fell in love with a rose (s.v. Maria Gowen Brooks). The Persian father's rage at the bird appears to result from the bird's singing to the rose but not for him.

from *Harper's New Monthly Magazine* (1899)

HEART'S-EASE OVER HENRY HEINE[35]

(In Montmartre Cemetery at Paris)

Here, with your leaf or two of literal laurel,
    (That rustles somewhat dryly, I suppose,)
One finds you silenced by the usual quarrel;
    And – oh, the irony of it! – a rose
    Out of your bosom, Henry Heine, grows.   5

If one may only pray for you, my brother,
    (Heart of the dead, yours was a ghastly wrong!)
Christ rest you in this grave, who in that other,
    In Paris there, awake in death so long,
    Shouted the world back your derisive song.   10

Well, up here in the sun, to-day, with beauty
    So dark of promise it might break her glass,
I saw a street child, one whose piteous duty
    To offer heart's-ease to the world it was –
    And, for your sake, I could not let her pass.   15

So, here is heart's-ease for you, bitter lover,
    O German poet in the German Land
Well known![36] and with it tears enough to cover
    The dust of all your woes – you understand?
    Reach me, in taking it, that hollow hand.   20

Heart's-ease, and for a heart of dust and ashes?
    Heart's-ease, and does the dead man care a whit? . . .
Into the empty eyes the old scorn flashes:
    About the mocking mouth the slow smiles flit:
    The still voice laughs, "Here I've too much of it!"   25

from *Independent* (1910)

A NEW THANKSGIVING

For war, plague, pestilence, flood, famine, fire,
    For Christ discrowned, for false gods set on high;
For fools, whose hands must have their heart's desire,
    We thank Thee – in the darkness – and so die.

HEART'S-EASE OVER HENRY HEINE
[35] Heinrich Heine (1797–1856), German poet. Heart's-ease means both peace of mind and a certain kind of wallflower or pansy. Both meanings are played with in the poem.
[36] Piatt's note: Heine's expression regarding himself.

For shipwreck: Oh, the sob of strangling seas! –   5
  No matter. For the snake that charms the dove;
And (is it not the bitterest of all these?)
  We thank Thee – in our blind faith – even for Love.

For breaking hearts; for all that breaks the heart;
  For Death, the one thing after all the rest,   10
We thank Thee, O our Father! Thou who art,
  And wast, and shalt be – knowing these are best.

from *Independent* (1911)

A DAFFODIL[37]

Look! – all the vales of all the world are bright
  With you, as that of Enna[38] was of old!
One sees the flutter of her apron light,
  All overflowing with your dew-dim gold!

Oh, shining memory of Persephone![39]   5
  Loosed from the dark of Dis,[40] in this her time,
The sadder for its sweetness, does not she
  Out of her under-realm, rejoicing, climb?

And should the Shadow-King, in anger, miss
  His fair, young, wandering Queen, as well he might,   10
Then let her take the lord of Hades this –
  For his dark crown – this flower of living light!

Christine Rutledge/The Carolina Singers (fl. 1870)

Spirituelles (Unwritten Songs of South Carolina) sung by The Carolina Singers during their Campaigns in the North in 1872–73, written for the first time, from memory, by Christine Rutledge, is a fading blueish-green pamphlet, maybe three by four inches, now lodged in the library of the American Antiquarian Society in Worcester, Massachusetts. It is all that remains of the high hopes of two men and five women, former slaves, who went North after the war to raise money to support the freedmen's schools in South Carolina.

A DAFFODIL

[37] This is Piatt's last published poem. In its striking emphasis on light even in darkness it represents a rare moment of healing in her œuvre.

[38] A city in central Sicily thought by some to be the location where Hades abducted Persephone. Enna was an ancient cult center of Demeter and her daughter.

[39] Demeter's daughter, later, after her abduction, Queen of the Underworld.

[40] An alternative name for Hades, the place and the person.

South Carolina schools were in need of support – as much as they could get. Where, according to G. D. Pike, the historian of the Jubilee Singers, the New England States could boast an average of one college for every 982 people, South Carolina, which was settled at about the same time, had one college for every 7,840. Without colleges there could be no teachers, without teachers no schools. Without schools, the great mass of newly liberated African Americans living in the South were as chained to lives of desperation and misery as they had been before the emancipation proclamation presumably set them free.

So like other groups before and after them, the Carolina Singers followed the example of the Jubilee Singers of Fisk University and headed North. With them they brought one of the great legacies which the slaves would leave their descendants and United States culture as a whole, a legacy without a price or a price too great to contemplate – what W. E. B. DuBois calls their "sorrow songs." As Pike explains, when the former slaves went North to sing, these songs were all that their white audiences wanted to hear. In the way of such things, however, only one group, the Jubilee Singers, was able to maintain the level of media interest and audience attendance necessary to fulfill its dream. What happened to the Carolina Singers (and to so many other groups) is not recorded.

Just as staging these songs in concert halls for white audiences tamed their wildness and to some extent "de-Africanized," so putting them into print here inevitably falsifies them. These poems were not meant to be read, let alone read in isolation. They grew out of a total group experience that involved the daily activities of the slaves' lives: their moaning and chanting, their work songs and mourning songs. Nor were they meant to be "fixed." Typically, the spirituals were constructed on a call-and-response pattern, with the lead singer (presumably Rutledge in the case of the Carolina Singers) carrying the main burden of the lyrics and the rest of the singers coming in with the chorus or with exclamations or lines of their own. The lyrics themselves are infinitely malleable, leaving plenty of room for spontaneous elaboration – and for the recuperation of errors. There is nothing to say that what Rutledge wrote down is necessarily what she and her group sang on any given night.

Yet the basic ideas in these songs remained constant, if not necessarily the exact wording itself. The slaves sang of their lives, their hopes and expectations, their fears, their faith, their humor, and their anguish. And they passed their songs along from one community and generation to the next, creating and enhancing a slave culture which they shared in common with each other across time and location. Often their songs had more than one application – most famously in "Go Down Moses" with its compelling refrain, and "Steal Away," which could serve as a code song to signal a slave's departure for the flight North on the underground railroad. The spirituals became, that is, a way for the slaves in the fields or in their cabins to communicate in public yet privately to each other; and to that extent what was said in the lyrics was fully as important as the melodies themselves.

Finally, whether viewed in terms of their music or their lyrics, these songs are also an essential part of American culture. Their influence is pervasive in United States music and literature, whether one looks to the works of blacks or whites or, indeed, as in Dvořák's music, to the works of those from outside the United States who have sought to define the specifics of an American difference. Wholly indigenous to American experience, yet indelibly shaped by their creators' African origins, they are part of the cultural glue that holds this country in its very diversity together. Beyond the United States they are also part of the contribution that African Americans have made to black Atlantic culture as a whole.

Primary Text

Spirituelles (Unwritten Songs of South Carolina) sung by The Carolina Singers during their Campaigns in the North in 1872–73, transcribed by Christine Rutledge, Philadelphia: Henry L. Acker, [1873?].

Further Reading

Frederick Douglass, *Narrative of the Life of Frederick Douglass, written by himself*, 1845; W. E. B. DuBois, *The Soul of Black Folk*, 1903; Miles Mark Fisher, *Negro Slave Songs in the United States*, New York: Citadel Press, 1990; Eugene Genovese, *Roll, Jordan, Roll: The World the Slaves Made*, New York: Pantheon, 1974; Charles Gilroy, *The Black Atlantic: Modernity and Double Consciousness*, Cambridge, Massachusetts: Harvard University Press, 1993; G. D. Pike, *The Jubilee Singers and their Campaign for Twenty Thousand Dollars*, Boston: Lee and Shepard, 1873; M. O. Wallace, "Spirituals," in *The Oxford Companion to Women's Writing in the United States*, eds Cathy N. Davidson and Linda Wagner-Martin, New York, Oxford: Oxford University Press, 1995: 841–3.

from *Spirituelles (Unwritten Songs of South Carolina)* (1873?)

THE GOSPEL TRAIN

The Gospel train is coming,
 I hear it just at hand;
I hear the car wheel moving,
 And rumbling through the land.

CHORUS:

Get on board poor sinners,
Get on board poor sinners,
Get on board poor sinners,
Get on board poor sinners,
There's room for many more.

I hear the bell and whistle,   5
 She's coming round the curve;
She's playing all her steam and power,
 And straining every nerve.

Oh see the engine banner,
 She's heaving now in sight,   10
Her steam valves they are groaning;
 The pressure is so great.

We soon shall reach the station,
 Oh how we then shall sing,
With all the heavenly army,   15
 We'll make the welkin ring.

We'll shout o'er all our sorrows,
   And sing forever more;
With Christ and all his army,
   On that celestial shore.   20

No signal for another train,
   To follow on the line;
Oh sinner you're forever lost,
   If once you're left behind.

Oh see the Gospel banner,   25
   She's fluttering in the breeze;
She's sprinkled with the Saviour's blood,
   But still she floats with ease.

This is the christians banner,
   The motto new and old;   30
Salvation and repentance,
   Are burnished there in gold.

I think she'll make a little halt,
   And wood upon the line;
And give you all a chance to go,   35
   But she'll make her time.

She's nearing now the station
   Oh sinner don't be vain;
But come and get your ticket,
   And be ready for the train.   40

The fare is cheap and all can go,
   The rich and poor are there;
No second class on board the train,
   No difference in the fare.

She's coming around the mountain,   45
   By the rivers and the lake;
The Saviour he's on board the train,
   Controling steam and brake.

This train has ne'er run off the track,
   She's pressed through every land;   50
Millions and millions are on board,
   Oh come and join the band.

There are Moses, Noah, Abraham,
   And all the Prophets too.
Our friends in Christ are all on board.   55
   Oh what a heavenly crew.

266 CHRISTINE RUTLEDGE/THE CAROLINA SINGERS

STEAL AWAY

Steal away, steal away,
   Steal away to my Jesus,
Steal away, steal away,
   And I ha'n't got long to stay here.

CHORUS:

   Steal away, steal away,
      Steal away to my Jesus,
   Steal away, steal away,
      And I ha'n't got long to stay here.

This ain't the home, this haint the home,   5
   This ain't the home for the christians to live in,
This ain't the home, this haint the home,
   And I ain't got long to stay here.

He calls me by the lightning,
He calls me by the thunder,   10
He calls me by the midnight cry,
   And I ha'nt got long to stay here.

Take warning by the lightning,
Take warning by the thunders,
Take warning by the midnight cry,   15
   And I ha'nt got long to stay here.

The Lord Almighty bless you,
And if I never see you,
King Jesus promised to show me the way,
   And I hain't got long to stay here.   20

SOUL SAYS TO THE BODY

The soul says to the body,
   Body, where have you been so long?
Been a lying over yonder in the plantation grave,
   Waiting for the trumpet to sound.

CHORUS:

   Where have you been so long?
   Where have you been so long?
   Where have you been so long?
   Been awaiting for the trumpet to sound.

The sinner see the mote in the christian's eye,   5
   And can't see the beam in his own;

You better go and sweep around your own house door.
And let all the other ones alone.

CHORUS:

Hail to the Lamb of God!
Hail to the Lamb of God!
Hail to the Lamb of God!
That takes away the sin of the world.

WHERE SHALL I GO?

Where shall I go? where shall I go?
  Where shall I go?
To ease my trouble in the mind.

I ran to the rocks for a hiding place,
  To ease my trouble in the mind;   5
And the rocks cried out, no hiding place,
  To ease my trouble in the mind.

CHORUS:

  Where shall I go? where shall I go?
    Where shall I go?
  To ease my trouble in the mind.

Oh, what shall I do when judgment comes,
  To ease my trouble in the mind?
I'll run to the rocks for a hiding place,   10
  To ease my trouble in the mind.

I went down the hill and tried to pray,
  To ease my trouble in the mind;
I went down the hill and tried to pray,
  To ease my trouble in the mind.   15

I'll ask my Jesus before I die,
  To ease my trouble in the mind;
I'll ask my Jesus before I die,
  To ease my trouble in the mind.

GOING TO WRITE TO MASTER JESUS

  Going to write to Master Jesus,
    To send some valiant soldiers,
    To turn back Pharoah's [sic] army,
    Hallelu.

CHORUS:

> To turn back Pharoah's army,
>   Hallelu.

Old Pharoah's army is coming,   5
    Hallelu, Hallelu,
Old Pharoah's army is coming,
    Hallelu.

If you want your soul converted,
    You'd better be a praying,   10
To turn back Pharoah's army,
    Hallelu.

You say you are a soldier,
    Fighting for your Saviour,
To turn back Pharoah's army,   15
    Hallelu.

RISE CHRISTIANS

Rise Christians, rise, and let's go home,
    I don't want to stay here no longer;
Some people go to meeting for to laugh and talk,
They don't know nothing about the Christian walk;
    I don't want to stay here no longer.   5

CHORUS:

> Rise Christians, rise, and let's go home,
>   I don't want to stay here no longer.

My sister you had better mind how you walk on the cross,
    Your right foot will slip,
And your soul get lost,
    I don't want to stay here no longer

If religion was a thing that money could buy,   10
    The rich would live and the poor would die,
I don't want to stay here no longer;
    But thanks, my Lord, it is not so,
If the rich don't pray, to hell they'll go.

SHOUT, INDEPENDENT

> Shout independent, shout bold,
>   Master in the field;

Shout independent, shout bold,
    Master in the field.

My sister carry the news home,   5
    Master in the field;
My sister carry the news home,
    Master in the field.

CHORUS:

Shout independent, shout bold,
    Master in the field;
Shout independent, shout bold,
    Master in the field.

If there are any gospel abusers here,
    Master in the field;   10
If there are any gospel abusers here,
    Master in the field;

My leader carry the news home,
    Master in the field;
My leader carry the news home,   15
    Master in the field;

My mother carry the news home,
    Master in the field;
My mother carry the news home,
    Master in the field.   20

KEEP ME FROM SINKING DOWN

O Lord, O my Lord, O my good Lord,
    Keep me from sinking down.

I looked up yonder, and what did I see?
    Keep me from sinking down;
I see the angel beckoning me,   5
    Keep me from sinking down.

CHORUS:

O Lord, O my Lord, O my good Lord,
    Keep me from sinking down.

I tell you what I mean to do,
    Keep me from sinking down;

I mean to go to heaven too,
  Keep me from sinking down.   10

When I was a mourner just like you,
  Keep me from sinking down;
I mourned and mourned, till I got through,
  Keep me from sinking down.

O SINNER MAN

O sinner man, O sinner man,
  O sinner, O which way are you going?

O come back sinner, and don't go there,
  Which way are you going?
For hell is deep and dark, despair,   5
  O which way are you going?

O sinner man, O sinner man,
  O sinner, O which way are you going?

Though days be dark and nights be long,
  Which way are you going?   10
We'll shout and sing till we get home;
  O which way are you going?

T'was just about the break of day,
  Which way are you going?
My sin forgiven and my soul set free,   15
  O which way are you going?

SWING LOW SWEET CHARIOT

Swing low sweet chariot,
  Coming for to carry me home;
Swing low sweet chariot,
  Coming for to carry me home.

I looked over Jordan, and what did I see,   5
  Coming for to carry me home;
A band of angels coming after me,
  Coming for to carry me home.

CHORUS:

  Swing low sweet chariot,
  Coming for to carry me home;
  Swing low sweet chariot,
  Coming for to carry me home.

If you get there before I do,
    While on your journey home;   10
Tell all my friends I'm coming too,
    I'm on my journey home.

The brightest day, that ever I saw,
    While seeking for a home,
Was when Jesus washed my sins away,   15
    And told me of that home.

CHORUS:

    I am sometimes up and sometimes down,
        While on my journey home;
    But still my soul feels heavenly bound,
        While on my journey home.

ROLL JORDAN ROLL

Roll Jordan roll, roll Jordan roll,
I want to go to heaven when I die,
To hear when Jordan roll.

Oh preacher you ought to been there,
    Yes my Lord, you ought to;   5
You ought to been sitting in the kingdom,
    To hear when Jordan roll.

CHORUS:

    Roll Jordan roll, roll Jordan roll,
    You ought to been sitting in the kingdom,
    To hear when Jordan roll.

Oh brother you ought to been there,
    Yes my Lord, you ought to;
You ought to been sitting in the kingdom,   10
    To hear when Jordan roll.

My sisters you ought to been there,
    Yes my Lord, you ought to;
You ought to been sitting in the kingdom,
    To hear when Jordan roll.   15

Mourners you ought to been there,
    Yes my Lord, you ought to;
You ought to been sitting in the kingdom,
    To hear when Jordan roll.

Seekers you ought to been there,   20
    Yes my Lord, you ought to;
You ought to been sitting in the kingdom,
    To hear when Jordan roll.

No More Horn Blow Here

No more horn blow here,
There's no more horn blow here,
There's no more horn blow here,
Going down to judgment bar.

There's no more peck of corn here, &c.   5

No more drivers' lash here, &c.

No more pint of salt here, &c.

No more mistress' call here, &c.

No more masters' call here, &c.

Sweet Turtle Dove

Sweet turtle dove, sing so sweet,
Muddy the water so deep,
And I had little meeting in the morning;
For to hear Gabriel's trumpet sound.

CHORUS:

    Jerusalem morning, Jerusalem morning
    By the light don't you hear Gabriel
        trumpet in that morning.

Old brother Philip took his seat,   5
And he want all his members to follow him,
And he had a little meeting in the morning,
For to hear Gabriel trumpet sound.

Didn't My Lord Deliver Daniel

Didn't my Lord deliver Daniel,
    Deliver, deliver Daniel,
Dident my Lord deliver Daniel,
    And why not every man?

He delivered Daniel from the lions' den;   5
    And Jonah when swallowed by the whale;

And the Hebrew children from the fiery furnace.
And why not every man?

CHORUS:

Dident my Lord deliver Daniel,
    Deliver, deliver Daniel,
Dident my Lord deliver Daniel,
    And why not every man?

I put my foot on the gospel ship,
    And the ship it began to sail;   10
It land my soul on Canaan shore,
    And I never come back any more.

The wind blow west, and the wind blow east,
    And it blow like a Judgment day,
And every poor soul that never did pray,   15
    Will be glad to pray that day.

GO DOWN MOSES

When Israel was in Egypt's land,
    Let my people;
Oppressed so hard he could not stand,
    Let my people go.

CHORUS:

Go down Moses, way down in Egypt land,
Tell old Pharaoh to let my people go.

Thus says the Lord, bold Moses said,   5
    Let my people go;
If not, I'll smite your first-born dead,
    Let my people go.

No more shall they in bondage toil,
    Let my people go;   10
Let them come out with Egypt's spoil,
    Let my people go.

Oh it was a dark and dismal night,
    Let my people go;
When Moses led the Israelite,   15
    Let my people go.

You'll not get lost in the wilderness,
    Let my people go;

With a lighted candle in your breast,
  Let my people go.   20

The devil thought he had me fast,
  Let my people go.
But I broke his chain, and free at last,
  Let my people go.

I do believe without a doubt,   25
  Let my people go;
That the Christian has a right to shout,
  Let my people go.

I'll tell you what I like the best,
  Let my people go;   30
It is the shouting Methodist,
  Let my people go.

RESURRECTION MORNING

In the resurrection morning,
  We will see our Saviour coming,
And the sons of God a shouting,
  In the Kingdom of our Lord.

CHORUS:

  Are your lamps a 'burning,
  Are your lamps a 'burning,
  Are your lamps a 'burning,
  And your vessels filled with oil?

In the midst of persecutions   5
  Daniel kept the same position;
And he waited for the glory
  Till the dawning of the day.

  Are your garments pure, &c.
  And unspotted from this world[.]   10

In the midst of earth's dominion,
  Christ has promised us the kingdom,
It shall not be left to others,
  Nor shall ever be destroyed.

  It shall stand forever, &c.   15
  And the saints possess the land.

We are a band of strangers,
   Traveling through this world of danger,
But Jesus heads the army,
   And we will surely gain the day.   20

   We will gain the victory &c.
   And we'll lay our armor down.

Oh what a happy meeting,
   When salvation is completed,
And the sons of God shouting,   25
   In the kingdom of our Lord.

We'll receive our crowns in glory, &c.
And we'll rest forever more, &c.

Elizabeth Stuart Phelps (1844–1911)

Named Mary Gray at birth in 1844, Elizabeth Stuart Phelps came, as biographers like to note, from a family of writers. Both grandfathers, and her father, authored religious tracts. As an instructor in sacred rhetoric at the Andover Theological Seminary in Andover, Massachusetts, her father also wrote pedagogical works. Under the pseudonym, "H. Trusta," her mother, Elizabeth Stuart Phelps, published children's stories and a number of novels, including one international "best-seller," *The Sunny Side, or the Country Minister's Wife*, 1851. Worn out by family and work, Elizabeth Stuart Phelps, senior, died shortly after the birth of her second son. As an act of fealty, her daughter Mary, all of eight at the time, took her mother's name and with it, the first Elizabeth Stuart Phelps's odd blend of nascent feminism, literariness, and religiosity.

Unable to enter Andover Seminary (for men), Phelps went to Mrs Edward School for Young Ladies. Here she received an unusually rigorous education, covering mental philosophy, English literature, Latin, astronomy, physiology, mathematics, history, and chemistry; but not Greek or trigonometry. The latter were reserved for Andover males. Phelps resented the exclusions, setting a pattern of injustice-collecting that would later blossom into a life of advocacy, not just for women's issues but for any number of related reforms, from antivivisection to temperance. Her devotion to these causes, which stood at curious odds with her strict Calvinist upbringing and her powerful idealization of her father, does much to explain many of the anomalies of her career.

Phelps's first story appeared in *The Youth's Companion* when she was thirteen. In 1868, her first serious recognition as a mature writer came with "The Tenth of January" published in the *Atlantic Monthly*. Influenced by Rebecca Harding Davis's "Life in the Iron Mills" (1861), Phelps's story was based on the devastating 1860 fire at the Pemberton Mills in Lawrence, Massachusetts. Also in 1868, Phelps published *The Gates Ajar*, a phenomenally successful novel (80,000 copies sold in the United States, nearly 100,000 in Britain). With its concrete depiction of heaven, *The Gates Ajar* established Phelps as a popular religious writer able to meet the needs of a society no longer content to leave religion to the clergy. Three more "Gates" novels would follow. But so, in the Phelps way of doing things, would more reformist literature, culminating in *The Story of Avis* (1877), a chillingly explicit feminist protest novel, drawing on her mother's life.

In 1888, Phelps, a woman well versed in women's wrongs, surprised friends and family alike by marrying Herbert D. Ward, seventeen years her junior. In a Pygmalion-in-reverse scenario, she apparently dreamed of shaping him into an author. But if so, their differences in age, talent, and professional status doomed her fantasy from the start. Made independent by virtue of his wife's earnings, Herbert Ward went his way. Phelps, who was by this time a semi-invalid, remained at home, doing what she did best, writing and making money. A moral teacher at heart, Phelps did not abandon her podium or her pen until death silenced her in 1911.

As the author of both *The Gates Ajar*, one of the major popular novels of the post-bellum era, and *The Story of Avis*, among the few unequivocally feminist novels of the century, Phelps's fiction has not suffered from critical inattention, either in her own day or ours. Her poetry, on the other hand, has been roundly ignored, this despite the fact that her best poetry is better crafted and more tightly controlled, and at the same time more elusive, than either of her two best known novels.

Phelps's poetic range is slight and many of her poems suffer from the same disability as her fiction – they preach too much. But when she focuses on inner division, as in "Divided" or "The Twain of Her," she is dealing with material on which, perhaps, she knew she had no right to preach. Here, as in other strong poems, her language is clean, the rhythms chastened, and the poems themselves speak directly without shouting the reader down. In poems such as "The Stone Woman of Eastern Point," she shows herself capable of deep and respectful sympathy for another woman's choices and does not attempt to answer all the questions she asks. Subtlety was not Phelps's strong suit, but in these poems, she exhibits a surprising capacity for it, and, as in "New Neighbors," an even more surprising capacity to make quiet fun of herself.

Primary Texts

The Gates Ajar, 1868; *The Silent Partner*, 1871; *Poetic Studies*, 1875; *The Story of Avis*, 1877; *Songs of the Silent World and Other Poems*, 1885; *Chapters from a Life*, 1896.

Further Reading

Susan Coultrap-McQuin, *Doing Literary Business: American Women Writers in the Nineteenth Century*; Lori Duin Kelly, *The Life and Works of Elizabeth Stuart Phelps: Victorian Feminist Writer*, Troy, New York: Witson, 1983; Carol Farley Kessler, "A Literary Legacy: Elizabeth Stuart Phelps, Mother and Daughter," *Frontier: A Journal of Women Studies* 5 (Fall 1980): 28–33; Harriet Spofford, ed., *Our Famous Women: An Authorized Record of the Lives and Deeds of Distinguished American Women of Our Times*, 1884.

from *Poetic Studies* (1875)

DIVIDED

If an angel that I know
Should now enter, sliding low
Down the shaft of quiet moonlight that rests upon the floor;

And if she should stir and stand
    With a lily in her hand,   5
And that smile of treasured stillness that she wore.

    Should I, falling at her feet,
    Brush or kiss her garments sweet?
Would their lowest least white hem upon me unworthy, fall?
    Or would she guarded, stand,   10
    Drop the lily in my hand,
And go whispering as she vanished, "This is all"?

from *Sunday Afternoon* (1879)

THE ROOM'S WIDTH

I think if I should cross the room,
    Far as fear;
Should stand beside you like a thought —
    Touch you, Dear!

Like a fancy. To your sad heart   5
    It would seem
That my vision passed and prayed you,
    Or my dream.

Then you would look with lonely eyes —
    Lift your head —   10
And you would stir, and sigh, and say —
    "She is dead."

Baffled by death and love, I lean
    Through the gloom.
O Lord of life! am I forbid   15
    To cross the room?

from *Harper's New Monthly Magazine* (1879)

SONG

The fire-light listens on the floor
    To hear the wild winds blow.
Within, the bursting roses burn,
    Without, there slides the snow.

Across the flower I see the flake   5
    Pass, mirrored, mystic, slow.
Oh, blooms and storms must blush and freeze,
    While seasons come and go!

I lift the sash — and live, the gale
  Comes leaping to my call.   10
The rose is but a painted one
  That hangs upon the wall.

from *Harper's New Monthly Magazine* (1881)

GEORGE ELIOT: HER JURY[1]

A Lily rooted in a sacred soil,
Arrayed with those who neither spin nor toil;
Dinah, the preacher, through the purple air,
Forever in her gentle evening prayer
Shall plead for Her — what ear too deaf to hear? —   5
"As if she spoke to some one very near."

And he of storied Florence, whose great heart
Broke for its human error; wrapped apart,
And scorching in the swift, prophetic flame
Of passion for late holiness, and shame   10
Than untried glory grander, gladder, higher —
Deathless, for Her, he "testifies by fire."

A statue fair and firm on marble feet,
Womanhood's woman, Dorothea, sweet
As strength, and strong as tenderness, to make   15
A "struggle with the dark" for white light's sake,
Immortal stands, unanswered speaks. Shall they,
Of Her great hand the moulded, breathing clay,
Her fit, select, and proud survivors be? —
Possess the life eternal, and not *She*?   20

from *Songs of the Silent World and Other Poems* (1885)

NEW NEIGHBORS

Within the window's scant recess,
  Behind a pink geranium flower,
She sits and sews, and sews and sits,
  From patient hour to patient hour.

As woman-like as marble is,   5
  Or as a lovely death might be —

GEORGE ELIOT: HER JURY
[1]   Mary Ann Evans (1819–80), widely admired British novelist. Her adulterous relationship with George Henry Lewes was judged harshly on both sides of the Atlantic.

Each stanza of the poem is devoted to a well-known figure in one of Eliot's works: Dinah in *Scenes of Clerical Life* (1858); Daniel Deronda in *Daniel Deronda* (1876); and Dorothea in *Middlemarch* (1871–2).

A marble death condemned to make
A feint at life perpetually.

Wondering, I watch to pity her;
   Wandering, I go my restless ways;   10
Content, I think the untamed thoughts
   Of free and solitary days,

Until the mournful dusk begins
   To drop upon the quiet street,
Until, upon the pavement far,   15
   There falls the sound of coming feet:

A happy, hastening, ardent sound,
   Tender as kisses on the air –
Quick, as if touched by unseen lips
   Blushes the little statue there;   20

And woman-like as young life is,
   And woman-like as joy may be,
Tender with color, lithe with love,
   She starts, transfigured gloriously.

Superb in one transcendent glance –   25
   Her eyes, I see, are burning black –
My little neighbor, smiling, turns,
   And throws my unasked pity back.

I wonder, is it worth the while,
   To sit and sew from hour to hour –   30
To sit and sew with eyes of black,
   Behind a pink geranium flower?

WON

Oh, when I would have loved you, Dear,
The sun of winter hung more near;
Yet not so sweet, so sweet, so sweet,
The wild-rose reddening at my feet.

Your lips had learned a golden word,   5
You sang a song that all men heard,
Oh, love is fleet, the strain is long.
Who stays the singer from her song?

Across my path the red leaves whirled.
Dared I to kneel with all the world?   10
How came I, then, to clasp you, Sweet,
And find a woman at my feet?

from *Harper's New Monthly Magazine* (1892)

THE STONE WOMAN OF EASTERN POINT[2]

At the turn of the gray and the green,
    Where the new road runs to the right
(For the summer people's ease),
    And on to the scarlet Light;

Where the tottering barn observes,   5
    And the old farm road looks down
The harbor, and out to sea,
    And back to the fishing-town;

Shapen of stone and of chance,
    Carven of wind and of time –   10
Stands the Woman of Eastern Point,
    Haunting my heart and my rhyme;

Stunted of stature and thin –
    Coast women alive look so –
Wrapped in her blanket-shawl,   15
    Wind-blown and cold, peering low

Past the shivering edge of the barn,
    Searching the bay and the sea
For the sail that is overdue,
    And the hour that never shall be.   20

Did she stand like that in the flesh,
    Vigilant early and late?
For the sake of a scanty love
    Bearing the blasts of fate;

Acquainted with hunger and pain;   25
    Patient, as women are;
Work, when he is at home;
    Pray, when he's over the bar;

Loving and longing and true;
    Gilding her idol of clay;   30
Bride, when the boat comes in;
    Widow, it sails away.

THE STONE WOMAN OF EASTERN POINT
[2] In Gloucester, Massachusetts, a major port for fishing
vessels and whalers.

Waiting and watching and gray;
   Growing old, poor, and alone; –
Was it worth living for? Say,   35
   Tell us, thou woman of stone!

Still she stands, face in her shawl.
   If it hide smiles, do they mock?
If the tears fall, are they sweet?
   Ask.   But you ask of the rock.   40

Dust unto dust taketh wing;
   Granite to granite is grown;
Seeking the sail overdue
   Turneth the heart to stone.

Wind-blown and grief-worn and brave,   45
   Gazing the sad sea o'er;
Dumb in her life and her death –
   Spirit of Gloucester shore!

from *Harper's Bazar* (1911)

THE TWAIN OF HER

Now the Martha[3] of her stiffened to her load
   Down-weighing, of relentless daily care.
Now she straightened upright, would not bend nor break,
   But held herself all iron standing there.

When the Mary of her called unto her soul,   5
   And made a moan, and cried to it in vain: –
["]Oh, this woman – look! She fretteth overmuch,
   And leaves no space for me, Lord, I complain."

But the Martha of her listened with the sigh
   Of those too weary or too strong to rest: –   10
"Tell who taketh then this burden if I cease,
   And empty both my hands upon my breast."

Oh, a soul divided is a soul forespent,
   She went still asking: –"Is it I? Or I?"
Low forever through the silence Mary spoke;   15
   And Martha, sad and sure, did make reply.

THE TWAIN OF HER
[3] In the Bible, the sister of Lazarus and friend of Jesus. She is mentioned in Luke 10:40, but her story was only elaborated in the Middle Ages when she came to symbolize the active life (of "toil"), as opposed to her sister Mary, who symbolized the contemplative life (of "prayer"). Here Phelps is suggesting that Martha and Mary represent two sides of the same woman.

Till the irony and harmony of death
    Made out of these a concord high and sweet.
When the Martha of the woman, toiling, passed,
    Estranged from ease, she sought her Master's feet.   20

"Now my turn has come, my turn at last!" she cried,
    "My time to worship, listening to Thy word."
Ah, but calm beyond her, fair above her still,
    The Mary of her knelt before the Lord.

Emma Lazarus (1849–1887)

Born on July 22, 1849 in New York City, Emma Lazarus was the fourth of seven surviving children of Moses and Esther Nathan Lazarus. Her father, who traced his descent to Sephardic Jews cast out of Spain and Portugal in 1492, was a successful sugar merchant. He and his family belonged to Congregation Shearith Israel, the oldest in New York City, but earlier family members had been part of the Newport congregation whose "disappearance" Longfellow mourns in "The Jewish Cemetery at Newport;" and which Lazarus subtly refutes with her own "In the Jewish Synagogue at Newport" (1871).

Although poems such as the latter testify to Lazarus's early concern with Jewish issues, her literary commitment to the Jewish community only flowered after Czar Alexander's pogroms caused a mass exodus of Russian Jews to the United States in the early 1880s. Until then, Lazarus's chief desire had been to win recognition from the East Coast literary establishment, in particular, Emerson, whom she deeply admired and to whom she sent a copy of her first book, *Poems and Translations: Written Between the Ages Fourteen and Sixteen* (1867). For a number of years thereafter Emerson "mentored" the young Jewish poet, their relationship only foundering when he failed to include any of her poems in his 1874 anthology, *The New Parnassus*.

By 1874, however, Lazarus had outgrown her need for a mentor in any case. A frequent contributor to the leading periodicals, she had become what she wanted to be – a well-established "mainstream" woman writer. Her second book of poetry, *Admetus and Other Poems*, appeared to admiring reviews in the United States and in England in 1871. Most of this poetry, which is deeply invested in the standard themes of late nineteenth-century polite literature, has been dismissed by scholars today. Writing it, however, gave Lazarus sound technical experience, and some poems, such as "The South" and "Off Rough Point," share qualities of sensuality and mysticism that link them to her later writing. Less happily, "The South" also sheds troublesome light on Lazarus's racial attitudes, attitudes which need further exploration.

In 1881, under the auspices of Rabbi Gustav Gottheil, Lazarus visited Jewish immigrants at their refuge on Wards Island and the experience was transformative. Although she had always been interested in Jewish authors and history, she now became an active advocate of Jewish political causes, using her pen and her presence to elicit support for refugee relief. By 1882, she was calling for a Jewish homeland in Palestine, making her an early forecaster of the Zionist movement; and she became sharply critical of Christians for their persecution of Jews through the ages. With the tellingly named *Songs of a Semite* (1882), Lazarus announced to the literary world her new identity as an explicitly Jewish-identified poet, an identity she reinforced through her exploitation of Jewish subject matter and biblical rhythms, as in the beautiful "Love Song of Alcharisi," among her most successful translations.

Between 1881 and her premature death from cancer in 1887, Lazarus became the best known English-speaking American Jewish writer of her day. Poetry and prose poured from her pen, as the long sordid history of Jewish persecution came alive to her in the present. No less important the United States as a refuge from persecution also came alive to her. However problematically stated, the sentiments of "The New Colossus," Lazarus's most famous poem, have had a powerful and enduring effect on the American cultural imaginary, probably beyond Lazarus's wildest dream of the influence her writing might some day wield. In thus contributing to the myth of national identity, Emma Lazarus achieved the fullest realization of her earliest ambitions, placing herself as a specifically Jewish writer at the very center of a culture to which her people had, up to that point, only the most tenuous of claims.

Primary Texts

Poems and Translations: Written Between the Ages Fourteen and Sixteen, 1867; *Admetus and Other Poems*, 1871; *Poems and Ballads of Heinrich Heine*, 1881; *Songs of a Semite: The Dance of Death and Other Poems*, 1882; *The Poems of Emma Lazarus*, 2 vols, 1889.

Further Reading

"Emma Lazarus," *Century* 36 (October 1888): 875–84; Diane Lichtenstein, "Words and Worlds: Emma Lazarus's Conflicting Citizenships," *Tulsa Studies in Women's Literature* 6 (1987): 247–63; Eve Merriam, *Emma Lazarus: Woman with a Torch*, New York: Citadel, 1986; Dan Vogel, *Emma Lazarus*, Boston: Twayne, 1980.

from *Scribner's Monthly* (1877)

OFF ROUGH POINT

We sat at twilight nigh the sea,
    The fog hung gray and weird.
Through the thick film uncannily
    The broken moon appeared.

We heard the billows crack and plunge,   5
    We saw nor waves nor ships.
Earth sucked the vapors like a sponge,
    The salt spray wet our lips.

Close the woof of white mist drew,
    Before, behind, beside.   10
How could that phantom moon break through,
    Above that shrouded tide?

The roaring waters filled the ear,
    A white blank foiled the sight.

Close-gathering shadows near, more near,   15
Brought the blind, awful night.

O friends who passed unseen, unknown!
O dashing, troubled sea!
Still stand we on a rock alone,
Walled round by mystery.   20

from *Lippincott's Magazine* (1878)

THE SOUTH

Night, and beneath star-blazoned summer skies
Behold the Spirit of the musky South,
A creole with still-burning, languid eyes,
Voluptuous limbs and incense-breathing mouth:
Swathed in spun gauze is she,   5
From fibres of her own anana tree.

Within these sumptuous woods she lies at ease,
By rich night-breezes, dewy cool, caressed:
'Twixt cypresses and slim palmetto trees,
Like to the golden oriole's hanging nest,   10
Her airy hammock swings,
And through the dark her mocking-bird yet sings.

How beautiful she is! A tulip-wreath
Twines round her shadowy, free-floating hair:
Young, weary, passionate, and sad as death,
Dark visions haunt for her the vacant air,   15
While noiselessly she lies
With lithe, lax, folded hands and heavy eyes.

Full well knows she how wide and fair extend
Her groves bright flowered, her tangled everglades,
Majestic streams that indolently wend   20
Through lush savanna or dense forest shades,
Where the brown buzzard flies
To broad bayous 'neath hazy-golden skies.

Hers is the savage splendor of the swamp,   25
With pomp of scarlet and of purple bloom,
Where blow warm, furtive breezes faint and damp,
Strange insects whir, and stalking bitterns boom –
Where from stale waters dead
Oft looms the great-jawed alligator's head.   30

Her wealth, her beauty, and the blight on these, –
   Of all she is aware: luxuriant woods,
Fresh, living, sunlit, in her dream she sees;
   And ever midst those verdant solitudes
     The soldier's wooden cross,   35
O'ergrown by creeping tendrils and rank moss.

Was hers a dream of empire? was it sin?
   And is it well that all was borne in vain?
She knows no more than one who slow doth win,
   After fierce fever, conscious life again,   40
     Too tired, too weak, too sad,
By the new light to be or stirred or glad.

From rich sea-islands fringing her green shore,
   From broad plantations where swart freemen bend
Bronzed backs in willing labor, from her store   45
   Of golden fruit, from stream, from town, ascend
     Life-currents of pure health:
Her aims shall be subserved with boundless wealth.

Yet now how listless and how still she lies,
   Like some half-savage, dusky Indian queen,   50
Rocked in her hammock 'neath her native skies,
   With the pathetic, passive, broken mien
     Of one who, sorely proved,
Great-souled, hath suffered much and much hath loved!

But look! along the wide-branched, dewy glade   55
   Glimmers the dawn: the light palmetto trees
And cypresses reissue from the shade,
   And *she* hath wakened. Through clear air she sees
     The pledge, the brightening ray,
And leaps from dreams to hail the coming day.   60

from *Songs of a Semite* (1882)

LOVE SONG OF ALCHARISI[1]

I.

The long-closed door, oh open it again, send me back
   once more my fawn that had fled.

LOVE SONG OF ALCHARISI
[1]   In later editions of this poem, it is attributed to Moses Ben Ezra, *c.* 1100. Ben Ezra was a twelfth-century Sephardic poet, writing in Hebrew. Lazarus made her translations from the German.

On the day of our reunion, thou shalt rest by my side,
there wilt thou shed over me the streams of thy
delicious perfume.
Oh beautiful bride, what is the form of thy friend, that
thou say to me, Release him, send him away?
He is the beautiful-eyed one of ruddy glorious aspect –
that is my friend, him do thou detain.

II.

Hail to thee, Son of my friend, the ruddy, the bright
colored one! Hail to thee whose temples are like
a pomegranate.   5
Hasten to the refuge of thy sister, and protect the son
of Isaiah[2] against the troops of the Ammonites.[3]
What art thou, O Beauty, that thou shouldst inspire
love? that thy voice should ring like the voices of
the bells upon the priestly garments?
The hour wherein thou desirest my love, I shall hasten
to meet thee. Softly will I drop beside thee like
the dew upon Hermon.[4]

from *Century* (1887)

FROM "BY THE WATERS OF BABYLON: LITTLE POEMS IN PROSE,"[5]

IV. The Test

1. Daylong I brooded upon the Passion of Israel.
2. I saw him bound to the wheel, nailed to the cross, cut off by the sword, burned at the stake, tossed into the seas.
3. And always the patient, resolute, martyr face arose in silent rebuke and defiance.
4. A Prophet with four eyes; wide gazed the orbs of the spirit above the sleeping eyelids of the senses.
5. A Poet, who plucked from his bosom the quivering heart and fashioned it into a lyre.
6. A placid-browed Sage, uplifted from earth in celestial meditation.
7. These I saw, with princes and people in their train; the monumental dead and the standard-bearers of the future.
8. And suddenly I heard a burst of mocking laughter, and turning, I beheld the shuffling gait, the ignominious features, the sordid mask of the son of the Ghetto.

---

[2] Hebrew prophet, *c.* 740 BCE.
[3] Followers of Amon, King of Judah (642–640 BCE).
[4] Mt Hermon, also called Mt Sion in the Bible.

FROM "BY THE WATERS OF BABYLON"
[5] During the reign of King Nebuchadnezzar, Hebrews were held in captivity in Babylon. To weep by the waters of Babylon became symbolic of the diasporic condition.

from *The Poems of Emma Lazarus* (1889)

THE NEW COLOSSUS[6]

Not like the brazen giant of Greek fame,
With conquering limbs astride from land to land;
Here at our sea-washed, sunset gates shall stand
A mighty woman with a torch, whose flame
Is the imprisoned lightning, and her name   5
Mother of Exiles. From her beacon-hand
Glows world-wide welcome; her mild eyes command
The air-bridged harbor that twin cities frame.
"Keep, ancient lands, your storied pomp!" cries she
With silent lips. "Give me your tired, your poor,   10
Your huddled masses yearning to breathe free,
The wretched refuse of your teeming shore.
Send these, the homeless, tempest-tost to me,
I lift my lamp beside the golden door!"

(1883)

VENUS OF THE LOUVRE[7]

Down the long hall she glistens like a star,
The foam-born mother of Love,[8] transfixed to stone,
Yet none the less immortal, breathing on.
Time's brutal hand hath maimed but could not mar.
When first the enthralled enchantress from afar   5
Dazzled mine eyes, I saw not her alone,
Serenely poised on her world-worshipped throne,
As when she guided once her dove-drawn car, –
But at her feet a pale, death-stricken Jew,
Her life adorer, sobbed farewell to love.   10
Here *Heine*[9] wept! Here still he weeps anew,
Nor ever shall his shadow lift or move,
While mourns one ardent heart, one poet-brain,
For vanished Hellas and Hebraic pain.

THE NEW COLOSSUS

[6] The Colossus of Rhodes, a bronze statue of the god
Helios, which was said to stand astride the entrance to
the harbor at Rhodes.

VENUS OF THE LOUVRE

[7] The Venus de Milo, the half-draped statue of
Aphrodite (*c.* 100 BCE), now in the Louvre Museum in
Paris. Perhaps the best known of all ancient sculptures,
it was found on the island of Melos in 1820.

[8] Aphrodite (Venus) was said to have been born of the
foam of the sea. (See Piatt, "A Sea-Gull Wounded.")

[9] Heinrich Heine (1797–1856) was a convert to Christianity, but the Jewish influence remained strong in his
work, and he is usually identified as a Jewish poet.

Manuscript Poem (date unknown; Vogel, 1980)

ASSURANCE

Last night I slept, and when I woke her kiss
Still floated on my lips. For we had strayed
Together in my dream, through some dim glade,
Where the shy moonbeams scarce dared light our bliss.
The air was dank with dew, between the trees,   5
The hidden glow-worms kindled and were spent.
Cheek pressed to cheek, the cool, the hot night-breeze
Mingled our hair, our breath, and came and went,
As sporting with our passion. Low and deep
Spake in mine ear her voice: "And didst thou dream,   10
This could be buried? This could be sleep?
An love be thrall to death! Nay, whatso seem,
Have faith, dear heart; *this is the thing that is!*"
Thereon I woke, and on my lips her kiss.

Henrietta Cordelia Ray (1849–1916)

Born in New York City in 1849, Henrietta Cordelia Ray was the daughter of Charles
Bennett Ray and his second wife, Charlotte Augusta Burrough. Ray's father was a former
blacksmith turned Congregational minister and an early abolitionist, who ran an Underground railroad station out of his New York home. He was a newspaper editor and a
community leader, active in various social reform movements, including suffrage and temperance. Ray was one of seven children, all talented. Her sister, Charlotte, had the distinction of being the first black woman lawyer to practice in the District of Columbia. Ray
herself received a Master of Pedagogy degree from the University of the City of New York.
Ray taught English in the New York City public school system for thirty years. She never
married and shared a home with her sister Florence, who was also a teacher, until her death.

Ray made her public debut as a poet in Washington, D.C., at the unveiling of the
Freedmen's Monument in April of 1876, when William E. Matthews read her eighty-line
ode to Lincoln before an assembled audience of dignitaries, including President Grant and
Frederick Douglass. Along with occasional appearances in black periodicals, Ray published
two books, *Sonnets* in 1893 and *Poems* in 1910. With Florence, she also co-wrote a biographical sketch of her father.

After noting Ray's mastery of poetic form, her modern editor, Joan Sherman, sharply
criticizes her for the excessive gentility of her writing, which, Sherman claims, like the
author herself "labor[s] under the blessing of a fine education." Unfortunately, this assess-
ment is not altogether off the mark. Ray is the strongest of a group of black women poets
publishing books at the end of the century; but for her, as for most of these poets, the desire
to demonstrate the rewards of a "fine" (genteel) education encouraged the wholesale absorption of white middle-class standards. Her drive is toward assimilation – of style, forms, and
themes. The result is, all too often, a lack of specificity that leads Sherman to speak

dismissively of "the wax flowers, stuffed birds, and canvas sunsets in her verse museum," as if that was all there were.

Yet Ray could also branch out on her own. Her "Vision of Eve," in particular, is a very modern re-visioning of Milton's *Paradise Lost*, both in terms of its feminist slant and in terms of its willingness to deliberately twist back upon itself the work of a "great" canonical writer. In the last two books of *Paradise Lost*, Milton puts Eve to sleep as Michael unfolds the future before Adam's wondering eyes (this, so that Adam can tell her the whole story later, mingling it with kisses, and accommodating it to her inferior mental powers). Ray, on the other hand, grants Eve a vision of her own, one referring, as Mary E. Ashe Lee says in "Afmerica," specifically to women as "the daughter[s] of futurity." This is a bold move on Ray's part and suggests a good deal about the hopefulness with which educated black women were prepared to greet the new century.

If, particularly with hindsight, Ray's vision of the future seems rose-tinted, as Sherman suggests, she was hardly alone in believing that finally for blacks in America "the world was all before them, where to choose." Nor was she alone, one suspects, in seeing it as part of her duty, therefore, to hide the "weight of woe," as she calls it in her sonnet on "Niobe," with which in fact her society had burdened her and every person of color living in the United States at that time. In this sonnet, which is, perhaps, the finest poem she wrote, Ray uses the classical figure of Niobe – the grieving mother – to express all the pain of sundered lives and suppressed "tears" that had been Africa's lot in this country for over two hundred years.

Primary Texts

Sonnets, 1893; *Poems*, 1910, facsimile reprint in *Collected Black Women's Poetry*, vol. 3, ed. Joan R. Sherman, 1988.

Further Reading

Hallie Q. Brown, comp., *Homespun Heroines and Other Women of Distinction*, Xenia, Ohio: Aldine, 1926; Leela Kapai, "Henrietta Cordelia Ray," *DLB* 50: 233–7; F. T. and H. C. Ray, *Sketch of the Life of Rev. Charles B. Ray*, New York: J. J. Little, 1887; Joan R. Sherman, *Invisible Poets: Afro-Americans of the Nineteenth Century*; "Introduction," in *Collected Black Women's Poetry*, vol. 3, New York, Oxford: Oxford University Press, 1988: xxix–xxxiv.

from *A. M. E. Church Review* (1893)

NIOBE[1]

O Mother-Heart! when fast the arrows flew,
Like blinding lightning, smiting as they fell,
One after one, one after one, what knell
Could fitly voice thine anguish! Sorrow grew
To throes intensest, when thy sad soul knew   5

NIOBE
[1] In Greek mythology, the wife of King Amphion of Thebes. Her excessive pride in her seven sons and daughters was punished by Apollo and Artemis, who destroyed all her children. Niobe herself was changed by Zeus into a marble statue whose face is continually wet with tears.

Thy youngest too must go.   Was it not well,
Avengers wroth, just one to spare?   Aye, tell
The ages of soul-struggle sterner?   Through
The flinty stone, O image of despair,
Sad Niobe, thy maddened grief did flow   10
In bitt'rest tears, when all thy wailing prayer
Was so denied. Alas! what weight of woe
Is prisoned in thy melancholy eyes!
What mother-love beneath the stoic lies!

from *Poems* (1910)

NOONDAY THOUGHT

The tranquil waters slept 'neath Nature's smile,
Watched by the sunlit skies, as, free from guile,
The tender infant sleeps, while o'er its bed
The mother, yearning dreamer, bends her head.

AT THE CASCADE

The waters rippled, gleamed and fell;
Sweet Jessie tripped adown the dell.
She heard his voice, their fond lips met;
The rocks with silver spray were wet.

THE VISION OF EVE[2]

When from the gates of Paradise fair Eve
Turned her reluctant steps with saddest mien,
A sense prophetic stayed her blinding tears,
And thus she yearning cried, her sobs between:
"Could I but see adown the coming days!   5
Yet, though I may not win that boon, alas!
One question haunts me with resistless charm,
What will my daughters be when aeons pass?"

She bowed her head, then as with rev'rence spoke:
"A hope has seized my spirit, e'en though late   10
It cometh. Ay! and will my fault be less
By what they may achieve of good or great?
Are all my cherished longings to be vain?
I cannot know what grander purpose lies
Beyond the misty verge that bounds my view."   15
She ceased, with supplication in her eyes.

THE VISION OF EVE
[2]   See John Milton's *Paradise Lost*, Books 11 and 12. At
the behest of God, the Archangel Michael gives Adam
a vision of the future up to Noah's Flood while Eve is
put into a deep sleep filled with gentle dreams inspiring
"quietness of mind and submission."

Again we see the Mother of mankind,
Yet not discrowned and mournful as of yore;
From amethystine battlements she leans,
Wide-eyed with wonder and admiring awe.   20
Far past the planets, past the swinging stars,
Past worlds on worlds that spin in ether there,
Her glances wander to the circling earth,
Lying below swathed by the purpling air.

Lo! what is it she sees? Forms like to hers,   25
When erst she paced fair Eden's flow'ry courts;
But on each brow there sits a something new,
A something mystical. Is it the thoughts'
Deep impress which the centuries have left?
The seal of alternating joy and woe,   30
Of care and grief, anon of hope and love,
Marked by the ages as they come and go?

And ever on and on the glances rove
Of our first mother. Now the marble yields
In Eve-like contours 'neath the skillful touch   35
Of one; another well the sceptre wields;
And one self-poised, regnant in dignity,
In philosophic councils holds the sway.
Upon the battlefield, one kneels to stanch
The crimson life-blood as it ebbs away.   40

And thus the dreamer spoke: "Are these my kin,
And has the world so grown since those sweet days
In glorious Paradise when Time was young?
Are these my daughters who with sweeping gaze,
Can scan the sheeny Heavens for a sign   45
Of God's deep wisdom writ upon the skies?
Are these indeed my children, all my own?
What strange, enchanting visions meet my eyes?"

She hears the rhythmic strains of one who caught
The Muse's most majestic melodies;   50
The lofty heights, the shining altitudes
Her latest children climb, with pride she sees.
"Ah! my prophetic hopes were not in vain,"
Cried Mother Eve with eager eyes aglow;
"Yet could I dream of this when Time began?   55
The deeds my daughters dare I could not know."

She paused, and soon her rapt soliloquy
Died like a zephyr o'er a leafy lawn;
She gazed once more from jeweled battlements

Far down the firmament, e'en as the Dawn   60
Blushed in the east; and when the magic hues
Began in mimic warfare to engage,
Throughout the spheres a chiming measure thrilled, –
The vibrant music of the newer age!

MY SPIRIT'S COMPLEMENT

Thy life hath touched the edges of my life,
All glistening and moist with sunlit dew.
They touched, they paused, – then drifted wide apart,
Each gleaming with a rare prismatic hue.

'Twas but a touch! the edges of a life   5
Alone encolored with the rose, yet lo!
Each fibre started into strange unrest,
And then was stilled, lulled to a rhythmic flow.

Perchance our spirits clasp on some fair isle,
Bright with the sheen of reveries divine;   10
Or list'ning to such strains as chant the stars,
In purest harmony their tendrils twine.

God grant our souls may meet in Paradise,
After the mystery of life's sweet pain;
And find the strange prismatic hues of earth   15
Transmuted to the spotless light again.

TO MY FATHER

A leaf from Freedom's golden chaplet fair,
We bring to thee, dear father!   Near her shrine
None came with holier purpose, nor was thine
Alone the soul's mute sanction; every prayer
Thy captive brother uttered found a share   5
In thy wide sympathy; to every sign
That told the bondman's need thou didst incline.
No thought of guerdon³ hadst thou but to bear
A loving part in Freedom's strife. To see
Sad lives illumined, fetters rent in twain,   10
Tears dried in eyes that wept for length of days –
Ah! was not that a recompense for thee?
And now where all life's mystery is plain,
Divine approval is thy sweetest praise.

TO MY FATHER
³ *Guerdon* a poetic word meaning reward or
recompense.

TOUSSAINT L'OUVERTURE[4]

To those fair isles where crimson sunsets burn,
We send a backward glance to gaze on thee,
Brave Toussaint! thou wast surely born to be
A hero; thy proud spirit could but spurn
Each outrage on thy race. Couldst thou unlearn   5
The lessons taught by instinct? Nay! and we
Who share the zeal that would make all men free,
Must e'en with pride unto thy life-work turn.
Soul-dignity was thine and purest aim;
And ah! how sad that thou wast left to mourn   10
In chains 'neath alien skies. On him, shame! shame!
That mighty conqueror who dared to claim
The right to bind thee. Him we heap with scorn,
And noble patriot! guard with love thy name.

Edith M. Thomas (1854–1925)

Edith M. Thomas was born on her family's farm in Chatham, Ohio, in 1854. Her father, a descendant of British and Welsh settlers, died when she was still quite young. Thereafter, her paternal uncle, James Thomas, was the most influential figure in her life, providing her with books and telling her about life outside Ohio. Thomas attended public school in Geneva, Ohio, and then went on to Geneva Normal Institute, where special classes in Greek had to be arranged for her. After briefly attending Oberlin College, she taught school for two years, only to abandon teaching for a typesetter's career – and writing.

In 1881, James Thomas took the young author, together with a scrapbook of poems she had published locally, to New York City, where she made her debut in East Coast literary society at a salon held by Anne Lynch Botta (s.v. Helen Hunt Jackson). Botta referred Thomas to Helen Hunt Jackson, who after some initial hesitation, supported her energetically. With Jackson's help, Thomas made contact with *Scribner's Monthly*. After her initial appearance in *Scribner's* caused something of a sensation, editors of all the leading periodicals began vying for her work.

Thomas's mother died in 1887, leaving Thomas free to move permanently to New York City. For ten years she enjoyed the patronage of Dr Samuel Elliot and his wife. A scientist and a musician, Elliot took Thomas under his wing, providing her with a home and introducing her to many of the nation's most notable intellectuals and artists, including Charles A. Dana, Parke Godwin, Elihu Vedder, and Edwin Booth. After Elliot's death, Thomas, by now very much a part of the New York literary scene, supported herself by working in publishing and by writing, voluminously. A sensitive, quiet woman, she became, according to all accounts, increasingly withdrawn and dependent on her own inner

TOUSSAINT L'OUVERTURE
[1]   François Toussaint L'Ouverture (1743–1803), leader of the Haitian independence movement. He led several rebellions on the island in the 1790s, aimed at emanci- pating Haiti's population of slaves. (See Sarah C. Bierce Scarborough's translation of an excerpt from Lamartine's "Toussaint Louverture" in Section II.)

life for sustenance. She died of a cerebral hemorrhage at seventy-one, passing away (to use her word) as "invisibly" as she had lived.

"Invisible" or not, Thomas is among the most interesting of the women poets who flourished in the final decades of the nineteenth century. The degree to which her early nature poems – not to mention the thematics of many of her later poems (poems on loss, hunger, etc.) – echo Dickinson's poems on similar subjects is almost uncanny. Although Thomas's diction can at times seem archaic, her word choice is clear, and her images are vital and precise. The last lines of "Harvest Noon" (1881), in particular – "By swimming dome and minaret, / And rich pavilion wove of cloud!" – could come right out of a Dickinson "sunset" poem. (See, for example, "How the old Mountains drip with Sunset" [291].) Yet, given this poem's date, it is unlikely that Dickinson influenced her directly, unless – tantalizing possibility – through Jackson.

At the same time, however, in her classicism and aestheticism, Thomas also anticipates the early modernists, Amy Lowell and the early H. D. Like theirs, hers is a poetry of the inner world, where a Keatsian concept of truth as beauty presides. Like Dickinson's, but unlike those of most nineteenth-century American women poets, Thomas's concepts of the moral and the spiritual are interior. Except for her occasional protests against the domination of money, the social world plays almost no role in her art. But unlike Dickinson, she also gives no role to religion. She is a poet speaking in secular terms of her interior life to a general audience of readers. This gives her poems a modern feel that those of Amherst's wayward Puritan daughter very much lack.

How important was Thomas? Certainly, like Lizette Woodworth Reese and Louise Imogen Guiney, she was one of the significant writers who helped change the public ear, preparing the way both for Dickinson's spectacular emergence in the 1890s and for the advent of free verse and imagism. Read thus against her precursors, she feels very modern and "necessary."

But read against the modernists themselves, she seems, particularly because of her metrics, old-fashioned, as if somehow she just missed, but missed fatally, where things needed to go. This is, one might say, the fate of the transition figure. She is liminal, belonging to neither world, yet serving as a bridge between them. Having served its purpose, need the bridge be remembered? How much audience develops for Thomas today will depend on how that question is answered as much as on the intrinsic appeal of her poetry when read for itself.

Primary Texts

A New Year's Masque and Other Poems, 1885; The Round Year, 1886; Lyrics and Sonnets, 1887; The Inverted Torch, 1890; Fair Shadow Land, 1893; The Dancers and Other Legends and Lyrics, 1903; The Guest at the Gate, 1909; The Flower from the Ashes, 1915; The White Messenger, 1915; Selected Poems of Edith M. Thomas, ed. Jessie B. Rittenhouse, 1926.

Further Reading

Fred Lewis Pattee, A History of American Literature since 1870, New York: Century, 1915; Jessie B. Rittenhouse, ed., "Memoir," in Selected Poems of Edith M. Thomas, New York: Harper's, 1926.

from *Scribner's Monthly* (1881)

FROST

How small a tooth hath mined the season's heart;
How cold a touch hath set the wood on fire,
Until it blazes like a costly pyre
Built for some Ganges emperor, old and swart,
Soul-sped on clouds of incense! Whose the art   5
That webs the streams, each morn, with silver wire,
Delicate as the tension of a lyre?
Whose falchion[1] pries the chestnut-bur apart?
It is the Frost; a rude and Gothic sprite,
Who doth unbuild the summer's palaced wealth,   10
And puts her dear loves all to sword or flight;
Yet in the hushed, unmindful winter's night,
The spoiler builds again with jealous stealth,
And sets a mimic garden, cold and bright.

from *Atlantic Monthly* (1881)

HARVEST NOON

Morn hath its matins, each morn new,
    The evening hath its vespers[2] meet;
Nor lacks the noon a service true,
    While crickets sing the song of heat.

An hour-long truce the reapers keep   5
    With the mute legions of the grain;
Through swath and stubble spiders creep,
    And web them with a filmy skein.

The bees forget their errantry,
    Lapped in the clover white and red;   10
The wind, grown faint with luxury,
    Leaves the ripe thistle-down unshed:

Still, yonder, on the long, gray road,
    It lives, – a momentary gust,
That drives along, with noiseless goad,   15
    A whirling phantom clothed in dust.

FROST
[1] *Falchion* a short broad sword having a convex edge curving sharply to a point.

HARVEST NOON
[2] Matins and Vespers are the names given to the morning and evening services in the Roman Catholic church.

The dreams of night? Noon, too, hath dreams;
   In fugitive, mysterious bands,
They launch their feet on quivering streams
   That flow above the sun-bright lands!   20

I see their prows are southward set;
   And soon their sails the haven crowd,
By swimming dome and minaret,
   And rich pavilion wove of cloud!

from *Century* (1891)

AD ASTRA[3]

(A. C. L. B.)[4]

Unto the stars the light they lent returned.
Seer of celestial order, – soother, guide, –
Be still such influence, though undiscerned,
Swept onward with the white sidereal[5] tide.

from *Fair Shadow Land* (1893)

THE TORCHES OF THE DAWN

Beneath the rough, black verge where ledgy isle
   And serried wave and fragment cloud are hurled,
      Swift through the underworld –
Lo where the torchmen of the Dawn defile!

Unseen they march beneath the rough, black verge,   5
   Unseen, save from the torches which they bear,
      Smoke and a crimson flare,
Wind-blown one way, show where their course they urge!

LOSSES

Speed had not served, strength had not flowed amain,
Heart had not braced me, for this journey's strain,
Had I foreseen what losses must be met;
But drooping losel[6] was I never yet!

So rich in losses through long years I've grown,   5
So rich in losses (and so proud, I own)
Myself I pity not, but only such
As have not had, nor therefore lost, so much.

AD ASTRA
3 Latin: to the stars, a motto for aspiration.
4 Anne Lynch Botta. This poem is written in response
to one by Botta.

5 *Sidereal* of or relating to the stars, starry, astral.
LOSSES
6 *Losel* a worthless person.

Behind me ever grew a hungry Vast
Which travelers fear to face, but call the Past;   10
So much it won from me I can but choose
To exult that I've so little left to lose.

When that shall go, as fain it is to go
(Like some full sail when winds of voyage blow),
At this late nick of time to murmur sore   15
Were idle, since so much I've lost before!

So much I've lost, lost out of hand – ah, yes!
But were that all, my fortune I could bless;
For whensoever aught has slipped away,
Some dearer thing has gone to find the stray;   20

And then, to find the finder loth or slow,
Yet dearer thing my wistful heart let go,
With hope like his whose glancing arrow gave
The clue to Pari-banou's[7] palace-cave.

Perchance one loss the more, regains the whole,   25
Lost loves and faith and young delight of soul:
I'm losing – what? ah, Life, join thou the quest;
It may be, to be lost, is not unblest!

from *The Dancers and Other Legends and Lyrics* (1903)

THE DEEP-SEA PEARL

The love of my life came not
  As love unto others is cast;
For mine was a secret wound –
  But the wound grew a pearl, at last.

The divers may come and go,   5
  The tides, they arise and fall;
The pearl in its shell lies sealed,
  And the Deep Sea covers all.

from *The Guest at the Gate* (1909)

EDEN-MEMORY

Now, when the Angel missioned with the sword,
  At Eden-gate his burning falchion drew,
  And when our sad first parents had passed through,

---

[7]   A fairy with magic powers in *The Thousand and One Nights*.

How did that garden mourn their fate untoward!
The fourfold rivers from their urns were poured   5
  With unconsoled repinings; and the dew
  Did stand like teardrops in the heart's-ease blue,
And waned the lilies' golden honey hoard.
The breathing air henceforth was but one sigh
  That all around that lonesome pleasance ran,   10
While Voices asked – and lapsed without reply. . . .
  Such wistful airs about my garden fan,
I dream, some grief of Eden still must lie
  At heart of every garden made by man!

from *Selected Poems of Edith M. Thomas* (1926)[8]

"Frost To-Night"

Apple-green west and an orange bar,
And the crystal eye of a lone, one star . . .
And, "Child, take the shears and cut what you will.
Frost to-night – so clear and dead-still."

Then, I sally forth, half sad, half proud,   5
And I come to the velvet, imperial crowd,
The wine-red, the gold, the crimson, the pied, –
The dahlias that reign by the garden-side.

The dahlias I might not touch till to-night!
A gleam of shears in the fading light,   10
And I gathered them all, – the splendid throng,
And in one great sheaf I bore them along.

In my garden of Life with its all-late flowers,
I heed a Voice in the shrinking hours:
"Frost to-night – so clear and dead-still . . ."   15
Half sad, half proud, my arms I fill.

Evoe![9]

"Many are the wand-bearers, few are the true bachanals."

  Many are the wand-bearers;
    Their windy shouts I hear,

---

from *Selected Poems of Edith M. Thomas* (1926)
[8]   According to Rittenhouse, of the poems that follow, "'Frost To-Night,'" "Evoe!" and "The Water of Dirce" all appeared in earlier volumes; but I have not been able to locate them. "The Etherial Hunger" and "To Walk Invisible" were among Thomas's uncollected poems at the time of her death.
Evoe!
[9]   The cry of the Bacchantes as it is given in classical literature. The Bacchantes were the female followers of

Along the hillside vineyard,
  And where the wine runs clear;
They show the vine-leaf chaplet,   5
  The ivy-wreathen spear;
But the god, the true Iacchus,
  He does not hold them dear.

Many are the wand-bearers,
  And bravely are they clad;   10
Yes, they have all the tokens
  His early lovers had.
They sing the master passions,
  Themselves unsad, unglad;
And the god, the true Iacchus –   15
  He knows they are not mad!

Many are the wand-bearers;
  The fawn-skin bright they wear;
There are among them maenads[10]
  That rave with unbound hair.   20
They toss the harmless firebrand –
  It spends itself in air;
And the god, the true Iacchus,
  He smiles – and does not care.

Many are the wand-bearers;   25
  And who (ye ask) am I?
One who was born in madness,
  "Evoe!" my first cry –
Who dares, before your spear-points,
  To challenge and defy;   30
And the god, the true Iacchus,
  So keep me till I die!

Many are the wand-bearers.
  I bear with me no sign;
Yet, I was mad, was drunken,   35
  Ere yet I tasted wine;
Nor bleeding grape can slacken
  The thirst wherewith I pine;
And the god, the true Iacchus,
  Hears now this song of mine.   40

---

the wine god Bacchus, or Iacchus, as Thomas calls him in this poem. Under the inspiration of the god, the Bacchantes roamed the hillsides and forests, adorned with ivy and animal skins, and waving the thyrsus or wand. The epigraph, drawn from Plato's *Phaedo* 69c, makes a distinction between true (divine) poetic inspiration and mere imitation (bearing the wand or playing the part). This is also the subject of Thomas's poem.

[10] Another name for the Bacchantes.

THE WATER OF DIRCE[11]

"If but the Gods, of their mercy,
        Would let me return ere I die,
To drink of the water of Dirce –
        On the cool sprinkled margin to lie!

"Yes, I drank of the Marcian waters,   5
        Of Bandusia's song-haunted spring;[12]
But not though Mnemosyne's daughters[13]
        The crystal of Helicon[14] bring –

"Not they, not the charm-weaving Circe,[15]
        Could make me forget or forego, –   10
I was used to the water of Dirce,
        I long for it, thirst for it so!

"The snows of Cithaeron have chilled it –
        I shall cease from this fever and pain,
If but the Gods have so willed it   15
        I taste that wild sweetness again!"

Then answered the Gods, of their mercy,
        "We give thee thy thirst and thy love,
But seek not the water of Dirce –
        For thy Youth was the sweetness thereof."   20

THE ETHERIAL HUNGER

I have been hungry all my days –
        (Oh, when shall I be fed?)
They saw my pinched and wistful gaze,
        And some there were gave wine and bread,
And some gave love and praise.   5

I was as hungry as before –
        (Oh, when shall I be fed?)
Good souls! they shared their choicest store,
        Another had been surfeited –
I did but hunger more.   10

THE WATER OF DIRCE
[11]   Dirce is a spring located on the side of Mt Cithaeron
in Thebes. Cithaeron was a mountain sacred to Dionysus,
the Greek god of wine and poetry (cf. Bacchus, his
Roman name), and Dirce was his votary. The spring
marks the spot where her body was thrown after she was
killed by Amphion and Zethus.

[12]   A spring near the birthplace of the Roman poet
Horace (65–8 BCE).
[13]   Mnemosyne is the goddess of memory. Her daughters are the nine Muses.
[14]   A mountain in ancient Greece supposedly sacred to
Apollo and the nine Muses.
[15]   A witch who appears in Homer's *Odyssey*. She serves
Odysseus's men a drink that transforms them into swine.

I am an ingrate in their eyes –
  (Oh, when shall I be fed?)
From their best feasts I famished rise,
  I dream of tables ampler spread –
O tables of the skies!   15

To Walk Invisible

"We have the receipt of fern-seed; we walk invisible."[16]

I smile – yet better might I sigh than smile –
  At my young waywardness that wished to try
"Receipt of fern-seed"; for some little while
  To walk unseen of any prying eye.
I said 'twas but detachment that I sought,   5
To better know my own good comrade, Thought.

I added, I had made, must keep, the tryst
  With Beauty, who had counseled Solitude –
I would be back again ere I was missed;
  Whoever loved me would indulge my mood,   10
Nor would they strive the veiling charm to break,
Nor turn aside my hidden path to take.

And then, I moved untroubled by the crowd.
  I softly stepped, and silence lapped me round.
I was but young – God knows I was not proud!   15
  My venture was to me enchanted ground
Where I might pass unseen, but, soon as fain,
Into my human world return again.

I went my way, I kept me far from sight,
  From jostling touch and ill-timed greeting free . . .   20
I, who was more beholden to the night
  Than any charm that could sequester me!
Now, deeper night and elder solitude
Begin to close around my errant mood.

And when I walk invisible, indeed,   25
  Who knows, I may the genius be of all
Who out of trodden ways their spirit lead?
  Then I will answer to their lonely call
Who, straying, have strayed wider than they wist,
Who walk invisible – and are not missed.   30

To Walk Invisible
[16] William Shakespeare, *Henry IV. Part 1*, II.i.12.

Lizette Woodworth Reese (1856–1935)

Lizette Woodworth Reese was born in January, 1856, in Huntingdon (now Waverly), Maryland, a border town in a border state. Her father, David Reese, had emigrated to the United States as a small boy from Wales. Her mother, Louisa Gabler Reese, came as a child from Germany. Reese and her twin sister Sophia, their two sisters and one brother, were all bilingual. David Reese fought on the Confederate side during the Civil War. Of the war, his daughter later recalled only a community torn apart and the tension and fear produced by Lincoln's assassination in 1865.

Reese attended the parish school of her church, St John of Huntingdon. She graduated from Baltimore's Eastern High School in 1873; and began teaching at St John's School when she was seventeen. For the next forty-six years she taught English and German in the Baltimore public school system. In 1874, Reese published her first poem, "The Deserted House," in the *Southern Magazine*. Her first volume of poetry, *A Branch of May*, appeared thirteen years later in 1887. A string of small, beautifully printed volumes followed, all stylistically and thematically of a piece, with very few poems deviating from her own self-imposed formal standard. (With its abrupt, broken lines and monosyllabic vocabulary, the free verse "Drought" is one of Reese's rare experimental poems.)

Having found her voice at the end of the nineteenth century, Lizette Woodworth Reese saw no reason to change it. As indifferent (apparently) to the lure of literary prestige as she was to the hype of mass appeal, she never joined any of the literary coteries flourishing in her day, nor did she emulate their up-and-coming early modernist fashions. Indeed, she ignored almost everything that was happening around her – at least in her art. As Maria Russo insists, in this way Reese had a good deal in common with Dickinson – insisting on stylistic autonomy and putting most of her energy into honing her considerable skills. Even her periodical publication is relatively limited for a poet of her talent, accessibility, and appeal.

Reese is a poet of nostalgia not tragedy. As a result, in this writer's opinion, she lacks the depth and scope to be a "great" poet. Nevertheless, she is probably the most consistently engaging woman poet of the second half of the century and, stylistically speaking, probably the most influential. At times she seems almost everything Piatt is not: ever careful and controlled, exquisitely sensitive to language, "early modernist" less in her irony *per se* (although she is ironic) than in the means she chooses to exercise it – her precise limpid "cool." Her range is narrow – nature poems, poems of mourning (she is one of the century's major elegiasts), poems on the art of poetry itself (perhaps, after nature, the subject to which she is most drawn), and poems to, on, and about women, especially women living gentle circumscribed lives in small rural communities. But if she does not do much, what she does, she does exceedingly well. Where, for example, Piatt wrote dozens of poems that are badly or crudely crafted (awkward, unclear, even grotesque), Reese wrote few if any. At worst she can seem school-marmish and dull. Taking her term from Reese herself, Russo argues that Reese practiced an aesthetic of "scarcity," or as the poet put it in another poem, reprinted here, "thrift." Like Frost, whom she strongly influenced, her verbal parsimony keeps both her craft and her sentiments in line.

Reese's most moving poems – "Early September," "Telling the Bees," "Emily," – possess an elegiac note that is specific to her and helps, perhaps, explain her enormous appeal. A Southerner who saw the genteel, slow-moving South of her early childhood ground down beneath the heel of war, she yearns, it seems, to go back in time, to stop change, and to let the outside world go its own way. In this sense she is what H. L. Mencken called her, the "last of the Victorians." Yet to this very "Victorian" nostalgia she brings a clarity and control that keep her laments from ever seeming mawkish.

Like the mullein with which she identified in the poem of that name, Reese offers "the sweet surety of the common air," but in a package ironic enough to still have bite. (The mullein is, after all, nothing but a roadside weed.) For those weary of breathing in the pollutions of the present, yet too "modern," or too cynical, to trust their own feelings of nostalgia without something there to limit them, she is sweet relief indeed.

Primary Texts

A Branch of May, 1887; *A Handful of Lavender*, 1891; *A Quiet Road*, 1896; *A Wayside Lute*, 1909; *Spicewood*, 1920; *Wild Cherry*, 1923; *Selected Poems*, 1926; *A Victorian Village*, 1929; *White April and Other Poems*, 1930; *Pastures and Other Poems*, 1933.

Further Reading

Hariette Cuttino Buchanan, "Lizette Woodworth Reese," *DLB* 54: 344–53; R. P. Harriss, "April Weather: The Poetry of Lizette Woodworth Reese," *South Atlantic Quarterly* 22 (1930): 200–7; Robert T. Jones, ed., *In Praise of Common Things: Lizette Woodworth Reese Revisited*, Westport, Connecticut: Greenwood Press, 1992; Carlin T. Kindilien, "The Village World of Lizette Woodworth Reese," *South Atlantic Quarterly* 61 (1957): 91–104; H. L. Mencken, "The Last of the Victorians," *The Smart Set* (October 1909); Maria Russo, "Lizette Woodworth Reese," *Encyclopedia of American Poetry*.

from *A Branch of May* (1887)

EARLY SEPTEMBER

The swallows have not left us yet, praise God!
And bees still hum, and gardens hold the musk
Of white rose and of red; firing the dusk
By the old wall, the hollyhocks do nod,
And pinks that send the sweet East down the wind.　　　　　　5
And yet, a yellowing leaf shows here and there
Among the boughs, and through the smoky air –
That hints the frost at dawn – the wood looks thinned.
The little half-grown sumachs, all as green
As June last week, now in the crackling sedge,　　　　　　10
Colored like wine burn to the water's edge.
We feel, at times, as we had come unseen
Upon the aging Year, sitting apart,
Grief in his eyes, some ache at his great heart.

AUGUST

No wind, no bird. The river flames like brass.
On either side, smitten as with a spell
Of silence, brood the fields. In the deep grass,

Edging the dusty roads, lie as they fell
Handfuls of shriveled leaves from tree and bush.   5
But 'long the orchard fence and at the gate,
Thrusting their saffron torches through the hush,
Wild lilies blaze, and bees hum soon and late.
Rust-colored the tall straggling brier, not one
Rose left. The spider sets its loom up there   10
Close to the roots, and spins out in the sun
A silken web from twig to twig. The air
Is full of hot rank scents. Upon the hill
Drifts the noon's single cloud, white, glaring, still.

from *A Quiet Road* (1896)

TELLING THE BEES

(A Colonial Custom)[1]

Bathsheba came out to the sun,
Out to our wallèd cherry-trees;
The tears adown her cheek did run,
Bathsheba standing in the sun,
Telling the bees.   5

My mother had that moment died;
Unknowing, sped I to the trees,
And plucked Bathsheba's hand aside;
Then caught the name that there she cried
Telling the bees.   10

Her look I never can forget,
I that held her sobbing to her knees;
The cherry-boughs above us met;
I think I see Bathsheba yet
Telling the bees.   15

IN TIME OF GRIEF

Dark, thinned, beside the wall of stone,
The box[2] dripped in the air;
Its odor through my house was blown
Into the chamber there.

Remote and yet distinct the scent,   5
The sole thing of the kind,

TELLING THE BEES
[1]   Upon a death in the family, a household member
would, according to old New England custom, "tell the
bees" lest they fly away.

IN TIME OF GRIEF
[2]   Boxwood tree.

As though one spoke a word half meant
That left a sting behind.

I knew not Grief would go from me,
And naught of it be plain,   10
Except how keen the box can be
After a fall of rain.

from *Spicewood* (1920)

A WAR MEMORY

1865

God bless this house and keep us all from hurt.
She led us gravely up the straight long stair;
We were afraid; two held her by the skirt,
One by the hand, and so to bed and prayer.
How frail a thing the little candle shone!   5
Beneath its flame looked dim and soft and high
The chair, the drawers; she like a tall flower blown
In a great space under a shadowy sky.
God bless us all and Lee and Beauregard. —[3]
Without, a soldier paced, in hated blue,[4]   10
The road betwixt the tents in pale array
And our gnarled gate. But in the windy yard
White tulips raced along the drip of dew; —
Our mother with her candle went away.

DROUGHT

Silence — and in the air
A stare.
One bush, the color of rust,
Stands in the endless lane;
And farther on, hot, hard of pane,   5
With roof shrunk black,
Headlong against the sky
A house is thrust;
Betwixt the twain,
Like meal poured from a sack,   10
Stirless, foot high —
The dust.

A WAR MEMORY
[3] General Robert E. Lee (1807–70) and General Pierre   [4] A Union soldier.
Gustave Toutant Beauregard (1818–93), leaders of the
Confederate army.

from *Wild Cherry* (1923)

THRIFT

To fast from wines, silks, anything,
Will spread you feasts indeed;
Still you possess the spring,
And still
The little, wealthy daffodil.   5

To choose and keep the straitened way,[5]
You serve, not without wage,
Your God, your race, your day;
You hold
Fast in your hand the ghostly gold.   10

WHITE FLAGS[6]

Now since they plucked them for your grave,
And left the garden bare
As a great house of candlelight,
Oh, nothing else so fair!

I knew before that they were white,   5
In April by a wall,
A dozen or more. That people died
I did not know at all.

EMILY

She had a garden full of herbs,
    And many another pleasant thing,
Like pink round asters in the fall,
    Blue flags, white flags a week in spring.

Housewives ran in each hour or so,   5
    For sprigs of thyme, mint, parsley too;
For pans to borrow, or some meal;
    She was the kindest thing they knew.

Tall, and half slender, slightly grey,
    With gay, thin lips, eyes flower-clear,   10
She bragged her stock was Puritan;
    Her usual mood was Cavalier.

THRIFT
[5]   An oblique allusion to Christ's statement: "Strait is
the gate and narrow is the way," Matthew 7:13–14.
Reese's concept of her craft as a quasi-religious calling

echoes that of Dickinson in "Publication – is the Auction" (709) and Guiney in "Deo Optimo Maximo."
WHITE FLAGS
[6]   White iris.

Ample of deed; clipped, warm of speech,
    Each day in some large-flowered gown,
She went the rounds to sad, to sick   15
    Saint, humorist to the faded town.

She died at sixty. For a while
    They missed her in each intimate spot —
Tall, and half slender, slightly grey —
    They ate, drank, slept, and quite forgot.   20

THE ROMAN ROAD[7]

(England)

As he went down the Roman Road
    In March or thereabout,
A slender, wild, unbroken gold,
    The daffodils were out.

Sudden along the Roman Road   5
    He saw the wind come down,
Behind the golden daffodils,
    And drive them into town.

A moment. Yet almost it seemed —
    That moment was of old;   10
A company of spears went by,
    All Roman, and all gold.

A PURITAN LADY

Wild Carthage held her, Rome,
    Sidon. She stared to tears
Tall, golden Helen, wearying
    Behind the Trojan spears.[8]

Towered Antwerp knew her well;   5
    She wore her quiet gown
In some hushed house in Oxford grass,
    Or lane in Salem town.[9]

THE ROMAN ROAD

[7] In whole or part, Britain was incorporated into the Roman Empire between 43 BCE and 410 CE, when the Roman legions were finally withdrawn. While in control of the island, the Romans built an extensive road system for military purposes.

A PURITAN LADY

[8] Carthage in North Africa, Rome, Sidon in Phoenicia (present-day Lebanon), and Troy near the mouth of the Dardanelles in Asian Turkey were all great cities of the ancient world.

[9] Antwerp, Belgium, Oxford, England, and Salem, Massachusetts, are all relatively modest-sized modern cities.

Humble and high in one,
    Cool, certain, different,   10
She lasts; scarce saint, yet half a child,
    As hard, as innocent.

What grave, long afternoons,
    What caged airs round her blown,
Stripped her of humor, left her bare   15
    As cloud, or wayside stone?

Made her as clear a thing,
    In this slack world as plain
As a white flower on a grave,
    Or sleet sharp at a pane?   20

Spring Ecstasy

Oh, let me run and hide,
    Let me run straight to God;
The weather is so mad with white
    From sky down to the clod!

If but one thing were so,   5
    Lilac, or thorn out there,
It would not be, indeed,
    So hard to bear.

The weather has gone mad with white;
    The cloud, the highway touch;   10
When lilac is enough;
    White thorn too much!

from *Selected Poems* (1926)

A Flower of Mullein[10]

I am too near, too clear a thing for you,
A flower of mullein in a crack of wall,
The villagers half-see, or not at all,
Part of the weather, like the wind or dew.
You love to pluck the different, and find   5
Stuff for your joy in cloudy loveliness;
You love to fumble at a door, and guess

A Flower of Mullein
[10]   *Mullein* a common wildflower that grows in waste
places. It belongs to a family of herbs possessing medicinal properties.

At some strange happening that may wait behind.
Yet life is full of tricks, and it is plain,
That men drift back to some worn field or roof, 10
To grip at comfort in a room, a stair;
To warm themselves at some flower down a lane:
You, too, may long, grown tired of the aloof,
For the sweet surety of the common air.

from *White April and Other Poems* (1930)

CROWS

Earth is raw with this one note,
This battered making of a song
Narrowed down to a crow's throat,
Above the willow-trees that throng

The crooking field from end to end. 5
Fixed as the sun, the grass, that sound;
Of what the weather has to spend,
As much a part as sky, or ground.

The primal yellow of that flower,
That tansy making August plain, 10
And the stored wildness of this hour,
It sucks up like a bitter rain.

Miss it we would, were it not here;
Simple as water, rough as spring,
It hurls us, at the point of spear, 15
Back to some naked, early thing.

Listen now. As with a hoof
It stamps an image on the gust:
Chimney by chimney, an old roof
Starts for a moment from its dust. 20

WHITE APRIL

The orchard is a pool, wherein I drown;
It is a very pool of loveliness.
I clutch the edge of a white world and press
To bottomless white billows down and down:
I clutch, I gasp, and all at once each spring 5
That I have known comes sharply to my mind,
Passes before me, and each one I find,
Stirs in me a packed, swift remembering.
Oh, pear-trees, ancient by an ancient lane,

A hundred at the delicate white start,⠀⠀⠀⠀⠀⠀⠀⠀10
Tall waves that roll and break upon a shore!
I struggle up, I am myself again:
Dripping with April, April to the heart,
I run back to the house, and bolt the door!

NINA

She was a woman like a candle-flame –
This stranger dead a score of years ago –
Tall, clearly dark. We loved, but said not so,
The slowness and the music of her name.
A widow. She was kind, the women knew,⠀⠀⠀⠀⠀5
And lent them patterns of her violet frocks;
And she had lovers. Past her high, crabbed box,
Went the sour judge, the rosy doctor, too.
Once, twice, a black word pricked the country-side.
She heard, and held a flower up to her lips,⠀⠀⠀⠀⠀10
Spoke brightly of our town, its small, close life:
On a wild morning of a sudden she died.
The next, a loud man, with the air of ships,
Stood at her coffin head: she was his wife.

from *Pastures and Other Poems* (1933)

THE WIDOWER

Half saint this dead girl was, yet her tight will
Rocked his dull house down to its doors. To think
How near at times she came to the dark brink
Of being a devil, makes him wonder still.
She was as cool as brambles after rain,⠀⠀⠀⠀⠀5
Clear of the dust of vulgar roads, and one –
Such delicate petals having need of sun –
To be forgiven, and to be loved again.
And like a bramble flower was her face,
With flash of fire beneath. He hated strife,⠀⠀⠀⠀⠀10
So ran back to his grey books on a shelf:
Yet can he set none other in her place.
She made a stir about the stems of life,
Kept April in him, being that herself.

TO A YOUNG POET

As fresh as are cowslips,
That blow the week-long,
The height of a finger,
Make you a song.

Of deep, simple things,   5
And near to your need
As the marrow to bone,
As the cowslip to seed.

Two pieces of wood
Made a cross one spring;   10
And is not a cross
A simple thing?

Charlotte Perkins Gilman (1860–1935)

Feminist, author, and lecturer, Charlotte Perkins Stetson Gilman was at the forefront of both asking and answering the "woman question" at the turn of the twentieth century. Although known today primarily for her psychological horror story, "The Yellow Wall Paper" (1892) and for her theoretical work, *Women and Economics* (1898), Gilman composed approximately five hundred poems. As with her prose works, Gilman uses her poetry to explore the social, political, and economic subjugation of women.

Charlotte Anna Perkins was born in Hartford, Connecticut, into a lineage of social reformers: Gilman's mother, Mary A. Finch, could trace her roots to the Puritan reformer Roger Williams; her father, Frederic Beecher Perkins, was the nephew of author and abolitionist Harriet Beecher Stowe. Shortly after Charlotte's birth, Frederic Perkins left his wife and family. He returned infrequently thereafter and provided little financial or emotional support to his family.

Gilman's early education consisted of readings from a list of books, mostly in history and the sciences, that her father sent home. At the age of eighteen, she enrolled in the Rhode Island School of Design. Even as she was in the process of gaining economic freedom, she met her first husband, Charles Walter Stetson. Worried over loss of independence, Gilman nevertheless agreed to marriage in 1884, only to find her new duties as stifling and depressing as she feared they would be.

With the birth of her daughter, Katherine Beecher Stetson, in 1885, Gilman's depression reached crisis proportions. When a trip west, without husband or child, gave her only temporary relief, Philadelphia "nerve specialist" S. Weir Mitchell was brought in. In what now must be one of the most famous misdiagnoses in women's literary history, Mitchell declared intellectual work the source of Gilman's problems and advised her "never touch pen, brush, or pencil" for the rest of her life. After a brief trial convinced Gilman that Mitchell's regime would only exacerbate her condition, she took the remaining option open to her. Taking Katherine with her, she departed for Pasadena, California, and a life of independence.

Once free to devote herself to her work, Gilman quickly became one of the most prominent feminist thinkers of her day, with *Women and Economics* her most important theoretical work. Her analysis of the role of economics in the social construction of gender is still considered relevant by feminist theorists today. In 1900, Gilman married her cousin, George Houghton Gilman. Unlike her first marriage, this one was based on equality and a recognition of the priority of Gilman's career. The years that followed were her most productive. Among the titles she published in this period were *Concerning Children* (1900),

The Home: Its Work and Influence (1903), and *Human Work* (1904). In 1932, Gilman was diagnosed with breast cancer. When her husband unexpectedly died in May of 1934, she moved back to Pasadena to live with her daughter Katherine and two grandchildren. On August 17, 1935, "preferring chloroform to cancer," Charlotte Perkins Stetson Gilman ended her life.

In many ways Gilman represents the lost love (or better, perhaps, the lost innocence) of second-wave feminism. The revival of interest in her work, first inspired by the Feminist Press's 1973 re-issue of "The Yellow Wall Paper," was quickly reinforced by admiration for *Women and Economics*. However, admiration for Gilman herself was cut short as scholars were forced to confront not just her racial eugenics, but the depth of her personal racism.

Yet as her poetry testifies, Gilman was a witty and accomplished writer, and as an author of feminist verse, she has a decidedly contemporary ring that can make her as relevant today as when she originally wrote. Whichever way one looks at her, she remains a highly significant figure in the history of American feminism, only now, perhaps, as much or more for what she says of feminism's limitations as of its strengths.

Robert Alsop with Paula Bennett

Primary Texts

"The Yellow Wall Paper," 1892; *In This Our World*, 1893, 1898; *Women and Economics*, 1898; *Herland*, 1915; *The Living of Charlotte Perkins Gilman: An Autobiography*, 1935; *The Later Poetry of Charlotte Perkins Gilman*, ed. Denise D. Knight, 1996.

Further Reading

Carol Farley Kessler, *Charlotte Perkins Gilman: Her Progress toward Utopia with Selected Writings*, New York: Syracuse University Press, 1995; Sheryl L. Meyering, ed., *Charlotte Perkins Gilman: The Woman and Her Work*, Ann Arbor: University of Michigan Research Press, 1989; Gary Scharnhorst, "Reconstructing *Here Also*: On the Later Poetry of Charlotte Perkins Gilman," in *Critical Essays on Charlotte Perkins Gilman*, ed. Joanne B. Karpinski, New York: G. K. Hall, 1992: 249–68.

from *In This Our World* (1893)

A NEVADA DESERT

An aching, blinding, barren, endless plain;
　　Corpse-colored with white mould of alkali;
Hairy with sage-brush, slimy after rain,
Burnt with the sky's hot scorn, and still again
　　Sullenly burning back against the sky.　　　　　　5

Dull green, dull brown, dull purple, and dull grey;
　　The hard earth white with ages of despair;
Slow-crawling, turbid streams where dead reeds sway;
Low wall of sombre mountains far away,
　　And sickly steam of geysers on the air.　　　　　　10

FALSE PLAY

"Do you love me?" asked the mother of her child,
  And the baby answered "No!"
Great Love listened and sadly smiled –
He knew the love in the heart of the child –
  That you could not wake it so.   5

"Do not love me?" the foolish mother cried;
  And the baby answered "No!"
He knew the worth of the trick she tried –
Great Love listened, and grieving sighed,
  That the mother scorned him so.   10

"O poor mama!" and she played her part
  Till the baby's strength gave way;
He [k]new it was false in his inmost heart
But he could not bear that her tears should start
  So he joined in the lying play.   15

"Then love mama!" and the soft lips crept
  To the kiss that his love should show;
The mouth to speak while the spirit slept!
Great Love listened, and blushed and wept
  That they blasphemed him so.   20

BABY LOVE

Baby [L]ove came prancing by,
Cap on head and sword on thigh, –
Horse to ride and drum to beat –
All the world beneath his feet. –

Mother Life was sitting there,   5
Hard at work and full of care, –
Set of mouth and sad of eye –
Baby Love came prancing by! –

Baby Love was very proud,
Very lively, very loud; –   10
Mother Life arose in wrath –
Set an arm across his path. –

Baby Love wept loud and long,
But his mother's arm was strong. –
Mother had to work, she said –   15
Baby Love was put to bed! –

from *In This Our World* (1898)

HOMES

A Sestina

We are the smiling comfortable homes
With happy families enthroned therein,
Where baby souls are brought to meet the world,
Where women end their duties and desires,
For which men labor as the goal of life,   5
That people worship now instead of God.

Do we not teach the child to worship God? –
Whose soul's young range is bounded by the homes
Of those he loves, and where he learns that life
Is all constrained to serve the wants therein,   10
Domestic needs and personal desires, –
These are the early limits of his world.

And are we not the woman's perfect world,
Prescribed by nature and ordained of God,
Beyond which she can have no right desires,   15
No need for service other than in homes?
For doth she not bring up her young therein?
And is not rearing young the end of life?

And man? What other need hath he in life
Than to go forth and labor in the world,   20
And struggle sore with other men therein?
Not to serve other men, nor yet his God,
But to maintain these comfortable homes, –
The end of all a normal man's desires.

Shall not the soul's most measureless desires   25
Learn that the very flower and fruit of life
Lies all attained in comfortable homes,
With which life's purpose is to dot the world
And consummate the utmost will of God,
By sitting down to eat and drink therein.   30

Yea, in the processes that work therein –
Fulfilment of our natural desires –
Surely man finds the proof that mighty God
For to maintain and reproduce his life
Created him and set him in the world;   35
And this high end is best attained in homes.

Are we not homes? And is not all therein?
Wring dry the world to meet our wide desires!
We crown all life! We are the aim of God!

THE BEDS OF FLEUR-DE-LYS[1]

High-lying, sea-blown stretches of green turf,
    Wind-bitten close, salt-colored by the sea,
Low curve on curve spread far to the cool sky,
And, curving over them as long they lie,
        Beds of wild fleur-de-lys.   5

Wide-flowing, self-sown, stealing near and far,
    Breaking the green like islands in the sea;
Great stretches at your feet, and spots that bend
Dwindling over the horizon's end, –
        Wild beds of fleur-de-lys.   10

The light keen wind streams on across the lifts,
    Their wind of western springtime by the sea;
The close turf smiles unmoved, but over her
Is the far-flying rustle and sweet stir
        In beds of fleur-de-lys.   15

And here and there across the smooth, low grass
    Tall maidens wander, thinking of the sea;
And bend, and bend, with light robes blown aside,
For the blue lily-flowers that bloom so wide, –
        The beds of fleur-de-lys.   20

THE HILLS

The flowing waves of our warm sea
    Roll to the beach and die,
But the soul of the waves forever fills
The curving crests of our restless hills
    That climb so wantonly.   5

Up and up till you look to see
    Along the cloud-kissed top
The great hill-breakers curve and comb
In crumbling lines of falling foam
    Before they settle and drop.   10

Down and down, with the shuddering sweep
    Of the sea-wave's glassy wall,

THE BEDS OF FLEUR-DE-LYS
[1] In her autobiography, *The Living of Charlotte Perkins Gilman*, Gilman comments of this "Burne-Jonesy poem," as she calls it, that it is "one of the very few poems among all my verses" (p. 188). She was in the Presidio area of San Francisco when she wrote it.

You sink with a plunge that takes your breath,
A thrill that stirreth and quickeneth,
   Like the great line steamer's fall.   15

We have laid our streets by the square and line,
   We have built by the line and square;
But the strong hill-rises arch below
And force the houses to curve and flow
   In lines of beauty there.   20

And off to the north and east and south,
   With wildering mists between,
They ring us round with wavering hold,
With fold on fold of rose and gold,
   Violet, azure, and green.   25

THE MOTHER'S CHARGE

She raised her head. With hot and glittering eye,
"I know," she said, "that I am going to die.
Come here, my daughter, while my mind is clear.
Let me make plain to you your duty here;
My duty once – I never failed to try –   5
But for some reason I am going to die."
She raised her head, and, while her eyes rolled wild,
Poured these instructions on the gasping child:

"Begin at once – don't iron sitting down –
Wash your potatoes when the fat is brown –   10
Monday, unless it rains – it always pays
To get fall sewing done on the right days –
A carpet-sweeper and a little broom –
Save dishes – wash the summer dining-room
With soda – keep the children out of doors –   15
The starch is out – beeswax on all the floors –

If girls are treated like your friends they stay –
They stay, and treat you like their friends – the way
To make home happy is to keep a jar –
And save the prettiest pieces for the star   20
In the middle – blue's too dark – all silk is best –
And don't forget the corners – when they're dressed
Put them on ice – and always wash the chest

Three times a day, the windows every week –
We need more flour – the bedroom ceilings leak –   25
It's better than onion – keep the boys at home –
Gardening is good – a load, three loads of loam –

They bloom in spring – and smile, smile always, dear –
Be brave, keep on – I hope I've made it clear."

She died, as all her mothers died before.   30
Her daughter died in turn, and made one more.

Louise Imogen Guiney (1861–1920)

Of Irish Catholic descent, Louise Imogen Guiney was born January 7, 1861, in Roxbury, Massachusetts, to Janet Margaret Doyle and Patrick Robert Guiney. The idol of his daughter's eye – "my *preux chevalier* of a father," Guiney called him – the Ireland-born Patrick Guiney rose to the rank of brigadier general in the Civil War. After being severely wounded, he retired from the military to take up a civilian career as lawyer and politician. His unexpected death in 1877 reduced his family to a state close to poverty, cutting Guiney's formal education short with her graduation from Elmhurst Academy, a Convent school in Providence, Rhode Island.

The need to support her family led Guiney into a number of unsuitable jobs that drained her physically and emotionally. In 1894, she assumed the position of postmistress in Auburndale, Massachusetts, a post from which militant anti-Irish and anti-Catholic sentiment in the community drove her three years later, but not before two physical breakdowns. She then tried working in the catalogue room of the Boston Public Library, a less personalized but no less deadening job. When not at the post office or the public library, she pieced together a living with an odd combination of hack work and scholarly writing. After several trips to Europe, one with her mother (1889–91) and another, a walking tour of England and Wales in 1895, she abandoned the United States altogether, and settled in Oxford, England in 1901. Although she hoped for greater success in Britain, it did not materialize. Unable to hold on to the money she made, she died on February 5, 1920, in Chipping Campden near Oxford, in poverty and attended only by her niece.

Like her life story, the story of Guiney's writing career is, at least on the surface, one of gallant failure. Despite early recognition and the approbation of the elite Boston and New York literary communities, Guiney, as Cheryl Walker notes, was never a popular poet, and her books sold poorly. Whether from lack of pecuniary encouragement or because the external circumstances of her life finally undermined her ability to write, her poetic vein ran out early, concluding with *Happy Ending* (1909, enl. 1927), her all-too-ironically named final volume.

Guiney herself recognized that she was finished. Calling the muse "a base baggage," she was honest enough as a writer not to go chasing hopelessly after her. As she so often did in her career, she turned to the comforts of esoteric scholarship instead: an edition of Henry Vaughan, a seventeenth-century British poet, and an anthology of Catholic recusant poets, never published. She had, as her close friend and memorialist, Alice Brown, observed, a way of making misfortune into a grace.

And it may be because she did that despite the slimness of her production, Guiney ranks among the most significant women poets of the *fin de siècle*, and one of the few to whom early modernists acknowledged a debt.

Guiney's poetry is a paradoxical blend of conservatism and daring that makes it fascinating to read today. She was a sensitive and careful poet with a fine ear, and an excellent control of tone. Her subtle dependence on cadence (as opposed to the metronome) helped pave the way for free verse, although she herself never experimented that way. Yet like Reese and Thomas, she also seems to have wanted to live in the past, this despite the apparent Bohemianism and the devil-may-care attitude of her personal life, and despite the aestheticism she cultivated in her writing and taste.

Much of Guiney's best work cannot be separated from her fervent Catholicism, or (simultaneously) from her deep love for and knowledge of the classics. It is typical that she saw herself like her father in terms of the "Cavalier" spirit and in terms of a gallantry and rebelliousness unassimilable to the time and place in which she lived. Even her choice of titles – from the loosely "pagan" "Alexandriana" to the sternly Catholic "Deo Optimo Maximo" – projects these conflicted yearnings.

Whether one looks to her life or her writing, Guiney exhibits, in short, the kinds of internal conflicts and multi-positionings that mark her distinctively as a woman of her era – a woman who stood on the brink of the modernist period, and who, without quite crossing over herself, helped make it possible for others to do so.

Primary Texts

Songs at the Start, 1884; *The White Sail and Other Poems*, 1887; *A Roadside Harp: A Book of Verses*, 1893; *The Martyrs' Idyl, and Shorter Poems*, 1899; *Happy Ending: The Collected Lyrics of Louise Imogen Guiney*, 1909, enl. 1927.

Further Reading

Alice Brown, *Louise Imogen Guiney*, New York: Macmillan, 1921; Bliss Carman, "Contemporaries IV: Louise Imogen Guiney," *Chap-Book* 2 (November 1894): 27–36; Henry G. Fairbanks, *Louise Imogen Guiney: Laureate of the Lost*, Albany, New York: Magi Books, 1972; T. J. Jackson Lears, *No Place for Grace*, New York: Pantheon, 1981; Michele J. Leggott, "Louise Imogen Guiney," *DLB* 54: 136–46; Barbara Ryan, "Louise Imogen Guiney," *Encyclopedia of American Poetry*; Sheila A. Tully, "Heroic Failures and the Literary Career of Louise Imogen Guiney," *American Transcendental Quarterly* 47–8 (Summer–Fall 1980): 171–86.

from *A Roadside Harp: A Book of Verses* (1893)

FLORENTIN[1]

Heart all full of heavenly haste, too like the bubble bright
On loud little water floating half of an April night,
Fled from the ear in music, fled from the eye in light,

Dear and stainless heart of a boy! No sweeter thing can be
Drawn to the quiet centre of God who is our sea;   5
Whither, thro' troubled valleys, we also follow thee.

FLORENTIN
[1] In later reprints of this poem Guiney added AD MDCCCXC (1890 CE) after the title, presumably a reference to the child's date of death. The striking similarity between this poem and Dickinson's elegy to her nephew, Gilbert (1564), has to be coincidental since the latter was not published until 1924, but like a number of such "coincidences" throughout this anthology it remains unnerving.

HYLAS[2]

Jar in arm, they bade him rove
Thro' the alder's long alcove,
Where the hid spring musically
Gushes to the ample valley.
(There's a bird on the under bough   5
Fluting evermore and now:
"Keep – young!" but who knows how?)

Down the woodland corridor,
Odors deepened more and more;
Blossomed dogwood, in the briers,   10
Struck her faint delicious fires;
Miles of April passed between
Crevices of closing green,
And the moth, the violet-lover,
By the wellside saw him hover.   15

Ah, the slippery sylvan dark!
Never after shall he mark
Noisy ploughmen drinking, drinking,
On his drownèd cheek down-sinking;
Quit of serving is that wild,   20
Absent, and bewitchèd child,
Unto action, age, and danger,
Thrice a thousand years a stranger.

Fathoms low, the naiads[3] sing
In a birthday welcoming;[4]   25
Water-white their breasts, and o'er him,
Water-gray, their eyes adore him.
(There's a bird on the under bough
Fluting evermore and now:
"Keep – young!" but who knows how?)   30

HYLAS
[2] In Greek mythology, a beautiful youth, beloved of
Hercules. While serving as an Argonaut, he was sent to
fetch water from a spring. There, the Naiads or nymphs
who lived in the spring, catching sight of his beauty,
dragged him in and his body was never found.

[3] *Naiads* nymphs inhabiting streams, rivers, and
lakes.
[4] Guiney appears to be suggesting that Hylas's "death"
in this life marked his rebirth (or "birthday") in the
next.

from "ALEXANDRIANA"[5]

VII.

Here lies one in the earth who scarce of the earth was moulded,
Wise Æthalides' son,[6] himself no lover of study,
Cnopus, asleep, indoors: the young invincible runner.
They from the cliff footpath that see on the grave we made him,
Tameless, slant in the wind, the bare and beautiful iris,   5
Stop short, full of delight, and shout forth: "See, it is Cnopus
Runs, with white throat forward, over the sands to Chalcis!"[7]

XII.

Cows in the narrowing August marshes,
Cows in a stretch of water
Motionless,   10
Neck on neck overlapped and drooping;

These in their troubled and dumb communion,
Thou on the steep bank yonder,
Pastora!
No more ever to lead and love them,   15

No more ever. Thine innocent mourners
Pass thy tree in the evening
Heavily,
Hearing another herd-girl calling.

XIII.

Praise thou the Mighty Mother for what is wrought, not me,   20
A nameless nothing-caring head asleep against her knee.

from Chap-Book (1896)

EMILY BRONTË[8]

What sacramental hurt that brings
The terror of the truth of things,
Had changed thee? Secret be it yet.

<hr>

FROM "ALEXANDRIANA"
[5]   Guiney is using this term to designate the kind of brief, epigrammatic poetry of varied line lengths and meters that forms the bulk of the *Greek Anthology*, a heterogeneous collection dominated by poets of the Hellenistic era. Her poems are sufficiently faithful to the spirit of this work that many readers mistook them for translations, much to her delight.

[6]   Both the "wise Æthalides" and his son, Cnopus, "the young invincible runner," are imaginary figures; but the garden they inhabit – the Greek view of death as metamorphosis – is, in this poem, exquisitely real.
[7]   Chalcis or Khalkis was the chief city and trading center of ancient Euboea, the largest of the Greek islands after Crete. Aristotle died there in 322 BCE.
EMILY BRONTË
[8]   Emily Brontë (1818–48), British novelist and poet.

'T was thine, upon a headland set,
To view no isle of man's delight   5
With lyric foam in rainbow flight,
But all a-swing, a-gleam, mid slow uproar,
Black-sea, and curved uncouth sea-bitten shore.

MONOCHROME

Shut fast again in beauty's sheath,
Where ancient forms renew,
The round world seems, above, beneath,
One wash of faintest blue.

And air and tide so stilly sweet   5
In nameless union lie;
The little far-off fishing fleet
Goes drifting up the sky.

Secure of neither misted coast,
Nor ocean undefined,   10
Our brooding sail is like the ghost
Of one that served mankind,

Who sad in space, as we upon
This visionary sea,
Finds Labour and Allegiance done,   15
And Self begin to be.

from *The Martyrs' Idyl, and Shorter Poems* (1899)

DEO OPTIMO MAXIMO[9]

All else for use, one only for desire;
Thanksgiving for the good, but thirst for Thee:
Up from the best, whereof no man need tire,
Impel thou me.

Delight is menace, if Thou brood not by,   5
Power is a quicksand, Fame a gathering jeer.
Oft as the morn, (though none of earth deny
These three are dear,)

Wash me of them, that I may be renewed,
Nor wall in clay mine agonies and joys: 10

DEO OPTIMO MAXIMO
[9]   Latin: "for God the best and greatest," motto of the
Benedictine religious order.

O close my hand upon Beatitude!
Not on her toys.

CHARISTA MUSING

Moveless, on the marge of a sunny cornfield,
Rapt in sudden revery while thou standest,
Like the sheaves, in beautiful Doric[10] yellow
Clad to the ankle,

Oft to thee with delicate hasty footstep   5
So I steal, and suffer because I find thee
Inly flown, and only a fallen feather
Left of my darling.

Give me back thy wakening breath, thy ringlets
Fragrant as the vine of the bean in blossom,   10
And those eyes of violet dusk and daylight
Under sea-water,

Eyes too far away, and too full of longing!
Yes: and go not heavenward where I lose thee,
Go not, go not whither I cannot follow,   15
Being but earthly.

Willing swallow poisèd upon my finger,
Little wild-wing ever from me escaping,
For the care thou art to me, I thy lover
Love thee, and fear thee.   20

from *Happy Ending: The Collected Lyrics of Louise Imogen Guiney* (1909)

ROMANS IN DORSET[11]

AD MDCCCXCV

A stupor on the heath,
And wrath along the sky;

CHARISTA MUSING
[10]   The Doric order (or style) was the oldest and simplest of the three major Greek architectural and musical modes. Guiney appears to want to associate Charista with classical Greek beauty and simplicity. Her name (Charista) derives from the Latin for love (as does the modern English, "charity") and there may also be a pun on "musing" ("Muse" or source of poetic inspiration, as in Greek mythology).
ROMANS IN DORSET
[11]   In southwest Britain. Dorset is famed for its Roman ruins. The date (1895 CE) probably refers to when the poem was written.

Space everywhere; beneath
A flat and treeless wold[12] for us, and darkest noon on high.

Sullen quiet below,   5
But storm in upper air!
A wind from long ago,
In mouldy chambers of the cloud had ripped an arras there,

And singed the triple gloom,
And let through, in a flame,   10
Crowned faces of old Rome:
Regnant o'er Rome's abandoned ground, processional they came.

Uprisen as any sun
Through vistas hollow grey,
Aloft, and one by one,   15
In brazen casques[13] the Emperors loomed large, and sank away.

In ovals of wan light
Each warrior eye and mouth:
A pageant brutal bright
As if once over loudly passed Jove's laughter in the south;   20

And dimmer, these among,
Some cameo'd head aloof,
With ringlets heavy-hung,
Like yellow stonecrop comely grown around a castle roof.

An instant: gusts again,   25
Then heaven's impacted wall,
The hot insistent rain,
The thunder-shock; and of the Past mirage no more at all,

No more the alien dream
Pursuing, as we went,   30
With glory's cursèd gleam;
Nor sin of Caesar's[14] ruined line engulfed us, innocent.

The vision great and dread
Corroded; sole in view
Was empty Egdon[15] spread,   35
Her crimson summer weeds ashake in tempest: but we knew

---

[12] *Wold* a piece of high open uncultivated land or moor.
[13] *Casques* helmets or military headpieces.

[14] Julius Caesar (102–44 BCE). His "line" served as the first emperors of Rome and became increasingly corrupt.
[15] The mythical heath in Thomas Hardy's novel, *The Return of the Native*.

What Tacitus[16] had borne
In that wrecked world we saw;
And what, thine heart uptorn,
My Juvenal![17] distraught with love of violated Law.   40

from "LONDON"

IX. Sunday Chimes in the City

Across the bridge, where in the morning blow
The wrinkled tide turns homeward, and is fain
Homeward to drag the black sea-goer's chain,
And the long yards by Dowgate[18] dipping low;
Across dispeopled ways, patient and slow,   5
Saint Magnus and Saint Dunstan[19] call in vain:
From Wren's forgotten belfries, in the rain,
Down the blank wharves the dropping octaves go.

Forbid not these! Though no man heed, they shower
A subtle beauty on the empty hour,   10
From all their dark throats aching and outblown;
Aye in the prayerless places welcome most,
Like the last gull that up some naked coast
Deploys her white and steady wing, alone.

from *Happy Ending: The Collected Lyrics of Louise Imogen Guiney* (1927)

DESPOTISMS

I. The Motor: 1905[20]

From hedgerows where aromas fain would be
  New volleyed odours execrably arise;
  The flocks, with hell-smoke in their patient eyes,
Into the ditch from bawling ruin flee:
Spindrift of one abominated sea   5
  Along all roads in wrecking fury flies
  Till on young strangled leaf, on bloom that dies,
In this far plot it writes a rune[21] for me.

---

[16] Tacitus (*c.* 55–*c.* 117 CE), a Roman historian best known for his history of the reigns of the Roman "Caesars" from Tiberius through the first years of Nero.
[17] Juvenal (fl. first to second century CE), a Roman satirist who vividly depicted the corruption of life under the empire.
FROM "LONDON"
[18] Dowgate Hill, a street in London below Southwark Bridge.
[19] Saint Magnus and Saint Dunstan, two London churches noted for their towers which were built by the

great British architect, Sir Christopher Wren, at the end of the seventeenth century.
DESPOTISMS
[20] The first self-propelled vehicle was built in Paris in 1789. By 1890, the internal combustion machine or horseless buggy was being manufactured in the United States by Henry Ford, Ransom E. Olds, and others.
[21] *Rune* an ancient character used in Teutonic, Anglo-Saxon, and Scandinavian inscriptions. The word is derived from an early Anglo-Saxon word meaning "secret" or "mystery."

Vast intimate tyranny! Nature dispossessed
 Helplessly hates thee, whose symbolic flare   10
Lights up (with what reiterance unblest!)
 Entrails of horror in a world thought fair.
False God of pastime thou, vampire of rest,
 Augur of what pollution, what despair?

II. The War: 1915

Speed without ruth, seedsman of vile success,   15
 Accustomed sight to ne'er-accustomed view!
 Am I not vindicate who strongly knew
Some portent there of pregnant ugliness?
The dooms are in; my soul hath won her guess.
 That which formed thee and franchised, had the cue   20
 To push all rudeness forward, and was due
To spawn ere long the sovereign menace.
 Yes,

Horror has come, has come! Horror set high,
 And drunk with boundless access, whirls amain: 25
Lost on the wind is Belgia's[22] holy cry,
 And Poland's hope shrinks underground again,
And France is singing to her wounds, where lie
 The golden English heads like harvest grain.

E. Pauline Johnson (Tekahionwake) (1861–1913)

Emily Pauline Johnson's (Tekahionwake's) father was George Henry Martin Johnson
(Onwanonsyshon), a Mohawk chief. She was born on March 10, 1861 at her father's estate,
"Chiefswood," on the Six Nation reserve in the county of Brant, Ontario. The Six Nations
of the Iroquois confederacy received this land after their loyalty to the British crown during
the American Revolution led to their expulsion from what is now upstate New York. Born
in Bristol, England, Johnson's mother, Emily Howells Johnson, came to the United States
with her family when she was eight years old. Her Quaker father, Henry Charles Howells,
was the great uncle of the American author and editor W. D. Howells, one of the late
nineteenth century's best known literary figures.

  Raised on the Six Nation reserve, Johnson's formal education was minimal – a governess
for two years, followed by two years at an Indian day school close to her home, and two
more years in the central school of the city of Brantford. She was, however, an avid reader,
especially of poetry, and before she was twelve, she had consumed large tracts of Scott,
Longfellow, Byron, and Shakespeare under her mother's guidance.

  Although she had already published a few poems, Johnson's first big break as an author
came when she recited "A Cry from an Indian Wife," before an assembled gathering of
Canadian literati at the Young Liberal Club of Toronto in 1892. The wildly positive

---

[22] Belgium.

response to her empathic presentation of the Indian side of the Northwest rebellion hit the newspapers the following morning, leading to requests that she perform her poems in public, and to calls for a book. Johnson's nearly two-decade career as a public performer of her own poetry, typically dressed in Indian costume for the "Indian" part of the evening, was launched.

Johnson's poetry was an inseparable part of her life as a performer and was largely shaped by it. Giving public recitals enabled her to earn enough money to travel to Britain, where she found a publisher for her first book, *The White Wampum* – and gave performances in the drawing rooms of the British nobility. Thereafter these recitals remained her primary source of income. Enormously popular though they were, however, they also destroyed her health and the stability of her personal life as she traversed the length and breadth of Canada staging her art. (She crossed the Rocky Mountains nineteen times under basically primitive conditions.)

In 1909, Johnson was forced to retire from the performance circuit for health reasons, despite the fact that this was how she made her living. Settling in Vancouver, she published *The Legends of Vancouver* (1911), a set of West Coast Indian legends, as told to her by Squamish Chief Joseph Capilano. Diagnosed with cancer, she published two more books to raise money for her own care, *Flint and Feather* (1912), her last poetry collection, and *The Shagganappi* (1913), a collection of twenty-two romantic adventure stories. Johnson died on March 7, 1913. Her last collection of stories, *The Moccasin Maker*, was published posthumously.

In her writing as in her life, Johnson used her liminal position as a mixed-blood to bridge differences between races and cultures, and insofar as she is one of Canada's best loved writers, she remains a bridge between peoples to this day. Yet it is not in her "Indian" poetry *per se* that Johnson speaks most effectively to many modern readers. For such readers, the current editor among them, these poems (for which she donned Indian garb to recite) seem often too close to "costume" poetry themselves. For all their moments of fire and anguish (the moving conclusion of "A Cry from an Indian Wife" is a good example), their very rhetoricality and the relative predictability of their content, for example their emphasis on Indian blood-thirstiness, reflect her period's tastes – and, unhappily, its stereotypes – too well.

Rather, Johnson is most impressive in those poems in which she speaks quietly of the dilemmas and pains characterizing the Indian present, poems such as "The Indian Corn Planter," which turns on the unstressed pathos of a hunter's conversion to farmer, and "The Cornhusker," which through the image of empty husks mourns the reality of Indian loss. In these poems, as in some of her more personal lyrics, where Johnson exhibits her deep sense of harmony with nature, or her own eroticism, she is fully able to escape the stage, creating poems as alive and immediate to readers now as on the day that they were written.

Primary Texts

The White Wampum, 1895; *Canadian Born*, 1903; *The Legends of Vancouver*, 1911; *Flint and Feather*, 1912; *The Moccasin Maker*, 1913.

Further Reading

Paula Gunn Allen, ed., *Studies in American Indian Literature: Critical Essays and Course Designs*, New York: MLA, 1983; Betty Keller, *Pauline: A Biography of Pauline Johnson*, Vancouver: Douglas & McIntyre, 1981; Marcus Van Steen, *Pauline Johnson: Her Life and Work*, Toronto: Hodder & Stoughton, 1965.

from *The White Wampum* (1895)

A CRY FROM AN INDIAN WIFE

My Forest Brave, my Red-skin love, farewell;
We may not meet to-morrow; who can tell
What mighty ills befall our little band,
Or what you'll suffer from the white man's hand?
Here is your knife! I thought 'twas sheathed for aye. 5
No roaming bison calls for it to-day;
No hide of prairie cattle will it maim;
The plains are bare, it seeks a nobler game:
'Twill drink the life-blood of a soldier host.
Go; rise and strike, no matter what the cost. 10
Yet stay. Revolt not at the Union Jack,
Nor raise Thy hand against this stripling pack
Of white-faced warriors, marching West to quell
Our fallen tribe that rises to rebel.
They all are young and beautiful and good; 15
Curse to the war that drinks their harmless blood.
Curse to the fate that brought them from the East
To be our chiefs — to make our nation least
That breathes the air of this vast continent.
Still their new rule and council is well meant. 20
They but forget we Indians owned the land
From ocean unto ocean; that they stand
Upon a soil that centuries agone
Was our sole kingdom and our right alone.
They never think how they would feel to-day, 25
If some great nation came from far away,
Wresting their country from their hapless braves,
Giving what they gave us – but wars and graves.
Then go and strike for liberty and life,
And bring back honour to your Indian wife. 30
Your wife?   Ah, what of that, who cares for me?
Who pities my poor love and agony?
What white-robed priest prays for your safety here,
As prayer is said for every volunteer
That swells the ranks that Canada sends out? 35
Who prays for vict'ry for the Indian scout?
Who prays for our poor nation lying low?
None – therefore take your tomahawk and go.
My heart may break and burn into its core,
But I am strong to bid you go to war. 40
Yet stay, my heart is not the only one
That grieves the loss of husband and of son;
Think of the mothers o'er the inland seas;
Think of the pale-faced maiden on her knees;

One pleads her God to guard some sweet-faced child   45
That marches on toward the North-West wild.
The other prays to shield her love from harm,
To strengthen his young, proud uplifted arm.
Ah, how her white face quivers thus to think,
Your tomahawk his life's best blood will drink.   50
She never thinks of my wild aching breast,
Nor prays for your dark face and eagle crest
Endangered by a thousand rifle balls,
My heart the target if my warrior falls.
O! coward self I hesitate no more;   55
Go forth, and win the glories of the war.
Go forth, nor bend to greed of white man's hands,
By right, by birth we Indians own these lands,
Though starved, crushed, plundered, lies our nation low. . . .
Perhaps the white man's God has willed it so.   60

The Camper

Night 'neath the northern skies, lone, black, and grim:
Naught but the starlight lies 'twixt heaven, and him.

Of man no need has he, of God, no prayer;
He and his Deity are brothers there.

Above his bivouac the firs fling down   5
Through branches gaunt and black, their needles brown.

Afar some mountain streams, rockbound and fleet,
Sing themselves through his dreams in cadence sweet,

The pine trees whispering, the heron's cry,
The plover's wing, his lullaby.   10

And blinking overhead the white stars keep
Watch o'er his hemlock bed – his sinless sleep.

Marshlands

A thin wet sky, that yellows at the rim,
And meets with sun-lost lip the marsh's brim.

The pools low lying, dank with moss and mould,
Glint through their mildews like large cups of gold.

Among the wild rice in the still lagoon,   5
In monotone the lizard shrills his tune.

The wild goose, homing, seeks a sheltering,
Where rushes grow, and oozing lichens cling.

Late cranes with heavy wing, and lazy flight,
Sail up the silence with the nearing night.   10

And like a spirit, swathed in some soft veil,
Steals twilight and its shadows o'er the swale.

Hushed lie the sedges, and the vapours creep,
Thick, grey and humid, while the marshes sleep.

THE IDLERS

The sun's red pulses beat,
Full prodigal of heat,
Full lavish of its lustre unrepressed;
But we have drifted far
From where his kisses are,   5
And in this landward-lying shade we let our paddles rest.

The river, deep and still,
The maple-mantled hill,
The little yellow beach whereon we lie,
The puffs of heated breeze,   10
All sweetly whisper – These
Are days that only come in a Canadian July.

So, silently we two
Lounge in our still canoe,
Nor fate, nor fortune matters to us now: 15
So long as we alone
May call this dream our own,
The breeze may die, the sail may droop, we care not when or how.

Against the thwart, near by,
Inactively you lie,   20
And all too near my arm your temple bends.
Your indolently crude,
Abandoned attitude,
Is one of ease and art, in which a perfect languor blends.

Your costume, loose and light,   25
Leaves unconcealed your might
Of muscle, half suspected, half defined;
And falling well aside,
Your vesture opens wide,
Above your splendid sunburnt throat that pulses unconfined.   30

With easy unreserve,
Across the gunwale's curve,

Your arm superb is lying, brown and bare;
Your hand just touches mine
With import firm and fine,   35
(I kiss the very wind that blows about your tumbled hair).

Ah! Dear, I am unwise
In echoing your eyes
Whene'er they leave their far-off gaze, and turn
To melt and blur my sight;   40
For every other light
Is servile to your cloud-grey eyes, wherein cloud shadows burn.

But once the silence breaks,
But once your ardour wakes
To words that humanize this lotus-land;   45
So perfect and complete
Those burning words and sweet,
So perfect is the single kiss your lips lay on my hand.

The paddles lie disused,
The fitful breeze abused,   50
Has dropped to slumber, with no after-blow;
And hearts will pay the cost,
For you and I have lost
More than the homeward blowing wind that died an hour ago.

from *Flint and Feather* (1912)

THE CORN HUSKER

Hard by the Indian lodges, where the bush
    Breaks in a clearing, through ill-fashioned fields,
She comes to labour, when the first still hush
    Of autumn follows large and recent yields.

Age in her fingers, hunger in her face,   5
    Her shoulders stooped with weight of work and years,
But rich in tawny colouring of her race,
    She comes a-field to strip the purple ears.

And all her thoughts are with the days gone by,
    Ere might's injustice banished from their lands   10
Her people, that to-day unheeded lie,
    Like the dead husks that rustle through her hands.
                                (*Canadian Born* 1903)

SILHOUETTE

The sky-line melts from the russet into blue,
Unbroken the horizon, saving where
A wreath of smoke curls up the far, thin air,
And points the distant lodges of the Sioux.

Etched where the lands and cloudlands touch and die   5
A solitary Indian tepee stands,
The only habitation of these lands,
That roll their magnitude from sky to sky.

The tent poles lift and loom in thin relief,
The upward floating smoke ascends between,   10
And near the open doorway, gaunt and lean,
And shadow-like, there stands an Indian Chief.

With eyes that lost their lustre long ago,
With visage fixed and stern as fate's decree,
He looks towards the empty west, to see   15
The never-coming herd of buffalo.

Only the bones that bleach upon the plains,
Only the fleshless skeletons that lie
In ghastly nakedness and silence, cry
Out mutely that naught else to him remains.   20

(Canadian Born 1903)

LULLABY OF THE IROQUOIS

Little brown baby-bird, lapped in your nest,
   Wrapped in your nest,
   Strapped in your nest,
Your straight little cradle-board rocks you to rest;
   Its hands are your nest;   5
   Its bands are your nest;
It swings from the down-bending branch of the oak;
You watch the camp-flame, and curling grey smoke;
But, oh, for your pretty black eyes sleep is best, –
Little brown baby of mine, go to rest.   10

Little brown baby-bird swinging to sleep,
   Winging to sleep,
   Singing to sleep,
Your wonder-black eyes that so wide open keep,
   Shielding their sleep,   15
   Unyielding to sleep,
The heron is homing, the plover is still,
The night-owl calls from his haunt on the hill,

Afar the fox barks, afar the stars peep, –
Little brown baby of mine, go to sleep.   20

(*Canadian Born* 1903)

THE CITY, AND THE SEA

To none the city[1] bends a servile knee.
  Purse-proud and scornful, on her heights she stands,
And at her feet the great white moaning sea
  Shoulders incessantly the grey-gold sands, –
One the Almighty's child since time began,   5
  And one the might of Mammon,[2] born of clods;
For all the city is the work of man,
  But all the sea is God's.

And she – between the ocean and the town –
  Lies cursed of one and by the other blest: 10
Her staring eyes, her long drenched hair, her gown
  Sea-laved and soiled and dank above her breast.
She, image of her God since life began,
  She, but the child of Mammon, born of clods,
Her broken body spoiled and spurned of man,   15
  But her sweet soul is God's.

(*Canadian Born* 1903)

THE TRAIN DOGS

Out of the night and the north;
  Savage of breed and of bone,
Shaggy and swift comes the yelping band,
Freighters of fur from the voiceless land
  That sleeps in the Arctic zone.   5

Laden with skins from the north,
  Beaver and bear and raccoon,
Marten and mink from the polar belts,
Otter and ermine and sable pelts –
  The spoils of the hunter's moon.   10

Out of the night and the north,
  Sinewy, fearless and fleet,
Urging the pack through the pathless snow,
The Indian driver, calling low,
  Follows with moccasined feet.   15

Ships of the night and the north,
  Freighters on prairies and plains,

THE CITY, AND THE SEA

[1] Vancouver, British Columbia, Canada. The largest
city in West Canada and a major port and manufactur-
ing center.

[2] *Mammon* Aramaic term meaning material wealth,
as in the biblical expression, "Ye cannot serve both God
and mammon" (Luke 16:9,11,13 and Matthew 6:24).

Carrying cargoes from field and flood
They scent the trail through their wild red blood,
The wolfish blood in their veins.   20

THE INDIAN CORN PLANTER

He needs must leave the trapping and the chase,
    For mating game his arrows ne'er despoil,
And from the hunter's heaven turn his face,
    To wring some promise from the dormant soil.

He needs must leave the lodge that wintered him,   5
    The enervating fires, the blanket bed –
The women's dulcet voices, for the grim
    Realities of labouring for bread.

So goes he forth beneath the planter's moon
    With sack of seed that pledges large increase,   10
His simple pagan faith knows night and noon,
    Heat, cold, seedtime and harvest shall not cease.

And yielding to his needs, this honest sod,
    Brown as the hand that tills it, moist with rain,
Teeming with ripe fulfillment, true as God,   15
    With fostering richness, mothers every grain.

Sophie Jewett (1861–1909)

Sophie Jewett was born on June 3, 1861 in Moravia, a small town in the lake country of central New York. Jewett's father, Dr Charles Carroll Jewett, was a country doctor. Her mother, Ellen Ransom Burroughs, died of acute neuralgia of the heart when Sophie was seven. Together with her three siblings, Sophie was wakened from sleep to witness her mother's death agony, an event whose impress remained with her all her life. Charles Jewett died two years later when Sophie was nine. After his death, the children moved to Buffalo, where they resided with their uncle and grandmother, both of whom died while Jewett was still in her teens.

In Buffalo, Jewett fell under the influence of her minister, Rev. Wolcott Calkins, whose daughter, Mary Whiton Calkins, remained Jewett's staunchest friend through life. The Calkinses provided a second home for the twice-orphaned young woman and Mary Calkins remembers Jewett and herself in her father's study, discussing "grave mysteries or bent together over books in strange tongues." As a last act of friendship, with Louise Rogers Jewett, the poet's sister, Calkins edited Jewett's posthumous volume of poetry and wrote the introductory memoir. This, and an obituary by Katherine Lee Bates are, to my know-ledge, the sole sources of biographical information extant on the poet.

Jewett was an imaginative child and a voracious reader. Without a formal higher edu-cation (her schooling appears to have ended with graduation from Buffalo Seminary), she became dependent on her own resources. In her early twenties, she supplemented her extensive reading with travel abroad. Later, after she became a teacher, she familiarized herself with the great libraries of London and Oxford, Florence and Rome. Her pursuit was the literature of the past, and although she always, according to Bates, questioned her fitness to teach, she made herself a competent specialist in Anglo-Saxon and medieval British literature.

Jewett began teaching English literature at Wellesley College in 1889, receiving tenure in 1899. At Wellesley, she also became part of the circle of unmarried women surrounding Bates, the chair of the Wellesley English department. Whether the women who composed this circle, which extended to Mount Holyoke and included Miss Jeanette Marks and Miss Mary Woolley, would have thought of themselves as lesbians is moot, but whether or not they would have, what is clear is that after Dickinson, Jewett is the nineteenth century's most accomplished writer of Sapphic verse. Other than scholarly translations, Jewett published two books of poetry in her lifetime, *The Pilgrim and Other Poems* (1896) and *Persephone and Other Poems* (1905). Neither attracted much attention, and with her premature death in 1909, she slipped from sight with as little notice as she had lived.

Written in the school of romantic friendship, Jewett's lesbian poetry has obvious affinities to that of Kemble, Fuller, Thaxter, Lazarus, and Dickinson, not to mention the many less well-known writers who seeded the century with poems in which one woman expresses passionate devotion to another. Yet the modernity of her style and of her awareness also ties her to Amy Lowell and H. D. Like so many late nineteenth-century figures, she was, in fact, a transition poet, opening the way for the more self-conscious work that would be the burden and pleasure of modernist lesbian women to produce.

Primary Texts

The Pilgrim and Other Poems, 1896; *Persephone and Other Poems*, 1905; *The Poems of Sophie Jewett*, eds Mary Whiton Calkins and Louise Rogers Jewett, 1910.

Further Reading

Katherine Lee Bates, "Sophie Jewett: the Passing of a Real Poet," Memorial article, Wellesley College Archives, [1909]; Mary Whiton Calkins, "Biographical Introduction," in *The Poems of Sophie Jewett*, eds Mary Whiton Calkins and Louise Rogers Jewett, Cambridge, Massachusetts: Thomas Y. Crowell, 1910; Lillian Faderman, *Surpassing the Love of Men: Romantic Friendship and Love Between Women from the Renaissance to the Present*, New York: Murrow, 1981.

from *The Poems of Sophie Jewett* (1910)

ENTRE NOUS[1]

I talk with you of foolish things and wise,
    Of persons, places, books, desires and aims,
Yet all our words a silence underlies,
    An earnest, vivid thought that neither names.

Ah! what to us were foolish talk or wise?   5
    Were persons, places, books, desires or aims,

ENTRE NOUS
[1] French: "between us," usually with the connotation of extreme privacy.

Without the deeper sense that underlies,
      The sweet encircling thought that neither names?
                      (MS 1882)

SEPARATION

Along the Eastern shore the low waves creep,
    Making a ceaseless music on the sand,
    A song that gulls and curlews understand,
The lullaby that sings the day to sleep.
A thousand miles afar, the grim pines keep   5
    Unending watch upon a shoreless land,
    Yet through their tops, swept by some wizard hand,
The sound of surf comes singing up the steep.

Sweet, thou canst hear the tidal litany;
    I, mid the pines land-wearied, may but dream   10
    Of the far shore; but though the distance seem
Between us fixed, impassable, to me
    Cometh thy soul's voice, chanting love's old theme,
    And mine doth answer, as the pines the sea.
                      (MS 1885)

A DREAM

Last night, what time dreams wander east and west,
    What time a dream may linger, I lay dead,
    With flare of tapers pale above my head,
With weight of drifted roses on my breast;
And they, who noiseless came to watch my rest,   5
    Looked kindly down and gentle sentence said.

One sighed "She was but young to go to-day;"
    And one "How fiercely life with death had striven
    Ere God set free her spirit, sorrow-shriven!"
One said "The children grieve for her at play;"   10
And one, who bent to take a rose away,
    Whispered "Dear love, would that we had forgiven."
                 (*Scribner's Magazine* 1888)

METEMPSYCHOSIS[2]

I watch thy face, Sweetheart, with half belief
    In olden tales of the soul's wayfaring;
    I marvel from what past thy young eyes bring
Their heritage of long entailed grief.

METEMPSYCHOSIS
[2] The theory that the soul is reincarnated in successive
births.

I watch thy face and soft as through a dream   5
   I see not thee, but some fair, fated Greek,
   Whose carven lips grow flesh straightway and speak
Stern words and sad, with perfect curves that seem

But as the cynic sweetness of thy smile,
   Set quivering over tears in self-despite.   10
   Again I watch by mystic taper-light,
Where a pale saint doth kneel a weary while;

I hear the murmured passion of her prayer,
   Imploring heaven for boon of sacrifice;
   I read behind the rapture of her eyes   15
A look which thou didst teach me unaware.

The visions pass; the light, but now so faint,
   Flames red and sudden over field and brook;
   Thy face is turned, full fronting me with look
Worn never yet of cynic nor of saint;   20

And now amid fierce Northern battle-glare,
   Where wounded heroes wait the gods' decree,
   The Valkyr[3] rides, and o'er her brow I see
The floating golden glory of thy hair.

Sweet spirit, pilgrim through the cycled years,   25
   Dear though thou art I may not bid thee stay;
   I bless thee whatsoever chartless way
Thou goest, God-impelled. I have no fears.

I know thou wilt surrender not to pain;
   Thou wilt look never forth from coward eyes;   30
   Thou would'st not barter truth for Paradise;
Thou could'st not think that ease and peace were gain.

Far off, I know, the darkness shall be light
   For him who scorneth to make terms with Fate;
   Far off for thee, Belovèd, there must wait   35
The answered question, and the finished fight.

                            (MS 1891)

Armistice

The water sings along our keel,
   The wind falls to a whispering breath;
   I look into your eyes and feel
      No fear of life or death;

---

[3] *Valkyr* in Norse mythology, a female warrior spirit.

So near is love, so far away 5
The losing strife of yesterday.

We watch the swallow skim and dip;
    Some magic bids the world be still;
Life stands with finger upon lip;
    Love hath his gentle will; 10
Though hearts have bled, and tears have burned,
The river floweth unconcerned.

We pray the fickle flag of truce
    Still float deceitfully and fair;
Our eyes must love its sweet abuse; 15
    This hour we will not care,
Though just beyond to-morrow's gate
Arrayed and strong, the battle wait.

(MS 1891)

I SPEAK YOUR NAME

I speak your name in alien ways, while yet
November smiles from under lashes wet.
    In the November light I see you stand
    Who love the fading woods and withered land,
Where Peace may walk, and Death, but not Regret. 5

The year is slow to alter or forget;
June's glow and autumn's tenderness are met.
    Across the months by this swift sunlight spanned,
        I speak your name.

Because I loved your golden hair, God set 10
His sea between our eyes. I may not fret,
    For, sure and strong, to meet my soul's demand,
    Comes your soul's truth, more near than hand in hand;
And low to God, who listens, Margaret,
        I speak your name. 15

(MS 1892)

"IF SPIRITS WALK"

*"I have heard (but not believed) the spirits of the dead
May walk again."*
                                        Winter's Tale[4]

If spirits walk, Love, when the night climbs slow
The slant footpath where we were wont to go,

"IF SPIRITS WALK"
[4] III.iii.16.

Be sure that I shall take the self-same way
To the hill-crest, and shoreward, down the gray,
Sheer, gravelled slope, where vetches straggling grow.   5

Look for me not when gusts of winter blow,
When at thy pane beat hands of sleet and snow;
    I would not come thy dear eyes to affray,
        If spirits walk.

But when, in June, the pines are whispering low,   10
And when their breath plays with thy bright hair so
    As some one's fingers once were used to play –
    That hour when birds leave song, and children pray,
Keep the old tryst, sweetheart, and thou shalt know
        If spirits walk.   15

                    (*Century* 1893)

SONG

"O Love, thou art winged and swift,
    Yet stay with me evermore!"
And I guarded my house with bolt and bar
    Lest Love fly forth at the door.

Without, in the world, 't was cold,   5
    While Love and I together
Laughed and sang by my red hearth-fire,
    Nor knew it was winter weather.

Sweet Love would lull me to sleep,
    In his tireless arm caressed;   10
His shadowing wings and burning eyes
    Like night and stars wrought rest.

And ever the beat of Love's heart
    As a chime rang at my ear;
And ever Love's bending, beautiful face   15
    Covered me close from fear.

Was it long ere I waked alone?
    A snow-drift whitened the floor;
I saw spent ashes upon my hearth
    And Death in my open door.   20

                    (MS 1893)

SONG

Lady mine, so passing fair,
Would'st thou roses for thy hair?

Would'st thou lilies for thy hand?
Bid me pluck them where they stand.
Those are warm and red to see,   5
These are cold. Are both like thee?
Brow of lily, lip of rose,
Heart that no man living knows!
If one knelt beside thy feet,
Would'st thou spurn, or love him, Sweet?   10
(The Pilgrim and Other Poems 1896)

WITH A DAFFODIL

Lady, I am pale and cold,
  Shivering without your door,
Yet my crown of winter-gold
  Poets loved and maidens wore
    In days of yore.   5

In a fairer spot of earth,
  Some dream-shrouded, sweeter year,
I, or mine, had other birth,
  Woke in fields of Warwickshire,⁵
  And laughed to hear   10

The boyish tread of Shakespeare's feet.
  Before the swallow, I and mine
Made spring for him. O Lady sweet!
  Welcome, as of an honored line,
    Your Valentine.   15
                        (MS 1900)

WITH A COPY OF WHARTON'S "SAPPHO"⁶

*And of Sappho few, but all roses. — Meleager*⁷

Roses, full-hearted as of old
  When Meleager garlanded
Blossom and bough of poets dead,
  Lie here, and with them, daintily,
Frail scattered petals, crimson, gold,   5
  Drift to the feet of you and me

WITH A DAFFODIL
⁵ Stratford-upon-Avon, Warwickshire, England, Shakespeare's birthplace.
WITH A COPY OF WHARTON'S "SAPPHO"
⁶ Henry Thornton Wharton's 1885 translation of the
Greek lyric poet Sappho (fl. early sixth century BCE).

Sappho is said to have run a school for young women on
her native island of Lesbos in the Adriatic. She is the
first known woman poet to write lyrics expressing deep
passion for women and the term lesbian, for the sexual
orientation, is derived from the name of her home island.
⁷ Meleager (fl. first century BCE), Greek lyric poet.

Unfaded, – even such vain, brief things
  (Roses of Paestum,[8] Helen's tears[9])
As lover loves, and poet sings,
  And wise earth hoards through myriad years,   10
  Careless when some star disappears.

Lover and poet, to your hands
  Red rose and golden rose I trust,
Attar[10] distilled in sunnier lands,
  Curled petal, sweet immortal dust.   15
                                    (MS 1904)

A SONG OF SUMMER

If I were but the west wind,
  I would follow you;
Cross a hundred hills to find
  Your world of green and blue;

In your pine wood linger,   5
  Whisper to you there
Stories old and strange, and finger
  Softly your bright hair.
                      (*Persephone and Other Poems* 1905)

Edith Wharton (1862–1937)

Ranked today among America's premier women novelists, Edith Newbold Jones Wharton was born in New York City on January 24, 1862. She was the youngest child of George Frederic and Lucretia Rhinelander Jones. Both parents were descended from New York's early Anglican and Dutch Reform settlers, qualifying Wharton for membership in "Old New York" – a tightly knit group of elite families whose wealthy ways and rigid social conventions provided Wharton with her richest source of fictional material.

In the economic depression that followed the Civil War, Wharton's father relocated his family in Europe as a money-saving gesture, residing there for the next six years. Both in Europe and after the family's return to the States, Wharton was privately tutored. She wrote her first fiction at age eleven. At her mother's instigation, Wharton's first book of poetry (*Verses*, 1878) was privately published when she was sixteen.

Wharton married Edward Robbins Wharton, a wealthy Boston banker thirteen years her senior, on April 29, 1885. The class-based marriage was characterized by a lack of sexual intimacy and by psychological incompatibility. Following her marriage, Wharton suffered several bouts of severe depression, which her husband nursed her through. Wharton had

---

[8] Paestum, in ancient times, a colony of the Greek city Sybaris (fl. sixth century BCE), known for its Doric temples and for the worship of Demeter, goddess of harvest.

[9] Helen of Troy.

[10] *Attar* perfume.

hardly recovered when Edward began to show signs of serious mental imbalance. The couple moved to France in 1910, where Edward's condition deteriorated to the point where he required hospitalization. His incurable mental condition, taken together with his flagrant infidelities, led to the Whartons' divorce in 1913.

Between 1907 and 1910, Wharton engaged in an extra-marital affair with Morton Fullerton, an American journalist who was a friend and protégé of Henry James. By her own account this was Wharton's first successful sexual relationship, allowing her to throw off the shackles of her "Victorian" upbringing. Wharton spent the years between 1905 and 1920 almost entirely in Europe. They were her most productive period, culminating in her Pulitzer prize-winning novel, *The Age of Innocence* (1920). She died in France at seventy-five, and was buried in the Protestant Cemetery at Versailles.

Although her reputation today rests solely on her fiction, Wharton wrote poetry throughout her career. Along with *Verses*, she published two other collections, *Artemis to Actæon and Other Verse* (1909) and *Twelve Poems* (1926). She also left some of her most passionate – and stylistically experimental – poetry in manuscript. The sonnet sequence, "The Mortal Lease," reproduced here, was written to celebrate her affair with Fullerton and is memorable from this perspective. However, it is also of interest as an example of a genre that has recently evoked considerable interest from women poets, possibly because the structure of the sonnet sequence creates a meditative framework through which poets can examine the significance of desire in their lives (see, for example, Adrienne Rich's "Twenty-One Love Poems" and Marilyn Hacker's *Love, Death, and the Changing of the Seasons*).

A tightly knit group of eight poems bound by image, theme, and sometimes wording, "The Mortal Lease" explores the meaning of Wharton's newly awakened eroticism against the speaker's knowledge of its adulterous nature and its inevitable ephemerality. The writing is heavily sensual and the view of love highly romanticized, as befits a speaker in the midst of an affair. The sequence breaks no new formal ground. Indeed, read against the poetry of other women of this period, it is in some respects strikingly old-fashioned. But taken in itself, it is a powerful statement of desire from one of America's most accomplished women writers.

Primary Texts

Verses, 1878; *The House of Mirth*, 1905; *Artemis to Actæon and Other Verse*, 1909; *The Age of Innocence*, 1920; *Twelve Poems*, 1926.

Further Reading

Shari Benstock, *New Gifts from Chance: A Biography of Edith Wharton*, New York: Scribner's, 1994; Gloria Erlich, *The Sexual Education of Edith Wharton*, Berkeley, California: University of California Press, 1992; Jennie A. Kassanoff, "Edith Wharton," *Encyclopedia of American Poetry*; R. W. B. Lewis, *Edith Wharton: A Biography*, New York: Harper and Row, 1975; Cynthia Griffin Wolff, *A Feast of Words: The Triumph of Edith Wharton*, New York: Oxford University Press, 1977.

from *Artemis to Actæon and Other Verse* (1909)

THE MORTAL LEASE

I.

Because the currents of our love are poured
Through the slow welter of the primal flood
From some blind source of monster-haunted mud,
And flung together by random forces stored
Ere the vast void with rushing worlds was scored —   5
Because we know ourselves but the dim scud
Tossed from their heedless keels, the sea-blown bud
That wastes and scatters ere the wave has roared —

Because we have this knowledge in our veins,
Shall we deny the journey's gathered lore —   10
The great refusals and the long disdains,
The stubborn questing for a phantom shore,
The sleepless hopes and memorable pains,
And all mortality's immortal gains?

II.

Because our kiss is as the moon to draw   15
The mounting waters of that red-lit sea
That circles brain with sense, and bids us be
The playthings of an elemental law,
Shall we forego the deeper touch of awe
On love's extremest pinnacle, where we,   20
Winging the vistas of infinity,
Gigantic on the mist our shadows saw?

Shall kinship with the dim first-moving clod
Not draw the folded pinion from the soul,
And shall we not, by spirals vision-trod,   25
Reach upward to some still-retreating goal,
As earth, escaping from the night's control,
Drinks at the founts of morning like a god?

III.

All, all is sweet in that commingled draught
Mysterious, that life pours for lovers' thirst,   30
And I would meet your passion as the first
Wild woodland woman met her captor's craft,
Or as the Greek whose fearless beauty laughed
And doffed her raiment by the Attic[1] flood;

THE MORTAL LEASE
[1]   Greek.

But in the streams of my belated blood   35
Flow all the warring potions love has quaffed.

How can I be to you the nymph who danced
Smooth by Ilissus[2] as the plane-tree's bole,
Or how the Nereid[3] whose drenched lashes glanced
Like sea-flowers through the summer sea's long roll –   40
I that have also been the nun entranced
Who night-long held her Bridegroom in her soul?

IV.

"Sad Immortality is dead," you say,
"And all her grey brood banished from the soul;
Life, like the earth, is now a rounded whole,   45
The orb of man's dominion. Live to-day."
And every sense in me leapt to obey,
Seeing the routed phantoms backward roll;
But from their waning throng a whisper stole,
And touched the morning splendour with decay.   50

"Sad Immortality is dead; and we
The funeral train that bear her to her grave.
Yet hath she left a two-faced progeny
In hearts of men, and some will always see
The skull beneath the wreath, yet always crave   55
In every kiss the folded kiss to be."

V.

Yet for one rounded moment I will be
No more to you than what my lips may give,
And in the circle of your kisses live
As in some island of a storm-blown sea,   60
Where the cold surges of infinity
Upon the outward reefs unheeded grieve,
And the loud murmur of our blood shall weave
Primeval silences round you and me.

If in that moment we are all we are   65
We live enough. Let this for all requite.
Do I not know, some wingèd things from far
Are borne along illimitable night
To dance their lives out in a single flight
Between the moonrise and the setting star?   70

---

[2] The stream that runs by Troy or Ilium.   [3] *Nereid* water nymph.

VI.

The Moment came, with sacramental cup
Lifted – and all the vault of life grew bright
With tides of incommensurable light –
But tremblingly I turned and covered up
My face before the wonder. Down the slope   75
I heard her feet in irretrievable flight,
And when I looked again, my stricken sight
Saw night and rain in a dead world agrope.

Now walks her ghost beside me, whispering
With lips derisive: "Thou that wouldst forego –   80
What god assured thee that the cup I bring
Globes not in every drop the cosmic show,
All that the insatiate heart of man can wring
From life's long vintage? – Now thou shalt not know."

VII.

Shall I not know? I, that could always catch   85
The sunrise in one beam along the wall,
The nests of June in April's mating call,
And ruinous autumn in the wind's first snatch
At summer's green impenetrable thatch –
That always knew far off the secret fall   90
Of a god's feet across the city's brawl,
The touch of silent fingers on my latch?

Not thou, vain Moment! Something more than thou
Shall write the score of what mine eyes have wept,
The touch of kisses that have missed my brow,   95
The murmur of wings that brushed me while I slept,
And some mute angel in the breast even now
Measures my loss by all that I have kept.

VIII.

Strive we no more. Some hearts are like the bright
Tree-chequered spaces, flecked with sun and shade,   100
Where gathered in old days the youth and maid
To woo, and weave their dances; with the night
They cease their flutings, and the next day's light
Finds the smooth green unconscious of their tread,
And ready its velvet pliancies to spread   105
Under fresh feet, till these in turn take flight.

But other hearts a long long road doth span,
From some far region of old works and wars,

And the weary armies of the thoughts of man
Have trampled it, and furrowed it with scars, 110
And sometimes, husht, a sacred caravan
Moves over it alone, beneath the stars.

CHARTRES[4]

I.

Immense, august, like some Titanic bloom,
    The mighty choir[5] unfolds its lithic[6] core,
Petalled with panes of azure, gules[7] and or,[8]
    Splendidly lambent in the Gothic gloom,
And stamened[9] with keen flamelets that illume 5
    The pale high-altar. On the prayer-worn floor,
By worshippers innumerous thronged of yore,
    A few brown crones, familiars of the tomb,
The stranded driftwood of Faith's ebbing sea –
    For these alone the finials[10] fret the skies, 10
The topmost bosses[11] shake their blossoms free,
    While from the triple portals, with grave eyes,
Tranquil, and fixed upon eternity,
    The cloud of witnesses[12] still testifies.

II.

The crimson panes like blood-drops stigmatise 15
    The western floor. The aisles are mute and cold.
A rigid fetich in her robe of gold,
    The Virgin of the Pillar, with blank eyes,
Enthroned beneath her votive canopies,
    Gathers a meagre remnant to her fold. 20
The rest is solitude; the church, grown old,
    Stands stark and grey beneath the burning skies.
Well-nigh again its mighty framework grows
    To be a part of nature's self, withdrawn
From hot humanity's impatient woes; 25
    The floor is ridged like some rude mountain lawn,
And in the east one giant window shows
    The roseate coldness of an Alp at dawn.

CHARTRES
1   Notre Dame Cathedral at Chartres, France, generally considered to be one of the greatest examples of Gothic architecture. Built in the twelfth and thirteenth centuries, it is famed for its spires and stained-glass windows.
5   The choir (individual box seats for the choir singers) terminated in the central nave of a Gothic cathedral.
6   *Lithic*   rock.
7   *Gules*   red.
8   *Or*   gold.

9   As in the stamens of a flower.
10   *Finials*   the upper extremities of a pinnacle, canopy or gable, often carved into foliage.
11   *Bosses*   ornamental blocks used as stops at the ribs in Gothic vaulting.
12   Hebrews 12:1: "Therefore, since we are surrounded by so great a cloud of witnesses, let us also lay aside every weight, and sin which clings so closely". Wharton is referring to the carved figures of saints which decorate the three great doors of the cathedral façade.

Elaine Goodale Eastman (1863–1953)

Elaine Goodale Eastman was born on October 9, 1863 at Sky Farm, in the Berkshire hills of western Massachusetts. According to the memoir introducing her last book of poetry, *The Voice at Eve* (1930), her father, Henry Sterling Goodale, was a romantic young man more comfortable with books than with money and better at writing than farming. As children, both she and her younger sister, Dora Read Goodale, were educated at home by their mother, Dora Hill Read Goodale. Reared in an environment of high idealism and self-sacrifice, the two sisters chose parallel life paths, abandoning the relative comfort of the East for lives of service among America's poor and disenfranchised. For both, the turn to social commitment was accompanied by a transformation in their writing that suggests much about the strengths (and, in Elaine's case, the limitations) of the nineteenth-century social reform ethos they imbibed.

Elaine Goodale Eastman and her sister were both precocious poets, publishing their first collection of poetry, *Apple-Blossoms: Verses of Two Children*, in 1878 when they were fifteen and twelve respectively. Two more co-written books quickly followed. Despite the authors' youth – and their youthful naiveté – these books were not vanity publications, nor were the sisters treated as curiosities (as, for example, Lucretia and Margaret Davidson were earlier in the century). On the contrary, by 1881, the Goodale sisters were regulars in the major periodicals, including *Scribner's Monthly*, *Harper's*, and *Sunday Afternoon*. Nor, for all its rose-tinted romanticism, is their early poetry without intimations of later power. Eastman's "The Wood-Chopper to his Ax," in particular, is stunningly effective in its deployment of a sadistic speaker as vehicle for the poem's bitter political thrust.

In 1883, a year after this poem was published, Eastman turned her politics into a life choice and accepted a teaching position at the Hampton Normal and Agricultural Institute in Virginia, a vocational school devoted to training Indian and African American students. The post-bellum inspiration of the American Missionary Association and Northern Quakers, the school was headed by Colonel Samuel Chapman Armstrong, a man who viewed forced assimilation (what today is thought of as "cultural genocide") as the only feasible solution to the "Indian problem." In 1885, Eastman traveled with Senator Dawes to observe the Indians of the Dakotas. Fully persuaded of the necessity for assimilation and the consequent need for land allotment, Eastman dedicated the remainder of her life to Indian (re-)education and to preserving the remnants of the culture she and her superiors did so much to help destroy.

In 1891, Eastman resigned her position as Supervisor of Indian Education in the Dakotas to become the helpmate and amanuensis of her new husband, Dr Charles Eastman (Ohiyesa), a full-blooded Santee Sioux. Despite its enormous productivity, both in books and offspring, the Eastmans' marriage came apart in 1921, presumably over money issues and rumors (possibly false) of Charles Eastman's infidelity. Elaine Goodale Eastman returned East with her children and never remarried. She continued to devote herself to Indian causes and to molding Indian cultural materials for white audiences until her death in 1953.

Whether Eastman ever fully understood the contradictions in her position *vis-à-vis* Indian culture is not clear. Like her writing, which returns to Indian themes again and again, without ever resolving her ambivalence toward Indians themselves, her life merely testifies to their existence. The powerful "The Cross and the Pagan" represents, perhaps, the closest she ever came to viewing her own reformist labors from what might fairly be called a Native American perspective. Its irony reverberates through the remainder of her work – and life.

Primary Texts

Apple-Blossoms: Verses of Two Children, with Dora Read Goodale, 1878; *In the Berkshires with the Wild Flowers*, with Dora Read Goodale, 1879; *Around the Years: Verses from Sky Farm*, with Dora Read Goodale, 1881; *Wigwam Evenings: Sioux Folktales Retold*, with Charles Eastman, 1909; *The Voice at Eve*, 1930; *Sister to the Sioux: The Memoirs of Elaine Goodale Eastman, 1885–91*, ed. Kay Graber, 1978.

Further Reading

Ruth Ann Alexander, "Elaine Goodale Eastman and the Failure of the Feminist Protestant Work Ethic," *Great Plains Quarterly* 8 (Spring 1988): 89–101; Kay Graber, ed., "Foreword," in *Sister to the Sioux: The Memoirs of Elaine Goodale Eastman, 1885–91*, Lincoln: University of Nebraska Press, 1978.

from *Scribner's Monthly* (1879)

INDIAN PIPE[1]

> Death in the wood, –
> Death, and a scent of decay;
>   Death, and a horror that creeps with the blood,
> And stiffens the limbs to clay;
>   For the rains are heavy and slow,   5
> And the leaves are shrunken and wan,
>   And the winds are sobbing weary and low,
> And the life of the year is gone.
>
> Death in the wood, –
> Death in its fold over fold,   10
>   Death, – that I shuddered and sank where I stood,
> At the touch of a hand so cold, –
>   At the touch of a hand so cold,
> And the sight of a clay-white face,
>   For I saw the corse of the friend I loved,   15
> And a hush fell over the place.
>
> Death in the wood, –
> Death, and a scent of decay;
>   Death, and a horror but half understood,
> Where blank as the dead I lay;   20
>   What curse hung over the earth,
> What woe to the tribes of men,
>   That we felt as a death what was made for a birth, –
> And a birth sinking deathward again!

INDIAN PIPE
[1] A leafless saprophytic herb native to Asia and the United States. It grows in mold and has a white waxy appearance that can make it seem ghost-like.

Death in the wood, —   25
In the death-pale lips apart;
　Death in a whiteness that curdled the blood,
Now black to the very heart:
　The wonder by her was formed
Who stands supreme in power;   30
　　To show that life by the spirit comes,
She gave us a soulless flower!

from *Overland Monthly* (1883)

THE WOOD-CHOPPER TO HIS AX

My comrade keen, my lawless friend,
When will your savage temper mend?
I wield you, powerless to resist;
I feel your weight bend back my wrist,
　Straighten the corded arm,   5
　Caress the hardened palm.

War on these forest tribes they made,
The men who forged your sapphire blade;
Its very substance thus renewed
Tenacious of the ancient feud,   10
　In crowding ranks uprose
　Your ambushed, waiting foes.

This helve, by me wrought out and planned,
By long use suited to this hand,
Was carved, with patient, toilsome art,   15
From stubborn hickory's milk-white heart;
　Its satin gloss makes plain
　The fineness of the grain.

When deeply sunk, an entering wedge,
The live wood tastes your shining edge;   20
When, strongly cleft from side to side,
You feel its shrinking heart divide,
　List not the shuddering sigh
　Of that dread agony.

Yon gaping mouth you need not miss,   25
But close it with a poignant kiss;
Nor dread to search, with whetted knife,
The naked mystery of life,
　And count on shining rings
　The ever-widening springs.   30

Hew, trenchant steel, the ivory core,
One mellow, resonant stroke the more!
Loudly the cracking sinews start,
Unwilling members wrenched apart —
Dear ax, your 'complice I   35
 In love and cruelty!

from *Frank Leslie's Popular Monthly* (1896)

THE MASTER OF THE HOUSE

Love came a-knocking at my door —
 I flung it wide without delay;
 He was so coaxing and so gay,
I bade him never leave me more!

Now in my house he's wont to dwell,   5
 So great have his exactions grown —
 So tyrannous that lisping tone,
I sometimes question, Was it well?

For I was strong, and now am weak,
 And I am bound, who once was free;   10
 I, too, since Love has mastered me,
Though I was proud, have grown so meek!

The rogue — he flouts me to my face!
 My sore complaint is food for smiles;
 He thinks to pay for all my toils   15
With one more boisterous embrace.

"See yonder virgin, spare and grave?
 Years past — ha, ha! — she *locked* her door —
 And now, if I should tap once more,
Doubt not she'd fly to be my slave!"   20

from *Independent* (1912)

THE CROSS AND THE PAGAN

As men in the forest, erect and free,
We prayed to God in the living tree;
You razed our shrine, to the wood-god's loss,
And out of the tree you fashioned a Cross!

You left us for worship one day in seven;   5
In exchange for our earth you offered us heaven;

Dizzy with wonder, and wild with loss,
We bent the knee to your awful Cross.

Your sad, sweet Christ – we called him Lord;
He promised us peace, but he brought a sword;   10
In shame and sorrow, in pain and loss,
We have drunk his cup;[2] we have borne his Cross!

from *The Voice at Eve* (1930)

THE END OF THE HUNT

The red man's lodges trespass for a night
Upon a white man's country – find it still
A barren and a treeless land, where he –
The rugged and unsmiling pioneer –
Heaps sod on sod for shelter – hardly wrings   5
From sandy wastes a scanty yield of corn.
Once more a ragged clump of smoke-stained tents
Proclaim the first possessors of the soil –
A race of hunters, a proud nation once
Who, dwindled to this petty, roving band,   10
Follow the ancient lure, pursuing still
The fleeing remnant of uncounted herds –
The last survivors of the stately deer!

At evening, gathered round the central blaze,
Loud jests and laughter, and the timely tale   15
Of the day's exploits fill a cheerful hour.
Nor is the curious alien turned aside
From this charmed circle, whose dark faces smile
A hospitable welcome; he, too, shares
The generous warmth, the smoking, savory meats   20
Hot from the chase.

                Hark to the leisured speech
Of the old chief, in accents musical!
"The white man's in a hurry – as for us,
We're in no haste. Why, 'tis not winter yet!   25
The cranes fly high – no promise yet of snow!
We'll journey slowly, tarry as we please
To rest our jaded ponies. In good time
We'll be at home."

THE CROSS AND THE PAGAN
[2]   Communion cup, Christ's blood.

There are few left like him,   30
And when these few are gone, there'll be no more;
None to succeed them, for their children bear
The mark, world-famous, of our conquering race;
And the last Adam, he who keeps alive
The memory of our common fatherhood,   35
The child-man, joying in all common things,
The wild, deep-hearted man – this separate type
Which Nature loved, she can no longer save!

Dora Read Goodale (1866–1953)

Poet-sister to Elaine Goodale Eastman, Dora Read Goodale was born in 1866 on Sky Farm, the Goodale family homestead in the Berkshires (s.v. Elaine Goodale Eastman). Like her sister she was educated at home by her mother, and began writing poetry at a very young age. Not surprisingly, her early poetry, with a few exceptions, tends to be weaker than that of Eastman's, showing fewer intimations of the power to come. Even more than her sister's, however, Dora Goodale's poetry matured under the impact of a life that was politically and socially committed. It is unfortunate, therefore, that, quite unlike Elaine, she seems to have left little in the way of explanation for the course her life and art took.

Were it not for Eastman, who wrote frequently of her childhood, almost nothing would be known of Dora's early life beyond the poetry itself. Effectively, she was one more "semi-anonymous" woman poet whose work appeared with such regularity in late nineteenth-century newspapers and periodicals. As it is, she all but "disappears from view" after 1883, when Eastman left the family farm (and her collaborative writing with her sister) for Hampton Institute in Virginia. A few ephemeral titles appear under Dora's name in the National Union Catalog after 1883, but it was not until fifty-seven years later that the seventy-five-year-old Dora Goodale, now a teacher and health care worker at Uplands Hospital, Pleasant Hill, Tennessee, finally made her literary mark.

Written entirely in free verse and in the mountain dialect of the Appalachian highlands (Tennessee, Virginia, Kentucky, and North Carolina), Dora Goodale's last book of poetry, *Mountain Dooryards* (1941, rev. and enl. 1946), is a moving testimony to the linguistic wealth and personal dignity of the rural poor. It is also a powerful testimony to the flexibility and genius of a woman who late in life made the transition to a twentieth-century (modernist) poetic even while retaining the best of early nineteenth-century sentimentalism's deep commitment to those who were socially powerless and in need.

Because of its inherent drive toward objectifying those whose language it claims to reproduce, dialect poetry has a fatal tendency to devolve into caricature, or as Goodale puts it, "burlesque." As her brief introductory comments to *Mountain Dooryards* make clear, Goodale was keenly aware of this problem and adjusted for it, refusing, as she says, to re-produce "inflections *literatim*." Her poems are not mimicry, but re-creations of the language and people whose speech and ways of thought she sought to preserve.

Far more fully, and far less ambivalently, than her sister, Dora Goodale became the recorder of a culture that was not her own and that was disappearing even as she wrote. "Her poetry," Chad Drake writes in his foreword to the 1958 edition of *Mountain Dooryards*, "has come as close to capturing the mountain spirit as we know." It is, as he maintains, the "finest flower" her "great gift bore."

Primary Texts

Apple-Blossoms: Verses of Two Children, with Elaine Goodale [Eastman], 1878; *Heralds of Easter*, 1887; *The Test of the Sky*, 1926; *Mountain Dooryards*, 1941, rev. and enl. 1946, 2nd edn 1958.

Further Reading

Richard Nunley, ed., *The Berkshire Reader: Writings from New England's Secluded Paradise*, Stockbridge, Massachusetts: Berkshire House Publishers, 1992.

from *Apple-Blossoms: Verses of Two Children* (1878)

OUR CHICKENS

A gentle pullet on the stoop, –
    A rooster where the cream is rising, –
A hen who doubtless likes our soup,
    And eats it without criticizing!

A mild-eyed chicken calmly stands   5
    And on the kitchen table lingers, –
And why? of course he understands
    The bread is fresh from mamma's fingers.

An angry "shoo!" – he thinks it vain,
    But then of course there is no knowing, –   10
He smashes thro' a window pane
    And fears it's time that he was going.

A pullet, *not* upon the stoop,
    But with cream gravy on a platter;
A hen who's grown so fat on soup   15
    That what she *makes* is no small matter.

Ah, chickens! 'tis no use to beg,
    Tho' you were bold, we, we are bolder, –
And mamma, will you take a leg?
    Or would you rather have a shoulder?   20

You make a most delicious pie!
    Your time is past and ours beginning, –
Not long upon my plate you'll lie, –
    This is the penalty of sinning!

from *Independent* (1884)

A WORKINGWOMAN

Life gives us armor for the fate we meet;
   Our sense is blunted when our pain is old;
A blacksmith's hand is hardened to the heat;
   A beggar's foot is torpid in the cold.
So every man develops incomplete   5
   You'd taste the tang in such a crust as mine,
   And be indifferent to your daily wine;
But to the starving palate, bread is sweet!

A woman gave me shelter from the rain;
   Her thrilling warmth was like a dumb caress;   10
No pang is like that pang of happy pain
   In souls unused to healing tenderness;
Such clay as ours grows callous toward disdain;
   We waste no anguish on perpetual slight;
   But, trust me, we can feel a sharp delight   15
Your deadened spirit will not know again!

I went at dusk a lonely watch to keep.
   A rough man stopped me, muffled to the chin;
I took his place; the way was long and steep,
   The wagon groaned, the white sacks hemmed me in;   20
In unwarmed hearts such kindnesses strike deep;
   That human touch uplifted and renewed
   Through long, laborious days of solitude
And feverish nights of unrefreshing sleep.

Where the wide hearth with rosy comfort glowed   25
   I drank new courage for advancing day;
In the bleak wind, against the dusty load,
   My swelling, overburdened heart gave way.
His silent figure kept the narrow road;
   I felt the panting horses heave and strain,   30
   Till night fell back from many a lighted pane
And through the fog the village steeple showed.

We laboring women are too early wise;
"Unformed" we are, by comfort, pleasure, care.
No wonder, then, we're crooked in your eyes,   35
   Too rudely shaped by trouble and despair.
You stare so hard the natural shrinking dies;
   We're fortunate and grow bold and suffer less,
   Being strongest in a power of happiness
That nothing this side Heaven satisfies.   40

from *Century* (1893)

MOONRISE FROM THE CLIFF

Rare nights have been, but never night like this!
　Never so softly breathed the ebbing gale
　Where, in locked slumber, rolls the intervale
　Under the brown edge of the precipice!
Oh, softly, from the purple hushed abyss   5
　With all its heavenly legions streaming pale,
　The moon, bright-orbed behind her crystal veil,
　Melts to this rude world in a stainless kiss!
Such is the hour when skyey forces hover;
　The prisoned spirit leaps to burst its bars,   10
　Earth's dullest mortal thrilling like a lover –
Poor shepherd dazed beneath that gulf of stars! –
　Till time and sense and rock and sand and sea
　Fade in the white glare of immensity.

from *Mountain Dooryards* (2nd edn 1958)

OF FROSTS IN MAY

Frostes in May – we call that Dogwood Winter.
Trees all tricked out[1]
Like maids in Sunday-best – and then come frostes!
I've knowed it frost with apples big as bird-eggs,
And black em same as fire . . .   5
That girl of mine – says now she hates young Hyman
That's moved up creek. Blast him, she looks downhearted!
It's just a dogwood squall though, don't you guess?

(1941)

MOUNTAIN DOORYARD

The timber's greenin –
Hit's a-greenin;
The oaktree in the dooryard's full of tossels[2] . . .
Ay, Winter, he's a bad un for old bones,
But I jest keep battlin on.   5

Past days was good days.
I've turned the ground a-many a time at sun-up
Hit a-sleetin and a-snowin and me bar-foot –

OF FROSTS IN MAY
[1] *Tricked out* dressed up.

MOUNTAIN DOORYARD
[2] *Tossels* fragile seedpods that appear on oaks at the beginning of spring.

But we was young then!
She had the say-so indoors and me out-doors;   10
She al'ays loved things nice and to go pleasant
And she kep em that-a-way.

I've cleaned the dooryard,
And left the lady-fingers in the corner
Like she al'ays had em. Yes, it's lonesome – lonesome,   15
But I jest keep battlin on.

                                                    (1941)

SPLINT BASKETS

You want a basket? . . .
No, the handle won't pull out –
It's put to stay.
If ever a one I made done lost its handle
I've yet to hear on 't –   5
I say, I've yet to hear on 't.

. . . But who's to swear, today'll run like yesterday?
– All his life my man had worked in the timber:
He'd felled a power o' trees
And not once missed by so much as the width o' your hand   10
To reckon the way they'd fall. And, come his hour,
A tree done felled him.

'Twas the time o' year the corn is puttin the silk on –
Hot nights,
And moonlight, bright like day. I'd got his supper ready   15
And I tuck my little Gladys by the hand
And went to meet him. . . .
And his mates, they come a-carryin him.

All day, they said, he'd ben more than common gay –
But hear me talk! It's like a leaky vessel   20
As goes a-strowin.[3]

'Twas quick as that!
Quick as that, I was left with five to raise
And bread em too:
All red-haired like their Pa, all but the youngest –   25
Crow-black, hers is,
To tell she picked the drap o' Cherokee blood[4]
My granny passed me down.

SPLINT BASKETS
[3] The speaker here seems to be comparing the sudden-
ness of her husband's death to a stove-in ship that sinks
unexpectedly.

[4] Prior to their forced removal to Oklahoma in 1838,
on the "Trail of Tears," the Cherokee nation inhabited
land throughout the mountain areas of what is now
Georgia, North and South Carolina, Alabama, and
Tennessee.

. . . You want a basket?
Little and big, same pattern, made o' splints   30
And handles put to stay. . . .
That time's gone by,
And now it's Gladys' younguns – out of school,
And in they come! Ain't women the endurinest?

No! No, I say!   35
If you want a gingercake, you go sweep the floor
And redd the room up first. And you, you Herschel,
Get shet o your jacket 'n split me up some kindlers.[5]
. . . *No, not today, I say, you won't make baskets,*
Not ary one of you!   40

. . . Lord love you, yes!
They're like a mess of acorns under a whiteoak,
All rarin to be oaktrees!

MAST[6] IN THE WOODS

Seven-eight days married,
And you'd ruther be back home!

Life's not all ruthers,
That's what my mammy told me
When I run off and got married   5
Like you
And come back home a-cryin.

Life's not all ruthers;
Good days and bad – it's like the mast in the woods,
Part sweet, part bitter.   10

Listen, my girl:
You pad it back to your man.
He's a good man; if he wants *his* way ever' time,
Let be! – there's times ahead.
Life's not all ruthers.   15
Some nights we cud step a tune; some we're that tarr'd
We feel like we'd been chewed up and spit out. . . .
What then?

I say, What then?
Ay, come foul weather, what then?   20
You take it,
And agin, it's fairin off.

---

[5] *Kindlers* kindling wood.

MAST IN THE WOODS
[6] *Mast* collective term for nuts, used especially as food for hogs and other animals, but also consumable by human beings. To the human palate acorns are bitter.

THE PORTRAITS

– That's her likeness, yes,
But I never knowed her. My daddy, he went first,
And she died a-birthing me.

My oldest brother,
I reckon he favored her. 'Twas him as raised us 5
And never quit
Till he'd saw the last one married.
He was more like a daddy than a brother.
He alays[7] had a kind look out of his eyes,
My brother had. . . . 10

That other likeness – that's my husband's mother.
I wasn't long married when she come to live with us
And we never had what you'd call a disagreeance –
Not really.
She holp me out a-many a time 15
Best way she could.
She was a good woman.
But *her*, my mother. . . . Well, it's like I said;
She died a-birthing me.

THE BLEEDING HEART[8]

My father's second –
'Twas her as fotched the root and her as planted it.
. . . 'Twas overnights away, the place she come from,
And she never went back more.

Seems like I can see her now, the way she stood there 5
And planted it deep
The day she married Pa. There was some man else, I reckon,
But she never told us:
Ma, she was quiet-turned.

Frances Densmore (1867–1957)/Owl Woman (Juana Manwell) (fl. 1880)

On April 25, 1952, ethnomusicologist Frances Densmore received a congressional tribute for her work in transcribing and preserving Native American song and poetry. In the

---

THE PORTRAITS
[7] Always.

THE BLEEDING HEART
[8] A graceful garden plant with drooping, heart-shaped, deep pink flowers.

address to the House of Representatives, the Honorable August H. Anderson pronounced Densmore "the greatest living authority on the music of the American Indian." Entombed today in the bulletins of the Bureau of American Ethnology, her literal transcriptions of Indian songs and poetry are the invaluable legacy of a woman who spent nearly forty years tracking down, recording, and analyzing the music of North America's myriad Indian tribes – not just for anthropological purposes but for the art itself.

Frances Densmore was born in Red Wing, Minnesota, on May 21, 1867. She was the daughter of Benjamin and Sarah Adalaide (Greenland) Densmore, and granddaughter of Judge Orrin Densmore. She studied music at Oberlin Conservatory from 1886 to 1889. Her course work was traditional; and she began her career as a piano teacher and lecturer in Wagnerian music. Personal interest and the model of Alice Cunningham Fletcher's pioneer studies of the music of the Omahas (1911) led Densmore to her life work.

Using portable cylinder equipment, Densmore recorded songs of individual Indian singers from the Chippewa in Minnesota to the Seminoles of Florida to the pueblo peoples of the American Southwest. In offering as far as she was capable literal translations of Indian poetry, Densmore was part of a sizable group of *fin-de-siècle* anthropologists and poets who were striving to render the lyrics of Native American songs more accurately than – in their opinion – their predecessors had. (See, for example, translations by Alice Fletcher (1838–1923) and Harriet Maxwell Converse (1836–1903) in Section II.) If Densmore's translations, in particular, with their "haiku-like" qualities, opened Indian poetry up for appropriation by early modernist writers interested in the primitive and searching for a new free verse poetic (s.v. Mary Hunter Austin), they also established Indian song as an independent self-legitimizing art form, thus helping provide a solid base for the Indian arts revival of the past thirty years.

This selection from Densmore's work limits itself to the sequence of poems which Densmore received from Owl Woman (Juana Manwell), an elderly Papago medicine woman living on the San Xavier reserve in Arizona. Owl Woman used her songs to cure sicknesses caused by Papago spirits. Sometime about 1880, the spirits had taken Owl Woman to the spirit land to console her after her husband's death. They showed her where the departed now lived and they decided that she should learn songs to cure the diseases the Papago spirits caused. They communicated this decision to her by the spirit of a man who had died near the Tucson area. He gave Owl Woman her first three songs, of which she was still using two when Densmore recorded her work in 1920 (Nos 72 and 73 below).

Thereafter, Owl Woman received hundreds of songs, in some cases from patients who had died in spite of her efforts to cure them, sometimes from people who had died years before or who had died under unusual circumstances far away. Thus, although these songs were hers by gift, she was not, in her own view, their author. According to her custom, she would sing four songs, then treat the sick person with a bunch of owl feathers on which she had sprinkled ashes, stroking the body "to get out the sickness." The alternation of songs and treatment would take place throughout the night, in four clearly marked intervals. By morning the patient either showed signs of improvement or Owl Woman knew she could not cure them.

Primary Text

Papago Music, Bulletin 90, Washington, D.C.: Smithsonian Institution Bureau of American Ethnology, 1929.

Further Reading

Mary Austin, "Introduction," in *American Indian Poetry: An Anthology of Songs and Chants*, ed. George W. Cronyn, New York: Fawcett, 1991; Kimberly M. Blaeser, "The Multiple Traditions of Gerald Vizenor's Haiku Poetry," in *New Voices in Native American Literary Criticism*, ed. Arnold Krupat, Washington, D.C.: Smithsonian Institution Press, 1993: 344–69; Frances Densmore, "Preface," in *Music of the Maidu Indians of California*, Los Angeles: Southwest Museum, 1958; Alice Fletcher, "Indian Songs and Music," *Journal of American Folk-Lore* 11 (April–June 1898): 85–104; Charles Hofman, *Frances Densmore and American Indian Music: A Memorial Volume*, New York: Museum of the American Indian, Heye Foundation, 1968; Arnold Krupat, *The Voice in the Margin: Native American Literature and the Canon*, Berkeley: University of California Press, 1989.

from *Papago Music* (1929)

Songs for Treating Sickness, Sung during the Four Parts of the Night

Parts One and Two: Beginning Songs and Songs Sung before Midnight

No. 72 "Brown Owls"[1]

Brown owls come here in the blue evening,
They are hooting about,
They are shaking their wings and hooting.

No. 73 "In the Blue Night"

How shall I begin my song
In the blue night that is settling?
I will sit here and begin my song.

No. 74 "The Owl Feather"[2]

The owl feather is rolling in this direction and beginning to sing.
The people listen and come to hear the owl feather
Rolling in this direction and beginning to sing.

No. 75 "They Come Hooting"

Early in the evening they come hooting about,
Some have small voices and some have large voices,
Some have voices of medium strength, hooting about.

No. 72 "Brown Owls"
[1] "Brown Owls" and "In the Blue Night" were given to Owl Woman by a man who was killed near Tucson, Arizona. She always began treatment with these songs. He encouraged her to become a healer.

No. 74 "The Owl Feather"
[2] Nos 74 and 75 were given to Owl Woman by a man whom she treated but who died.

No. 76 "In the Dark I Enter"[3]

I can not make out what I see.
In the dark I enter.
I can not make out what I see.

No. 77 "His Heart is Almost Covered with Night"[4]

Poor old sister, you have cared for this man and you want to see him again,
but now his heart is almost covered with night. There is just a little left.

No. 78 "I See Spirit-Tufts of White Feathers"[5]

Ahead of me some owl feathers are lying,
I hear something running toward me,
They pass by me, and farther ahead
I see spirit-tufts of downy white feathers.

No. 79 "Yonder Lies the Spirit Land"

Yonder lies the spirit land.
Yonder the spirit land I see.
Farther ahead, in front of me,
I see a spirit stand.

NN/NT[6]

Sadly I was treated, sadly I was treated,
Through the night I was carried around,
Sadly I was treated.

No. 80 "Song of a Spirit"

A railroad running west,
He travels westward.
When he gets a certain distance
He flaps his wings four times and turns back.

No. 76 "In the Dark I Enter"
[3] No. 76 was given to Owl Woman by Nonka Simapere. He died at an advanced age.
No. 77 "His Heart is Almost Covered with Night"
[4] No. 77 was give to Owl Woman by her brother. She had been caring for an old man named Marciano. As she was going to treat him, her brother's spirit told her Marciano would die. When she arrived at Marciano's home, he was already dead.

No. 78 "I See Spirit-Tufts of White Feathers"
[5] Nos 78 and 79 were given to Owl Woman by Jose Louis two days after his death, around 1912.
NN/NT
[6] This poem and No. 80 were given to Owl Woman in 1914 by Ciko, who had been killed two years before in a drunken bar fight. His body was carried around in a buggy and finally laid on some railroad tracks to make it appear that he had died in a train accident.

No. 81 "We Will Join Them"[7]

Yonder are spirits laughing and talking
>> as though drunk.
They do the same things that we do.
Now we will join them.

No. 82 "My Feathers"

I pity you, my feathers,
I pity you, my feathers, that they make fun of,
They must mean what they say,
Or perhaps they are crazy in their hearts.

No. 83 "The Women are Singing"[8]

On the west side people are singing as though drunk. The women are singing
as though they were drunk.

NN/NT

In the great night my heart will go out,
Toward me the darkness comes rattling,
In the great night my heart will go out.

NN/NT

On the west side they are singing, the women hear it.

No. 84 "I am Going to See the Land"[9]

I am going far to see the land,
I am running far to see the land,
While back in my house the songs are intermingling.

No. 85 "I Run Toward Ashes Hill"

Ashes Hill Mountain, toward it I am running,
I see the Ashes Hill come out clearer.

No. 86 "The Waters of the Spirits"

They brought me to the waters of the spirits.
In these waters the songs seem to be stringing out.

No. 81 "We Will Join Them"

[7] Nos 81 and 82 were taught to Owl Woman by a man who had died eight years before and who had returned to look at his house.

No. 83 "The Women are Singing"

[8] This song and the two that follow it were given to Owl Woman by Jose Gomez, who died around 1918. According to Owl Woman "Jose was not a lively boy, he was slow and sleepy headed" and that was why his songs were not very interesting. Densmore did not record their music.

No. 84 "I am Going to See the Land"

[9] According to Densmore, Nos 84 through 86 were the final songs in this group and sung just before midnight. She does not identify their source.

Parts Three and Four: Songs Sung between Midnight and Early Morning

NO. 87 "THERE WILL I SEE THE DAWN"[10]

A low range of mountains, toward them I am running.
From the top of these mountains I will see the dawn.

NO. 88 "I RUN TOWARD THE EAST"

I am not sure whether I am running west or east but I run on and on.
I find that I am running east.

NO. 89 "I DIE HERE"[11]

I am dead here, I die and lie here,
I am dead here, I die and lie here,
Over the top of *Vihuliput* I had my dawn.

NO. 90 "I COULD SEE THE DAYLIGHT COMING"

Black Butte is far. Below it I had my dawn.
I could see the daylight coming back of me.

NO. 91 "THE DAWN APPROACHES"

I am afraid it will be daylight before I reach the place to see.
I feel that the rays of the sun are striking me.

NO. 92 "THE OWL FEATHER IS LOOKING FOR THE DAWN"

The owl feather is likely to find the daylight.
He is looking for it.
He is looking to see the dawn shine red in the east.

NO. 93 "THE MORNING STAR"

The morning star is up.
I cross the mountains into the light of the sea.

NO. 94 SONG OF A MEDICINE WOMAN ON SEEING THAT A SICK PERSON WILL DIE[12]

I think I have found out.
I think I have found out.
With the owl songs I have found out and I will return home.

NO. 87 "THERE WILL I SEE THE DAWN"
[10] Nos 87 and 88 were both given to Owl Woman by Francisco Pablo, an old man who died around 1913.
NO. 89 "I DIE HERE"
[11] Nos 89 and 90 were given to Owl Woman by the spirit of a man who fell down a well. According to Densmore, the "dawn" mentioned in both poems "is the light seen by the spirits." Black Butte and *Vihuliput* were two Buttes relatively close to each other. The man had traveled from one to the other.
NO. 94 SONG OF A MEDICINE WOMAN ON SEEING THAT A SICK PERSON WILL DIE
[12] Owl Woman only sang this song if she knew her patient was going to die. Then she would talk with his relatives, telling them he would not recover.

Mary Hunter Austin (1868–1934)

Mary Hunter Austin was born in Carlinville, Illinois, on September 9, 1868, the fourth of six children. Mary's father, George Hunter, immigrated from Yorkshire, England in 1851. In 1861, he married Susannah Graham, a descendant of one of Illinois's original settler families. Service in the Civil War seriously impaired Hunter's health, and he died of malaria in 1878. Two months later, Austin's younger sister, Jennie, died of diphtheria. Already a difficult child, given to mystical experiences (she is said to have declared that "God happened to Mary under the walnut tree" when she was five), with these deaths, Austin, age ten, lost her only supports within the family.

Lonely, unloved, and fretting over gender restrictions, Austin spent her remaining childhood unhappily, turning inward for support. Recognizing what she thought was a second personality inside herself – an "I-Mary" – she identified it by various names: "Inknower," "Genius," "Wakonda" (from the Native American "Wakan" or power), and "the presence of God." In adulthood, Austin attributed her creativity to this intuitive personality, viewing it as the source of her art.

In 1888, after graduating from college in Carlinville, Austin moved with her family to a desert homestead near Fort Tejon, California. In 1891, she married Stafford Wallace Austin, a man of "good family" but little business acumen. The union was unsuccessful and they separated in 1904. Austin's first book, *The Land of Little Rain*, a collection of desert sketches, appeared in 1903, bringing her immediate recognition. For the next twenty years, she shuttled between Carmel, California, where she lived in an artists' colony, and New York City. The bulk of Austin's work emerged in this period, including *A Woman of Genius* (1912). This novel, together with her nature writings and her autobiography, *Earth Horizon* (1932), are generally considered her best writing. These years also saw the publication of Austin's one contribution to American poetry, *The American Rhythm* (1923, rev. and enl. 1930).

As the two sections dividing *American Rhythm* indicate (one devoted to Native American poetry, the other to poetry "in the American Manner"), Austin viewed Native American poetry as both a legitimate part of American poetry and apart from it – a channel running, as it were, below and beside it. Searching for indigenous roots for free verse form, she found them in what she viewed as the earth-based rhythms of Native American song. In the book's long introductory essay, Austin discusses her ideas. Similar to Whitman in her nativism and in her self-taught mysticism, Austin believed that America's lyric heart could be found within the continent itself and in the poetic forms to which the land "spontaneously" gave rise. Influenced by Densmore, among others, she believed she found these rhythms in Native American song.

Was she also exploiting this song and its Native American makers? Austin is not the scrupulously literal translator Densmore is. Rather, she sought to "interpret" (for white audiences) the spirit of the material she "reëxpressed." Alert to *fin-de-siècle* stylistic trends, she recognized that the concise, intense imagery of Native American poetry and its apparently free metrical structure were qualities that would appeal to the poets – and audiences – of her own day. So, like other women poets from Sigourney on, she sought to build a bridge between alien cultures by stressing more the commonalties than the differences between them. As the term "reëxpressions" indicates, hers was a bastard art from the outset – a matter less of direct translation than of re-creation – and she admitted it.

How Austin's "Native American" poetry is judged today may say more finally about present positions on race and ethnicity than it does about her. Do cultural forms "belong" to particular groups? Or are they always in process, always subject to influence, absorption, growth, and change? How does one go about defining a national poetry in a multicultural (or, from a Native American perspective, multi-national) society such as the United States? And what role has this continent, with its lush environmental bounty and its enormous distances and differences, played in shaping "American" culture and art? Even as Austin and her family moved West (from Illinois to California), was the cultural center of the United States shifting also? Or was it simply being dispersed among different geo-political cultural centers: the Northeast, the South, the West, and the Midwest? And as it shifted or was dispersed, did it free itself sufficiently from "Eastern" influence to absorb more deeply the lives of native peoples? Or has it simply exploited them more fully?

Like a number of women in this anthology, Austin sought to play the role of "translator/interpreter" as well as poet and, like them, she was committed to cultural reform as well as to the reformation of art. To attempt to move between cultures is always risky. To seek to intervene in one's own culture by bringing it into contact with other ways of being and thinking can easily brand one a traitor to one's people or one's class, or an "exploiter" of someone else's.

As "On Hearing Vachel Lindsay Chant His Verse" makes clear, Austin knew from whence she came and owned the "slab-sided," Bible-thumping men who were her "forebears." But in the tradition of women's writing that has been so strikingly alive throughout this volume, she also opened up her writing and her self to the voices of others, changing who she was even as she sought to listen and to give voice to what she was not.

Primary Texts

The Land of Little Rain, 1903; *A Woman of Genius*, 1912; *The American Rhythm*, 1923; *The American Rhythm: Studies and Reëxpressions of American Songs*, 1930; *Earth Horizon*, 1932.

Further Reading

Helen McKnight Doyle, *Mary Austin: Woman of Genius*, New York: Gotham, 1939; Beth Harrison, "Zora Neale Hurston and Mary Austin: A Case Study in Ethnography, Literary Modernism, and Contemporary Ethnic Fiction," *MELUS: The Journal of the Society of the Multi-Ethnic Literature of the United States* 21 (1996): 89–106; Mark T. Hoyer, "Weaving the Story: Northern Paiute Myth and Mary Austin's *The Basket Woman*," *American Indian Culture and Research Journal* 19 (January 1995): 133–5; Karen S. Langlois, "Marketing the American Indian: Mary Austin and the Business of Writing," in *A Living of Words: American Women in Print Culture*, ed. Susan Albertine, Knoxville: University of Tennessee Press, 1995: 151–68; John P. O'Grady, *Pilgrims of the Wild*, Salt Lake: University of Utah Press, 1993; James Ruppert, "Discovering America: Mary Austin and Imagism," in *Studies in American Indian Literature: Critical Essays and Course Designs*, ed. Paula Gunn Allen, New York: MLA, 1983: 243–58.

from *The American Rhythm* (1923)

Amerindian Songs

SONG OF THE BASKET DANCERS[1]

I.

We, the Rain Cloud callers,
Ancient mothers of the Rain Cloud clan,
Basket bearers;
We entreat you,
O ye Ancients,   5
By the full-shaped womb,
That the lightning and the thunder and the rain
Shall come upon the earth,
Shall fructify the earth;
That the great rain clouds shall come upon the earth   10
As the lover to the maid.

II.

Send your breath to blow the clouds,
O ye Ancients,
As the wind blows the plumes
Of our eagle-feathered prayer sticks,   15
Send, O ye Ancients,
To the Six Corn Maidens.
To the White Corn Maiden,
To the Yellow Corn Maiden,
To the Red Corn Maiden,   20
To the Blue Corn Maiden,
To the Many Colored Maiden,
To the Black Corn Maiden,
That their wombs bear fruit.

III.

Let the thunder be heard,   25
O ye Ancients!

SONG OF THE BASKET DANCERS

[1] Austin's note: The Song of the Basket Dancers was taken down from a verbal translation offered me by a young man at the pueblo of San Ildefonso where the dance was being performed. I have no way of checking up the translation as there is no existing record of the San Ildefonso dance, and no other person could be found who was willing to vouch for it. It seems necessary to offer this explanation, since Miss Lowell has also published a song of the Basket Dancers which differs materially in content from mine. It is quite impossible that what my interpreter gave me could have been improvised, though it is possible that he may have been giving me some other than the Basket Dancer's Song. I have had that happen when the interpreter for superstitious reasons wished not to translate, and was too anxious to please to refuse me altogether. However, the Basket Dance is undoubtedly a fertility rite and this is quite certainly a fertility song. Whether the dance and the song belong together is a matter of interest only to the ethnologist.

Let the sky be covered with white blossom clouds,
That the earth, O ye Ancients,
Be covered with many colored flowers.
That the seeds come up,   30
That the stalks grow strong
That the people have corn,
That happily they eat.
Let the people have corn to complete the road of life.
                                        (San Ildefonso Pueblo)

Lament of a Man for his Son

Son, my son!

I will go up to the mountain
And there I will light a fire
To the feet of my son's spirit,
And there will I lament him;   5
Saying,
O my son,
What is my life to me, now you are departed!

Son, my son,
In the deep earth   10
We softly laid thee in a Chief's robe,
In a warrior's gear.
Surely there,
In the spirit land
Thy deeds attend thee!   15
Surely,
The corn comes to the ear again!

But I, here,
I am the stalk that the seed-gatherers
Descrying empty, afar, left standing.   20
Son, my son!
What is my life to me, now you are departed?

Papago Love Songs

I.

Early I rose
In the blue morning;
My love was up before me,
It came running to me from the doorways of the Dawn.

On Papago Mountain   5
The dying quarry
Looked at me with my love's eyes.

II.

Do you long, my Maiden,
For bisnaga[2] blossoms
To fasten in your hair?   10

I will pick them for you.
What are bisnaga spines to me
Whom love is forever pricking in the side?

GLYPHS[3]

I.

A girl wearing a green ribbon, –
As if it had been my girl.
– The green ribbon I gave her for remembrance –
Knowing all the time it was not my girl,
Such was the magic of that ribbon,   5
Suddenly,
My girl existed inside me!

II.

Your face is strange,
And the smell of your garments,
But your soul is familiar;   10
As if in dreams our thoughts
Had visited one another.

Often from unremembering sleep
I wake delicately glowing.
Now I know what my heart has been doing.   15

Now I know why when we met
It slipped
So easily into loving.

III.

Truly buzzards
Around my sky are circling!   20

For my soul festers,
And an odor of corruption
Betrays me to disaster.

PAPAGO LOVE SONGS
[2] *Bisnaga* any of several thorny cacti growing in Southern California and adjacent regions.
GLYPHS
[3] *Glyphs* symbols, typically on a sign, that impart information nonverbally. For Austin, Native American song functioned as glyphs, their intense impact condensed within their imagery, rather than achieved through discursive elaboration.

Meanness, betrayal and spite
Come flockwise,   25
To make me aware
Of sickness and death within me.
My sky is full of the dreadful sound
Of the wings of unsuccesses.

(from the Washoe-Paiute)

Neither Spirit nor Bird

Neither spirit nor bird;
That was my flute you heard
Last night by the river.
When you came with your wicker jar
Where the river drags the willows,   5
That was my flute you heard,
Wacoba, Wacoba,
Calling, Come to the willows!

Neither the wind nor a bird
Rustled the lupine blooms.   10
That was my blood you heard
Answer your garment's hem
Whispering through the grasses;
That was my blood you heard
By the wild rose under the willows.   15

That was no beast that stirred,
That was my heart you heard,
Pacing to and fro
In the ambush of my desire,
To the music my flute let fall.   20
Wacoba, Wacoba,
That was my heart you heard
Leaping under the willows.

(from the Shoshone)

Songs of the Seasons[4]

I.

All these I have mentioned
    With Wawanut;
I have mentioned all the seasons and the stars
    To Wawanut.

Songs of the Seasons

[1]   Austin's note: This and the ensuing numbers of this group are rather saturations than reexpressions. There is a cycle of Songs of the Season among the Luiseno of Southern California, which concludes with the magic formula of belief as I have closed this, but the rest is largely inferred.

In every other song, no matter how free the rendering, I had some specific Amerind composition as a foundation. In this last group, I have only Amerindian thought.

All the little steadfast stars   5
And the Walkers of the Night,
Where the flying light of sun is caught and hidden,
I have named them to Wawanut.

I have named the Thunder,
With his moccasins of dark cloud   10
Walking on the mountain.
I have named the Tovukmal,
The clean March water
Washing down the last year's leaves.
And the little silver rains,   15
The many footed rains
Dancing with the meadowlarks
Round the roots of the rainbow.

II.

I have named the Pahoyomal
    With Wawanut,   20
Now the ant has her hill and her house,
The spider opens her door, dew shining;
White butterflies emerging
In their spotted robes
From their sacred dance enclosure.   25
The wind tosses
The white blossom cones of the chamise,[5]
    And the sea's white foam flowers.

Now the sky is ashamed
Of what he did to the maiden summer;   30
Retreating afar and on high
He tugs at the four world quarters.

The elk brings forth in the north,
The wild sheep at Temucula,[6]
The horned lizard on the hot sands   35
Around Turtle Rock
With his young is dancing.

All these I have mentioned in my songs.
I have made a twine of songs
To bind them to Wawanut.   40

---

[5] *Chamise* probably the chamiso plant, a saltbush having grayish foliage, native to the southwest United States.

[6] Possibly Temuco, a city in south-central Chile.

III.

I have named the summer
       To Wawanut.
I have mentioned earth's contented noises.
I have named the Star Chief, Kukilish
And the lovely Light-Left-Over-from-the-Evening-to-the-Morning.[7]   45

I have named the ripe wild oats
Moon white on the sea-fronting ranges.
Arrows twanging in the white oak browse,
Women stripping deer meat,
All these I have mentioned to Wawanut,   50
Women winnowing *chia*.[8]

I have made them songs.
With a net of songs I bind them
       To Wawanut.

On the silver-glimmer path   55
My songs are walking
       With Wawanut.

I am proud of my songs,
I have believed my songs.
I have made the seasons and the stars   60
Work together with Wawanut.

BLACK PRAYERS

There is a woman
Has taken my man from me.

How was I to know,
When I gave him my soul to drink
In the moon of Corn Planting,   5
When the leaves of the oak
Are furred like a mouse's ear,
And the moon curls like a prayer plume
In the green streak over Tyuonyi.[9]

When I poured my soul to his   10
In the midst of my body's trembling,
How was I to know
That the soul of a woman was no more to him

---

[7]   Austin's note: The planet Venus.
[8]   *Chia* an aromatic annual plant in the mint family
with edible seed-like fruit.

BLACK PRAYERS
[9]   Large southwestern pueblo that was deserted *c.* 1550.

Than sweet sap dripping
From a bough wind-broken?   15

If I had known
I could have kept my soul from him,
Even though I kept not my body.

That woman, with her side-looking eyes.
Whatever she takes from him,   20
It is my soul she is taking.
Waking sharply at night
I can feel my life pulled from me,
Like water in an unbaked olla.[10]
Then I know he is with her,   25
She is drinking from his lips
The soul I gave him.

    Therefore I make black prayers for her
    With this raven's feather,
    With owl feathers edged with silence,   30
    That all her days may be night haunted;
    Let blackness come upon her
    The Downward road
    Toward Sippapu,[11]
    Let her walk in the shadow of silence.   35

Would I had kept my soul
Though I gave my body.
Better the sly laugh and the pointed finger
Than this perpetual gnawing of my soul
By a light woman.   40

Now I know why these witches are so fair,
They are fed on the hearts of better women.
Who would not take another's man,
Knowing there is no untying
The knot of free-given affection.   45

    Let darkness come upon her.
    Let her feet stumble
    Into the Black Lake of Tears.
    Let her soul drown.
    Let Those Above not hear her.   50
    By the black raven's plume
    By the owl's feather.

---

[10] *Olla* earthenware pot.

[11] Entrance to the underworld, the hole in the ground
from which the pueblo people originally emerged.

Songs in the American Manner

ON HEARING VACHEL LINDSAY CHANT HIS VERSE[12]

I have remembered whence I came. . . .

Sleek, silt-charged rivers,
Fat loam, slow yielding to the share,
Slithering yellow clay,
Tenacious as the heavy farmer stuff   5
Cold on the withers of your stallion fancy, Lindsay.

I remember the lush bottoms,
The basson blare of the trumpet creepers,
The glassy air
Shattered by insect glitter.   10
Slow-moving summer creeks
Laced in light rings
By obscene water moccasins;
And straight as a wound bleeding inwardly,
The red streak of the cardinal.   15

I remember the towns,
Slab-sided, smug,
Impounding Pegasus[13] among the cockleburs;
The slab-sided men, my forebears,
Bearded like prophets,   20
But setting a clean-shaven upper lip
Against prophesying in the name of any God but theirs.
Songs I remember. . . .
"Tenting To-night," and "Nicodemus"[14]
Haunting my childhood like gray gulls   25
Blown inland from deep-sea commotion,
Sung by deep-breasted women,
Large-armed for the cradling of States.
And like a child's dream of a star,
High on a heaven-whitened hill   30
Old John Brown[15] and his seven sons
Making with God a majority.

Witchfires, outside the window, in the cold twilight,
The beckoning dance, fragmentary, of Old-World Wonder,

ON HEARING VACHEL LINDSAY CHANT HIS VERSE
[12]   Vachel Lindsay (1879–1931), American poet.
[13]   In Greek mythology, the winged horse, symbol of poetic inspiration. The image of an impounded Pegasus suggests the constraints placed by middle-class, genteel society on the poetic imagination. Dickinson uses the same image in her letters (*Letters* 144).

[14]   Hymns popular at revival meetings.
[15]   John Brown (1800–59), zealot leader of the unsuccessful raid on the arsenal at Harper's Ferry, Virginia (1859).

And that dim shouter in the offing of my mind,   35
(You, Lindsay, on your stallion fancy?)

All these I have remembered,
As a man wearing the king's tinsel,
Suddenly sees in the throng gathered to celebrate him,
Strong peasant faces,   40
Knowing, at once and past any shaming,
How he has climbed by their sinews,
Throws his cockade[16] to the king's lackeys,[17] and declares
There, there alone, are my kinsmen!

Alice Ruth Moore Dunbar-Nelson (1875–1935)

Like so many end-of-the-century poets, Alice Ruth Moore Dunbar-Nelson can be viewed either as a late nineteenth- or as an early twentieth-century writer. Born July 19, 1875 in New Orleans, Louisiana, she arrived somewhat too soon for the Harlem Renaissance, in which she nevertheless participated, yet too late (and too modernist in inclination) to be considered a nineteenth-century poet proper. The liminal position of her poetics reflects something of the liminality of her own position, as a member of the first generation of "new" black women — women for whom issues of modernity (equality, professionalism, agency within the culture) could claim equal attention with those of race and civil rights.

The daughter of Patricia Wright, a mixed-blood seamstress and former slave, and Joseph Moore, a Creole seaman, Dunbar-Nelson received an unusually solid education for a woman of her day, including a teacher-training degree from Straight University in New Orleans, and an M.A. in English Literature from Cornell University, plus courses in psychology and educational testing at the University of Pennsylvania and at Columbia University. The breadth of her educational experience mirrors the breadth of her interests and accomplishments as teacher, writer, public speaker, club woman, political activist, and community organizer. Light-skinned and auburn-haired, Dunbar-Nelson used her ability to pass to gain educational and cultural advantages that would otherwise have been denied her. However, unlike many who passed, she never turned her back on the community from which she sprang.

In March 1898, Dunbar-Nelson married the celebrated African American poet Paul Laurence Dunbar. Despite its Browningesque trappings, theirs was not a match made in poet-heaven. On the contrary, Dunbar-Nelson's family felt that she had degraded herself in joining with a laundrywoman's son who was much darker than herself, and a dialect poet to boot. Alice also had problems on the latter point, berating her husband in private for his willingness (as she saw it) to provide whites with images that played heavily into stereotypes of black uneducatability. This conflict, taken together with Paul Dunbar's addiction to medicinal alcohol, his ill health, constant traveling, and alleged infidelity, not to mention Alice's own strong will and unapologetic self-confidence, brought the marriage to a premature and stormy end in 1902, four years before Paul's death at thirty-four. Alice

---

[16] *Cockade* a rosette or knot of ribbon, usually worn on the hat as part of a uniform or badge of office.

[17] *Lackeys* footmen or liveried manservants, also applied to servile followers or toadies.

Dunbar-Nelson took a number of women lovers and two more husbands after Paul's decease but, historically speaking, she remains "Paul Dunbar's wife," enhanced and overshadowed by him simultaneously.

Alice Dunbar-Nelson was not the poet her first husband was. By her own account she lacked the imagination. She certainly lacked the devotion. Her writing life, which included stories, essays, speeches, textbooks, and journals, was simply too full to make poetry more than a side occupation. Yet such poetry as she produced is of substantial merit and clearly places her among the most accomplished black women writing poetry before the Harlem Renaissance.

Today the sonnet "Violets" (1917) is, perhaps, her best known work and often referred to as her signature poem. It is a sensitive rendering of lost romanticism in a modern urban setting. But Dunbar-Nelson's political poems – from the World War I "I Sit and Sew" (1920) to the powerful "Harlem John Henry Views the Airmada," written on the brink of World War II – are at least of equal interest. The latter poem, in particular, which alternates snatches from the spirituals (written in dialect!) with brief overviews of American history and the history of blacks in America, is a poem worthy of sustained study (and of fruitful comparison both to Lucy Larcom's "Wild Roses of Cape Ann" and to M. E. Ashe Lee's "Afmerica" in Section II).

Despite awkward moments, "Harlem John Henry Views the Airmada" suggests a complex perspective on American history that brings together many of this society's warring elements, even as it disavows war itself. Through the figure of John Henry, the legendary and archetypal black laborer, Alice Dunbar-Nelson sought reconciliation with her people's (and her own) past and hope for a better future for the country as a whole. Read in terms of her life-long struggle to accept the dark side of her own blackness – as she found it both in Paul Dunbar's dialect poetry and in her own discomfort with those who were "too dark" – "Harlem John Henry Views the Airmada" is Alice Dunbar-Nelson's poem to America about itself.

Primary Texts

Violets and Other Tales, 1895; *The Goodness of St. Rocque and Other Stories*, 1899; *The Dunbar Speaker and Entertainer*, ed. with contributions by Alice Dunbar-Nelson, 1920; *The Works of Alice Dunbar-Nelson*, ed. Gloria T. Hull, 4 vols, 1988.

Further Reading

Gloria T. Hull, "Dunbar-Nelson, Alice Ruth Moore," in *Black Women in America: An Historical Encyclopedia*, ed. Darlene Clark Hine, 2 vols, New York: Carlson, 1993: 359–63; "Introduction," in *The Works of Alice Dunbar-Nelson*, 4 vols, Oxford: Oxford University Press, 1988; Ora Williams, "Alice Moore Dunbar-Nelson," *DLB* 50: 225–33.

from *The Works of Alice Dunbar-Nelson* (1988)

VIOLETS

I had not thought of violets of late,
The wild, shy kind that springs beneath your feet
In wistful April days, when lovers mate
And wander through the fields in raptures sweet.
And thought of violets meant florists' shops,   5

And bows and pins, and perfumed paper fine;
And garish lights, and mincing little fops
And cabarets and songs, and deadening wine.
So far from sweet real things my thoughts had strayed,
I had forgot wide fields, and clear brown streams;   10
The perfect loveliness that God has made –
Wild violets shy and heaven-mounting dreams.
And now – unwittingly, you've made me dream
Of violets, and my soul's forgotten gleam.

                           (*Crisis* 1917)

I SIT AND SEW

I sit and sew – a useless task it seems,
My hands grown tired, my head weighed down with dreams –
The panoply of war, the martial tred of men,
Grim-faced, stern-eyed, gazing beyond the ken
Of lesser souls, whose eyes have not seen Death,   5
Nor learned to hold their lives but as a breath –
But – I must sit and sew.

I sit and sew – my heart aches with desire –
That pageant terrible, that fiercely pouring fire
On wasted fields, and writhing grotesque things   10
Once men. My soul in pity flings
Appealing cries, yearning only to go
There in that holocaust of hell, those fields of woe –
But – I must sit and sew.

The little useless seam, the idle patch;   15
Why dream I here beneath my homely thatch,
When there they lie in sodden mud and rain,
Pitifully calling me, the quick ones and the slain?
You need me, Christ! It is no roseate dream
That beckons me – this pretty futile seam   20
It stifles me – God, must I sit and sew?

            (*The Dunbar Speaker and Entertainer* 1920)

YOU! INEZ!

Orange gleams athwart a crimson soul
Lambent flames; purple passion lurks
In your dusk eyes.
Red mouth; flower soft,
Your soul leaps up – and flashes   5
Star-like, white, flame-hot.
Curving arms, encircling a world of love.
You! Stirring the depths of passionate desire!

                    (MS 1921)

THE PROLETARIAT SPEAKS

I love beautiful things:
Great trees, bending green winged branches to a velvet lawn,
Fountains sparkling in white marble basins,
Cool fragrance of lilacs and roses and honeysuckle.
Or exotic blooms, filling the air with heart-contracting odors;   5
Spacious rooms, cool and gracious with statues and books,
Carven seats and tapestries, and old masters
Whose patina[1] shows the wealth of centuries.

And so I work
In a dusty office, whose griméd windows   10
Look out in an alley of unbelievable squalor,
Where mangy cats, in their degradation, spurn
Swarming bits of meat and bread;
Where odors, vile and breath taking, rise in fetid waves
Filling my nostrils, scorching my humid, bitter cheeks.   15

I love beautiful things:
Carven tables laid with lily-hued linen
And fragile china and sparkling iridescent glass;
Pale silver, etched with heraldies,
Where tender bits of regal dainties tempt,   20
And soft-stepped service anticipates the unspoken wish.

And so I eat
In the food-laden air of a greasy kitchen,
At an oil-clothed table:
Plate piled high with food that turns my head away,   25
Lest a squeamish stomach reject too soon
The lumpy gobs it never needed.
Or in a smoky cafeteria, balancing a slippery tray
To a table crowded with elbows
Which lately the bus boy wiped with a grimy rag.   30

I love beautiful things:
Soft linen sheets and silken coverlet,
Sweet coolth of chamber opened wide to fragrant breeze;
Rose shaded lamps and golden atomizers,[2]
Spraying Parisian fragrance over my relaxed limbs,   35
Fresh from a white marble bath, and sweet cool spray.

And so I sleep
In a hot hall-room whose half opened window,
Unscreened, refuses to budge another inch;

THE PROLETARIAT SPEAKS   [2] *Atomizers* instruments used for reducing perfumes
[1] *Patina* the sheen on an antique surface.   to a fine spray.

Admits no air, only insects, and hot choking gasps,   40
That make me writhe, nun-like, in sack-cloth sheets and lumps of straw.
And then I rise
To fight my way to a dubious tub,
Whose tiny, tepid stream threatens to make me late;
And hurrying out, dab my unrefreshed face   45
With bits of toiletry from the ten cent store.

                                                        (*Crisis* 1929)

HARLEM JOHN HENRY VIEWS THE AIRMADA[3]

Harlem John Henry mused into the sky,
"Beauty must be, must be, else life is dust."
Outspread white wings that cleave the sullen gray,
Myriads of double wings, swooping on in threes,
Darting trilineate,[4] far, near, in threes,   5
Twelve, thirty, sixty. And converges now
A flock of eagles, zooming crescendo roars;
In threes and twelves, thrice tens, and six times ten;
Six hundred more make dark the air, and cloud
That lone sarcophagus commemorative of him   10
Who cried in pain of soul, "Let us have peace!"[5]

Beauty must be. But is this threat beauty?
Harlem John Henry hears the sinister drone
Of sextuples of planes. Sings jeeringly —

    "I've got wings,   15
    You've got wings,
    All God's chillen got wings!"

Lowers his gaze from dun rain-clouds of May,
Where scarring wings insult the quiet of spring,
And laughs aloud at that white pediment,   20
On whose Corinthian beauty blazons tall
The hope-fraught words that make the Hudson sneer,
And Harlem John Henry rock with mirthless mirth.

Beauty and peace? Beauty and War? Yet no.
Beyond the clouds that drift athwart the wings,   25

HARLEM JOHN HENRY VIEWS THE AIRMADA

[3] John Henry was a highly popular Bunyanesque hero of folksong and legend. The best known aspect of his story has to do with his competition with a steamdrill (that is, his assertion of human worth over that of a machine). Airmada is a portmanteau coinage, made from combining airplanes and armada. In this poem John Henry, now relocated on Manhattan's upper west side, views an airshow from Grant's tomb, and meditates on American history, the machine age, and the possibilities opening up for African Americans in the new world that wars and advances in technology had, for better *and* worse, made for them

[4] *Trilineate* marked with three usually longitudinal streaks.

[5] Words Grant wrote in a letter accepting the presidency. They are inscribed on his tomb.

An ancient scene seeps in John Henry's soul.
Above the crashing zoom of mighty sound,
John Henry hears a throbbing, vibrant note –
    "Boom ba boom boom
      Boom ba boom boom   30
        Boom ba boom!"

Jungle bamboula beats the undertone
To all that fierce hoarse hiss above the sky.
Cruel corsairs[6] of foul, slave-weighted ships;
Deep-throated wails from black, stench-crowded depths –   35

      "Sometimes I feel like a motherless child,
      Sometimes I feel like a motherless child,
      Sometimes I feel like a motherless child,
          A long ways from home!"

Beauty must be, must be, beauty, not death.   40
Harlem John Henry shivers. A gusty blast,
March winds benumbing Boston streets of old;
Crispus,[7] the mighty, gone Berserk again,
Cursing his rage at red-coats' insolence,
Smiting a first wild blow for Liberty,   45
Dying, his face turned to the bullets' spirt.

      "Joshua fit de battle of Jericho, Jericho, Jericho!
      Joshua fit de battle of Jericho,
      An' de walls come tumblin' down!"

Surcease of weary strife. An infant land   50
That marched erect to wealth on lowly backs.
Harlem John Henry's soul flowed to the past;
Zoom-zoom, resounding from the lowering sky,
Throbs like the base-viol in the symphony –

      "Go down, Moses, way down in Egypt's land,   55
      Tell ol' Pharaoh, let my people go!"

"Peace will be served by this, this airmada,
For me and mine, they said," John Henry mused.
"We helped build beauty tall unto the skies."
But years ere towers could rise of steel or stone,   60

---

[6] *Corsairs* privateers along the Barbary coast of North Africa, but the word carries a number of submerged echoes: airships, coarse/air, and possibly corse (body)/ corpse.

[7] Crispus Attucks (*c.* 1723–70), one of the first to die in the so-called Boston massacre, March 5, 1770, one of the events leading up to the American Revolution. He is said to have been a runaway mulatto and a leader on the colonists' side.

Structures that clutched the rocks beneath the sea –
Boom-boom, drum beats of seventy years agone,
Boom-boom, answering the zoom of circling wings –

> "We are coming, Father Abraham,[8]
> One hundred thousand strong!"   65

And in the camp fires' glow o'er Wagner's heights,[9]
A thousand black throats hurl their melody –

> "Dey look like men,
> Dey look like men,
> Dey look like men of war;   70
> All dressed up in deir uniforms,
> Dey look like men of war!"

Let us have peace! and weary warriors
Echoed the clatter of dropped pen that wrote
Fulfilment of three centuries of hope –   75

> "Sometimes I feel like an eagle in de air,
> Some-a dese mornin's bright an' fair
> I'm goin' to lay down my heavy load,
> Goin' to spread my wings an' cleave de air!"

Who thought of beauty? Money marts and trade,   80
Argosies[10] on seas, schools, churches, trusts and rings,
Politicians, wealth, cotton, wheat, machines,
Steel tracks, flung spider-like o'er continent.
Harlem John Henry hears a tiny voice,
Piping a thin thread through that turgid roar,   85
"Get money, get trades, be thrifty, be compliant!"

> "We are climbin' Jacob's ladder,
> We are climbin' Jacob's ladder,
> Every roun' goes higher, higher,
> Every roun' goes higher, higher,   90
>   Soldiers of de Cross!"

Beauty is lost in smugness, sordidness,
Harlem John Henry sights a bombing plane,
Flashing white shafts across the lowering sky,

---

8   President Abraham Lincoln as well as the biblical patriarch. "We are coming, Father Abraham" was a song written by James Sloan Gibbons in response to President Lincoln's call for 300,000 more volunteers to join the Union army in July 1862. The music was written by Stephen Foster, an obscure musician at the time.

9   Fort Wagner located at the mouth of the Charleston harbor in South Carolina. Site of a battle in which Robert Gould Shaw (1837–63) and nearly half the Negro Troops of the 54th Massachusetts were killed on July 18, 1863.
10   *Argosies* a group of merchant vessels, connotes great wealth.

As back in Ninety-eight there gleamed cruel steel   95
Of jingo[11] jabs, and little children sang
About a ship called Maine,[12] that sank too soon.
Surging up a red-hot Cuban hill,[13]
A medieval charge in khaki garb –

    "There'll be a hot time in the old town to-night!"   100

Beautiful the feet of them that bring us peace!
Beauty in wings that cleave th' uncharted air!
Zoom-zoom, by three, by twelves, six hundred more,
Etching their path from cruel past to now.
Harlem John Henry stands with lifted face,   105
Ruthless star-shells[14] are shattering round his feet;
He staggers through the muck of No-Man's Land[15] –

    "Singin' wid a sword in my han',
    Singin' wid a sword in my han',
        Purties' singing evah I heard,   110
        Way ovah on de hill,
    De angels shout an' I sing too,
    Singin' wid a sword in my han'!"

Stumbles again from France and Flanders Field,[16]
Back from the mire and rats and rotting dead,   115
And that wild wonder of a soundless world,
When death ceased thundering that November day.[17]

    "My Lord what a mornin',
    My Lord what a mornin',
    My Lord what a mornin',   120
        When de stars begun to fall!"

Back o'er the sea and home – that soon forgot,
Lustily singing, as he ever sang –
    "Goin' to lay down my burden,
        Down by the river-side   125
        Down by the river-side
    Goin' to study war no more!"

---

[11] An allusion to jingoism, the advocacy of a policy of aggressive nationalism.
[12] The US battleship destroyed in Havana harbor February 15, 1898, helping to precipitate the Spanish-American War.
[13] San Juan Hill in East Cuba, where Theodore Roosevelt led the Rough Riders in their charge in July 1898.
[14] A military term referring to shells timed to burst in midair in a shower of bright particles that light up the surrounding terrain.

[15] Term for the unoccupied, shell-devastated land between the trench lines held by the Central Powers (Germany and its allies), on the one side, and the Allies (France, England, and their allies) on the other, during World War I (1914–18).
[16] Major battle areas in World War I. There may also be an allusion here to the poem "In Flanders Fields" by John McCrae.
[17] November 11, 1918, Armistice day (now Veterans' day), when the peace ending World War I was signed.

Now, o'er the Hudson[18] on this day in May,
Circling six hundred wings, sinister, strange.
Harlem John Henry asks, was that in vain?   130
Beauty and peace? Must beauty die once more,
Slain o'er and o'er in stupid, senseless rage?
But from the throats of all those millions dusk,
Harlem John Henry hears that beauty's cry,
Beauty from pain, triumphant over hate –   135

    "Great day! Great day! Great day, de righteous marchin',
    Great day! Great day! God's goin' to build up Zion's walls,
De chariot rode on de mountain top;
God's goin' to build up Zion's walls!
My God he spoke an' de chariot stop,   140
God's goin' to build up Zion's walls!
Great day! Great day!"

                          (*Crisis* 1932)

---

18   Major river marking the west side of Manhattan.

Section II

Poems from Regional, National, and Special Interest Newspapers and Periodicals, arranged chronologically

from *Weekly Museum* (1800)

Sonnet to a Mop-Stick
by "Deborah"

Straight remnant of the spiry birchen bough,
　　That o'er the streamlet wont perchance to quake
Thy many twinkling leaves; and, bending low,
　　Behold thy white rind dancing on the lake;

How doth thy present state, poor stick! awake　　　　　　　　5
　　My pathos; for, alas! e'en stript as thou,
May be my beating breast, if e'er forsake
　　Philisto[1] this poor heart, and break his vow.

So musing, on I fare with many a sigh,
　　And meditating then, on times long past,　　　　　　　　10
To thee, torn pole! I look with tearful eye,
　　As all beside the floor-soil'd pail thou'rt cast;
And my sad thought, while I behold thee twirl'd,
Turn on the twirlings of this troublous world.

Woman's Hard Fate[2]
By a Lady

How wretched is poor woman's fate!
　　No happy change her fortune knows:
Subject to man in every state,
　　How can she then be free from woes?
In youth, a father's stern command,　　　　　　　　5
　　And jealous eyes, control her will;
A lordly brother watchful stands,
　　To keep her closer captive still.

The tyrant husband next appears,
　　With aweful and contracted brow;　　　　　　　　10
No more a lover's form he wears:
　　Her slave's become her sov'reign now,
If from this fatal bondage free,
　　And not by marriage chains confin'd,
If, blest with single life, she see　　　　　　　　15
　　A parent fond, a brother kind –

Sonnet to a Mop-Stick
[1] *Philisto* Greek, loosely "he who loves" – a generic name for a (shepherd) lover in neoclassical literature, in particular the pastoral.

Woman's Hard Fate
[2] To my knowledge, the earliest American reprinting of this popular poem is in 1743 in the *South Carolina Gazette*, where it is followed by "The Answer: by a Gentleman," elsewhere titled, "Man's Hard Fate." In the *Weekly Museum*, however, the "Lady's" poem stands alone, without its palinode.

Yet love usurps her tender breast,
    And paints a phoenix to her eyes;
Some darling youth disturbs her rest;
    And painful sighs in secret rise.   20
Oh cruel pow'rs, since you've design'd,
    That man, vain man, should bear the sway,
To slavish chains add slavish mind,
    That I may thus your will obey.

from *Ladies' Monitor* (1801)

By a Lady Whose Infant Lay Sleeping in the Cradle
by "Maria"

    Sweet sleeps my babe! but ah! how soon
Will life's bleak aspect change the scene.
So changing, as the changing moon
Will be her prospects in the main.

    Sleep on, my babe, thy mother's care   5
Extends itself to guard thee well,
Oh? lay thee still – thou canst not share,
In troubles which I dare not tell.

    With time comes thought, and thought too well
Will stir that little beating heart,   10
When with a mother's tender tale
I shall my grief to thee impart.

    But why call forth the tender tear?
Why stir thy sympathy for me?
For thee, life will its troubles wear;   15
Its changes will be bleak for thee!

    Say, why that sigh! – Oh! baby say?
Dos't now anticipate thy doom?
Dos't feel that friendship will betray?
Dos't feel, that love, is life's drear tomb?   20

    It must be thus; or in thy state
Of infancy, thou could'st not be,
Thus restless, sighing, as if fate
Set his peculiar mark on thee.

    A female babe – this stamps thy woe!   25
Oppression's wand in time will wave!
Fair reason hence will prove thy foe!
Nor sense – tho' God-like can thee save!

Sleep on, sleep sweet, thou baby dear;
Nor shall a whisper 'scape by me,   30
Experience will its terrors wear
This may be teacher unto thee.

from *Lady's Magazine and Musical Repository* (1801)

EPITAPH ON A BIRD
by Anonymous

Here lieth,
aged three months and four days,
the body of
RICHARD ACANTHUS,[3]
a young person of unblemished character.   5
He was taken, in his callow infancy, from the wing
of a tender parent,
By the rough and pitiless hand of a two-legged animal
without feathers.
Though born with the most aspiring disposition & unbounded   10
love of freedom,
he was closely confined in a grated prison,
and scarcely permitted to view those fields,
to the possession of which he had an undoubted charter.
Deeply sensible of this infringement of   15
his natural and unalienable rights,
he was often heard to petition for redress,
not with rude and violent clamours,
but in the most plaintive notes of harmonious sorrow!
At length tired with fruitless efforts to escape,   20
his indignant soul
burst the prison which his body could not,
and left a lifeless heap of beauteous feathers.
Reader!
if suffering innocence can hope for retribution,   25
deny not to the gentle shade of this
unfortunate captive,
the humble, though uncertain, hope of animating
some happier form;
or, trying his new-fledged pinions   30
in some happy elysium, beyond the reach of
MAN,
the tyrant of this lower world!

EPITAPH ON A BIRD
[3] *Acanthus* a thistle-like plant, with lobed, often spiny leaves, found in the Mediterranean area. Its leaves were used as a decorative motif for Corinthian columns in classical architecture.

THE OLD MAID'S APOLOGY
by Anonymous

I determine'd the moment I left off my bib,
 I would never become any man's crooked rib,
And think you to fright me, when gravely you tell
 That Old Maids will surely lead apes when in hell?

I'll take the reversion, and grant 'twill be so   5
 But yet I shall keep to my vow,
For I'd rather lead apes in the regions below,
 Than be led by a foolish ape now.

from *Boston Gazette* (1801)

CACŒTHES SCRIBENDI
by "Constantia" (Judith Sargent Murray)[1]

"CACŒTHES Scribendi,"[5] is the rage,
And she's a genius, who can fill a page.
All to the field with conscious strength repair,
With brains congenial to the arms they wear;
"Fire in each eye, and papers in each hand,   5
"They rave, recite, and madden round the land,"
Alike professing all the self same end,
Vice to reform, and Virtue to defend;
Alike all strive each other to excell,
And most do *ill*, who *seem* intending well,   10
To whom is given a moderate share of sense,
To spell and write (tho' badly) shall commence
An "Author," and the better to succeed,
In the first essay publishes a creed,
That passes current, and by which we guess   15
The principles, this riddle *would* express.
But so desultory seems the motley scrawl,
The maudlin meaning so equivocal,
That we might well these farrago's regard
As written, and baptized afterward.   20
Writers like these would sooner gain their end
By writing 'gainst the cause they would defend.

CACŒTHES SCRIBENDI
[1] Judith Sargent Murray (1751–1820), feminist and essayist.   [5] *Cacœthes Scribendi* Latin: "the rage for writing."

from *Boston Gazette* (1802)

An Unfortunate Mother, to Her Infant at the Breast[6]
by Anonymous

Unhappy child of Indiscretion!
    Poor slumb'rer on a breast forlorn;
Pledge and reproof of past transgression,
    Dear, tho' unwelcome to be born.

For thee, a suppliant wish addressing   5
    To heaven, thy mother fain would dare;
But conscious blushes stain the blessing,
    And sighs suppress my broken prayer.

But spite of these my mind unshaken,
    In parent duty turns to thee;   10
Tho' long repented, ne'er forsaken,
    Thy days shall lov'd and guarded be.

And, lest the injurious world upbraid thee
    For mine, or for thy father's ill,
A nameless mother oft shall aid thee,   15
    A hand unseen protect thee still.

And though, to rank and place a stranger,
    Thy life an humble course must run;
Soon shalt thou learn to fly the danger,
    Which I too late have learn'd to shun.   20

Mean time in these sequestered vallies,
    Here may'st thou rest in safe content,
For innocence may smile at malice,
    And thou, O! thou, art innocent.

Here to thine infant wants, are given   25
    Shelter and rest, and purest air,
And milk as pure – but, mercy, heav'n!
    My tears have dropt, and mingled there.

An Unfortunate Mother, to Her Infant at the Breast
[6] The following letter to the editor accompanied this poem:
  Gentlemen. I hand you the following lines for publication in your Gazette. – They were written by a young lady. once lovely and virtuous. but now plunged in the deepest gulph of misery. by a most perfidious wretch – "one whom God denies." The simplicity of the following. and forceful expression throughout the whole lines – the feeling manner in which they are written. are the reasons of my offering them to you.
                      PHILO.

from *Boston Gazette* (1804)

The Tiger Hunter
by Sappho

Where the red sun casts forth a sickly heat,
    And scarse a zephyr fans the laurid[7] air;
Where no cool rills the fainting traveller greet,
    But sandy whirlwinds 'whelm him with despair.

Where the ruth tiger, in dark ambush lies,   5
    Ready to dart upon his lonely prey;
Thro' knotted trees fix'd stare his sea-green eyes,
    And meet the fear-struck wand'rer on his way.

There, drear o'er Afric's wild the Negro roams,
    Wielding his spike, pointed with sharpen'd steel,   10
And seeks the savage who with vengeance foams,
    Then, springing, makes his sable hunter reel.

Adroit the lance deep wounds his speckled throat,
    Roaring he writhes upon its crimson'd blade;
His glaring eyes fierce on the Negro glote,[8]   15
    But vain – the gri[n]ding steel a gap has made.

The savage yells – and horrid struggle both;
    The lance transfixes still the vital part,
Now spinning round the sanguine stream bursts forth,
    And pangs convulsive tear his bleeding heart.   20

At length with howls tremendous he expires,
    And life forth issues as he prostrate lays;
The gleaming Negro with the conquest fires,
    And whilst still warm, the spotted victim flays.

But ill-starr'd hunter! should fate prove averse,   25
    If in thy hardy palm, should *break* the spear,
Then would thy springing foe, with howlings fierce,
    Thy sable body into atoms tear.

from *Boston Gazette* (1805)

The Hot-House Rose
by Anonymous

An early rose borne from her genial bower
    Met the fond homage of admiring eyes,

The Tiger Hunter
[7] Laurid may be a printer's error for "humid."   [8] *Glote* gloat.

And while young zephyr⁹ fann'd the lovely flower
    Nature and Art contended for the prize.

Exulting Nature cried, I made the fair,   5
    'Twas I that nursed thy tender buds in dew;
I gave the fragrance to perfume the air,
    And stole from Beauty's cheek her blushing hue.

Vainly fastidious novelty affects
    O'er Alpine hei[gh]ts, and untrod wilds to roam,   10
From rocks and swamps her foreign plants collects
    And brings the rare but scentless treasure home.

Midst Art's factitious¹⁰ children let them be
    In sickly state by names pedantic known,
True Taste's unbiased eye shall turn to thee   15
    And Love and Beauty mark thee for their own.

Cease, Goddess, cease, indignant Art replied,
    And ere you triumph, know that but for me
This beauteous object of our mutual pride
    Had been no other than a vulgar¹¹ tree.   20

I snatch'd her from her tardy mother's arms,
    Where sun-beams scorch and piercing tempests blow;
On my warm bosom nursed her infant charms,
    Pruned the wild shoot, and trained the straggling bough.

I watched her tender buds and from her shade   25
    Drew each intruding weed with anxious care,
Nor let the curling blight her leaves invade,
    Nor worm, nor noxious insect harbour there.

At length, the Beauty's loveliest bloom appears,
    And, Art from Fame shall win the promised boon,   30
While wayward April, smiling through her tears,
    Decks her fair tresses with the wreaths of June.

Then, jealous Nature, yield the palm to me,
    To me thy pride its early triumph owes,
Though *thy* rude workmanship produced the tree   35
    'Twas *Education* formed the perfect rose.

THE HOT-HOUSE ROSE
⁹ *Zephyr* breeze.   ¹¹ *Vulgar* common.
¹⁰ *Factitious* not natural or genuine, artificial, unspont-
aneous, with homophonic pun on fractious, or difficult.

from *Weekly Inspector* (1806)

"YOU SAY WE'RE FOND OF FOPS, – WHY NOT?"[12]
by "Volina"

You say we're fond of fops, – why not,
When men of sense cannot be got?
A woman, *something* must admire,
Or else with *ennui* expire.

O Doctor! listen to my prayer –   5
A lesson for proud man prepare;
There is a fault you must confess,
Most men of wit and worth possess.

They seem to think in woman's mind,
But very little sense to find;   10
And therefore when they condescend,
Perchance an hour with us to spend –

Think it impossible to please,
With their profound sublime ideas;
But sit in silence, most heroic,   15
Plodding, like philosophic stoic.

Upon my word, I do not know,
Aught more provoking here below;
Than thus to see a man, who might,
Fill every soul with pure delight,   20

Sit pondering with thought profound,
On follies of each female 'round;
Then wonder at our want of spirit,
And blindness to his worth and merit.

Now in my mind, pert prattling beaus,   25
Are more amusing, far, than those;
I grant sometimes a man you find,
With reason, wit, and genius join'd;

With each united charm and grace,
Which fascinate the female race;   30
One whom no prejudice controls,
To think us destitute of souls.

"YOU SAY WE'RE FOND OF FOPS, – WHY NOT?"
[12] This poem was written in response to satirical
comments made by "Dr. Caustick," the publisher of the
Weekly Inspector, about fops in the preceding issue.

Should such a man as this advance,
The fop would stand but little chance;
Believe me, sir, our sex you'll find,   35
To mental worth is never blind.

The man of mind we more admire,
Than perfect forms, or fine attire:
Most women will the fop despise,
When men of sense shall be so wise   40

As to discard, Turk-like opinions,
That women are but Nature's minions;
Made for a while to please the eye,
To nourish man, and then to die!

When you do this we'll bid adieu,   45
To lap-dogs, fops, and monkies too;
Reserving all our admiration,
For MAN, THE GLORY OF CREATION.

from a Broadside (between 1810 and 1814)

THE YOUNG GIRL'S RESOLUTION
by Anonymous

I am a brisk, young lively lass,
    A little under twenty,
And by my comely air and dress,
    I can get sweethearts plenty;
But I'd beware of wedlock's snare   5
    Though dying swains adore me,
The men I'll teaze, myself to please,
    My mamma did so before me.

In rich brocades, and diamonds bright,
    Like gayest springs delighting,   10
My parts and humor shall unite,
    To make me more inviting:
For I'll advance and learn to dance,
    To please shall be my glory,
I'll learn to trace each step with grace,   15
    My mamma did so before me.

I'll dress as fine as fine can be,
    My pride shall be my pleasure,
And though my neighbours envy me,
    To mind them I've no leisure;   20

I will delight by day and night,
    To be talk'd of in story,
I'll have it said there shines a maid,
    My mamma did so before me.

To park and play I'll often go,   25
    And spend a leisure hour:
I'll walk and talk, with every beau,
    And make him feel my power;
But if a dart, should pierce my heart,
    From one that does adore me,   30
We'll wed and kiss, what harm's in this?
    My mamma did so before me.

Then I will manage, when I've wed,
    My husband to perfection;
For, as good wives have always said,   35
    Keep husbands in subjection;
No snarling fool shall e'er me, rule,
    Nor e'er eclipse my glory,
I'll let him see, I'll mistress be,
    My mamma did so before me.   40

from *New York Weekly Museum* (1814)

THE FIRST IDEAL OF BEAUTY
by Anonymous

The babe, emerging from its liquid bed,
Now lifts in gelid[13] air its nodding head;
The light's first dawn, with trembling eyelids hails,
With lungs untaught arrests the balmy gales;
Tries its new tongue in tones unknown, and hears   5
The strange vibration with unpractis'd ears,
Seeks with spread hands the bosom's velvet orbs,
With closing lips the milky fount absorbs;
And, as compress'd, the dulcet streams distill,
Drinks warmth and fragrance from the living rill;   10
Eyes with mute rapture every waving line,
Prints with its coral lips the Paphian shrine,[14]
And learns, ere long, the perfect form confest,
Ideal beauty, from its mother's breast.

THE FIRST IDEAL OF BEAUTY
[13] *Gelid* extremely cold, frozen.

[14] *Paphian* of or pertaining to Paphos, an ancient city in Cyprus, with a famous temple of Aphrodite, the goddess of love, hence, pertaining to love, especially illicit love.

from *Intellectual Regale or Ladies' Tea Tray* (1815)

THE WILD GAZELLE
by Anonymous

"The wild Gazelle on Judah's hills
    Exulting yet may bound,
And drink from all the living rills
    That gush on holy ground;
Its airy step and glorious eye   5
May glance in tameless transport by: –
"A step as fleet, an eye more bright,
    Hath Judah witness'd there,
And o'er her scenes of lost delight
    Inhabitants more fair.   10
The cedars wave on Lebanon,
But Judah's statelier maids are gone.
"More blest each palm that shades those plains,
    Than Israel's scatter'd race;
For, taking root, it there remains   15
    In solitary grace;
It cannot quit its place of birth,
It will not live on other earth
"But we must wander, witheringly,
    In other lands we die,   20
And where our father's ashes be,
    Our own may never lie;
Our temple hath not left a stone,
And mockery sits on Salem's[15] throne."

from *Literary Voyager* (1827)

INVOCATION TO MY MATERNAL GRANDFATHER ON HEARING HIS DESCENT FROM CHIPPEWA ANCESTORS MISREPRESENTED
by "Rosa" (Jane Johnston Schoolcraft)[16]

Rise bravest chief! of the mark of the noble deer,
    With eagle glance,
    Resume thy lance,

THE WILD GAZELLE
[15] Salem was the city of Melchizedek, equated with Zion or Jerusalem. Salem means peaceful, alluding to the messianic "prince of peace."

INVOCATION TO MY MATERNAL GRANDFATHER ON HEARING HIS DESCENT FROM CHIPPEWA ANCESTORS MISREPRESENTED
[16] Jane Johnston Schoolcraft (Ojibwa) (1800–41), folklorist, translator, wife of Henry Rowe Schoolcraft, and granddaughter on her mother's side of Waub Ojeeb (White Fisher) (d. 1793), an important chief of the Chippewa Ojibwas. She also celebrates his deeds in "Otagamiad."

And wield again thy warlike spear!
    The foes of thy line,   5
    With coward design,
Have dar'd, with black envy, to garble the truth,
And stain, with a falsehood, thy valorous youth.

They say, when a child, thou wert ta'en from the Sioux,
    And with impotent aim,   10
    To lessen thy fame
Thy warlike lineage basely abuse,
    For they know that our band,
    Tread a far distant land,
And thou noble chieftain! art nerveless and dead,   15
Thy bow all unstrung, and thy proud spirit fled.

Can the sports of thy youth, or thy deeds ever fade?
    Or those ever forget,
    Who are mortal men yet,
The scenes where so bravely thou'st lifted the blade,   20
    Who have fought by thy side,
    And remember thy pride,
When rushing to battle, with valor and ire,
Thou saw'st the fell foes of thy nation expire.

Can the warrior forget how sublimely you rose?   25
    Like a star in the west,
    When the sun's sunk to rest,
That shines in bright splendor to dazzle our foes:
    Thy arm and thy yell,
    Once the tale could repel   30
Which slander invented, and minions detail,
And still shall thy actions refute the false tale.

Rest thou, noblest chief! in thy dark house of clay,
    Thy deeds and thy name,
    Thy child's child shall proclaim,   35
And make the dark forests resound with the lay;
    Though thy spirit has fled,
    To the hills of the dead,
Yet thy name shall be held in my heart's warmest care,
And cherish'd, till valor and love be no more.   40

                (MS 1823)

SONNET[17]
by J[ane] S[choolcraft]

The voice of reason bids me dry my tears,
        But nature frail, still struggles with that voice;
Back to my mind that placid form appears
        Lifeless, – he seemed to live and to rejoice,
As in the arms of death he meekly lay.   5
        Oh, Cherub Babe! thy mother mourns thy loss,
Tho' thou hast op'd thine eyes in endless day;
        And nought, on earth, can chase away my grief
But Faith – pleading the merits of the Cross,
        And Him, whose promise gives a sure relief.   10

from *Ladies' Garland* (1827)

THE BROKEN PROMISE
by "Estelle"

I knew men kept no promises – or none
At least, with women – and yet, knowing this,
With credulous folly, still I trusted one,
Whose word seemed so like TRUTH, that I forgot
The lessons I had learned full oft before –   5
And I believed, because he *said* he'd come,
That he *would* come – and then, night after night,
I watched the clouds, and saw them pass away
From the bright moon – and leave the clear blue sky,
As spotless, and serene, and beautiful   10
As if no promises were broken e'er
Beneath it. – Man forgets, in busy hours,
What in his idle moments he has said,
Nor thinks how often woman's happiness
Hangs on his lightest words. – It is not things   15
Of great importance which affect the heart
Most deeply – trifles often weave the net
Of misery or of bliss in human life.
There's many a deep and hidden grief, that comes
From sources which admit of no complaint –   20
From things of which we cannot, dare not speak –
And yet they seem but trifles, till a chain,
Link after link, is fastened on each thought,
And wound around the heart – they do their work

SONNET
[17]   William H. Schoolcraft, the son of Jane and Henry
Rowe Schoolcraft, died of croup March 13, 1827. He
was two years, eight months old.

In secrecy and silence – but their power   25
Is far more fatal than the open shafts
Of sorrow and misfortune; for they prey
Upon the health and spirits, till the bloom
Of hope is changed to fever's hectic flush. –
They break the charm of youth's first, brightest dreams,   30
And thus wear out the pleasures of the world –
And sap, at length, the very spring of life.
But this is *woman's* fate. It is not thus
With proud, aspiring *man* – his mind is filled
With high and lofty thoughts – and love, and hope,   35
And all the warmest feelings of his heart,
Are sacrificed at cold ambition's shrine.
He feels that the whole world was made for *him*;
And if some painful disappointments cross
His path of life, he does but change his course;   40
Nor broken promises, nor hopes destroyed,
Are e'er allowed a place on memory's page.
'Tis only woman, in her loneliness,
And, in her silent, melancholy hours,
Who treasures in her heart the idle words   45
That had no meaning – and who lives on hope
Till it has stolen the colour from her cheeks –
The brightness from her eyes; who trusts her peace
On the vast ocean of uncertainty –
And if 'tis wrecked, she learns her lot to bear,   50
Or she may learn to *die* – but not *forget*.
It is for her to hoard her secret thoughts,
To brood o'er broken promises, and sigh
O'er disappointed hopes – till she believes
There's less of wretchedness in the wide world   55
Than in her single heart.

from *Ladies' Magazine* (1833)

THE CHILD ON THE BEACH
by Hannah Gould[18]

Mary, a beautiful artless child,
    Came down on the beach to me,
Where I sat, and a pensive hour beguiled,
    By watching the restless sea.

I never had seen her face before;   5
    And mine was to her unknown,

THE CHILD ON THE BEACH
[18]   Hannah Gould (1789–1865), Massachusetts-born
popular poet.

But we each rejoiced on that peaceful shore,
    The other to meet alone.

Her cheek was the rose's opening bud,
    Her brow of an ivory white;   10
Her eyes were bright as the stars that stud
    The sky of a cloudless night.

To seek my side as she gaily sped,
    With the step of a bounding fawn,
The pebbles scarce moved beneath her tread,   15
    Ere the little light foot was gone.

With the love of a holier world than this
    Her innocent heart seemed warm,
While the glad young spirit looked with bliss
    From its shrine, in her sylph-like form.   20

Her soul seemed spreading the scene to span,
    That opened before her view,
And longing for power to look the plan
    Of the universe fairly through.

She climbed and stood on the rocky steep,   25
    Like a bird, that would mount, and fly
Far over the waves, where the broad blue deep
    Rolled up to the bending sky.

She placed her lips to the spiral shell,
    And breathed through every fold,   30
And she looked for the depth of its pearly cell
    As a miser would for gold.

Her small white fingers were spread to toss
    The foam as it reached the strand –
She ran them along in the purple moss,   35
    And over the sparkling sand.

The green sea-egg, by its tenant left,
    And formed to an ocean-cup,
She held by its sides, of their spears bereft,
    To fill, as the waves played up.   40

But the hour went round, and she knew the space
    Her mother's soft word assigned: –
She seemed to look with a saddening face
    On all she must leave behind.

She searched 'mid the pebbles, and finding one,   45
    Smooth, clear, and of amber dye;
She held it up to the morning sun,
    And over her own mild eye.

Then "here," said she, "I will give you this,
    That you may remember me;"   50
And she sealed her gift with a parting kiss,
    And fled from beside the sea.

Mary, thy token is by me yet,
    To me 'tis a dearer gem,
Than ever was brought from the mine, or set   55
    In the loftiest diadem.

It carries me back to the far-off deep,
    And sets me upon the shore,
Where the beauteous child who bade me keep,
    Her pebble, I meet once more.   60

And all that is lovely, pure and bright,
    In a soul that is young and free
From the stain of guile, and the deadly blight
    Of sorrow, I find in thee!

I wonder if ever thy tender heart   65
    In memory meets me there,
Where thy soft, quick sigh when we had to part
    Was caught by the ocean air.

Blest one! over time's rude shore on thee,
    May an angel guard attend,   70
And *a white stone bearing a new name*, be
    Thy passport when time shall end!

from *Knickerbocker* (1833)

MY HEAD[19]
by Anonymous

"The day is come I never thought to see!
Strange revolutions of my farm and me." – Dryd. Virg.

MY HEAD
[19] *Knickerbocker*   editor's note: "This article from a fair
lady is too good a hit on our cranium to be rejected
from our pages."

My head! my head! the day is come
    I never, never thought to see;
When all with fingers and a thumb,
    May to thy chambers have a key!

That is, if thou wouldst but submit   5
    To come beneath the learned touch,
And let the judge in judgment sit
    Upon thy bumps, that prove so much.

I used to think our heads might let
    Their own contents, at will, be shown;   10
I never thought mankind could get
    An outward way to make them known.

But now the sapient hand has cut
    The matter short, and all may tell
Thy value, as they'd prize a nut,   15
    And know the kernel by the shell.

If half the light that has been thrown
    On heads, were only poured *within*,
Thou wouldst not thus, be left to own
    The darkness that is now thy sin.   20

But, while the world is in a blaze
    Of purely phrenologic light,
Thou, wildered thing! art in a maze,
    And destitute of faith and sight.

They use a thousand meaning words   25
    Thou could'st not utter or define,
Of which, to tell the truth, three thirds,
    Were gravel, in a mouth like thine.

They hold me out an empty skull,
    To show the powers of living brains;   30
'Tis just like feeling of the hull
    To tell what goods the ship contains.

And whether nature or mishap
    Have raised the bump, 'tis all the same;
The sage's crown or dunce's cap   35
    Must be awarded as its claim.

The hobby that so many sit,
    And manage with such ease and grace
I dare not try with rein or bit,
    It seems so, of the donkey race.   40

And yet, my head, no doubt, 'tis all
    A fault of thine, a want of sight,
That so much said by Combe and Gall,
    And Spurzheim[20] cannot turn thee right.

I know not what thy case may be,   45
    If thou art hollow or opaque;
I only know thou canst not see,
    And faith declines one step to take.

This burst of light has turned thee numb,
    Depriving thee of every sense!   50
So now, if tried, thou must be dumb,
    Nor say one word in self-defence!

A BELLE'S PHILOSOPHY[21]
[From a Lady's Album]

Yon mountain's side hath a crystal stream,
Which laughs along in the sunshine free,
And its rippling course and the splintering gleam
Of its diamond falls are a joy to see.
Shall we turn it aside from its sparkling way,   5
To slake for a summer a garden's thirst,
That buds may have life, and that flow'rets gay
In its fostering dews may be born and nurs'd.
Oh no, philosopher, no,
Utility must not mislead us so.[22]   10
We must always strive
To preserve alive
A little romance in this world below.

There's a statue beneath yon humble shrine,
'Tis the Queen of the Graces in virgin gold,   15
Instinct[23] with a beauty, as like divine,
As poet or painter could feign of old.
Shall her smiling and gentle presence be
Coined down[24] like a common and sordid thing,
To bear to the ends of the earth and sea,   20
The stupid impress of a foolish king,
Oh no, philosopher, no, &c.

---

[20] George Combe (1788–1858), Franz Joseph Gall (1758–1828), and Johann Caspar Spurzheim (1776–1832), well-known names in phrenology or the pseudo-science of reading head-bumps.
A BELLE'S PHILOSOPHY
[21] *Knickerbocker* editor's note: "Supposed to be the only one now extant."

[22] The hit here is at Jeremy Bentham (1748–1832), English philosopher and political theorist. He was the founder of Utilitarianism.
[23] *Instinct* imbued or filled; charged.
[24] *Coined down* melted down and turned into money.

There's another shrine where the votary[25] sues
To the glorious life of that sculptured form;
And where in the light that her smiles diffuse,   25
The iciest bosoms grow soft and warm.
Shall the fatal spell of the parson drown
In the rights of one mortal, the hopes of all.
Shall the queen of the belles lay the sceptre down,
And yield to a homely domestic thrall.   30
Oh no, philosopher, no.
Utility must not mislead us so.
We must always strive
To preserve alive
A little romance in this world below.   35

from *Knickerbocker* (1834)

THE WITCHES' REVEL
by E[lizabeth] F. E[llet][26]

On with the dance! Let the echoing earth
From the depth of its caverns resound to our mirth,
'Tis the blithe hour of revel! the hated moonlight
Is quenched in the scowl of the tempest-winged night!
The spirits of death and of vengeance are nigh,   5
And their voice of wail moans to the darkened sky!

On with the dance! On the far battle field
Dimmed with gore is the glitter of helmet and shield,
The fell stream of carnage still reeks on the air –
And the raven stoops earthward, his banquet to share: 10
Let him feast! The last breath from the vanquished is sped –
But our song shall exult o'er the festering dead!

On with the dance! Of the red lightning's gleam
We will twine us a wreath that in triumph shall beam;
For the pale flowers of earth, in that garland to shine,   15
Of our victim's torn limbs, gasping trophies we'll twine!
For the rich mantling wine cup, of victory to tell,
With the heart's drained life-blood, our goblets shall swell!

Sisters – rejoice! On yon foam-crested wave
There are ships going down with the fair and the brave!   20
As the storm petrel flaps his wing fitfully there,
Ye may hear in the wild blast the curse and the prayer!

---

[25] *Votary* a devoted adherent, with a religious connotation.

THE WITCHES' REVEL
[26] Elizabeth Ellet (1818–77), author, editor, scholar, and historian of women's lives.

Ye may hear the last groan as the victim sweeps by –
Ye may catch the last gleam of the quivering eye!

Wake the loud revel! The roar of the sea,   25
And the drowning one's death-shriek, our music shall be!
While our beacon of vengeance illumines the night,
And the deep thunder peals from his mantle of light –
While the freed winds rejoice, and the fierce lightnings glance –
'Tis the blithe hour of revel! On – on with the dance!   30

from *National Enquirer* (1836)

THE STRANGER IN AMERICA
by Ella (Sarah Mapps Douglass)[27]

*"They tie our feet, and seal our mouths, and then exclaim, 'See how superior
we are to these people!'"* – *J. Forten, Jr.*

I come from a far country, where I dwelt
With friends and kindred in a quiet vale.
Of distant scenes we knew not; and I now
Find some *most* strange – incomprehensible
    I hear the Negro spoken of, as one   5
Who wears the form of man, – but who has not
Hs intellectual powers.   Can this be so?
    "It is! – 'tis true he wears the form of man,
Else could he not perform the labor done
Here by the grov'ling whites.   He was so formed,   10
To execute the tasks allotted him.
The work your horses and your oxen do,
Is done by him; but walking upright, he
Can other tasks perform."
                        And is that all;   15
Has he not intellect, – a mind – a heart?
    "He has no intellect! – Phrenologists[28]
Will tell you that his skull is not like ours:
He is a link between us and the brutes,
F[ound?] more than half way down."[29]   20

THE STRANGER IN AMERICA
[27] Sarah Mapps Douglass (1806–82), black abolitionist
and author, who wrote under the pseudonyms "Ella"
and "Sophronisba." The author of the epigraph, James
Forten, Jr, is Sarah Louisa Forten's brother. I wish to
thank Professor Julie Winch for calling my attention to
this poem.
[28] For two more responses to phrenology, see Fuller's
"Governor Everett Receiving the Indian Chiefs" (1844)
and "My Head" (1833).

[29] Anticipations of Darwin's theory of evolution (1859)
linking human beings to "lower" orders of animal life
were widespread in the early nineteenth century, which
was seeking a scientific explanation for inter-species
differences and similarities. Also widespread was the
abuse of this theory, which led pro-slavery apologists to
argue on "scientific" grounds that Africans were not fully
human. Unfortunately, the advent of Darwinism itself
only intensified this belief, laying the foundations for
the scientific racism (racist eugenics) that is one of the
hallmarks of the early twentieth century.

'Tis very strange!
No intellect – no mind – and has he not
A *soul* to save, or lose?
                    "Young stranger, come,
Such enquiries may not be answer'd *here*,   25
Where gloomy superstition[30] reigns.
Come with me to the *South*, where freedom dwells,
There shall you see the truth of all I've told."
Oh! can it be, that I have lived till now,
Nor known of such misery and crime –   30
Such stain upon a world I deem'd so fair?
The Negro! – why his limbs are manacled!
He can but use them as a tyrant wills;
And on his mind, his senses, and his soul,
Are fetters heavier still. Proud Southron, yes!   35
He *has* a soul; but he will not be judged, –
Surely unerring justice will not judge
His soul as thine – *he* knows not what he does;
The voice of conscience silenced by the lash,
Will not the crimes that he may perpetrate,   40
Be charged to *thy* account?

from *Liberator* (1836)

LINES,

Suggested on Reading "An Appeal to Christian Women of The South," By A. E. Grimke
by Ada (Eliza Earle?)[31]

My spirit leaps in joyousness tow'rd thine,
My gifted sister, as with gladdened heart
My vision flies along thy 'speaking pages.'[32]
Well hast thou toiled in Mercy's sacred cause;
And thus another strong and lasting thread   5
Is added to the woof[33] our sex is weaving,
With skill and industry, for Freedom's garb.
Precious the privilege to labor here, –
Worthy the lofty mind and handy-work
Of Chapman, Chandler, Child, and Grimke[34] too.   10

---

[30]   That is, religious scruples.
LINES
[31]   Eliza Earle (1807–46), schoolteacher, abolitionist
poet (s.v. Sarah Louisa Forten).
[32]   Quoted from Grimké's peroration.
[33]   *Woof* the threads that cross the warp in a woven
fabric.
[34]   Maria W. Chapman (1806–85), Elizabeth Margaret
Chandler (1807–34), Lydia Marie Child (1802–80), and
Angelina Grimké Weld (1805–79), prominent female

abolitionists. Chandler and Chapman were also poets.
Grimké's "Appeal to the Christian Women of the South"
(1836) argued that women had a moral duty to speak
out against slavery since it was against God's law. Her
pamphlet is one of the foundational texts for American
feminism and the Ada poet follows her in making wom-
en's literary empowerment a consequence of their moral
duty as defined by abolitionist politics and spiritual
beliefs.

There's much in woman's influence, ay much,
To swell the rolling tide of sympathy,
And aid those champions of a fettered race,
Now laboring arduous in the moral field.
We may not 'cry aloud,' as they are bid,   15
And lift our voices in the *public* ear;[35]
Nor yet be mute. The pen is ours to wield,
The heart to will, and hands to execute.
And more the gracious promise gives to all –
Ask, says the Saviour, and ye shall receive.   20
In concert then, Father of love, we join,
To wrestle with thy presence, as of old
Did Israel, and will not let thee go
Until thou bless. The cause is thine – for 'tis
Thy guiltless poor who are oppressed, on whom   25
The sun of Freedom may not cast his beams,
Nor dew of heavenly knowledge e'er descend.
And for their fearless advocates we ask
The wisdom of the serpent – above all,
Our heavenly Father, clothe, oh clothe them with   30
The dove-like spirit of thine own dear Son:
Then are they safe, tho' Persecution's waves
Dash o'er their bark, and furious winds assail –
Still they are safe.

       —— Yes, this *is* woman's work,   35
Her own appropriate sphere; and nought should drive
Her from the mercy seat, till Mercy's work
Be finished.

       Whose is that wail, piercing the ear
Of night, with agony too deep for words   40
To give it birth? 'Tis woman's – she of Ramah[36] –
Another Rachel,[37] weeping for her babes,
And will not be consoled, for they are not.
Oh! slavery, with all its withering power,
Can never wholly quench the flame of love,   45
Nor dry the stream of tenderness that flows
In breasts maternal. A *mother's love!* deep grows
That plant of Heaven, fast by the well of life,
And nought can pluck it thence till woman cease

---

[35] The Ada poet is drawing a line between public speech and writing that other more radical women abolitionists, such as Frances Wright and Maria W. Stewart, had already violated, marking her as more conservative on women's issues than some of her peers. The Grimké sisters would soon break this barrier also in their speaking tour of the late 1830s.

[36] 1 Samuel 1:1; 1:19. Like the better known Rachel, Hannah, the mother of Samuel, was originally unable to conceive.

[37] Genesis 30:1. Rachel, wife of Jacob and mother of Joseph.

To be. — Then, long as mother's hearts are breaking   50
Beneath the hammer of the auctioneer,
And ruthless Avarice tears asunder bonds,
That the fiat of the Almighty joined,
So long should woman's melting voice be heard,
In intercession strong and deep, that this   55
Accursed thing, this Achan[38] in our camp,
May be removed.

from *Liberator* (1837)

[PETITIONING CONGRESS][39]
by Ada (Eliza Earle)

*"We also respectfully announce our intention to present the same petition
yearly, before your honorable body, that it may, at least, be a memorial of
us, that in the holy cause of human Freedom we have done what we could."*

The scroll is open — many a name is written —
    The ink is flowing from the lifted quill —
Say, is that lily hand with palsy smitten,
    That it should disobey the writer's will?

Her free consent already has been given,   5
    Why should she then thus hesitating stand?
Fears she the wrath of an offending Heaven,
    Its righteous judgments on a guilty land?

No! — but that sneer — should female christians fear it,
    And from their holy purposes be swayed?   10
The world's dread laugh — they surely well may bear it,
    Tho' "firm philosophers" may be dismayed.

What tho' they call us "Female Politicians,"
    And many an ill-timed epithet bestow?
Shall they thus stem the tide of our petitions?   15
    And shall we steel our hearts to human woe?

To woman is assigned her proper station,
    To pluck life's thorn, and strew its path with flowers,
Exempted from the cares of legislation,
    No Amazonian prowess should be ours.   20

---

[38] Joshua 6:17–19 and 7:1–26. Achan hid loot from the battle of Jericho in his tent and brought down God's wrath on Israel.

[PETITIONING CONGRESS]

[39] This title only appears in the *National Enquirer* reprint of the poem in February, 1837. The use of petitions to flood Congress was a tactic of women abolitionists who were otherwise debarred from speaking in public (s.v. Lydia Huntley Sigourney, "The Cherokee Mother"). There is no specific source for most of the quotations that pepper this poem. They were phrases "in the air."

Yet "MORAL COURAGE" has been freely given,
    By Him whose wisdom never yet has erred,
And shall we trample on this gift of Heaven,
    For high and holy purposes conferred?

Ours be the "Duty," not the "Rights of woman,"[40]   25
    Knowing the strength of nature's dearest ties,
May we yet "prove that ours are feelings human,"
    Holy affections, kindly sympathies.

Are we disheartened? Shall our footsteps, falter?
    Lonely and weeping are we seen to stand,   30
Like Israel's priests, between the porch and altar,
    Sad and dispirited, a fearful band?

No – perseverance yet may safely bear us,
    O'er opposition's overwhelming tide;
We still will trust that they may deign to hear us,   35
    And our petitions may not be denied.

Oh! there is one tribunal, where we fear not,
    Humbly to bend the knee in fervent prayer,
And, tho' earth's magnates our petitions hear not,
    They shall ascend in blest acceptance there.   40

Then in each high and holy aspiration,
    With frequent intercession let us pray,
That those foul sins which stigmatize our nation,
    From her escutcheon[41] may be washed away;

That Freedom's gift may yet to man be given,   45
    That he, disfranchised, yet may walk abroad –
Each shackle broken, every fetter riven –
    Erect and free, the image of his God.

from *National Enquirer* (1837)

THE BOAST OF AMERICANS
by Ella (Sarah Mapps Douglass)

"In other lands, we read in story,
Are Kings and Thrones, but 'tis our glory
That we are free: no tyrant's frown
We fear – no man who wears a crown."

---

[10] Earle's note: Alluding to the works of M. Wolstone-craft [*sic*], the latter written while she was yet an Infidel – the former, after she embraced the Christian religion.

[11] *Escutcheon* a shield on which armorial bearings are depicted.

No! – *Free born Americans* fear not the frown
That may darken the brow which is wreathed by a crown;
But happier thousands, aye, millions, might be,
If bending to monarchs and princes the knee,
Than here in "the land of the brave and the free."   5
What mock'ry to prate of the *free* and the *brave!*
'Tis the land of the tyrant, the coward, and slave, –
The "bye-word of nations," – deep sunk in disgrace,
Which no boast of *our glory* can ever efface.
Shall the record be kept, that in future may tell   10
How our country was blest, how it flourished – and fell!
The record for struggles of freedom – and then
Of oppress'd, and degraded, and manacled men? –
Of *Americans* stolen, and barter'd for gold, –
To bondage and death *by Americans* sold?   15
Shall the record be kept? – But not as of yore;
It is hidden by *pictures* of freedom no more;
It is written and spoken, and mountain and vale
Re-echo the dark, the soul-harrowing tale.
It is lisped in the nurs'ry; (the Southron may sneer   20
At "*women and children*," – their feelings are dear
To the high soul'd and gen'rous, the gifted and kind;)
And *now* are the labors of thousands combin'd –
The noblest, the purest, and fearless, extend
Their efforts, the chain of oppression to rend,   25
Ere long 'twill be broken! – Not vainly hath striv'n
The "*Genius*" of Freedom, and favor'd by Heaven.
With spirits unshrinking, the friends of the slave,
Prepared all the power of tyrants to brave,
Their actions, their motives, the feelings they cherish,   30
Draw blessings from those who are "ready to perish."
They have pass'd through the gloom of "a long weary night,"
But their path is illumin'd by Heaven's own light.
From that light shall the spirit of tyranny flee.
And Americans *really* be "equal and free."   35

from *Knickerbocker* (1837)

To a Bride
by Mary E. Hewitt[42]

I.

He hath wooed thee with those wildering[43] words which maidens blushing
   heed,
He hath won thee, ere thy heart might well its own pure language read;

To a Bride
[42]   Mary E. Hewitt (1808–94), poet.   [43]   *Wildering* bewildering.

He hath wed thee at the altar, with the vow and with the token,
Which bind ye, till the cord be loosed, and the golden bowl be broken.[44]

II.

He will love thee for a season – ay! more than tongue can speak –   5
While the orange wreath is on thy brow, and the rose upon thy cheek:
He will wear thee like a festal robe – then fling thee careless by –
Light holds the wayward heart of man sworn oaths of constancy.

III.

Are they not all of love and hope, the dreams of thy young years?
It will fade, the blissful vision – thou wilt awake in tears!   10
They will change, those wreaths for future hours which thy bright spirit
    weaves,
Like the genii gold of the eastern tale, to a heap of withered leaves.

IV.

The lot is on thee! – woman's lot – in loneliness to pine,
That thy gods he doth not worship – his people are not thine;
To find earth's pleasant places unto thee made desolate,   15
Thy path all sand, yet 'mid the waste, to wrestle with thy fate.

V.

Wear broidered robe and costly gem – light be thy laugh and jest –
Lead the gay dance – none look for wo beneath the glittering vest;
Hide deep thy thoughts – yet thy young heart back from itself will quail,
From all the hideousness which lies beneath its silver veil.   20

VI.

Thou may'st not bend at other shrines – thy vow is on the first –
Thou may'st not at another fount quaff to allay thy thirst:
O drooping reed! no draught for thee may earthly hand prepare –
Yet there is 'balm in Gilead'[45] – seek thy physician there!

from *Colored American* (1840)

LINES

Written on Visiting the Grave of a Venerated Friend
by Ann Plato[46]

Deep in this grave, her bones remain, –
She's sleeping on bereft of pain, –

---

[44]   That is, at death. See Ecclesiastes 12:6.
[45]   *Gilead* a fertile mountainous region northeast of the Dead Sea; it was noted for its spices, myrrh, and balm or healing salve.

LINES
[46]   Ann Plato (b. 1820?), black poet, educator, and essayist.

Her tongue in silence now does sleep,
And she no more times call can greet.

She lived as all God's saints should do,   5
Resigned to death and suffering too;
She feel[s] not pain, nor sin oppress'd,
Nor is of worldly cares possess'd.

White were the locks that thinly shed
Their snows around her honor'd head,   10
And furrows not to be effaced,
Had age amid her features traced.

I said, my sister, DO tread light,
Faint as the star that gleams at night,
Nor pluck the tender leaves that wave   15
In sweetness o'er this sainted grave.

The rose I've planted by her side,
It tells me of that fate decried,
And bids us all prepare to die,
For that our doom is hast'ning nigh.   20

Oh! that the gale that sweeps the heath
Too roughly o'er your leaves should breathe,
Then sigh for her, – and when you bloom,
Scatter your fragrance o'er her tomb.

Alone I've wander'd through the gloom   25
To pour my lays upon her tomb:
And I have mourn'd to see her bed
With brambles and with thorns o'erspread.

O! surely, round her place of rest
I will not let the weed be blest,   30
It is not meet that she should be
Forgotten or unblest by me[.]

My sister said, "tell of this grave;"
Go ask, said I, the thoughtless wave,
And spend one hour in anxious care,   35
In duty, penitence, and prayer.

Farewell! let memory bestow,
That all may soon be laid as low,
For out of dust we were composed,
And turn to dust, to sleep, repose.   40

from *Southern Literary Messenger* (1842)

MY MUSE
by Lydia Jane [Pierson]

Born of the sunlight and the dew,
 That met amongst the flow'rs,
That on the river margin grew
 Beneath the willow bow'rs;
Her earliest pillow was a wreath   5
 Of violets newly blown,
And the meek incense of their breath
 Became at once her own.

Her cradle hymn the river sung
 In that same liquid tone,   10
With which it gave, when earth was young,
 Praise to the Living One;
The breeze that lay upon its breast
 Responded with a sigh,
And the sweet ring-dove from her nest 15
 Warbled her lullaby.

The only nurse she ever knew
 Was Nature, free and wild:
Such was her birth, and so she grew
 A moody, wayward child,   20
Who loved to climb the rocky steep,
 To wade the mountain stream,
To lie beside the sounding deep
 And weave the enchanted dream.

She lov'd the paths with shadows dim 25
 Beneath the dark-leav'd trees,
Where Nature's feathered seraphim
 Mingled their melodies;
To dance amongst the pensile[47] stems
 Where blossoms bright and sweet, 30
Threw diamonds from their diadems
 Upon her fairy feet.

She lov'd to watch the day-star float
 Upon the aerial sea,
Till morning sunk his pearly boat   35
 In floods of brilliancy;

MY MUSE
[17] *Pensile* hanging, pendant.

To see the angel of the storm
    Upon his wind-wing'd car,
With dark clouds wrapt around his form
    Come shouting from afar;   40

And pouring treasures rich and free,
    The pure refreshing rain,
Till every weed and forest tree
    Could boast its diamond chain;
Then rising with the hymn of praise   45
    That swell'd from hill and dale,
Leave a rainbow-sign of peace –
    Upon his misty veil.

She lov'd the wave's deep uttering,
    And gaz'd with frenzied eye   50
When night shook lightning from his wings,
    And winds went sobbing by.
Full oft I chid the wayward child
    Her wanderings to restrain,
And sought her airy limbs to bind   55
    With prudence's worldly chain.

I bade her stay within my cot
    And ply the housewife's art;
She heard me, but she heeded not;
    Oh who can bind the heart!   60
I told her she had none to guide
    Her inexperienced feet
To where, through Tempe's[48] valley, glide
    Castalia's[49] waters sweet.

No son of fame to take her hand   65
    And lead her blushing forth,
Proclaiming to a laurel'd band
    A youthful sister's worth;
That there was none to help her climb
    The steep and toilsome way,   70
To where, above the mists of time
    Shines genius' living ray.

Where wreath'd with never-fading flow'rs
    The Harp immortal lies,
Filling the souls that reach those bow'rs   75
    With heavenly melodies.

---

[18] *Tempe* a valley in Thessaly celebrated for its beauty.   [19] *Castalia* a spring sacred to the Muses on the lower slope of Mt Parnassus in Greece.

I warn'd her of the cruel foes
        That throng that rugged path,
Where many a thorn of misery grows,
        And tempests wreak their wrath.   80

I told her of the serpent's dread
        With malice-pointed fangs,
The yellow-blossom'd weeds that shed
        Derision's maddening pangs;
And of the broken mouldering lyres   85
        Thrown carelessly aside,
Telling the winds with shivering wires
        How noble spirits died.

I said her sandals were not meet
        Such journey to essay,   90
There should be gold beneath the feet
        That tempt Fame's toilsome way.
But while I spoke, her burning eye
        Was flashing in the light
That shone upon that mountain high,   95
        Insufferably bright.

And soft upon the balmy air
        Castalia's murmurs came,
And gentle spirits hymning there
        Breath'd forth her humble name.   100
And bending from the dizzy height
        The blossom'd laurel seem'd,
And wreaths of bloom divinely bright
        Like crowns of glory gleamed;

While streaming from the Eternal Lyre,   105
        Like distant echoes, came
A strain that wrapp'd her soul in fire,
        And thrill'd her trembling frame.
She sprang away, that wayward child,
        The Harp! the Harp! she cried.   110
And still she climbs and warbles wild
        Along the mountain's side.

from *Southern Literary Messenger* (1845)

LOVE AND FLOWERS
by E[lizabeth] J. E[ames]

I.

I do remember now
That green and sloping bank, whereon we sat,
A bank of mossy grass, as delicate
As Tempe e'er for Io's[50] slumber spread;
While through each woven bough   5
Of the old tree 'neath which we sat, were shed
Touches of silver light, that changeful stirr'd
With the soft-dallying zephyr's faintest whisper'd word.

II.

Yes, I remember it.
That cool, delicious stream which, sparkling, wound   10
Its way the baselet of that bank around; –
How beautiful its glossy mirror spread,
Just where we two did sit –
And pictur'd in its glass the bright gold-thread,
Green-fern fringe, moss-bell, and blue-lily bent,   15
While bird, and brook, and branch, their broken murmurs blent.

III.

'Twas in the sweet June-time,
That thou and I together *there* last sat –
And thou had'st gather'd for my gypsy-hat,
Bell, bud, and blossom, and fair flowret wild –   20
While to a quaint old rhyme,
My thoughts kept time; meanwhile, tho' but a child
And scarcely conscious in those careless hours –
I knew that thou would'st tell thy boyish love [in f]lowers.

IV.

Well – so thou didst – and well –   25
I had a cousin's kindness for thee then,
And may be something more; but thou dost ken
That *flowers will* fade, and *love*, too, *can* decay
Beneath the stronger spell
Of chance, and change; and thus it pass'd away,   30
That fickle fondness, from thy heart, and mine.
We both are wiser *now*, yet kneel, each at a falser shrine.

LOVE AND FLOWERS

[50] *Io* the daughter of the river god, Inachus, beloved by Zeus and transformed into a heifer by his jealous wife, Hera. While in heifer shape she wandered throughout Greece.

from *Lowell Offering* (1845)

HOME
by A. M. S. (Mary Anne Spaulding?)

I dream of home, and much rejoice,
For then I hear my father's voice
    Ascend again in prayer;
I see again my mother's face,
Return each sister's kind embrace,   5
    And meet a brother there.

And then I wake alone, alone,
And hear no kind familiar tone,
    Nor form of kindred see;
They vanish all with that sweet dream,   10
For hills and vales now lie between
    My distant home and me.

And Autumn winds shall cease to wail
Among the groves of that fair vale
    Where rolls the Chicopee;[51]   15
And Winter stern, all pale and cold,
About the earth his robe shall fold,
    Ere I my home shall see.

But when shall come the vernal queen,
With floral crown and mantle green,   20
    To bid rude Winter flee,
Then all my weary exile o'er,
I'll seek with joy my home, where roar
    The falls of Chicopee.

from *North Star* (1848)

THE TIMES THAT TRY MEN'S SOULS[52]
by [Maria W. Chapman]

Confusion has seized us, and all things go wrong,
    The women have leaped from "their spheres,"
And, instead of fixed stars, shoot as comets along,

HOME
[51] A river in Massachusetts found approximately sixty miles west of Boston in the Springfield area.

THE TIMES THAT TRY MEN'S SOULS
[52] According to *Littell's Living Age*, which also reprints this poem, Elizabeth W. McClintock read it for Maria W. Chapman (1806–85) at the Seneca Falls' Women's Rights Convention in July, 1848. Chapman was a prominent feminist and abolitionist.

And are setting the world by the ears!
In courses erratic they're wheeling through space,   5
In brainless confusion and meaningless chase.

In vain do our knowing ones try to compute
    Their return to the orbit designed;
They're glanced at a moment, then onward they shoot,
    And are neither to "hold nor to bind;"   10
So freely they move in their chosen ellipse,
The "Lords of Creation" do fear an eclipse.

They've taken a notion to speak for themselves,
    And are wielding the tongue and the pen;
They've mounted the rostrum, the termagant[53] elves,   15
    And, oh horrid, are talking to *men!*
With faces unblanched in our presence they come,
To harangue us, they say, in behalf of the dumb.

They insist on their right to petition and pray –
    That St. Paul, in Corinthians, has given them rules   20
For appearing in public;[54] despite what those say
    Whom we've trained to instruct them in orthodox schools.
But vain such instruction, if women may scan,
And quote texts of Scripture to favor their plan.

Our grandmothers' learning consisted of yore,   25
    In spreading their generous boards;
In twisting the distaff,[55] or mopping the floor,
    And *obeying the will of their lords.*
Now, *misses* may reason, and think, and debate,
Till unquestioned submission is quite out of date.   30

Our clergy have preached on the sin and the shame
    Of woman when out of "her sphere,"
And labored, *divinely*, to ruin her fame,
    And shorten this horrid career;
But for spiritual guidance no longer they look,   35
To Folsom, or Winslow, or learned Parsons Cooke.[56]

Our wise men have tried to exorcise in vain –
    The turbulent spirit's abroad;

---

[53] *Termagant* when said of woman, a froward, shrewish individual.
[54] 1 Corinthians 14:34. "Let your women keep silent in the churches for they are not permitted to speak; but they are to be submissive, as the law also says."
[55] *Distaff* the staff for holding a bunch of wool or cotton from which yarn or thread is drawn.

[56] Nathaniel Smith Folsom (b. 1806), Hubbard Winslow (1799–1864), and Parsons Cooke (1800–64) were all Congregational ministers who had protested vehemently against abolitionist women speaking in public.

As well might we deal with the fetterless main,
  Or conquer ethereal essence with sword,   40
Like the devils of Milton,[57] they rise from each blow,
  With spirit unbroken insulting the foe.

Our patriot fathers, of eloquent fame,
  Waged war against tangible forms;
Ay, *their* foes were men, and if ours were the same,   45
  We might speedily quiet their storms;
But ah! Their descendants enjoy not such bliss –
The assumptions of Britain were nothing to this.

Could we but array all our force in the field,
  We'd teach these usurpers of power,   50
That their bodily safety demands they should yield,
  And in presence of manhood should cower;
But, alas! for our tethered and impotent state,
Chained by notions of knighthood, we can but debate.

Oh! shade of the prophet Mahomet,[58] arise,   55
  Place woman again in "her sphere,"
And teach that her soul was not born for the skies,
  But to flutter a brief moment here.
This doctrine of Jesus, as preached up by Paul,
If embraced in its spirit, will ruin us all.   60

                    LORDS OF CREATION

from *Cherokee Advocate* (1850)

MISSPENT LIFE
by The Cherokee Poetess

E'n now on heights of age I sit,
  My soul enwrap'd in grief;
In vain my thoughts on past I let,
  In search of sweet relief.

How killing to my trembling heart,   5
  The thought of murder'd youth,
When racking pains, in every part,
  Confirm the fatal truth.

Had I my life again to live
  As you, my youth, do now –   10

---

[57]   John Milton (1608–74), British poet, author of *Paradise Lost*. (See Ray's "Vision of Eve.")

[58]   Muhammad (570?–632 CE), the prophet of Islam. Islamic doctrine on the fate of women's souls in the afterlife is unclear.

Would I my hopes to ruin drive,
 And at the coffer[59] bow?

While death beats high in ev'ry pulse,
 Urged on by ragged age,
The thoughts of youthful hope insult,   15
 And in my bosom rage.

Oh death! death! thou most cruel king,
 Why on my vitals prey,
And to the grave untimely bring,
 These locks now growing gray?   20

But ah! too late, the gale has past,
 That fan'd my healthy face.
The chains of death are on the fast,
 And I conclude my race.[60]

O now, ye merry children, view   25
 A picture of yourselves,
When all the joys you ever knew,
 Have formed you into elves.[61]

My breath grows short; my strength now fails;
 To you I bid adieu.   30
My spirit soon shall ride the gales;
 But this I leave with you,

That you in age may be secure,
 Though I'm o'erwhelmed in fault.
Eternal heaven, my troubles cure –   35
 I tumble in the vault.[62]

from *Louisville Weekly Journal* (1850)

TO MY CHILD
by S.

Farewell! I will not part from thee in sadness and in tears,
Nor darken this, our parting hour, with vain and fruitless fears;
Though long and weary years may pass, ere we shall meet again,
I will not lose the present hour in tears as weak as vain.

MISSPENT LIFE
[59] *Coffer* a chest or trunk usually holding valuables, hence, treasure. There is a subtle pun on coffin, a secondary meaning for "coffer."
[60] *Race* life history. There may be a pun on people or kind.

[61] *Elves* a small person, a child, especially a mischievous child.
[62] *Vault* a burial chamber; secured place to store valuables.

Sweet baby! come and lean thy head upon my aching heart,   5
And let me look into thine eyes, one moment, ere we part,
And smile as thou art wont to smile in thy young childish glee,
That so thy joy may reach the heart that bleeds to part from thee.

No grief shall mark my death-cold brow, no sorrow dim my eye,
In bidding thee a last adieu when other eyes are by;   10
But *here*, with none but God and thee to witness, let me tell
How bleeds the heart, that seems so cold, in bidding *thee* farewell!

We are alone, my sweetest child, no friend is left us now,
Save Him who blesses every tear that falls upon thy brow;
And He *will* bless thee evermore, for He has sworn to be   15
"A father to the fatherless" – then will He care for *thee*!

I leave thee with a breaking heart, a dry and aching eye,
For none may know the thoughts that swell within my soul so high;
I press thee in a last embrace – and *can* it be the last?
Can all the love I felt for thee be but as shadows past?   20

I have bent o'er thy little form, when cradled on my breast,
Thy dark eye softly folded in its sweet, unbroken rest,
And my wild heart has gone above in gratitude to God,
And I have bowed in spirit there, and kissed His chastening rod!

My child! if in this breaking heart one feeling lingers still,   25
Which anguish hath not changed to gall, nor wrong hath made an ill,
It is the deep, redeeming love that fills my heart for thee,
And forms the last link, yet unrent, between my God and me!

from *Occident* (1850)

HULDAH THE PROPHETESS

From Female Scriptural Characters, No. IX
by Mrs R[ebekah] Hyneman[63]

There are sounds of complaint in a lordly hall;
        What grieveth the spirit of Judah's king?
Hath a mystical finger portrayed on the wall
His prophetic doom, or his kingdom's fall,
        Or whence does that sorrow spring?   5

Have his cities been wasted by sword and by flame?
        Are his treasures engulphed by the sea?

HULDAH THE PROPHETESS

[63] Rebekah Gumpert Hyneman (1812–75), Jewish American poet. Huldah is an Old Testament prophet-ess, consulted by Josiah on the finding of the Law. See 2 Kings 22:14–20; 2 Chronicles 34:22–8.

Does his heart lie crushed by a weight of shame,
That stains his kingdom and sullies his name,
      And causes his misery?   10

Oh! a heavier doom than these has spread
      A shadow o'er heart and brain,
A weightier grief has bowed his head,
And though few and low were the words he said,
      They betokened his inward pain.   15

"Go ask," he said, "of the good and wise
      If this doom may pass away;
If lowly prayer and the sacrifice
Of our penitent hearts may yet arise
      To avert the evil day."   20

And whom shall they seek in that trying hour?
      What bearded sage or deep-learned seer,
Whose prophetic words have a magical power
To point the right path when dark tempests lower,
      And the strong man shrinks with fear?   25

Oh, how can a *woman's* soft voice foretell
      The heavy doom they dread to know?
Or how can she pierce through the mystic veil
Of the shadowy future, and breathe a spell
      Like that which her lips breathe now?   30

"Ye ask me what answer the Lord hath given?
      Thus say to him who sent you here:
For the deep transgressions of those who have striven
To call down the judgment and vengeance of heaven,
Both they and theirs shall from hence be driven,   35
      And their spirits shall quail with fear.

"A terror and blight in field and on flood
      Shall descend unto all who have fled from me,
Who have bowed themselves to a god of wood,
And polluted their hands with innocent blood;   40
Let the reptile crawl where their palace hath stood,
      And their name be a mockery.

"Go bear ye hence, to an erring race,
      The answer God in his wrath hath sent,
And say to the hardened and shameless of face,   45
That henceforth the wide world has no resting-place
To screen them from terror and deep disgrace,
      Until all His anger is spent."

When, when will thy anger be spent, Oh, God!
    And thy children's sufferings past?   50
Oh lead then their steps where the righteous have trod,
That the bigot's chain and the tyrant's rod
May pollute no longer that sacred sod,
    And thy chosen be free at last.

from *Frederick Douglass's Newspaper* (1852)

STORY TELLING
by Annie Parker

The winter wind blew cold, and the snow was falling fast,
But within the cheerful parlor none listened to the blast;
The fire was blazing brightly, and soft lamps their radiance shed
On rare, and costly pictures, and many a fair young head.

The father in the easy chair, to his youngest nestling dove,   5
Whispered a wondrous fairy tale, such as all children love;
Brothers and sisters gathered round, and the eye might clearly trace
A happiness too deep for words, on the mother's lovely face.

And when the fairy tale was done, the blue-eyed Ella said,
"Mama, please tell a story too, before we go to bed,   10
And let it be a funny one, such as I like to hear
'Red Riding Hood,' or 'The Three Bears,' or 'Chicken Little dear.'"

A smile beamed on the mother's face, as the little prattler spoke,
And kissing her soft, rosy cheek she thus the silence broke,
"I will tell you, my own darlings, a story that is true,   15
Of a little Southern maiden, with a skin of sable hue.

"Xariffe, her mother called her, a child of beauty rare,
With soft gazelle-like eyes, and curls of dark and shining hair,
A fairy form of perfect grace, and such artless winning ways
That none who saw her, e'er could fail her loveliness to praise,   20

"She sported mid the orange-groves in gleeful, careless play,
And her mother as she gazed on her, in agony would pray,
'My Father, God! be merciful! my cherished darling save
From the curse whose sum of bitterness is to be a female slave.'

"God heard her prayer, but often He, in wisdom doth withhold   25
The boon we crave, that we may be pure and refined like gold;
And the mother saw Xariffe grow in loveliness and grace,
Till the roses of five summers blushed in beauty on her face.

"At length, one day, one sunny day, when earth and heaven were bright,
The mother to her daily toil went forth at morning light;   30
At evening, when her task was done – how can the tale be told?
She came back to her empty hut, to find her darling sold.

"Come nearer, my own precious ones, your soft white arms entwine
Around my neck, and kiss me close, sweet Ella, daughter mine.
Five years in beauty *thou* hast bloomed, of my happy life a part,   35
Oh, God! I guess the anguish of that lone slave mother's heart.

"Now, darlings, go and kiss papa, and whisper your good night,
Then hasten to your little beds, and sleep till morning light;
But oh! before you close your eyes, God's care and blessing crave,
On the saddest of His children, that poor heart-broken slave."   40

from *Louisville Daily Journal* (1854)

A WARNING[64]
"By an Old One"

"Behold the woes of matrimonial life
And hear with reverence an experienced wife."[65]

Come all ye maidens fair and young;
    Whose fate is yet uncertain –
Come, while it yet is time, and take
    A peep behind the curtain.
Come, you who think the marriage state   5
    A Paradise on earth,
And you who trust in lover's vows –
    I'll show you what they're worth,
And what sweet figures you will cut,
    Unangeled, and *ungoddessed*,   10
And somewhat of your chosen ones,
    The tender, fond, and modest.

Know, as each object still must have
    A sunny side and shrouded,
Of man the lover is the *bright*,   15
    The husband is the *clouded*,
This is, alas! too sadly true,
    And ah! it makes it sadder
To think, the fairer fell the light
    The deeper seems the shadow;   20

A WARNING
[64] I want to thank Pamela Kincheloe for giving me
this poem.

[65] Free translation of the opening lines of the Wife of
Bath's Prologue in Geoffrey Chaucer's *Canterbury Tales*
(begun 1386).

That those, whose vows such fervor showed
  You could not but receive them,
Will be the first to break their oaths
  And laugh that you believe them.

When once they have you safe at home   25
  And get you to house-keeping,
No more they'll tremble at your frown
  Or melt before your weeping.
You'll find yourself a household drudge –
  A sort of upper servant –   30
Cook, nurse, and seamstress, all in one,
  Obliged to be observant
Of all his whims – a real slave
  In every word and action,
Without the power to leave the place   35
  Or to give satisfaction.

In him, who once so meekly bore
  Your humors and caprices,
You'll find to wake resentment now
  How slight a cause suffices –   40
He'll make a fuss if dinner's late,
  Or he should chance to put on
A coat you have forgot to mend
  Or shirt without's button;
Forgetting as he blames the hands   45
  That should have made or mended,
How oft and fondly he has sworn
  They were only intended
For love's soft pressure, flowers to twine,
  Or music's strain to waken –   50
Alas! that woman should believe
  And be so much mistaken!

Oh! why should fingers, that might wield
  The chisel, pen, or pencil,
Be thus condemned to needle, broom,   55
  Or other vile utensil?
In pickling and preserving peas
  Their days, and the creation
Of puddings, pies, or, now and then
  By way of variation,   60
In boxing squalling brats? (a part
  I can't forbear to mention –
A *crying evil*, which I hope
  The "Woman's Rights convention"

Will utterly eradicate   65
  When it reforms the nation)
But husbands are my theme, the "great
  First cause" of all vexation.

There is a dream of happiness –
  Each maiden's heart doth bear it –   70
A vision of a pleasant home
  And a kindred soul to share it.
But ah! it is a dream indeed,
  And one that passes fleetly,
For with the waning honey-moon   75
  It vanishes completely;
Then vainly will you strive to please
  With many a fond endeavor,
And hide your cares to lessen his –
  The charm is gone forever.   80

He lingers long or comes depressed
  By business, wrath, or gloom –
Clouds from the world to dim the light
Around your heart and home –
And your inquiring, timid looks   85
  And gentle, shy advances
Are met with silent sulleness
Or coldly careless glances,
When at a stranger's step, perchance,
  The frowning brow will brighten,   90
And heartless voices chase the gloom
  Not all your cares could lighten;
While sadly thinking of the past,
  You strive in vain to smother
The sigh for times when you were all   95
  The world unto each other.

Now, tho' this list of grievances
  I have enumerated
Should be sufficient to deter
  "The uninitiated,"   100
Yet they are only gentle hints
  Or "warnings to the young,"
And nothing, when compared to those
  Which "yet remain unsung."[66]

---

[66] Milton, *Paradise Lost* 7:21.

from *A Wreath of Cherokee Rose Buds* (1855)

LITERARY DAY AMONG THE BIRDS
by Lily Lee

Dark night at last had taken its flight,
Morn had come with her earliest light;
Her herald, gray dawn, had extinguished each star,
And gay banners in the east were waving afar.

That lovely goddess, Beautiful Spring,   5
Had fanned all the earth with her radiant wing;
"Had calmed the wild winds with fragrant breath,"
And gladden'd nature with an emerald wreath.

Within the precincts of the Bird Nation,
All was bustle and animation;   10
For that day was to witness a literary feast,
Where only Birds were invited guests.

The place of meeting was a leafy nook,
Close by the side of a sparkling brook.
Soon were assembled a merry band,   15
Birds from every tree in the land.

Mrs. DOVE came first, in soft colors drest;
Then Mr. CANARY, looking his best.
The family of MARTINS, dressed in brown,
And Mr. WOODPECKER, with his ruby crown.   20

The exercises opened with a scientific song,
By the united voices of the feathered throng.
Then was delivered a brilliant oration,
By 'Squire RAVEN, the wisest bird of the nation.
Master WHIP-POOR-WILL next mounted the stage,   25
Trying to look very much like a sage.

Eight pretty green PARROTS then spoke with art;
Though small, with credit they carried their part.
Again an oration by Mr. QUAIL,
Spoken as fast as the gallop of snail.   30
And lastly, Sir BLACKBIRD whistl'd off an address,
Of twenty odd minutes, more or less.

Then came the applause, so loud and long,
That the air echoed the joyous song.
But the sun was low, so soon they sped   35
To their quiet nests and their grassy beds;

And rocked by the breeze, they quietly slept,
Ere the firstling star in the blue sky crept.

from *National Anti-Slavery Standard* (1856)

SOUVENIR OF THE NIGHT OF THE FOURTH OF DECEMBER, 1851[67]

From The French of Victor Hugo

Translated by Maria Weston Chapman

His little head all cloven by their bullets,
We bore the infant to his humble home.
A bough the priest had blessed hung o'er a portrait
Where the old grandmother stood by and wept.
His helpless arms hung heavily from his shoulders;   5
His little beech-wood top was still upon him.
You've seen the mulberry bleeding in the hedges? –
One might have laid a finger in his wounds.
Silently we undressed him, while his pale
Half-opened lips fell lifelessly apart,   10
And death was swimming in his ghastly eye.
The poor old mother watched as we went on:
"How white he is!" she said; "bring near the lamp!
How his poor curls are clotted to his temples!" –
And when we had finished, took him on her lap.   15
The night was wild and dark – and still we heard
The musket-shots of murder in the street.
"The poor child must be buried," then we said;
And took a white sheet from the walnut press.
The poor old mother brought him to the fire   20
As if to warm the limbs already stiffened.
Alas! – what death has touched with his cold fingers
May never more be warmed by mortal hearth!
She bowed her head and drew his stockings off,
And held the cold feet in her withered hands.   25
"Now is it not a thing to break one's heart?"
She said; "Ah, Sirs, he was not eight years old!
His masters, for he went to school, all praised him;
And when I had a letter to be sent,
'Twas always he that wrote it out for me.   30
And now they set to work to murder babies!
And ah! my God! What are they, then, but ruffians?

SOUVENIR OF THE NIGHT OF THE FOURTH OF DECEMBER, 1851

[67] On December 2, 1851, a coup largely engineered by Louis Napoleon Bonaparte's half-brother, the Duc de Morny, put Bonaparte in control of the Second Republic with dictatorial powers. Louis Napoleon was crowned Emperor of France the following year. Louis Napoleon, a nephew of Napoleon I, reigned as Napoleon III from 1852 to his deposition in 1870. See Piatt's "The Palace-Burner" for the aftermath.

He prayed this morn before the window there!
And they have murdered the poor little thing!
They fired upon him passing in the street! 35
Sir, he was good and kind as the child Jesus!
For me, I am old: 'tis time that I should go.
No harm had come if Monsieur Bonaparte
Had but killed me in place of my poor baby."
Her voice was choked by sobbing, and we all 40
With one accord wept with her, who stood round.
"What will become of me, alone!" she said:
"Some of you, tell me that before you go!
Ah! he was all I had left of his mother.
Tell me, for I *will* know! – why did they kill him! 45
He never cried, *Vive la République!* "[68]
Silent and still we stood, with heads uncovered,
Trembling before this inconsolable anguish.

Mother! you don't see into politics!
Monsieur *Napoleon*[69] (*that's* his name to-day) 50
Is poor; a prince too. He loves palaces;
It likes him to have horses and gay laqueys;[70]
Gold for his games, his table, his shameless bed!
His hunting too; and by that same occasion,
He saves the family, the Church, the State. 55
He must have St. Cloud with its summer roses,
Where mayors and prefects may go worship him.
Therefore it is, the poor old mother
Must sadly fold, with her pale trembling fingers,
The seven years' infant in his bloody shroud. 60

from *Atlantic Monthly* (1858)

MERCEDES
by Elizabeth Stoddard[71]

Under a sultry, yellow sky,
On the yellow sand I lie;
The crinkled vapors smite my brain,
I smoulder in a fiery pain.

Above the crags the condor flies; 5
He knows where the red gold lies,

---

[68] French: "Long live the Republic!"
[69] Having his followers call him "Mr" ("Monsieur") and use his first name was presumably Bonaparte's gesture toward populism; but the "Napoleon" itself also served as a reminder of his uncle.

[70] *Laqueys* lackeys, obsequious servants or hangers-on.
MERCEDES
[71] Elizabeth Drew Stoddard (1823–1902), Massachusetts-born novelist and poet.

He knows where the diamonds shine; –
If I knew, would she be mine?

Mercedes in her hammock swings;
In her court a palm-tree flings   10
Its slender shadow on the ground,
The fountain falls with silver sound.

Her lips are like this cactus cup;
With my hand I crush it up;
I tear its flaming leaves apart; –   15
Would that I could tear her heart!

Last night a man was at her gate;
In the hedge I lay in wait;
I saw Mercedes meet him there,
By the fire-flies in her hair.   20

I waited till the break of day,
Then I rose and stole away;
I drove my dagger through the gate; –
Now she knows her lover's fate!

from *Knickerbocker* (1859)

"THE BEAUTIFUL SNOW"[72]
by Annie Keely?

Oh! the snow, the beautiful snow,
Filling the sky and the earth below;
Over the house-tops, over the street,
Over the heads of the people you meet,
    Dancing,   5
        Flirting,
            Skimming along,
Beautiful snow! it can do nothing wrong,
Flying to kiss a fair lady's cheek;
Clinging to lips in a frolicsome freak,   10
Beautiful snow from the heavens above,
Pure as an angel, and fickle as love!

"THE BEAUTIFUL SNOW"

[72]   When reprinting this poem in the "Editor's Table," the *Knickerbocker* editor comments: "Late the other afternoon, hurrying at night-fall for the last boat to the 'Cottage,' in a soft, warm, *clean* snow-storm, we thought of these lines, and wished that we knew who wrote them." In the *Irish Nationalist* (1873), the poem is attributed to Annie Keely of Annaghs, New Ross, who is said to have published the poem first in the United States, before emigrating there herself. Whoever wrote "The Beautiful Snow," it is an exceptionally effective example of a very popular genre – the fallen woman poem. Most of these poems were written by men.

Oh! the snow, the beautiful snow!
How the flakes gather and laugh as they go!
Whirling about in its maddening fun,   15
It plays in its glee with every one,
    Chasing,
        Laughing,
            Hurrying by,
It lights up the face, and it sparkles the eye;   20
And even the dogs, with a bark and a bound,
Snap at the crystals that eddy around;
The town is alive, and its heart in a glow,
To welcome the coming of beautiful snow.

How wild the crowd goes swaying along,   25
Hailing each other with humor and song!
How the gay sledges, like meteors flash by,
Bright for a moment, then lost to the eye;
    Ringing,
        Swinging,   30
            Dashing they go
Over the crust of the beautiful snow:
Snow so pure when it falls from the sky,
To be trampled in mud by the crowd rushing by:
To be trampled and tracked by the thousands of feet.   35
Till it blends with the filth in the horrible street.

Once I was pure as the snow – but I fell:
Fell, like the snow-flakes, from Heaven – to hell:
Fell, to be trampled as filth of the street:
Fell, to be scoffed, to be spit on and beat,   40
    Pleading,
        Cursing,
            Dreading to die,
Selling my soul to whoever would buy,
Dealing in shame for a morsel of bread,   45
Hating the living and fearing the dead.
Merciful GOD! have I fallen so low?
And yet I was once like this beautiful snow.

Once I was fair as the beautiful snow,
With an eye like its crystals, a heart like its glow: 50
Once I was loved for my innocent grace –
Flattered and sought for the charm of my face.
    Father,
        Mother,
            Sister, all,   55
GOD, and myself I have lost by my fall.
The veriest wretch that goes shivering by

Will take a wide sweep, lest I wander too nigh:
For of all that is on or about me, I know
There is nothing that's pure but the beautiful snow.   60

How strange it should be that this beautiful snow
Should fall on a sinner with no where to go!
How strange it would be, when the night comes again,
If the snow and the ice struck my desperate brain!
    Fainting,   65
       Freezing,
          Dying alone!
Too wicked for prayer, too weak for my moan
To be heard in the crash of the crazy town,
Gone mad in their joy at the snow's coming down;   70
To lie and to die in my terrible woe,
With a bed and a shroud of the beautiful snow!

from *Atlantic Monthly* (1859)

BLOODROOT[73]
by Emily S. Forman

"Hast thou loved the wood-rose, and left it on its stalk?"[74]

Beech-trees, stretching their arms, rugged, yet beautiful,
Here shade meadow and brook; here the gay bobolink,[75]
High poised over his mate, pours out his melody.
Here, too, under the hill, blooms the wild violet;
Damp nooks hide, near the brook, bellworts that modestly,   5
Pale-faced, hanging their heads, droop there in silence; while
South winds, noiseless and soft, bring us the odor of
Birch twigs mingled with fresh buds of the hickory.

Hard by, clinging to rocks, nods the red columbine;
Close hid, under the leaves, nestle anemones, –   10
White-robed, airy and frail, tender and delicate.

Ye who, wandering here, seeking the beautiful,
Stoop down, thinking to pluck one of these favorites,
Take heed! Nymphs[76] may avenge. List to a prodigy; –
One moon scarcely has waned since I here witnessed it.   15

BLOODROOT
[73] An early spring woodland plant, having a pretty white flower. Its name derives from the red sap in its root.
[74] The epigraph is from Ralph Waldo Emerson's "Forbearance."
[75] North American songbird.
[76] In classical mythology nymphs are guardian spirits of the woodland.

One moon scarcely has waned, since, on a holiday,
I came, careless and gay, into this paradise, –
Found here, wrapped in their cloaks made of a leaf, little
White flowers, pure as the snow, modest and innocent, –
Stooped down, eagerly plucked one of the fairest, when   20
Forth rushed, fresh from the stem broken thus wickedly,
Blood! – tears, red, as of blood! – shed through my selfishness!

from *Cincinnati Israelite* (1859)

THE GRAVE OF RACHEL
by Magga Kilmer

"Joseph was sold for a servant,"[77] *&c. Psalms cv, 17.*

The day had passed; and Night, descending, laid
          Her shadowy mantle on the slumbering earth;
The soft wind stirred the long, tall grass, and played
          Gently among the trees; the voice of mirth,
And song, and revelry were hushed, and quiet reigns,   5
Unbroken, undisturbed, on Bethlehem's plains.

Night! holy Night! when the earth-weary rest,
          Forgetting, in sweet dreams, the hours of care!
When Peace comes gently to the troubled breast,
          And calms the spirit like the voice of prayer!   10
When Sleep, with magic wand, drives care away,
And brings new strength to meet the coming day!

The tents were spread upon the grassy plain,
          And while, o'er all, the moon her vigil kept
In peaceful rest, a toil-worn, weary train,   15
          The camels and their dark-browed masters slept;
But, hark! low stealing through the evening air,
A deep-toned voice is heard, a voice in prayer.

'T is he, the captive youth! thus doomed to roam,
          A bondman vile, freeborn, yet slave to those;   20
Torn from his father's arms, his friends, his home,
          By brothers' hands, whom envy changed to foes!
He now, in loneliness and grief, has sought
His mother's grave, earth's dearest, holiest spot!

Heart-broken, crushed, his weary head he lays   25
          In woe's dark dreariness upon the cold, hard sod;

THE GRAVE OF RACHEL
[77]   Genesis 37:28.

And groans with anguish deep, and weeps, and prays,
    And asks, in grief's despair, his father's God,
For strength to conquer, courage to withstand,
The toils, and trials, in a stranger land!   30

    "My son!" a low, soft voice falls on his ear!
        A shadowy presence stands beside the boy!
    "Is it some angel, from a holier sphere,
        To bring me words of comfort, hope and joy?"
"My son!" that voice, that form, he can but know!   35
He whispers, "Mother!" and his head bows low!

    ["]Peace be with thee, my son! thy prayers and tears
        Have reached the throne of God, and lo! I bring
    Tidings of hope to thee, to banish fears,
        And change to joy thy bitter sorrowing: 40
A vision passed before my face, behold!
A glorious future unto thee unrolled!

    A slave to-day – to-morrow crowds shall bow,
        In reverence to thee, as the great and wise!
    To-day a cloud – to-morrow, o'er thy brow,   45
        The sunshine of prosperity shall rise!
For though His face is hidden from thee now,
The God of Israel will redeem His vow!

    He lifted up his head – the form was gone;
        But to his heart a quiet peace had stole,   50
    That made him feel, though friendless, not alone,
        And a glad thankfulness new filled his soul,
As now, reclining on the grassy sod,
He slept in peace, as one who trusted God!

from *Atlantic Monthly* (1860)

THE "CATTLE" TO THE "POET"[78]
by Frances Sophia Stoughton Pratt

How do *you* know what the cow may know,
    As under the tasselled bough she lies,
When earth is a-beat with the life below,
When the orient mornings redden and glow,

THE "CATTLE" TO THE "POET"

[78] The original poem to which this is a response ("The Poet's Friends," *Atlantic Monthly* V [1860]:185) assumed that cows were too "stupid" to understand the bird's song.

When the silent butterflies come and go, –   5
    The dreamy cow with the Juno[79] eyes?

How do *you* know that she may not know
    That the meadow all over is lettered, "Love,"
Or hear the mystic syllable low
In the grasses' growth and the waters' flow?   10
How do *you* know that she may not know
    What the robin sings on the twig above?

from *Harper's New Monthly Magazine* (1860)

BEFORE THE MIRROR
by Elizabeth Drew Stoddard

Now, like the Lady of Shalott,[80]
    I dwell within an empty room,
And through the day, and through the night,
    I sit before an ancient loom.

And like the Lady of Shalott,   5
    I look into a mirror wide,
Where shadows come, and shadows go,
    And ply my shuttle as they glide.

Not as she wove the yellow wool,
    Ulysses's wife, Penelope;[81]   10
By day a queen among her maids,
    But in the night a woman, she,

Who, creeping from her lonely couch,
    Unraveled all the slender woof:
Or with a torch she climbed the towers,   15
    To fire the fagots on the roof!

But weaving with a steady hand,
    The shadows, whether false or true,
I put aside a doubt which asks,
    "Among these phantoms what are you?"   20

---

[79] In Roman mythology, Juno, the wife of Jupiter, was associated with a cow and she is frequently referred to as "Ox-eyed." She was the goddess of women and childbirth.

BEFORE THE MIRROR

[80] Eponymous heroine of Tennyson's Arthurian romance, "The Lady of Shalott" (1833). Because of a curse placed on her, she must spend her life in a closed tower weaving, viewing the external world only in the images presented to her by her mirror.

[81] Besieged by suitors during Odysseus's ten-year trip home from Troy, Penelope, his loyal wife, manages to hold them off by promising to wed one of them when she completes her father-in-law Laertes's burial robe; but each night she unravels what she wove during the day.

For not with altar, tomb, or urn,
    Or long-haired Greek with hollow shield,
Or dark-prowed ship with banks of oars,
    Or banquet in the tented field;

Or Norman knight in armor clad,   25
    Waiting a foe where four roads meet;
Or hawk and hound in bosky[82] dell,
    Where dame and page in secret greet;

Or rose and lily, bud and flower,
    My web is broidered. Nothing bright   30
Is woven here: the shadows grow
    Still darker in the mirror's light!

And as my web grows darker too,
    Accursed seems this empty room;
I know I must forever weave   35
    These phantoms by this hateful loom.

from *Saturday Evening Post* (1860)

ŒNONE[83]

A Statue by Miss H. Hosmer[84]
by Emma Alice Browne[85]

The golden moss beneath her spread,
The June around her, white and red,
(And life beyond her wasting and dead!)
Where – tangling ever to and fro
Its silver hands among the snow   5
And blush of all the flowers that grow

In Ida's[86] fountain nursing breast –
A wild brook runs in sweet unrest
Toward the blue rivers of the West –
She leans upon a listless hand,   10

[82] *Bosky* wooded or bushy.
ŒNONE
[83] In Greek mythology, a nymph skilled in healing whom Paris deserted. When he was wounded in the Trojan War, she refused to heal him, but committed suicide after his death.
[84] Harriet G. Hosmer (1830–1908), highly popular expatriate sculptor of mixed racial background.
[85] Dates unknown. Although she never published a book, Browne was a highly popular newspaper poet whose career flourished in the 1850s and 1860s. She lived in St Louis and, like Sarah Piatt and Rosa Vertner Jeffrey, published heavily in the *Louisville Journal*.
[86] Mt Ida, the highest mountain in Greece, located in central Crete. Paris, the son of King Priam of Troy, was abandoned as an infant on Mt Ida, after a prophesy warned his parents that his actions would destroy Troy. Here he tended sheep and fell in love with the nymph Œnone.

Her great eyes sorrow-smitten, grand,
With sight turned death-ward! All the land

That southward from Dardania[87]
Rolls to the purple bordered sea,
Lies dim before pale Œnone!   15
For that sweet way *he*, wounded, came –
(Where'er his rich blood fell, the same
Kindled the Crocus' golden flame.)

For once to Ilian[88] Œnone
A sudden gift of prophecy   20
Foreshadow'd him dying by the sea –
And how alone *her* subtle skill
Compell'd thro' woman's loving will
Had power to work him good – or ill.

And she, remembering slighted pain,   25
Forgot her true heart – and in vain
The Trojans knelt for Paris slain!
Breathless she leans above the clay
That erst in youth's sweet holiday
Blushed with her kisses like a May –   30

Till memories of that golden prime –
Like some dead poet's saddest rhyme
Touching the heart of after-time –
Hold her all breathless – powerless – pale –
With the dumb agony of a wail   35
Dying out in her soul. The tale

Hath won a high interpreter
In the strong, womanly heart of her
Who carved this antique legend for
The truth's and beauty's sake. Oh, eyes   40
Full of the old Greek mysteries –
Oh, lips of unsung melodies!

Oh, marble dream, divinely wrought,
Embodying a master-thought,
Whose grief eternal life hath caught!   45
Pale type of many a voiceless heart,
Wasting in agony apart
From human sympathy, thou Art!

---

[87]   Troy. Dardanus, son of Jupiter, was the mythical   [88]   Trojan.
ancestor of the royal family of Troy.

ROCK ME TO SLEEP
by Florence Percy (Elizabeth Akers Allen)[89]

Backward, turn backward, oh, Time, in your flight,
Make me a child again, just for to-night!
Mother, come back from the echoless shore,
Take me again to your heart as of yore, –
Kiss from my forehead the furrows of care,   5
Smooth the few silver threads out of my hair –
Over my slumbers your loving watch keep –
Rock me to sleep, mother – rock me to sleep!

Backward, flow backward, oh, tide of the years!
I am so weary of toil and of tears –   10
Toil without recompense – tears all in vain –
Take them, and give me my childhood again!
I have grown weary of dust and decay,
Weary of flinging my soul-wealth away –
Weary of sowing for others to reap; –   15
Rock me to sleep, mother – rock me to sleep!

Tired of the hollow, the base, the untrue,
Mother, oh, mother, my heart calls for you!
Many a summer the grass has grown green,
Blossomed and faded, our faces between –   20
Yet, with strong yearning and passionate pain
Long I to-night for your presence again; –
Come from the silence so long and so deep –
Rock me to sleep, mother – rock me to sleep!

Over my heart, in the days that are flown,   25
No love like mother-love ever has shone –
No other worship abides and endures
Faithful, unselfish and patient, like yours;
None like a mother can charm away pain
From the sick soul and the world-weary brain;   30
Slumbers soft calms o'er my heavy lids creep –
Rock me to sleep, mother – rock me to sleep!

Come, let your brown hair, just lighted with gold,
Fall on your shoulders again as of old –
Let it drop over my forehead to-night,   35
Shading my faint eyes away from the light –

ROCK ME TO SLEEP
[89]   Elizabeth Akers Allen (1832–1911), New England poet. Allen's authorship of this enormously popular poem was hotly contested, but E. C. Stedman in *An American Anthology* asserts that it was unequivocally hers. Set to music by at least thirty different composers in the US and in Britain, it was especially popular among soldiers in the Civil War, the Cuban War, and the Spanish-American War.

For with its sunny-edged shadows once more,
Haply will throng the sweet visions of yore;
Lovingly, softly, its bright billows sweep –
Rock me to sleep, mother – rock me to sleep!   40

Mother, dear mother! the years have been long
Since I last listened your lullaby song –
Sing then, and unto my soul it shall seem
Womanhood's years have been only a dream; –
Clasped to your heart in a loving embrace,   45
With your light lashes just sweeping my face,
Never hereafter to wake or to weep –
Rock me to sleep, mother – rock me to sleep!

from *Atlantic Monthly* (1861)

THE WILD ENDIVE
by Annie Fields[90]

Only the dusty common road,
    The glaring weary heat;
Only a man with a soldier's load,
    And the sound of tired feet.

Only the lonely creaking hum   5
    Of the Cicada's song;
Only a fence where tall weeds come
    With spiked fingers strong.

Only a drop of the heaven's blue
    Left in a way-side cup;   10
Only a joy for the plodding few
    And eyes that look not up.

Only a weed to the passer-by,
    Growing among the rest; –
Yet something clear as the light of the sky   15
    It lodges in my breast.

THE WILD ENDIVE
[90] Annie Fields (1834–1915), poet, memoirist, and wife
of James T. Fields, editor of the *Atlantic Monthly*. When
publishing this poem in *The Singing Shepherd and Other
Poems* (1895), Fields renamed it "Blue Succory."

from *National Anti-Slavery Standard* (1861)

THE HARVEST-FIELD OF 1861
by Mrs James Neall[91]

Lo! the fields of Harvest whiten with the heavy bending grain:
Hither bring the patient oxen, yoke them to the empty wain;
Call the Reapers; for the Summer has put on her crown again.

And her minister of Plenty stands with overflowing horn,
While the serried[92] ranks in waiting, of the fully ripened corn, 5
Gaily wave their golden tassels in the soft midsummer morn.

Fair Pomona[93] bendeth lowly 'neath the chrism[94] of her hope,
Summer has fulfilled the promise of the Spring-times' horoscope,
For her fruit is ripe and mellow over many a sunny slope.

Rounded are the rich grape clusters, for the vintage time is near, 10
Let them fall in purple glory when the vintagers appear;
Press the juices warm and glowing from each perfect pulpy sphere.

Lo! the fields of Harvest whiten – and the plains are dry and hot,
And the golden fruit is mildewed, and the grain is garnered not,
And the maidens sit in silence, while the grapes are left to rot. 15

Listening to the tread of armies, and the clanging noise of War,
Ploughshares into swords are beaten, and the scythe is wet with gore,
For the Harvesters are gathered, where the smoking cannons roar.

And the reapers reap together, spear on spear-top falling low,
And the serried ranks are parted, be it friend or be it foe, 20
While the Summer days are waning and the Harvest-moon is low.

And the dust lies on the vintage. Ah! the tendrils torn away,
For the crimson wine is flowing, which no human hand may stay,
And the stain is darkly resting on the sad hearts far away.

Lo! the empty field of Harvest! tread the rank grain in the soil, 25
Cover all with "dust and ashes," let the gleaners take the spoil,
Call the Mowers and the Reapers, thus to rest them from their toil,

Listening to the glad evangel, "Freedom for the coming years!"
While the Nation shouts in triumph. And the broad world rings with cheers
That the Spring-time brings in gladness, what the Autumn sowed in tears. 30

THE HARVEST-FIELD OF 1861
[91] Mrs James Neall was probably the wife of James Neall (1820–1903), a western writer. This poem originally appeared in the *California Farmer*.

[92] *Serried*   pressed together.
[93] Pomona, California is an agricultural area located in Los Angeles County.
[94] *Chrism*   consecrated oil, used for sacred rites.

from *Independent* (1861)

CHURCH AND STATE
by Caroline Cheseboro (Caroline Cheseborough)[95]

Brave old Leonidas[96]
  Cumber'd with cares,
Wearies of worship
  And doubts through his prayers.
  "Ho, from the sacrament   5
  Wine for our brother!
Bread for his bivouac!
  Hearest thou, mother?"

Church of the Ages
  She listened aghast.   10
Bold son, Leonidas,
  Pierced her, and pass'd.
  "Wine from the sacrament
  Stronger the flood
Men thirst for in battle . . .   15
  Unsymbol'd the blood!"

Blood for Leonidas!
  Not His he pour'd
Naming the crucified
  Jesus adored!   20
Blood of the men he led
  Up to the Master.
"Tears," then, "befit," he said –
Now, "blood runs faster."

Red robes for garments   25
  Priestly and white,
Deadly surprises
  For vigils by night.
  "Schism and murder,
  And pestilent death,   30
Send us to fight for
  The slaves' sake," he saith.

Blood for Leonidas,
  Warrior athirst!

CHURCH AND STATE
[95]   Caroline Cheseborough (1825–73), domestic novelist.
[96]   Leonidas Polk (1806–64), bishop of the Protestant Episcopal Church and fiery pro-slavery lieutenant-general in the Confederate army. Polk's name inevitably recalls Leonidas, King of Sparta (d. 480 BCE). With a small force of Spartans, he sacrificed his life to hold the pass at Thermopylae against Xerxes's invading army. Subsequently his name has become a watchword for duty and self-sacrifice to the State.

Blood of the Mother   35
   Who bore him and nursed!
Blood of the Brotherhood!
   (Strong grows the draught) –
Life-blood of Liberty . . .
   – Lucifer laughed.   40

from *Southern Literary Messenger* (1862)

THE SNOW STORM
by E. A. C.

The day was bitter cold, she said,
   'Twas very long ago;
The North winds rushed with withering tread,
And, hurrying on before them fled
   The shivering flakes of snow.   5

But 'midst the storm-field's wild alarms,
   I sat so warm and still,
And, smiling, thought, "within his arms,
No evil spells, nor wicked charms,
   Can ever work me ill."   10

He kissed my lips and hands that day,
   And held me warm and still,
'Till in the wintry twilight ray,
The snowy gleam had died away
   Upon the distant hill.   15

The snow falls fast again, she said,
   It lies in drifted waves;
Beneath, the church-yard willows spread,
How close it wraps the sleeping dead
   Within their quiet graves!   20

The frost-wreaths cluster white and chill,
   Around each sculptured tomb;
My heart, she said, is colder still,
And ghastly memories ever fill
   Its spectre-haunted gloom.   25

from *Galaxy* (1867)

HER ANSWER
by Mrs W. H. Palmer

Speak? If you will. But I have learned to bear
Your silent moods without the wear and tear
And rack and torture of the old despair,

And have no right to lead you to believe
I care to listen, still less to retrieve   5
The past, for which, to-day, I do not grieve.

I ask no explanation. You may prate
Of misconstruction, temperament, or fate,
But anything you say now, comes too late.

If this is wrong I ask of heaven, not you: 10
Of God, who knows what suffering I've been through,
And whether still more suffering is my due.

Exacting? Am I? Other wives have kept
Their faith in patience? Well, I grant I wept,
Implored, entreated, even basely crept   15

Up to that last appeal, and knelt and sued
For Love's poor pretence smeared by passion's mood,
Taking Desire's dry husks for Hope's true food,

And could not own your love lost! Glad to die
If you just once by tender word or sigh   20
Should prove your marriage pledge was not a lie.

But you denied me. Cold and still with me,
(Using "ungenial habit" as your plea –
Genial enough with others, I could see!)

Till the sham would not cheat me; and I saw   25
The jewel that had bought me, one great flaw;
While still you kept the letter of the law.

I gave up then; learned by-and-by to live
Without you. To forget or to forgive
Slipped with life's other gold grains, through the sieve.   30

And yet I'll do my duty; keep your name
High as the stars are above any shame;
Your home well ordered, nothing left to blame.

But do not talk of loving! It is vain
To think that words can cure this sort of pain,   35
Or bring a stone-dead heart to life again.

from *Colored American* (1865)

ETHIOPIA'S DEAD

*A tribute to the memory of her sons who have fallen in the great struggle for
liberty and independence.*

by Sarah E. Shuften[97]

Brave hearts! brave Ethiopia's dead
   On hills, in vallies lie,
On every field of strife, made red
   With gorey victory.

Each valley, where the battle poured   5
   It's purple swelling tide,
Beheld brave Ethiopia's sword
   With slaughter deeply dyed.

Their bones bleach on the Southr'n hill,
   And on the Southern plain,   10
By [brook], and river, lake and rill,
   And by the roaring main.

The land is holy where they fought,
   And holy where they fell;
For by their blood, that land was bought   15
   That land they loved so well –
Then glory to that valiant band,
   The honored saviors of the land.

Oh! few and weak their numbers were,
   A handful of brave men,   20
But up to God they sent their prayer,
   And rushed to battle, then
The God of battle heard their cry,
   And crowned their deeds with victory.

From east to west, from hill to vale,   25
   Then be their names adored –

ETHIOPIA'S DEAD
[97] Shuften was apparently the wife of John T. Shuften, editor of the *Colored American*, Augusta, Georgia. Her name does not appear in Yellin and Bond. To my knowledge, this poem represents the sole surviving example of her work.

Europe, with all thy millions, hail!
　　The Peace bought by their sword.

Asia, and Africa shall ring
　　From shore to shore, their fame;　　　　　　　　30
And fair Columbia shall sing,
　　Their glory, and their name.

Peace, with her olive branch, shall spread
　　Her wings, o'er sea and shore,
And hearts no more with terror dread　　　　　　　35
　　The battle's clashing roar.

Fair Afric's *free* and valiant sons,
　　Shall join with Europe's band,
To celebrate in varied tongues,
　　Our *free* and happy land　　　　　　　　　　40

Till freedoms golden fingers trace,
　　A line that knows no end,
And man shall meet in every face,
　　A brother and a friend.

from *Overland Monthly* (1868)

LONGING
by Ina Coolbrith[98]

O Foolish wisdom sought in books!
　　O aimless fret of household tasks!
O chains that bind the hand and mind –
　　A fuller life my spirit asks!

For there the grand hills, summer-crowned,　　　　5
　　Slope greenly downward to the seas;
One hour of rest upon their breast
　　Were worth a year of days like these.

Their cool, soft green to ease the pain
　　Of eyes that ache o'er printed words;　　　　10
This weary noise – the city's voice,
　　Lulled in the sound of bees and birds.

For Eden's life within me stirs,
　　And scorns the shackles that I wear;

LONGING
[98] Ina Coolbrith (1841–1928), the first poet laureate
of California. She earned her living as a librarian.

The man-life grand – pure soul, strong hand,   15
  The limb of steel, the heart of air!

And I could kiss, with longing wild,
  Earth's dear brown bosom, loved so much,
A grass-blade fanned across my hand,
  Would thrill me like a lover's touch.   20

The trees would talk with me; the flowers
  Their hidden meanings each make known –
The olden lore revived once more,
  When man's and nature's heart were one!

And as the pardoned pair might come   25
  Back to the garden God first framed,
And hear Him call at even-fall,
  And answer, "Here am I," unshamed –

So I, from out these toils, wherein
  The Eden-faith grows stained and dim,   30
Would walk, a child, through nature's wild,
  And hear His voice and answer Him.

from *The Land We Love* (1869)

"MAMMY"

(A Home Picture of 1860)
by L. Virginia French[99]

Where the broad mulberry branches hang a canopy of leaves
Like an avalanche of verdure, drooping o'er the kitchen eaves,
And the sunshine and the shadow dainty arabesques have made
On the quaint, old oaken settle, standing in the pleasant shade;
Sits good "Mammy" with "the child'un" while the summer afternoon   5
Wears the dewy veil of April, o'er the brilliancy of June.
Smooth and snowy is the 'kerchief, lying folded with an air
Of matron dignity above her silver-sprinkled hair;
Blue and white the beaded necklace used "of Sundays" to bedeck
(A dearly cherished amulet,) her plump and dusky neck;   10
Dark her neatly ironed apron, of a broad and ample size,
Spreading o'er the dress of "homespun" with its many colored dyes.

"MAMMY"

[99] L. Virginia French (1830–81), literary editor and apologist for the Old South. This poem concludes a long nostalgic portrait by French on life in the Old South that particularly concerns itself with the vital role that "Mammy" played in running her master's household. Writing from the point of view of an isolated white child on a plantation, Piatt tells a very different story in "A Child's Party."

True, her lips are all untutored, yet how genially they smile,
And how eloquent their fervor, praying, "Jesus bless de chile!"
True, her voice is hoarse and broken, but how tender its replies;   15
True, her hands are brown and withered, yet how loving are her eyes;
She has thoughts both high and holy tho' her brow is dark and low;
And her face is dusk and wrinkled but her soul as white as snow!

An aristocrat is "Mammy" – in her dignity sedate,
"Haught as Lucifer" to "white trash" whom she cannot tolerate;   20
Patronizing too, to "Master" for she "nussed 'im when a boy;"
Familiar, yet respectful, to "the Mistis" – but the joy
Of her bosom is "de child'un," and delightedly she'll boast
Of the "born blood" of her darlings – "good as kings and queens a'most."

There she sits beneath the shadow, crooning o'er some olden hymn,   25
Watching earnestly and willingly, altho' her eyes are dim;
Laughing in her heart sincerely, yet with countenance demure
Holding out before "her babies" every tempting little lure, –
Noting all their merry frolics with a quiet, loving gaze,
Telling o'er at night to "Mistis" all their "cunnin' little ways."   30

Now and then her glance will wander o'er the pastures far away
Where the tasselled corn-fields waving, to the breezes rock and sway,
To the river's gleaming silver, and the hazy distance where
Giant mountain-peaks are peering thro' an azure veil of air;
But the thrill of baby voices – baby laughter, low and sweet,   35
Recall her in a moment to the treasures at her feet.

So "rascally," so rollicking, our bold and sturdy boy
In all his tricksy way-wardness is still her boast and joy,
She'll chase him thro' the shrubberies – his mischief-mood to cure,
"Hi! whar dat little rascal now? – de b'ars will git 'im shure!"   40
When caught she'll stoutly swing him to her shoulder, and in pride
Go marching round the pathways – "jus to see how gran' he ride."

And the "Birdie" of our bosom – Ah! how soft and tenderly
Bows good "Mammy's" mother-spirit to her baby witchery!
(*All* to her is dear devotion whom the angels bend to bless,   45
All our thoughts of her are blended with a holy tenderness;)
Coaxing now, and now caressing – saying with a smile and kiss –
"Jus' for Mammy – dat's a lady – will it now?" do that, or this.

On the sweet white-tufted clover, worn and weary with their play,
Toying with the creamy blossoms, now my little children lay;   50
Harnessed up with crimson ribbons, wooden horses side by side
"Make believe" to eat their "fodder" – (blossoms to their noses tied!)
Near them stands the willow wagon – in it "Birdie's" mammoth doll,
And our faithful "Brave" beside them, noble guardian over all.

Above them float the butterflies, around them hum the bees,   55
And birdlings warble, darting in and out among the trees;
The kitten sleeps at "Mammy's" side, and two brown rabbits pass
Hopping close along the paling, stealing thro' the waving grass;
– Gladsome tears blue eyes are filling and a watching mother prays –
"God bless 'Mammy' and my children, in these happy, halcyon days!"   60

from *Hearth and Home* (1870)

THE ACCEPTED

(From Heine's Song of the Oceanides[100])
Translated from the German by Mignonette

Ah! she loves me! she loves me! the beautiful maiden!
   Even now she is thinking of me, I know,
As she stands, perhaps, by her vine-wreathed window,
   Looking down on the blooming roses below.

Or she leans like a lily into the twilight,   5
   Eager to see my well-known form;
And as vainly she gazes she seeks the garden
   With the breath of Summer so sweet and warm.

And, sighing, she wanders beneath the lindens,
   Or pauses, and speaks to the blossoms so pure,   10
And tells them how I deserve her affection,
   And am *so* agreeable – she is sure!

And when in her bed she softly slumbers,
   And the moonlight over her blonde hair streams,
There flits around her my well-loved presence –   15
   Floating and mingling with all her dreams.

E'en in the light of the morn – at breakfast,
   In the omelet's gold and the muffin's snow,
She sees my dear, sweet-smiling features,
   And she eats them up out of love, I know!   20

from *Golden Age* (1871)

IN ITALY
by Grace Greenwood (Sara Jane Clarke Lippincott)[101]

Night lies between us, and unpitying sea –
And for all path, the light the moon may fling

THE ACCEPTED
[100] Heinrich Heine (1797–1856), German poet.

IN ITALY
[101] Sara Jane Clarke Lippincott (1823–1904), poet and essayist.

On shifting waves – yet in my dreams, O love,
All firm and proud I tread such ways to thee, –
As though I walked o'er floors of porphyry,   5
With roses strewn, and purple-draped above, –
As Sheba's queen sought Israel's youthful king; –[102]
Thou like to him, makest glad haste to rise
And half way down the steps toward the throne
Of thy high manhood, stand'st, with welcoming eyes!   10
But here the likeness ends, – we are not shown
How that grand prince bepraised the cheeks and lips
Of that dark lady, calling her his own;
Or said her love-dewed orbs might well eclipse
The midnight stars that burned o'er Lebanon, –   15
Or hung upon the sweetness of her tone,
With hunger still renewed – declaring oft
His father's golden harpings[103] were less soft;
From her dusk forehead laid the locks apart,
And smoothed their blackness down with fingers white;   20
The while she leant against his royal heart,
There most a queen – and felt his eyes' keen light
Flame on her thought, and read it as a scroll –
And felt his kiss sound deep her crystal soul.

Not royal our dream-trysting, – for I hold   25
'Tis lik[e]liest that from his jasper throne,
He blazed upon her, like the sun at noon;
While she shone on him, like a dusky moon
That reddens up the East – 'twas bronze for gold.
Proud at his feet barbaric gifts she cast –   30
He lavished gems, and silks of wondrous dyes –
But naught so human, sure, as love-words passed
Between such grandeurs and high sovereignties.

O love, if here, through dim immensity,
My soul thy soul so surely, safely seeks, –   35
Through darkness pillared on vast Alpine peaks,
And sleeping on a thousand leagues of sea;
May not *all* change, *all* distance be defied?
Shall starry spaces cold, a barrier be?
Shall deeps of mystery and death divide?   40
Shall whitest heights of God shut thee from me?

---

[102] Lippincott is alluding to the well-known story of the Queen of Sheba's visit to King Solomon as told in 1 Kings 10, and which is thought to have occurred in the tenth century BCE. Sheba is the biblical name for S. Arabia. Later interpretations of the Bible assumed that the "Song of Solomon," a heterogeneous group of erotic poems, some dating as late as the third century BCE, was written by King Solomon for the Queen, his "dark lady." The Song of Solomon (Canticles) is one of the primary texts for women's erotic poetry in the nineteenth century and, as this text demonstrates, its stunning imagery was easily woven into contemporary poetry.
[103] King David (c. 972 BCE), father of Solomon. As a boy he harped for King Saul.

from *Galaxy* (1872)

THE HEART OF JUNE
by Constance Fenimore Woolson[104]

Down in the heart of the June, my love,
    Down in the heart of the June;
The gold, gold sun, like a bridegroom proud,
Lifts the fair sky's veil of summer cloud,
While the green, green earth laughs out aloud   5
    In the heart of the red, red June.

This is the best of the world, my love,
    This is the best of the year;
Behind is the springtime, cold and sweet,
Forward the summer's feverish heat;   10
Stay, then, my darling, thy hurrying feet,
    For the best of our life is here.

Sip the red wine of the June, my love,
    Sip the red wine of the June,
In May it was white as the fading snow,   15
August's deep purple will darken its glow;
Then, with lingering lip and kisses slow,
    Sip the red, red wine of the June.

The roses, June roses, are red, my love,
    They hang from your lattice high.   20
Faint was the May-blossom's gentle breath –
The orange-flower will be strong unto death;
But the rose is sweet, and its sweetness saith,
    "There are none so lovely as I."

Then live in the heart of this June, my love,   25
    Live in the heart of this June.
Once we were friends – oh, cold, barren dearth!
Soon must our wedded life prove its own worth;
But now we are lovers – are gods on earth,
    In the heart of this red, red June.   30

THE HEART OF JUNE
[104] Constance Fenimore Woolson (1840–94), fiction
writer, great-niece of James Fenimore Cooper.

from *Vindicator* (1872)

THE BAGGAGE WAGON
by Ethel Lynn (Ethelinda Beers)[105]

In from the ferry's pulsing door,
    In by the railroad gate,
Comes all day long the baggage home,
    Mighty in size and weight.

Trunks with their canvass quite unfurled;   5
    Boxes in woeful trim,
With garments dried in country sun,
    Tumbled and tossed within.

Under the locks what finery
    Lies travel-stained and worn;   10
Limp muslins with the sea kiss on,
    Flounces on fences torn.

(For how could Kitty stop to think
    Of dress on sea-sand wet,
When Fred was whispering the while   15
    A vow she don't forget?

Or how could Lily spare her flounces,
    Scrambling in breathles[s] fright,
When silvertop[106] was coming near
    To woe her, if he might?)   20

Methinks mamma will open wide
    Her pretty eyes to see
How schoolboy Fred has packed his trunk
    With trophies recklessly:

Risking, by Bramah Poofra eggs,   25
    The shine of Sunday clothes;
A tortoise in the collar box,
    Bird's nests on satin bows.

But oh! there's baggage coming home
    In yonder jostled pile;   30
Packed, outward bound, not long ago,
    With jest and happy smile;

THE BAGGAGE WAGON
[105] Ethelinda (Eliot) Beers (1827–79), popular poet and author of "The Picket Guard." Beers wrote under the pen name "Ethel Lynn."

[106] *Silvertop* probably an alternative or printer's error for "silvertip," a male grizzly bear.

Seeking out now stricken heart,
    Hands that shall softly move
The folded garments with the touch   35
    We give to things we love.

Oh, solemn garments needed not;
    Oh, childish treasures, dearer far,
For wear of little baby heads,
    Than jewels newly burnished are.   40

Oh, empty glove and kerchief smooth;
    Oh, idle shoe, that treads no more
Life's measure to the tune of Time;
    Oh, treasures dropped on Jordan's shore.

I dream to-day, as dreamers must,   45
    I see dim shadows come,
Claiming their own with smile and tear
    As noisy wheels bring baggage home.

from *Overland Monthly* (1873)

THE SEA-SHELL
by Ina D. Coolbrith

"And love will stay — a summer's day!"
    A long wave rippled up the strand;
She flashed a white hand through the spray.
    And plucked a sea-shell from the sand.
And, softly: "Let thy heart have peace.   5
    Mine shall not fail in aught to thee,
Until this little shell doth cease
    To sing its love — the sea."

Ah, well! sweet summer's past and gone,
    And love, perhaps, dreads winter weather.   10
And so the happy dears are flown
    On careless wings together!
And yet I smile: this pearly-lined,
    Rose-veinèd shell she gave to me,
With foolish, faithful lips to find   15
    Still singing of the sea!

from *Irish Nationalist* (1873)

ADIEU TO INNISFAIL[107]
by a Lady from Cork

I'm lonely to-night, as I stand on the deck,
    And think of the days gone by;
Of the friends I have left; of my ivy-clad home,
    And the blue mountains clustering nigh.

I'm lonely – the night sky is brilliant with stars –   5
    A light breeze is snuffing the sea –
Each white sail is full, and the ship dashes on
    That's bearing me further from thee.

I'm lonely – the moonlight is silvering the sea –
    The southern cross bends on high –   10
There is music, and dancing, and laughter around,
    But my heart seeks relief in a sigh.

Oh! bird of the white foam, when morn is dawning,
    Extend thy bright pinions and soar;
Stay not till thou'st found that sweet isle far away,   15
    Where the waves kiss the EMERALD SHORE.

Pass on, where the heather empurples the hill –
    Where the sky is so brilliantly blue –
Where the stream rushes on past the velvet lawn,
    And the roses are brightest in hue.   20

'Tis there! My sweet home! Thou'st found it at last!
    Go, peep through the casement and see!
Oh, say, are they joyous – oh, say, are they sad –
    Oh, say, are they speaking of me?

When night steals apace o'er the mountains' dark brow,   25
    And the moonbeams my lone chamber steep,
Do they think of the absent one – far, far away –
    Far away – far away on the deep.

ADIEU TO INNISFAIL.
[107] A poetical name for Ireland.

from *Woodhull & Claflin's Weekly* (1874)

MY FASHIONABLE MOTHER[108]
by Anonymous

Who feared my birth might her annoy,
Did many sinful arts employ,
My embryo being to destroy?
My fashionable mother.

And who, at fashion's stern behest,   5
Kept me from her maternal breast
In a wet-nurse's arms to rest?
My fashionable mother.

Who left her pleasures twice a week,
Who deigned my nursery realms to seek,   10
And coldly kissed my rosy cheek?
My fashionable mother.

And who, through all my early days,
Ne'er mingled with my childish plays,
Or hushed my cries with nursery lays?   15
My fashionable mother.

Who dressed me, fashion's whim to please,
In frocks much shorter than my knees,
Which caused my limbs to nearly freeze?
My fashionable mother.   20

Who taught my childish lips to pray,
That I in beauty day by day,
Might grow, and lead in fashion's sway?
My fashionable mother.

Who taught me with maternal care   25
Of every suitor to beware,
Unless he was a millionaire?
My fashionable mother.

And now my charms begin to fade,
If I remain a lone old maid,   30
Whom shall I blame for hopes delayed?
My fashionable mother.

MY FASHIONABLE MOTHER
[108] Woodhull and Claflin took this poem from the *Sunday Union*, Detroit, Michigan. If it is by a woman, then it is an extremely rare instance of a nineteenth-century woman poet attacking a mother, made even rarer by its first stanza allusion to abortion.

from *Galaxy* (1875)

THE SEA PEOPLE
by Lillie Devereux Blake[109]

The pale white chargers of the sea
  Toss back their foam-white hair,
As swift they plunge beneath the waves
  With mist-robed sea-nymphs fair.

Far down in dim-lit coral caves   5
  The mermaids coil and glide,
Or with fish-monsters, filmy-eyed,
  Through walls of water glide.

While whirling up from darkling deeps,
  With hurrying leap and reach,   10
The great wave Tritons[110] dance and dash
  Along the echoing beach.

from *Scribner's Monthly* (1875)

WHITE AZALEAS
by Harriet McKewen Kimball[111]

Azaleas – whitest of white!
  White as the drifted snow
Fresh-fallen out of the night,
  Before the coming glow
Tinges the morning light,   5
  When the light is like the snow,
    White,
And the silence is like the light; –
  Light, and silence, and snow, –
    All – white!   10

White! not a hint
Of the creamy tint
  That a rose will hold
  (The whitest rose) in its inmost fold,
Nor a possible blush;   15

THE SEA PEOPLE
[109] Lillie Devereux Blake (1835–1913), author and women's rights reformer.
[110] *Tritons* in classical mythology, a triton was a sea demi-god, son of Poseidon and Amphitrite, represented as having the lower half of his body fish-like.

WHITE AZALEAS
[111] Harriet McKewen Kimball (b. 1834), poet and hymn writer.

White as an embodied hush;
   A very rapture of white,
   A wedlock of silence and light.
White, white, as the wonder undefiled
   Of Eve just wakened in Paradise;   20
Pure as the angel of a child
   That looks into God's own eyes.

from *Atlantic Monthly* (1875)

POSSESSION
by Mary B. Cummings

I.

Summer and blossoms are lavish, my dearest;
   See this red rose!
Look how its buds press upon you; the nearest
Tries for your mouth with the gayest, sincerest
   Wish to unclose!   5

You were always a little neglectful, my brother,
   But why are you cold?
Take my word for it, Francis, there is n't another
To equal this roselet, for any flower-lover
   To have or to hold.   10

II.

Yes, but I've had it so long, and it bores me;
   What is its name?
Lifting its head in that way, it implores me
To care for it, look at it; see! it adores me
   Always the same!   15

from *Shaker* (1875)

MOTHERLAND
by Cecelia Devyr

Daughters of the nation listen!
   Liberty to you appeals!
Tearful eyes around you glisten,
   While she supplicating kneels.
To their homes your fathers brought her   5
   Through the flood and fire of war;
Through the thunderstorm and slaughter
   Rolled her fair triumphal car.

And they said, "All men are equal,
    With inalienable rights;"   10
Little dreaming of the sequel,
    That has filled the land with blights.
For a while their sons defended
    That great heritage with power;
Sought the good that was intended,   15
    For the country's lasting dower.

But the demon, *slavery*, flourished;
    Half approved and half ignored;
At her founts his life was nourish'd,
    Till he grew to be her lord.   20
Boldly took not heavy duty
    On such articles as tea;
His, not taxes, but rich booty;
    Even pearls of liberty.
Then a lofty manhood crumbled,   25
    Like a soulless mass of clay;
For its spirit had been humbled,
    And its honor swept away.

Droop'd the flag, the stars were broken
    As by clouds of inky hue!   30
And the stripes disclosed in token,
    Blood and tears that bondage drew.
When, at length, its folds were lifted,
    By the soldier's dying breath,
Was the nation's harvest sifted,   35
    From the bitter seeds of death?
Do not intrigue, sloth and plunder
    Still destroy her ripening grain,
While the world is struck with wonder
    At her turmoil, loss and pain?   40
Is there yet no hope for nations?
    Must all constitutions fail,
And the heart's uplifted patience,
    Sink and let despair prevail?

Safe between two veiling oceans,   45
    God had kept a land to show,
When the Church and State commotions,
    Blacken'd earth with crushing woe.
When the hells that *priests* created
    Lit the inquisition's flame,   50
And the flesh was satiated
    In the Holy Spirit's name.
From Republican Genoa
    To the tortured Spanish land,

Came a man,[112] impress'd like Noah,   55
    With the rescue God had plan'd.
Europe had no aid to furnish;
    Tyrants heard no pleading tone;
They had thrones and arms to burnish,
    Schemes for prowess, all their own.   60

But a woman heard the story[113]
    Of a land beyond the sea;
And bright visions of its glory,
    Gifted were her eyes to see.
She the jewel treasure offer'd,   65
    That adorned her as a queen;
And the gems thus freely proffer'd
    Bridged the waves to shores unseen,
Where shall be a declaration,
    That will make all *women* free!   70
Where our eyes shall see a nation,
    That is fit for liberty!

Where the rights, divine and human,
    Shall forever be secure.
In the land first bought by women,   75
    And by her made good and pure.
For a government parental
    Soon will bring true *order* forth:
Place whate'er is accidental,
    Build "new heaven and new earth."[114]   80
Heavy is the task before us;
    But it takes no winding course,
Cloudless light is shining o'er us,
    In this day of vital force.

from *Shaker and Shakeress* (1876)

SPIRIT VOICES[115]
by Anna White[116]

Voices sweet as angel whispers,
    Come to us from yonder clime,

MOTHERLAND
[112] Christopher Columbus (1451–1506), Italian explorer.
[113] Queen Isabella I of Spain (1451–1504), who financed Columbus's exploratory mission. The role of women in founding visionary communities was, of course, part of Shaker reality insofar as their US founder and chief popularizer was Ann Lee (1736–84), or "Mother Ann" as she was called.

[111] Revelations 21:1.
SPIRIT VOICES
[115] This hymn was accompanied by music when initially published.
[116] Anna White (1831–1910), Shaker eldress in the New Lebanon community, Lebanon, New Hampshire.

Gentle as the evening zephyrs,
    Is their song of love divine.
Tarry with us blest immortals,   5
    We will learn the heavenly song,
Press toward the shining portals,
    Whence the melody was borne.

Living souls with hope resplendent,
    And a spirit formed anew,   10
Catch the joyous notes triumphant,
    Swell the chorus rich and true.
These have left the world forever,
    Turned from darkness unto light,
Thus renouncing every error,   15
    That the spirit's growth would blight.

Ye who still are waiting – watching,
    For the bright and morning star,
See, the dawn is fast approaching,
    And the gates are left ajar.   20
And the Bridegroom[117] now appeareth,
    With his Bride in raiment white,
Hear ye what the Spirit sayeth,
    Come receive the truth, the light.

Not in measured form 'tis given,   25
    Nor in dogmas of the past,
Word of life flows down from heaven,
    Void of priestly cant or caste.[118]
'Tis the "Rock of Revelation,"[119]
    'Tis the gift of God to man,   30
Showing all whence comes salvation,
    The established, gospel plan.

from *New Century for Women* (1876)

TO GEORGE ELIOT[120]
by Constance Fenimore Woolson

O wondrous woman! Shaping with thy pen
As Michael Angelo[121] did shape from stone,

---

[117]   Christ.
[118]   The Roman Catholic Church, a favorite butt of
Shaker poets.
[119]   This well-known phrase is not in the Bible but
may derive from Christ's reference in Matthew 7:24–5
to a rock whose firmness resembled the foundation upon
which believers built.

TO GEORGE ELIOT
[120]   Mary Ann Evans (1819–80), the British novelist.
Guiney and Phelps also wrote poems to Eliot.
[121]   Michelangelo Buonarroti (1475–1564), Italian Renaissance painter and sculptor.

Colossal forms of clear-cut outline, when
We dwell upon thy pages, not alone
The beauty of thy rose, we see, as finely traced   5
As roses drawn by other woman-hands
Who spend their lives in shaping them, but faced
We find ourselves with giant's work, that stands
Above us as a mountain lifts its brow,
Grand, unapproachable, yet clear in view   10
To lowliest eyes that upward look. O, how
Hast thou shed radiance as thy finger drew
Its shapes! A myriad women light have seen,
And courage taken, because *thou* hast been!

from *Sunday Afternoon* (1879)

AT HOME FROM CHURCH
by Sarah Orne Jewett[122]

The lilacs lift in generous bloom
    Their plumes of dear old-fashioned flowers;
Their fragrance fills the still old house
    Where left alone I count the hours.

High in the apple-trees the bees   5
    Are humming, busy in the sun, –
An idle robin cries for rain
    But once or twice and then is done.

The Sunday-morning quiet holds
    In heavy slumber all the street,   10
While from the church, just out of sight
    Behind the elms, comes slow and sweet

The organ's drone, the voices faint
    That sing the quaint long-meter hymn –
I somehow feel as if shut out   15
    From some mysterious temple, dim

And beautiful with blue and red
    And golden lights from windows high,
Where angels in the shadows stand
    And earth seems very near the sky.   20

The day-dream fades – and so I try
    Again to catch the tune that brings

AT HOME FROM CHURCH
[122] Sarah Orne Jewett (1849–1909), fiction writer.

No thought of temple nor of priest,
    But only of a voice that sings.

from *Pilot* (1880)

THE WORK-GIRL'S REST
by Lizzie Ward O'Reilly

Dead – and it sounded not sadly
    To those who had known her best;
Dead – not a summons of sorrow,
    Only a much needed rest. –

Fold the scant robe close about her,   5
    Lay the fair head gently down,
'Tis but the workshop closed early,
    The work-girl claiming her crown.

Naught of this world but its sorrows,
    Naught but its work did she know;   10
Is it strange that she welcom'd the summons?
    Is it strange she wanted to go?

No more shall the slumb'ring streets echo
    The sound of her weary tread;
No more shall we mark the pale woman   15
    Who toiled for her daily bread.

From the sneer, the jest of the work-room,
    She is safe in her Father's breast,
With her pearl of life unsullied,
    She has lain her down to rest.   20

Would you sing of the brave and the valiant,
    The battles of life amid;
Go! look at the pale little toiler
    Under the poor coffin-lid.

Weep not! For her there's no morrow.   25
    See her still hands on her breast;
Death, and death only hath pity,
    He giveth the work-girl rest.

Then fold the scant robe close about her,
    Lay the fair head gently down,   30
Place on the fair brow the lilies,
    The work-girl deserveth her crown.

from *Californian* (1880)

IN A NEW ENGLAND GRAVEYARD
by Milicent W. Shinn[123]

Beside these crumbling stones – where saints of old
    Were laid to rest two hundred years ago,
    And where the quaint, still village, nestled low,
Lives gently 'mid its elms, and seems to hold
In thought the warning o'er this archway told,   5
    "*Memento mori*"[124] – where the feet have trod
    Of later saints, akin to these in blood –
I think of *their* rest by the mart of gold,
The wild-pulsed city that the sea-winds beat,[125]
    Where, on its bare, round hill uplifted high,   10
Far-seen from beating seas and eager street,
    Watching the graves where alien thousands lie,
A stark, lone cross – the dead about its feet –
Lifts its white protest to the windy sky.[126]

from *Daily Eastern Argus* (1880)

MY ANTONY'S AWAY
by Olive Harper (Mrs Helen Burrell D'Apery)[127]

The passion vine in masses dark
    Sweeps low against my window pane,
And roses drink the nectared dew
    Dropped from the chalice of the rain;
Tall cypress trees all trembling lay   5
Upon my roof their shadows gray.

IN A NEW ENGLAND GRAVEYARD
[123] Milicent Washburn Shinn (1858–1940), poet and editor of the *Overland Monthly*.
[124] Latin: "Remember you must die."
[125] San Francisco, California, after 1849, a primary trading center for gold due to its proximity to the "motherlode."
[126] This is probably a reference to an early version of a cross still found on Mt Davidson today on the southern point of the Twin Peaks area overlooking the city. From the site of the cross, one can see a number of different ethnic cemeteries in the city of Colma below, including a Chinese cemetery. This suggests that "white" carries a racial meaning in this poem and that the poem itself, sited in a New England graveyard, is pointing quite explicitly to concerns over racial national identity which were reaching fever pitch during the 1880s as successive waves of immigration from Asia and Europe eroded the country's Anglo-Saxon base. By 1867 there were some 50,000 Chinese in California and by 1877 there were anti-Chinese riots in San Francisco. The Chinese Exclusion Act was passed in 1882, banning immigration from China for ten years. It or later versions were in force until 1943.
MY ANTONY'S AWAY
[127] Mrs Helen Burrell D'Apery (1842–1915), author of penny novels. She wrote a longer poem on the Mark Antony–Cleopatra material which is mildly pornographic. I want to thank Professor Kenneth Collins for giving me this poem.

Like a white angel, on my wall
    Through the lone window glides the moon;
The crystal panes are silver rayed
    Where golden bright they seemed at noon,   10
When brightened by the light of day;
But now, my Antony's away.

A tiny vase of fragrant flowers
    Give perfume sweet, like his sweet breath;
A string of pearls that car[e]le[s]s lie   15
    Are white and even as his teeth.
My lowly couch, ah, whose fair brow
Is like that pillow's polished snow?

The passion vine droops darkly low,
    Weighed down by heavy purple flowers,   20
The fleur de lys with fragrance fills
    All the oppressive, loitering hours.
I sit and wish and wait for day,
Though day is dark while he's away.

The night is dead – cold morning's born   25
    From chilly clouds of ghostly gray;
I hate the morning's empty hours,
    For he I love is still away.
Draw close the blinds, shut out the light;
Oh, sun, go down; send back the night.   30

from *Scribner's Monthly* (1881)

IRREVOCABLE
by Mary L. Ritter[128]

I did not know that thou couldst grow still dearer,
With every passing hour.
I did not dream that thou couldst draw still nearer,
Consume, absorb, devour,
Till life without thee is a barren thing, –   5
A fig-tree cursed, and done with blossoming.

I thought that summer of idyllic pleasure,
For us, was "summit line";[129]
I said, the vintage grapes that give such measure
Must ripen on a vine,   10

IRREVOCABLE
[128] Mary L. Ritter (b. 1860), Californian poet.   [129] As high as one can get.

Clinging to some volcanic rock, whose heart
Sends through each branch its fiery counterpart.

But oh, these days of more than tropic beauty,
These sweet and bitter days,
When passion drags the loosened chain of duty,   15
And every sense betrays,
When, all the outposts stormed, enforced retreat
Is victory more cruel than defeat.

These days when all the starved and orphaned senses,
That through long years have cried,   20
Are filled and fed with heavenly recompenses,
Rested, and satisfied,
When asking lips, and eyes, and hands confess
The living love, and the lost loneliness.

These days where sin is not, nor selfish feeling,   25
But two souls made as one
See, in the light of this strange self-revealing,
Their birthright sold and gone –
Behold around them arid desert sand,
Beyond their reach the blessed Promised Land.   30

Dearest, the wasted years are unreturning,
Give, then, as spendthrifts give.
What if the oil consumes itself in burning?
We die that we may live.
Living or dead, in essence we shall prove   35
The indivisibility of love.

from *Pilot* (1882)

AFTER DEATH
by Fanny Parnell[130]

Shall mine eyes behold thy glory, O my country?
     Shall mine eyes behold thy glory?
Or shall the darkness close around them, ere the sun-blaze
     Break at last upon thy story?

When the nations ope for thee their queenly circle,   5
     As a sweet, new sister hail thee,

AFTER DEATH
[130] Fanny Parnell (1854–82). The *Pilot*'s note: "This beautiful and sadly prophetic poem was written by Miss Fanny Parnell nearly one year ago, on August 27th, 1881." Parnell was the sister of the renowned Irish nationalist leader, Charles Stewart Parnell; at the time of her death she was living with her mother in New Jersey.

Shall these lips be sealed in callous death and silence,
    That have known but to bewail thee?

Shall the ear be deaf that only loved thy praises,
    When all men their tribute bring thee?   10
Shall the mouth be clay, that sang thee in thy squalor,
    When all poets' mouths shall sing thee?

Ah! the harpings and the salvos and the shoutings
    Of thy exiled sons returning!
I should hear, though dead and mouldered, and the grave-damps   15
    Should not chill my bosom's burning.

Ah! the tramp of feet victorious! I should hear them
    'Mid the shamrocks and the mosses,
And my heart should toss within the shroud, and quiver
    As a captive dreamer tosses.   20

I should turn and rend the cere-clothes[131] round me.
    Giant-sinews I should borrow,
Crying, "O my brothers, I have also loved her,
    In her lowliness and sorrow.

"Let me join with you the jubilant procession[,]   25
    Let me chant with you her story;
Then contented I shall go back to the sham[rocks,]
    Now mine eyes have seen her glory."

from *Californian* (1882)

WAITING FOR DAY
by Mrs Henrietta R. Eliot[132]

        I slept and woke,
And instant knew, by some more subtle sense,
That day was near: although the soft and velvet dark
Hung heavy in the room, and from the eaves
The steady drip of night-fog seemed to make more still   5
The else unbroken hush.
        A little space
I waited in the quiet gloom; and then afar
A shrill-voiced cock awoke the silent air,
And then another, and another, near at hand;   10
I felt the darkness thinning in the room,

---

[131] *Cere-clothes*   waxed cloths used as a winding sheet.   WAITING FOR DAY
        [132] Henrietta R. Eliot (b. 1845), poet.

And saw, or thought I saw, my window bars show dim
Against a lesser dark.
       With that I rose,
And throwing wide my window, turned me toward the east;   15
And there, between a low black line of cloud
And blacker line of hills, there glimmered to my view
The whitening ribbon of the dawn.

from *Century* (1884)

A Marriage
by Mary Ainge De Vere[133]

They stood together, he and she,
    As tenderly as lovers may
Who know the breaking dawn will be
    Their wedding day.

His flashing eyes told half his bliss;   5
    But hers seemed full of silent prayer,
As if a mightier voice than his
    Had named her there.

Behind the altar and the ring,
    Behind the brimming cup love holds,   10
Her timid soul sought, wondering,
    The future's folds.

His eyes were sweet; she looked beyond
    Through waiting years of sun and rain.
His clasp was dear; she felt the bond   15
    That might be pain!

Yet he all gladness, she half fear,
    Gave kisses only of delight.
Love touched and brought them close and near
    That happy night.   20

Long afterward he waked to doubt –
    But she, with care-worn matron grace,
Shut patience in and passion out,
    And held her place.

And never thought, nor word went wild –   25
    Content if only she could see

A Marriage
[133] No dates exist for Mary Ainge De Vere, but she
was a frequently published Irish poet and humorist.

His features in the sleeping child
Across her knee.

Her doubt had end where his begun;
She smiled, nor knew the bitter cost   30
At which his prison calm was won –
His freedom lost!

from *Century* (1886)

PAST
by Winifred Howells[131]

There, as she sewed, came floating through her head
Odd bits of poems, learned in other days
And long forgotten in the noisier ways
Through which the fortunes of her life now led;
And looking up, she saw upon the shelf   5
In dusty rank her favorite poets stand,
All uncaressed by her fond eye or hand;
And her heart smote her, thinking how herself
Had loved them once and found in them all good
As well as beauty, filling every need;   10
But now they could not fill the emptiness
Of heart she felt ev'n in her gayest mood.
She wanted once no work her heart to feed,
And to be idle once was no distress.

from *Southern Workman* (1886)

AFMERICA
by M[ary] E. Ashe Lee[135]

With che[ek]s as soft as roses are,
And yet as brown as chestnuts dark;
And eyes that borrow from a star
A tranquil, yet a brilliant spark;
Or face of olive, with a glow   5
Of carmine on the lip and cheek;
The hair in wavelets falling low,
With jet or hazel eyes, that speak;
Or brow of pure Caucasian hue,

PAST
[131] Winifred Howells (1863–89), poet-daughter of
W. D. Howells, novelist and editor.

AFMERICA
[135] Mary E. Ashe Lee (no dates), black educator, wife
of Bishop B. F. Lee. This important poem was reprinted
at least three times (see Yellin and Bond, 1991).

With auburn or with flaxen hair;   10
And eyes that beam in liquid blue,
A perfect type of Saxon fair, –
Behold this strange, this well-known maid,
Of every hue, of every shade!

We find this maiden everywhere, –   15
From wild and sun-kissed Mexico
To where the Rocky Mountains rear
Their snow-peaked heads in Idaho.
From East to West, she makes her home;
From Carolina's pine-clad State,   20
Across the plains, she still doth roam
To California's golden gate.
Yet roaming not as gypsy maid,
Nor as the savage red-man's child,
But seeking e'er the loving shade   25
Of home and civil habits mild.
A daughter of futurity,
The problem of the age is she.

And why should she be strange to-day?
Why called the problem of the age?   30
Not so when slavery held its sway,
And she was like a bird in cage.
She was a normal creature then,
And in her true allotted place;
Giving her life to fellow-men,   35
A proud and avaricious race.
But now, a child of liberty,
Of independent womanhood,
The world in wonder looks to see
If in her there is any good;   40
If this new child, Afmerica,
Can dwell in free Columbia.

" 'Twas mercy brought me here,["][136] said one,
E'en Phillis Wheatly [*sic*], child of song,
Who, born beneath an Afric sun,   45
In her kind mistress found no wrong.
Though maid and mistress, they were true
Companions, both in mind and heart.
No sad impression Phillis knew,
She was content to play her part,   50

---

[136] From "On Being Brought from Africa to America" (1768) by Phillis Wheatley (1753?–84), African slave and poet. Her mistress, Susanna Wheatley, and Susanna's daughter, Mary, taught Wheatley to read and encouraged her writing.

In her is found the purest type
Of Afric intellectual might,
Which fast will grow and soon will ripe,
When nourished by the Christian light.
'Tis like Egyptian wheat that slept   55
In mummy graves, while ages crept.

When first America began
To give the world a nation new,
Then this strange child, called African,
Began to make her history, too,   60
In New York's Knickerbock[137] days,
As she would in the corner sit,
She sang with glee her cheerful lays,
And joined the family's mirth and wit.
New England even took her in   65
As servile at her own fireside;
But when convinced that it was sin,
And wounding to a Christian's pride,
To hold a fellow-man in chains,
She washed her hands from slavery's stains.   70

The warm affections of her heart,
Her patience and fidelity,
Adapted her in every part
A Washington's[138] fit nurse to be.
And other children, too, of state   75
Were nurtured on her trustful breast:
Their wants she would alleviate,
And solace them when in distress.
Full well she filled her humble sphere
As cook or drudge or ladies' maid;   80
For all the varied household care
Was on her docile shoulders laid;
While in *ennui* her mistress fair
Was burdened with herself to bear.

Her lot grew harder year by year;   85
For she was called from household care,
And forced within the fields t' appear,
The labor of the men to share.
In purple fields of sugarcane,

---

[137]   A term used to refer to early New York, *c.* seventeenth century, when the state was largely under the control of Dutch immigrants.

[138]   George Washington (1732–99), first President of the United States. The hit here is at wealthy whites who entrusted their most precious possessions, their children, entirely to the fostering care of otherwise despised black servants (typically slaves) – one of many startling inconsistencies which white Americans have exhibited over the years towards people of color.

At early morn, her task began   90
In regions of the Pontchartrain.[139]
She did the hardy work of men
From Florida to Maryland,
In cotton, rice, and fields of corn.
Such work as calls for masculine hands,   95
All weary, overtasked, and worn,
Subdued, she was compelled to do.
She helped in clearing forests, too.

The cultivation through her toil,
The literal labor of her hands,   100
Brought to pe[r]fection Southern soil
And swelled the commerce of those lands.
But as she toiled she prayed and longed
For freedom and for womanhood.
No Jewess, when in Goshen[140] wronged,   105
In trusting God e'er firmer stood
Than sad Afmerica, who, through
The thick'ning of the midnight gloom,
Looked steadfast on the North Star true,
And knew Jehovah held her doom.   110
So thus for twice a century
She sang the song of jubilee.[141]

Nor did she wait on God in vain.
No disappointment comes to those
Who ever strong in faith remain   115
And in God's confidence repose.
At last, a signal crisis came.
When on the first of sixty-three
Brave Lincoln made the bold proclaim:
'Twas but a war necessity,   120
Which Heaven did potentiate.[142]
That he on that day did decree
In every fighting Southern State
Afmerica forever free.[143]
God wrought this glorious victory,   125
Triumphant swelled the Jubilee.

Well did she use her chances few.
Each opportunity she prized

---

[139] Lake Pontchartrain, located in southeastern Louisiana.

[140] Goshen was the section of northeastern Egypt where Jacob and his family settled at the behest of the pharaoh's prime minister, Joseph (Genesis 46:28).

[141] Jubilee refers to those years (once in fifty) in biblical times when alienated property and land were restored, slaves manumitted, debts forgiven. In African American literature jubilee came to refer to the day of complete emancipation.

[142] *Potentiate* to make possible.

[143] The Emancipation Proclamation, put into final effect January 1, 1863.

As silvery drops of falling dew,
Sent to her from benignant[144] skies.   130
So freedom found her not without
Fair education in the North.
In Southern cities, too, no doubt
Her acquisitions proved her worth.
In many of her homes were found   135
Refinement true, and some degree
Of culture there, too, did abound,
Ere she was absolutely free.
Her small one talent was not hid,[145]
Whate'er she found to do she did.   140

O turbulent America!
So mixed and intermixed, until
Throughout this great Columbia
All nationalities at will
Become thine own, thy legal heirs, –   145
Behold, this colored child is thine!
Deny it, if there's one who dares,
Amid these glaring facts that shine
Upon the face of this ripe age.
As history doth record thy good,   150
We trace these facts on every page, –
These facts cry out like Abel's[146] blood;
And "I am vengeance," saith the Lord;
"I will repay."[147] Hear his own word.

This hardest of all problems hard,   155
Which baffles wit of every school
And further progress doth retard,
Is solved but by the Golden rule.[148]
Be calm and think, sublimity –
Have ye not learned, America? –   160
Is only sweet simplicity.
Cease *working out* Afmerica;
Most simple and sublime is truth.
A truth divine points out to you
The duty owed e'en from thy youth;   165
One which you need not *solve*, but do.
Acknowledge and protect thy child,
Regard her not as strange or wild.

---

[144] *Benignant* beneficial, favorable.
[145] A reference to Jesus's parable of the talents, Matthew 25:14–30.
[146] Genesis 4:2 and 4:10. In the Bible, Abel's blood is said to cry out for vengeance against his brother Cain, who murdered him.

[147] A loose rendition of Romans 12:19 and Hebrews 10:30. "'Vengeance is mine, I will repay,' saith the Lord."
[148] Matthew 7:12 and Luke 6:31, the precept loosely stated: do unto others as you would have them do unto you.

Afmerica! her home is here;
She wants or knows no other home;   170
No other lands, nor far nor near,
Can charm or tempt her thence to roam.
Her destiny is marked out here.
Her ancestors, like all the rest,
Came from the eastern hemisphere: 175
But *she* is native of the *west*.
She'll lend a hand to Africa,
And in her elevation aid.
But here in brave America
Her home, her only home, is made.   180
No one has power to send her hence;
This home was planned by Providence.

Whatever other women do
In any sphere of busy life,
We find her, though in numbers few,   185
Engaged heroic in the strife.
In song and music, she can soar;
She writes, she paints and sculptures well:
The fine arts seem to smile on her.
In elocution, she'll excel;   190
In medicine, she has much skill.
She is an educator, too;
She lifts her voice against the *still*.[149]
To Christ she tries man's soul to woo.
In love and patience, she is seen   195
In her own home, a blessed queen.

O ye, her brothers, husbands, friends,
Be brave, be true, be pure and strong!
For on your manly strength depends
Her firm security from wrong.   200
Oh, let your strong right arm be bold!
And don that lovely courtesy
Which marked the chevaliers of old.
Buttress her home with love and care;
Secure her those amenities   205
Which make a woman's life most dear;
Give her your warmest sympathies:
Thus high her aspirations raise
For nobler deeds in coming days.

---

[149]   This is probably a pun on distillery – i.e., a temperance reference as well as a breaking of silence.

from *Harper's New Monthly Magazine* (1887)

NOON IN A NEW ENGLAND PASTURE
by Margaret Deland[150]

With scattered birch the pasture's slope is crowned;
   The sunburnt grass that clings to mountain-sides,
   Cropped by small mouths of timid sheep, scarce hides,
Like a scant coverlet, the hard dry ground,
Through which, with stony ledge or rocky knee,   5
   The strong world breaks. The ragged ferns that fill
   Each dimple on the shoulders of the hill
Rustle with faint sharp sound if but the bee
Slips through their stems to find his mossy nest.
   With soft, thick, wilted leaves the mulleins grow,   10
   Like tall straight candles with pale yellow glow,
Their stalks star-flowered toward the cloudless west.
The crooning cricket with an endless song
   Jars the hot silence. The crumbling fence is grayed
   By the slow-creeping lichen, held and stayed   15
By arms of wandering rose, that, tough and strong,
Bind firm its slipping stones. The rusty brier
   And scarlet fingers of the bitter-sweet
   Cast a light shade that shelters from the heat
A thousand voiceless little lives. Higher   20
Than maiden birch or solitary pine,
   Poised in the brooding blue, on speckled wings,
   A hawk hangs motionless: so straight he flings
His shadow to the earth, like plummet-line
It drops through seas of air. As in a swoon   25
   Of light, the great world lies, and life stands still,
   Wrapped in a breathless hush; till up the hill
Drift dappled shadows of the afternoon.

from *Lippincott's Magazine* (1887)

FROM "THE DILEMMA OF THE NINETEENTH CENTURY"
by Rose Elizabeth Cleveland[151]

I.

Judith Von Stump[152] fell sick, or fell to ailing, –
   That was as clear as day to any one, –

NOON IN A NEW ENGLAND PASTURE
[150] Margaret Deland (1857–1945), well-known novelist.
FROM "THE DILEMMA OF THE NINETEENTH CENTURY"
[151] Rose Elizabeth Cleveland (1846–1918), poet, educator, youngest sister of President Grover Cleveland.

[152] Judith's given name may be meant to suggest the biblical heroine, Judith, slayer of Holofernes; but her patronymic suggests (1) the confusion that has "stumped" her and left her unable to move forward; and (2) her resulting sense of "castration." In the deleted portion of

And it was settled Judith's health was failing,
 That something was the matter, something must be done;
And so a meeting of the wise physicians   5
 Of either sex was called upon to sit
In counsel upon Judith's sad condition
 And charged to find a speedy cure for it:
From far and near they came, and saw, and – sat!
Of conquering I speak not: you shall judge of that.   10

II.

'Twas marvelous indeed how many doctors,
 Of every school and age, of either sex,
Came at the call, – from fierce concocters
 Of potions blue the gastric juice to vex,
To those exponents of a dispensation   15
 Whose sugar-coatings, redolent with ease,
Soothing and pleasant in their application,
 Outside or in, can never fail to please.
Nor lacked there those astute manipulators
Who charge upon disease like gladiators.   20

III.

Well, after some profound investigation,
 The following were found to be the leading facts
In Judith's case. Her education,
 Life subsequent, her birth, and other acts,
Were found to be correct, and well conducted,   25
 And after the approved, accepted plan.
Mamma Von Stump herself was well instructed,
 Papa Von Stump was no unlettered man.
She kept the house, he kept the store: together
They went to the right church in pleasant weather. 30

V.

In such an atmosphere was Judith nourished,
 And, at the proper age, to school was led,
Where all that genteel ladies learn was flourished
 In pleasant breezes round her youthful head;
And that no native airs or foreign graces   35
 Should Judith lack, which fashion can invent,

----

the poem, Cleveland offers her prescription for the
future woman, but it is very vaguely and unpersuasively
worded, suggesting that Cleveland herself was unsure
what Judith's fate would or should be. That is, she
herself was "stumped."

To dancing-school (quite moral), where the paces
    And bows of polite life are taught, she went;
And, as a finish to her education,
To boarding-school was sent for graduation.   40

VII.

And then the august day of graduation
    Drew up the curtain on the pretty scene
Where Judith reads with nice articulation
    Her *Vale*,[153] tied with ribbons in between.
Mamma Von Stump weeps fondly at its pathos,   45
    Papa Von Stump looks all around with pride,
And Judith bends her pretty head, while gracious
    Dr. Trigelgus[154] hands the sheepskin tied.
The bouquets rustle, every one's elated:
The curtain falls, Judith is educated!   50

VIII.

It next appeared, the relatives decided,
    The proper time for Judith to appear
In social life had come: so she presided
    At a grand fête given for her eighteenth year.
The iron gates of upper-tendom[155] tingled   55
    At Judith's graceful knock, and open rolled;
For from her taper jewelled fingers jingled
    Distinct suggestions of her papa's gold.
Judith's first season was a royal heyday,
She was crowned queen, and every day was May-day.   60

IX.

A year passed on, and Judith still was reigning,
    Her empire just a little less, 'twas said;
Young rivals said her beauty fast was waning,
    And old ones called her auburn ringlets red.
'Tis true that Judith (naughty Judith!), flirting   65
    Implacably, had cracked a dozen hearts
And broke a couple; "didn't mean to hurt 'em,"
    She said, and always gathered up the parts
And gave them back; and, singular, but true,
They all turned out again as good as new.   70

---

[153] *Vale* Latin for farewell, referring here to the valedictory address, usually given by the most accomplished student in the class on graduation day.

[154] A nonsense name, suggesting a medieval alchemist such as Hermes Trismagistus, a purveyor of occult knowledge.

[155] *Upper-tendom* slang for the social elite.

X.

Another year found Judith's empire shaken:
    The sceptre was departing, – that was clear.
The Grundys[156] said (and when were they mistaken?)
    That Miss Von Stump's unparalleled career
Was at an end, and Judith now or never   75
    Must change her base, or abdicate in full;
No longer beautiful, now to be clever
    Was her last rope, and she must sink or pull.
She could no longer rule by beauty's part:
What now she gained must be by wit or art.   80

XI.

Here testimony all agreed, Judith was clever,
    And found her tongue as potent as her face,
With different results; for the endeavor
    To scathe with wit diminished from her grace.
At least the Grundys said that it was certain   85
    People began to think her sharp and queer;
Society considered her a burden,
    Too smart by half, – that truth was very clear.
So much for facts. Judith is twenty-one,
And our review of her past life is done.   90

XII.

What time was taken in the rapid mention
    Of these *few facts*, the doctors all sat round
With faces grave, in eager, rapt attention,
    Some dubious, some shrewd, and all profound.
The crowd was calm, save that I saw a very   95
    Young man at one time feeling of his heart;
I noticed, too, just then, a missionary
    Look somewhat shocked and give a little start.
After a pause, what next my tale discloses
Is the announcement of a diagnosis.   100

XIII.

And thus it briefly ran: "We find this woman
    Existing without life, at twenty-one;
Possessing all those forces which a human
    Nature can boast. The patient should be one

---

[156] Originally an imaginary character in *Speed the Plough* (1798), a comedy by Thomas Morton, the name "Mrs Grundy" came to represent narrow conventionalism and morality.

In robust health. Upon investigation,   105
      We find the nervous centres and the brain
A little strained; local ossification
      Threatens the heart, and yet no trace of pain
Is to be found. In fact, we are not sure
Of cause, and therefore find, as yet, no cure."   110

XIV.

On this a doughty doctor rose, and, calling
      For silence, said, "The cause, sir, was a fall.
The woman fell in love, sir, and, in falling,
      Got hurt a little in the head, – that's all.
And as to all your stuff about the heart, sir,   115
      Nonsense! Among all woman-kind you can't
Single out one who don't possess the art, sir,
      To make her heart as hard as adamant
If it suits her. Now bother all this chatter!
The woman is in love, – that's what's the matter."   120

XV.

In a great heat and much exasperation,
      A little burly doctor then cried out,
"You're wrong, sir, – wrong! The proper explanation
      Is quite the contrary, I have no doubt:
The woman's not in love, and *that's* the trouble.   125
      Give her a husband, sir, a house to keep,
Children to rear, and this romantic bubble
      Will soon collapse. Why, you must be asleep!
A woman, sir, is an absurd anomaly
Found anywhere but in the house and family."   130

XVI.

At this a murmur of shrill indignation
      Arose from where the crinoline was dense.
A female here cried with determination,
      "Sir, we insist on *truth* and *common sense*
And *science*, sir. The musty old traditions   135
      Left to us by the elders will not do.
In seeking to improve the sad condition
      Of our sick sister, we must learn to view
Her case in the broad light of progress, which advances
Beyond the pale of these effete romances."   140

XVII.

Amidst the tumult, one, with face exuding
      With fat complacence, smiling pleasantly,

Said, "My dear friends, I hope I'm not intruding.
        Our fair friend's sickness, it is clear to me,
Is one caused by unwholesome agitation   145
        Of thought: in truth, her history
Makes clear that fact: it is an aberration
        From woman's law. The patient must be free
From all brain-labor. It is foul, inhuman,
And out of nature, sir, for lovely woman."   150

XVIII.

Then up there jumped, with jovial air and bustle,
        A little man, rubbing his hands with glee,
Who said, "The cause of all disease is lack of muscle.
        Turn out the patient; let her climb a tree;
Feed her with bran; teach her to roar with laughter   155
        All day; pack her in air at night;
Burn up her books, spill all her ink, and after
        Ten months I'll warrant her all right.
A woman's proper sphere is vegetation
In air and sunshine, with good cultivation."   160

XIX.

The next who gained a hearing was a woman
        Of visage resolute and purpose fell,
Who now proclaimed, in accents superhuman,
        "The true cause of this illness I can tell,
And will. Our patient is a wretched sufferer   165
        From man's injustice: you will please to note
The cause, 'tis soon explained, and 'tis enough, sir,
        To make a woman sick, sir, not to VOTE.
She never told her grief, yet how it cankers!
Give her the ballot, sir: for this she hankers."   170

XX.

Immense applause, tremendous acclamation,
        Followed the speaker. Quickly then arose
Another voice, which said, "This explanation
        Is good enough, and true, as far as it goes.
Our Radical Committee of Research, however,   175
        Are happy to assure you that they can
Announce the final cause. Our patient never
        Can hope for perfect health until she is a MAN;
Which metamorphosis our noble science
Hopes soon to reach, bidding to doubt defiance.   180

XXI.

"Since in all sciences exact investigations
    Have made it clear that a desired end
May be attained by close approximations,
    We feel quite confident our female friend
Will soon have reached the last round of the ladder   185
    Reaching from woman's up to man's estate.
In truth, if Miss Von Stump long since had had her
    Feet free to climb, we do not hesitate
To say, this piece of ailing femininity
Would have attained a robust masculinity."   190

XXII.

The speaker ceased, and furious applauses
    Closed in about her, – or, I should say, him.
'Twas evident at last that the first causes
    Were reached. I heard, indeed, a dim
And insignificant remonstrance blowing   195
    From certain parts: the missionary men
Looked somewhat pale, but that, no doubt, was owing
    To change of air, – a little strong for them.
One glance at the reporters made me dizzy
With admiration, they appeared so busy.   200

XXIII.

The case being made clear, just how to treat it
    Was next the subject of prolonged discourse.
Some clamored, "Teach her medicine: you cannot beat it
    For making an already bad thing worse."
Others cried loudly, "Put her on a rostrum;   205
    To talk is woman's chief necessity;
It makes her comfortable; and no other nostrum
    Is suited to her taste so perfectly."
And others cried, with vehemence still madder,
"Just let her vote, and soon she'll climb the ladder."   210

XXIV.

Just then, amid the murmur and outcrying,
    Nature gave out. I slept, and, sleeping, dreamed
I stood at one end of a ladder lying
    Level across a gulf which without bottom seemed.
With purpose fell and step unhesitating,   215
    This perilous bridge from round to round I stepped.
The shore I left from sight was fast abating,
    And yet the farther one as distant kept,

Or seemed to keep, – an optical delusion,
I thought, and with this wise conclusion   220

XXV.

I still kept stepping on, and fondly hoping
    The longed-for shore soon with my feet to press;
Yet ever farther seemed its blue hills sloping,
    While still the one behind grew less and less.
On, on I went, yet by no footstep nearing   225
    The shore beyond; and then the night drew on;
Backward I could not turn: trembling and fearing,
    I fell, and, falling, woke. My dream was gone!
Gone were the doctors, – gone the crowd. All over!
And of the patient naught could I discover.   230

XXVI.

Yet, I have heard it said, the woman-tinkers
    Still wrangle o'er her case most faithfully,
And still it baffles the profoundest thinkers.
    "Who shall decide when doctors disagree?"
Ah, Judith! wheresoe'er we turn we see you,   235
    Your pretty, puny face, your helpless hands
Lying in graceful ease, while still to free you
    From chains yourself has forged, fermenting bands
Of yeasty quacks prescribe without a fee
For this sick woman of the nineteenth century!   240

---

from *Century* (1887)

SOLACE
by Julie M. Lippmann[157]

What though you lie, like the still pool of rain,
    Silent, forgotten in some lowly place;
    Or if remembered, in your being to trace
But the remainder of a past storm's pain?
What though the storm-drops, falling fast again, –   5
    Call we them "years" that hasten down apace, –
    Smite your still breast, as if they would efface
All sign of peace, and leave but blot and stain?

SOLACE
[157] Julie M. Lippmann (b. 1864), poet and novelist.

Look! even now the reaper-beams appear,
    And gather in the clouds' spare aftermath,   10
    With glancing scythes, of silver every one.
While in the pool's still bosom, mirror-clear
    Is Heaven pictured; and a mystic path
    Strikes from it heart's clear center to the Sun.

from *A. M. E. Church Review* (1888)

GOOD NIGHT
by Mrs N. F. Mossell (Gertrude E. H. Bustill)[158]

Good night! Ah no, that cannot be
Good night that severs thee from me;
To dwell with thee in converse sweet,
And evermore thy presence greet,
Filling thy life with cheer and light,   5
Then each hour lost would bring good night.

To listen for thy footstep's fall,
To answer when thy voice doth call,
To feel thy kisses warm and sweet,
Thy downward glance my lifted eye to greet,   10
To feel love's silence, and its might,
Then evermore 't would be good night.

To dwell with thee shut in, and all the world shut out,
Close clasped in love's own clasp,
And thus to feel that I to thee belong   15
And thou to me;
That nevermore on earth shall parting come,
But only at the bidding of that Loving One,
With will, power and hope to show love's might,
Then, and not till then, can come good night.   20

To know thy every helpful thought,
To look upon the universe and think God's thoughts after him,
To see the mystic beauty of music, poetry and art,
To minister unto thy every want,
To fill thy life with all the joy that woman's love can bring,   25
To shield thy life from evil, to bring thee good with loves in sight,
This daily life would surely bring to each
The best good night.

GOOD NIGHT
[158] Gertrude E. H. Bustill (1855–1948), black educator and author.

from *Lamartine's "Toussaint Louverture"*[159]

Translated from the French by Sarah C. Bierce Scarborough

TOUSSAINT

Advance,
My children, friends, brothers in ignominy,
Whom nature seems to hate and man disowns;
In whom the milk from breasts bruisèd by chains
Has formed in bodies thin but hearts of gall;   5
You, like in all to that which makes the brute!
    Reptiles!
Of whom I'm venom and the head! –
The moment's come with us to sting in heel
Th' oppressor race now crushing us – Come then!   10
They are advancing, and in proud disdain
Are 'bout to set their white feet on our turf;
The day of judgment rises 'twixt us two!
Hoard up all ills they've bro't on you:
The scorn and hate, the shame and injury,   15
The torture, sweat, hunger and nakedness;
The marks of lash and rod upon your skin,
The tainted food, vile refuse of the flocks;
Your naked children suckling at dry breasts,
Your maidens from their mothers, husbands, torn   20
As tiger tears her darlings from her breast
To gratify its brutal appetite;
Your limbs, devour'd by insects vile, unclean,
In prison rotting on infectious chaff;
Your unions base, 'thout offspring and 'thout wife,   25
And e'en the earth refus'd unto your bones! –
All this in order that the black, proscribed
And solitary ev'rywhere, might be
'Thout brother 'neath the sun, 'thout God on earth.
Recall, I say, all names they've branded us,   30
All epithets of baseness, scorn, disgust;
Count o'er and tell them, and in memory,
In these – the whites' insults – let us take pride!
It is the bloody goad thrust in its skin
Which makes the bull against the driver kick;   35

FROM LAMARTINE'S "TOUSSAINT LOUVERTURE"

[159] Scarborough's note: "This extract is Toussaint Louverture's address to his army on the mountain heights of Hayti, where they are awaiting the approach of the French army. Time: – The treacherous invasion of Hayti by the French expedition commanded by General Leclerc, under the Consulate of Bonaparte, in December, 1881." Although she does not seem to have published anything else, Scarborough's translation of Lamartine suggests she was an accomplished poet as well as linguist. Alphonse de Lamartine (1790–1869), French poet and politician. An idealist and a democrat, Lamartine retired from politics after losing the election of the French presidency to Louis Napoleon Bonaparte, later Napoleon III. See Chapman's translation of Hugo's "Souvenir of the Night of the Fourth of December."

At last he turns his dull and stupid head
And gores his tyrant's body with his horn.

You have seen cannon-dust made, pounded fine
With the saltpetre and the charcoal black –
Together on a hollow stone they're kneaded;   40
We load, ram down and fire! a shot – earth reels!
With worthless rubbish of the earth, and fire,
We have God's thunderbolt with which to kill!
Well then! as powder's made, so ram your hearts;
You're the saltpetre, charcoal – thunderbolt!   45
And I – I'll be the fire, the whites the mark.
You wretched refuse both of earth and heaven,
You, race aveng'd at last, show, blazing forth,
With what explosive pow'r has time charged you.

They're there! – quite near! – your coward oppressors!   50
The cursed hunters of the poor black game!
Toward hidden snare my hand has laid for them,
With dull'd steps they ascend, thinking surprise.
But tho' they speak so low, my ear is keen,
And from the sea's edge hears their steps mount up.   55
Hush! – Now their horses drink from the cascades,
In strong ambushes they their troops divide,
And one by one ascend our rugged stairs. –

'Fore long, by thousands they'll go down again!

How long to place this rock upon the peak?   60
To roll it down, how long? – a minute's all!
Are you afraid of them – the whites? – Afraid!
And why? I also was afraid. – But hear:
When I was fleeing with the fugitives,
No refuge was obscure enough for me,   65
So, one night, that I might take sleep, I sought
That field where death places the white near black –
The cemetery, far from village huts,
Where trembling moonbeams glided 'neath the leaves;
There 'neath the cedar branches' outstretch'd arms,   70
My hammock scarce had been suspended safe
Than 'peared a tiger huge, whetting his teeth,
Wand'ring from grave to grave scenting his prey.
Op'ning the dead's low bed with his sharp claws,
Two human corpses were disclosed to view –   75
One that of master, the other of a slave.
My ear heard him feasting upon the two;
Then, when he'd finished his dismal repast,
Licking his lips, he left with lengthen'd strides.

Colder than marble, trembling more than leaf,   80
When day dawned I descended from the tree,
Wishing to cover 'gain with holy earth
Our brother's bones exhumed beneath my eyes.
Desires and efforts vain! the tiger'd left
Those hideous skeletons with frames complete,   85
And, gnawing those two bodies from head to toe,
Their skin removing had made both alike.
O'ercoming horror, said I to myself:
"Let's see where God the limit puts 'twixt them;
By what nerve-bundles, organs separate,   90
Did nature make them like and different;
Whence comes the diff'rence great between their lot –
Why does the one obey, other command."
Into that human mystery I plunged;
From sole of foot to fingers of the hand,   95
Each membrane by itself in vain compared;
Like openings pierced the walls of either skull –
Same bones, same senses, equal all – alike!
Said I: "The tiger made of them same feast,
And with the same contempt, worms of the tomb   100
And of decay made of them, too, their food!
Where, then, the diff'rence 'twixt the two? – *In fear* –
The one more cowardly is the inferior!"
Cowards! shall it be we? Will you still fear
The one whom worms dissect, jacka[l]s devour? –   105
Then put out your two hands, and, like them, crawl.
Both beasts and worms have more manhood than you!
But if God made your fibres of their heart
Obtain to-day the freeman's paradise!
The weapon's in your hands, your dest'ny shape!   110

from *Overland Monthly* (1889)

THE PATH TO THE SEA
by Mary Leland Adams

Across the russet pastures to the sea
Our pathway led. In buoyant sunlit air
The blue waves tossed, roughed by the north wind's glee,
And leaped in foam where the black reef lay bare.

From wind-swept pasture-ridges, rugged, high,   5
We turned aside, and kept the easier track
Around a ledge, pale brown with grasses dry,
And gray with lichens on its rocky back:

When lo! the grass was green – the ground was wet
With springs that trickled from the cloven ledge;   10
The fragrant meadow orchid there had set
Its snowy spikes among the rustling sedge.

Beyond, the pathway threaded out and in
Through a young spreading growth of fir and spruce,
Wherein the wind sang softly, and wherein   15
The sweet sun-extracts from the resinous juice

Filled all the air. The treetops pricked the blue;
On either side the branches shut us in.
Where was the sea? The bird that upward flew
Was not the white-winged gull, which o'er the din   20

Of the loud breakers wheeled and flashed, but brown
And small; his hurried gay cadenza, flung
In a glad rush from boughs above us, down,
Was of green fields and sun-warmed valleys sung, –

Of his shy partner, and his meadow-nest –   25
Not of the broad horizon of the sea, –
Small vistas, – little pleasures, – evening rest, –
Not of immensity – eternity.

from *Harper's Bazar* (1889)

THE CHILD THAT GAVE TROUBLE
by Anonymous

A tease for a kiss, for a story, a song;
    You must make her a doll, you must blow her a bubble;
She was under your heels almost all the day long;
She was climbing and falling, and bumping and bawling,
    And crying and calling – the child that gave trouble.   5

She was sliding down-stairs with a shout and a shock;
    Flying all ways at once till you thought you saw double;
She was filling the vase, she was winding the clock;
She was slopping and slipping, and prancing and skipping,
    And dancing and tripping – the child that gave trouble.   10

If the water was running, the bath-room afloat;
    If the fence was afire, and was burning like stubble;
If the rope had been cut of the leaky old boat
That down-stream was trailing, with weeping and wailing –
    You knew without failing 'twas the child that gave trouble.   15

That was she if the croup gave a gasp in the night;
  It was hers if a forehead was bruised on the rubble;
It was hers, too, the clamor that filled you with fright;
And she talked till you maddened, and cried till you saddened,
  And laughed till you gladdened – the child that gave trouble.   20

How still is the house now! how darkling the hearth!
  Oh, what is our joy – for that breaks like a bubble?
Is there pleasure or music so sweet on the earth
As the voice that once gushed so, the face that once flushed so,
  The child that we hushed so – the child that gave trouble?   25

from *Chautauquan* (1890)

THE TOUCH OF THE FROST
by Lucy E. Tilley[160]

Summer advancing through the unwaked day
Turns slowly, knowing some strange fingers stay
Her garments trailing through the lowland corn.
"Who in this blinding press of leaves hath shorn
The strength and vigor from my swift-pulsed heart?   5
The darkness hides thee, but soon Dawn shall part
Her curtains." While she spoke the waiting earth
Was thrilled and quickened by a day's new birth,
And in the sudden light she bent her face
That this strange, numbing guest she now might trace.   10
But only in the low-cropped grass the sheen
Of filmy whitened footsteps might be seen,
And with the shadows in her deep, still eyes,
Of coming pain, she turns in startled wise
And sadly lifts an aster's drooping stem   15
And smitten corn leaves from her garment's hem.

from *Century* (1890)

A DAMASCUS GARDEN
by Margaret Preston[161]

Amid the jostling crown, she dwells apart,
  Girt by it, but not of it. To and fro
  She watches the world's commerce come and go,

THE TOUCH OF THE FROST
[160] Lucy E. Tilley (1859–90), author.

A DAMASCUS GARDEN
[161] Margaret Junkin Preston (1820–97), Northern-born pro-Confederate novelist. Damascus, capital of modern Syria, is reputedly the oldest continuously occupied city in the world and a strategically placed trading center.

With laden caravans for every mart
That craves such traffic. Hers the mystic art   5
   To keep unparched by desert winds that blow, –
   By skies that burn, and sands that scorch below,
All the lush freshness of her tropic heart.

Find but the gate of entrance: turn the key,
   And gaze within. What fountains leaping bright! –   10
   What palm-like aspirations, rich with bloom
Of lofty passion! What a mystery.
   Of pure emotion hidden in fragrant gloom!
   What a Damascus garden of delight!

from *Century* (1891)

LOVE AND THE WITCHES
by Mary E. Wilkins [Freeman][162]

It was a little, fearful maid,
   Whose mother left her all alone;
Her door with iron bolt she stayed,
   And 'gainst it rolled a lucky stone –
For many a night she'd waked with fright
   when witches by the house had flown.   5

To piping lute in still midnight,
   Who comes a-singing at the door, –
That showeth seams of golden light, –
   "Ah, open, darling, I implore"?
She could not help knowing 't was Love,
   although they'd never met before.   10

She swiftly shot the iron bar,
   And rolled the lucky stone away,
And careful set the door ajar –
   "Now enter in, Sir Love, I pray;
My mother knows it not, but I have watched
   for you this many a day."   15

With fan and roar of gloomy wings
   They gave the door a windy shove;
They perched on chairs and brooms and things;
   Like bats they beat around above –
Poor little maid, she'd let the witches in with Love.   20

LOVE AND THE WITCHES
[162]   Mary E. Wilkins Freeman (1852–1930), highly regarded regionalist fiction writer.

from *Far and Near* (1891)

SUNSET AFTER A RAINY WORK-DAY
by Ruth Huntington Sessions[163]

The skies are dark, the rain drops fast,
The dreary ranks of toil file past,
The work-room's hum sounds tired and slow,
The hand moves listless to and fro;
Even our needles seem imbued   5
With rustily rebellious mood,
And dull revolt against our will.
Like teasing sprites, to work us ill,
Envy and discontent steal in,
Whispering to us thro' the din.   10
None but ourselves, say they, must climb
Rough paths, while others have free time
For all life's joys, its beauties rare,
Its music soft, its flowers fair,
Knowing no tasks for whose hard sake   15
Tired heads must throb and curved spines ache:
We hail the whistle's blatant scream
That wakes us from this bitter dream,
Break off the thread, and fold away
Our work, to wait another day,   20
Plod homeward thro' the darkening street,
With chilly hands and mud-soiled feet.

   ———————

The clouds seem frowning heaviest,
When lo! they open in the West;
A faint pink touches smoke and mist,   25
One spire, its crowning cross atwist
With golden rays, points upward to
A vapor-edged, rare glimpse of blue,
And thro' a narrow, brick-framed space
Smiles suddenly the sun's dear face.   30
Life looks so liveable again;
Where are the long-drawn hours of rain?
Courage and confidence draw near,
Whispering to us calm and clear,
None but ourselves, say they, may know   35
The fulness of this sunset glow,
For we alone, who drudged all day

SUNSET AFTER A RAINY WORK-DAY
[163] Ruth Huntington Sessions (b. 1859), novelist and
memoirist.

'Twixt streets of mud and skies of gray,
Can read the symbol fair aright,
'At evening-time it shall be light' –   40
Back to the heart comes, Heaven-sent,
That guest it cannot spare, – Content.

from *Journal of American Folk-Lore* (1891)

THE THANKSGIVINGS (IROQUOIS)
Translated by Harriet Maxwell Converse[164]

We who are here present thank the Great Spirit that we are here to
praise Him.
We thank Him that He has created men and women, and ordered that
these beings shall always be living to multiply the earth.
We thank Him for making the earth and giving these beings its
products to live on.
We thank Him for the water that comes out of the earth and runs for
our lands.
We thank Him for all the animals on the earth.   5
We thank Him for certain timbers that grow and have fluids coming
from them for us all.[165]
We thank Him for the branches of the trees that grow shadows for
our shelter.
We thank Him for the beings that come from the west, the thunder
and lightning that water the earth
We thank Him for the light which we call our oldest brother, the sun
that works for our good.
We thank Him for all the fruits that grow on the trees and vines.   10
We thank Him for his goodness in making the forests, and thank all
its trees.
We thank Him for the darkness that gives us rest, and for the kind
Being of the darkness that gives us light, the moon.
We thank Him for the bright spots in the skies that give us signs,
the stars.
We give Him thanks for our supporters, who have charge of
our harvests.[166]
We give thanks that the voice of the Great Spirit can still be heard
through the words of Ga-ne-o-di-o (by his religion).[167]   15

THE THANKSGIVINGS (IROQUOIS)

[161] Harriet Maxwell Converse (1836–1903), a poet and
ethnologist. In her commentary, Converse explains that
these lyrics accompanied the "Great Feather Dance,"
which she viewed as one of the most imposing dances of
the Iroquois. Each "thanks" was followed by a moder-
ately quick dance.

[165] Maple trees, whose sap can be boiled down to make
maple syrup, a sweetener.

[166] In Iroquois mythology, the "supporters" were three
sisters who serve as spiritual guardians of the corn, the
beans, and the squash.

[167] Handsome Lake (fl. 1799), the Senecan prophet
under whose leadership the Iroquois remaining in New
York State after the American Revolution experienced a
major spiritual and cultural revival.

We thank the Great Spirit that we have the privilege of this
pleasant occasion.[168]
We give thanks for the persons who can sing the Great Spirit's music,
and hope they will be privileged to continue in his faith.
We thank the Great Spirit for all the persons who perform the
ceremonies on this occasion.

from *Atlantic Monthly* (1891)

SWEET PEAS
by Julie M. Lippmann

A crowd of butterflies (white-emblemed souls . . .
Pale Psyches[169]) leashed together by a stem.
Most fragrant-breathed, but trembling with deep doles
Lest Love come not apace to rescue them.

A NOVEMBER PRAIRIE
by Katharine T. Prescott

The sun rose up in drear and sullen state
And gazed remote upon a withered world;
One slow, cold, distant glance, one pale unfeeling gaze,
Then drew the gray clouds close, and veiled his face from view
From east to west the tall bleached grass stretched out   5
A wide and level monotone of gray.
No sign of life was there, nor tree, nor living thing;
A frozen earth spread 'neath an ashen sky,
And all between was silence and the cold.

The day draws on, the cold still fiercer grows,   10
Upon the gray a darker gray appears;
A writhing, seething mass of angry clouds
Sweeps on with fearful force and snowy breath;
The ghostly grass bows down with one great moan of pain,
And all the shuddering air is filled with strife.   15

from *Arena* (1892)

A PRAYER OF THE HEART
by Julia Anna Wolcott

Thy pity, Lord, for those who lie
And watch their years go, fruitless, by,

---

[168] Converse notes that especially vigorous dancing
followed this verse.

SWEET PEAS
[169] In Greek mythology, Psyche, the personification of
the soul, was a lovely maiden usually represented with
butterfly wings emblematic of immortality.

With folded hands and weary eye;
    Yet know not why!

Who long, with spirit valiant still,   5
To work with earnest hand and will;
Whose souls for action strive and thrill –
    Yet must be still!

Who smell in dreams the clover sweet,
And crush the wild fern 'neath the feet,   10
And seek each well-loved haunt and seat, –
    Each old retreat;

And mark again the birds' quick flight,
The river glancing in the light,
The blue hills melting from the sight,   15
    The starry night, –

The fields aglow with sun and bloom,
The cloudless sky, the leafy gloom;
Then wake to low and darkened room, –
    Their world! – a tomb!   20

Dear Lord, forgive! if as they lie,
And sadly watch their lives drift by,
Pain-torn, in anguish sore, they cry
    I would know why!

from *Overland Monthly* (1892)

IN A VALLEY OF PEACE
by Ella Higginson[170]

This long green valley sloping to the sun,
    With dimpling, silver waters loitering through;
    The sky that bends above me, mild and blue;
The wide, still wheat-fields, yellowing one by one,
And all the peaceful sounds when day is done –   5
    I cannot bear their calm monotony!
    Great God! I want the thunder of the sea!
I want to feel the wild red lightnings run
Around, about me; hear the bellowing surf,
    And breathe the tempest's sibilant, sobbing breath;   10
    To face the elements, defying death,

IN A VALLEY OF PEACE
[170]   Ella Higginson (1862–1940), poet laureate of Washington State.

And fling myself prone on the spray-beat turf,
    And hear the strong waves trampling wind and rain,
    Like herds of beasts upon a mighty plain.

POINT LOBOS
by Virna Woods[171]

Above the sea the crags rose wild and gray;
    And in their chasms dashed the foaming tide;
    Before us stretched the waters dark and wide;
And on the breakers dim and heavy lay
The deepening mists; the headlands stretched away   5
    Steep and precipitous, on either side;
    Shrill in the windy roar a sea-gull cried,
And dipped his snowy pinions in the spray.

The slender column of Cathedral Spire
    Pierced the dark skies; back from the shore the breeze   10
    Stirred the light mosses hanging from the trees;
The waters foamed and billowed, mounting higher
    On the great rocky walls and in the caves
    Hollowed by thundering footsteps of the waves.

from *Century* (1892)

COMATAS
by Annie Fields

And he shall sing how, once upon a time, the great chest prisoned the living
goatherd by his lord's infatuate and evil will, and how the blunt-faced bees,
as they came up from the meadow to the fragrant cedar-chest, fed him with
food of tender flowers because the Muse still dropped sweet nectar on his lips.
                                          – Theocritus[172]

        Lying in thy cedarn chest,
        Didst thou think thy singing done,
        Comatas? And thyself unblest,
        Prisoned there from sun to sun?

        Through the fields thy blunt-faced bees   5
        Sought thy flowers far and away,
        And gathered honey from thy trees –
        Thou a prisoner night and day.

POINT LOBOS
[171] Virna Woods (1864–1903), dramatist and poet.
Point Lobos is located on the northern California seacoast.

COMATAS
[172] Theocritus (*c.* 270 BCE), Hellenistic poet, believed
to be the originator of the pastoral form.

Heavy with their honeyed store,
Seeking west and seeking east   10
Thee whose absence they deplore,
Late they found and brought their feast.

Grief no more shall still thy song,
Loss, privations, fortunes dire!
Servants of air about thee throng,   15
And touch thy singing lips with fire.

Love, art thou discomforted
In thy narrow lot to lie?
See how divinely thou art fed
By the creatures of the sky!   20

from *Harper's New Monthly Magazine* (1893)

THE CADET
by Rose Hawthorne Lathrop[173]

Oh, I'm a fellow, my good sir,
Who never knew a breath of fear;
My back is straight as any spear;
My shoulders stretch a good three span.
To say I'm right you'll not demur.   5
Hurrah! I'm an American!

I wear the uniform, my friend,
That strikes me as the best on earth.
Though wildly gay, my fiercest mirth
Ne'er hinted at the drummer's ban.   10
Let revel die ere I offend
The flag! I'm an American!

To run and leap, to ride and spar,
To swim, make love, and catch a sword
Flung round my head like flaming cord,   15
I'm usually first, my man.
Keen-eyed, steel-pulsed, and muscular:
Ha! ha! I'm an American!

Six feet of spring and joy and pride;
Six feet for victory or a shell;   20

THE CADET
[173]   Rose Hawthorne Lathrop (Mother Alphonsa) (1851–1926), author, religious superior, and daughter of Nathaniel Hawthorne. This poem, written at the beginning of the 1890s, reflects the jingoism that accompanied the growth of American imperialism in the post-bellum period, leading ultimately to the annexation of the Hawaiian Islands and to the Spanish-American War in 1898.

A voice to mate with wine, or yell
Orders from Beersheba to Dan;[174]
Six feet with nothing base to hide,
Thank God! I'm American!

You know I'm not a vain young blade;   25
The best I say is not enough
When speaking of such human stuff,
That in no age turned face and ran.
I did not make it, when all's said,
For I was born an American!   30

from *Overland Monthly* (1893)

RHODODENDRON CALIFORNICUM
by Lillian H. Shuey[175]

In Mendocino,[176] where tall redwoods grow,
    The Rhododendron lifts its clusters bright,
    Soft gleams of radiance in the solemn light
Of forest aisles. In dim cathedral arches, so
Gleam out the faces our devotions know;   5
        Nor in Saint Mary's face more beauties speak,
        Or live in softness on her waxen cheek,
Than in these pink-hued clusters sweetly glow.

When first I saw this beauteous pink-browed saint,
    Sweet to my soul came its beatitude;   10
    My heart its gracious mission understood;
And while I breathed the forest incense faint,
I laid before the shrine my heart's complaint,
        And bowed for blessing in the silent wood.

from *Independent* (1895)

THE SEA-BIRDS
by Irene Putnam

An hour in the calm the boat lay rocking
    On the mild and awful Pacific sea,
And the beautiful birds of the deep came flocking;
    They cried in their salt, wild tones to me.

---

[171] Beersheba was a town located in the southernmost area of ancient Palestine; Dan was located in the northernmost region. Hence, "from Beersheba to Dan" was used to indicate the whole of ancient Palestine.

RHODODENDRON CALIFORNICUM
[175] Lillian H. Shuey (1853–1921), author of western romances and poetry.
[176] Area in northern California. Today there is a national state forest located in Mendocino.

They were billed with amber, and silver-breasted,   5
    With long gray wings with a band of snow;
Like fans snow-white, as their red feet rested
    Fleet on the slippery swell below.

They circled high in the calm, veiled heaven,
    They glided low to the solemn sea,   10
They swung in the long wave's hollow haven,
    And called with their salt, hoarse tones to me.

And I flung white bread on the glassy waters,
    My heart grew laughing for love and pride
That the infinite Ocean's sons and daughters   15
    Out of my palm could be gratified.

I felt the approval of sky soft-laden,
    Of lapping wave and of lonely isle, –
I felt the approval of fond mermaiden,
    The sun's and the moon's and the ocean's smile.   20

They fled away and forgot their lover, –
    Beautiful wave like, wind-like things!
But I will remember, the wide world over,
    Their silvery breasts and their swirl-bent wings.

And my heart is glad, when the blue rim dances   25
    On and under the sun flame-red,
Or the great mild sea in the morning glances,
    I have shared with the wild sea-children bread!

from *Century* (1895)

SPRING SONG
by Elizabeth C. Cardozo[177]

In the recurrent pauses of the night
    Not all unmeet is pain,
But how shall I endure it when the light
    Of morning comes again?

When the black clouds of winter hedge me round   5
    Grief is no alien thing.
But how shall I support the sight and sound
    And ardor of the spring?

SPRING SONG
[177]   Elizabeth Clayton Cardozo (b. 1867), poet.

from *Symposium* (1896)

LACE
by Maud Louise Fuller

Warm frost of fine-spun thread,
Whereon my rose so red
Doth rest its blushing head!

The hands that made thee so
Are dust, and none may know   5
Who wrought thee, long ago.

But at the final Day,
Some angel-voice may say,
"Ye singers great, make way."

And through that throng shall go   10
The peasant poor and low
Who wove this song in snow!

from *Chap-Book* (1896)

"OF THE EARTH"
by Alice Katherine Fallows[178]

When celestial tasks grow dull, perfection dreary,
Do the angels ever feel heaven-weary?
When a cherub or a seraph, less or more,
Seems as futile as a sand-grain on the shore?

EVOLUTION
by Dorothea Lummis Moore

Chaos and Night and Silence: these.
   Then moving masses in a mystery.
Sudden a globule leaps to space and flees
   To light and law and history.

CREATION
by Eleanor B. Caldwell

Aeons of time, infinite space,
Blackness and chaos interlace.
Sudden, a streak of light shot through –
On a pin-head of earth, a red cock crew.

"OF THE EARTH"
[178] Alice Katherine Fallows (1872–1932), poet, editor.

ILLUSION
by Ella Wheeler Wilcox[179]

God and I in space alone,
  And nobody else in view.
And "Where are the people, O Lord," I said,
"The earth below and the sky o'erhead
  And the dead whom once I knew?"   5

"That was a dream," God smiled and said:
  "A dream that seemed to be true.
There were no people living or dead,
There was no earth and no sky o'erhead –
  There was only Myself and you."   10

"Why do I feel no fear," I asked,
  Meeting YOU here this way?
"For I have sinned, I know full well;
And is there heaven, and is there hell,
  And is this the Judgment Day?"   15

"Nay! those were but dreams," the great God said;
  "Dreams that have ceased to be.
There are no such things as fear, or sin;
There is no you – you never have been –
  There is nothing at all but me!"   20

AN IMPRESSIONIST PICTURE
by Ethel Balton

I. "Golden Hair in Shadow"

A group of cotton clouds, a brilliant pinkish sea,
A mass of golden hair beneath a purple tree,
And far across the emerald land
There lies a wealth of orange sand.

She of the yellow hair throws down her book at last,   5
She views the gorgeous scene and is amazed, aghast.
"This cannot be the world," she said;
"I am afraid that I am dead."

"Oh, stay," the artist said; "sweet maiden, do not move."
She cried: "I will not stay for money or for love.   10
"It is too strange, and you would find
"That soon I would be color-blind."

ILLUSION
[179] Ella Wheeler Wilcox (1850–1919), phenomenally
popular poet, best known for *Poems of Passion* (1883).

The maiden rose to go. In vain the artist plead;
She left the purple tree, and maiden-like she fled.
The artist wept; then thought awhile;   15
Then changed the title with a smile.

II. "After the Husking"

A group of cotton clouds, a brilliant pinkish sea,
A mass of yellow corn-shucks beneath a purple tree,
And far across the emerald land
There lies a wealth of orange sand.   20

from *Frank Leslie's Popular Monthly* (1896)

TWO PRAYERS
by Ella Higginson

Lord, I have often prayed
    One deep wrong to forget;
And Thou hast granted me that prayer,
    And I should thank Thee, yet —

To-night, O God, I kneel,   5
    Of conscience-torment free,
And with a clearer knowledge make
    A later, stronger plea:

Let me *remember*, God,
    Though that drive peace from me!   10
To rise above myself, I need
    The scourge of memory.

from *Philistine* (1896)

BEHOLD THE LILIES
by Sarah Norcliffe Cleghorn[180]

Drowsy weather, eleven o'clock;
    Tall white daisies blow in the sun,
And dust blew lightly on Martha's[181] frock;
    (Morning Service must have begun).

BEHOLD THE LILIES
[180] Sarah Norcliffe Cleghorn (1876–1959), socialist poet and memoirist.
[181] In the Bible, Martha and Mary are the sisters of Lazarus, a friend of Jesus, briefly mentioned in Luke 10:40; their story was only elaborated in the Middle Ages when they came to symbolize the active life (of "toil") and the contemplative life (of "prayer"), respectively.

> The anthem sounded along the street;   5
>   Winds breathed up from the fresh-cut hay.
> She lingered a little: the fields are sweet,
>   They toil not, neither do they pray.[182]

from *Time and the Hour* (1896)

THE SINNER
by Anne Throop

After the storm the lyre-strung forest sullen booms, till, in the
    rain-drenched glooms,
Its gold strings – for the Wind to better find, and so perchance more
    sweetly strike them – one by one
Light from the Sun.

And as he strikes, he soon doth laughing hear – whom his late storm
    offended – the capricious Sea
Sing to his lyre's new melody.   5
If upon that he make the quest with speed, she – gentle captured –
    will accede
To him forgiveness, and will squander on him
Her skimming, soft wave-kisses,
Quickly won.

from *Quartier Latin* (1897)

from *Songs of the Forest Beautiful*,
from the French of Catulle Mendès[183]
translated by Mary Kent Davey

THE LITTLE DEAD LEAF

They run, run, run, The little dead leaves, And they
disappear, And others follow them, And no one knows
whence they come, Nor whither they go . . . They
run, run, run, The little dead leaves.

This one that runs, runs, runs, Poor little dead leaf,
Did it fall from an oak, Did it fall from a birch, Or from
the willow that leans o'er the brook? Did it fall from an
aspen, This one that runs, runs, runs, Poor little dead
leaf?

---

[182]   Matthew 6:26.
FROM *QUARTIER LATIN* (1897) ·
[183]   Catulle Mendès (1841–1909), French poet and critic
of the Parnassian school, identified with the doctrine of

"art for art's sake," a late nineteenth-century reaction to
the looseness of romanticism.

Because they are all withered, All, all, all, The little
dead leaves, Sad withered and torn, We know them no
longer; They do not resemble the branches of spring-
time! Now they are all alike, Because they are all
withered, All, all, all, The little dead leaves.

They run, run, run, The little dead leaves, But lo!
there is one which resembles no other; It is sadder, more
withered, more torn, And I know it at once; It is my
heart that in autumn fell, From the tree of my love
. . . They run, run, run, The little dead leaves.

from *Century* (1897)

ENNUI
by Grace Denio Litchfield[184]

A wide, bare field 'neath blinding skies,
Where no tree grows, no shadow lies,
Where no wind stirs, where no bee flies.

A roadway, even, blank, and white,
That swerves not left, that swerves not right,   5
That stretches, changeless, out of sight.

Footprints midway adown its dust;
Two lagging, leaden feet, that just
Trail on and on, because they must.

from *Chap-Book* (1897)

AN ELECTRIC-LIGHT POLE[185]
by Ann Devoore

O Boughless tree, that bars the sky,
     All naked, grim, and stark,
Your blossoms, in a hundred homes,
     Bloom out and light the dark!

ENNUI
[184]   Grace Denio Litchfield (1849–1944), author, poet.

AN ELECTRIC-LIGHT POLE
[185]   Carbon-arc street lamps were first produced by the
American scientist Charles F. Brush in Cleveland, Ohio,
in 1879 and soon spread to other cities.

A VISION
by Ellen Glasgow[186]

I died and passed from earth and went my way;
    I trod the starry gulf from sphere to sphere;
I felt the breath of God upon my brow
        As I drew near.

I paused above Infinity's abyss,   5
    Scanning the upward path my spirit trod;
A million silver planets spun between
        Myself and God.

Yet, scarlet on the ether's inky wave
    The crooked orbit of the earth was cast,   10
Dark silhouettes against that lurid light,
    I saw its creatures pass.

I saw the human shadows stumble on,
    Rising in anguish, passing in a breath,
Blind atoms, treading their predestined doom   15
        From birth to death.

I saw the smiling mask that Nature wears
    Blurred by the blasphemy of human wills;
I saw man's bloody footprint on the shore,
        His hand upon the hills.   20

I heard his laughter as he passed along;
    I heard the mortal boast immortal breath;
I saw the earth in tragic irony
        Plunge to its death.

Then low into Jehovah's listening ear   25
    I spoke: "O God of Gods, – the life you gave
Is but a lying travesty, whose lie
        Ends with the grave.

"Look on the lives that you have made and marred,
    Filing black phantoms in a bloody train;   30
The stronger finds your heaven; the weaker finds
        An endless pain.

"O God, within the hollows of whose hand
    A million worlds are tossed to win or lose,

A VISION
[186]   Ellen Glasgow (1873–1945), best-selling Southern
novelist, still well regarded today.

You choose the stronger for salvation, – but   35
        The damned I choose.

"I take my stand upon the weaker side,
    I grasp the sinner's hand, I share his fate;
The Hell of those who failed I choose, or those
        Who win too late."   40

God smiled; across the inky ether way
    A flash that lighted worlds supernal fell;
"It is the damned you look upon," God said;
        "The earth is Hell."

from *Time and the Hour* (1897)

THE SHADOW-SONG OF THE HYPER-BOREAN[187]
by Anne Throop

Come with me into the Northland.
That is my Mother, the Witch, in the Fire in the Sky.
She beckons to me, –
She is the Quickener of the Earth.
What is that sound? – It is the *tss* of the frost under my feet.   5
Ho, – for the cold! – the glint, glint of the snow!
But the cold is my breath of life –
It is the new breath of all life –
It is the breath of the Sky-Fire –
That is why my Mother is the Witch, – is the Quickener of Life!   10

The breath of my Mother sweeps over the Earth.
She keeps the ships to their courses,
And we of the land find our way against her blowing.
But the life of her blowing is in me, and warms me,
And in its whispering, – to her children, listening, – are the secrets of her
    Land.   15
My Mother is the Witch, the Witch of the Fire of the Sky!

The cold seas, with a great roar, rush and lap about her feet
And she draws another great breath.
– Ah! – That is the breath of her life,
And she sends it forth again –   20
My Mother is the Witch, the Witch of the Fire of the Sky!

THE SHADOW-SONG OF THE HYPER-BOREAN
[187] According to Greek mythology, the Hyperboreans were a people dwelling in perfect bliss in the far north. They lived above the North Wind in perpetual sunshine. Throop attributes a gynocentric religion and world view to them in this poem.

Her fingers are very beautiful,
She spreads them along the sky.
They are transparent, – and colors shine through them.
She is the Witch, is the Witch of the Fire of the Sky!   25

Her hair is very beautiful.
She spreads it out with her thin fingers over the sky,
And it blows with the life-wind above her head.
White it is – the colors play upon it like fire –
My Mother is the Witch, the Witch of the Sky-Fire!   30

Yellow are the borders of the garments that are over her arms, – like light
    and like the colors of the flames –
And they fly in beautiful folds; –
Like fire are the colors that play about my Mother, – my Mother is white –
    white!
Who shall say if it be hot or cold, – that fire that plays about my Mother?
See – her hair stirs in it like a live thing   35
And plays about in the sky! –
She is the Witch, the Witch of the Fire of the Sky!

Listen, – do you hear the "crackle, crackle"?
That is her children clapping their hands as they sing and dance together in
    the Land of my Mother.
There she keeps them till they must come here to be my brothers and
    sisters.   40
Stay, Little Children, till you must come into this Land!
The birds of the North have small wings that they shall not fly and tell its
    secrets.
I have forgotten the land of my mother;
I have wandered far from it.
Oh – the little birds of the North have small wings that they shall not fly
    and tell its secrets!   45
I have come away from the land of my mother,
But now I know her glory –
She is the Witch, the Witch of the Sky-Colors!

Hark – to the great beasts that plunge in the cold seas!
They are her children likewise.   50
Bellowing with a strange gladness
They climb upon the ice-floes
And their coats shine glossy in the hollow gloom.

The Shadow is even and unending till the Great Light comes, –
He shines upon my Mother   55
And her joy is the Fire of the emptied Dark.
Then it is in the Dark that the Little Children of the Fire sing and clap
    their hands, that the Great Light may not forget them and may soon return.

The Sea that is unfathomable is blue, blue, – when he shines upon it, – and
   the beasts bring their young into his light with strange croonings.
The ice shines with the secret colors of my Mother's Sky – her secret
   message it has learned from my Mother in the Dark,
And the snow remembers the light for the Time of the Shadow.   60
Then in the light I know again of the Land of my Mother – but the Great
   Light is winged and can fly to her, but I cannot find the way over the
   reaches of the snow.
My Mother and her children love the Great Light, as the children of my
   Mother are lonely away from her Land.

But in the unending Shadow all is clear;
The snow stretches out in the Dark
And the edges of the ice-floes are smooth in the black water, –   65
The lighted edges of the waves move up and down;
– They are never still, – restless as the children of my Mother beyond her
   Land, –
And the coats of the glossy beasts shine as they plunge and curve about.

They are warm, the great creatures, – warm through their bodies, even in
   the icy water, –
It is the breath of my mother that warms them through their lithe, glad
   bodies!   70
Hark! – they bellow again in their ununderstood gladness!
– That was the gladness I knew in the Land of my Mother, – the Land of
   the Fire. –

> Oh, – she is my Mother, the Witch
>   Of the Fire of the Sky!
> I am the Child of the Witch, –   75
>   Of the Fire of the Sky!

from *Midland Monthly* (1897)

A WINTRY NIGHT
by Maude Morrison Huey

No moon, no stars, only the threatening gray;
   And night down-swooping o'er the ice-capped ledge,
As yon dark eagle swoops to meet the sea.
   Cold snow-drifts heaped along the leafless hedge,
Where birdless nests sway weirdly to and fro.   5
   Wild north winds howling o'er the frozen heath,
Like hungry wolves, sharp-fanged and ravenous,
   Haunting the night with greedy, famished breath.

My cottage window throws a feeble light
    Into the snow-flecked darkness. Dismal sounds   10
Wail from the naked orchard trees outside.
    Each empty gloom-encurtained room resounds
With ghost-like whisperings. Strange fingers tap
    My broken lattice-slats, – a frozen vine
That angry winds have loosed; a straggling stem,   15
    Ice-burdened, that the trellis bars entwine.

from *Scribner's Magazine* (1897)

WITH A BIT OF GORSE FROM CARNAC
by Lilla Cabot Perry[188]

This bit of yellow gorse I plucked for thee
By a huge Menhir, where, on Carnac's shores
The long waves murmur dirges evermore
For men dead ere the birth of history.
Here once they lived whom Time's immensity   5
Had quite o'erwhelmed, and blotted out their page
From the world's book! On them may learned sage
Descant, and poet dream here by the sea!
But none may know what were their thoughts, their lives,
None e'er may know! None living or unborn! –   10
Were these their tombs built where the strong sea strives
In vain to hold the warm elusive sands?
Were these hard by their altars where forlorn
They stretched to Heaven imploring empty hands?

from *Chap-Book* (1898)

GODDESS OF LIBERTY,[189] ANSWER
By Ella Wheeler Wilcox

Goddess of Liberty, listen! listen, I say, and look
To the sounds and sights of sorrow this side of Sandy Hook![190]
Your eye is searching the distance, you are holding your torch too high
To see the slaves who are fettered, though close at your feet they lie.
And the cry of the suffering stranger has reached your ear and your breast,   5

WITH A BIT OF GORSE FROM CARNAC
[188] Lilla Cabot Perry (1848–1933), impressionist painter and poet. Gorse is a spiny evergreen shrub with yellow flowers common through Europe. Carnac is a neolithic site in Brittany, France, noted for its megalithic monuments, particularly the menhirs or rough upright stones.

GODDESS OF LIBERTY, ANSWER
[189] The Statue of Liberty. This poem appears to be a response to Lazarus's "The New Colossus."
[190] Sandy Hook, a spit of land on the New Jersey coast, opposite the south end of Manhattan. It marked the boundary beyond which lay the open ocean and Europe, source of the immigrant populations to whom Lazarus's poem is addressed.

But you do not heed the wail that comes from the haunts of your own
  oppressed.

Goddess of Liberty, follow, follow me where I lead;
Come down into sweat-shops and look on the work of greed!
Look on the faces of children, old before they were born!
Look on the haggard women, of all sex graces shorn!   10
Look on the men – God, help us! if this is what it means
To be men in the land of freedom and live like mere machines!

Goddess of Liberty, answer! how can the slaves of Spain
Find freedom under your banner, while your own still wear the chain?
Loud is the screech of your eagle and boastful the voice of your drums,   15
But they do not silence the wail of despair that rises out of your slums.
What will you do with your conquests, and how shall your hosts be fed,
While your streets are filled with desperate throngs, crying for work or
  bread?

from *Journal of American Folk-Lore* (1898)

"THE MOTHER'S VOW TO THE THUNDER GODS"
by Anonymous, translated by Alice Fletcher[191]

> Flying, flying, sweeping, swirling,
> They return, the Thunder gods.
>   To me they come, to me their own.
>   Me they behold, who am their own!
>   On wings they come, –   5
> Flying, flying, sweeping, swirling,
> They return, the Thunder gods.

from *Poet-Lore* (1898)

LONGING
by Florence Earle Coates[192]

> The lilacs blossom at the door,
>   The early rose
> Whispers a promise to her buds,
>   And they unclose.

"THE MOTHER'S VOW TO THE THUNDER GODS"
[191] Alice Cunningham Fletcher (1838–1923), American
ethnologist. According to Fletcher's commentary, the
woman to whom this song belongs had vowed her first-
born child to the Thunder after the god spoke to her in

a vision. When she was unable to fulfill her promise the
Thunder took her child anyway. Fletcher does not identify the woman's tribe, nor does she supply her name.
LONGING
[192] Florence Earle Coates (1850–1927), poet.

There is a perfume everywhere,   5
    A breath of song,
A sense of some divine return
    For waiting long.

Who knows but some imprisoned joy
    From bondage breaks: 10
Some exiled and enchanted hope
    From dreams awakes?

Who knows but you are coming back
    To comfort me
For all the languor and the pain,   15
    Persephone?[193]

O come! For one brief spring return,
    Love's tryst to keep;
Then let me share the Stygian[194] fruit,
    The wintry sleep!   20

from *Atlantic Monthly* (1898)

SUMMER DIED LAST NIGHT
by Maude Caldwell Perry[195]

Summer died last night,
Lady of Delight, –
Summer died last night;
    Look for her no more.

In the early gray   5
Of this golden day,
In the early gray
    By the mirrored shore

I saw leaves of red, –
So I knew her dead, –   10
I saw leaves of red
    Wreathed upon her door.

---

[193] In Greek mythology, the daughter of Demeter, goddess of the earth. She was abducted by Hades, the Lord of the Greek Underworld, and – as a consequence of eating some pomegranate seeds while his prisoner – spends an equivalent amount of time each year as his Queen. During this period, Demeter (the earth) goes into mourning, causing winter.

[194] *Stygian* from the river Styx. The Styx marks the boundary of the Greek underworld. Once having crossed it, the dead can never return to the land of the living.
SUMMER DIED LAST NIGHT
[195] Maude Caldwell Perry (1873–1963), poet.

from *Century* (1899)

"When Loud My Lilac-Bush with Bees"
by Muriel Campbell Dyar

O Horace,[196] through all days 't is sweet
To taste from thy wide Sabine jar
The mellowed breath of glorious wine;
Whether my old Soracte[197] far
Gleams whitely with its gathered snows,   5
Whether the flails of summer beat
The hot earth, or the purple grapes,
At vintage, yield to rhythmic feet.
Yet most I love it that fair time
When loud my lilac-bush with bees,   10
And, dreaming, I hear leagues away
A sea 'twixt shining Cyclades.[198]

"When Loud My Lilac-Bush with Bees"
[196] Quintus Horatius Flaccus (65–8 BCE), Roman poet
and satirist. His patron, Maecenas, gave him the famous
Sabine farm near Tivoli, a pleasure resort near Rome.
He celebrated a rural life characterized by good food,
good wine, and good conversation.

[197] Isolated mountain in Latium in central Italy, celebrated in the poetry of Virgil and Horace.
[198] An island group that is part of the Greek archipelago in the Aegean sea. The name was originally used to indicate those islands that formed a rough circle around Delos, birthplace of Apollo and Artemis.

List of Serials

(Information in the following list is based principally on the *Union List of Periodicals* and the Library of Congress computer catalog, supplemented by the index for the American Periodical Series, 1800–1900, and Frederick Winthrop Faxon's *"Ephemeral Bibelots:" A Bibliography of the Modern Chap-Books and their Imitators*. All information on women editors comes from the appendix to Patricia Okker's *Our Sister Editors: Sarah J. Hale and the Tradition of Nineteenth-Century American Women Editors*.)

A. M. E. Church Review, 1884–present, Nashville, Tennessee, published by the African Methodist Episcopal Church, religion, literature. Alice Ruth Moore Dunbar-Nelson among associate editors.

Arena, 1889–1910, Boston, Massachusetts, New York City, New York, Trenton, New Jersey, social and political reform. Helen Hamilton Gardener, associate editor and briefly co-editor. Owner: Mrs Gideon F. T. Reed.

Atlantic Monthly, 1857–present, Boston, Massachusetts, general interest, premier literary journal of the Northeast.

Beadle's Monthly: A Magazine for To-Day, 1866–7, New York City, New York, literature, general knowledge.

Boston Gazette, 1719–1816, Boston, Massachusetts, semi-weekly, commercial and political news.

Boston Pilot, Pilot, 1858–present, Boston, Massachusetts, published by the Archdiocese of Boston, religious news.

Californian and Overland Monthly, 1880–2, San Francisco, California, general knowledge, literature with western slant. Managing editor: Milicent Washburn Shinn.

Capital, Sunday Capital, 1870–90, Washington, D.C., weekly newspaper published and edited by Donn Piatt between 1871 and 1879, domestic and foreign political news, reviews.

Century, see *Scribner's Monthly*.

Chap-Book, 1894–8, Cambridge, Massachusetts and Chicago, Illinois, semi-monthly miscellany and review of *belles lettres*, poetry, fiction. The premier "ephemeral bibelot."

Chautauquan, 1880–1914, Jamestown, New York, official publication of the Chautauqua Institution. Ida Minerva Tarbell, member of editorial staff.

Cherokee Advocate, 1844–1906, Tahlequah, Oklahoma, "Our Rights, Our Country, Our Race," bilingual weekly in Cherokee syllabary and English, news of interest to Cherokee Nation.

Cherokee Phoenix, 1828–34, New Echota, Cherokee Nation (Georgia), weekly in Cherokee syllabary and English, news of interest to Cherokee Nation. National and international news.

Cherokee Rose Buds, A Wreath of Cherokee Rose Buds, 1854–7, Female Seminary, Park Hill, Oklahoma, Cherokee Nation, Cherokee Territory, school newspaper with some articles in the Cherokee syllabary.

Christian Parlor Magazine, 1844–55, New York City, New York, religious monthly, family magazine.

Cincinnati Israelite, Israelite, 1854–74, Cincinnati, Ohio, weekly, news and literature relevant to the Jewish population in the Midwest and South.

Colored American, 1837–42, New York City, New York, published by Robert Sears, abolition, news of interest to African Americans.

Colored American, 1865–6, Augusta, Georgia, edited by James T. Shuften, general news of interest to African Americans.

Daily Eastern Argus, 1863–1921, Portland, Maine, "Independent Democratic," domestic and foreign news.

Dial: A Magazine for Literature, Philosophy, and Religion, 1840–4, Boston, Massachusetts, monthly periodical of the transcendental movement, edited by Margaret Fuller, 1840–2.

Family Magazine or the General Abstract of Useful Knowledge, 1833–41, New York City, New York, monthly family magazine, general useful knowledge on "the wonders of the world."

Far and Near, 1890–4, New York City, New York, published under the direction of the Auxiliary Society of the Association of Working Girls, concern with women's employment. Editor: Maria Bowen Chapin. Assistant editor: Emily Malbone Morgan.

Frank Leslie's Popular Monthly, American Magazine, 1876–1904, New York City, New York, literary (fiction and poetry) and general interest. On editorial staff: Miriam Florence Squier Leslie.

Frederick Douglass's Newspaper, see *North Star*.

Galaxy, 1866–78, New York City, New York, a premier Northeast literary journal and general interest "magazine of entertaining reading."

Golden Age, 1871–5, New York City, New York, weekly newspaper.

Good Company, see *Sunday Afternoon*.

Graham's Magazine, Graham's American Monthly Magazine of Literature, Art, and Fashion, 1839–58, Philadelphia, Pennsylvania, literature and general interest to women. Editors: Edgar Allan Poe, 1841–2; Emma Catherine Embury, nominal editor. Co-editor: Ann Sophia Winterbotham Stephens.

Harper's Bazar, Harper's Bazaar, 1867–present, New York City, New York, women's fashion magazine, some literature and poetry. Editor of women's department: Ida A. Husted Harper. Editors: Mary Louise Booth, Margaret Elizabeth Munson Sangster.

Harper's New Monthly Magazine, 1850–present, New York City, New York, a leading Northeast literary periodical and magazine of general knowledge.

Harper's Weekly, 1857–1916, New York City, New York, "a journal of civilization," and weekly illustrated review.

Hearth and Home, 1868–75, New York City, New York, women's general interest newspaper, "for the farm, garden and fireside," covering domestic and cultural matters. Editor: Harriet Beecher Stowe. Associate editor, Mary Elizabeth Mapes Dodge. Assistant editor: Margaret Elizabeth Munson Sangster.

Independent, 1848–1921, New York City, New York, religious and literary weekly, Congregationalist, foreign and domestic news, abolition, progressive politics, women's rights. Literary editor: Susan Hayes Ward.

Intellectual Regale or Ladies' Tea Tray, 1814–15, Philadelphia, Pennsylvania, literary miscellany for women. Editor: Mary Clarke Carr.

Irish Nationalist, Nationalist, 186?–187?, San Francisco, California, news and literature of interest to Irish community on the West Coast.

Journal of American Folk-Lore, c. 1888–present, New York City, New York, published for the American Folk-Lore Society, articles and news.

Knickerbocker, Federal American Monthly, New York Monthly Magazine, 1833–62, New York City, New York, a premier ante-bellum literary magazine.

Ladies' Magazine, American Ladies' Magazine, 1828–36, Boston, Massachusetts, containing original tales, essays, literary and historical sketches, poetry, music, etc. Editor: Sarah J. Hale.

Ladies' Monitor, 1801–2, New York City, New York, fashion, travel, sketches, and literature.

Lady's Magazine and Musical Repository, 1801–2, New York City, New York, literary magazine and political essays, national and international news.

Ladies' Garland, 1824–8, Harper's Ferry, Virginia, domestically oriented women's literary magazine.

Ladies' Repository: A Monthly Periodical, Devoted to Literature, Art, and Religion, 1843–73, Boston, Massachusetts, a Universalist periodical. Editors: Henrietta A. Bingham, Phebe Ann Coffin Hanaford, Caroline Mehitable Fisher Sawyer. Associate editor: Sarah Carter Edgarton Mayo. Western editor: Caroline Augusta White Soule.

Ladies' Weekly Museum, see *Weekly Museum*.

The Land We Love: A Monthly Magazine devoted to Literature, Military History, and Agriculture, 1866–9, Charlotte, North Carolina, Southern apologist, articles on antebellum life, the Civil War, literature.

Liberator, 1831–65, Boston, Massachusetts, abolitionist newspaper. Editors: William L. Garrison, Maria Weston Chapman.

Lippincott's Magazine of Literature, Science, and Education, Lippincott's Monthly Magazine, and other titles, 1868–1916, Philadelphia, Pennsylvania and New York City, New York, literary monthly. Associate editor: Lucy Hamilton Jones Hooper.

Literary Voyager, or Muzzeniegun, 1826–7, Sault Ste Marie, Michigan, manuscript magazine, literature of interest to Ojibwas. Editor: Henry Rowe Schoolcraft. Susan Johnston (Ozha-guscoday-way-quay) and her daughter, Jane Johnston Schoolcraft, possibly assistant editors.

Louisville Daily Journal, 1830–68, Louisville, Kentucky, local, national, and international news. Editor: George Prentice, 1831–62.

Louisville Weekly Journal, Louisville Courier-Journal, 1831–68, Louisville, Kentucky. Domestic and foreign news.

Lowell Offering, New England Offering, 1840–5, Lowell, Massachusetts, literary magazine devoted to the work of Lowell and Lawrence textile mill operatives. Co-editors: Harriot F. Curtis, Harriet Farley, and Harriet Lees.

Massachusetts Spy, 1770–1904, Worcester, Massachusetts, general and local weekly newspaper, John Milton Earle, proprietor/editor, 1825–37. Quaker and abolitionist during his tenure.

Midland Monthly Magazine, 1894–9, Des Moines, Iowa, general interest and literary periodicals, with special emphasis on Midwestern life and authors.

Mother's Assistant and Young Lady's Friend, 1841–63, Boston, Massachusetts, religion, child-rearing and education, some literature.

National Anti-Slavery Standard, National Standard, 1840–72, n.p., organ of the American Anti-Slavery Association, a journal of reform and literature, abolition, temperance, women's rights. Editor: Lydia Marie Child, 1841–3.

National Enquirer, Pennsylvania Freeman, 1830–60?, Philadelphia, Pennsylvania, abolitionist newspaper. Editors: Benjamin Lundy and John Greenleaf Whittier.

New Century for Women, 1876, Philadelphia, Pennsylvania, women's rights newspaper for centennial exhibition. Editors: Mrs R. C. Hallowell, Louise Stockton.

New National Era and Citizen, 1870–5, Washington, D.C., news, literature of interest to African Americans. Published by Frederick Douglass and the Douglass brothers.

North American Daily, 1847–8, Mexico City, Mexico, Spanish and English weekly newspaper serving the American military colony in Mexico.

North Star, Frederick Douglass's Newspaper, 1848–60, Rochester, New York, abolition, women's rights, general news, some poetry. Owner and editor: Frederick Douglass.

Occident and American Jewish Advocate, 1843–69, Philadelphia, Pennsylvania, Jewish issues and literature.

Overland Monthly, 1868–1935, San Francisco, California, premier Western literary magazine. Editors: Ina Coolbrith, Milicent Washburn Shinn.

Pennsylvania Freeman, see *National Enquirer*.

Philistine: "a Periodical of Protest," 1895–1903, East Aurora, New York, a monthly published by the Society of the Philistines. Avant-garde literature.

Poet-Lore, 1889–1953, Philadelphia, Pennsylvania and Boston, Massachusetts, "A Magazine of Letters." Co-founders and co-editors: Helen Archibald Clarke and Charlotte Endymion Porter.

Quartier Latin, 1896–9, Paris, London, monthly illustrated magazine of the arts, catering to expatriate Americans. Published by the American Art Association of Paris.

Saturday Evening Post, 1821–, Philadelphia, Pennsylvania, literature, articles of general interest.

Scribner's Magazine, 1887–1939, New York City, New York, literary magazine.

Scribner's Monthly, Century Illustrated Magazine, 1870–81, 1881–1930, New York City, New York, founded by Josiah Holland, literature and general interest. Assistant editor: Sophia Bledsoe Herrick.

Shaker, Shaker and Shakeress, 1871–99, Shakers, New York and E. Canterbury, New Hampshire, official news and literary publication of the Shakers. Co-editor: Antoinette Doolittle.

Southern Literary Messenger, Devoted to Every Department of Literature and the Fine Arts, 1834–64, Richmond, Virginia, the premier ante-bellum Southern literary magazine. Editorial staff included L. Virginia French and Virginia Otey Minor.

Southern Workman, 1872–1939, Hampton, Virginia, published by the Hampton Normal and Agricultural Institute, literature and general knowledge, focus on the cultural contributions of African Americans and Native Americans.

Sunday Afternoon, Good Company, 1878–81, Springfield, Massachusetts, "a monthly magazine for the household."

Symposium: A Monthly Literary Magazine, 1896, Northampton, Massachusetts, monthly literary magazine.

Time and the Hour, 1896–1900, Boston, Massachusetts, *belles lettres* review.

Vindicator, Atoka Vindicator, 1872–6, Atoka, Indian Territory [New Boggy, Oklahoma], catering to the Choctaws and Chickasaws. A commercial weekly in English with some Choctaw.

Weekly Inspector, 1806–7, New York City, New York, "a vehicle of intelligence, which shall be principally devoted to the political interests of our country." Weekly promoting Federalist viewpoint, with some literature, foreign and domestic news.

Weekly Museum, Ladies' Weekly Museum, New York Weekly Museum, 1788–1817, New York City, New York. "A repository of amusement and instruction, being an assemblage of whatever can interest the mind, or exalt the character of American fair." General interest.

Wide-Awake, 1875–93, Boston, Massachusetts, children's monthly periodical, contains illustrated stories and poetry. Editor: Eliza Anna Farman Pratt. Associate editor: Sophia Mariam Swett. Department editor: Mary Virginia Hawes Terhune ("Marion Harland").

Woodhull & Claflin's Weekly, 1870–6, New York City, New York, advocating suffrage, free love, workers' rights, and spiritualism. Co-publishers and co-editors: Victoria Claflin Woodhull and Tennessee Celeste Claflin.

A Wreath of Cherokee Rose Buds, see *Cherokee Rose Buds*.

Index of Titles and First Lines